PERSONALITY THEORIES

PERSONALITY THEORIES

Bem P. Allen
Western Illinois University

Allyn and Bacon
Boston • London • Toronto • Sydney • Tokyo • Singapore

Vice President, Publisher: Susan Badger
Executive Editor: Laura Pearson
Editorial Assistant: Marnie Greenhut
Production Coordinator: Marjorie Payne
Editorial-Production Service: Chestnut Hill Enterprises, Inc.
Cover Administrator: Linda Dickinson
Composition Buyer: Linda Cox
Manufacturing Buyer: Louise Richardson

Copyright © 1994 by Allyn and Bacon
A Division of Simon & Schuster Inc.
160 Gould Street
Needham Heights, MA 02194

Library of Congress Cataloging-in-Publication Data

Allen, Bem P.
  Personality theories / Bem P. Allen
    p. cm.
  Includes bibliographical references and index.
  ISBN 0–205–13774–1 (alk. paper)
  1. Personality. I. Title.
BF698.A3614 1994
155.2—dc20   93–14051
                                                      CIP

PHOTO CREDITS   p. 24: Courtesy of the National Library of Medicine; p. 48: North Wind Picture Archive; p. 49: The Granger Collection; p. 54: Lyrl C. Ahern; p. 78: Lyrl C. Ahern; p. 105: Lyrl C. Ahern; p. 131: The Granger Collection; p. 157: Lyrl C. Ahern; p. 183: Lyrl C. Ahern; p. 211: Lyrl C. Ahern; p. 241: Lyrl C. Ahern; p. 243: Lyrl C. Ahern; p. 245: The Bettmann Archive; p. 251: The Bettmann Archive; p. 253: The Granger Collection; p. 261: The Bettmann Archive; p. 268: Lyrl C. Ahern; p. 315: Lyrl C. Ahern; p. 330: Lyrl C. Ahern; p. 354 (left): The Granger Collection; (right): North Wind Picture Archives; p. 361 (both): Lyrl C. Ahern; p. 409: David Dempster; p. 421: Courtesy of Dr. Raymond Cattell; p. 422: The Bettmann Archive; p. 439: Lyrl C. Ahern; p. 455: The Bettmann; p. 456: The Bettmann Archive.

Printed in the United States of America

10 9 8 7 6 5 4 3 2 1   99 98 97 96 95 94

To the memory of my mother

BRIEF CONTENTS

CONTENTS

PREFACE

Of the theories attempting to explain psychological phenomena, those applied to understanding personality are among the most fundamental. They are also among the oldest and most enduring psychological theories, with origins dating to the ancient Greeks. Despite being "long in the tooth," these venerable points of view are still being pursued by modern theorists, researchers, and practitioners. In fact, few groups of theories that focus on a single, complex phenomenon have survived as well as theories of personality. For example, personality theories have gained many new advocates, while theories of conditioning (instrumental and classical) have recruited relatively few enthusiasts.

Why the longevity of these notions? They have served psychology well in terms of generating fruitful ideas, leading to means of helping people with psychological problems, and providing the grist for psychological researchers' scientific mills. Thus, one basic assumption is that personality theories are central to psychological thinking. I have woven this assumption into the fabric of the text.

A second basic assumption is wrapped up in the answer to the question, "At what level of difficulty can a broad range of college students be expected to function successfully?" Personality theories do not have the reputation for difficult and arcane structures by which physicists' theories of time and space are known. They do, however, involve complexities and abstractions that can be quite challenging. Nevertheless, the question can be answered in an optimistic fashion: Typical students attending every kind of school, ranging from community colleges to Ivy League universities, can learn even intricate and daunting material, provided it is presented in a manner that will excite their imaginations and relate to their lives. Therefore, I have tried to make each personality theory come alive by showing how it relates to the personality of the individual who composed it, by indicating how solutions to life's puzzles may be better approximated through understanding it, and by using it to inspire some thoughts that most students have yet to think.

A third basic assumption of *Personality Theories* involves notions of objectivity. Although perfect objectivity is probably unobtainable, even-handedness can be achieved. *Personlity Theories* assumes that students should come away from a thorough consideration of personality theories with a sense that each has its merits and deficiencies and that none can be reasonably called "the best" or the "the worst." Students can achieve this goal by taking the perspective of each theorist while maintaining an informed outsider's perspective, viewing the merits and deficiencies of each thoery in relation to the field of personality as a whole. These perspectives are complementary, allowing me to write about theorists major contributions with great enthusiasm, sometimes bordering on zealousness. At the same time, I am able to step back and caution students that the apparent weaknesses of even the most laudable ideas as well as the holes in theories left by failures to consider important matters of personality.

Audience

Personality Theories is designed for undergraduate students, regardless of level. It is written to be easily read, but does include sentences of a moderate level of complexity/length, and it contains many words that are not common. Although some students may be advised to occasionally use a dictionary, care is taken so that context usually defines uncommon words. These practices will ensure that students who are unintimidated by any readings, even the most difficult, will find that *Personality Theories* holds their interest. At the same time, students who are not so widely read can manage *Personality Theories* without undue trouble and can improve their ability to read more challenging literature.

Organization

The organization of chapters of *Personality Theories* is unique and consistent throughout. All chapters have basically the same format, allowing students to learn quickly what to look for—a lesson that will make reading more comfortable and rapid. Because the organization is so important to students, it is detailed in the first chapter where it will not be missed. Here, I have provided only a brief rationale for the various chapter sections that constitute the organization. Readers of the Preface who want more information are referred to Chapter One.

An *introductory statement*, designed to link a given chapter to preceding ones, is followed by a *biography* of the theorist under consideration. Here each theorist is humanized and the groundwork is laid for linking his or her personality to the theory in question. These biographies provide students with "memory hooks" upon which to hang components of theory.

A *view of the person* section follows and orients students by providing them with the philosophical underpinnings of each theory. This section answers such questions as "To what degree is the theory scientific?", "Does the theory attempt to understand the person by reference to the past, present, or future?", "Are external or internal determinants of psychological functioning emphasized?", and "Do inborn or acquired determinants explain personality?"

The *basic concepts* section lays out the fundamental constructs of each theory. The critical elements of each theory are linked so that students may understand their interrelationships and, where possible, are organized according to some familiar schema. For example, the theory may fit the "stage theory" mold and, thus, its concepts are presented within the framework of its sequential stages. In any event, an effort is made to begin with more global concepts where such concepts can be identified and proceed to more specific ones.

Evaluation of each theory is organized into "contributions" and "limitations" subsections. Two broad categories of criteria applicable to both subsections are used to assess aspects of each theory. A given criterion may be used for one theory to illuminate contributions, and, for another, to point out limitations. Alternatively, a theory may meet a given criterion to some degree therefore revealing a contribution, or it may fail to meet the criterion, indicating a limitation. None of these criteria is relevant to every theory; thus, a given one may be used to evaluate one theory but not another. One of these broad categories is "science criteria." These criteria address such questions as "Is the theory constructed in logical fashion?", "Are the concepts interrelated?", "Do the concepts tend to be distinct or are they overlapping?", "Are common labels for concepts used or are obscure labels used?", "Does each label give precise meaning to its concept or does it have multiple meanings?", "Do concepts imply testable predictions?", and "Do research studies support the validity of concepts." "Nonscience criteria," the other category, raise such questions as "Does the theory inspire psychologists to experience new insights and clarify their thinking?", "Does the theory lead to a useful method of therapy?", and "Have the theorist's writings been interesting and helpful to laypersons?"

A few sections are found in only some chapters. These include "personality development" and "supporting evidence." For example, only some theories address "personality development" or have generated enough contemporary research to warrant a "supporting evidence" section.

Content and Chapter Organization

Personality Theories is comprehensive. A first step in developing a plan for the book was to informally survey the range of theories apparently deemed most central to instructors of personality theory. Every theory that has been of interest to even a substantial minority of personality instructors is included in this text. Few if any other texts cover as many theories and none cover a better representation of mainstream theories. It is, therefore, likely that most personality instructors will find the theories they want to cover within the pages of *Personality Theories*.

The chapters are grouped in representative clusters and ordered within clusters in popular fashion. For example, Chapters Three through Eight are devoted to theorists who modified Freud's point of view (Chapter Two) and reacted against it. Freud's closest associates are considered in early chapters of this cluster (Jung and Adler), and those more removed from direct influence by him are considered in later chapters (Horney, Sullivan, Erikson, and Fromm). Consideration of Fromm, who may be regarded as an early humanist, provides a bridge to the second cluster, chapters on modern humanists, Rogers and Maslow. A chapter on the cognitive approach (Kelly) is followed by chapters on the social/cognitive point of view (Rotter/Mischel and Bandura). Next come the ideas of the self-proclaimed, anticognitive theorist Skinner. Then a chapter on Murray's theory addresses the Freudian tradition, often contrasting it with the humanistic, cognitive, and behavioral orientations, and lays the groundwork for the trait theories. Cattell's and Eysenck's theories are next and emphasize sophisticated statistical approaches to trait definition. Finally, ending the book is Allport's more humanistic and socially flavored theory of traits that focuses on personality development and prejudice.

Alternative Uses of the Book

I have always found comprehensive texts more attractive than ones with specialized content because they invariably include the chapters I want to cover. Only some of them, however, are written so that I can "unplug" the chapters I want to consider without concern that I have eliminated material essential for understanding covered chapters. In composing *Personality Theories* I have taken great care to interrelate chapters, while, at the same time, making sure that each chapter can stand alone should any instructor want to consider only a subset of all chapters. I believe that personality instructors will find they can readily skip some chapters of *Personality Theories* and focus on others without fear that students will be unduly troubled by lack of exposure to eliminated material.

Special Features

Each chapter begins with some "teaser questions" that are designed to alert students to the critical issues considered in the chapter and to arouse their curiosity regarding the theory. The presence of these questions at the beginning of each chapter primes students to consider new material that is dissimilar to that discussed in previous chapters. The questions are always answered in the text of the chapter.

Immediately following the text for each chapter, students will find some *Summary Points* that will allow them a quick review of the chapter. These "points" are synopses of ten major considerations. They are not an attempt to reiterate the entire chapter. Students can expect that the "points" will trigger their memories concerning major issues in the chapter and the details surrounding them, *if they have carefully read the text*. The "points" are not a substitute for perusal of the chapter.

All too often some students will read a chapter—or, more likely, a set of chapters over which they are to be tested—and then forget about chapter content as soon as they will no longer be evaluated based on their knowledge of it. The *Running Comparison* that follows the "points" is constructed so that students are continually reminded of material in earlier chapters. This goal is accomplished by comparing the theory currently under consideration with theories of previous chapters. Also, the "comparison" helps students anticipate future theories by occasionally comparing the current theory with ones yet to be considered. Should instructors want to give a comprehensive, final exam, the "comparison" will help students greatly, because it will ensure that they are continually reviewing material from all chapters. In addition, the comparison further sharpens students' understanding of a given theory by contrasting it with other theories.

The last section in each chapter is designed to promote critical thinking. While these *Critical Thinking* questions can be used as essay-test items, alternatively they can be used as a basis for class discussions. In addition, they are good review questions, but, more important, they can be used by students to expand their thinking by conjuring up implications of theories that reach far beyond the text. Many of these questions will be challenging even to the best students, partly because they require analysis, not "rote memory."

A complete glossary of all concepts comprising covered theories is presented at the end of the book. The listing is alphabetical and each entry clearly specifies its concept. Concepts are also listed with page number under each theorist's name in the subject index.

A comprehensive test-item-file is available. Multiple-choice items thoroughly cover each chapter's material. There are an average of more than 75 items per chapter providing instructors with approximately 1,300 items total, more than enough for several tests during the semester and a final exam. As I have years of experience in contributing multiple-choice items to text manuals, instructors can be assured that items are carefully and professionally selected. Alternatives such as "all of the above," "none of the above," and "both a & b" are avoided because they confuse students. Each item, therefore, has only one correct alternative. All incorrect alternatives are written to be highly plausible so that students must make thoughtful choices. They are often statements that are true of other aspects of a theory but are incorrect in terms of the main body of the question. These alternatives require students to discriminate among concepts of a theory. Concepts from other theories are also used to require intertheory discrimination.

I have always believed that tests are learning experiences, not just occasions for evaluation. Accordingly, items are written to engage students in analytic thinking. Most items require that students employ their reasoning powers rather than merely recognize the correct alternative.

The instructor's manual accompanying this text is designed so that instructors may enhance their lectures with interesting and edifying classroom discussions and exercises. As a member of a national college teacher's organization, and a frequent participant in its conventions, I have become convinced that spending the entire class period in a straight lecture format is not ideal for either students or instructors. Students can obtain basic information from the text. Class time can be used to get students excited about the course content, to go over difficult material, to provide the latest hot-off-the-press information about course content, and to cover issues about which the instructor is expert in greater depth than text space allows.

Acknowledgments

Sincere thanks are due to Susan Badger, Vice-President and Publisher, for her helpful insights and suggestions during the planning and much of the writing of *Personality Theories*. Laura Pearson, Executive Editor, was brand new at Allyn and Bacon when she took on *Personality Theories*. Despite the burden of becoming familiar with a new and challenging list of books, she devoted a great deal of time to helping with the refining of *Personality Theories*. Given that it is the high quality, professional product that I believe it to be, she deserves much of the credit. The members of the Allyn and Bacon production team are also due accolades for their outstanding creative efforts.

These colleagues are much appreciated for their constructive and thoughtful reviews during the writing of *Personality Theories:* Maxine Warnath (Western Oregon State University), Gordon M. Becker (University of Nebraska), John Vitkus (Barnard College), George Boeree (Shippensburg University), Richard Logan (University of Wisconsin-Green Bay), James Johnson (Illinois State University), Dennis Elsenrath (University of Wisconsin-Stevens Point), Joseph Horvat (Weber State University), and Ursula White (El Paso Community College).

1

INTRODUCTION

- Is there a "best" definition of personality?
- Do case studies qualify as "scientific?"
- If two factors are correlated, does it mean that one causes the other?
- Do personality researchers often do experiments?
- What kinds of tests do personality psychologists use?

One goal of this first chapter is to give you a preliminary answer to the question, What is Personality? by providing a working definition. Another is to consider how personality is studied and the kinds of tests *personologists*, personality psychologists, use. A final goal is to lay out the logic behind the structure of chapters. To facilitate reading chapters and comparing one with another, the sections of the different chapters are virtually identical.

Working Definition of Personality

The parts of the working definition of personality include individual differences, behavioral dimensions, traits, and profiles.

Individual differences is a key psychological phrase generally referring to the observation that people differ in a variety of ways. In the study of personality, the important differences involve **personality traits**, internally based psychological characteristics that often correspond to adjectival labels such as "shy," "kind," "mean," "outgoing," "dominant," and so forth. Several theorists covered in this book will have more specific definitions of traits.

Each trait corresponds to one end of a **behavioral dimension**, a continuum of behavior analogous to a yardstick. Just as one end of a yardstick is anchored by

0 inches and the other end by 36 inches, one end of a behavioral dimension is anchored by one behavioral extreme and the other end is anchored by the opposite extreme. For example, *affiliativeness, assertiveness,* and *conscientiousness* are labels for behavioral dimensions. Each has anchors representing behavioral extremes. The following diagram illustrates a behavioral dimension.

assertive   :1:2:3:4:5:6:7:   unassertive

One end of the assertiveness dimension is anchored by *assertive,* the tendency to stand up for one's rights and say *no* when it seems appropriate to do so. The other end is anchored by *unassertive,* the tendency to allow one's rights to be trampled by others. Likewise, *affiliative* means desiring social relations with others, while *unaffiliative* refers to shunning relations with others. *Conscientious* involves careful attention to duties and obligations and *unconscientious* entails failure to meet obligations and to perform duties. For the sake of convenience and simplicity, the example has only seven degrees. In reality the number of degrees of a dimension is difficult or impossible to determine. In any case, only behaviors falling near the extremes of dimensions have much meaning for personality. If a person's behavior can be represented on the assertiveness dimension by a degree close to the anchor *assertive,* it can be inferred that he or she possesses the trait *assertive.* On the other hand, if an individual displays behavior indicative of the other extreme, *unassertive* is inferred. Degrees near the middle of dimensions are too ambiguous to allow inferences on which one can rely.

Traits are directly related to profiles. A **personality profile** is represented by the line that connects the degrees on the behavioral dimensions associated with various traits that a person possesses. In a real sense, a profile is a graphic summary of an individual's personality.

Having defined the parts of the working definition, it is time to consider the whole. An individual's **personality** is a set of degrees falling along many behavioral dimensions, each degree corresponding to a trait, resulting in a unique profile, different from that of other individuals. Note that although some people may share a particular trait, there are individual differences in possession of the trait. Some people have it and others do not. However, sharing does not apply to profiles. There are individual differences in profiles such that no two personalities are exactly alike. As is the case with traits, several theorists covered in this book will have more specific definitions of personality.

A Portrait of Three Personalities

Next, consider a concrete illustration of the working definition in the form of a portrait of personalities belonging to three imaginary people—Jane, John, and Julie. To see what traits are possessed by these people, one can observe them operating in some sample social situations as they perform behaviors belonging to some sample dimensions. Classroom, work, and party were chosen as social situations, because you are highly likely to encounter them. The illustrative behavioral dimensions are assertiveness, affiliativeness, and conscientiousness. Remember, however, that no individual's personality is limited to traits corresponding to such a small number of behavioral dimensions. Neither are corresponding behaviors performed in just three social situations. It is necessary to simplify. Assume that observations of behaviors have been made in each situation on a number of occasions.

Now turn to Table 1.1 and look at Jane's entries under assertiveness. Her behavior is extremely assertive across occasions in the classroom (degree 1), less so across occasions at work (degree 2), and extreme again at parties (degree 1). The average assertiveness (see mean column) across situations is 1.33. One can make the strong inference that Jane possesses the trait *assertive*. In fact, one could say, "Jane is really a very assertive person." Similarly, John is unassertive and Julie is so neutral on the assertiveness dimension, she cannot be meaningfully characterized in terms of it.

Turning to the other behavioral dimensions, one can see that Jane possesses the trait unaffiliative. On the other hand, John and Julie are both clearly affiliative. John is conscientious, but not Jane and Julie. In examining Table 1.1, please remember that you are looking at an ideal picture. Real people's behaviors do not fall so neatly at the extremes or in the middle of behavioral dimensions.

Next consider concrete examples of Jane's, John's, and Julie's profiles. Figure 1.1 shows the profiles of Jane, John, and Julie. For each person, the line connect-

TABLE 1.1   Behavioral Dimensions

	Assertiveness (1 = assertive)			
	Classroom	Work	Party	Mean
Jane	1	2	1	1.33
John	6	6	6	6.00
Julie	4	3	4	3.67

	Affiliativeness (1 = affiliative)			
	Classroom	Work	Party	Mean
Jane	5	5	5	5.00
John	1	1	1	1.00
Julie	1	1	1	1.00

	Conscientiousness (1 = conscientious)			
	Classroom	Work	Party	Mean
Jane	6	7	7	6.33
John	2	1	2	1.67
Julie	5	6	5	5.33

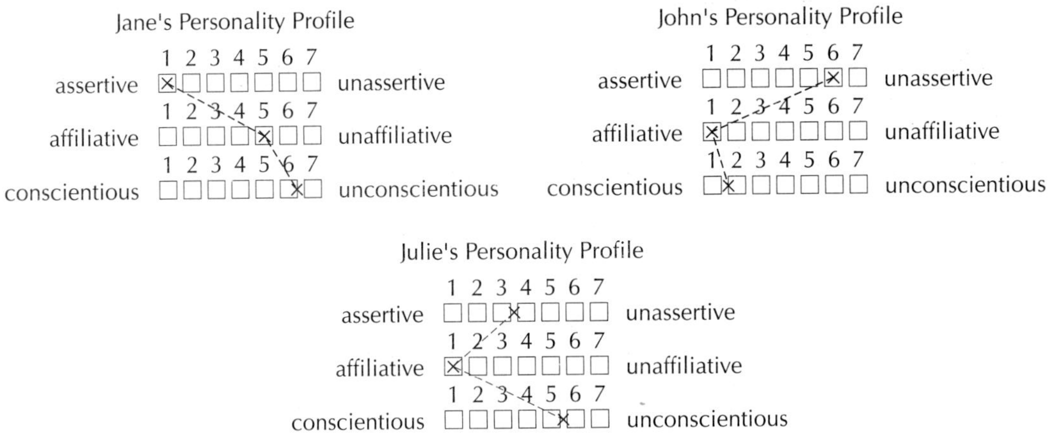

Jane's Personality Profile

1 2 3 4 5 6 7
assertive ☒☐☐☐☐☐☐ unassertive
1 2 3 4 5 6 7
affiliative ☐☐☐☐☒☐☐ unaffiliative
1 2 3 4 5 6 7
conscientious ☐☐☐☐☐☒☐ unconscientious

John's Personality Profile

1 2 3 4 5 6 7
assertive ☐☐☐☐☐☒☐ unassertive
1 2 3 4 5 6 7
affiliative ☒☐☐☐☐☐☐ unaffiliative
1 2 3 4 5 6 7
conscientious ☐☒☐☐☐☐☐ unconscientious

Julie's Personality Profile

1 2 3 4 5 6 7
assertive ☐☐☐☒☐☐☐ unassertive
1 2 3 4 5 6 7
affiliative ☒☐☐☐☐☐☐ unaffiliative
1 2 3 4 5 6 7
conscientious ☐☐☐☐☒☐☐ unconscientious

FIGURE 1.1   Personality Profiles

ing points on the behavioral dimensions represents a summary of the individual's personality. It is clear that the line is different for the different people. It is easy to see that individual differences along the behavioral dimensions, each corresponding to a trait, result in individual differences in profiles. Picturing Figure 1.1 in "your mind's eye" will allow you to remember the working definition of personality and, more important, to understand it thoroughly.

Implications and Cautions

The simplified illustrations in Table 1.1 and Figure 1.1 highlight a coincidence of personologists' beliefs about personality and the common sense notions held by nonprofessionals or laypersons. First, as represented in Figure 1.1, many personologists and laypersons believe that people are quite consistent across different situations (remember the consistency is exaggerated here for the purpose of illustration). Second, where single dimensions are involved, individuals can be very similar or even identical. That is, two or more people can on average exhibit about the same degree of a behavior, and thus possess the same trait. Julie and Jane are unconscientious to a similar extent, while John and Julie are affiliative to the same degree. Therefore, Julie and Jane both possess the trait unconscientious and John and Julie both possess the trait affiliative.

Third, the overriding agreement between personologists and the people they study is the shared belief in individual differences that is reflected in Table and Figure 1.1. That belief is at the core of conceptions about personality (Lamiell, 1981). Because there are individual differences along every behavioral dimension, given enough dimensions, personalities must differ. One respected estimate put the number of traits and corresponding dimensions at 17,000+, thereby guaranteeing that each person's profile is different from that of other persons and, thus, each person has a unique personality (Allport and Odbert, 1936).

Methods of Studying Personality

Now that you have an answer to the question, What is personality? it is possible for you to consider how personality is studied. First, however, there is a need to specify a set of criteria for evaluating those methods. *Science* provides the needed criteria. The minimum requirement for a research method to be called **scientific** is that it involve unbiased observations that are quantified so that systematic analyses can be performed (Allen, 1990). Methods can properly be called scientific if they allow researchers to make observations without regard to their personal biases, and permit the assignment of numbers to those observations so that systematic analysis is possible. By contrast, users of unscientific methods base selection of observations on convenience—whatever happens to be handy is observed. Or observations are based on personal bias—the researchers arbitrarily believe that selected observations are more important than other observations they might have made. In addition, users of unscientific methods may draw conclusions about what they have observed based solely on intuition, as opposed to assigning numbers and doing a systematic analysis. However important such efforts may be for some purpose or another, the methods involved would not ordinarily qualify as scientific.

The Case Study Method

The **case study method** involves collecting background data about and making intensive observations of a single individual in order to discover how to treat that person or to obtain information that may apply to other people (Carson & Butcher, 1992). The case study method may be scientific in that observations can be unbiased. It is possible for psychologists to lay aside their own personal biases concerning personality functioning. However, unbiased observations may be difficult for them because the person under observation may be a patient with whom they are personally involved. Also, observations made on a single individual may not be applicable to other persons. A given individual may be quite unusual and, therefore, not at all representative of other people. Further, although it may be possible to assign numbers to observations, systematic analysis may be difficult or impossible. For example, a psychologist may give personality tests to an individual and then derive some scores. Still systematic analysis may be impossible because scores from more than one person are ordinarily needed to conduct a meaningful analysis.

Obviously the case study method does not necessarily qualify as scientific. Nevertheless, information derived from it may be useful. Reports based on observations of single individuals, sometimes called *case histories* or just *cases*, often are valuable as illustrations of personality functioning. At a number of points in this text, real or contrived cases will be used to concretely illustrate some aspect of personality functioning. Bearing these cases in mind will help you remember some of the important patterns that relate to personality theories.

The Correlational Method

The term **variable** refers to variation in quantity specified by numbers. The numbers associated with a variable are called *values*. Weight is a variable, because it can take on different values. Some people weigh 100 lbs., some weigh 200 lbs., others 140 lbs. and still others 250 lbs. For adults, weight can vary from well under 100 lbs. to well over 500 lbs. Likewise, height is a variable. Adults vary in height from under three feet to well over seven feet. Other example variables include anxiety, intelligence, and kindness. In each case, observations can assume values that vary over some range.

The correlational method is used to determine whether variations in certain variables tend to occur together. Any two variables are said to be **correlated** if variations in one correspond closely with variations in the other. To illustrate the correlational method, suppose some researchers are interested in the relationship between just two variables, the number of alcoholic drinks people consume per day and the number of psychological complaints they register per day. Assume that for the researchers' sample of subjects, the greatest number of drinks consumed per day, averaged over a ten-day period, was 20, and the least was none. Thus, for the variable "number of drinks per day," values varied from 0 to 20. The list of psychological complaints that subjects could check off included "felt anxious," "felt irritated," "felt depressed," "felt worthless," "felt lonely," "felt humiliated," "felt stupid," "felt unmotivated," "felt pressured," and "felt persecuted." For the variable "psychological complaints," values could vary from 0 to 10 (complaints were also averaged over 10 days). Table 1.2 shows the number of drinks per day and the number of complaints registered per day (the numbers presented are whole numbers in order to keep things simple). Figure 1.2 depicts a plot of the relationship between number of drinks per day and number of psychological complaints per day. Look at them before going on.

In Table 1.2, notice that the variation in number of drinks closely matches the variation in the number of complaints. For a given subject, if the number of drinks per day is high, the number of complaints tends also to be high. If the number of drinks is low, the number of complaints is low. You can clearly see this pattern in Figure 1.2.

When using the correlational method, researchers are usually interested in the degree to which the variables they are investigating are related in straight-line or *linear* fashion. In the example shown in the Table and Figure 1.2, the relationship is quite linear.

Relationships that tend to fit a straight line can conform to one of two patterns. Two variables are said to be **positively correlated** when high values on one variable correspond to high values on the other, and low values correspond with low values, as in Table 1.2 and Figure 1.2. This and the other pattern of relation-

TABLE 1.2　Positive Correlation

Subjects' Initials	# Drinks/Day	# Complaints/Day
JJ	2	1
PC	6	4
RM	3	2
LD	15	9
RC	2	1
MP	10	7
IN	4	2
MA	7	5
BC	9	6
KI	5	3
MZ	11	8
PS	6	4
CC	16	9
BT	3	1
LL	8	6

ship can be represented by a **correlation coefficient**—an index, represented by the letter r, of the degree to which a relationship is linear. For positive correlations, the coefficient varies from 0 to 1.00. In this example case the correlation coefficient is $r = +.975$.

To consider the second pattern, it is necessary to make different assumptions. In Table 1.3, notice that variation in the number of drinks corresponds closely with variation in the number of complaints, therefore, the relationship is approximately linear. However, Figure 1.3 shows that the relationship is inverse, rather than

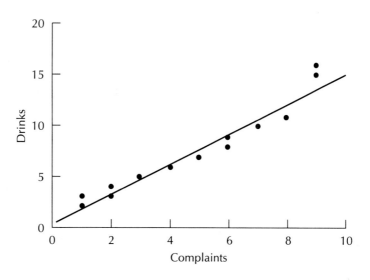

FIGURE 1.2　Positive Correlation

TABLE 1.3   Negative Correlation

Subjects' Initials	# Drinks/Day	# Complaints/Day
JJ	10	3
PC	4	8
RM	5	7
LD	14	1
RC	8	4
MP	5	8
IN	2	10
MA	11	3
BC	1	10
KI	16	1
MZ	3	8
PS	12	3
CC	7	6
BT	5	7
LL	10	2

direct, as in the positive correlation. Notice that the line in Figure 1.3 is almost perpendicular to the one in Figure 1.2. A given subject who has only a few drinks a day reports many complaints. One who reports few complaints has many drinks per day (remember that this relationship is hypothetical). This case illustrates a **negative correlation**—high values on one variable correspond to low values on the other variable. The correlation coefficient is $r = -.968$.

The relationship between variables may fail to fit either type of linear relationship. Table 1.4 displays such a case. There is no clearly discernable pattern. It

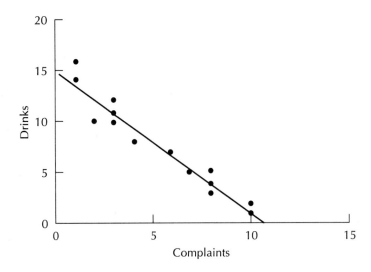

FIGURE 1.3   Negative Correlation

TABLE 1.4   Nil Relationship

Subjects' Initials	# Drinks/Day	# Complaints/Day
JJ	10	10
PC	9	1
RM	15	2
LD	8	7
RC	7	9
MP	9	3
IN	6	8
MA	16	10
BC	4	2
KI	1	10
MZ	1	10
PS	2	4
CC	5	3
BT	18	9
LL	2	10

is not true that as the number of drinks go up the number of complaints go up. Nor is it true that as the number of drinks go up the number of complaints go down. Figure 1.4 depicts this lack of pattern. Notice that the line drawn to represent the values is nearly parallel to the axis for complaints. Whenever the line is parallel to an axis, the correlation is nil. The correlation coefficient for the data in Table 1.4 and Figure 1.4 is nearly zero, $r = -.045$.

The correlational method can qualify as scientific. Observations can be unbiased. Generally, bias is avoided by selecting subjects, and therefore observa-

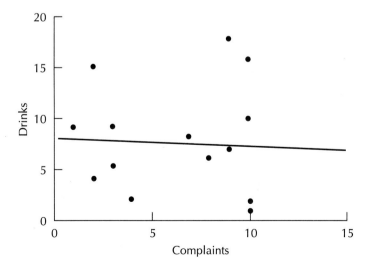

FIGURE 1.4   Nil Correlation

tions, at random. If we pursue the "drinking and complaints" example a bit farther, we find that random selection prevents getting too many alcoholics or too many people with serious psychological problems in the sample. Either one of these two biased selections would obviously make results difficult to interpret (if the sample had mainly people with serious psychological problems, maybe results would apply only to such people).

The correlational method also involves quantification and systematic analysis. In our example, numbers are associated with both the observations of drinking and the observations of complaints. These numbers were plotted to depict the relationship between variables, and the degree of relationship was represented by a correlation coefficient.

While the correlational method can readily qualify as *scientific,* like the other methods, it has its problems. Chief among them is the fact that while it can indicate whether there is a relationship between two variables, it cannot indicate whether one variable determines variation in another. This weakness is best expressed in the statement "correlation is not causation." That is, just because two variables are correlated does not mean one "caused" variation in the other. A few examples will illustrate the point. There is a high, positive correlation between the inseam length of pants and the height of wearers, but buying longer jeans will not make a person taller. Nor will increases in height cause jeans to grow. Similarly, a researcher once found a high, positive correlation between the amount of rainfall in Arizona and the rate of suicide in Canada. However, no one was willing to argue that rain in Arizona "causes" suicides in Canada, or vice versa.

It often happens that when one of two correlated variables seems to have caused variation in the other, a third or fourth variable actually is a more likely candidate as the "cause." One winter in another country, there was a high correlation between the presence of storks on roofs and the births of babies the following summer and fall. Assuming that storks do not bring babies, something else accounted for the obtained relationship. The storks roosted on the roofs near chimneys to keep warm, and the people, having no TV and tiring of card games, resorted to other forms of evening recreation. "Escaping the cold" both led the storks to the chimneys and confined the people inside where they became bored.

Even with new, sophisticated techniques, it is accurate to say that the correlational method generally cannot tell us what variables determine variation in what other variables. Nevertheless, the correlational method can be very useful. First, sometimes it does not matter which of two variables "causes" variation in the other. If intelligence is highly, positively correlated with doing well in school, college recruiters will not care whether high intelligence "causes" doing well in school or doing well in school "causes" high intelligence. They may recruit those who score high on some test of intelligence, and rest easy in the belief that these people will succeed in college. Second, correlational methods may suggest a causal relationship between variables, thereby alerting researchers to apply other methods to confirm the existence of the causal relationship. The persistent positive correlation between cigarette smoking and lung cancer certainly suggests that smoking causes lung cancer. Use of another kind of method has confirmed that, indeed, cigarette smoking does determine lung cancer.

That method is considered next, but first it is worth mentioning that a sophisticated technique built on correlation—called *factor analysis*—is very important to the study of personality. It will receive considerable attention in the chapter on Raymond Cattell and Hans Eysenck.

The Experimental Method

When psychologists use the experimental method, the variables they deal with are classified into two different categories. **Independent variables** have variation that is arranged by the person who uses the experimental method, called the *experimenter*. Through certain manipulations, the experimenter assigns values to independent variables, thereby dictating their variation. **Dependent variables** have values that are free to vary so that they are open to influence by the independent variables. The experimental method involves performing an **experiment**, a procedure whereby an experimenter *first* sets the variation in some independent variable(s) and *then* ascertains whether variation in some dependent variable(s) is influenced. In contrast to use of the correlational method, with the use of the experimental method it may be possible to assert that, when variation in two variables corresponds, variation in one determined or "caused" variation in the other. The claim is possible because the experimenter, not some third variable, dictated the variation in the independent variable that, in turn, corresponds with variation in the dependent variable. With the correlational method, there is no *prior* manipulation of one variable followed by verification of whether the other variable was influenced.

The following experiment illustrates the experimental method. Researchers Edward Diener and Mark Wallbom (1976) hypothesized that people are more honest when they are *self-aware*, made to pay attention to themselves and their values. They made some subjects highly self-aware by placing them in front of a mirror. Others were not self-aware, because they were placed at an angle to the mirror so they could not see themselves in it. This procedure was an independent variable manipulation, because prior research had shown that people placed in front of mirrors had high self-awareness ratings, whereas those not looking into a mirror had relatively low ratings. (For the sake of simplicity, an additional self-awareness manipulation is not considered.)

Regardless of whether they were self-aware or not, all subjects were told that they would be completing an "intelligence test." Actually they were given a task that was impossible to do in the five minutes they were allotted. Subjects were to complete the task while alone. After explaining about the "intelligence test" to each subject, the experimenter put a timer next to the subject. The experimenter told all subjects that the timer's alarm was set to go off in five minutes and that they must stop when it sounded. Finally, subjects were lead to believe that the experimenter would be detained for ten minutes.

Obviously, subjects could cheat by continuing to work after the alarm sounded. Unknown to them the mirror that they were either looking into or not was "one-way": An observer seated behind the mirror could see subjects, but they could not see the observer. This observer could: (1) ascertain the percentage of subjects in the two awareness conditions who cheated; and (2) count the number of responses each subject made after the alarm sounded. These two sets of values constituted the two dependent variables for the experiment.

Results were, well, alarming. Fully 71 percent of subjects cheated in the low-self-awareness condition. By contrast, only 7 percent of those in the high-self-awareness condition cheated. This result was **statistically significant**—it reflected a difference between conditions that is so large it is very unlikely to occur solely by chance. Subjects in the low-self-awareness condition also made more responses after the alarm went off than high-self-awareness subjects. This result was also significant. Using the experimental method Diener and Wallbom showed that it is possible to arrange for conditions that promote honesty.

While the experimental method may be the most powerful scientific procedure, it too has its problems. Its most serious fault may be that, in order to have the control researchers need to carry out manipulations of independent variables, experiments must be performed in laboratories or other artificial settings. As a result, experimental outcomes must be generalized to real life with considerable caution.

Because it is generally assumed that behavior corresponding to traits is consistent across situations, experiments are a relatively rare form of personality research. Why manipulate circumstances to create different situations if behavior is not going to be differentially affected by those situations? Nevertheless, experimental research is done by some personologists, such as Albert Bandura and Hans Eysenck. They show that behavior corresponding to traits is affected by experimental manipulations that amount to the creation of different situations. Further, one theorist, George Kelly, even used the experimental method in psychotherapy to help people get a better grip on their lives.

Personality Tests: Personologists' Tools

Reliability and Validity

Like other scientists, personologists also have their instruments. Their tools, or assessment tests, come in a variety of forms, all of which are evaluated on two important dimensions. First, tests must demonstrate **reliability**, the degree to which test results are repeatable. If people take a test on one occasion and then again a short time thereafter, *test-retest reliability* is demonstrated if the scores on the two occasions are highly similar. If people score similarly on two forms of the same test *reliability of parallel forms* is demonstrated. Second, tests must demonstrate **validity**, the degree to which a test measures what it was designed to measure. A test can be said to have *content validity* if its items actually sample the behaviors of interest, such as typing skills or arithmetic computation. A test of shyness versus outgoingness should have items such as "Do you tend to blush and look away when people introduce themselves to you?" rather than "Is your room neat and clean?" *Predictive validity* refers to a test's capacity to make predictions about people's behavior. A test of the trait *aggressiveness* in children that accurately predicts pushing and shoving on the playground would have this kind of validity. *Construct validity* is the degree to which a test measures a defined concept. If a test measures the construct *consciousness,* several of its items should be highly intercorrelated and, together, represent consciousness. Finally, a valid personality trait test should correlate positively with tests of dissimilar format that assess the same trait (*convergent validity*), but not at all with tests of similar format that assess different traits (*divergent validity*). A multiple choice test of "helpfulness" and a true/false test of the same trait should be positively correlated, but two true/false tests, one measuring "helpfulness" and the other "ambition," should be uncorrelated.

Projective and Objective Tests

Most personality tests fall into one of two categories. **Projective tests** present people with test items that are unstructured, ambiguous, or open-ended, thus allowing them a wide range of freedom in making responses. A prime example of the projective test are the inkblots designed by Rorschach (1942/1951). His test consists of ten cards on which there are inkblots, five in black and white and five in color. A respondent is asked to look at each inkblot and say what it looks like or what it might be. The idea for the inkblot test came from spilling ink on a blotter, then folding it over so that the two sides of the resultant smear are symmetric: they look the same (see Figure 1.5). Because the inkblot is a randomly determined stimulus, respondents "project" themselves onto the "blank screen" of this neutral test stimulus in ways that reflect their individual backgrounds, perceptions, and fantasies (Frank, 1939). Responses are scored in various ways according to what a person said about the inkblot: what part of it is emphasized, what shape is seen, whether the person's response is typical of what other people say or is original, how organized their response is, and how they use color. Scoring is rather subjective: it is up to the peculiar interpretation of the particular psychologist who looks at responses. Consequently, reliability is rather low as is agreement between interpreters (Potkay, 1971). Whenever reliability is low, validity is difficult to demonstrate, as it has been for the Rorschach test.

The Thematic Apperception Test (TAT) developed by Henry A. Murray, one of the theorists covered in this book, has also been popular. Because the TAT is considered in detail later, for now it is sufficient to say that the test consists of 20 cards each containing a black-and-white drawing, painting, or photograph of a human situation, such as a boy playing a violin. A person is asked to look at each card and make up a short story about it, which the personologist writes down. These stories are then analyzed to identify dominant themes or patterns of inner needs and external forces important for understanding the individual's personal-

FIGURE 1.5   Ink Blot

ity. In other kinds of projective tests respondents are asked to complete partial sentences, add an ending to a story, or draw a picture such as "your house."

Validity is difficult to demonstrate for any projective test. Nevertheless, the Rorschach, TAT, and other projective tests still have many advocates who find them useful for gaining a more intuitive sense of the patient's mental processes than is allowed by the type of test considered next.

Objective tests are highly structured paper-and-pencil questionnaires such as true/false or multiple-choice, each of which can be scored with a key so that scorers all agree on the scores. They are considered "structured" because they allow people very little freedom of response in answering items. People typically are instructed to read a number of statements and indicate which of the statements best applies to them or which are true of them and which are false. A sample item on an objective personality test might be "When I go to a party (check the statement that best applies to you): (1) "I am a wall-flower"; (2) "I am the life of the party"; (3) "I just blend in with the others"; (4) "I tend to throw a wet blanket on other people's fun." Alternatively an item might simply be "I am the life of the parties I attend" (indicate true of you or false). To appreciate the difference in structure between objective and projective techniques, contrast the format and degree of response freedom you have in answering true/false and multiple-choice examinations with those of open-ended essay exams. The scoring of objective tests is straightforward. Each possible response to an item is assigned some numerical value and the values of items are simply totaled to yield an overall score. Because objective tests, being highly structured, can be quantified in a concrete, non-arbitrary fashion, they show high reliability and validity relative to projective tests. There are several examples of objective personality tests presented in the pages to follow.

A Final Word about "Science"

All this talk of science should not leave you with the impression that it is good and other approaches are bad. It is neither good or necessarily better than other orientations; science just is. However, because personality psychologists generally claim to have scientific theories, it is reasonable to use scientific criteria to evaluate those theories. Therefore, those criteria will be applied to the theories covered in this text. Some covered theories will meet the scientific criteria better than others. Theories that fail to meet the criteria well will be subjected to appropriate criticism—so will more scientific theories that are flawed in other ways. But no theories will be dismissed solely on the basis of failure to meet scientific criteria. There are good reasons to include theories that do not meet scientific criteria well. In fact, strengths in the non-scientific realm may make these theories more valuable than some more scientific theories. Sometimes a well-thought-out philosophical position, though it is too abstract to be tested scientifically, can have more merit than a "hard science" point of view.

Chapter Sections

Chapter sections are virtually the same for all chapters. After you have read a few chapters, you will know what to expect from the rest. The remainder of this introduction is devoted to familiarizing you with the chapter format.

Introductory Statement

Brief introductory sections at the beginning of each chapter are designed to provide a transition from the previous chapters to the current one. Contrasts between previous theorists and their theories and the theorist/theory presently under consideration will allow you to "shift gears" in preparation for a new orientation. How you may expect to benefit from the chapter is also often a part of this first section.

The Person: Biographies

Just as oppression suffered during his youth led former Supreme Court Justice Thurgood Marshall to pursue racial justice throughout his illustrious career, psychological interests born of theorists' peculiar backgrounds have sometimes influenced the development of their personality theories. Some theorists covered in this book suffered personal difficulties during childhood, adolescence, or young adulthood that influenced the personality issues in which they became interested.

In turn, how they framed their ideas about those issues was determined by their own reactions to their difficulties. Knowing something about a theorist's life can tell you something truly meaningful about where that person "is coming from."

In addition, knowing about the life of a theorist can transform a sometimes alien name and a curious picture in the text into an image of quite a fascinating person. Indeed, by any standard, many of the theorists covered in this text are remarkable individuals. Some have overcome enormous obstacles to win the fame and make the contributions credited to them. Others are notable for devoting themselves to making other people's lives better, not only through their theories, but also through their personal efforts including freely donated time and money. Some theorists have escaped from territories controlled by the Nazis, others have overcome the handicap of poverty, and still others have conquered psychological disorders or the aftermath of childhood trauma.

All this information will provide you with "memory hooks." Many people have no trouble remembering details of individuals' personal lives, but sometimes do have some difficulty remembering abstract theories. After grasping a theorist's personal background and how it may relate to her or his theory, you can more easily get a grip on that person's basic ideas. Ideas are like articles of clothing that lie around in disarray if there is nothing to "hang them on," but become easy to organize and relate one to another, if an "apparel rack" with plenty of hooks is available. Extending the analogy to advances in brain science, if you have a "neurological network" composed of information about computers, it is a memory rack upon which you can "hang" newly encountered ideas about computers. Should you lack such a network, you are forced to use cumbersome and inefficient rote memory.

Memory hooks come from more than just details of theorists' lives. Very often the personality traits of a theorist, as distinguished from life events or accomplishments, play a large role in determining his or her personality theory. The traits of theorists can provide a rack for hanging ideas about their theories. One theorist's personality may dictate the assumption that conflict in interpersonal relations is the rule, not the exception. Another theorist's personality may yield the assumption that harmony characterizes interpersonal relations. Some theoretical ideas about personality hang easily on the network of a theorist's personality traits.

View of the Person: General Philosophical Orientation

Before getting into theorists' basic concepts or other elements of their theories, it is beneficial to consider their underlying assumptions. It is difficult to understand basic concepts of a theory without knowing the theorist's orientation to people and how their personalities function. Trying to absorb a theory without grasping the theorist's orientation is a little like going to the polling booth without knowing politicians' positions on critical issues.

There are a number of questions one needs to answer to discover a theorist's orientation. Is a theory founded on the belief that all people can solve their own problems if offered adequate support? Is a theory predicated on the presumption that normal and abnormal personality are on the same continuum or that the two are quite separate so that the theory deals with one or the other, not both? Is the theorist a "scientist" who quantifies personality data so that correlational and experimental methods can be used or a "non-scientist" who relies on intuition and qualitative information produced by the case study method? Does the theorist look to the person's past in attempting to understand her or his personality, or to the present (or to the future)? Does the theory assume that personality can be understood only by examining circumstances *outside* the person or by looking at processes *inside* the individual? Does what the person is born with largely determine personality, or do events after birth shape personality? The *view of the person* section will tackle these and other questions, so that you can get into the mind of the theorist you are considering before you entertain his or her theory.

Basic Concepts: The Heart and Soul of a Theory

The *basic concepts* section is the centerpiece of each chapter. It contains a presentation of a theory's elements fitted into the structure of the theory. Whenever possible, the theory's framework, which may be in a form such as stages of personality development or kinds of traits, is used to organize concepts. If appropriate, the description of a given theory is constructed pyramid fashion, with more global concepts at the top and more elemental concept forming the foundation. In any case, connections among concepts are emphasized so that learning can take the form of understanding relations among concepts, rather than just memorizing disconnected ideas.

Evaluation: Placing a Theory in Perspective

Each evaluation section is divided into *contributions* and *limitations* subsections. It is sort of a pluses and minuses organization. Because the positive and negative aspects of a theory are often at opposite ends of the same continuum, contributions and limitations are presented together here, rather than in separate subsections. Thus, a criterion for evaluation of theories may be viewed as a pole with contrasting endpoints.

Various criteria are used to evaluate theories. Because not all of them are relevant to all theories, only some are used in the examination of a given theory. These criteria are organized here into two categories.

Science Criteria

For a theory to be scientific, it must be structured in a logical fashion. Concepts may bear a definite relationship to one another. Some may be seen as more central than others and some may build on others. Thus, one criterion can be stated "Is the theory coherent, so that the relationship among concepts is clear and overlap among them is minimal or is the theory chaotic so that some concepts are disconnected from others while some overlap?" Some theories may be tightly bound networks with each concept having a definite place relative to others. Conversely, some may be a collection of isolated concepts or a group of minitheories, each not well related to the other.

Are labels for concepts common terms, each with several meanings, or are they words, common or not, that have precise and specific meanings? Words with several meanings, such as hot, cool, or gay, are a nuisance when used as labels for concepts. When trying to relate such labels to those of other concepts, the irrelevant meanings get in the way. By contrast, words with precise and specific meanings are easy to grasp and relate one to another, because there are no irrelevant meanings that one must forget. *Experience,* a word often used by personologists, may be a confusing label for a concept because, invariably, each theorist defines it differently. Also non-professional people use it in different ways. *Competency,* on the other hand, is a helpful word, because it always refers in some way to a person's skills, talents, or abilities.

One axiom of science is that if two notions account for something equally well, choose the simpler one. Concepts with short definitions that are "given away" by their labels are to be preferred to those with lengthy definitions seemingly unrelated to their labels. *Positive-self-regard* is an example of a label preferable to *sizothymia*. The latter word roughly means "reserved," though most people would not know why. Sizothymia brings up another issue. Theorists may resort to Greek or Latin words to avoid multiple meanings, but in so doing, enshroud their concepts in unnecessary mystery. A well-known word is best, so long as it does not have a surplus of meaning.

Do concepts imply definite predictions that can be confirmed or disconfirmed by some method or another, or do they yield no clear expectations that can be evaluated through systematic observation? On the one hand, high "self-efficacy" refers to confidence in one's ability to perform some feat and predicts enhanced performance. If one has high self-efficacy for picking up a snake, it is predicted that one will be able to grasp the reptile and lift it aloft with no signs of hesitancy. On the other hand, *proprium* is "me as felt and known," but what predictions can be derived from the concept?

Does a theory have a body of data to support it, or is there little empirically derived evidence to confirm implications of its concepts? To modify the rule offered earlier, if two theories are equally coherent and equally simple, choose the one that is most strongly supported by evidence. Some of the theorists covered in this book have inspired many researchers to produce much current data that supports their theories, but others' theories suffer from lack of evidential support. Those theories that catch the attention of each new generation of researchers are more likely than the others to maintain a place in future books like this one.

Non-science Criteria
In tune with the contention that science is not everything, there are criteria for evaluating theories that are not strictly scientific. Theorists may inspire not just researchers, but others as well. If second generation theorists or practitioners make careers of pursuing a given theory, the impact of the theory will be ensured.

Some theories covered in this book have failed to stimulate a great deal of research. Still, among them are theories of such great interest to professionals that they have generated a lively discourse in journals devoted solely to them. There have been psychotherapies derived from some of these same theories that have been embraced by thousands of practitioners.

In turn, these same practitioners have used the theory-based therapies to help thousands of people. Nevertheless, therapies arising from theories are not the only ways that theorists' ideas may have positive impact on people. There are personality theorists who have written books that have been read by many thousands of people, many of whom have experienced increased understanding of themselves and increased fulfillment as a result of exposure to the theories. Some theorists covered in this book have a large following among laypeople, if not among researchers and other theorists.

Occasional Sections
Aside from the sections that appear in every chapter, there are a couple that appear only in some chapters. A separate section entitled *Supporting Evidence* will appear in a chapter devoted to the theories that have generated important, current research. It will contain contemporary studies that address the theory. A few theories include especially strong ideas regarding *personality development*. Thus, the chapters covering them include a separate section on personality development. These sections map out the development of personality in relatively great detail.

Summary Points

1. The working definition of personality is founded on the notion of: individual differences, people differ in a variety of ways; traits, internal characteristics corresponding to labels such as "shy" and "kind"; and behavioral dimensions, continua, like yardsticks. A personality profile is a line connecting degrees of behavioral dimensions, each representing a trait. Personality, therefore, is a set of points falling along several behavioral dimensions, each corresponding to a trait, resulting in a unique profile.

2. Jane, John, and Julie, three hypothetical people followed in "classroom," "work," and "party" situations, share same traits in common. However, their personality profile lines reflect differences in overall personality. The scientific method involves quantification of observations. The case study method involves intensive observations of a single person. Unbiased observations may be difficult, because the observer, often a psychotherapist, is frequently involved with the observed. Also, the observed may be atypical and a meaningful analysis is difficult to conduct on the data of one person.

3. A variable assumes different values. Two variables are correlated if variation in one closely corresponds to variation in the other. Two variables are positively correlated when high values on one correspond to high values on the other.

They are negatively correlated when high values on one correspond to low values on the other. When the relationship between variables is not *linear,* meaning there is no pattern to it, it is called *nil.* With random selection of observations the correlational method can be scientific, but correlation does not mean causation.

4. In an experiment, variation in an independent variable(s) is set, and it is ascertained whether variation in a dependent variable(s) is influenced. In an experiment by Diener and Wallbom, self-awareness was varied by placing subjects in front of a mirror or not. The dependent variable, honesty, was affected: there was a statistically significant difference in cheating, with the subjects not in front of the mirror cheating more. Unfortunately results obtained with the experimental method may not generalize well to the real world.

5. Personality tests must demonstrate reliability, repeatability, and validity, actually measure what they are designed to measure. Reliability can be determined by the test-retest or the parallel forms techniques. Methods for determining validity include content validity, criterion-related validity, and convergent versus divergent validity. On projective tests, people respond to ambiguous, unstructured, or open-ended stimuli. With the Rorschach test, people describe what they see in some inkblots. Scoring is rather subjective, so reliability and validity are low. In the TAT, people view ambiguous pictures and tell stories about them.

6. Objective tests employ multiple choice or true/false formats and, thus, are highly structured. They have relatively high reliability and validity. The several sections of each chapter begin with an introductory statement that ties the theory(s) to be covered to previously considered theories. A biography section forms a link between a theorist's personality and background and her or his theory. Knowing about the lives of theorists makes them real. It also provides "memory hooks" on which to hang theoretical principles.

7. Getting to know the philosophical orientation of a theorist lays the groundwork for understanding his or her basic concepts. Does the theorist believe people can solve their own problems? Is she or he scientific or intuitive? Is the past emphasized or the present? Is the "inside" what matters or the "outside"? Is nature more important or nurture? With answers to these questions, basic concepts can be fitted into a theoretical framework such as stages of development.

8. Scientific criteria for evaluating a theory include: Is it structured in a logical fashion? Do labels for concepts each have many common meanings, or highly specific meanings? Do the labels "give away" the meanings of the concepts? Do the concepts imply definite predictions that can be confirmed or disconfirmed? Have theorists' ideas inspired researchers to produce supportive data?

9. Non-scientific criteria include: Have second generation theorists and practitioners been inspired to pursue the theory? Have lay readers of the theory embraced its principles to the betterment of their lives? Occasional supporting evidence sections are included as is the case in chapters presenting especially heavily researched theories and personality development sections in those chapters featuring theories particularly strong in charting the evolution of personality.

Essay/Critical Thinking Questions

1. What did the term *personality* mean to you before you encountered a formal definition? What do you think that it means to most people?

2. Could you make up some behavioral dimensions that seem relevant to you and "score" yourself on them? That is, could you draw your profile line?

3. Prior to encountering a formal definition of "scientific" what did it mean to you? What do you think it means to other people?

4. Could you do a case study of someone you know well?

5. If you found that the correlation between physical attractiveness and grade point average was positive and high, what would you conclude?

6. Could you design a simple experiment to determine whether a certain drug cured a certain disease?

7. If you developed a personality test, how would you go about showing that it was reliable and valid?

8. Could you conceive of a format for a projective test that is different from any mentioned in the text?

9. Could you build an argument that science *does not* provide the most appropriate criteria for the evaluation of personality theories? Mention some shortcomings that are not covered in the text.

10. You will be evaluating the personality theories covered in the pages to follow (whether you intend to or not!). What criterion would you consider to be the most important for a theory to meet if it is to be acceptable to you?

2

CLASSICAL PSYCHOANALYSIS: FREUD

- To what degree can we control our behavior, thoughts, and feelings?
- How much of what we call our "minds" is unconscious?
- What is the impact of childhood experiences on later personality development?
- What is the true meaning and purpose of dreams?
- Can a "talking therapy" change personality?

When asked questions about personality, Sigmund Freud typically gave very definite replies. Some of his answers are timeless contributions to our understanding of personality. Others were less helpful, but Freud clung to all of them with great tenacity. He was suspicious of those who disagreed with any of his ideas. During a speech at a Massachusetts university, Freud accused his most esteemed student, Carl Jung, of being interested in archeology—the discipline that often studies long-dead cultures—because of an unconscious wish that Freud, the father figure, be dead. Jung and many other early followers soon split with Freud as their ideas began to deviate from those of "the father figure." Nevertheless, all were influenced by him, whether they admitted it or not. More important, it is possible that none of them would have developed meaningful theories had Freud's ideas not provided stimuli for their own.

Freud, the Person

Sigmund Freud was born on May 6, 1856, in Moravia, a Germanic area that is now in the center of the former Czechoslovakia. He was the oldest of Amalie and Jakob

Sigmund Freud

Freud's eight children. Amalie was Jakob's second wife, 20 years his junior, who bore her "golden Sigi" at age 21. She had a lively personality and sharp-witted mind. Jakob, a wool merchant, was devoted to his wife. He had a good sense of humor and was a liberal thinker. They were Jewish.

Sigmund was only 17 when he entered medical school at the University of Vienna. He was an excellent student of neurology, with a photographic memory. Young Freud was most influenced by Professor Ernst Brucke, a respected and disciplined physiologist with an uncompromising spirit and a stare that could terrorize students. Brucke believed that the only active forces in living organisms were physical-chemical ones interacting in a closed energy system, a viewpoint that later influenced Freud.

During medical school, Freud was preoccupied with becoming well-known and economically secure by making some important discoveries (E. Jones, 1953; Parisi, 1987). His research as a student included: (1) dissecting 400 male eels to show, for the first time, that they had testes; (2) discovering new characteristics of neurons (nerve cells) in fish; and (3) developing the first gold-chloride technique of staining nervous tissue. It is also noteworthy that Freud's notion of "contact barriers" anticipated the concept *synapse* or space between neurons (Parisi, 1987). His discovery that cocaine could be used as an anesthetic may also have been motivated by the desire for fame and economic security (Parisi, 1987). He arrived at this discovery by directly observing the effects of cocaine on himself. This episode highlights one of Freud's most significant characteristics. Confronted with an isolated fact or experience, Freud "could not dismiss it from his mind" until he had found an explanation (E. Jones, 1953, p. 97).

Throughout his life, Freud never ceased self-analysis, using the last half-hour of each day to explore himself as "the single fact." He found it uncanny when he was unable to understand someone else's behavior in terms of himself. His most important book, *The Interpretation of Dreams* (1900/1958), was based on analyses of his own dreams. Freud believed that dreams allow people to fulfill wishes that they could not fulfill in real life (Dement, 1976). His *Psychopathology of Everyday Life* (1901/1965) also was derived from self-analysis and dealt with the psychological meanings of apparent "mistakes" in memory, speech, reading, and writing. Both works assumed the influence of **psychological determinism**, a belief that nothing about human behavior occurs by accident or chance. For Freud, everything about personality is *determined* or has a psychological cause. One need only uncover these causes and examine them. However, contrary to a popular belief, he was not an advocate of biological determinism (Parisi, 1987). In fact, in attempting to discover why people do what they do, Freud emphasized psychological rather than biological determinism. He wrote "consciousness knows nothing of . . . neurons" (quoted in Parisi, 1987, p. 240). This comment meant that while consciousness could not exist without nerve cells, what emerges from those cells transcends them and cannot be explained by them.

Unlike some of us, Freud was able to confront his own personal experiences, secrets, and conflicts through self-analysis. Using himself as a primary subject, he traced his own behaviors back to their hidden origins. He was a theoretical pioneer who was able to overcome intense personal fears as he explored the closeness of his relationship with his mother, as well as hostile feelings toward his father. In fact, Freud's explorations of his own childhood experiences were important contributors to his belief that boys want to "kill" their fathers in order to "marry" their mothers. Among Freud's earliest memories, "one was of penetrating into his parents' bedroom out of [sexual] curiosity and being ordered out by an irate father" (E. Jones, 1953, p. 7). Consistent with his theory, these feelings toward his father may have created guilt when Jakob died during Freud's fortieth year. About the time of the funeral, he wrote his friend Wilhelm Fliess: "By one of those dark pathways behind the official consciousness the old man's death has affected me deeply. . . . I now feel quite uprooted" (quoted in Bronfen, 1989, p. 963).

Freud lived most of his life in Vienna, where he established a private practice for the treatment of nervous disorders. His home and offices were located at

---

BOX 2.1   Freud: Target of Nazi Persecution

They burned his books, stole much of his fortune, drove him from his home country, and sent three of his four sisters to the infamous gas chambers (a fourth sister died of internal bleeding, probably due to starvation suffered while in a concentration camp; Leupold-Loewenthal, 1989). Ostensibly, the Nazis persecuted Freud because he was Jewish. Indeed, Hitler distrusted everything Jewish, even the theories of Einstein—a mistake that helped to hasten his defeat (Shirer, 1960). However, one can speculate about other reasonable possibilities. Freud taught that people are controlled by inner forces that are beyond their access or control. Hitler, by contrast, believed in the "triumph of the will." Willpower could dominate not only one's mental processes and behavior, but also one's environment, given, of course, that one is a member of the "master race" rather than a Jew or a person of color. Just as he could not allow the presence of Jehovah's Witnesses, a religious sect who refused to submit to the power of the state, Hitler could not tolerate the works or presence of someone who held that mysterious internal forces control people (Toland, 1976). Such an individual and his writings could corrupt the people and make them weak. Also, Hitler felt rather uncomfortable with sexuality. He kept his affair with Eva Braun a secret partly because he did not want the German people to think of him as sexually involved. A theory that was popularly considered to be founded on sex was probably alien to him.

Berggasse 19, now a world famous address and a museum in his honor. He enjoyed his role as father to six children, one of whom, Anna, became an important psychoanalyst, specializing in the treatment of children. Shortly after the Nazi invasion in 1938, Freud had to be persuaded by friends to leave Vienna because of the oppression of Jews. In fact, he was never an avid believer in Judaism, considering all religion an illusion used by civilization to cope with feelings of infantile helplessness. At the time of his departure, the Gestapo, Nazi secret police, attempted to obtain an endorsement from him, which was something Freud said he could not do. Box 2.1 contains more information about his tragic relationship with the Nazis.

Freud survived only a year and a summer after he migrated to London on June 3, 1938. He died from cancer of the jaw and mouth on September 23, 1939. The malignancy undoubtedly stemmed from his lifelong addiction to cigars, which he chain-smoked from early morning to late evening. You may find this addiction quite interesting when you read about Freud's theory of orality later.

During his last years he experienced pain, fatigue, and difficulties in speaking and eating caused by repeated surgery and a mechanical device that separated his nasal cavity from his mouth. Essayist Stefan Zweig (1962) wrote of Freud's "gloomy" perspective, which became all the more evident during the autumn of his years: ". . . So long and so abundantly has Sigmund Freud been a physician that he has gradually come to look upon mankind at large as ailing. His first impression, therefore, when he looks forth from his consulting-room into the outer world, is a pessimistic one. However, to the very end, Freud's instinct for life still was greater than that for death: 'I prefer a mechanical jaw to no jaw at all. I still prefer existence to extinction' " (quoted in Golub, 1981, p. 195).

Freud's View of the Person

Probably you are already familiar with some of the fundamental notions of Freudian theory. Freud painted a vivid portrait of human nature as dominated by instinctual, unconscious, and irrational forces. To him, the human organism is selfish, at war internally and externally, aggressive, and sexual, even during periods when childhood innocence was supposed to prevail. Determined by events outside of conscious control, the person is covered with a thin crust of civilization, but exists in a constant state of frustration. People are religious only out of fearfulness and illusion.

To get a preliminary view of some of the ideas discussed in this chapter, I invite you to complete the pretest in Box 2.2. The items are based on Freudian concepts, although they are somewhat simplified for teaching purposes. By indicating your agreement or disagreement, you can begin to identify some of your own basic assumptions about human nature. Later in the chapter, you will be asked to compare your answers with those that Freud would have given.

BOX 2.2   Freud's View of the Person

Answer each question true or false according to your own point of view.

1. My basic personality is the same today as when I was about 5 years old.
   TRUE   FALSE
2. I have little knowledge of my real personality or its development.
   TRUE   FALSE
3. I choose to lead my life in a self-directed manner.
   TRUE   FALSE
4. My basic motivations are sex and aggression.
   TRUE   FALSE
5. Many of my behaviors are irrational, in that I repeatedly do things that make little logical sense.
   TRUE   FALSE

6. I have had few inner conflicts in my life.
   TRUE   FALSE
7. I am afraid to know my true self, and I keep unpleasant aspects of my personality hidden from myself.
   TRUE   FALSE
8. As a child, I had sexual wishes and feelings about my opposite-sex parent.
   TRUE   FALSE
9. Women and men are psychological equals.
   TRUE   FALSE
10. The best way for me to change my personality is to enter long-term therapy with a trained expert who will provide insight into my early childhood experiences.
   TRUE   FALSE

Basic Concepts: Freud

Personality Structure: Three Interacting Systems

Structure refers to how something is put together. Most things have a readily definable structure: atoms, dormitories, families, and business organizations. For Freud, personality also has a definable structure with three basic components. One can be thought of as the personality's biological side, a second represents the psychological side, and a third reflects society's contribution to personality. These are not "parts" of personality in a physical sense, nor do they have any specific, physical location in the person. Rather, they are processes or systems of the mind. Their "job" is to organize mental life and interact with one another in a dynamic way so that personality is influenced and changed.

Id

For Freud, the origin of personality is the id, the most basic of the three systems. **Id is beyond conscious awareness and comprises whatever is present at birth, including everything that relates to the satisfaction of physical drives, such as sex and hunger, or primitive psychological needs, such as for comfort and for protection from danger. Id operates according to what Freud termed the pleasure principle,** the achievement of pleasurable feelings as quickly and immediately as possible through the reduction of discomfort, pain, or tension. Id satisfies its needs through the **primary process**, a continual flow of events involving infantile images and wishes that demand immediate and direct satisfaction. It demands satisfaction of its needs without consideration of what is right or wrong or "good" for the person.

Among its other important functions, id is the reservoir of **instincts**, inborn forces with characteristics that are both physical (bodily needs) and psychological (wishes). In Freud's writings, id and the other two systems were described as powered by **libido**, an energy variously described as "psychical desire," "erotic tendencies," "sexual desire in the broadest sense," and the "motive forces of sexual life" (Freud quoted in Rychlak, 1981, p. 54). After career-long deliberation, Freud (1940/1949) assumed the existence of only two basic categories of instincts, those of life and those of death. Instincts toward life, called **Eros**, represent energy for preserving oneself (love of self) and one's species (love of others). In other writings, Freud subsumed the several meanings of libido under "love," thereby tying libidinal energy to Eros.

Thanatos is the instinct toward destructiveness and death that is aimed at returning living things to their original non-living state. The most important aspect of Thanatos is that it promotes aggressiveness. Life and death instincts may fuse together or work against each other, giving rise to "vicissitudes" or frequent changes in a single personality, as well as to individual differences across personalities.

To understand the operation of id, think of the behaviors of a baby just a few days old. It sleeps, it awakens, it cries for milk and comfort, it urinates and defecates, it fusses, or its hand finds its mouth. However, it does nothing at all for its parents, or anyone for that matter, at least not intentionally. Since the baby's personality is dominated by id, its preoccupation is with itself and its primarily physical needs and comforts. The behavior of the infant corresponds with a popular song lyric, "I want what I want when I want it."

Ego

Infant behaviors are one-sided and preoccupied with inner states of tension, because id is entirely isolated from the external world. Id has no means of directly establishing contact with the world outside itself. While able to detect changes in internal tension, such as hunger or cold, it has no way of relieving them. It experiences only pain/discomfort and pleasure.

It should be obvious that humans equipped only with ids would have difficulty surviving. It is dangerous to satisfy a need as soon as it arises with whatever apparently gratifying object happens to be available. For example, hungry babies who are a few months of age will stuff anything into their mouths that appears edible and is within reach, including poisonous or otherwise dangerous objects. There is a clear need for another structure that will satisfy id needs without getting the baby in trouble (Freud, 1923).

Ego is a coherent organization of mental processes that develops out of id energy, has access to consciousness, and is devoted to contacting reality for the purpose of satisfying id needs. Ego strives to allow adaptation of the personality to the world outside itself. Id is subjective, directed inward in the interests of its wants and demands. By contrast, ego is objective, or directed outside itself. Ego has the task of satisfying id needs in a manner that promotes self-preservation.

Whereas id is governed by the pleasure principle, ego operates according to the **reality principle**: ego has the capacity to delay satisfaction of id's demands until an appropriate object is found that will allow gratification without harmful side-effects. Ego is guided by a higher level of mental functioning, called **secondary process**, intellectual operations such as thinking, evaluating, planning, and decision-making that test reality to determine whether certain behaviors are beneficial. Ego thus serves as a bridge to reality. It plans for actions in the real world that will satisfy id. Unlike id, ego has the capacity to appreciate the difference between food-producing breasts or bottles and ineffective objects such as thumbs or dangerous ones such as sharp objects. The functions of ego increase the likelihood that id will experience satisfaction of its demands while avoiding the dangers associated with choosing an inappropriate real-world object.

While ego has contact with reality, it is not totally conscious (see Figure 2.1). It also "suffers" from secondary status: it is an arm of the id rather than an independent entity. Ego's operations on both the conscious and unconscious levels, along with its secondary status, makes it vulnerable to stresses from both internal and external dangers. For this reason, ego constantly has to be on guard. External dangers include insufficient food, water, and physical comfort to sustain life, as well as threats of physical or psychological injury, and loss of parental love. Internal dangers include uncontrollable increases of instinctual energies, particularly sex and aggression. Freud (1923) liked to use the metaphor of a horse and rider: the superior strength of the horse (id) must be held in check by its rider (ego).

Ego's reaction to threatening surges of instinct is to experience **anxiety**, a state of extremely unpleasant emotional discomfort. To minimize this anxiety, ego calls upon various **defense mechanisms**, internal, unconscious, and automatic psychological strategies for coping with or regaining control over threatening id instincts. Defense mechanisms protect the personality by keeping unacceptable urges or ideas from ever reaching conscious awareness. Freud believed that exaggerated

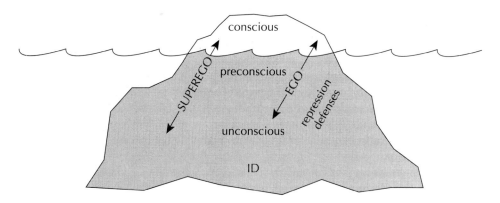

FIGURE 2.1   Personality as an Iceberg

use of such defense mechanisms results in **neuroses**, anxiety driven patterns of abnormal behavior related to an over-control of instincts. One such pattern is **hysterical neurosis**, in which, for example, a person who feels angry may develop a "paralyzed" arm to lessen the chances of hitting someone. These neuroses often assume metaphorical form (White, 1989). One of Freud's patients who felt "stabbed in the heart" by important persons in her life developed chest pains in the heart region. Another who experienced lack of feeling in the face declared that her husband's remarks were ". . . like a slap in the face" (p. 1042).

Superego

The third major force in personality is **superego**, the representation of society in personality that incorporates the norms and standards of the surrounding culture. It may be thought of as operating according to a **morality principle**, a code that concerns society's values regarding right and wrong. One of its aspects is equivalent to **conscience**, the internal agent that punishes us when we do wrong. Like ego, superego develops from id energy and is irrational in its influence. Although it is a specialized system operating in coordination with ego, it often functions below the level of ego's awareness. Superego's most important function is to help control id impulses by directing energy toward entirely inhibiting id's expression of its sexual and aggressive instincts.

The specific content of each personality's superego results from **introjection**, a process by which personality incorporates the norms and standards of its culture through identification with parents or other admired persons in society, such as clergy and teachers (Freud, 1977). As the primary interpreters of society's rules of proper conduct, parents convey these values to their children by showing them love for being "good" and punishing them for being "bad." A child's immature ego is especially sensitive to potential losses of love when parental standards are not being adopted internally.

Superego can become a relatively independent and dominating force in personality. It can work against both id and ego by making personality excessively conforming to social norms. The result is patterns of anxiety-driven behavior such as illogically striving for 100-percent perfection in absolutely everything one does. It can observe and influence ego directly, taking it to task, giving it orders, or correcting it. Superego can also threaten ego with unpleasant emotional experiences when perfectionistic, parental standards—represented by its "conscience" aspect—are not being satisfied. These unpleasant emotions include **guilt**, an intense feeling of regret over having done something wrong, and evaluations of oneself as an undeserving, inadequate person. It is as if the maturing personality never outgrows the role of child in relation to parents. As children grow toward adulthood they substitute internal scolding for the verbal punishment once meted out by parents: "That's a bad feeling. It's wrong to think that. Always do what your parents have told you to do. Be perfect in everything." This process of substitution is the main mechanism behind internalization of parental values.

On the other hand, superego can offer the personality favorable emotional experiences when another of its aspects comes into play. The superego can result in feelings of pride and self-respect through the influence of the **ego ideal**, positive standards in the form of internal representations of idealized parental figures (Freud, 1977). These favorable feelings can take the form of statements about one-self that substitute for parental statements: "You're a good child. You make your parents proud and happy. They love you."

Freud conceived of personality as an internal battleground where the combat-ants are id, ego, and superego. Id, ego, and superego are in a constant struggle to dominate the personality. One of the spoils of this war is energy captured from one of the three systems by another. The victor can then use this plundered energy for its own purposes. Sometimes there is a temporary truce: one system forms an alliance with another. The ego may "say," in effect, "Superego, let me satisfy this aggressive need; then you may have your revenge." Table 2.1 compares the three major structural systems of personality identified by Freud.

Personality Development: Five Sequential Stages

Development refers to the processes by which something grows from a beginning state to a later one. Development is seen in plants, animals, and solar systems. Per-sonality also develops over time, from states of early childhood immaturity to those of later adult maturity. Freud hypothesized a series of five sequential stages of personality development. Four of the stages are closely associated with **eroge-nous zones**, sensitive areas of the body from which instinctual satisfactions can be obtained (Freud, 1920/1977). In the order of their appearance as focal zones, these zones are the mouth, anus, penis or clitoris, and penis or vagina. Freud assumed the clitoris to be a miniature penis, because both structures are outer sexual organs that become erect during sexual stimulation.

TABLE 2.1   Comparisons of Freud's Three Systems of Personality

	Id	Ego	Superego
Nature	Represents biologi-cal aspect	Represents psy-chological aspect	Represents societal aspect
Contribution	Instincts	Self	Conscience
Time Orientation	Immediate present	Present	Past
Level	Unconscious	Conscious and unconscious	Conscious and unconscious
Principle	Pleasure	Reality	Morality
Purpose	Seek pleasure Avoid pain	Adapt to reality Know true and false	Represent right and wrong
Aim	Immediate gratification	Safety and compromise	Perfection
Process	Irrational	Rational	Illogical
Reality	Subjective	Objective	Subjective

Freud defined "sexual" very generally to encompass any pleasurable feeling associated with stimulation of the erogenous zones, whether or not the stimulation involved the mouth, anus, penis, clitoris, or vagina. Libido was used as a substitute term for sexual cravings or satisfactions, which also are reflections of Eros, the instinct toward life. One example of libidinous satisfaction is the release of tension associated with defecation. Given this view of sexuality, it is easy to see why Freud referred to the developmental stages as **psychosexual**, stages conceived of as "sexual" only in the broadest sense of the word, because some stages involve organs ordinarily seen as "sexual" and others organs not popularly regarded as "sexual."

Freud's statement that "the child is father to the man" represents his firm belief that every person's basic personality is established by the age of 5. In short, important psychological aspects of the personality you have today are basically the same as those you had when you were just entering kindergarten. This idea is grounded in Freud's unique notion of determinism, which allows little room for personal freedom, conscious purpose, or routine changes in one's personality or behavior.

Suppose you were asked to think of the name of a person, any person. You may feel you were making a free choice or decision about the name you came up with, but Freud would say your feeling is simply an illusion. To Freud, every decision you display during your lifetime—your "choices" of hobbies or a mate—results from influences present in your unconscious.

Oral Stage: Phase One

During the **oral** or **narcissistic (self-centered) stage** which begins at birth, the organism's psychic activity focuses on satisfying the needs of the mouth and digestive tract, including the tongue and lips (Freud, 1920/1977; 1977). Narcissus is a Greek mythological figure who saw his reflection in a pool of water and fell in love with himself. Eros' aim of self-preservation is met in part by the production of energy, made possible by nourishment received through the mouth. Independent of nourishment, an infant's sucking movements also provide it with pleasure. "Thumbsucking shows that the pleasure gained from breast or bottle is based not alone on the gratification of hunger but on the stimulation of the erogenous oral mucous membrane as well; otherwise the infant would disappointedly remove his thumb, since it produces no milk" (Fenichel, 1945, p. 63).

The importance of stages in understanding adult personality is manifested in Freud's concept of **fixation**, the impairment of development at a particular stage because satisfactions appropriate for the stage are frustrated, resulting in permanent investment of libidinal energy in the stage. When under stress the fixated person is likely to show **regression**, retreating to behaviors, feelings, and thoughts characteristic of the earlier fixated stage (soldier under fire cries "Mama!").

Freud referred to two personality types related to fixation at the oral stage. The **oral-receptive** personality type is derived from childhood pleasures of receiving food in the mouth and ingesting it. Persons with this trait form relationships characterized by dependency on others, who are expected to care for them. Psychologically, such persons are more suggestible and gullible than others. It is as if they are willing "to swallow" anything. They are also interested in receiving information and knowledge and acquiring material goods. Persons especially fond of candy, sweets, smoking, and oral sex, and those who are obese, are often identified in the psychoanalytic literature as oral-receptive.

The **oral-aggressive** type is also derived from childhood pleasures associated with the mouth, food, and eating, but with greater chewing, biting, and use of the teeth (Freud, 1977). Persons of this type would be expected to favor rock candy and jawbreakers to gumdrops and marshmallows, and hard-stemmed pipes to cigarettes. They are orally aggressive in their relationships with others, as if "to bite the hands that feed them." Their manner of talking is sarcastic and argumentative. They also seek to hold firmly onto others, as if to possess them or incorporate them internally.

Anal Stage: Phase Two

During the **anal stage** (age of 2–3 years) sexual gratification occurs when defecation relieves the tension of a full bowel and simultaneously stimulates the anus. "There are many people who retain a voluptuous feeling in defecating all through their lives and describe it as being far from small" (Freud, 1920/1977, p. 316).

An important aspect of the anal stage is toilet training, which involves children and parents in issues of social interaction and conflict. From the parents' point of view, the issue is social control: "Will my child 'go' on the toilet or not?" The child's point of view, on the other hand, is one of power: "Should I do what I want to do or what they want me to do?" Individual differences are shown in the manner in which parents and children answer these questions behaviorally. Some parents are rigid and demanding, expecting their child to "Go right here! Right now!" These interactions can lead to a struggle of wills, with the child experiencing conflict and social pressures to perform for Mommy and Daddy. Such experiences can carry over to later situations in life, even building to rebellion against other authority figures in society—schoolteachers, principals, police, and bosses. On the other hand, some parents are highly permissive in accepting their child's preferences and schedule, reacting favorably to the child's personal needs and self-expressions: "Take as long as you want. Oh, you did it! We're so proud." Such reactions can foster positive self-esteem.

Fixation at the anal stage may produce the **anal-retentive** personality type which is characterized by delay of final satisfactions to the last possible moment. Individuals who fit this personality type constantly "save" for the future, whether the reference is to money or gratification of some need. Other characteristics related to this "constipated" orientation include orderliness, stinginess, and stubbornness. In a famous case study called *The Wolf Man* (1963), Freud traced an adult's interests in gifts and money to childhood defecation experiences.

In contrast, the **anal-expulsive** type involves a "diarrhetic" orientation. Anal-expulsive people react against other's attempts to restrict them by doing whatever they want, just as, during childhood, they defecated whenever and wherever they wanted. Characteristics of these people include messiness—their adult lifestyle is sloppy and slovenly, just as they often "messed their pants" as rebellious children. They may also show aggressive destructiveness, temper tantrums, explosive emotional outbursts, and even sadistic cruelty.

Phallic Stage: Phase Three

During the **phallic stage** (4–5 years of age), satisfaction is gained primarily by stimulation of the penis or clitoris, through masturbation (Freud, 1920/1977). The phallic stage is central to Freud's theoretical ideas for several reasons:

1. It is the last of the infantile stages of psychosexual development.
2. It provides the context in which two important *complexes*, formations having ideational content, operate and the critical issues of castration anxiety and penis-envy become relevant.
3. It forms the basis of psychological and social identification for all children.
4. It results in psychological and sex-role differences between boys and girls.
5. It determines the development of superego.

Physical and fantasy pleasures experienced through masturbation are important aspects of the phallic stage. However, satisfaction of libidinous needs is only one part of this developmental experience, because the phallic stage is dominated by the realization that boys have penises whereas girls do not.

The question then becomes, "Why don't girls have penises?" According to Freud, answers to this question are accompanied by negative emotions of fear in boys, jealousy in girls, and changes in all children's relationships with their parents. He theorized that boys, at this stage of development, have feelings of possessive love for their mothers and see their fathers as rivals. His thinking was influenced by the Greek myth of Oedipus Rex, immortalized by Sophocles. In this tragedy, fate determines that Oedipus will kill his father and marry his mother. To Freud, the scenario reflects an internal psychological process characteristic of everyone. Freud termed this dynamic the **Oedipus complex**, the constellation of feelings, desires, and strivings revolving around the boy's desires for his mother and his fearful/hateful orientation to his father. The corresponding dynamic for girls, involving love of father and hatred of mother, is called the **Electra complex**. The significance Freud attached to issues surrounding the Oedipus complex is evident in his famous assertion that "if psychoanalysis could boast of no other achievement than the discovery of the repressed Oedipus complex, that alone would give it a claim to be counted among the precious new acquisitions of mankind" (1940/1949, p. 97).

Freud saw boys as experiencing **castration anxiety**, a generalized fear that they might lose their highly prized organ of pleasure (Freud, 1977; see Box 2.3). They "reason" that "if Father discovers that I want to love Mother the way he does, he might cut 'it' off." Girls, on the other hand, supposedly display **penis envy**, feelings of inferiority over not having the male organ and compensatory wishes to someday obtain one of their own. They may blame their mothers for their lack of a penis—"after all she doesn't have one either . . . maybe in a fit of jealousy she cut mine off so we'd be alike. I must find a way to have a penis."

At this point, the foundations of socialization are set. Faced with fantasized threats of either "losing my penis" or "giving up my desire to love Mama like Daddy does" boys choose the latter. They react to the imagined threat of castration by accepting their father's dominant status and power. They identify with father, becoming "just like Dad" for safety's sake. Just as tigers get other species, not their own, the boy reasons that if he becomes like his father, his father will not get him. Also, if he becomes like his father, it is almost as if he is his father. Therefore, when his father possesses and physically loves the mother, so does he. Finally, if he becomes like his father he will adopt the masculine characteristics that are apparently pleasing to his mother. In this process of becoming "like Dad," he also introjects the father's values and rules. Thus, the superego is formed as an inner moral code based on the father's translation of society's taboos, rights, and wrongs. The formation of the superego is the final step in resolving the Oedipal complex.

Failure to identify appropriately and, thus, failure to resolve the Oedipal complex, has important implications for the male, adult personality (Rychlak, 1981). The male who is fixated at the phallic stage may become a Don Juan as an adult, devoting his life to sexual promiscuity in a quest for the sexual gratification denied him as a child. Alternatively, he may fail to take on the masculine characteristics due to weak identification with the father. The result could be a feminine orientation and possibly attraction to men.

If libidinous feelings toward mother, the first object of childhood phallic pleasure, are not entirely eliminated, they will be actively kept buried deep in the unconscious. This occurs through the ego defense mechanisms which operate automatically and unconsciously. The most important defense mechanism is **repression**, a selective type of memory in which threatening material is unavailable for recall, because it has been pressed down into the unconscious. Repression protects the personality by allowing ego to be conscious only of those thoughts and urges that it deems to be "safe" or that do not relate too closely to threatening material. Other defense mechanisms can be called upon as well. **Projection** protects us from threat by allowing us to literally project our own unacceptable traits onto other people—"Those filthy Abagarians; unlike me, all they can think about is sex!" **Rationalization** allows us to excuse our threatening and unacceptable behavior and thoughts—"So what if I stole from my employer; they don't pay me enough." Other mechanisms allow us to **deny** whatever is too hard to bear by refusing to think about it or otherwise address it. We **intellectualize**, talk and think at an intellectual rather than an emotional level, about what we do or contemplate that is threatening to us (a smoker says "the link between cancer and smoking is unproven; I've seen the studies"). We may also attempt **undoing** "bad" behavior by displaying behavior designed to reverse the effects of the undesirable behavior ("Forgive me for hitting you! Let me grovel at your feet, and proclaim my undying love for you, and buy you flowers").

Freud saw the socialization process as different for girls. On the average, they resolve their complex less completely than boys. Boys are motivated to work through their complex by castration anxiety, but girls, lacking a penis, lack the appropriate motivation. Girls do identify with the same-sex parent and do so for roughly the same reasons as boys, but there are two reasons why identification is more difficult for them. First, girls experience ambivalence toward the mother. Pre-phallic love mixes with Electra hostility, because girls may blame mother for their "missing" penis and devalue her for not having a penis of her own. Second, girls' Electra complex turns them toward father in hopes of obtaining the missing penis from him, perhaps by having him all to themselves. Mother not only has too little with which girls might identify, she is also the object of her daughter's jealousy in relation to father. These difficulties in completing the process of identification led Freud to believe that females' superegos would develop less completely than males'. Further, fixation at the phallic stage accompanying

---

BOX 2.3   The Case of Little Hans

Freud's (1909/1963) case study of Little Hans provided the cornerstone for his ideas about the Oedipus complex. Hans was a 5-year-old boy who was afraid to go outdoors because of a *phobia*, an exaggerated fear that a horse would bite him. Freud agreed that Hans was afraid, but not of horses. For Freud, the origin of all phobias is fear that has its source in the unconscious. He believed Hans had resorted to the ego defense mechanism of **displacement**, finding a new target for some feelings, one that is less threatening than the original. The boy's fear had been redirected away from its original source, father, onto horses. Freud hypothesized "Hans was really a little Oedipus who wanted to have his father 'out of the way,' to get rid of him, so that he might be alone with his handsome mother and sleep with her" (1909/1963a, p. 148). He supported this hypothesis with the following observations:

1. Hans said he wanted to sleep in his mother's bed, caress her, be married to her, and have children "just like Daddy."
2. Hans experienced castration anxiety. His parents had told him that if he continued to play with his "widdler" (penis), it would be cut off. Hans saw that his younger sister had no "widdler."
3. Hans wanted his mother all to himself, was jealous of his father, and feared that his mother would prefer

father's bigger widdler, which was "like a horse's." Hans had dreamed of two giraffes, a "big" one and a "crumpled" one. Freud inferred that Hans had a death wish regarding his father. Hans' dream is a good example of *wish fulfillment* through dreams (Dement, 1976).
4. Hans showed greatest fear of horses with black muzzles, similar to his father's black mustache.
5. Horses were symbolic substitutes for Hans' father. When Hans saw a horse fall down, he sensed his own aggressive wish that father fall down and die, an idea too threatening to be consciously recognized.

Psychoanalysis helped remove Hans' phobia. Unconscious fears were brought into the open, and through the process of insight, the unconcious was made concious.

It should be noted that Freud's analysis of Little Hans was based on information provided by the boy's father who was biased in favor of Freud's theory. Several alternatives to Freud's interpretation of Little Hans have been suggested. Marsha Garrison (1978) observes that Hans seemed to fear castration more from his mother than from his father. Joseph Wolpe and Stanley Rachman (1960) concluded that Hans' "cure" was simply desensitization, a way to modify behavior that depends on repeated discussions of his obvious fear, horses.

incomplete resolution of the Electra complex ensures that women will have, on average, less *ego-strength*, the ability of the ego to successfully interact with reality on behalf of the id and inhibit id impulses until "safe" satisfactions are found. (Freud, 1977). Deficient ego-strength results because fixation ties up libidinal energy, leaving less of it available to the ego for use in its attempts to deal with reality.

Latency Stage

Freud's fourth stage of psychosexual development is notable for its absence of dominant erogenous zones and readily visible events or outcomes. As its name implies, **latency** is a quiet period between ages 6 and 12 during which children lay aside their attraction to parents and become sexually disinterested. Libidinous instincts previously seeking expression are reduced in intensity or more deeply buried in the unconscious through repression. They are transformed through **sublimation**, a process that reorients instinctual aims in new directions that are more personally and culturally acceptable. For example, an adolescent psychologically fixated at the anal stage of development might, unconsciously, become interested in sculpting with clay. This would be an acceptable substitute (sublimation) for earlier desires to play with feces.

Genital Stage

Freud's final stage of development is called **genital**, the stage of mature sexual love, including both feelings of lust and of affection directed toward another person, that begins at puberty. It differs from the first three (pregenital) stages. The difference revolves around **cathexes**, investments or attachments of the personality's libidinous energy either to real objects in the external world or to fantasized images in the inner world. Pregenital-stage cathexes are typified by the self-centered quality of maximizing pleasure from one's own body, supported by one-sided "me first" relationships with parents or peers. In contrast, genital-stage cathexes are directed less selfishly and more altruistically toward something other than oneself.

These externally directed energies are represented by two psychoanalytic ideals of mature, normal-personality functioning: to love and to work. Thus, loving and caring relationships with other people develop during adolescence and young adulthood, along with interests and activities related to productive, cooperative work within society. The successful pursuit of these goals contributes to the fulfillment of Eros' instinctual aim, preservation of self and species. Persons unable to make psychological attachments during their early years will show abnormal personality patterns during this later stage: immaturity, sexual deviation, and neurosis.

Another characteristic of this stage is the final resolution of the phallic-stage identification difficulties theorized for women. Supposedly, women who are able to mature successfully accept the absence of a penis and identify with the vagina. With this change to "femininity," the clitoris "should wholly or in part hand over its sensitivity, and at the same time its importance, to the vagina" (Freud,

TABLE 2.2   Summary of Freud's Stages of Psychosexual Development

Stages	Ages	Zones	Activities	Task
Pregenital (infantile)				
Oral	0–1/2	Mouth	Sucking Biting	Weaning
Anal	2–3/4	Anus	Expelling Retaining	Toilet training
Phallic	4–5/6	Penis Clitoris	Masturbating	Identifying
Latency	6–12/13		Repressing	Transforming
Genital	13+	Penis Vagina	Being sexually intimate Sublimating	Loving another Working

1901/1965, p. 118). This view supported Freud's belief in vaginal orgasm as the standard of mature, normal, sexual experience for women.

Table 2.2 summarizes the five stages of psychosexual development identified by Freud.

Freud and Sexism

Because of the different socialization processes for girls and boys, Freud believed girls are more dependent on the defense mechanism of repression. Further, because of their assumed weaker superego development, "for women the level of what is ethically normal is different from what it is in men" (Freud, 1925/1959, p. 196). The fact that this opinion is still very much alive and well is seen in the work of leading moral development theorist Lawrence Kohlberg, who allegedly also consigned women to a relatively low level of moral functioning (Kohlberg, 1981; Gilligan, 1982).

Elisabeth Young-Bruehl (1990) recently outlined the reasoning behind Freud's view of women in her book concerning "Freud on women." Her point was to show that Freud did not wish to confine women to the status of lesser men. Rather he wanted to account for his observation that women were "innately bisexual" (p. 22). Freud reasoned that to be sexual females had to be masculine. Thus, girls engage in sex like boys: they manipulate the clitoris just as boys stroke the penis. But at about adolescence they must come to accept their femininity and the lack of a penis by becoming sexually passive. Maturing girls must renounce clitorial stimulation and embrace the passive sexual mode: penis in vagina. By this "logic," females are first masculine and then feminine, therefore, bisexual. In transition from masculine (clitorial pleasure) to feminine (vaginal pleasure), females must repress their sexuality. In turn, the switch accounts for their greater

---

BOX 2.2 Revisited   Freud's Answers to the
Preliminary Self-Test

Following the review of Freud's basic concepts, you may find it interesting to compare your assumptions about personality with those of Freud. Determine how closely your answers in Box 2.2 agree with what Freud might have indicated and compare your results with those of other students in class.

1. My basic personality is the same today as when I was about 5 years old.
   TRUE: "The child is father to the man."

2. I have little knowledge of my real personality or its development.
   TRUE: Personality is largely unconscious, similar to an iceberg submerged in water.

3. I choose to lead my life in a self-directed manner.
   FALSE: We are not in control of our own fates. "Man is not master in his own house."

4. My basic motivations are sex and aggression.
   TRUE: Human behavior is governed by the two basic instincts of life (generalized "sexual" pleasure) and death (destructiveness).

5. Many of my behaviors are irrational, in that I repeatedly do things that make little logical sense.
   TRUE: People are dominated by their instincts and emotions, not by logic and intellect, and they compulsively relive their past.

6. I have had few inner conflicts in my life.
   FALSE: Psychological conflict is a fact of life. Only the dead have no conflicts.

7. I am afraid to know my true self, and I keep unpleasant aspects of my personalty hidden from myself.
   TRUE: Personality is a complicated system of psychological avoidance and defense, triggered by feelings of anxiety.

8. As a child, I had sexual wishes and feelings toward my opposite-sex parent.
   TRUE: Inevitably, all sons live through the Oedipus complex of "killing" father and "marrying" mother, and all daughters live through the Electra complex, "wanting" father.

9. Women and men are psychological equals.
   FALSE: Women are "failed men" and differ from men in their weaker moral development.

10. The best way for me to change my personality is to enter long-term therapy with a trained expert who will provide insight into my early childhood experiences.
    TRUE: There is nothing better than psychoanalysis for making conscious that which is unconscious, thereby minimizing personality conflicts and problems.

---

tendency to neurosis. Thus, concluded Young-Bruehl, the negative traits Freud assigned to females arose out of the necessary transition from masculinity to femininity dictated by their anatomy, not to female inferiority per se. However, a reviewer of Young-Bruehl's book declared that "Her unconvincing introduction to this chronologically organized anthology of Freud's essays, case material and letters reads like an apology" (Stuttaford, 1990, p. 54). Indeed, Young-Bruehl merely reiterates Freud's point of view, offering nothing new. She does not effectively rebut critics of Freud on women; she simply offers a plea for a different interpretation.

If Freud were alive today, he would almost surely not retreat from his position on women. His final pronouncement on the subject was that he refused "to be deflected from [my conclusions about women] by the denials of the feminists, who are anxious to force us to regard the two sexes as completely equal in position and worth" (1925/1959, p. 197).

Evaluation

Contributions

To talk of unconscious aspects of personality is one thing; to observe or measure such phenomena is quite another. How can psychologists possibly get at something that, by definition, is not directly available to consciousness? Freud suggested a number of avenues to the unconscious: free association, slips of the tongue, certain events occurring during psychoanalytic therapy, waking fantasy, and interpretation of dreams.

Free Association
Freud's primary assessment technique for getting at the unconscious was **free association** in which the person adopts a mental orientation that allows ideas, images, memories, and feelings to flow spontaneously, without external guidance or suppression. It allows patients to experience **catharsis**, a process by which inner feelings are openly expressed in words or behaviors. If one idea—apple—suggests an associated idea—worms—one is free to pursue thoughts about worms. The fundamental rule of free association is to allow expression of anything and everything that comes to mind, no matter how senseless, illogical, trivial, embarrassing, unpleasant, or absurd it may seem. Free association is important because it provided Freud with clues about the person's unconscious.

Interpretation of Dreams
According to Freud (1900/1958), dreams are "the royal road to . . . the unconscious . . ." (p. 608). It is not simply dreams in and of themselves that are important, but their interpretation. Freud believed that the **manifest content** of dreams, what the dreamer remembers about the dream when awakened, is deceptive and should not be taken at face value. Dreams originate in unconscious, primary processes of the id. Id forces gain strength during sleep, when conscious suppression is less than during wakefulness. Through working in dreams, the ego lessens the threat of id's instinctual impulses and images clearly revealing themselves by modifying and distorting them. It uses such mechanisms as censorship, symbolic substitution, and defensive elaboration. Consequently, the true content of dreams is sel-

dom what it appears to be on the surface; everything is in disguise and mysterious. Skilled interpretation is required to get at **latent content**, the underlying meaning of each dream.

Freud assumed that every dream has a meaning that can be interpreted either symbolically or through decoding. Symbolic interpretation focuses on the dream as a whole and seeks to replace disguised manifest content with some reasonable latent parallel. For example, in a biblical account from Genesis, a Pharaoh dreamed of seven plump ears of corn on a single stalk, followed by seven diseased ears that devoured the first seven. Joseph offered a symbolic interpretation of this perplexing dream: the ears of corn symbolically represented seven future years of good harvest for Egypt, followed by seven years of famine.

A **dream symbol** is dream content that represents some person, thing, or activity involved in unconscious processes. Freud agreed that symbols can sometimes have common meanings for people in general. Table 2.3 illustrates this point. However, his stronger belief was that symbols are more highly personal than universal. All symbols need to be interpreted individually, because they are determined by unconscious forces in the individual's own personality: "The same piece of content may conceal a different meaning when it occurs in various people or in various contexts" (Freud, 1900/1958, p. 105).

Typically Freud preferred a decoding method of dream interpretation in which each part of the dream is analyzed separately from the others. Correct analysis deciphers all dream elements, including symbols, that are then put together to uncover each dream's hidden meaning. The final result is certain to involve the discovery of some wish-fulfillment for the dreamer, which Freud saw as the primary purpose of dreaming (Dement, 1976). Other functions served by dreams include guarding sleep (keeping the dreamer from waking), releasing emotional energy, lessening the shock of traumatic events, and aiding problem-solving.

TABLE 2.3   Some Freudian Dream Symbols

Dream contents	Symbolic meanings
Knife, umbrella, snake	Penis
Box, oven, ship	Uterus
Room, table with food	Woman
Staircase, ladder	Sexual intercourse
Water	Birth, mother
Baldness, tooth removal	Castration
Left (direction)	Crime, sexual deviation
Children playing	Masturbation
Fire	Bed-wetting
Robber	Father
Falling	Anxiety

Psychoanalysis

Free association quickly became the basic technique of Freud's "talking treatment" (Breuer & Freud, 1895/1950). As a treatment technique, **psychoanalysis** refers to Freud's systematic procedures for providing a patient with the insight necessary to rid the personality of its neurotic conflicts. The recall of childhood experiences is central to these procedures especially involving memories of sex and aggression in relation to one's parents. Through **insight**, personally unacceptable and socially "taboo" experiences buried in the person's unconscious can be made conscious.

Free association substituted for Freud's earlier use of hypnosis as a treatment technique. Unlike the supposedly unconscious "trance" state traditionally linked to hypnosis, free association enabled patients to consciously recall everything they said. One reason Freud decided to use a couch in psychoanalysis was that it helps patients settle into the mental state needed for effective free association. Use of the couch led patients to adopt a passive posture and relaxed attitude for experiencing a more preconscious state of fantasy than usually occurs during normal consciousness. Freud sat behind his patients, away from their direct view, partly to minimize his influence on their psychological explorations. He wanted to be like "a neutral, blank screen," so that his patients would feel free to verbalize their associations without looking for his facial reactions or fearing criticism and disapproval.

Eventually, patients would project their unconscious images onto Freud, "the mirror." They would also display **transference** relating to the psychoanalyst as if he were some other person from their past with whom they were continuing to experience psychological conflict. The origin of these unrealistic transformations is the patient's unconscious. It is as if the patient needs to remake the analyst in the image of the patient's father, mother, or some other significant person in order to work through the psychological fixations of childhood. Use of the couch partly contributed to transference by fostering the patient's dependent, child-like relationship with the psychoanalyst, who quickly becomes a superior parent-expert. **Countertransference** occurs when analysts project their own unconscious needs onto their patients.

A Theory of Personality, a Philosophy about Human Nature

Freud summarized his contributions to psychology in a brief, recorded statement, the year before he died (Lawrence, 1938):

> *I started my professional activity as a neurologist trying to bring relief to my neurotic patients. Under the influence of an older friend, and by my own efforts, I discovered some important new facts about the unconscious in psychic life, the role of instinctual urges, and so on. . . . I had to pay handily for this bit of good luck. People did not believe in my facts and thought my theories unsavory. Resistance was strong. . . . In the end I succeeded in acquiring . . . an international psychoanalytic association. But the struggle is not yet over.*

Freud's statement identifies two of his major contributions to psychology: a theory of personality and a philosophy of human nature.

To appreciate Freud's contributions to personality theory you need only recall his basic theoretical concepts of unconscious motivation in personality, the three-part structure of personality, the five psychosexual stages of personality development, the Oedipus complex, defense mechanisms, and the importance of early childhood experiences. One area where his ideas had truly great impact was providing inspiration for much creative thinking during the first half of the 20th century. As you will see, several theorists considered in this book were strongly influenced by him. Other theorists who have disagreed sharply with classic psychoanalytic thinking have nevertheless had to reckon with Freud's ideas.

Freud's summary statement refers indirectly to a second contribution: a philosophy of human nature. Freud "had to pay" for his discovery of "important new facts." The pessimistic picture he painted of human nature clashed with the romanticized ideals of religion, free will, and scientific rationality popular in his time. In the 19th century, Darwin's theory of evolution had removed humans from a category of special creation to a species with a line of development no different from that of related creatures. Then, in the 20th century, Freud removed humans from the psychological center of their own personal universe to a sphere in which unconscious forces dominated over illusions of personal freedom and rational choice. No wonder public resistance was high. Freud was telling people what they needed to hear, but refused to listen to.

Supporting Evidence

Empirical support for Freud's ideas has accumulated over the years, although it has often been qualified. J. McVicker Hunt (1979) assessed evidence from different streams of investigation flowing from Freud's ideas. He found that the studies "lent support" to Freud's general proposition about "the special importance of early experience" (p. 119), but not to the specific psychosexual experiences hypothesized by Freud. Salvatore Maddi (1968) reviewed empirical studies and concluded that there was qualified support for two Freudian concepts. First, while not all behavior is defensive, the general concept of ego defense is "tenable," supported by a "rather convincing" number of studies related to repression. Second, "there is more evidence of castration anxiety among men than women" (p. 392).

Lloyd Silverman (1976) summarized two 10-year research programs bearing on specific Freudian concepts. Results of these independent, laboratory studies support the relationship between certain types of abnormal behavior and certain types of unconscious conflict over libidinal and aggressive wishes. One series of studies involved 39 groups, some comprised of stutterers, others of depressives, homosexuals, or schizophrenics. Subjects were asked to view flickers of light through the eyepiece of a *tachistoscope*, a machine that exposes visual stimuli for fractions of a second. Visual information relevant to the participants' psychological conflicts was presented to subjects subliminally, below their level of conscious awareness (Dixon, 1971). Psychoanalytic theory (PT) predicts that information relevant to a particular fixation or inner conflict would affect persons with that fixation/conflict, but information related to other kinds of fixations/conflicts would have no effect on them. The prediction was generally confirmed. Persons with oral-aggressive conflicts were stirred up by the message "Cannibal eats person" but not by "Murderer stabs victim." Persons with oral-receptive conflicts showed decreased anxiety with the wishful message "Mommy and I are one" but not with "I am losing Mommy."

A number of research studies on castration anxiety in men and penis envy in women have been reported. Blum (1949, 1950, 1962) assessed psychosexual fantasies in college students who were asked to tell stories to the Blacky Test, a series of cartoon pictures about a dog named Blacky. In the 1949 study, differences in test responses of 119 men and 90 women agreed with "some aspects" of PT. In the 1962 study, men who were high and low in castration conflict told contrasting stories in response to a picture of Blacky looking on as a knife falls toward sibling Tippy's tail. One example of a "low castration anxiety" response is as follows:

> *Tippy, Blacky's little brother, is about to have his tail chopped off unknowingly. Blacky is about to bark and warn him of his danger. Physically there is nothing he can actually do, but he will also try to push him away from the block. (p. 135)*

Compare the preceding with the following example of a "strong castration anxiety" response:

> *Blacky doesn't like the looks of this at all, and he's very conscious of his big black tail out behind him. . . . The expression on Tippy's face is worried, and Blacky's beginning to think that way. (p. 135)*

In a study by Hall and Van de Castle (1965), three groups of college students, 20 men and 20 women per group, recorded their dreams as part of a class project. All of the 1,909 dreams were scored by two judges to determine the presence of castration anxiety (CA), castration wishes (CW), and penis envy (PE). The majority of male dreamers had higher CA scores, and the majority of female dreamers had higher CW and PE scores. Zero CA scores were observed for 50 percent of the women but only 13 percent of the men. Findings were replicated using an additional sample of men aged 37–54, suggesting a stable rate of castration anxiety from young adulthood to middle age. Nevertheless, caution should be exercised. Hall and Van de Castle's research has been severely criticized because of the procedure they used and because more efficient explanations of their results may be provided by non-Freudian theories (Daly & Wilson, 1990).

Raskin and Shaw (1988) reported research outcomes that could be interpreted as evidence for Freud's narcissistic or oral stage. People fixated at this stage might continue to be self-centered just as they were during infancy. In confirmation of that possibility, subjects whose tape-recorded monologues reflected heavy use of first person singular pronouns ("I" and "me") scored high on a narcissism test of tendency to be self-centered and self-absorbed.

Much of the research has attempted to support the existence of Freud's most central idea, the unconscious. Freud found evidence for the existence of the unconscious in **slips of the tongue**, verbal errors that seem to replace neutral words with ones that supposedly emanate from the unconscious. However, researcher Michael Motley (1985; 1987), believes that most such slips are due to the misfirings of the brain and its verbal mechanisms. For example, consider the following scenario: young man approaches attractive woman with whom he has plans to spend the evening and exclaims, "I'll pick you up at sex. . . . I mean six!" According to Motley, the most efficient and verifiable way to explain this error is in terms of word retrieval mechanisms. The words "six" and "sex" share two of three letters, and are thus probably stored in the same neural network. Therefore, the young man's brain "went looking for" the word "six," but "found" "sex" instead, because their structural near-identity caused them to be stored "close to" one another.

Motley believes, however, that notions about the unconscious are not entirely without merit. In fact, his work has shown that sometimes the unconscious actually may rear its ugly head, much to our embarrassment. In one of his studies, he and his colleagues tested three groups of college men. One group was fitted with electrodes and warned that they would receive an electric shock at some point in the experiment. A second group performed in the presence of a provocatively dressed female experimenter. Both groups and some control subjects were asked to speak a set of word pairs designed to elicit verbal foul-ups that Freud would interpret as spill-over from the unconscious. Males threatened with electric shock tended to say "damn shock" for "sham dock" and "cursed wattage" for "worst cottage" rather than commit sexual slips. The group in the presence of the female experimenter tended to make mistakes like "fast passion" for "past fashion" and "nude breasts" for "brood nests." Control subjects were no more likely to make sexual than electricity-related slips. Thus, when the environment contains cues relating to certain motivations that we tend to harbor in our unconscious minds, words that represent these forbidden motivations may pop out.

More generally, it can now be asserted that there is an unconscious (see *American Psychologist*, June, 1992). That unconscious, however, may not be the analytic, manipulative, and smart entity that Freud assumed. Instead, it may be simple, straightforward, and unanalytical compared to consciousness (Greenwald, 1992).

Limitations

The Uncertain Status of Psychoanalytic Theory (PT)
Freud's view of psychoanalytic theory (PT) as "a new science" may have been partly justified during psychology's youth at the turn of the century. It certainly was Freud's intent to make PT the basis of a scientific psychology that would integrate, once and for all, the psychological and physical events of mind and body. However, after three-quarters of a century, the scientific potential of PT has not been realized, despite occasionally supportive research and attempts to integrate PT with other areas of psychology such as learning (Dollard & Miller, 1950), development (Wolff, 1960), and cognition (G. Klein, 1970). Because of the problems to be considered next, PT cannot be considered a fully scientific theory.

As you have seen, there is considerable, qualified support for some of Freud's ideas, but it is not great considering the large number of researchers who have tried for so many years to confirm his concepts. One reason is that the concepts of PT, even when clearly defined, are not open to direct observation (Stanovich, 1989; Daly & Wilson, 1990). Thus, they are hard to test scientifically. How is a researcher to quantify energy that is "psychological" or get at events that are "unconscious" and "repressed"? Unfortunately, the answer is "indirectly, uncertainly, and often, not at all."

Again, considering the number of researchers who have for so long attempted to support PT, it has shown little ability to predict behavior. Psychoanalytic concepts work best when applied backward, accounting for an individual's past behavior after the facts have been gathered (Stanovich, 1989). They seldom indicate the person's future behavior.

The primary setting for gathering data relevant to PT has been the clinic, not the laboratory. In the clinic, events that are irrelevant to diagnosis and treatment act on patients and analysts but cannot be controlled: interruptions, chance moods of patient and analyst, temporary health status of both, events in the setting (baby crying next door), and unknown events occurring just before the session (a lover's quarrel). One of Freud's patients, a psychiatrist, wrote that during treatment sessions Freud's dog was "sitting quietly . . . at the foot of the bed . . . a big chow" (Wortis, 1954, p. 23). Obviously, it did not occur to Freud that the presence of this possibly threatening, at least distracting, animal may have affected his patient's thoughts, verbalizations, and behaviors, and, in turn, Freud's interpretations. If Freud thought this patient's discomfort was due to touching on sensitive, unconscious material, he might have been incorrect.

The analyst, as data gatherer, is a potential determinant of the behavior, not just an observer. Analysts influence the very processes they wish to observe objectively (Joseph, 1980). Attempts have been made to overcome this limitation by requiring analysts to undergo psychoanalytic treatment, so that they may better understand their own personalities and influences on patients. However, total objectivity in human relationships is never fully achieved.

The typical research method of PT is the case study. You will recall the limitations of this procedure outlined in Chapter 1. Aside from these problems, in PT, emphasis is placed on a particular person's early development, responses to interviews and tests, and personal ideas, feelings, and experiences. Much of what the analyst values in this clinical work is not assessable in any objective or reliable way (Stanovich, 1989). Because the individual's experiences are so private, he or she may have difficulty communicating them or be reluctant to do so. In turn, these events are interpreted by yet another individual, the psychoanalyst, who, though trained, is still subject to limitations in ability to make interpretations. In all cases, the important reality is subjective rather than objective and verifiable.

Samples of subjects used by Freud and other psychoanalysts as the basis of their observations are unrepresentative of people in general. For example, persons seen in clinical settings typically are unrepresentative precisely because, unlike most people, they have serious problems requiring treatment. Further, Freud's major case studies were of persons seen in Victorian Vienna (probably 100 percent) between the years 1889 and 1900 (50 percent) who showed abnormal behaviors (50 percent hysterical neuroses; Brody, 1970). This sample was heavily biased in favor of upper-class (100 percent) women (67 percent) between the ages of 18 and 20 (75 percent) who were single (75 percent). Such a selective sampling biased the theory and calls into question the generalizability of Freud's observations.

Freud's ideas relied heavily on experiences related to early childhood development: psychosexual stages, Oedipus and Electra complexes, castration anxiety, penis envy, real or fantasized sexual seductions, and so on. However, Freud actually had few patients who were children (Daly & Wilson, 1990). He obtained most of his information about children through everyday experience, reading, his own recollections of his childhood, and the recollections of adult patients who were well aware of Freud's belief in the sexual origins of maladaptive behavior and just as subject to memory distortion as anyone.

A number of Freud's assumptions about children have been called into question by later research (Daly & Wilson, 1990). In two separate studies, only 50 percent of children between 4 and 6 years of age showed knowledge of genital sex differences, and those who did showed little evidence of emotional trauma (Conn & Kanner, 1947; Katcher, 1955). According to Kohlberg (1966), a more plausible alternative to castration anxiety is the general childhood fear of bodily injury, not the specific fear of losing the sex organ. Social-learning explanations involving sex roles also have offered supportable alternatives to Freud's overemphasis on physical anatomy as the basis of sex differences (Rohrbaugh, 1979). Referring to a research example of castration anxiety in dreams, Hall and Van de Castle (1965) recognized explanations other than penis envy. For example, sex-role expectations can account for women dreaming of weddings and babies more often than men.

Finally, the very foundation of psychoanalytic theory has been attacked (Daly & Wilson, 1990). Critic Jeffrey Masson (1984) was fired from his post as projects director of the Sigmund Freud Archives because of his assault on PT. With the reluctant cooperation of Freud's daughter Anna, Masson tracked down some of Freud's lost correspondence, principally his letters to Fliess. Comparing these letters with an 1896 lecture to the Society for Psychiatry and Neurology in Vienna led to an "alarming discovery" (the lecture, "The Aetiology of Hysteria," is reprinted in its entirety by Masson, 1984). On April 21, 1896 Freud confidently presented his seduction thesis, his belief that his early female patients actually had been sexually molested by their fathers, as they claimed, and these traumas were the source of their adult hysterical neuroses. Scarcely a year and a half later, he wrote Fleiss that he had abandoned the seduction thesis of the 1896 lecture. Among his reasons for the change was ". . . in all cases, the father, not excluding my own, had to be accused of being perverse . . ." (Masson, 1984, p. 108). He went on to explain that the frequency of such "perversion" would have to be improbably high to account for all the observed cases of hysteria. Thus Freud asserted that these early patients had fantasized the alleged molestations. In turn, these fantasies were supposedly manifestations of "lust for the father" that they had submerged into their unconscious minds.

Charles Darwin

If Masson's interpretations are correct, Freud may be guilty of intellectual underhandedness and submission to fear of censure by colleagues (his 1896 "seduction" lecture was received in silence and immediately condemned). He may also be accused of callous insensitivity to the suffering of untold millions of sexually abused children. On the theoretical side, if Masson is right, Freud's theory may be wrong. The theory is based in large part on the idea that young children are attracted to the parent of the opposite sex and desire to possess that parent sexually. The "fantasies" supposedly confirm this desire and, according to Freud's theory, the remainder of children's psychological development rests largely on the existence of the alleged desire. If the molestations are real, the fantasy notion vanishes and, along with it, support for the claim that children desire their parents sexually. Remove that claim and Freud's entire theoretical structure is in danger of tumbling down.

However, Masson must be considered with caution. He acknowledges that Anna Freud believed that her father had an honest change of heart and that most psychoanalysts agree with her. While the comparison between the 1896 lecture and the 1897 letter to Fleiss is provocative, it does not prove anything. It is not necessarily the case that Freud, being fearful of disapproving colleagues and unable to accept that fathers—even his own—are perverse, abandoned the "truth" about sexual molestation and literally adopted a fantasy upon which to base his theory. Instead he may have done what good theorists often do: changed his mind after reflection and consideration of new evidence.

Conclusion

Despite the limitations of PT as a scientific theory, Freud's genius is commonly accepted. No history of psychology could be written "in the next three hundred years" without mentioning this "man with the attributes of greatness" (Boring, 1957, p. 706). He was the right person at the right time, a synthesizer with strong leadership ability. As a psychological detective, he left no stone unturned and no thread unraveled in arriving at analytic conclusions of certainty to himself. He was a thorough observer of his own experience and that of his Victorian community. His professional integrity led him to pursue original and unpopular ideas even when under harsh, personal attack by colleagues. He not only identified important psychological causes of abnormal behavior arising during childhood, he was the leader in showing how abnormal behaviors could be systematically changed.

Freud's vast writings are still being mined to discover new fuel for thought. For example, Freud was ahead of his time with regard to attitudes toward homosexuals. Years ago he wrote "We surely ought not to forget that . . . the sensual love of a man for a man was not only tolerated by a people so far our superiors in cultivation as were the Greeks, but was actually entrusted by them with important social functions" (quoted in Young-Breuhl, 1990 p. 14). Although he has been gone for more than fifty years, Freud still has much to teach us.

Freud was one of the most influential thinkers of the late 19th and early 20th centuries, along with Charles Darwin and Albert Einstein. The theoretical ideas he developed have had major impact in the fields of psychiatry, social work,

Albert Einstein

psychology, literature, and history. His ideas have had a direct impact on each and every one of us, by increasing our awareness of childhood influences on our behavior and our understanding of our own expressions of unconscious and irrational behavior.

Summary Points

1. Freud was born (1856) of Jewish parents in the Germanic area of Moravia. He made a number of notable discoveries while a young medical student. *Interpretation of Dreams* (1900) set the tone for later break-through concepts, such as libido. Freud was banished from Vienna by the Nazis and died in London of cancer in 1939.

2. Freud pictured humans as under the control of instincts that fall into two categories: Eros and Thanatos. Consistent with this orientation, he posed a primitive first structure of personality, id, that operates according to the pleasure principle and the primary process. The ego holds the id in check with its reality principle and secondary process. The superego operates according to the morality principle and comes into existence through the process of introjection.

3. The oral stage involves pleasure from ingesting food that stimulates the mouth area. Fixation can lead to either oral-receptive or oral-aggressive adult personality types. During the anal stage, pleasure is achieved by dispelling the feces. Harsh toilet training can produce anal-retentive or anal-expulsive adult personality types.

4. During the phallic stages, boys lust after their mothers. Fear of their fathers takes the form of castration anxiety. They resolve their Oedipal complexes by identifying with their fathers, a process that leads to superego development if it succeeds and over-use of defense mechanisms as well as adult promiscuity or feminization if it fails.

5. Girls lust after their fathers and hate their mothers; but a girl's lack of castration anxiety, due to lack of a penis (penis envy), makes resolution of her Electra complex difficult. As a result she may have lowered ego strength and superego development relative to males. An apologist for Freud contends that he did not intend to degrade women; the negative traits he attributes to them are merely his attempt to explain their personalities.

6. The latency stage involves no focal, genital area, but entails the process of sublimation. The genital stage involves cathexes that are more altruistic and less self-centered than earlier ones. Freud's psychoanalytic free association technique depended on use of a couch that induced patients to cathartically pursue insight. It replaced hypnosis and involved transference and countertransference. Freud examined dreams for both manifest and latent content.

7. Freud felt people are controlled from within, by primitive, unconscious forces, a position that challenged popular notions. Some research results that support Freud include evidence for the importance of early experience, ego defense, oral aggressive and oral receptive types, castration anxiety in men but not women, narcissistic tendencies, and the operation of the unconscious when cued by the environment.

8. Problems with his psychoanalytic theory include concepts that are difficult to measure, relatively low predictive validity, use of uncontrolled clinical settings, problems because the analyst/observer participates in observations, over-reliance on case studies, sampling bias, and limited experience with children.

9. Perhaps the strongest challenge to Freud's ideas in recent years was served up by Masson, who accused Freud of abandoning an earlier seduction theory in favor of a fantasy position. If Masson is correct, Freud wrote off real sexual abuse as a fantasy and, therefore, his theory was founded on a fantasy of his own making.

10. Freud has been described as one of the greats of this century. His brave challenge to the Victorian period in which he theorized led to the timeless discoveries relating to the unconscious and early childhood. Because Freud's writings are so vast, he may yet teach us more.

Essay/Critical Thinking Questions

1. What was it about the era in which Freud lived that so shaped his point of view?

2. Freud wrote of the instincts as if they were present at birth, and also writes of such as the Oedipal and Electra complexes as if we are all predisposed to these conditions from birth. What's the problem with suggesting that these factors are present at birth?

3. Hysterical neuroses are rather strange. Come up with two that are not discussed in the text and specify an origin for each.

4. There are descriptions of the oral-receptive and oral-aggressive adult types in the text. Expand on the text and provide a more complete description of these types; this could involve coming up with additional traits that are implied by the text.

5. The apologists for Freud's view of women have failed to be convincing. Try to support the argument that Freud's view of women really was not a condemnation of them.

6. "Sublimation" is an interesting concept. Invent some unacceptable needs or desires on the part of some hypothetical people and indicate how they might sublimate those needs or desires.

7. Free association is the basis of Freud's psychoanalysis. What other forms might it take, similar to but not identical to those described in the text.

8. Based on Freud's point of view, analyze a dream that you have had recently (or one someone has told you about).

9. Sketch a scenario in which an analyst displays countertransference.

10. What is a Freudian contribution, possibly implied by the text, but not actually covered in it, that might be influential in years to come.

3

A STEP BEYOND FREUD AND BACK INTO THE PAST: JUNG

- Did you inherit your mind?
- Are you an introvert or an extravert?
- Where is the "self" located?
- Are your dreams related to one another?
- How do UFO reports reveal the workings of the unconscious?

On the occasion of his former mentor's death, Carl Jung described Freud's work as "surely the boldest attempt ever made . . . to master the riddle of the unconscious psyche. For us young psychiatrists, it was a source of enlightenment . . ." (quoted in Wehr, 1989, p. 29). These words were written despite the fact that Freud's view of Jung had changed from that of a loving father to one of a betrayed patriarch. In the early years of their collaboration, Freud pleaded with Jung, "My dear Jung, promise me never to abandon the sexual theory. That is the most essential thing of all. You see, we must make a dogma of it, an unshakable bulwark" (p. 34). Later he wrote, to his "number one man, the 'crown prince' " (p. 34): "I therefore don once more my hornrimmed paternal spectacles and warn my dear son to keep a cool head. . . . I also shake my wise gray locks . . . and think: Well, that is how the young folks are; they really enjoy things only when they need not drag us along with them . . . " (p. 36). But, unfortunately for Freud, Jung could not endorse dogma nor could he drag along someone else's theoretical baggage. He had his own ideas including a conception of an unconscious that is dominated by the ancestral past of humans, not sexuality however broadly defined. It was the beginning of the end when Jung's interest in paranormal phenomena led him to declare his "father" wrong. While in Freud's presence, Jung

Carl Jung

had a curious sensation in his diaphragm which was followed by a loud "detonation" in a nearby bookcase. When he labeled the experience a "catalytic exteriorization phenomenon" and Freud responded "sheer bosh," Jung exclaimed, "You are mistaken Herr Professor" (p. 35). Then Jung proceeded to add insult to injury by successfully predicting a second "detonation."

By 1913, such insubordination had become too much for Freud. He wrote Jung suggesting "that we give up our private relationship altogether. I lose nothing by this, since . . . I have been bound to you only by the thin thread of . . . previously experienced disappointments. . . . Assume complete freedom and spare me the supposed 'duties of friendship' " (p. 39). The thread had indeed worn thin, as Jung wondered whether he was ever really a student of Freud. Thereafter, he went his own way.

Jung, the Person

Carl Gustav Jung (1875–1961) was born in Kesswil, Switzerland, the son of a minister and the grandson of a professor and a clergyman (Wehr, 1989). One of those grandfathers was rumored to be the bastard son of Goethe, the famed German author of *Faust*, a play about a magician who sold his soul to the devil in return for magic powers (Lebowitz, 1990). Jung nurtured this rumor because he liked to view himself as a person with ties to mysticism.

As a boy, he experienced numerous "visions" and marveled at the mysteries around him. He recalled a dark and dreary funeral during which men in black clerical gowns lowered a coffin into a deep hole and repeated the phrase "Lord Jesus" over and over. This phrase scared him thereafter. He called the experience a trauma. Another event, a recurrent dream, haunted Jung for years. It also involved a dark hole.

> *I ran forward and peered into it . . . I saw a stone stairway. . . . At the bottom was a doorway . . . closed off by a green curtain. . . . I pushed it aside [and] saw a rectangular chamber . . . a red carpet ran from the entrance to a low platform. On this platform stood a . . . golden throne. . . . something was standing on it. . . . It was a huge thing, reaching almost to the ceiling . . . it was made of skin and flesh, and on the top was something like a rounded head with no face and no hair. On the very top of the head was a single eye, gazing motionlessly upward. (Wehr, 1989, p. 13)*

Jung could still recall this dream even in his later years. One can only wonder whether the obvious phallic symbolism of this dream so intrigued Jung that it led him to Freud's door.

Jung spent much of his youth by himself, in "extreme loneliness," talking out his innermost thoughts to a small mannequin he had carved and secreted away under the floorboards of the family's "forbidden attic."

> *I am a solitary, because I know things and must hint at things which other people do not know, and usually do not even want to know (Jung, 1963, p. 42). Loneliness does not come from having no people about one, but from being unable to communicate the things that seem important to oneself, or from holding certain views which others find inadmissible. (p. 356)*

Following medical training at the University of Basel, Jung became aware of Freud's work and began to defend him from critics (Wehr, 1989). When Jung's *Studies in Word Association* was published in 1905, he sent a copy to Freud, only to be informed that the famous psychoanalyst had, "out of impatience," already acquired a copy. Freud's blunt message arrived in April of 1906. Seven years later, the two had exchanged 350 letters. Freud had looked on Jung as heir apparent to the psychoanalytic throne. Jung's presence at Freud's side would assure an intolerant world that psychoanalysis was not a Jewish movement. When Freud's disappointment with Jung's rejection of the sexual theory ended their relationship, Jung suffered what would now be called a mid-life crisis. Visions of apocalypse overwhelmed him. "I saw a monstrous flood covering all the northern low-lying lands between the North Sea and the Alps. . . . I realized that a frightful catastrophe was in progress. I saw the mighty yellow waves, the floating rubble of civilization, and the drowned bodies of uncounted thousands. Then the whole sea turned to blood" (Wehr, 1989, p. 41). That was October 1913. The next year, World War I broke out.

That premonition must have shaken Jung. It was followed by, in his words, a struggle with the "building blocks of psychosis" (p. 44). The turmoil within him would not cease. His mind was flooded with images and fantasies, many of them containing mythological symbols and figures. One day when gripped with the feeling that he was in the "land of the dead" Jung glimpsed two human forms (p. 45). One was an elderly sage "Elijah" and the other was a blind beauty who called herself "Salome." It was the beginning of his unique conception of the unconscious. He would later transform these Biblical figures into important components of the collective unconscious, "wise old man" and a representation of womanhood.

Jung's View of the Person

Jung and Freud did share ideas and even theoretical concepts. Like Freud, Jung talked about the psyche, ego, consciousness, and unconsciousness. Jung's theory included analogies to id and "insight." Their theories even share some of the same shortcomings. But the common ground ended there. Although they used the same terms, Jung's definitions were different from Freud's. Further, Jung offered alternate explanations for "penis envy" and viewed dream content quite differently than Freud. Jung's conception of the impact that mothers and fathers have on their children was markedly different. Finally, Jung's rejection of Freud's sexualism guaranteed that his theory would be fundamentally different.

Jung's orientation to people was different not only from Freud's, but also that of other theorists covered in this book. There are some ironies here. Freud was more controlling as a therapist. In contrast, Jung sometimes participated in therapy sessions as an equal partner with the patient. Freud never did, but he would allow patients to "free associate." By comparison, Jung frequently offered less freedom; association was less free and more structured. Jung would often suggest what patients should think and talk about.

Jung's greater trust in people's ability to contribute to their own "cure" was evidenced in his willingness to suggest that they "self-analyze." His greater trust in other points of view was reflected in his occasional use of other people's ideas and methods. Further, he felt that people's minds were not limited by the size of their craniums. A person's mind can expand beyond his or her skull into the mental space of other people. He believed that there is *connectedness* between the minds of people. It is seen in parapsychological phenomena such as ESP. Jung thought that minds could communicate with other minds. In addition, as seen in Jung's claims to have anticipated "detonations," minds can communicate with non-human entities. Because of these beliefs, Jung was labeled a "mystic," which lowered his status among some of his colleagues, but raised it among much of the public who became aware of his thinking.

Jung anticipated other theorists' ideas about people when he abandoned Freud's rather pessimistic conception of humans in favor of a refreshingly optimistic position. He believed that people are capable of being more than they are. In fact, to Jung, one of the major tasks of life is to develop the "self" so that it acknowledges all aspects of the psyche. In this developmental process people not only are able to become all they potentially can be. In addition, they can relate more completely to others and to realms of experience that are beyond our restricted and meager physical reality.

He also believed that humans are multifaceted beings who, if they wish to be fully functioning, have to accept all aspects of themselves, the bad as well as the good. We have to reconcile the opposing forces in our psyches. In fact, the very essence of human mentality is the clash of opposites. Jung believed that for every facet of our mental life there is an opposing aspect. In every male there is femaleness; in every female there is maleness. Consciousness opposes unconsciousness and we all have a shadowy side that opposes our good side. A nonviolent person will dream of violence; a chaste person will dream of sexual wantonness. If we acknowledge these opposing forces and bring them into communication with one another, we can become fulfilled, complete persons.

Basic Concepts: Jung

Consciousness and Unconsciousness

For Jung, unconsciousness refers to two distinct entities. His **personal unconscious** which "is made up essentially of contents [that] have at one time been conscious but which have disappeared from consciousness through having been forgotten or repressed . . ." did resemble Freud's unconscious (Jung, 1959a, p. 42). As with the Freudian unconscious, each individual's personal unconscious is unique to him or her. Jung also wrote of "complexes" and located them in the personal unconscious. However, he devoted a lion's share of his attention to the **collective unconscious**, a storehouse of ancestral experiences dating to the dawn of humankind and common to all humans. This unconscious belongs to the collective, not just to a single person. It has "never been in consciousness, and therefore [has] never been individually acquired, but owe[s its] existence exclusively to heredity" (p. 42).

Jung's conception of the collective unconscious crystallized as he pursued scholarly interests in a variety of fields: archeology, history, religion, mythology, and even alchemy, a now discredited precursor of chemical science that was prevalent during the Middle Ages. In addition, he dabbled in anthropology, traveling to the United States to investigate artifacts of Native Americans. During these pursuits he was struck by remarkable consistencies in comparative studies of different cultures, religions, literature, and art forms, spanning thousands of years. Despite differences in time, geography, culture, and historical development, people everywhere seemed to express their life experiences in highly similar ways. The similarities encompassed many forms of human experience: attitudes, ideas, feelings, actions, fantasies, and dreams. Jung saw much of human experience as being communicated through common, age-old symbols, artistic figures, myths, legends, fairy tales, and folklore. These images would crop up century after century, even among cultures isolated from those that had previously displayed these universal symbols of human experience. Jung attributed the consistent appearance and reappearance of these ancient motifs and figures to the mechanisms of the collective unconscious.

Like Freud, Jung wrote of a **psyche**, or total mentality, all of consciousness and unconsciousness. But **ego** is what we think of as ourselves, the genuine us, and is the "centre of the total field of consciousness" (Jung, 1959b, p. 3). It is not Freud's servant of unconscious urges. Ego, however, has communion with the collective unconscious.

That the ego is not entirely equivalent to consciousness is confirmed by the existence of another facet of consciousness, **persona**, or mask, the identities we assume because of the socially prescribed roles we play. Jung wrote:

> *Every calling or profession, for example, has its own characteristic persona. It is easy to study these things nowadays, when the photographs of public personalities so frequently appear in the press. A certain kind of behavior is forced on them by*

*the world and professional people endeavour to come up to these expectations.
Only the danger is that they become identical with their personas, the professor
with his text-book, the tenor with his voice. (Jung 1959a, p. 122–123)*

Rychlak (1981) dubbed the persona the "collective conscious" because we all
share knowledge of the prescribed behaviors that are associated with the various
roles people play. In a sense, personas are stereotypes associated with various
roles: the dumb jock, the nurdy student, the straightlaced accountant.

Consciousness and unconsciousness may be welded into a unified whole by
the development of the **self**, the "total personality," the unifying core of the psyche
that ensures a balance of conscious and unconscious forces (Jung, 1959b, p. 5).
When properly and fully developed, it is a fulcrum located at the center of the psyche, like the one that *balances* the playground teeter-totter or seesaw. However, the
self is a potentiality that may not become actual. In the poorly developed self, the
balance of the conscious and unconscious is disrupted. The result could be various
psychological ills.

Jung often wrote in terms of balancing opposing forces or opposites. Like
Freud, he referred to psychic energy, which he believed to be guided by the principle of **equivalence**, energy consumed to accommodate one intention—"say
something nice"—is balanced by energy fueling an opposite intention—"say
something nasty." **Entropy** is the equalization of differences in order to bring
about a balance or equilibrium. Balancing maleness with femaleness is an example.

Archetypes

The contents of the collective unconscious are called **archetypes**, or ancient types,
pre-existent forms that are innate and represent psychic predispositions that lead
people to apprehend, experience, and respond to the world in certain ways (Jung,
1959a). Jung explains their nature as analogous to Freud's biological instincts, but
more psychological. The existence of archetypes is due exclusively to heredity.
Therefore, the mind of the newborn infant is not a *tabula rasa,* or blank slate, but is
imprinted with forms from the past experience of humans. What is inherited are
not specific ideas or images but *potential,* general types of inner patterns and functioning. Archetypes often may be cast in terms of human forms, but many are most
accurately perceived by the mind's eye if pictured as non-human symbols, such as
numbers for "order." They may be thought of as magnets that attract ancestral
experiences which all relate to a common theme. For example, the mother archetype is constituted by ancient experiences common to all humans such as nurturance, warmth, love, and protection.

One prominent archetype comes as close to Freud's id as Jung gets. The
shadow is the dark side of the personality, the inferiorities of the person that are
emotional in nature and too unpleasant to willingly reveal (Jung, 1959a). Jung
believed that the shadow is a moral problem for the ego because it may resist
moral control. This resistance may be bound up in projection—the person sees

some of their unsavory qualities in other people. Jung was sometimes evasive when writing about the shadow. Although he refused to clearly indicate that its contents included Freud's primitive, biological instincts, it does apparently contain the physical urges. However, there was more to it. The shadow is manifested as the crude, bumbling, immature, incomplete side of us. It is the worst of us; it is what causes us to do what we do when "the devil made us do it." But the shadow is important. If the self is to evolve from potential to actual, it must fully acknowledge and deal with the contents of the shadow, as well as the ego and persona (Rychlak, 1981).

The archetype **anima** is the representation of woman in man. It is the accumulation of men's ancestral experiences of relating to women. Jung conceived of this presence in genetic terms. "It is a well-known fact that sex is determined by a majority of male or female genes, as the case may be. But the minority of genes belonging to the other sex does not simply disappear. A man therefore has in him a feminine side, an unconscious feminine figure—a fact of which he is generally quite unaware" (Jung, 1959a, p. 284). **Animus** is the corresponding man in woman. It is constituted by ancestral experiences of women relating to men. Anima is to Eros (sexual allure) as animus is to Logos (rational thinking). In women, animus may "show up" in argumentativeness, opinionation, and insinuation. In men, anima may make an appearance in the form of faithlessness, sentimentality, and resentment. When the two archetypes "meet" they clash: "the animus draws his sword of power and the anima ejects her poison of illusion and seduction" (Jung, 1959b, p. 15).

The result of a man's anima meeting a woman's animus can be quite humorous. Initially the man, under the influence of anima, may be seductive. When the woman, at the behest of animus, counters with arguments, he may become resentful. In turn, she may make insinuations. According to Jung "no man can converse with an animus for five minutes without becoming the victim of his own anima. Anyone who still had enough sense of humour to listen objectively to the ensuing dialogue would be staggered by the vast number of commonplace, . . . misapplied truisms [and] cliches . . ." (p. 15). On the positive side, anima gives men a sense of relatedness to others that may help them interact with people more smoothly. Animus provides women with the capacity to reflect and deliberate which may help them understand themselves and their surroundings. By extrapolation, it seems reasonable to assume that the presence of woman in man and man in woman allows each to better understand the other.

While Jung believed that there is an indefinite number of archetypes, he did consider several in addition to shadow, anima, and animus. Table 3.1 lists a sample of these.

Jung likened the process by which archetypes affect us to the experience of "love at first sight." Love "can suddenly seize you." Imagine that a person has been carrying "a certain eternal image" of a potential partner, without necessarily knowing it. Another person then appears who meets that inner image and "instantly you get the seizure; you are caught" (quoted in Evans, 1964, p. 51). Archetypes may seize you in a similar fashion. It may occur when you are strolling

TABLE 3.1   Some Jungian Archetypes

Name	Qualities
Trickster (also clown)	Characterized by unconsciousness and ability to change forms
Child	Beginning and the end; invincible
Mother	Sacred motherness (as in the Virgin Mary)
Father	Dynamism, form, and energy; like the cerebrum
Wotan	Warrior-god
Animal	Horse or snake
Quarternity	Squared circle with cross: four-fold division of ideal completeness
Order	Number; the numbers 3, 4
Hermaphrodite	Union of opposites

through a museum and happen upon a suit of armor that was worn by a medieval warrior. It may occur when you show unusual interest in a pregnant women. You may experience the grip of an archetype when you gaze at a symbol rendered in stone or wood—such as a representation of the quarternity—even though you have never encountered it before.

It will be déjà vu: you will feel that you have been there before. Indeed Jung would say you have, or rather your ancestors have. Thus, the roots of your experience are embedded in your collective unconscious in some archetypal form.

Jung (1978) speculated that 20th-century interest in unidentified flying objects (UFOs) may reflect the archetype of wholeness or totality. He noted that the sightings of flying saucers began toward the end of World War I, a time of intense conflict and strife. The psychic basis of these sightings is a splitting apart, which is then projected outward. The opposite of splitting apart is wholeness, symbolized by a **mandala**, or magic circle, a round object often including an inner spiral that draws the eyes to the center of its surface. Therefore, the "many thousands of individual testimonies" involving round flying bodies may be a *compensation* on the part of the collective unconscious as it seeks to bring about order and "heal the split in our apocalyptic age by means of the symbol of the circle" (Jung, 1964, p. 285). UFOs are often reported as luminous disks that come to earth from another planet (the unconscious) and contain strange creatures (archetypes) (Hall & Nordby, 1973).

Archetypes seem present always and everywhere in the psyche. While predominantly emotional, they also have intellectual elements. However, no archetype has itself ever been present in any individual's consciousness (Jung, 1959a). Archetypes manifest themselves only secondarily, through symbols, images, and behavior. Their pure form is not concrete. They exist as potentials or dispositions, similar to genetic dispositions. When they are manifested in consciousness, they are not themselves, but some representation of themselves that is manufactured by consciousness. For example, if one has a dream or daydream of the Christ Child, the archetype of the child has not entered consciousness. Rather a manifestation of it has been developed by consciousness into a recognizable form. It is possible for archetypes to become so powerful that they constitute a separate personality system, as sometimes occurs in certain mental disorders.

An archetype may manifest itself in one's experience and, at about the same time, in an external event. To explain this phenomenon, Jung introduced **synchronicity**, the simultaneous occurrence of two happenings that are correlated but have no direct cause-and-effect connection. Jung sought to understand "meaningful coincidences . . . or meaningful cross-connections," a falling into pattern that cuts across chains of causally connected events (quoted in Rychlak, 1981, p. 204). He used the concept of synchronicity to explain, without implying causality, simultaneous occurrences of inner images and outer events relating to some archetype. Inner images may be manifested in dreams, visions, forebodings, and hunches. Outer events may include any observable occurrences from the past, present, or future. Here are a few everyday examples: "It's weird that you telephoned about the birth of your baby, because I was talking about babies with my wife."; "Grandfather had flashbacks of his World War I experiences just as he turned on the radio to hear that World War II had begun."; "I dreamed of the Devil last week and the next day a friend offered me her copy of *Faust.*"

Jung also linked synchronicity to *parapsychology*, a subfield of psychology in search of acceptable scientific explanations for extrasensory perception (ESP) such as mental telepathy and clairvoyance. You may be experiencing ESP when you have the same thought as someone else (telepathy; "I was thinking about Michael Jackson just as you said his name out loud!") or successfully predict a future event (clairvoyance; you have a feeling that a relative is coming to visit and he or she shows up shortly thereafter).

Dreams as Messages from a Wise Unconscious

Jung was highly respectful of dreams and fantasies. Dreams were a primary vehicle of his approach to therapy. "I have spent more than half a century in investigating natural symbols, and I have come to the conclusion that dreams and their symbols are not stupid and meaningless" (Jung, 1964, p. 93). He was convinced that dreams contained important messages from the "wise" unconscious. The task was to decipher these messages, a job that was much more straightforward than Freud thought.

Jung did not distinguish between "manifest" and "latent" content of dreams as did Freud. He wrote, "The 'manifest' dream-picture is the dream itself and contains the whole meaning of the dream. When I find sugar in the urine, it is sugar and not just a facade for albumen. What Freud calls the 'dream-facade' is the dream's obscurity, and this is really only a projection of our own lack of understanding" (quoted in Rychlak, 1981, p. 246). To Jung, the symbols of the collective unconscious are undisguised in a dream, ready for interpretation. Nevertheless, interpretation may be difficult because of the complex and abstract nature of the

BOX 3.1   The Case of Little Anna

"About the time when Freud published his report on the case of 'Little Hans,' I received from a father who was acquainted with psychoanalysis a series of observations concerning his little daughter, then four years old" (Jung, 1954, p. 8). So Jung introduced his analysis of a bright little girl who was virtually obsessed with what the casual observer might view as the age-old childhood question "where do babies come from?"

Anna's curiosity was stimulated by the impending arrival of her new sibling. Before Anna was told that her brother had been born, she was asked, "What would you say if you got a little brother tonight?" She promptly answered, "I would kill it." This seemingly shocking response might have been interpreted by Freud as indicating that Anna was showing natural jealousy of her new brother's anatomy, or "worse," if he were dead, maybe she could take his penis. However, Jung characteristically had a much milder interpretation: Anna did not mean "kill it" literally, but "just get rid of it," perhaps because she was jealous of the attention it would receive or maybe because it was something new and new "things" are nuisances with which one must cope.

Some of Anna's behaviors and experiences did seem "Freudian." She saw some carpenters working and then dreamed that one of them cut off her genitals. She played a game in the tool house which involved "getting rid of mother." She became very curious when she saw the gardeners and her father urinating outdoors. Jung's response to the "sliced genitals" comment was a reference to Anna's curiosity regarding the purpose of her genitals. "Getting rid of mother" was merely to keep her from interfering with the children's games

(they enjoyed defecating in the corner of the tool house, a practice that Mother wished to terminate). However, watching the men urinate had greater significance, but not in the Freudian sense.

To Jung, Anna was curious about the men urinating because she had a burning interest in how babies are formed, how they "get out" of mothers, and more relevant to the present concern, what role do fathers play in all of this. She wanted to know "what fathers do," that is, how do father's contribute to the birth of babies. The interest was not mere childish curiosity. Anna's collective unconscious was at work. The ancient and never ending cycle of birth and rebirth was manifesting itself in her consciousness.

Anna was fond of her uncle and once asked if she could sleep with him (think of what Freud would make of that!). While making this request she was clinging to her father's arm as her mother often did. Later she dreamed that she crept into her uncle and aunt's bedroom and peeked under the covers to discover ". . . Uncle lay on his stomach, and joggled up and down on it" (p. 31). Still later she frequently crawled into her father's bed, lay on her stomach—arms and legs stretched out—and joggled back and forth while exclaiming "this is what father does" (p. 32). According to Jung all this was in pursuit of knowledge concerning what "father does" in the whole process of birth and death.

Evidence of rumblings in the unconscious regarding the life-death cycle were more clearly displayed when Anna asked whether her mother would die when the baby was born. This question suggests that death is exchanged for life. The cycle is also evident in a conversation Anna had with her grandmother:

BOX 3.1   *Continued*

"Granny, why are your eyes so dim?"

"Because I am old."

"But you will become young again?"

"Oh dear, no. I shall become older and older, and then I shall die."

"And what then?"

"Then I shall be an angel."

"And then you will be a baby again?" (p. 9).

To Jung, many childhood games have meaning related to the collective unconscious. When, like children of today, Anna stuffed pillows under her clothes and incessantly queried adults about "where do babies come out" she was not just playing games or satisfying childish curiosity. Nor was she being controlled by psychosexual urges when she spoke or dreamed of "sleeping with uncle," or "getting rid of mother," or genitals being cut off. In all cases she was under the spell of the collective unconscious.

symbols, each of which has at least two meanings. However, one need not dig through some protective crust to get at those symbols. They are naked, out in the open, and in plain sight.

One type of message, mentioned earlier in relation to flying saucers, is **compensation**, a basic law of the psyche referring to observations that a dream's meaning is often just the opposite of the person's conscious experience. In this sense, the collective unconscious represents the second of "two sides to every story," reflecting functions that are autonomous and compensatory. As you have seen and will see again, the balance of opposites is a constant theme in Jung's writings. Jacobi (1962) offers an example and interpretation of a compensation:

> *Someone dreams that it is spring, but that his favourite tree in the garden has only dry branches. This year it bears no leaves or blossoms. What the dream is trying to communicate is this: Can you see yourself in this tree? That is how you are, although you don't want to recognize it. Your nature has dried up, no green grows within you. Such dreams are a lesson to persons whose consciousness has become autonomous and overemphasized. Of course the dreams of an unusually unconscious person, living entirely by his instincts, would correspondingly emphasize his "other side." Irresponsible scoundrels often have moralizing dreams while paragons of virtue frequently have immoral dream images. (p. 76)*

Another type of message is **prospective**, or anticipatory, through which dreams may "foretell" future events and outcomes. A friend of mine told of a dream he had during his high school years. He was riding a bicycle, with his brother on the handlebars, when a hole suddenly opened in the street, toppling both of them. Two days later, the mishap of the dream occurred in real life. Jung's favorite example illustrates how dreams may prepare a person for the future . . . if they pay attention to dream-meaning. A friend described a dream about climbing a steep mountain and experiencing exhilaration upon reaching the top. When Jung advised caution in the future, the friend scoffed. Later he fell to his death during a climb.

Personality Typology

Two Psychological Attitudes: Extraversion and Introversion

After 20 years of observing people "of all classes from all the great nations," Jung theorized that human beings could be divided into two groups based on "two fundamentally different general attitudes," extraversion and introversion (Jung, 1921/1971, p. 549). He defined **attitude** as "a readiness of the psyche to act or react in a certain way" to experience (p. 414). He defined **type** as a habitual attitude, or a person's "characteristic way." Although extraversion and introversion are discussed at length later in this book, it would be remiss not to introduce Jung's version of these two psychological types, which many psychologists consider his best-known contribution to personality theory (Evans, 1964).

Jung also assumed that the psyche runs on **libido** or psychic energy. According to his theory (1921/1971), **extraversion** is an "outward-turning" of libido that involves a positive movement of interest away from one's inner experience toward outer experience. The extravert is characterized by

> interest in the external object, responsiveness, and a ready acceptance of external happenings, a desire to influence and be influenced by events, a need to join in and get "with it," the capacity to endure bustle and noise of every kind, and actually find them enjoyable, constant attention to the surrounding world, the cultivation of friends and acquaintances, none too carefully selected, and finally by the great importance attached to the figure one cuts, and hence by a strong tendency to make a show of oneself. (p. 549)

Introversion is an "inward-turning" of psychic energy and involves a negative movement or withdrawal of subjective interest away from outer objects and toward one's inner experience. Jung, a self-acknowledged introvert, believed that introverts have more problems with social relations than extraverts (Lebowitz, 1990). The introvert

> holds aloof from external happenings, does not join in, has a distinct dislike of society as soon as he finds himself among too many people. In a large gathering he feels lonely and lost. The more crowded it is, the greater becomes his resistance. He is not in the least "with it," and has no love of enthusiastic get-togethers. He is not a good mixer. What he does, he does in his own way, barricading himself against influences from outside. He is apt to appear awkward, often seeming inhibited ... His own world is a safe harbour, a carefully tended and walled-in garden, closed to the public and hidden from prying eyes. His own company is the best. He feels at home in his world, where the only changes are made by himself. His best work is done with his own resources, on his own initiative, and in his own way. (Jung, 1921/1971, pp. 550)

Four Psychological Functions: Sensing, Thinking, Feeling, and Intuiting

Jung also theorized that there are four *orientations*, or basic psychological functions, in personality: sensing, thinking, feeling, and intuiting. The first and second are considered "rational," while the last two are "irrational." These functions may combine with introversion or extraversion, making eight possible combinations. **Sensation** determines that *something is present*; it is the same as sensory perceptions of sight, sound, smell, taste, and touch. The sensation function is especially characteristic of children, with emphasis placed on actual observations or "facts." **Thinking** determines *what is present* and interprets its meaning; it connects ideas with one another to form intellectual concepts or reach solutions. **Feeling** evaluates *how experiences strike us*, whether they are suitable to us or not; it is a kind of judgment that is entirely subjective. **Feeling** imparts a definite value, of acceptance-rejection or of like-dislike. It also includes mood. **Intuition** suggests where something *seems to have come from* and where it may be going. It is a kind of "instinctive apprehension," of unconscious origin, with no tangible basis. You display intuition when you understand something but cannot explain how or why you understand.

It should be noted that Jung was not primarily interested in classifying people into distinct categories. His aims were to (1) understand dimensions of individual differences, (2) guide research, and (3) aid clinical evaluation of patients.

Personality Development

Individuation

For Jung, the direction of personality development is **individuation**, "the process by which a person becomes a psychological 'in-dividual,' that is, a separate, indivisible unity or 'whole' " (Jung, 1959a, p. 275). It is a process of self-realization in which the totality called "self" is differentiated from the various parts of the personality, including the collective unconscious (Rychlak, 1981).

It is union of opposites represented by the archetype Hermaphrodite. It is confronting what we are not as well as what we are. Through individuation, animus is

---

BOX 3.2   What Combination Are You?

The attitudes and functions combine as follows: extraverted-thinking, extraverted-feeling, extraverted-sensing, extraverted-intuiting, introverted-thinking, introverted-feeling, introverted-sensing, introverted-intuiting. Carefully go over each of the eight possibilities. Put together the attitude and function definitions of each attitude/function combination, referring back to the text as needed. Then determine which combination best fits you. Later your choice will become even more meaningful as you read about a famous test that classifies people as you have done with regard to yourself.

balanced with anima and conscious with unconscious. This bringing together of opposites has a name, **transcendental function**, the process of rising above what we are through our tendency "to combine consciousness and unconsciousness into a balanced whole" (Rychlak, 1981, p. 218). Thus, individuation may be thought of as the process by which the self emerges from the psyche through the operation of the transcendental function.

At first, the person refuses to accept the unconscious within. However, the person may eventually begin to accept what is within as part of his or her personality, rather than "projecting" it outside the self, onto others, as "not me." In this process, personality development is expressed through the archetypes, as the person comes to terms with each, in sequence (Hogan, 1976). The proposed steps are as follows: (1) the persona dissolves when the person recognizes the artificiality of society's goals; (2) the shadow is integrated with other psychic units when there is awareness of one's selfish and destructive "dark side"; (3) acceptance of the anima or animus is achieved by recognition of opposite-sex components in one's personality; and (4) commitment to an archetype that is symbolic of spiritual or creative meaning allows one to tackle the final stage of individuation.

Recognition of unconscious contents leads to *synthesizing* archetypes to consciousness, a process of blending conscious and unconscious into a whole, resulting in self-knowledge (Freud's "insight"). Recognition allows projections to be withdrawn from the external world, thereby releasing energy for use in continued personal development.

The process of individuation proceeds slowly, in stages covering the entire life span. Fulfillment of individuation is "a favor that must be paid for dearly." Archetypes need to be recognized every step of the way, which is no easy task. However, the process is not simply one of struggling with the collective unconscious, but a continuing adaptation to it. Think of a plant that must first be able to grow in soil (recognition of the collective unconscious) before it can unfold its own particular fullness (development of the self). In its ultimate adult form, individuation shows characteristics not found during childhood: definiteness, fullness, and maturity. As you will see, the notion of individuation of the self anticipates Carl Roger's ideas about self-acceptance and Abraham Maslow's thoughts about self-actualization.

Four Stages of Life-Span Development

Jung discussed four stages of personality development: childhood, youth, middle age, and old age (Hall & Nordby, 1973).

Childhood (birth to adolescence) is a relatively problem-free period that is dominated by instincts, dependency, and a psychological atmosphere provided by parents. Development of an ego occurs gradually, as does one's separation from the protective "psychic womb" of home when schooling starts. These ideas are in keeping with Jung's assumption of the collective unconscious. The infant has no real ego, or separate identity, and is almost totally dependent on its parents. The infant's unconscious is not personal, only collective.

Youth (adolescence through young adulthood) begins at puberty, at which time physiological changes are accompanied by "psychic revolution." The demands of life dictate that people make their own decisions. At the same time they find it difficult but necessary to give up the illusions and fantasies of childhood. "Psychic birth" occurs as the psyche begins to take on its own character, although experiences of sexuality and inferiority may create problems. The person begins to establish vocational, marital, and community roles.

Middle age (age 40 to old age) brings with it the task of building a whole personality. Jung observed many of his adult patients dealing with issues of lost zest and meaning in life. Their focus was on inner, spiritual values, different from earlier adaptations that were more external and materialistic. Contemplation becomes more important than activity. Opposite psychological processes, such as introversion-extraversion or feeling-thinking, may be synthesized. This blending process may be stimulated by a symbol that represents ascendancy of the spirit above worldly matters. One example involves the symbol of *yin* and *yang*, which may be interpreted as the female-like and male-like forces in nature according to ancient Oriental philosophy. Appreciation of this symbol may lead to synthesis of the male and females aspects of the person.

The period of **old age** parallels childhood because of a return to submersion in the unconscious. The figure of a snake biting its own tail is symbolic of life coming full circle. Death is as important as birth. Jung found belief in a hereafter so universal that he considered it to be a manifestation of the unconscious (see Campbell, 1975). Perhaps psychic life does not end with bodily death because the psyche continues an endless quest for self-realization.

A Different View of Maternal and Paternal Influence

One aspect of Jung's view of interpersonal relationships differs quite markedly from those of Freud and other theorists considered later. Jung sees individuals as relating psychologically to others more on the basis of universal inner archetypes than on others' individual characteristics. Jung attributes only "limited [causative] significance" to a child's personal mother and father. The influences mothers reportedly have on their children "do not come from the mother herself, but rather from the archetype projected upon her" (1959a, p. 83). In effect, children respond less to their parents than to the archetypes they have of "mother" and "father." The mother archetype is a composite of humans' experiences with *all* mothers down through the ages. It has "an almost infinite variety of aspects": mother, grandmother, stepmother, mother-in-law, nurse, governess, "good" mother, "bad" mother, Mother of God, Great Mother, fertility, fruitfulness, cooking vessels, rose, cow, witch, dragon, deep water, and so on. On the other hand, parents do have an influence on the child's development of other archetypes. A boy's interactions with his own mother and father affect the functioning of his anima and shadow, respectively. Similarly the girl's relationship with her own father and mother affects the functioning of her animus and shadow, respectively.

Evaluation

Contributions

Jung's Psychological Types

Later in this book I will return to introversion/extraversion and the literally hundreds of studies that support this seminal contribution by Jung. Here the concentration is on the combination of this central dimension with the four functions. This eight-fold typology has been the focus of a number of research studies.

A particularly good example of research on the typology was an investigation by Gorlow, Simonson, and Krauss (1966). The subjects were 98 introductory psychology students at Pennsylvania State University, two-thirds of whom were male. The results supported the hypothesis that subjects using a self-report technique would order themselves into the eight types postulated by Jung. However, extraverted types emerged much more clearly than introverted types in the sample studied. Evidence was strongest for the extraverted-feeling type, followed by the extraverted-thinking type ("a man . . . who make[s] all his activities dependent on intellectual conclusions, which in the last resort are always oriented by objective data . . ." Jung, 1921/1971, p. 346). The significant relationship observed between extraverted-feeling type and sex of subjects supported Jung's assertion that this type of personality is more commonly female than male.

The most popular psychological measure of Jung's typology is the Myers Briggs Type Indicator (MBTI) (Myers, 1962). The MBTI is a self-report questionnaire that has been used in at least 400–500 studies (Carlyn, 1977; Carskadon, 1978).

Carskadon (1978) has used the MBTI to predict the quality of contributions made by students to discussions in undergraduate psychology classes at Mississippi State University. Carskadon noticed that self-described MBTI extraverts made "very infrequent discussion contributions," whereas introverts made "frequent and thought-provoking contributions." However, this pattern seemed to be related less to the extraversion-introversion dimension than to the sensation-intuition dimension. Carskadon tested the hypothesis that the best classroom contributions come from intuitive types. At the end of a semester, 65 students in three psychology courses were asked to rate every class member on quality of discussion contributions during the course. A 3-point rating scale was used (3 = excellent, 2 = good, and 1 = fair to poor). Carskadon also rated the students independently. The correlation of .84 between class means and instructor ratings was statistically significant. Results for both sets of rating data also proved significant. Students with high intuitive scores obtained the highest discussion ratings, while students with high sensation scores obtained the lowest ratings (peer ratings = 2.05 and 1.62, respectively; instructor ratings = 2.06 and 1.26, respectively). Other comparisons were non-significant, indicating that intuiting/sensing was critical to contributions to class discussion compared to extraversion-introversion in combination with the functions. By way of general advice to instructors, Carskadon noted, "Too many extraverts can give all action but little thought; too many introverts all thought and no action. Too many thinking types can use all logic and no human values; too many feeling types, all subjective values and no critical analysis" (p. 141).

In brief, some research showed that extraversion emerged more clearly than introversion. However, a more thorough discussion later in this book generally supports both extremes of Jung's typology. Use of the most popular measure of types, the MBTI, yields the result that it is introverts, not extraverts, who contribute most to discussions and that a better understanding of discussion processes may be achieved by attention to the four functions than to introversion/extraversion.

Jung's Analytic Psychotherapy

Jung's approach to therapy was flexible, open-minded, and eclectic, showing a willingness to use whatever methods seemed most workable with individual patients, including the methods of other therapists (Hall & Nordby, 1973). He felt that Freud's and other theorists' methods may work just as well as his own methods in dealing with psychological problems as he saw them (Rychlak, 1981). He was even known to send his Catholic patients to confession as he thought their knowledge of that "method" might lead them to use it effectively in ferreting out unconscious influences. Further, unlike Freud and other theorists, Jung maintained a more or less equal relationship with his patients. As you will see, he sometimes participated in some types of therapy right along with the patient. This innovation may have influenced Carl Rogers and some other psychotherapists.

Roazen (1974) writes that Jung "successfully pioneered short-term psychotherapy" and promoted the development of self-help programs like Alcoholics Anonymous (p. 284). Initially, he might see patients four times a week. Then he would cut back to one to two hours a week. Finally, he would encourage patients to do self-analysis and would serve only as their consultant (Rychlak, 1981).

Jung also initiated the use of projective tests, like the ones discussed in Chapter 1. He often encouraged patients to express their experiences through drawing and painting, a technique that has been adopted by others, especially therapists who work with children. The waking-imagery techniques he developed have become popular with current-day professionals working with terminally ill cancer patients (Achterberg & Lawlis, 1978; Simonton & Simonton, 1975). However, a discussion of his main methods of psychotherapy must await a consideration of his general approach to therapy.

Jung tended to see older patients than Freud (Rychlak, 1981). Of course, he wished to help them toward individuation and the further development of the self. Often, however, they were troubled in such a way that individuation was arrested. A major source of these troubles were **complexes**, mental contents in the psyche that agglutinate or stick together like the clumping of red blood cells and eventually take up residence in the personal unconscious. For example, a person's strong religious faith may lead to the agglutination of religious beliefs into a complex that may overwhelm the identity of the person. Complexes may be thought of as clogs in the pipeline of the psyche that block commerce between the conscious and collective unconscious. A frequent goal of Jungian analytic psychotherapy was to identify these complexes and "dissolve them"—in the sense of de-centralizing them—so that the conscious and collective unconscious might better relate to one another.

An illustrative case involves a mother complex (Jung, 1959a). The core of this complex might be the mother archetype. As the complex develops it migrates from the collective unconscious, the realm of the archetype, to the personal unconscious where experiences with the person's mother agglutinate to it. A boy with this complex, for example, may as an adult become a Don Juan, unconsciously seeking his mother in every woman he encounters.

The existence of the mother complex may be confirmed by one of the first personality tests, an instrument developed by Jung (1910). It was one of the first personality tests used in clinical settings. When using the **Word Association Test** Jung instructed persons to say the first word that came to mind after hearing each of 100 words from a standardized list. He then analyzed these associations according to content, commonness or uniqueness, time lapse between list word presentation and patient's response, later recall, and accompanying behavior (facial expressions, postural shifts, voice changes, laughing, crying). He paid particular attention to responses given to emotionally arousing words, such as the one relevant to our example, mother. Strong reactions to the word "mother" would inform Jung that a mother complex may exist. An analysts' knowledge that a mother complex exists, however, may do little by way of solving the patient's problem. For dissolution of the complex to occur, the patient must have insight. This critical event will likely require deeper probing all the way to the heart of the matter, in this case, the mother archetype. Other techniques are needed for this plunge into the depths of the collective unconscious.

Interpreting Dreams in a Series

Unlike Freud, Jung generally saw dreams as having little to do with worldly concerns and much to do with the meaning of life. Jung's approach to dream interpretation was one of *amplification*, broadening and enriching dream or other image content through a process of directed association (Rychlak, 1981). Jung's interpretations were guided by images and analogies related to the dream's emotional nucleus or hub. His method differs from Freud's free association in three ways: (1) Instead of deducing meaning by working backward from present to past, Jung sought to understand meaning by progressing forward, from present to future; (2) Jung provided dreamers with his vast knowledge of universal archetypal symbols and meanings, orienting them in certain directions and actively guiding their interpretations (in our example, he would introduce the patient to symbols of "mother"); and (3) Jung offered his own associations to dream content, sometimes simultaneously engaging in the association process with the patient. The goal was to aid patients in deriving the meanings of symbols themselves. Once they were acquainted with those meanings, dissolution of troublesome complexes becomes possible.

Amplification could also occur apart from the exploration of dream content. In this case Freud's free association would be used, except that "freedom" was restricted by Jung's interventions to keep a patient oriented to a particular image or to join in the associations.

Jung did not use any standard, cookbook approach to interpreting dream symbols. His approach was also highly individualized, taking into account different personalities, circumstances, and contexts. For example, while for many individuals sexual intercourse might symbolize union with another human being, for a particular person it might well signify lustful needs. He sought to increase his patients' ability to interpret dreams by encouraging them to keep a log of all dreams and interpretations, and to pursue their own interpretations whenever possible.

Jung was the first theorist to investigate large numbers of dreams in succession, or **dream series** (Jacobi, 1962). Jung did not find interpretations of single dreams generally representative of the dreamer, but he did find later dreams helpful in correcting misinterpretations of earlier ones. He also recognized that the meaning of dreams in a sequence is not necessarily chronological, but radial. Imagine a wagon wheel having spokes that extend outward from a central hub. Different dreams would be represented by the spokes, but all would be related to the hub which could be a complex of the dreamer.

Waking-Dream Fantasy

Another technique frequently used by Jung was **active imagination** through which patients are encouraged to simulate dream experiences by actively engaging in imagination while fully awake (Watkins, 1976). For example, a patient may be asked to close his eyes in a darkened room and imagine himself descending a succession of stairways. While so doing (symbolically going down into the unconscious), the patient is also asked to detail his sensations, perceptions, experiences, thoughts, and behaviors as vividly as possible. It frequently happens that the patient finds himself next to water, perhaps a lake, the most common symbol of unconscious psychological spirit. To pursue our example further, "deep water" is a mother symbol.

Limitations

Jung's theory shares several shortcomings with that of Freud. Many of his concepts are not amenable to scientific testing. How does one get at an archetype so that some hypothesis regarding it can be tested? How does one understand a Jungian symbol when each symbol has *at least* two meanings? What is the *real* meaning of each?

Aside from these problems, some of Jung's notions seem mixed up with others. The anima and the shadow sometimes get mixed up in his writings, as do the shadow and the trickster. In fact, his writing is sometimes confusing: for example, some concepts are never clearly defined—complex is a case in point—and others are defined in obscure fashion or defined differently in different writings—individuation is an illustration (Rychlak, 1981). Even the central concept "collective unconscious" is sometimes treated ambiguously. It is not entirely clear whether there is initially anything in the collective unconscious except archetypes. Jung (1959a) does mention simple unconscious elements in the collective unconscious—such as fire and water—but does not make it clear whether these elements stand alone or exist only as parts of archetypes.

These problems are relatively minor compared to Jung's ideas concerning how the collective unconscious comes into being. Like Freud, Jung was influenced by Charles Darwin's contemporary Chavalier De Lamarck who believed that animals and plants can change their forms during their lifetimes in adapting to their environments and these changes can be passed on to future generations. In other words, Lamarck believed in the inheritance of acquired characteristics. If a seagoing animal loses it front feet and that loss helps it survive better in the sea, the lack of feet might be passed on. Unfortunately, Lamarck's ideas are suspect.

Broadly speaking, the "mind" (psyche) can be thought of as composed of "ideas." There are problems related to associating "inheritance" with the "mind" and its components. First, inheritable traits are normally thought of as physical, but the mind is not physical. Second "ideas" are acquired during people's lifetimes and thus are not inheritable.

There is a strong flavor of "inherited ideas" in Jung's notion that the collective unconscious consists of elements which originated in the experiences of ancient humans and then were genetically passed to the present generation. He writes, "We must assume that [mythological types] correspond to certain *collective* (and not personal) structural elements of the human psyche in general, and, like the morphological elements of the human body, are *inherited*." (Jung, 1959a, p. 155; emphasis in original). That any characteristic can be acquired during a lifetime and then passed on to future generations has now been thoroughly discredited, a fact known to Jung, at least in his later life. In defense of the collective unconscious, Jung argued that what is inherited are not ideas per se and certainly nothing concrete, but "experiences" that are merely dispositions. These dispositions may ready a person for certain experiences, but never are present themselves in any observable form (remember, archetypes become transformed when their representations appear in consciousness). Yet, Jung was never able to explain how experiences differ from ideas or how any trait whatsoever can be acquired during lifetimes and then passed on. The stigma of "inheritance of acquired characteristics" is branded on notions of the collective unconscious and remains the most serious weakness of Jung's theory.

Conclusion

Although Jung's contributions to the psychology of personality have had less impact than those of Freud, appreciation of his ideas is likely to increase over time. Jung was not a theorist "in the right place at the right time." He was often overshadowed by the dominating presence of Freud, a circumstance he shared with others considered in this book. Following his break with Freud, Jung (1963) found even his professional acquaintances dropping away—"I was a mystic, and that settled the matter" (p. 167). However, the breadth of Jung's perspective on personality remains unrivaled. It encompasses the collective unconscious of antiquity as well as futuristic ideas about synchronicity and extrasensory perception. More important, Jung introduced the timeless notion of introversion/extraversion—now a part of our language—and popularized the central idea "self." Further, as you will see in subsequent chapters, his openness to the use of many different kinds of procedures in therapy and his willingness to accept equal status with patients set precedents that are still being followed today. More specifically, several theorists have endorsed Jung's assumptions about dream-series interpretation (Perls, 1969), self-realization (Horney, 1950), the holistic nature of human experience (Rogers, 1961), and the biological origin of spiritual meaning (Maslow, 1967).

Clinically, Jung worked more with normal persons than did Freud, covering the full range of life-span development, including adults undergoing mid-life crises. Also, his therapeutic work was undertaken not only with neurotic patients but with more seriously disturbed people. Thus, ideas derived from his clinical experience are likely to be more generally representative than those of Freud. Scientifically there is support for Jung's concepts of introversion and extraversion, the four functions, and for applications of the Word Association Test (Cramer, 1968). Although Jung's popularity is greater in Europe than the United States, the journal devoted to his view, *The Journal of Analytical Psychology*, has an American as well as a British version.

Jung's collected works total some 20 volumes. Like Freud's writings, Jung's vast works contain many undiscovered insights. His orientation to the mystical and to the past history of humans may have more appeal to young people of today than to the youth of Jung's own time. You can look forward to increased interest in Carl Jung during the next century.

Summary Points

1. Jung was born (1875) in Kesswill, Switzerland, the son of a minister and possibly the great grandson of Goethe. As a lonely, reclusive boy, he had many visions, including one of a phallic symbol. These mystical interests carried over into adulthood as indicated by the theme of his post-M.D. research. His break with Freud was traumatic, but led to a creative mid-life "crisis."

2. Jung's personal unconscious is different for different people, but his collective unconscious is the same for all people. The psyche is all of mentality. The ego is associated with consciousness. Persona is the mask that corresponds to any one of the roles that society thrusts upon us. The self is the core of the psyche. The collective unconscious contains the archetypes.

3. Jung emphasized the archetypes shadow, anima, and animus. Archetypes can suddenly "seize you" and have been used to explain reports of UFOs. Archetypes may be manifested in synchrony with external events and synchronicity has been used to explain ESP.

4. Little Anna was obsessed with "where babies come from." She sometimes displayed behaviors that appeared to support Freud's notions of psychosexuality. However, Jung discounted Freudian explanations in favor of Anna's archetypical obsession with the cycle of birth and rebirth. Unlike Freud, Jung did not distinguish between latent and manifest dream content—the symbols of the collective unconscious and its archetypes are displayed directly in dreams. Dreams anticipate the future and compensate for a conscious process by manifesting its unconscious opposite.

5. Jung's most enduring contributions are "extraversion" and "introversion." Also important are his four psychological functions: thinking, feeling, sensing, and intuiting. Individuation is the "process by which a person becomes a psychological in-dividual." It differentiates the self from the psyche with the aid of the transcendental function. Jung postulated four stages of development. He viewed the impact of relations between children and their parents differently than Freud.

6. Some research regarding Jung's psychological types seems to indicate clearer support for extraversion than introversion, and, in the case of classroom discussion, stronger support for the importance of his four functions than for introversion/extraversion. Jung's analytic psychotherapy is unique in that patient and therapist have relatively equal status, therapy tends to be relatively short term, and different techniques associated with different theories are seen as relatively equivalent.

7. Jung pioneered use of projective tests and popularized the concept "complex." Dissolving troublesome complexes was a main goal of psychotherapy. A boy with a mother complex is a case in point. Jungian therapeutic and diagnostic techniques include the Word Association Test, dream and waking amplification, dream series analysis, and active imagination.

8. Jung's limitations are much like Freud's: his concepts are often poorly or ambiguously defined, some of his concepts are mixed up with others, some concepts are defined differently in different writings, and the contents of the collective unconscious are not clearly specified.

9. The most serious problem with Jung's point of view is that assumptions behind the collective unconscious have the flavor of "inheritance of acquired characteristics." Jung's impact may have been less than Freud's because he stood in the "master's" shadow and was identified with mysticism.

10. Jung's innovations, such as extraversion/introversion and self, as well as his flexibility and contribution to others' theories make him a major contributor. Undoubtedly, Jung's vast writings will yield new insights when they are more fully examined. In the meantime, his more mystical point of view may receive increased attention as time passes, especially among young people.

Running Comparison

Theorist	Jung in Comparison
Freud	Jung also used psyche, ego, consciousness, unconsciousness, and analogies to id and insight. He and Freud even shared shortcomings. But Jung rejected sexualism, criticized

penis envy, made no distinction between latent and manifest dream content, and viewed the impact of parents differently.

Carl Rogers	Jung anticipated Rogers' concern with self-acceptance and his more egalitarian relations with patients.
Abraham Maslow	Jung anticipated Maslow's concern for self-actualization.

Essay/Critical Thinking Questions

1. Can you argue that the mystical, magical, parapsychological orientation is, as Jung would have it, an important part of understanding personality?

2. List and describe three personas that are not mentioned in the book. How does each impede the development of persons who manifest it?

3. Can you make up an archetype different from any discussed by Jung? Chose it from the mythology of ancient culture. For example—but not for your use—the swastika is an ancient Germanic and Native American symbol.

4. Can you reconsider the case of Little Hans and reinterpret it in Jungian terms?

5. Can you write four items for a test of introversion/extraversion, two that would be endorsed by introverts and two that would be endorsed by extroverts?

6. Reconsider a dream of your own, briefly describe it, then analyze it in Jungian terms. Can you indicate the symbols for ancient archetypes and interpret their meaning?

7. Are you a sensation, thinking, feeling, or intuition person (or none of the above)? Indicate why you are one or more of the four functions and not the other varieties.

8. Pretend that you are a Jungian analyst hunting for a complex that is troubling a patient. Can you describe the complex, how you would confirm its existence, and what you would do to dissolve it?

9. Several contributions of Jung are described in the book. Can you come up with one missed by the author and indicate why it is important?

10. Several criticisms of Jung's ideas and methods are described in the book. Can you come up with one missed by the author and indicate why it is important?

4

STRIVING FROM A MINUS TO A PLUS CONDITION: ALFRED ADLER

- Do you believe that it is only human to feel inferior?
- Does it matter whether you are born first, second, middle, last, or are an only child?
- Are people destined to be social beings, or do they have to work at it?
- Is your lifestyle temporary—forced on you by your current circumstances—or does it have deeper meaning?
- Do the earliest memories that you can recollect say anything about you as a person?

Although Freud stands by himself in pioneering new ideas and methods for understanding personality, one of his continuing contributions has been to show others how to think in new ways about personality. It was not just a matter of the content of Freud's ideas—*what* to think. It was also a matter of procedure—*how* to think. Some of Freud's psychiatric followers adhered closely to his orthodox tradition (Deutsch, 1945; Fenichel, 1945). Others began to elaborate entirely new concepts, to question and even abandon some of the tenets of classical psychoanalysis. These *neo-Freudians* include the theorists covered in this and four subsequent chapters: Alfred Adler, Karen Horney, Harry Stack Sullivan, Erik Erikson, and Erich Fromm. Although these theorists were influenced by Freud, all departed from Freud's ideas. They abandoned Freud's "overemphasis" on infantile sexuality and elaborated new concepts about parent-child relationships, social experiences, and cultural patterns of behavior.

Jung's split with Freud was painful and not really desired by either party. Mutual respect and personal warmth had characterized their relationship. By

Alfred Adler

contrast, Alfred Adler's fatal rift with Freud was more due to a clash of wills (Rychlak, 1981). When Adler brazenly refused to embrace Freud's sexual instinct, and openly rejected the Oedipus complex, he came to be regarded as a renegade. At the urging of his followers, Freud decided to force Adler out of the psychoanalytic camp. As both individuals were editors of a psychoanalytic journal, Freud devised a showdown. He wrote the journal staff a "him or me letter": he would resign if Adler remained on the editorial board. Adler promptly quit and thereafter became the enemy. During the period that followed, some of Freud's communications with Jung were diatribes against Adler.

Adler, the Person

Alfred Adler was born in Vienna in 1870 to a middle-class Jewish family. Because he did not grow up in a Jewish neighborhood, he never developed a strong identity as a Jew. Accordingly, he converted to Protestantism in his youth and thereafter considered himself a Christian.

The fact that he was the second of six children was to have a profound affect on Adler. He felt that he would always be in the shadow of his successful, older brother. Despite some successes of his own, Adler regarded his childhood as rather unhappy. His childhood illnesses, however, proved to be assets. He suffered from rickets during infancy, and nearly died of pneumonia at age five. Following a miraculous recovery, young Adler vowed to become a physician and save others. Later he was to theorize about the implications of being an invalid.

In a lecture given when he was more than 60 years old, Adler talked about the importance of his early physical ailments:

> *I was born a very weak child suffering from certain weaknesses, especially from rickets which prevented me from moving very well. Despite this obstacle, now, nearly at the end of my life, I am standing before you in America. You can see how I have overcome this difficulty. Also, I could not speak very well early in my life; I spoke very slowly. Also, though you are probably not aware of it in my English, I am supposed to be a very good orator in German. I have also overcome this difficulty. (Stepansky, 1983, p. 9)*

Adler was more of a father's son than a mother's boy. The fact that he felt closer to his father may in part explain why he found Freud's Oedipal complex so alien. A boy who cherishes his father and is somewhat distant from his mother is not likely to accept the belief that boys wish their fathers would disappear so they could be in sole possession of their mothers.

Adler did not distinguish himself as a student. In grade school he was average. The University of Vienna did grant him a medical degree in 1895, but he failed to impress any professor enough to develop the close mentor-student relationship enjoyed by Freud and Jung. During this period he flirted with Marxism and became something of a student revolutionary. Among the rebellious youths who shared his socialist inclinations was an intellectual revolutionary from a wealthy Russian family who especially interested him. She eventually became Raissa Adler.

Adler began his medical career as a general practitioner. Among his typically poor patients were some who showed outstanding physical abilities. For example, some were acrobats. What intrigued Adler the most was his observation that some of these strong performers had been victims of physical weakness or accidents as children. Coupled with his own experience of childhood weakness, it appeared that early handicaps can, through compensation, lead to adult accomplishments.

Adler had a strong social conscience. His tendency to support the underdog may explain his initially friendly overtures to Freud and his ideas. Like Jung, at first Adler defended Freud. Despite the irreconcilable differences they developed later, Adler never totally rejected all of Freudianism. Even after his resignation from the joint editorship with Freud, Adler recommended that his students become thoroughly acquainted with Freud's "meritorious" theory of dreams (Adler, 1964). Like Jung, he was more open to Freud than Freud was to him.

Unlike Jung, the formation of Adler's major ideas followed rather than preceded his split with Freud. It was after serving as an army physician during World War I that Adler framed perhaps his most useful concept. During this period he witnessed firsthand the suffering of wounded soldiers and the despair of children damaged by war. These human tragedies and some people's altruistic responses to them led him to theorize about *Gemeinschaftsgefuhl*, development of a deep-seated concern for others and a need to associate with them (Ionedes, 1989). Later it was translated as "social interest," a concept that was to become central to his theory.

After he established his own point of view, Adler endured rebellion among the socially conscious radicals he attracted. He also suffered the deprivation that came with serving the "common folk" rather than the "well to do" who gathered in Freud's waiting room. While serving the working class did not create a bulging wallet, it did swell Adler's pride in being the champion of the underdog.

Adler was probably the only well-known personality psychologist who held political office (Rychlak, 1981). As vice-chairman of the workers committee in Vienna, he gained some influence with the Social Democrats. Using the leverage associated with this post, he and his students installed Adlerian clinics into the thirty state run schools of Vienna. These mental health facilities prospered from 1921 until 1934 when they were closed by the Nazis. The clinics scored many successes. For example, the Viennese delinquency rate dropped during the clinics' existence.

Later Adler began to emphasize adult education, making him a pioneer in applied psychology. He made his first trip to the United States in 1926. In 1934 he and his wife fled Nazi-infested Austria for the United States. Here Adler became known as an "indefatigable lecturer" to parents and teachers, as well as a "constant advisor" to child-guidance clinics (Alexander & Selesnick, 1966). His remaining life combined great energy, enjoyment, and capacity for work. You will learn in later chapters that he had significant influence on other personality psychologists during his time in the United States.

Adler has been described as "a most democratic, friendly, hospitable person with a love for informal sociability, music, and all the arts, including gardening" (Ansbacher 1964, p. xxii). Two of his four children, Alexandra and Kurt, became psychiatrists in their father's tradition. Like their father, they were devoted to helping people overcome handicaps and enjoy life more fully. It was on this worthy mission that Adler traveled to Scotland as a part of his 1937 speaking tour. While on an after-breakfast walk, he suffered a heart attack and died. Adler was 67 years old.

Adler's View of the Person

As you may have already gathered, Adler did not like to think of humans as collections of ids, egos, and complexes. Rather he saw the person as a whole individual with aspects that are too interconnected for meaningful examination apart from one another. The lives of people were seen as flowing from immaturity to maturity without the discrete breaks that characterized Freud's stages of psychosexual development. People were viewed as largely deciding for themselves what direction their lives would take—sometimes wisely, sometimes not. Whatever direction people's lives took, Adler saw them as striving for "perfection" as they conceived of the term.

Unlike Freud, Adler changed his view of the person over the years (Ansbacher & Ansbacher, 1964). At first he emphasized natural feelings of inferiority that supposedly appear very early in the person's life and require compensation for the rest of his or her life. Eva Dreidurs Ferguson (1989) called this orientation the first stage in the development of Adler's thinking. She defined a second stage that emphasized striving for power and superiority. Finally, more near the end of his career, "Adler made it explicit that humans as a species strive to belong and that the goal . . . is to contribute to human welfare" (p. 354).

Dinkmeyer and Sherman (1989) list five principles that might be regarded as basic Adlerian assumptions about people and their psychological functioning. Understanding them will move you closer to appreciating Adler's view of the person.

1. *All behavior has social meaning.* A social group, such as a family, has its own social system, including methods of relating and ways by which power is communicated. "All behavior has meaning inside this social context. Behavior can best be understood and changed when seen within the social context" (p. 148).

2. *All behavior has a purpose and is goal-directed.* Adler firmly believed that all behavior is **teleological**, or performed with a purpose. He also believed that people are always moving toward some significant goal. To understand a person's goal is to take a giant step toward understanding that person.

3. *Unity and pattern.* As indicated already, Adler was a pioneer in viewing people holistically. He saw people as unified, indivisible wholes, each with his or her unique pattern of behaviors that are designed to reach a goal.

4. *Behavior is designed to overcome feelings of inferiority and to move toward feelings of superiority.* "We are continuously working from a feeling of being less, toward a feeling of being more. This is the striving for significance" (p. 149).

5. *Behavior is a result of our subjective perceptions.* "We all create unique meanings for our experiences. We actually create our script, produce, direct, act and act out our roles" (p. 149). The way we see ourselves in relation to others is from our own unique perspectives.

Basic Concepts: Adler

Developing Social Feeling: Society, Work, and Love

Alfred Adler's commitment to "individual differences" is seen in the label he affixed to his point of view, **individual psychology**, an attempt to conceive of a unique human being as a interconnected whole, biologically, philosophically, and psychologically (Adler, 1971). Given this uniqueness and wholeness, the same situations, experiences, and life problems have different meanings for and effects on different people. While recognizing the existence of in-born differences among people, Adler warned against over-stressing them: the important thing is "not what one is born with, but what use one makes of that equipment" (1956, p. 176). He viewed the basis of individual differences as psychosocial, not hereditary. The psychosocial factor of ultimate importance to civilization is **social feeling**, concern for the community and need to associate/cooperate with people (Adler, 1964).

The cornerstone of individual psychology is Adler's belief that there are three unavoidable tasks each person must address in life: society, work, and love. The solution to all three tasks requires childhood preparation for **social interest**—individuals' efforts to develop social feeling (Rychlak, 1981). Although "social feeling" is a potential and "social interest" involves efforts to make it actual, Adler often used the terms interchangeably (Rychlak, 1981).

First, social feeling relevant to society is revealed in the individual's capacity to develop and maintain friendships. It involves preparation for cooperation in school, sports, and choice of a partner. Also the development of interest in state, country, and humanity is involved. Second, the individual must show an ability to be interested in *work*. Social feeling here takes the form of cooperative activity for the benefit of others. Individuals who perform useful work not only provide themselves with a livelihood but obtain a sense of worth to society, which values industry over laziness. It is through work that individuals assist in the progress of their developing community. Third, is an interest in *love:* the ability to be more interested in a partner than in oneself. Social feeling here is concerned with a task that requires the cooperation of two persons, as both help perpetuate the human species by caring for offspring. Prerequisites of love include childhood preparation for a two-person task, continuing consciousness of the equal worth of both partners, and a capacity for mutual devotion.

Style of Life

According to Adler, an individual's attitudes toward society, work, and love are summarized in a **style of life**, the individual's unique but consistent movement toward self-created goals and ideals developed beginning in childhood (Adler, 1964). The style of life is an original, psychological orientation that contains the individual's relatively permanent **law of movement**, the direction taken by the person that originates in his or her ability to exercise free choice in fully exploiting personal capabilities and resources (Adler, 1933a).

You have likely noticed the coincidence of style of life and "lifestyle," a currently popular phrase. "Lifestyle" probably originates from Adler's "style of life." It is another example of how our language has been influenced by the major personality theorists.

Adler illustrated style of life by reference to a couple of pine trees, one growing in a valley and one growing on a mountaintop. Although they are both pine trees, thus the same species, each shows a distinct style of life, with individuality "expressing itself and molding itself in [a unique] environment" (1956, p. 173). In human terms, the style of life is the medium through which each of us interprets the facts of our existence and through which our lives unfold. It dominates personal experience and guides dreams, fantasies, games, and recollections of childhood. It even selects images to serve its own ends and it determines thinking, feeling, and behaving.

In forming a style of life, we are not passively molded by our environment. Personality results from the activity of the **creative power of the individual**, the process by which we each make original conceptions of ourselves and our world as we develop a style of life for solving the three great problems of life (Adler, 1932). Thus, each of us is the sculptor of our own personality. Childhood beliefs, typically developed between the ages of 3 and 5, are particularly influential in the process that nurtures the developing style of life. Once these beliefs have been held for a short time, experiences out of tune with them have little influence. Behavior springs from a person's ideas about self and life.

Future Goals versus Past Events

It is also during childhood that each person establishes a **prototype**, the "complete goal" of the style of life that is a fiction conceived as a means of adapting to life and includes a strategy for its achievement (Rychlak, 1981, p. 128). Development of this concept was suggested by Hans Vaihinger's (1925) philosophy that people create fictional ideas for themselves "as if" they were objectively true. Under Vaihinger's influence, Adler conceived of **fictional finalism**, a fictional goal toward which all psychological currents flow, thereby unifying the personality (Adler, 1933b). This notion later became virtually synonymous with "prototype," which took over the title of "fictional goal."

A goal orients the individual's personality toward future expectations, not the past. It provides direction for promised security, power, and perfection, and awakens feelings consistent with one's anticipations. Freudian instincts, mechanisms, impulses, and childhood traumas are far less important in this process than Adlerian teleology or purposiveness. One's prototypical goal appears

> *in one's attitude toward others, toward one's vocation, toward the opposite sex. Thus we find concrete, single purposes, such as: to operate as a member of the community or to dominate it, to attain security and triumph in one's chosen career, to approach the other sex or to avoid it. We may always trace in these special purposes* what sort of meaning the individual has found in his existence, *and how he proposes to realize that meaning. (Adler, 1930, p. 400)*

The attitude we adopt toward solving the "three great problems of existence" is necessarily reflected in our personality. Because personality is a unity, the direction of our capacity for living life in common with others is manifested even in the "slightest" of our expressive movements. Our beliefs, misconceptions, social interest, or failure to achieve social interest, characterize all forms of personal expression, including our memories, dreams, bodily postures, and physical ailments. This framework underlies Adler's personality-assessment technique of collecting and interpreting early recollections.

Further, an individual's style of life is best seen in new situations, especially those that confront the person with difficulties. This is because one's stylistic "gait"—whether it is best characterized as a trot, a canter, or a gallop—is more clearly displayed during crises than during untroubled times. Problems result when the individual's fictions clash with reality, thereby "disclosing his wrong meaning—the mistaken significance he has foisted on life" (Adler, 1964, pp. 40–41). A type of psychological **shock** may be experienced when a person's fiction runs head-on into reality. It results in a narrowing of the person's field of action or path of advance, an exclusion of threatening tasks, and a retreat from problems for which the person is not prepared. Disillusionment, disappointment, and isolation may occur. In fact, Adler defines **neurosis** as an extreme form of reaction to shock, "a person's automatic, unknowing exploitation of the symptoms resulting from the effects of a shock" (1964, p. 180).

The general level of social feeling is not high among neurotics, who likely have been pampered as children. At the lowest level, negative personality traits such as shyness, anxiety, and pessimism indicate a "defective inclination and preparation of the whole personality" in its relations with other persons (p. 112). The essence of Adlerian therapy is to increase the neurotic's awareness of this lack of cooperative power. A technique he found helpful in working with neurotics is to bring out the "courage" and "optimism" aspects of social feeling still existing within the neurotic personality.

Overcoming Inferiority

Adler believed in the thesis that to be human means to feel inferior, insufficient, and helpless. As mentioned earlier, this orientation became deemphasized in his later writing, but if one considers his writings as a whole, it is quite central. The universal human experience of inferiority generates a struggle for perfection. Individuals are "always possessed and spurred on by a feeling of inferiority," brought about by their perpetual comparisons of themselves with unattainable ideals of perfection (Adler, 1964, p. 37). As in evolution, there is a "great upward drive" toward perfection or a "compulsion" to carry out a better adaptation. In essence, all personality develops from **inferiority,** the persistent feeling that one does not measure up to society's ideals or to one's own fictional standards. The individual's movement in life is from a minus to a plus condition.

Inferiority complex is Adler's term for the consequences of an exaggerated, persistent form of inadequacy that is partly explained by a deficiency in social interest (Adler, 1964). Adler discussed three childhood handicaps contributing to inferior feelings and a resultant lack of social feeling: inferior organs, neglect, and overindulgence (Adler, 1933a).

Inferior Physical Organs

To Adler, an "organ" could be any physical attribute. His study of organ inferiority led him to conclude that feelings of psychological inferiority might be due to a person's physical limitations (Adler, 1907/1917). This is because children born with organ weaknesses are necessarily required to **compensate**, to overcome their weaknesses by striving to become superior in some way (Adler, 1971). They may even **overcompensate**, bend over backwards to do or become whatever their weaknesses have denied them. Demosthenes, the ancient Greek, had weak lungs and a weak voice, yet he became a famous orator. Pianist Klara Schumann overcame childhood hearing problems. In this context, I am reminded of a colleague's blind student who ended a classroom talk about personal career plans by indicating all the possibilities open to him, including becoming an astronomer. Adler saw human development as "blessed with inferior organs" (1930, p. 395) because of the achievements that can be traced to the efforts aimed at overcoming physical inferiorities.

Parental Neglect: The Unwanted or Hated Child

The neglected child does not experience love, cooperation, or friendship, and seldom finds a trustworthy other-person. Throughout life, problems are overrated as "too difficult" and personal resources for problem solving are underrated as being too limited. Neglected children may be described as cold, suspicious, untrusting, hard, envious, and hateful.

Parental Overindulgence: A Harmful Practice That Often
Produces a Pampered or Spoiled Child

Adler proposed overindulgence as an alternative to Freud's "misinterpretation" of observations surrounding the Oedipus complex (Adler, 1964). To Adler, the Oedipus complex is not a universal fact but something that occurs infrequently. It is an abnormality, the unnatural outcome of overindulgence by the child's opposite-sex parent. The basic pattern is one in which the pampered child is allowed contact mainly with the person doing the spoiling, thereby excluding others.

Striving for Superiority and the Superiority Complex

During the transition from emphasizing inferiority to stressing service to society, Adler wrote of **striving for superiority**, a universal psychological phenomenon that parallels physical growth and involves the goal of bringing about perfection, security, and strength. It is represented by the dictates "Achieve! Arise! Conquer!" Specific paths to conquest are as different "in a thousand ways" as the chosen goals. **Superiority complex** is Adler's term for an exaggerated, abnormal form of striving for superiority that involves "overcompensation" for personal weakness. Like other severe psychological problems, this one is partly explained by an unaccepted deficiency in social interest. The neurotic person may present a false front of superiority as a method of escaping from social difficulties. Normal people do not have superiority complexes. Their strivings for superiority are aimed at common ambitions for success, expressed through work, love, and cooperation in society. By contrast, a superiority complex "invariably" stands in opposition to social cooperation.

As the concept "superiority complex" implies, Adler's theory has something to say about braggarts. They are people who may irritate us with their constant claims of superiority. Many of us probably assume that braggarts believe themselves to be superior. However, Adlerians would be inclined to a different interpretation. The more people brag about themselves, the more an Adlerian might see them as just compensating for feelings of inferiority. That is, braggarts may actually be people who feel inferior and are boasting to cover up their problem.

Whether or not it is to cover up inferiority, braggarts' behavior may reflect on us, making us look inferior by contrast to them. When people make very positive statements about themselves in our presence, they may make us look bad by comparison. Dismissing braggarts' exaggerated claims and assuming they are just trying to cover-up their inadequacies would seem to save us from feeling inferior relative to them. If, in fact, people adopt this logic they should describe braggarts in negative terms. Tucibat (1986) did a study to see how people respond to a braggart. Surprisingly, he found that subjects in his experiment tended to use favorable terms to describe a braggart who boasted about doing very well *in the future.*

If Adler had known of these results he might have asserted that our acceptance of other's boastfulness may be an indication that we assume our own inferiority relative to them. However, final conclusions await additional research. Future studies may show that when braggarts boast about *past accomplishments* we tend to reject their attempts to exalt themselves over us.

Family Influences on Personality Development

Of the several family influences on personality development discussed by Adler, the most important is the mother (Adler, 1964). Contact with her probably makes the largest contribution to the social interest of the child. Two tasks are involved. One is encouraging social feeling by providing the greatest experience of love and fellowship the child will ever possess. Another is spreading this connectedness, trust, and friendship to others in the form of displaying a cooperative attitude toward working with others. Adlerian therapists perform these tasks for patients who are deficient in social interest.

Second in importance for personality development is experience with the father. Adler offered a number of specific suggestions concerning how fathers may contribute to their children's development: allow children freedom to speak and ask questions; encourage children to pursue their own interests; do not ridicule or belittle; do not seek to supplant the mother; make mealtimes pleasant; be supportive.

Third in importance is **birth order**, the child's birth position relative to other siblings (Adler, 1964; see Table 4.1). In addition to birth order in and of itself, Adler's theory addresses the impact of family size and sex of siblings on personality. He deemed it a "superstition" to believe that a given family situation is the same for each individual child. This qualification helps to account for cases where circumstances may be psychologically similar for children in seemingly inconsistent birth order positions. Thus, it is not birth order itself that accounts for differences among siblings, but the psychological situation resulting from it. Additional developmental factors discussed by Adler include illness and school entry.

TABLE 4.1   Some Adlerian Hypotheses about Birth Order

Birth Order	Hypotheses
Only child	The center of attention, dominant, often spoiled because of excessive parental timidity and anxiety
Firstborn	Dethroned from a central position, has negative attitudes and feelings toward the second child and a passion for domination, but protective and helpful toward others
Second-born	Actively struggling to surpass others, with success related to competition with the firstborn, restless
Last-born	The most pampered (the smallest and weakest), not unhappy, able to excel over others by being different, often a problem child
Only girl/boy	Extreme feminine or masculine orientation

The "birth order" factor has been heavily researched in the decades after it was posed by Adler (Falbo & Polit, 1986). For example, reviews of the literature indicate a total of 391 studies on birth order between 1963 and 1971 alone (Miley, 1969; Vockell, Felker, & Miley, 1973). Birth order was also the sole topic of the May 1977 issue of *Individual Psychology.* After all these investigations, it is now clear that most of the differences, in so far as they exist, are between firstborn (or only) and later-born individuals. Research suggests that firstborns and only children are higher in achievement motivation and actual success than later borns. Such may be the case, because their environment contains only adults, mature people who are capable of creating an achievement-oriented atmosphere. On the other hand, later borns have an atmosphere that is less mature, because it is composed of children as well as adults (Zajonc & Markus, 1975). Thus, one is more likely to find firstborns rather than later borns in the U.S. Senate or the executive board room. However, firstborns are not better in every way. For example, later borns are less self-centered (Falbo, 1981).

Robert Zajonc and his colleagues have focused on the dilution of the home intellectual atmosphere by mixing later-born children with firstborns and the adults who constitute the firstborn's mature environment. Zajonc and Markus (1975) have related family size to intellectual development. Using data on nearly 400,000 Dutch 19-year-old males, they found larger family size detrimental to intellectual development. They explained this result by reasoning that each later-born child added to a family of increasing size dilutes the intellectual atmosphere for all children. Further, the larger the family, the more compressed the spacing between children, which leads to a decline in average age of family members, and, in turn, a more immature intellectual atmosphere for each child. In sum, large families immerse children in a later-born intellectual atmosphere, one created by cognitively primitive people, a sharp contrast to the adult atmosphere that exists for firstborns.

Some more contemporary studies also appear to support Adler's notions about birth order. For example, Parrish (1990) investigated teachers' evaluations of 94 students' support systems (a support system is composed of friends and relatives who provide aid and comfort in times of distress). He found that firstborns experienced fewer dysfunctional support systems than later borns. Parrish also reported that firstborns experienced fewer support system failures than later borns when both were from divorced and remarried families. The two birth order positions did not differ if both were from intact families or from divorced-nonremarried families.

In line with earlier results, Cherian (1990) found that among 1021 South African school children, the later were children born into their families, the lower was their academic achievement. An additional study by Ishiyama, Munson, and Chabassol (1990) produced logically related results. Among 194 Canadian high school students, compared to later borns, firstborns showed less fear of the possible negative consequences of academic success (an example negative consequence would be facing higher expectations after scoring a success).

BOX 4.1   Frankenstein and His Monster Reconsidered: An Adlerian Analysis

When R. John Huber, Joan Widdifiel, and Charles Johnson (1989) recently took another look at Mary Shelley's classic novel about a brilliant scientist who creates life in the laboratory, they made two important discoveries. First, the Hollywood rendition of Frankenstein's creation and its aftermath is largely an inaccurate translation of the original novel. Second, they noted remarkably clear illustrations of Adler's major principles and conceptions. Huber and colleagues contend that Frankenstein was *not* a scientist interested in advancing his discipline and benefiting humanity who was victimized by laboratory manipulations gone wrong. Rather he was a man overwhelmed with compensatory strivings for god-like superiority because of inferior feelings dating to his pampered childhood. Further, his "monster" began life with human qualities, including the desire to be a loved member of the community, and might have developed his natural propensity to social feeling had it not been for the neglect of his "father," Frankenstein. An examination of the two main characters in Shelley's misunderstood novel provide helpful illustrations of Adler's most critical concepts.

Victor Frankenstein: The pampered child becomes the adult seeker of grandiosity. The first five years of his life, Victor Frankenstein was an only child, the recipient of his parents' "inexhaustible stores of affection from a very mine of love" (Shelley, 1965, p. 32). He was his parents' "innocent and helpless creature bestowed on them by heaven," their "plaything and idol," and their "only care" (p. 32). When his parents adopted a daughter, Frankenstein was not threatened. His new sister was presented to him as his "pretty present." He came to regard her as a possession. During what

was for him an idyllic childhood, Frankenstein had only his family and one friend all of whom regarded him as the center of the universe. However, at maturity, having ventured forth from his privileged realm and arrived at the university, he felt immediately alienated from the other students, a sure sign of deficient social interest. Neither did he seek the help and cooperation of his professors. Frankenstein earned his own way into the halls of science. Throughout his early adult years, he yearned only for those who had pampered him during childhood. Finally, the longing became so strong that he partially transferred his childhood universe to his new galaxy by marrying his adopted sister!

You may wonder how a pampered child harbors feelings of inferiority and resultant strivings for superiority as Adler has claimed and as Huber and colleagues extrapolated to Frankenstein. Pampering may promote inferiority because coddled children do not recognize their feelings of inferiority, much less feel the need to struggle with those basic emotions. Rather they respond to exaggerated attention by assuming their superiority and letting close relatives grapple with their problems. In conformance with these ideas, Frankenstein grew to adulthood laboring under the delusion that he was a superior being.

Then, suddenly, he was at the university, facing the shock of being surrounded by people who, by their inattention, challenged the fiction of his genius. [To Adler a true genius is one who creates a timeless contribution to all of humanity, not a memorial to her or his presumed superiority]. His response to shock was withdrawal into plans to rise above all students, all people. Through the creation of life, Frankenstein

BOX 4.1 *Continued*

expected to transcend mere mortals. Instead he suffered the fate of all those who are dominated by the superiority complex, self-destruction.

Frankenstein's creation: Unsupported attempts to develop social feeling yield monstrous results. In complete contradiction to movie depictions, Frankenstein's "monster" began life with clear signs of social interest. His "life" is a profound testimony to the truth of Adler's belief that social feeling is a potential common to us all that may or may not become actual. The "monster," whose strength and intelligence were extraordinary, showed the need for upward striving by immediately displaying an intense desire to learn. In particular, he strove to learn language, a definite sign of emerging social feeling. A still clearer mark of social interest was his need for companionship and desire to relate to others. He peered from his miserable hovel at the villagers as they passed by and longed to become one of them. When they were joyful so was he; when they were unhappy he was depressed. "The creation wept with sensitivity when he observed displays of affection, heard of injustices to mankind, or heard beautiful music" (Huber et al., 1989, p. 275).

Despite this evidence that social feeling was blooming in the "monster," events began to remind him of his inferiority. When he visited a blind priest from whom he expected sympathy, all went well until others arrived on the scene and recoiled in horror at his appearance. It was the first time that others' abhorrence of his organ inferiority fully registered on him. When he saw his own image in a pool of water for the first time, he was able to understand their revulsion at the mere sight of him.

The final blow was struck when "the creation" read an abandoned copy of *Paradise Lost* and contrasted his own existence with that of Adam. Adam was loved; Adam had a mate; he did not. When he revealed the agony of his loneliness to his creator and pleaded for a mate, Frankenstein at first expressed intentions to sculpture a wife for him. But when the scientist began what was to be his second creation, he was overcome with guilt and concern. If the monster had a mate, they would have offspring that might terrorize the world. Was this concern a vestige of social interest? Huber and colleagues think so. Was his guilt a sign of his genuine affinity for people and love of community? The authors thought not. His display of guilt was merely an attempt to appear more sensitive and thoughtful than others.

Extreme strivings for superiority end in self-destruction. When guilt led Frankenstein to destroy his laboratory, "the creation" realized that his "father" had abandoned him. The scientist's rash act made him apperceive that he had visited catastrophe on the world rather than heaped glory on himself. His creation, realizing that his desire to join the community and experience acceptance had been dashed forever, declared ". . . if I cannot inspire love, I will cause fear" (Shelley, 1965, p. 147). Truly there is no hatred so intense as that born of unrequited love. The enraged monster went on an unmerciful rampage. He stalked Frankenstein, leaving the mangled bodies of the scientist's loved ones in his wake. Finally, they adopted a mutual goal: destroy the other. In the end, Frankenstein's desperate striving to overcome inferiority due to a pampered childhood, and the monster's struggle to compensate for the repulsive appearance that constituted his organ defect, led to the demise of both. Each was a victim of failure to develop social feeling.

Evaluation

Contributions

Early Recollections: A Useful Measurement Technique

Adler employed a simple method to assess aspects of people's lifestyles (Hyer, Woods, & Boudewyns, 1989). **Early recollections (ERs)** indicate how a person views her or himself and other people and reveal what the person strives for in life, what he or she anticipates, and, more generally, his or her conception of life itself. ERs also index present attitudes, beliefs, and motives. That is, ERs are more important for what they say about a person as she or he is now, than for what the person was like as a child.

The best way to appreciate an ER is to do one. Read the instructions in Box 4.2 concerning how to do an ER. Do one, then read on to find out how to interpret your ER.

The technique of asking people to state their earliest recollection (ER) was dear to Adler. Adler would "never" investigate a personality without asking for the first memory, which he considered one of the "most trustworthy" ways of exploring personality. In essence, ERs are summary statements about personality, closely tied to the person's style of life.

Adler's reliance on ERs reflects his special brand of determinism: *the present determines the past*, exactly the opposite of Freud's determinism. According to Adler, we are necessarily "forced" to select precisely those events from our past

---

BOX 4.2   Doing and Interpreting ERs

To do an ER, simply think back to the earliest time in your life that you can remember. Write down this earliest recollection as completely as you can. After you are finished, return to the next paragraph.

You can interpret your ER by answering some questions concerning it (Manaster & Perryman, 1979). Answer each question fully.

1. Who is present? Mother, father, siblings, grandparents, friends?
2. Who is not present?
3. How are different people portrayed? What are the basic thoughts, feelings, words, and actions of all present?
4. What is the world like? Friendly?

Hostile? Cooperative? Uncooperative? Unfamiliar?
5. What is your role or behavior? Active? Passive? Independent? Dependent? Sick?
6. What is the outcome of your behavior? Success? Failure? Uncertainty? Good? Bad? Right? Wrong?
7. What is your primary social attitude? "I" or "we"?
8. What is your dominant emotion? Happy? Sad? Fearful? Worried? Guilty? Proud?
9. What is your primary motive? To gain attention, power, revenge, or to be left alone?
10. What is the underlying "story" of your life?

that best represent our current personality. We have little choice in the matter. Also, it makes no difference whether the events appearing in our ER really occurred. It is only important that we *believe* such events happened, in the particular way we remember them.

> *Among all psychological expressions, some of the most revealing are the individual's memories. His memories are the reminders he carries about with him of his own limits and of the meaning of circumstances.*
>
> *There are no "chance memories": out of the incalculable number of impressions which meet an individual, he chooses to remember only those which he feels, however darkly, to have a bearing on his situation. Thus memories represent his "Story of My Life"; a story he repeats to himself to warn him or comfort him, to keep him concentrated on his goal. . . . A depressed individual could not remain depressed if he remembered his good moments and his successes. He must say to himself, "All my life I was unfortunate," and select only those events which he can interpret as instances of his unhappy fate. Memories can never run counter to the style of life. (Adler, 1956, p. 351)*

Sanitioso, Kunda, and Fong (1990) recently produced results consistent with Adler's belief that people's current conceptions of themselves influence their recollections of the past. These researchers first informed some subjects that it is better to be introverted. Others were told that being extraverted is better. It may be assumed that subjects in the first group would come to see themselves as introverted, and those in the second group would see themselves as extraverted. Then subjects read a message on a personal computer screen and pressed a key to signify "yes" as soon as they had a memory related to the message. Each message pertained to introversion or to extraversion. Subjects who were made to feel "introverted" were quicker to come up with a memory when cued by an introverted message than those who were led to feel "extraverted." The analogous results occurred for those led to feel extraverted. Thus, as Adler would have predicted, individuals whose current conception of themselves was "extravert" were relatively quick to retrieve extraverted memories and those whose conceptions were "introvert" were relatively quick to recollect introverted memories.

Two examples of ERs follow, accompanied by Adler's (1956) interpretations of them.

> #1. *When I was three years old, my father purchased for us a pair of ponies. He brought them by the halters to the house. My sister took one strap and led her pony triumphantly down the street. My own pony, hurrying after the other, went too fast for me and trailed me face downward in the dirt. It was an ignominious end to an experience which had been gloriously anticipated. The fact that I later surpassed my sister as a horsewoman has never mellowed this disappointment in the least. (pp. 354–355)*

Adler offered a "blind interpretation" of this memory, which means he knew nothing about the person who gave it. He assumed the person to be a girl who was more interested in her father than her mother, just as he had been. There is triumph for the older sister, who may have been the mother's favorite. The girl is unable to keep up with her older sister. She believes she must be careful or her sister will always win, resulting in the girl's being left behind "in the dirt," defeated. The girl's attitude conveyed in the ER is "If anyone is ahead of me, I am endangered. I must always be first."

> *#2. When I was about four years old I sat at the window and watched some work-men building a house on the opposite side of the street, while my mother knitted stockings. (p. 356)*

This memory was provided by a 32-year-old man, an eldest sibling whom Adler identified as the "spoiled son of a widow." His life was characterized by severe anxiety attacks, except when he was at home. Past school and professional work had proved difficult for him. While good-natured, he had found it difficult to make social contact with others. Although his ER may seem "rather insignificant," it is not. Support for his having been a pampered child is present in his recall of a situation that includes his solicitous mother. More important, his preparation for life is that of being an onlooker: "he looks on while other people work." Once his anxiety has been eliminated through therapy, planning for future work could be guided by his natural dispositions toward seeing and observing. Adler recommended a business dealing with art objects.

Adler's measure of ERs has received much attention and proven quite useful (Mosak, 1969). Olson (1979) estimates that 100 articles have been written about ERs. Using ERs, Burnell and Solomon (1964) were able to predict success or failure in basic military training of Air Force recruits. Jackson and Sechrest (1962) reported more ER themes of fear in anxiety neurotics, abandonment in depressed clients, and illness in psychosomatic patients. In a study by Hafner, Fakouri, and Labrentz (1982), more alcoholics than non-alcoholics remembered threatening situations and showed themes of being controlled externally rather than internally. Hyer, Woods, and Boudewyns (1989) report ER evidence that Vietnam veterans suffering from Posttraumatic Stress Disorder (PTSD) are low in social interest, pursue goals in a devious manner, are vigorously acted upon by others, and pursue more negative outcomes and themes. Mosak and Kopp (1973) interpreted the ERs of Adler, Freud, and Jung and concluded that Adler related to people through inadequacy, Freud through provocation, and Jung through helplessness.

Measures of Social Interest

In recent years measures of social interest have been developed and validated. Most prominent among them is the Social Interest Scale (SIS) developed by James E. Crandall (1980). In deriving the SIS, Crandall attempted to account for Adler's conceptions of healthy and unhealthy striving for superiority that involve social interest (Ansbacher & Ansbacher, 1964). Healthy striving involves a blending of superiority needs with social interest requirements such that the individual's development and accomplishments are integrated with concern for others. Unhealthy striving entails a decided lack of social interest.

Crandall found that the SIS is reliable: a typical subject's score tends to be similar from one occasion to the next. It was also valid: it related to measures that assess certain aspects of social interest. In particular, the SIS correlated well with several measures of psychological adjustment and well-being: well-adjusted individuals and people with positive senses of well-being scored high on the SIS.

Recent investigations provide further evidence that measures of social interest are both valid and useful. Leak and Williams (1989a) used three measures of social interest, finding their own measure and one by Greever, Tseng, and Friedland (1973) to correlate better with family environment than the SIS. For these two superior measures, the greater the social interest, the greater the family cohesion and expressiveness and the less the family conflict. Also, the greater the social interest, the greater the degree of interest in political, social, intellectual, and cultural activities and the greater the emphasis on ethical and religious issues and values. Finally, Leak and Williams found that the higher the social interest, the more positive were perceptions of the family environment.

A second study by the same researchers related social interest to hardiness and alienation (Leak & Williams, 1989b). Hardiness consisted of three factors: commitment, challenge, and control. "Commitment involves an active approach to coping with life's challenges . . . because of a sense of courage and psychological tolerance" (p. 370). "Challenge entails a perception that novel events and changing circumstances offer an opportunity for development" (p. 370). Control "refers to a belief in personal, internal control over the events in one's life" (p. 370). Subjects received alienation scores on alienation from work, alienation from self, alienation from others, alienation from family, and total alienation. Across two studies, the SIS was significantly and inversely related to all four alienation scales and total alienation: the greater the social interest, the less the alienation. Social interest was significantly and positively related to total hardiness (sum across the three scores): the greater the social interest the greater the hardiness. A breakdown of hardiness into its three scales revealed a more specific outcome: the greater the social interest the higher the commitment and control scores, but challenge was unrelated to social interest.

Although research on social interest is just beginning, the outlook is quite hopeful. At present it appears that social interest is positively related to psychological adjustment and hardiness and inversely related to alienation. Social interest also is meaningfully related to a number of family environment factors. It may well be that social interest measures will one day take a place alongside such measures as introversion-extraversion on the list of primary psychological indexes.

Adlerian Therapy: A Going and Growing Concern
While the psychoanalytic brand of therapy developed by Freud may be fading in popularity, it appears that Adlerian therapy is gaining popularity. An entire journal devoted to Adlerian theory and therapy has been thriving for years. It is *Individual Psychology*, a major contributor to this chapter.

A survey of 32 Adlerian therapists, conducted by Kal (1972), contains many insights into the nature of Adler's therapeutic methods. He found that Adlerians are more likely to view people in terms of wishes, expectations, goals, convictions, and mistaken apperceptions, not in terms of needs, conflicts, drives, and pleasure. Their primary question in relation to patients is "What purpose does the symptom serve?", not "What caused the symptom?" Therapists' interest is forward-looking, not backward-looking. One of the questions in Kal's survey was "What in your practice do you consider most typically Adlerian, in contrast with other schools?" Respondents indicated the following beliefs, rank-ordered according to the frequency with which they were mentioned:

1. Social nature of man
2. "Soft determinism": freedom of choice
3. Purposefulness of all behavior
4. Therapist's optimism
5. Therapist's effectiveness
6. Holistic approach
7. Stress on reason and understanding vs. instincts and emotions
8. Active role of the therapist
9. Cooperative, egalitarian aspect of therapy
10. Use of early recollections

One practical problem with some therapies, such as psychoanalysis, is the large number of sessions assumed to be required. The greater the number of sessions, the more the time and money invested. In light of this problem, Adlerian therapy seems to have a definite advantage over some others therapies. It seems especially easy to adapt Adler's methods to the *brief therapy approach*, techniques that are able to address and solve clients' problems in a specifiable and relatively small number of sessions.

Carlson (1989) illustrates brief therapy of the Adlerian type in the case of a patient, Jim, who wished to stop smoking. Jim's mother and stepfather were married when he was two years old. When he learned of his "real" father at age nine, his entire life changed. Up to that point he had been a rather typical child. Thereafter he became a "hellraiser."

Background information collected upon Jim's first appearance for therapy indicated that he smoked for some 20 years, consuming in the order of 150,000 cigarettes at an estimated cost of $15,000. Despite drinking too much coffee—about 10 cups a day—and having had past problems with alcohol, Jim's general health was good. To assess his lifestyle, Carlson gave Jim the Kern Life-style Scale (Kern, 1986). It revealed that Jim's two lifestyle priorities were perfectionism and being a victim. ER data was also collected and indicated that Jim was a thrill seeker and bent on oral gratification. More specifically, at six or seven years of age, he remembered running down a hill toward the ocean too enthralled by the roar of the water to heed his mother's terrified pleas for him to stop. At age seven Jim recalled being at a large family gathering during which someone pushed him off a tree stump, breaking his arm. He ran around howling in pain unable to stop even when others attempted to intervene.

Putting together the background information, the ERs, and the lifestyle data, Carlson indicated that Jim was "an excellent candidate to stop smoking" (p. 222). After all, he had managed to keep his weight down and beat his alcohol problems. Carlson went on to inform Jim that he would need to work on his *self-efficacy*, the perception of one's ability to perform a specific task, such as losing ten pounds. This useful notion is covered more fully in the chapter on the work of Albert Bandura that occurs later in the book.

The discussion of self-efficacy was preliminary to the first step in therapy, the education phase. To begin this step, Carlson asked Jim why he wanted to stop smoking. Jim answered that he knew it was bad for this health—he was experiencing morning coughing and shortness of breath. He also indicated that smoking was offensive to his friends—their "kidding" caused him to hide in the bathroom when he needed to smoke.

Carlson's first suggestion was that Jim write his reasons for not smoking on a card and refer to it when he had the urge to smoke. The therapist's second suggestion regarded diet. Jim was advised to eat sunflower seeds when he felt the need to smoke. These seeds are botanically related to the tobacco plant and curb the urge to smoke because they generate "a glandular reaction very similar to that caused from tobacco" (p. 223). Thus, sunflower seeds would ease his craving for cigarettes.

Carlson's third suggestion revolved around the observation that nicotine raises the alkaline level in the body, thus shifting the PH balance: the alkaline and acidic levels relative to one another. When an individual stops smoking, the PH balance is shifted again. The problem of a changed PH balance after smoking cessation is minimized by the consumption of fruits and vegetables. Jim agreed to increase his consumption of apples and oranges.

Carlson also suggested that Jim cut down on meat, eggs, sugar, and caffeine: consumption of these substances also makes smoking cessation difficult. To lower caffeine intake, it was suggested that Jim use a smaller mug and mix in decaffeinated coffee. Because smokers are also deficient in vitamins C and B, Jim was asked to consider taking vitamins for a few weeks after quitting.

Next Jim was given some psychological techniques that are useful in combatting the stress associated with giving up cigarettes. Carlson outlined a simple, deep-breathing method: one hand is placed on the belly, one on the chest, and the patient is told to practice breathing such that the hand on the belly moves, not the one on the chest. This is diaphragmatic breathing and is an effective stress reducer. Jim was also taught some simple stretching exercises and encouraged to continue his walking and recently initiated bicycling.

Carlson also equipped Jim to avoid situations that elicit smoking behavior. Jim was instructed to avoid the chair he typically sat in during smoking. He was also advised to discard ashtrays, clean his car thoroughly to eliminate smells, and brush his teeth regularly, following professional teeth cleaning. Finally, Jim was given an audiotape containing a hypnosis routine and told to play it at least once a day. The tape was designed to reinforce the points made in the initial session.

True to Adler's orientation, Carlson focused on Jim's present problems, using ERs only to assess his current characteristics. In contrast to psychoanalysis, Jim was not just encouraged to "talk things out in order to gain insight," he was given some tasks to do. Also, in line with the Adlerian assumption that people need to enhance self-esteem, Jim was encouraged to build his self-efficacy, a very specific kind of self-esteem. Finally, Jim's need to accommodate his friends at work, a community concern, thus, a show of social feeling, was encouraged.

Jim would need only to check back with Carlson on a few additional occasions to assess his progress. The brief therapeutic method had equipped him to handle his smoking problem on his own. To support the success of his practices, Carlson reported that 70 percent of research patients who adopted the suggested activity changes were still not smoking one year after initial sessions. Other therapists report success in adapting Adlerian methods to brief therapy. In just ten sessions, Dinkmeyer and Sherman (1989) helped a disturbed family to become more functional and showed them how to support one another in coping with personal problems.

Limitations

Birth Order Research: A Big Boondoggle?

The vast number of studies concerning birth order are beginning to create more confusion than enlightenment. Contradictory findings plague research, often resulting from the absence of a coherent theoretical rationale, a disregard of family size, and inattention to sex of siblings (MacDonald, 1971; Schooler, 1972). In one illustrative study, MacDonald (1971) explored relationships between birth order and six personality variables in 1262 college students. The mean differences among birth-order groups were slight, and the relationships uncovered were complicated: firstborns appeared rigid, firstborns and only children appeared socially responsible, only females appeared high in need for approval, and later borns appeared to be controlled more by external than by internal factors. Havassy-De Avila (1971) urged that greater attention be paid to psychological processes underlying birth-order differences, rather than looking at the simplistic fact of birth order itself. In support of this position, Jordan, Whiteside, and Manaster (1982) evaluated seven different schemas for measuring birth order effects among 467 business majors. The only schema that predicted academic achievement was the one that included information on sex of subject and sex of siblings rather than birth position alone. Competitive desire to succeed and career strivings were highest in only-child males. Relative indifference to negative interpersonal consequences of achievement was highest in only-child females.

Discouragement with the birth order effect has become epidemic, even spreading to the popular literature. Kohn (1990) interviewed some leading researchers on the topic and concluded that birth order probably does not matter unless parents take it seriously. Among the experts interviewed was Toni Falbo whose work was cited earlier. Falbo now concedes, "Birth order doesn't really explain a whole lot. . . . But people like it. It's much like astrology. It says, 'I'm not to blame for the way I am' " (Kohn, p. 34).

Much of the criticism has been aimed at the Zajonc and Markus (1975) assertion that large family size, which produces large numbers of later borns, has a negative effect on intellectual development. The June, 1988 *American Psychologist* included several letters concerning Zajonc's (1986) article in which his earlier moderation in regard to the potency of the birth order factor was replaced by new claims for the power of "position in the family." Basically these letters, some of which contained original data, indicated that Zajonc had overstated his case. The writers, all researchers and theorists, felt that birth order was a weak determinant of intellectual development, at best. Nevertheless, into the early 1990s, researchers are still finding birth order useful in understanding other factors (Newman, Higgins, & Vookles, 1992).

ERs Revisited

While ERs are interesting, they are also open-ended and abstract, thus, subject to various interpretations (Carlson, 1989). Because of their nature, they are also difficult to quantify: it is hard to find valid and reliable ways to score them. As a case in point, Hyer and colleagues (1989) attempted to quantify some subjects' ERs and relate them to several personality measures. Their results were notable for displaying an almost complete lack of relationship between ER variables and many different personality factors.

Conclusion

I think you will find in the chapters ahead that Alfred Adler's influence on other theorists is very great, if not widely recognized. His effect on others was not just in terms of theory or the practice of psychotherapy. Adler was a model of the responsible, humanitarian professional. As a person who fervently sought world peace and fought for more humane treatment of people, especially children, he almost certainly had great impact on the many psychologists who followed him, including some of the ones covered in subsequent chapters.

Recently, a section of the *Psychologists for Social Responsibility Newsletter* was devoted to Adler's contribution to the cause of world peace and just treatment of all people (Rudmin & Ansbacher, 1989). The authors of this piece indicated that "Adler was a social activist in theory and practice. He opposed violence of all forms and promoted social interest in the individual and in the group. To him mental health implied `socially affirmative action' . . . and social responsibility was fundamental to the practice of psychology . . ." (p. 8). Adler himself was quoted as saying, "The honest psychologist cannot shut his eyes to social conditions which prevent the child from becoming a part of the community and from feeling at home in the world, and which allow him to grow up as though he lived in enemy country. Thus, the psychologist must work against nationalism . . . against wars of conquest . . . against unemployment which plunges people into hopelessness; and against all other obstacles which interfere with the spreading of social interest in the family, the school, and society at large" (1956, p. 454).

In 1928 Adler, along with such notables as Mohandas Gandhi, contributed an article to *Violence and Non-violence: A Handbook of Active Pacifism*, edited by Franz Kobler for War Resisters International. In it he wrote, "War is not the continuation of politics with other means, but the greatest social crime against the solidarity of humanity . . ." (Rudmin & Ansbacher, 1989, p. 8). Later he expanded this point of view, revealing greater sensitivity and enlightenment regarding women than was displayed by his former colleagues Freud and Jung. "He theorized that it was war, with its high valuation on physical strength, that led to the original subjugation of women, and he claimed that the 'inequality of women is greater in warlike countries'" (Adler, quoted in Rudmin & Ansbacher, 1989, p. 8). Though a socialist, Adler was vehemently anti-communist. The reasons were twofold. First, the Bolsheviks, Soviet communists, embraced violence and sought power for its own sake. He wrote of them, "The rule of Bolshevism is based on the possession of power. Thus its fate is sealed . . . the intoxication of power has seduced them. . . . Cheap reasons are given to justify action and reaction. Fair becomes foul, foul becomes fair!" (Adler, 1956, p. 457). "He likened Bolshevism to a puppet without a soul, and argued that it will be worthless if it succeeds . . ." (Rudmin & Ansbacher, 1989, p. 8). His words were obviously prophetic. Bolshevism has failed.

His second reason for hating the communists was the arrest of his daughter Valentine during the Stalinist purges of 1937 (she had fled to the Russia of her mother to escape the Nazis). In April of the same year he wrote that "Vali" caused him sleepless nights and that he did not know whether he could endure the thought of her incarceration. Later when he had exhausted his last means of freeing Vali, he reported that he could neither eat nor sleep for worrying about her. It was a few days after making this declaration, on May 28, 1937, that he died of a heart attack.

Summary Points

1. In 1870, Adler was born the second of six children. He was a "father's son" who overcame childhood weaknesses. At school he was average and at the University, he failed to develop a close relationship with a professor. Adler met his wife, Raissa, among the rebellious company he kept at this time. During his early medical career, he favored poor patients. After his bitter break with Freud, Adler began to blossom as a theorist.

2. During a minor political career, he established children's clinics. After these were closed by the Nazis, he fled to the U.S. and devoted his time to applied psychology. He viewed the person as an indivisible whole. Over the years, Adler changed his view of the person, at first emphasizing inferiority, and finally stressing contributions "to human welfare." His basic assumptions included: all behavior has social meaning; all behavior has a purpose and is goal directed; all behavior has unity and pattern; behavior is designed to overcome feelings of inferiority and move toward feelings of superiority; behavior is a result of our subjective perceptions.

3. Adler's most useful concept, social interest, the development of social feeling, is directed to three life tasks: society, work, and love. Individuals' unique movements toward self-created goals are their styles of life. Their "laws of movement" are the directions they take. The "creative power of the individual" is the process by which we each make original conceptions of ourselves as we develop our styles of life.

4. During childhood we develop *prototypes*, fictional goals. This point of view illustrates the teleological nature of Adler's theory. Shock occurs when the individual's fiction runs head-on into reality. Neurosis is an extreme reaction to shock. An extreme reaction to inferiority is the inferiority complex that may require overcompensation, rather than the usual compensation. Inferiority and its aftermath take different forms depending on whether the person has been neglected or over-indulged during childhood.

5. Striving for superiority is a reaction to inferiority and can lead to the superiority complex. People with this complex may brag to cover up inferiority. That we give braggarts high marks may say much about our own feelings of inferiority. Mothers are most important in the development of their children, but fathers are close behind.

6. Adler believed only children tend to be dominant and are often spoiled. Firstborns are disturbed by a new arrival and strive for domination. Second-borns struggle to surpass others and last-borns are pampered. Much research suggests that the difference between first/only and later-borns exists, as does the tendency for many later-borns (large family size) to have a negative effect on intellectual development. Frankenstein and his misunderstood "monster" provide good illustrations of Adlerian principles. Their lack of social interest was their downfall.

7. An ER simply involves recalling an early childhood event. Adler believed that ERs are indexes of a person's present conceptions of self and style of life. Sanitioso and colleagues did a memory study that confirmed Adler's view. Supportive studies show ERs' ability to predict the success of military training, the effects of post traumatic stress syndrome, and alcoholism's affect on personality.

8. A measure of social interest (SIS) by Crandall is based on the assumption that there are healthy and unhealthy ways to pursue superiority. Crandall found the SIS to be well related to psychological adjustment. Leak and Williams report that two additional measures of social interest are negatively related to alienation and positively related to favorable family environment and hardiness. Adlerian therapists emphasize wishes and goals, purposiveness, freedom of choice, holism, social factors, ERs, and an active therapist. Carlson led "Jim" to quit smoking by developing self-efficacy, changing his diet, using deep breathing, cleaning out traces of cigarettes from his life, and using hypnosis and exercise.

9. Limitations of Adlerian theory and practice include that birth order studies show mixed results, no results, or results that contradict conceptions of birth order. Even the popular press has taken up the cause against birth order. The prestigious *American Psychologist* recently contained several negative responses to

Zajonc's claim that the birth order factor, family size (including spacing), affects intellectual development.

10. Despite these limitations, Adler will long be remembered, especially when psychologists reflect on the roots of their social activism and the source of many of their ideas. Adler's life set the stage for today's attention to the needs of disadvantaged children, oppressed people—including women—and the necessity of eliminating war.

Running Comparison

Theorist	Adler in Comparison
Freud	He rejected sexualism and the universality of Freud's Oedipus complex. He focused on community (social) factors, rather than intrapsychic ones. Consciousness and the present were more emphasized than in psychoanalytic theory (PT). He believed that people are pulled by goals rather than pushed by instincts. Unlike PT, personality was viewed holisticly and people have freedom of choice. To Adler, insight is not enough; people have to have the courage to act.
Abraham Maslow and Carl Rogers	Striving for superiority has the flavor of "self-actualization."
Albert Bandura	Like Bandura, anticipations of the future rather than motivations rooted in the past determine behavior.

Essay/Critical Thinking Questions

1. Knowing what you now know about Adler, and recalling what you learned about Freud a short time ago, contrast the two as people. How were they different as people?

2. What were the essential differences between Freud's view of people and Adler's view? Indicate the five most basic philosophical differences that separated Freud and Adler.

3. Adler believed that people have free will. What does his assumption predict about the kind of therapy that Adler would be expected to develop? Describe aspects of Adlerian therapy that are consistent with "free choice."

4. What is your style of life? Outline your style of life, being careful to include how your prototype has developed and how you have evolved since childhood.

5. What was the *shock* of your life? Using Adler's definition of the term, indicate the clearest instance of "shock" that has occurred to you.

6. How does *healthy* and *unhealthy* "striving for superiority" differ? Indicate examples of both kinds, being sure to clearly differentiate between them.

7. How do you spoil a child the Adlerian way? Map out the child-rearing techniques parents would use to develop a spoiled child. Remember to stick with Adler's theory, not your own.

8. What could Frankenstein have done to make a *super good* human being of his creation? Where did he go wrong as a "parent" and how would you correct his course? Use Adlerian terms in this discussion.

9. How well have you developed social feeling? Look at the state of your social interest by indicating factors in your history that would or would not promote development of social feeling.

10. Could you come up with a measure of social interest? Try it. Write a ten-item questionnaire that would be designed to assess people's social interest, or lack of it.

5

MOVING TOWARD, AWAY FROM, AND AGAINST OTHERS: HORNEY'S SOCIAL PSYCHOANALYSIS

- How basic is anxiety? Does everyone suffer from it?
- What makes people jealous?
- If some women are "castrating," why are they?
- What is your orientation to others, toward them, away from them, or against them?
- What are the reasons for various sexual behaviors?

Recall that Freud saw personality largely as a function of instinctive influences. Jung's "collective unconscious" was intimately tied to humans' ancestral past and Adler's point of view was anchored by present strivings for superiority. In comparison, Karen Horney's most central concepts emerge from explorations of parent/child relationships. Thus, her theory refers to early childhood. However, interactions between parents and children are the critical consideration, not repressed attraction to the opposite sexed parent, early experiences with remnants of humans' ancestral past, or strivings to overcome inferiority that date to early childhood. Nevertheless, Freud was important to Horney. She used his theory as a framework upon which she built a new more social psychoanalysis that reinterpreted Freud's orientation to females and reconceived his hypotheses about parent-child relationships.

Horney, the Person

Karen Clementina Theodora Danielsen was born on September 15, 1885, in Eilbek, Germany, a community near Hamburg (Quinn, 1988). However, she was not really German. Her father, Berndt Henrik Wackels Danielsen, was a Norwegian sea captain working for a Hamburg-based shipping line, and her mother, Clothilde Marie Van Ronzelen, was born to a well-regarded Dutch-German family. Clothilde, called Sonni, was the beautiful and commanding daughter of Dutch architect Jacob Van Ronzelen, born during the second of his three marriages. Sonni's mother died giving birth to her and she was reared by Van Ronzelen's third wife.

Captain Danielsen was 18 years older than Sonni and had four children by a previous marriage. Karen was the second child of his second marriage. Her feelings toward him were always mixed. She apparently admired her father, but he was stern, a man of strong religious fervor who attempted to control her life. There was a time when she felt attracted to men like her father, "brutal and . . . forceful men" (Quinn, 1988, p. 160). Perhaps to establish some bond with him, she even claimed that they made an extended sea voyage together, an assertion that Quinn doubts. However, she also expressed loathing for him and they had many conflicts, one of which involved the educational arena.

Because Karen was very bright, and early on expressed an interest in pursuing an advanced education, the Captain's conventional belief that education was for men predicted a clash. When the inevitable happened and he opposed her educational aspirations, Karen's mother stood by her. While Sonni's support was important, Karen's determination to be an educated person may have come from knowledge of her maternal step-grandmother's unusual childhood. Wilhelmine Lorentz-Mayer Van Ronzelen, or Minna, who reared Sonni as her own, was educated by her father along with her seven brothers, very unusual treatment at that time (Quinn, 1988). Fortunately, Captain Danielsen was at sea so often that he proved a paper barrier in Karen's path to academic success.

Having thus escaped from under the thumb of her father, she submitted to the protection of her mother. Consequently her sense of security was undermined, a state that was enhanced by a self-perceived lack of physical beauty (Quinn, 1988). As a remedy, Horney immersed herself in her studies and seemed to assert that if she could not be beautiful, she would be smart.

At about this time Horney began to overtly display a concern for *human relationships* and the *role of women*. In her adolescent diaries, she displayed both of these orientations: "I think very highly of men who can bear to love a woman just as she is without demanding that she be in one certain uniform" (Horney, 1980, p. 177).

Horney's goal to study medicine was clear to her at age 14. Though encouraged by her intelligent and freethinking mother, it was unconventional for a woman of her day. However, Karen proved to be in the right place at the right time. Social changes in Germany allowed her to move to the forefront of new circumstances favorable to women's rights: secondary education and medical training. At the age of 20 she became one of a very few women immersed in a sea of first-year, male, medical students at the University of Freiburg. During this first semester, she met Oscar Horney, with whom she maintained a lively correspondence after he left almost immediately to pursue a law degree (Quinn, 1988). Some four years later they were married. She had the first of their three daughters during the second part of her medical training. While Oscar was becoming a success as the rapidly promoted manager of an investment firm, Karen was trying to balance mother, homemaker, and medical student roles. She succeeded at this early attempt to fit the superwoman image and completed her final requirements for the M.D. degree in 1915.

Karen Horney

Possibly stresses involved with her complex life pursuits partly explain the depression and an alleged suicide attempt that Horney experienced during her medical training. Her melancholy condition may have initiated her interest in Freudian therapy. In any case she began analysis with Dr. Karl Abraham in 1910. Eventually she attended weekly meetings on psychoanalysis at Abraham's house and he became her mentor, the same role he played for Erich Fromm. These excursions into psychoanalysis lead to the founding of the Berlin Psychoanalytic Institute of which Horney was an active member from 1918 to 1932. They also planted the seeds of doubt in Horney's mind. Her criticisms of Freud's point of view began to blossom at this time.

Horney's early letters to Oskar reflected the personal questioning and deep exploration mentioned earlier. The Alfred Adler concepts of inferiority and striving for superiority, especially regarding women in social relationships, were prominent in Horney's thinking at this time. When her marriage began to dissolve in 1926, writing in search of the "truth" became her passion. She could think of nothing more unbearable than "disappearing quietly in the great mass of the average" or "of being told one is a nice, friendly, average person" (Horney, 1980, p. 245).

Horney emigrated to the United States in 1932, perhaps to escape the possibility that the Nazis would seize power and probably to escape the remnants of her marriage. Almost immediately she became associated with the Psychoanalytic Institute. However, after Institute members criticized her for questioning Freudian theory, she and her followers left the organization and founded the Association for the Advancement of Psychoanalysis. They also started a training institution, the American Institute of Psychoanalysis. Horney was a founding editor of the Association's official organ, the *American Journal of Psychoanalysis*. While in the United States, she had the opportunity to associate with Erich Fromm, Harry Stack Sullivan, Margaret Mead, and other luminaries of the time. Karen Horney died of cancer in 1952.

Horney's View of the Person

Though retaining what I considered the fundamentals of Freud's teachings, I real-
ized . . . that my search for a better understanding had led me in directions that
were at variance with Freud. If so many factors that Freud regarded as instinctual
were culturally determined, if so much that Freud considered libidinal was a neu-
rotic need for affection, provoked by anxiety and aimed at feeling safe with others,
then the libido theory was no longer tenable. Childhood experiences remained
important, but the influence they exerted on our lives appeared in a new light.
(Horney, 1945, p. 13)

As you can see, Horney parted company with Freud and his more pessimistic
and instinctionally based point of view. However, she did agree with him on the
importance of anxiety-provoking childhood experiences in the development of
psychological maladjustment. Anxiety became a central aspect of Horney's theory,
accounting for the operation of various defensive and security operations in personality. Along with Freud, Horney saw neuroses, which are anxiety-based, as the
predominant form of maladjustment in the early 20th century.

There are other similarities with Freud as well. Like the founder of psychoanalysis, Horney saw motivation as active and dynamic. She agreed that personality is changeable through psychotherapeutic treatment that provides insight into
the development and maintenance of problem behaviors. Horney, like the psychoanalysts, drew support for her theory from clinical observation and case-study
analyses rather than scientific research. Thus, her approach was more fundamentally human than the animal-research orientation that dominated psychology in
her day. Finally, she believed that the global and abstract topics of human nature
and values merit discussion.

At the same time, there are irreconcilable differences with Freud. Horney discarded Freud's theory of instincts as the explanation of human behavior. She
openly declared, " . . . the libido concept is unproved" (Horney, 1939, p. 52). In addition, Horney pointed out that oral, anal, genital, and aggressive drives do not exist
in all human beings (1937). To her the aim of compulsive drives is not to satisfy sexual instincts but to provide safety from feelings of isolation, helplessness, fear, and
hostility. Her conviction, "expressed in a nutshell," was that psychoanalysis should
outgrow the limitations characteristic of instinctivistic psychology (1939).

Horney declared that Freud's Oedipus complex was not universal or even central to understanding personality. In fact, she rejected his over-emphasis on sexuality: "But the one-sided emphasis Freud has given sexual factors may tempt many
people to single them out above others. . . . To be straight in sexual questions is
necessary; but to be straight only with them is not enough" (1942, p. 295). At best,
psychosexuality is relevant to some cases of neurotic jealousy in parent/child relationships (Horney, 1937).

Horney also took issue with Freud's view of the differences between the sexes.
She (1937) began her questioning in response to Freud's biased postulations about
the psychology of women, especially his concept of "penis envy." While she

acknowledged that in some cultures women may be jealous of men's anatomy, in other cultures it is the other way around (1937). In this way she chastised Freud for generalizing from his perception of his own culture to all other cultures. In regard to our culture, that is, Euro-American culture, envy of male anatomy may be limited to neurotic women. Horney used this point to criticize Freud and other psychoanalysts for extrapolating from their biased samples of disturbed patients to all people.

Horney linked "penis envy" to women's alleged "castrating tendencies." This inclination to excise the male organ, often associated with Freud's point of view, supposedly derives from women's need to take from men what the feminine gender lacks. Horney's response was straightforward: "Much of what in psychoanalytic literature is regarded as castrative tendencies in women and is traced back to penis envy, is in my opinion the result of a wish to humiliate men" and, one might add, not the desire to take the symbol of masculinity from men (Horney, 1937, p. 199).

Most important, Freud was seen as lacking a social orientation. Beyond ignoring other cultures, he showed a "total" disregard of cultural factors as influences on personality. As Horney (1937) remarked:

> *Freud sees a culture not as the result of a complex social process but primarily as the product of biological drives which are expressed or sublimated, with the result that reaction formations are built up against them. The more complete the suppression of these drives, the higher the cultural development. . . . Historical and anthropological findings do not confirm such a direct relation between height of culture and the suppression of sexual or aggressive drives. (pp. 282–283)*

Freud's view was contrary to social experience. For example, when Horney (1945) first came to the United States in 1932, she noted important differences between the behaviors of persons in this country and in some European countries that "only the difference in civilizations" could account for.

Horney, along with the other social psychoanalysts, developed alternative, social concepts. The real forces motivating human attitudes and actions were believed to be social ones: dependency, cooperation, interpersonal anxiety, hostility, love, jealousy, greed, competitiveness, inferiority, and work. Even a newborn's first experience, feeding, is one of social cooperation. The collective emphasis is clearly on human interactions in cultural and interpersonal contexts: parents, siblings, peers, significant social figures, and one's total society. This broader social perspective may be seen as compensating for Freud's theoretical deficiencies.

In general, and in contrast to Freud, Horney placed greater emphasis on conscious processes. Thus, id influences recede into the background. The influence of superego (conscience aspect) remains important. However, it is tied to the process of *socialization*, learning one's particular culture, not just the identification process. The primary vehicle of socialization is the family, which passes culture from generation to generation. The family's importance as a psychosexual unit—children lusting after parents—is of secondary importance.

There were also some differences in regard to the origin of human values. Horney believed there is "no such thing" as a universal trend in human nature or a "normal" psychology that holds true for all humankind. Nevertheless, she did endorse a view of healthy persons as having the capacity to bestow "a good deal of genuine friendliness and confidence" on people (1937, p. 95).

BOX 5.1   Horney on Adult Sexuality

Although Horney largely bypassed or reconceived of Freud's psychosexuality, she had much to say about adult sexuality, an unusual propensity for a woman of her era.

Horney regarded masturbation as normal, but compulsive masturbation was a different matter. Individuals who masturbate compulsively—engaging in this activity frequently and without the ability to stop themselves—are attempting to release anxiety through a sexual "safety-value" (Horney, 1937, p. 52).

In the realm of sexual relations with other people, Horney saw four types of troubled individuals. All of these types primarily seek sex for reasons other than physical gratification. The first variety crave sexual interaction because it allows them to establish human contact. Unfortunately, malevolent motivation lies behind their desire to have relations with others: ". . . it is not so much a need for affection as a striving to conquer, or more accurately, to subdue others" (1937, p. 154).

The second type " . . . are prone to yield to sexual advances from either sex, [and] are driven by an unending need for affection, especially by a fear of losing another person through refusing a sexual request, or through daring to defend themselves against any requests made upon them, whether just of unjust" (p. 154). These people have interpersonal problems that go far beyond sexuality. They become slaves of others because they cannot bear the thought of losing them. Horney is quick to point out that these people are not genuine bisexuals, people who have a real attraction to both sexes. Rather they will submit to anyone in order not to lose that person.

The third type experience increased sexual excitement because " . . . it is an outlet for anxiety and for pent-up psychic tensions" (p. 155). When these individuals find themselves in a context that provokes their anxiety, they become attracted to the most prominent individual present. It is among these people that patients who become infatuated with their analysts are found. They either become passionately attracted to their analysts or they are highly aloof, unconsciously preferring to transfer the need for sexual closeness to an "outside" person who resembles the therapist. Alternatively, individuals in this category may manifest their need to establish sexual contact with the therapist exclusively in dreams. Ironically they have a "deep disbelief in any kind of genuine affection" and feel that the analyst is interested in them only for "ulterior motives" (p. 156).

The fourth type, homosexuality of the neurotic variety, is due to fear of competitiveness. This type is composed of individuals who (1) withdraw from attempts to attract the opposite sex so that they may avoid competition with their own sex, and (2) deal with the anxiety that competitiveness with the same sex engenders by seeking the sense of reassurance that only affection from the same sex can provide.

Horney's views on two other issues are worth brief consideration. Horney, in characteristic straightforward fashion, dismisses the Freudian allegation that women are masochistic—desire to be hurt, even physically, a probable source of the myth that women wish to be raped (Allen, 1990). In a major section on masochism, which goes well beyond sexuality, Horney used only masculine pronouns and examples. She closed this discussion with a general statement that makes no reference to gender: "Masochistic drives are neither an essentially sexual phenomenon nor the result of biologically determined processes, but originate in personality conflicts" (1937, p. 280).

Finally, Horney addressed women's alleged sexual frigidity by first acknowledging that, with the close of the Victorian era, frigidity was no longer considered a "normal condition in women" (1937, p. 199). Still it may occur as a "deficiency" for two reasons. First women may display frigidity, not because they have no sexual desire, but because they wish to humiliate the men in their lives. This explanation is especially applicable if their men have a neurotic fear of being humiliated by women. Second, women may display frigidity because of ". . . a feeling of being abused, degraded, and humiliated by sexual relations." Sex was, and to some degree still is, something that is done to them, even against their wills, as in the popular male exclamation "I put the make on her"; that is, "I tried to make her do it." Marriage gave women license to have sex, but many still felt the obligation to be frigid in order to avoid the feeling that they were willingly submitting to humiliation.

Horney felt comfortable with her own sexuality. To her sex was a normal, natural, and enjoyable experience. She was known to have had meaningful extramarital affairs before, during, and after her marriage to Oscar Horney (Quinn, 1988).

In sum, Horney reminds us that sex is rarely, if ever, just to achieve physical orgasm. Almost always there are psychological reasons behind sexual expression that are far more important than physical gratification. In turn, we are reminded that any sexual interaction is complex, a human relationship not to be taken lightly or to be engaged in thoughtlessly.

Basic Concepts: Horney

Basic Anxiety: Infantile Helplessness in a Parental World

According to Horney (1950), normal personality development occurs when factors in the social environment allow children to develop "basic confidence" in themselves and other people. This is most likely to result when parents convey genuine and predictable warmth, interest, and respect toward their child. Abnormal development occurs when environmental conditions obstruct a child's natural psychological growth. Instead of developing confidence in self and others, the child develops **basic anxiety**, "an insidiously increasing, all-pervading feeling of being lonely and helpless in a hostile world" (Horney, 1937, p. 89). The child feels "small, insignificant, helpless, deserted, endangered, in a world that is out to abuse, cheat, attack, humiliate, betray, envy" (Horney, 1937, p. 92). Basic anxiety is an irrational emotional experience involving a pervasive, unpleasant feeling of extreme discomfort.

A wide range of factors in the family environment contribute to this fundamental insecurity: parental domination, belittling attitudes, indifference, unkept promises, overprotection, a hostile home atmosphere, encouraging the child to take sides in parental disagreements, isolation from other children, and lack of respect for the child's individual needs (Horney, 1945). Perhaps Horney's sensitivity to these conditions comes from the observation that some of them existed in her own childhood home: her father was domineering, her mother somewhat overprotective, and her family divided, with Karen, Sonni, and beloved brother Brendt taking sides against her father and his other children (Quinn, 1988). However, "the basic evil is invariably a lack of genuine warmth and affection" because of the parents' own incapacity to give it (Horney, 1937, p. 80). Horney saw neurotic persons as requiring excessive amounts of reassurance, and as incapable of loving. In the final analysis, disturbances in human relationships are expressed in *neuroses*— "psychic disturbance[s] brought about by fears and defenses against these fears, and by attempts to find compromise solutions for conflicting tendencies" (1937, pp. 28–29).

Coping by Way of Ten Neurotic Needs

The child's methods of adjusting to basic anxiety form enduring motivational patterns which crystallize into important aspects of personality. These patterns are called **neurotic needs**, the coping techniques that are initiated in childhood and composed of excessive, insatiable, and unrealistic demands developed in response to the basic anxiety that dominates the person (Horney, 1950). Their aim is not instinctual satisfaction, as Freud believed, but social safety or security.

Needs are considered neurotic (1) when a person adheres to them more rigidly than do other people in the culture and (2) when there is a discrepancy between the person's potentialities and actual accomplishments. Neurotic people lack flexibility in reacting to different situations. For example, most people in our culture are likely to react indecisively or suspiciously when there are appropriate reasons for doing so. It is reasonable to be somewhat indecisive in response to having to make a difficult choice or in reaction to evidence of insincerity from another person. However, neurotic individuals tend to be indecisive or suspicious most of the time, regardless of the circumstances and persons involved. They usually are unable to make up their minds, or repeatedly indicate how impossible it is to trust anyone because "everyone" is out to get whatever they can. They experience a discrepancy between their potential and their actual productivity or enjoyment. Even though they seem to have everything going for them, their feelings point to an inappropriate sense of inferiority and an absence of happiness. They sense that they stand in their own way. Table 5.1 presents Horney's ten neurotic needs, together with some illustrative behaviors.

TABLE 5.1   Ten Neurotic Needs Identified by Horney

Excessive needs for	Shown in behaviors
1. Affection and approval	Striving to be liked and pleasing to others, to live up to the expectations of others dreading self-assertion and hostility
2. Having a "partner"	Seeking to be taken over by another, through "love"; dreading being left alone
3. Narrowly restricting one's life	Trying to be inconspicuous, undemanding, and modest; contented with little
4. Power	Seeking domination and control over others; dreading weakness
5. Exploiting others	Taking advantage of others, using others, dreading being "stupid"
6. Social recognition or prestige	Seeking public acceptance; dreading "humiliation"
7. Personal achievement	Striving to be best; defeating others; ambitious; dreading failure
8. Personal admiration	Self-inflating; not seeking social recognition, but admiration for their idealized self-image (I'm a saint)
9. Self-sufficiency and independence	Trying to not need others; maintaining distance; dreading closeness
10. Perfection and unassailability	Being driven toward superiority; dreading flaws and criticism

Moving toward, against, and away from People

According to Horney, identifying the characteristics of an individual's dominant needs can reveal the relative direction the person is likely to take in relationships with other people. The overall pattern of needs also suggests the form intrapsychic conflict is likely to take. For Horney (1945), contradictory dispositions toward other people constitute a critically important form of conflict. She called attention to the dramatization of one such contradiction, the story of Dr. Jekyll and Mr. Hyde. One side of Dr. Jekyll is "delicate, sensitive, sympathetic, helpful," while a second side is "brutal, callous, and egotistical." Horney did not imply that the Jekyll/Hyde story is the precise form that intrapsychic conflict takes, only that the central character shows a basic incompatibility of interpersonal dispositions.

"Conflict" is an essential aspect of Horney's description of neurosis. All normal people experience conflict, however, conflict of neurotic proportions is an excessive deviation from the cultural norm. Eventually, neurotic conflict comes to involve contradictory orientations to the self, pervading the entire personality "as a malignant tumor."

Horney (1945) has discussed three generalized trends that individuals may show in regard to others and themselves. These trends may be thought of as a synthesis of the neurotic needs. Each trend is "a whole way of life," including thinking, feeling, and behaving. A given trend results from different combinations of the ten needs summarized in Table 5.1.

Moving toward people reflects neurotic needs for a partner and for affection; it also involves compulsive modesty. This trend is associated with the first three needs listed in the table. The predominant direction is one of helplessness and compliance. In fact, people in this category may be regarded as *compliant* types. Such a person

> . . . *accepts his own helplessness, and in spite of his estrangement and fears tries to win the affection of others and to lean on them. Only in this way can he feel safe with them. If there are dissenting parties in the family, he will attach himself to the most powerful person or group. By complying with them, he gains a feeling of belonging and support which makes him feel less weak and less isolated.* (p. 42)

Moving against people is associated with needs 4, 5, 6, and 7 in Table 5.1. This trend reflects compulsive cravings for power and prestige, as well as personal ambition. There is such an overemphasis on hostility that these people may be thought of as suffering from "basic hostility." One may think of these people as *aggressive* types. In this case, the person

> . . . *accepts and takes for granted the hostility around him, and determines, consciously or unconsciously, to fight. He implicitly distrusts the feelings and intentions of others toward himself. He rebels in whatever ways are open to him. He wants to be the stronger and defeat them, partly for his own protection, partly for revenge.* (p. 43)

Moving away from people reflects a person's concern with self, as seen in needs for admiration and perfectionism. This attitude is associated with needs 8, 9, and 10 in Table 5.1. The predominant direction is one of isolation. These people are *detached* types. The individual in this category

> . . . *wants neither to belong nor to fight, but keeps apart. He feels he has not much in common with them, they do not understand him anyhow. He builds up a world of his own—with nature, with his dolls, his books, his dreams.* (p. 43)

These orientations can exist within a single person. Basic conflict involves contradictory orientations to move toward, away from, and against others all existing within a neurotic.

Developing an Idealized versus a Real Image of Self

Once firmly established, basic anxiety gives rise to additional feelings of alienation toward one's real self and growing self-hatred. Genuine self-realization is sacrificed to an **idealized image of self,** an artificial pride system that the person creates to give the personality a sense of unity that does not exist. Horney (1945)

BOX 5.2   Which Is Your Orientation

Table 5.1 may be regarded as a rough test of whether people show one trend or another. Go back to the table and pick the four (4) entries that fit you best. It is "forced choice": even if it is difficult to make up your mind, force yourself to choose four entries. If three of your choices include the first three needs in the table, your dominant trend tends to be "moving toward people." Should your choices include any three of 4, 5, 6, and 7, your trend tends to be "moving against people." Finally, if you chose a foursome including 8, 9, and 10, your

trend is "moving away from people."

For many, if not most of you, your choices failed to fit any of the patterns: choices did not include three entries fitting one of the trends. This outcome is a reminder that fitting one of these extreme trends is unusual. However, if it does turn out that your choices do fit one of the trends, interpret the outcome with caution. Do not regard yourself as "neurotic." To do so would be to assume the validity of Horney's trends, which still await empirical confirmation.

---

refers to a cartoon she once saw in *The New Yorker*. A heavyset, middle-aged adult is depicted as looking in a mirror and seeing the image of a trim, young adult. Such an idealized image serves five functions: (1) It substitutes for the absence of realistic self-confidence and pride, through an inflated but ungrounded feeling of significance and power; (2) it counteracts the presence of real inner weakness and self-contempt, by falsely allowing the person to feel better or more worthy than others; (3) it compensates for a lack of genuine ideals, the absence of which otherwise would lead the person to feel quite lost; (4) it represents an idealized, private mirror upon which to rely so that one's most blatant faults and handicaps disappear or take on an attractive coloration; and (5) it offers the appearance of reconciled conflicts and inconsistencies within the individual's personality, even though such is not the case. By contrast, the **real self** is the potential for growth beyond the artificial idealized image of self.

Creation of an idealized self takes place unconsciously. It also may be accompanied by other forms of pretense, such as **externalization**, the tendency to experience internal processes as if they occurred outside oneself and to hold these "exterior" factors responsible for one's difficulties. Externalization serves to eliminate oneself as the cause of personal problems by projecting or shifting blame onto entities "outside" oneself, especially other people. Externalization is not just shifting responsibility. "Not only one's faults are experienced in others but to a greater or lesser degree all feelings" (1945, p. 116). One externalizes many aspects of oneself.

"Another inevitable product of externalization is a gnawing sense of emptiness and shallowness" (p. 117). Along with it comes an *externalization of self-contempt* in which one either despises others or feels "that it is others who look down upon oneself" (p. 118). Finally, rage results and is itself externalized in three ways. First, anger is "thrust outward" either as general irritability or as "specific irritation directed at the very faults in others that the person hates in himself" (p. 120). Second, rage is externalized in the form of an ever-present expectation that the faults "which are intolerable to oneself will infuriate others" (p. 121). As an illustration, Horney referred to a former patient whose idealized self-image was as saintly as the priest in Victor Hugo's *Les Miserables*. When she deviated from this angelic image and became angry, she was amazed to find that others liked her better. The patient had *expected* that others would have contempt for her real self so she hid it behind a "holier than thou" facade. The third way to externalize rage is to channel it into physical ills. Individuals who use this form of externalization are incessantly complaining of various vague maladies, from headaches to fatigue.

"The discrepancy between a *neurotic's actual behavior* [dictated by flaws in the real self] and his *idealized picture of himself* can be so blatant that one wonders how he himself can help seeing it" (Horney, 1945, p. 132; emphasis added). The inevitable trauma of the brutal collision between these two forces is akin to *shock*, the term Adler reserved for "fiction running head-on into reality." However, the individual can postpone the clash by resorting to one or more of seven defenses (Horney, 1945).

A **blind spot** is an area of contradiction about which the individual manages to remain unaware. As an example, Horney referred to a patient who never saw the contradiction between his "game" of figuratively killing colleagues at a meeting by "gunning them down" with an index finger and the "Christlike" idealized image he maintained. In **compartmentalization**, individuals separate key aspects of themselves and their life situations into "logic-tight" compartments. "There is a section for friends and one for enemies, one for the family and one for outsiders, one for professional and one for personal life, one for social equals and one for inferiors. Hence what happens in one compartment does not appear to the neurotic to contradict what happens in another" (p. 133).

Rationalization "may be defined as self-deception by reasoning" (p. 135). Here the individual attempts to excuse socially unacceptable actions by passing them off as laudable behavior (Allen, 1990). By mental gymnastics the individual makes despicable behavior into benevolent deportment. Horney refers to someone who sees himself as helping another, when, in fact, "strong tendencies to dominate are present" (p. 135).

Excessive self-control arises in reaction to a flood of contradictory emotions and involves holding feelings and behavior in a vice-grip. "Persons who exert such control will not allow themselves to be carried away, whether by enthusiasm, sexual excitement, self-pity, or rage" (p. 136). **Arbitrary rightness** is the strategy of people who see life as a merciless battle and, therefore, feel they must be definite and "right" about everything lest "foreign influence" control them. For these people, doubt is a dangerous weakness. In the event of a conflict, they can feel "in control" only if they can declare themselves "in the right."

Diametrically opposed to "rigid rightness" is **elusiveness**, the ability to slither away from conflicts by refusing to ever take an identifiable stand. People "inclined to this kind of defense often resemble those characters in fairy tales who when pursued turn into fish; if not safe in this guise, they turn into deer; if the hunter catches up with them they fly away as birds. You can never pin them down to any statement" (p. 138). If one of their pronouncements is challenged, people who use this defense deny having said whatever they said, say they did not really mean it, or reinterpret it.

Cynicism is "the denying or deriding of moral values" because of a deep-seated uncertainty with regard to moral values (p. 139). These people's response to moral uncertainty is skepticism about morality. To them, wrong can be twisted into right and right can be transformed into wrong. All that matters is doing what they please and looking good in the process. Those who reason and behave otherwise are thought to be either hypocrites or stupid.

A Psychology of Women

> Women lived for centuries under conditions in which she was kept away from great economic and political responsibilities and restricted to a private emotional sphere of life. This does not mean that she did not carry responsibility and did not have to work. But her work was done within the confines of the family circle and therefore was based only on emotionalism, in contradistinction to more impersonal, matter of fact relations. Another aspect of the same situation is that love and devotion came to be regarded as specifically feminine ideals and virtues. Still another aspect is that to woman—since her relations to men and children were her only gateway to happiness, security and prestige—love represented a realistic value, which in man's sphere can be compared with his activities relating to earning capacities. Thus not only were pursuits outside the emotional sphere factually discouraged, but in woman's own mind they assumed only secondary importance. (Horney, 1939, pp. 114–115).

Horney made significant contributions to the psychology of women by questioning Freudian assumptions about women. She was an influential critic of Freud and his "boy's eye" view of physical anatomy as the basis of psychological differences between men and women. Horney challenged Freud's theoretical speculations that lacking male anatomy led women to (1) envy men for their penises; (2) feel shame over biological "deficiency"; (3) resent their mothers, who were to blame for their anatomical deficiency; (4) overvalue relationships with men, including having male babies as a way of possessing male anatomy; (5) become jealous of other women as competitors for men and the anatomical superiority they supposedly represent; (6) seek sexual stimulation through the clitoris because it is penis-like; and (7) pursue desires for submissiveness, dependency, and masochistic abuse that are allegedly unique to women.

There were several reasons why Horney viewed Freud's underlying assumptions about gender as suspect. First, Horney considered it illogical that persons built for specific biological functions should be obsessed with obtaining the biological attributes of the other sex. "It would require tremendous evidence to make it plausible" (1939, p. 104). Second, Horney saw no evidence of universal support for Freud's conjectures. As mentioned earlier, cross-cultural investigations failed to demonstrate the universality of the supposed female wish for male anatomy. In fact, there are societies whose males show "womb envy."

Third, Horney (1926) asserted that a psychological theory "written" by men may not be wholly relevant to women. Psychoanalysis was created by "a male genius," almost all of whose followers were men. In fact, the masculine point of view pervades all science and most of Euro-American thought. "Like all sciences and all valuations, the psychology of women has hitherto been considered only from the point of view of men" (Horney, 1967, p. 56).

Horney endorsed philosopher Georg Simmel's view that Euro-American culture is dominated by masculine ideology. For centuries, women have been enmeshed in social systems that have promoted a "too exclusive" concentration on, and "overvaluation" of, men. Women's lives have been structured around political, economic, and psychological dependency on men. The specific social vehicle contributing to female dependency is the development of "love" relationships, based on the belief "I must have a man" that is foisted on women (1942). Horney saw this belief as motivating women to unconsciously conform to the wishes and demands of men and then assume, erroneously, that the behavior and feelings they adopt at the behest of men represents true feminine nature.

From a social perspective, Horney saw women's submission to the control of men as "cultivated" through a process of systematic selection by men. Male selectivity fosters the development of relationships with certain types of conforming women. Women are selected whose willingness to please would compensate for specific male deficiencies such as vulnerable self-esteem. The selection process instills in women the dispositions of dependency, inconspicuousness, frailty, suffering, emotionality, and jealousy of other women, traits that serve men well. In sum, systematic selection promotes a self-fulfilling prophecy in which women became what men want them to be.

Psychologically speaking Horney felt that society's "masculine tendency" conveys demeaning attitudes toward women. Women are then led to compensate for the consequent heightened sense of inferiority by further increasing their over-valuation of relationships with "superior" men. The net result is, once again, a strengthening of male dominance. More generally, Horney's reconceptualization of Freudian theory redirects attention away from the instinctive position that favors the masculine gender, to a trend that is more sociocultural in nature.

Horney's impact was important in her day as well as now. Then, it was great enough to elicit Freud's (1925/1959) direct opposition—and that of American psychoanalysts—as well as the support of Adler and Fromm. Adler, for example, addressed the myth of women's inferiority when he asserted that decisions about birth control and abortion are best left entirely to women (1982, p. 63). Recall that he also regarded macho, war-mongering nations as most likely to oppress women. Nowadays, there is renewed interest in the work of Horney, associated with ongoing development of the women's movement and specific interest in psychology of women (Rohrbaugh, 1979; Williams, 1983). She continues to be cited as an important figure on the issue of culture and sex roles.

Evaluation

Contributions

Help with Everyday Problems

Horney was noted for working with neurotics, but there was another side of her. She had much concern for the everyday problems of normal people. Horney promoted self-exploration by presenting her theoretical and clinical ideas in popular, "plain language" books. She wrote expressly for interested laypeople "who want to know themselves and have not given up struggling for their own growth" (1945, p. 8). Her purpose was not to offer clear-cut answers or cures for neurotic conflicts, which would be unrealistic as well as unprofessional, but to offer information useful for self-examination. Her books include *The Neurotic Personality of Our Time* (1937), *Self-Analysis* (1942), *Our Inner Conflicts* (1945), and *Are You Considering Psychoanalysis?* (1946).

Consistent with her interest in helping normal people with normal problems, Horney wrote extensively about issues that concern the typical person. Her books are filled with discussions of ambition, depression, self-confidence, dependency, greed, and other concepts from the everyday language of everyday people. Her consideration of these common concerns is illustrated by her treatment of "jealousy."

Horney defines **jealousy** as the fear of losing a relationship that is seen as the best available means of satisfying an insatiable concern for affection and incessant demands for unconditional love (Horney, 1937). She recognized that jealousy is fully in evidence even in early childhood. A child can be jealous of siblings. She or he can also be jealous of a parent who seems to be receiving more attention from the other parent than is the child. Furthermore, Horney acknowledged that jealousy of the Oedipal type may also exist: a child may be jealous of the parent of the same sex for monopolizing the physical (sexual) and emotional attention of the opposite-sex parent. However, here she reiterates that Oedipal jealousy is not found in all cultures and may be confined to neurotic people in this culture.

Some degree of jealousy is true of all of us and may be a quite reasonable reaction to the real but generally remote possibility that an important love-relationship may end. However, the kind of jealousy considered here—the sort that Horney concentrated on in her writings—is exaggerated beyond the bounds of reason. Morbidly jealous people show fear of losing someone's love that is way out of proportion to the actual danger. The fear of these people is so great that any other interest not revolving around themselves is a threat to them. "This kind of jealousy may appear in every human relation—on the part of parents toward their children who want to make friends or to marry; on the part of children toward their parents; between marriage partners; in any love relationship" (p. 129).

According to Horney, morbid adult jealousy can be a carry-over from childhood neurosis in that both spring from the same source: an insatiable appetite for love arising from unresolved basic anxiety. In recognizing a possible tie between jealousy involving childhood relationships and jealousy in adult relationships

Horney was ahead of her time. Philip Shaver and his colleagues have established a link between the way children relate to their parents and how they later relate to important people in their adult lives, most especially lovers (see Shaver and Hazan, 1987). Certain insecure people whose childhood needs were not consistently met by their parents show, as adults, the same kind of insatiable need for unconditional love that Horney alluded to. Because they cannot get enough assurance of love, they are morbidly jealous of anyone who is a rival for the attentions of their loved ones.

Box 5.3 contains information relevant to Shaver's theory and also a jealousy scale. Read and follow the instructions in the box before going on.

Anticipating Popular Psychological Mechanisms

"Jealousy" was not the only idea conceived by Horney that was ahead of its time. As will be apparent, she anticipated many beliefs of the humanists whose theories are considered in later chapters. Like Adler, Horney's therapy was not just for gaining what Freud called "insight." It was for growth.

Another of Horney's notions anticipated a popular idea of psychotherapist Albert Ellis, the psychologist who is known for his assumption that people are basically irrational. As reflected in Ellis' concept "musturbation," Horney believed that some people are subject to the **tyranny of the shoulds**, the belief that one should do this and that, whatever a good person *should do*, whatever is expected by others, rather than whatever one feels it is his or her nature to do. People afflicted with this malady think of themselves as miserable worms who must forever wriggle forth in pursuit of the elusive perfection that evades them. Horney wrote, "Forget about the disgraceful creature you actually are; this is how you *should* be; and to be this idealized self is all that matters. You should be able to endure everything, to understand everything, to like everybody, to be always productive . . ." (Horney, 1950, pp. 64–65). The shoulds dominate the individual, so that not to do what one "should" generates anxiety and guilt. "He should be the utmost of honesty, generosity, considerateness, justice, dignity, courage, unselfishness. He should be the perfect lover, husband, teacher . . . he should love his parents, his wife, his country . . . he should never feel hurt, and he should always be serene and unruffled" (p. 65). He should be whatever others deem to be the "right kind of person," never himself. Needless to say, many of us are bound by the chains of the "shoulds." Horney believed that the first step in working free of this bondage is to recognize the tyrant who has tied us up. Then we may begin to acknowledge that the ideal of perfection we pursue is impossible to obtain, and in fact, detracts us from being who we really are.

Developing New Clinical Techniques: Self-Analysis

One of Horney's contributions was the development of clinical and therapeutic techniques. She was oriented toward "new ways in psychoanalysis" (1939). Martin (1975) has characterized Horney's therapeutic approach as one of trust, confidence, respect for each person's individual uniqueness and inner constructive resources, and adherence to the principle that exploration always precedes expla-

BOX 5.3   Attachment Styles and Jealousy

First read the three descriptions of attachment styles and choose the one that fits you best. Then respond to the Interpersonal Jealousy Scale. Finally, refer to the information at the end of the box to learn of the relationship between the two exercises.

Part 1: Attachment Styles

An attachment style is the mode of relating to important people in your life that you developed through your relationships with your parents. Now follow the instructions.

Attachment Styles

Read the statements below and simply check the one that is most applicable to you. If you are not sure, check the statement that is more applicable than the others.

1. I find it relatively easy to get close to others and am comfortable depending on them and having them depend on me. I don't often worry about being abandoned or about someone getting too close to me.

2. I find that others are reluctant to get as close as I would like. I often worry that my partner doesn't really love me or won't want to stay with me. I want to merge completely with another person, and this desire sometimes scares people away.

3. I am somewhat uncomfortable being close to others; I find it difficult to trust them completely, difficult to allow myself to depend on them. I am nervous when anyone gets too close, and often, love partners want me to be more intimate than I feel comfortable being.

Quoted from Shaver (1986, p. 31), with permission.

Part 2: The Interpersonal Jealousy Scale

In responding to each item, place the name of your boyfriend or girlfriend in the blank of each item. Then use the scale below to express your feelings concerning the truth of the item. For example, if you feel the item is "absolutely true" of you, place a 9 in the blank before the item. If it is only definitely true place an 8 in the blank, etc.

9 = absolutely true; agree completely
8 = definitely true
7 = true
6 = slightly true
5 = neither true or false
4 = slightly false
3 = false
2 = definitely false
1 = absolutely false; disagree completely

1. If___were to see an old friend of the opposite sex and respond with a great deal of happiness, I would be annoyed.

2. If___went out with same sex friends, I would feel compelled to know what he/she did.

3. If___admired someone of the opposite sex I would feel irritated.

4. If___were to help someone of the opposite sex with his/her homework, I would feel suspicious.

5. When___likes one of my friends I am pleased.

6. If___were to go away for the weekend without me, my only concern would be with whether he/she had a good time.

7. If___were helpful to someone of the opposite sex, I would feel jealous.

8. When___talks of happy experi-

Continued

BOX 5.3 *Continued*

ences of his/her past, I feel sad that I wasn't part of it.

9. If___were to become displeased about the time I spend with others, I would be flattered.

10. If___and I went to a party and I lost sight of him/her, I would become uncomfortable.

11. I want___to remain good friends with the people he/she used to date.

12. If___were to date others I would feel unhappy.

13. When I notice that___and a person of the opposite sex have something in common, I am envious.

14. If___were to become very close to someone of the opposite sex, I would feel very unhappy and/or angry.

15. I would like___to be faithful to me.

16. I don't think it would bother me if___flirted with someone of the opposite sex.

17. If someone of the opposite sex were to compliment___, I would feel that the person was trying to take___away from me.

18. I feel good when___makes a new friend.

19. If___were to spend the night comforting a friend of the opposite sex who had just had a tragic experience, ___'s compassion would please me.

20. If someone of the opposite sex were to pay attention to___, I would become possessive of him/her.

21. If___was to become exuberant and hug someone of the opposite sex, it would make me feel good that he/she was expressing his/her feelings openly.

22. The thought of___kissing someone else drives me up the wall.

23. If someone of the opposite sex lit up at the sight of___, I would become uneasy.

24. I like to find fault with___'s old dates.

25. I feel possessive toward___.

26. If___had previously been married, I would feel resentment towards the ex-wife/husband.

27. If I saw a picture of___and an old date I would feel unhappy.

28. If___were to accidentally call me by the wrong name, I would become furious.

Note: To calculate your score, put minuses in front of the scale numbers you assigned to items 5, 6, 11, 16, 18, 19, and 21, then add these numbers. Next add the numbers for the other items. Your score is this total minus the negative total. The higher it is, the more the jealousy.

Reprinted with the permission of Eugene Mathes

Part 3: Relationship Between the Exercises

About 55 percent of the respondents surveyed by Shaver checked the first statement in Part 1. Twenty percent endorsed the second statement and 25 percent checked the third statement. The last two statements indicate insecure attachment styles. People with these two styles, especially the second, would be expected to be unusually jealous. Notice that Shaver's second statement indicates high need for assurance of love. It could have been made by one of Horney's patients with "an insatiable need for affection."

Assume that scores on the Interpersonal Jealousy Scale of 100 or above indicate high jealousy, and scores of 25 or below indicate low jealousy. If Horney and Shaver are correct, those of you who checked the last two statements, especially the second, would be expected to score close to 100, while those who endorsed the first statement would be expected to score close to 25. More realis-

BOX 5.3 *Continued*

tically, those of you who checked the last two statements should score relatively high on the Interpersonal Jealousy Scale, compared to those of you who checked the first statement.

There are a couple of points to remember in evaluating your responses to the two exercises and the relationship between them. First, both the research associated with Shaver's statements and Mathes' scale are oriented to romantic involvements, but Horney's point of view relates to a broader range of relationships (see Mathes, Adams, & Davies, 1985). Thus, whether or not your attachment style choice matched your jealousy score reflects only partially on Horney's theory. Second, as always, do not take a single score or outcome on any psychological instrument very seriously. Much more information about you would be needed before solid conclusions could be drawn concerning whether or not you are a particularly jealous person and concerning what your attachment style might be.

Before leaving this box, go back to the Interpersonal Jealousy scale again and look for items that fit Horney's conception of jealousy well. For example, items 7 and 17 are clear examples of what Horney meant by "morbid jealousy."

nation. The goal is to become a better person, not to discover some awful problem and correct it somehow.

One of her contributions that has been relatively ignored and has not been widely adopted is **self-analysis**, a process whereby people come to understand themselves better through their own efforts, often outside the context of psychotherapy (Horney, 1942). It is apparently rare that theorist/therapists trust people under their care to probe their own psyches in the hope of useful self-discovery without their psychologist, psychiatrist, or counselor being present. But Horney was a rare theorist/therapist.

In Horney's view, self-analysis apparently is not analogous to self-hypnosis, a process that a person takes over after training, and continues to use without any further professional assistance. It certainly is not the same as "self-help," which is typically done by people with no assistance, except possibly that provided by a popular book. Rather it is a step that a person takes in the direction of **self-recognition**, coming to know one's neuroses, idealized self-image, and real self, including positive and negative attributes. It is also a step taken under supervision. The patients on whom Horney concentrates in her 1942 book may have tried "self-analysis" (the book title) while not in therapy, but they likely had received therapy and would have it again. As you will see, there are problems with self-analysis that make it risky without supervision.

To illustrate self-analysis, I have chosen the case of Clare, because, of the several case-histories covered in the book *Self Analysis*, it is the most detailed. Reading it will not only tell you something about self-analysis, it will partially reiterate Horney's theory.

Clare was unwanted by her mother who unsuccessfully attempted to abort her. Her father simply was uninterested in any of the children. However, Clare was intelligent and received a good education. By the time she entered therapy at age 30 she had been married—her husband died—and had become an apparently successful magazine editor. During analysis she was involved with Peter, a businessman and the focus of her problems. Clare was morbidly dependent, lacking in self-confidence, and in the grip of an insatiable need for reassurances of love. This account concentrates on instances of self-recognition that occurred to Clare.

Clare's whole life was wrapped up in Peter. She wanted to be with him all the time. When he failed to keep a promised date with her, which happened often, she was devastated. A light bulb went on for Clare and illuminated both herself and her relationship with Peter when she awoke on a Sunday morning intensely irritated at an author who broke his promise to submit an article for her magazine. While reflecting on this puzzling incident, it occurred to Clare that she was not really angry with the author, nor at people who fail to keep promises. Rather, she was angry because Peter had frustrated her desire to be with him by failing to show up on that weekend as promised. This realization caused her to remember the heroine of a novel who lost her feelings for her husband while he was away at war. In turn, she wondered whether she wanted to sever her emotional ties with Peter, but dismissed the thought "because I love him so much" (p. 194). Thus, despite the correct recognition that she was really angry with Peter, an important opportunity to break away from Peter was lost.

Clare "managed to shake off the whole problem," fell back to sleep, and dreamed she was lost in a foreign city where people spoke an unknown language and had left her luggage and money at the train station (p. 196). Then she was at a fair where there was gambling and a freak show. Reflecting on this dream she realized that counting on the unreliable Peter was a "crap shoot," and that he was something of a freak. However, this shallow analysis was as far as she was able to go. She missed the symbolism of being lost without luggage and money: she had "invested" everything in Peter, and it all had been lost.

One morning a notice of a shipwreck brought back a dream in which she was adrift on the waves. Being in danger of drowning, a "strong man put his arms around her and saved her" (p. 202). She had the feeling of belonging and of endless protection. "He would always hold her in his arms and never leave her" (p. 202). In turn this dream reminded Clare of another nocturnal revelation in which she was hand in hand with Bruce, an older writer who had promised to be her mentor. He was a "hero" whose interest in her was described as a "blessing." These experiences moved Clare closer to realizing that she wanted everlasting love and protection. She also recognized that Bruce was not as brilliant as her dream implied. Unfortunately, she did not generalize her revelation about Bruce to the "superior" man in her life, Peter. It was to be some time before she fully admitted to Peter's many deficiencies. However, it was the first time she truly recognized that Peter was not giving her what she wanted and that she was dissatisfied with the relationship.

Clare's mood hinged on every nuance of Peter's behavior. An instance of his lateness plunged her into deep depression. The smallest favor granted to her generated disproportionate joy. When he gave her a scarf, she reacted as if he had presented her with the Hope diamond. If he relented and said that he would go somewhere with her after all, her gratitude was that of a dying patient saved by the surgeon. She was like a robot controlled by a less than benevolent scientist.

Later Clare recalled a dream of a large bird flying away. It was glorious in color and grace, not unlike Peter who was handsome and a fine dancer. It meant that Peter, under whose "wing" she wanted to hide, had flown away, or was about to.

Reflecting on her tearfulness during a movie, Clare noticed that she had cried not when "the girl in the movie was badly off but when her situation took an unexpected turn for the better" (p. 211). She then coupled this realization with two other recollections concerning friends' comments about love: (1) a confirmed bachelor asserted that "woman's love is merely a screen for exploiting men" and (2) another friend, Susan, had proclaimed that love was nothing more than an "honest deal" in which each partner did his or her share to create "good companionship" (p. 213). She wondered, was her love nothing more than "sponging on somebody else!" (p. 212). She begin to realize that her need for Peter was based on something other than affection.

Eventually, Clare recognized that she desperately needed Peter for the protection and reassurance that she hoped he would provide, not because he was a great hero or because she had true affection for him. Fortunately she was in the process of weaning herself from him when the rumor mill told her he was having an affair. When his subsequent letter asking for a separation confirmed what others were telling her, she averted the emotional collapse that would have occurred earlier. Instead she got through the crisis and later came to the realization that her problem was broader than Peter: "her picture of herself was determined entirely by the evaluation by others" (p. 245). The revelation almost made her faint. When Clare returned to therapy later, she executed the final stroke to excise Peter from her psyche, but Horney acknowledged that she probably could have done it on her own in continued self-analysis.

While self-analysis is valuable, it has definite shortcomings, according to Horney. During self-analysis, patients: (1) may perceive something about themselves that is not true, but see it as accurate; (2) may come up with correct information about themselves, but misinterpret it; (3) may have a partial and accurate realization about themselves, but fail to extend it to core personality dispositions; and (4) may analyze an incident correctly with regard to its implications for themselves, but not know what to do with the result. These are all reasons why self-analysis is better done under supervision. Clare made all four errors. Nevertheless, self-analysis is certainly a first bold step on the path to self-recognition.

Limitations

Horney's theory shares two major limitations with classical psychoanalysis: (1) an absence of controlled research studies testing theoretical concepts, and (2) an emphasis on pathology. Relatively little systematic or programmatic research activity concerning her theory has been reported. In fact, the lack of research effort to support her theory is quite unprecedented; few other prominent theories are so neglected. Also, few theorists have had so few followers. The scarcity of scientific literature can be traced to the observation that a number of Horney's concepts related to personality are difficult to define and measure. These concepts include such broad, external influences as parents, siblings, significant others, family, society, and culture.

Horney's theory, like classical psychoanalysis, focuses a great deal on human pathology—on what is maladaptive in human functioning and what goes wrong in human relationships. Recall Horney's concept "basic anxiety." There is also an overriding emphasis on "neurosis." This is most obviously seen in Horney's "ten neurotic needs."

A review of the many factors contributing to basic anxiety and insecurity in children highlights Horney's emphasis on the disturbed side of humans. Sometimes it seems impossible for any parent to behave as a healthy, stabilizing influence on children. Personality development becomes a fretful phenomenon. So many things can go wrong in the parenting process that it is difficult to imagine more than marginal success in raising children. It is amazing that adjustment occurs at all.

Horney's basic deficit as a theorist was shared by all the theorists covered so far and also the two to be considered in the next couple of chapters: she, like the others, was trained as a physician and psychiatrist, not a psychological scientist. She and the others were simply not equipped to conduct the scientific research that might have confirmed or disconfirmed their points of view. Further, none of these theorists seemed able to recognize contradictions to their theories found in their own writings. For example, according to Horney's notions of "need for assurance of love" and "jealousy," Clare ought to have been an especially jealous person. In fact, there are few, if any, lines in the description of her case that can be clearly interpreted as references to jealousy.

Conclusions

Despite the observation that some of Horney's concepts are too broad and general "to get a handle on," some of them are not too global to deal with scientifically. Among these are many concepts that are defined in crystal clear fashion. While other theorists are evasive, Horney is refreshingly straightforward.

To take these credits a step further, Horney is an outstanding writer, probably the best among the theorists covered in this book. Unlike the case of some other theorists, I can recommend her books as both an enjoyable read and a useful source of information. Further, the popular idea that Horney dwelled on the neurotic, maladjusted side of people may be overblown. Though she did make constant reference to neurosis, she also designed some of her books for normal people. As illustrated above, she, more than some others, addressed the considerations that are of interest to normal people and are embedded in their language.

Also, the alleged untestability of her concepts may also be overstated. If it is true that she defined her concepts clearly, they should be testable. In fact, her ideas about jealousy in relation to need for reassurances of love are quite testable. Actually, in the jealousy/attachment styles exercises you considered earlier, you tested her views. So also did Shaver in some of his research.

Given that Horney's ideas are more testable than has been commonly believed, one may ask why they have not often been subjected to scientific scrutiny. The answer may well be that the only woman theorist taken seriously by modern personality psychologists is taken less seriously than male theorists. A reconsideration of Horney's writings seems in order.

Finally, Karen Horney was a fascinating person. Even as an adolescent she wrote literate, often poetic lines about herself that were extraordinarily candid. If she seemed to be more troubled during her early life than other theorists, it may be because she was more honest and self-disclosing than the others. Reading her adolescent diaries (1980) and her life story (Quinn, 1988) is more than the act of perusing biographies of a famous figure. It will allow you to get under the skin of an interesting human being and also follow the development of a significant contributor to understanding the human condition.

Summary Points

1. Karen Clementina Theodora Danielsen was born to Norwegian and Dutch/German parents in a community near Hamburg, Germany. Her father, a sea captain, was often gone, but attempted to dominate her life when he could. In response she clung to her mother. Despite paternal resistance, Karen received a good education and entered medical school at age 20. There she met Oscar Horney, her eventual husband. Balancing school with typical homemaker "obligations" was stressful. Depression led to therapy and gained exposure to psychoanalysis. Overcoming these early hardships, Horney grew to be a forceful and well-known figure in the area of personality.

2. Freud and Horney both oriented to childhood experiences and both saw motivation as active and dynamic. Both thought that personality was changeable through therapy and both relied on case studies. However, Horney questioned the sexual instincts, Oedipal theory, Freud's view of gender differences, and the psychosexual stages. Penis envy was deemed not generally true and, in this culture, is confined to neurotic women. "Castrating tendencies" were also snubbed and Freud's inattention to social matters criticized.

3. Horney regarded masturbation as normal when not compulsive and identified four sexually troubled types. She also dismissed the Freudian allegation of female masochism and frigidity. Basic anxiety, an all-pervading feeling of being lonely and helpless in a hostile world, was due to a number of family-background factors. Horney's neurotic needs include affection and approval; having a "partner;" narrowly restricting one's life; power; exploiting others; social recognition or prestige; personal admiration; personal achievement; self-sufficiency and independence; and perfection and unassailability.

4. Neurotic conflict stems from contradictory attitudes the person holds toward other people. The three orientations are moving toward others (compliant type); moving against people (aggressive type); and moving away from people (detached type). The idealized image of self is an artificial pride system that substitutes for realistic confidence and counteracts real inner weakness and self-contempt. Along with the idealized self comes externalization. People can postpone the inevitable clash between actual behavior and idealized self by resorting to blind spots, compartmentalization, rationalization, excessive self-control, arbitrary rightness, elusiveness, and cynicism.

5. Horney threw out the Freudian assumption that women long for male anatomy and the several implications of that alleged need. She noted the illogical nature of women's alleged desire for male anatomy, the lack of evidence for the universality of Freud's assumptions about the sexes, the irrelevance to women of a theory written by men for men, and the false belief "I must have a man." Finally, Horney condemned male selection processes that create a self-fulfilling prophesy and the socially conveyed attitudes that demean women.

6. Horney wrote plain language books for everybody. She also showed an unusual interest in concepts that are important to rank and file people. For example, jealousy begins in childhood, can include Oedipal jealousy, and, in adults, can be reasonable and normal. However, morbidly jealous people show fear of losing someone's love that is way out of proportion to the actual danger. Their excessive jealousy which may be a hold-over from childhood is due to an insatiable need for love caused by unresolved basic anxiety.

7. Horney's views of jealousy anticipated the work of Philip Shaver who proposed three attachment styles dating to parent-child interactions, two of which predict inordinate jealousy. Mathes's jealousy scale has the flavor of Horney's views and may relate to the attachment styles. Horney's idea—the tyranny of the shoulds—clearly conveys the currently important picture of people who feel they should do this and that, whatever is demanded by the idealized self.

8. She also revamped psychoanalysis making it more concerned with "being a better person," rather than discovering something awful in the psyche. She uniquely recommended self-analysis, during which one can begin to gain self-recognition. Clare, a self-analysis case, was unwanted by her parents and grew to be a dependent, assurance-seeking adult. She was morbidly dependent on her lover, unreliable Peter, whose every mood determined her own.

9. Several dreams, fantasies, and other revelations showed approximations to self-recognition: Clare realized that anger at an author's lateness was really directed to Peter; she had a dream including symbols of Peter being like a "crap shoot" and a "freak"; she dreamed of being "cast adrift" and rescued, symbolizing her need for everlasting love and protection; a bird dream made her feel that Peter was about to "fly the coop;" and friends' cynical views of love made her wonder if her love was just "sponging." Peter left and Clare survived, coming to realize that her picture of herself was determined by others.

10. Horney's theory has received little scientific support and heavily emphasizes the psychological ills of people and the near impossibility of being a successful parent. A lack of scientific training limited her ability to test her theory or even recognize contradictions in her writings. But, she often defined her concepts with such relative clarity that they could be adequately tested by others. Thus, it appears that lack of scientific attention to her ideas by others may be due to their lack of respect for her gender. Horney was a fascinating person whose writings should be reconsidered and who is well worth reading.

Running Comparison

Theorist	Horney in Comparison
Freud	Agreed with Freud on the *importance* of anxiety-provoking childhood experiences on adult personality, neurosis, gaining insight, dynamic view of motivation, conscience, instincts, and case histories vs. scientific research. But they disagreed on libido (she said "unproven"), sexual motivation ("over-emphasized"), Oedipus complex ("not true of all people"), penis envy ("rare worldwide"), culture ("Freud ignored"), consciousness ("Freud neglected"), and women (rejected his treatment of them).
Adler	She agreed with him on the importance of social cooperation and her discovery of conflict between the idealized and real self is akin to his "shock." Also, she acknowledged his concept "striving for superiority."

Essay/Critical Thinking Questions

1. What was it about Horney's childhood that made her a different person as a child and adolescent than as a adult?

2. What was it that so upset American psychoanalysts with Horney's criticisms of Freud? Was it the criticisms themselves? Her gender? The particular "soft spots" she picked on? All of these? Explain your answer.

3. What are some reasonable criticisms of Horney's hypotheses concerning the sexual types who are (1) ". . . prone to yield to sexual advances from either sex" and (2) homosexuals?

4. What is a parent to do in order to be a good parent in Horney's eyes? (Try to respond to the criticism that it is difficult or impossible to be an effective parent from Horney's point of view.)

5. Horney makes it "bad" to show any of her three trends. How could you transform one of them so that it would be adaptive rather than maladaptive?

6. Could you write a paragraph describing a person who would likely be the jealous type according to Horney's point of view?

7. Look at yourself. Can you isolate some instances in which you have been victimized by the "tyranny of the shoulds?" Describe a couple of them.

8. We are all prone to externalizing to some degree. Can you provide a couple of examples of externalizing on the part of friends of yours?

9. You have probably done self-analysis, even if you are not aware of it. There have been times when something unusual that happened to you has caught your attention and you have used the occurrence to better your understanding of yourself. Can you provide an example?

10. Horney's theory has been unjustifiably neglected. Can you find among her concepts one that can be easily tested (excluding jealousy)? Tell how it could be tested.

6

THE INTERPERSONAL APPROACH TO PERSONALITY: HARRY STACK SULLIVAN

- Can a person with his or her own severe psychological problems give useful advice to others?
- Was your mother or father a "good parent" or a "bad parent" (or neither one)?
- Was there a time during your early infancy when you had no sensations or feeling or any thoughts?
- What is more important in determining your personality, your genes, what happens to you, or who you interact with?
- How important is physical contact with other human beings in the development of the infant?

The chapters in the first half of this book may be thought of as starting with Freud and withdrawing from him gradually. Jung was most closely tied to Freud. He maintained a relationship with Freud longer than the others and made the strongest statements acknowledging a debt to the founder of psychoanalysis. Adler quarreled with Freud, but wrote a theory that was clearly a reaction to Freudian thought. Horney never had personal contact with Freud. She did found her theory on his, but was noted for rebelling against his dogmatic ideas, especially those regarding psychosexuality and women. Harry Stack Sullivan also had no personal relationship with Freud. One of his mentors even warned him against Freud and encouraged him to be critical of psychoanalysis (Perry, 1982). Yet Sullivan was heavily influenced by Freud, and, like Horney, used the framework of psychoanalytic theory to build his own point of view. Nevertheless, he joined the others in deserting the sexual emphasis. To Sullivan, the critical consideration in attempts to understand personality is **interpersonal relations**, the relationships between a person and each other important person in his or her life. These crucial twosomes or dyads were behind much of what Sullivan wrote and theorized about. His emphasis on them distinguishes his theory.

Sullivan, the Person

Harry Stack Sullivan is sometimes considered "America's psychiatrist" (Perry, 1982). Born in 1892 to recent Irish immigrant families in the rural New York town of Norwich and raised on a nearby farm, Sullivan was traditionally American through and through. The people in the area where he grew up were "farm folk," hard workers who came to America for a better life. Area residents did, however, show some peculiarities. The surrounding region was known for its high suicide rate, with isolated farm wives most often taking their own lives, and sometimes taking their children with them.

Sullivan was an only child, idealized by his mother, Ella Stack, but considered by his father "no good to work, for he has his nose stuck in a book all the time" (Perry, 1982, p. 85). Although Harry was prone to greatly overstate their accomplishments, the Stack family was well regarded in the community. The same could not be said for the Sullivans. This comparison is an example of the "social law of relativity": the Stacks had relatively high status compared to the Sullivans in a very humble community. In fact, Sullivan's family background is among the most ordinary and pedestrian of the theorists covered in this book. Horney's name on her mother's side, Ronzelen, began with *Van*, a mark of nobility. By contrast, the Sullivans were pretty much "fresh off the boat" and "working class."

One of the factors that may have spurred Sullivan to fame may have been his desire to rise above his background. Alternatively, his delusions about the accomplishments of Mother Ella Stack's family may have driven him to "live up to her standards." The name changes he displayed may be interpreted as supporting the contention that Ella's influence was behind his drive to achieve. When he entered medical school, he was Harry Francis Sullivan, or H. F. Sullivan (Francis was given to him at age thirteen, upon his confirmation). Later he used a variety of combinations, for example, Harry F. Sullivan and just plain Harry Sullivan. But eventually, Francis dropped out in favor of the maternal surname, Stack. This indecisiveness regarding his name may also be interpreted as indicative of identity confusion, a trait he shared with Erik Erikson.

As a person, Sullivan was lonely, somewhat reserved, rather fatalistic about his health, and a user of alcohol "to combat anxiety" (Perry, 1982, p. 175). He had the vulnerable, haunted look of movie actor James Dean. During childhood, Sullivan was isolated, a loner at school, and conveyed a sense of ambiguous sexuality during preadolescence that lingered into adulthood. Supposedly he was involved in a homosexual relationship during preadolescence. Later he wrote that he entered puberty late, possibly as late as age seventeen.

In college he did report "lust" for a girl in one of his classes, but Perry (1952) indicates that people close to the adult Sullivan were never quite sure about his sexual orientation. Friends indicated that they thought Sullivan had sexual contact with both men and women during his adulthood. Whether these speculations were true or not Sullivan was known to long for marriage and to lament his bachelorhood. Perry even suggests that Sullivan may have sent proposals of marriage to astounded women with whom he was merely acquainted. At one point, he was reported to be "attentive" to Karen Horney (Perry, 1982, p. 335). Nevertheless, sustained love for women was probably directed exclusively to his mother and his Aunt Maggie, possibly his first sexual interest. Clara Thompson, a beloved colleague, apparently was not sexually involved with Sullivan.

Harry S. Sullivan

Suggestions of personal difficulties were present throughout Sullivan's life. Sullivan was apparently in trouble with the law while a student at Cornell University. Allegedly he was involved in "mail fraud," supposedly as a part of a "criminal gang" (Perry, 1982). Scant detail of the relevant incidents led Perry to speculate that Sullivan and "the gang" were using the mail to obtain "chemicals" from a drugstore (1982). Yet the penalty meted out to Sullivan was slight: he was suspended from Cornell for a year and could have returned to school (but he never did).

Between his suspension in 1909 and his arrival at medical school in 1911, Sullivan disappeared. It was remotely possible that he was in jail—maybe he was "sprung" by his uncle, a judge. More likely, Sullivan suffered a psychotic break during this period and was receiving treatment. In any case, the youthful Sullivan was known to have had bouts of *schizophrenia*, profound disturbances in reality relationships as well as thoughts, feelings, and behaviors. These episodes probably explain his burning interest in the disorder.

Sullivan was admitted to the Chicago College of Medicine and Surgery (CCMS) despite the absence of credits from Cornell where he did poorly as a physics student (Chapman, 1976; Perry, 1982). Though valedictorian in high school, his record in medical school was dismal. While living in poverty and working as an elementary physics teacher and a Chicago Elevated Railway conductor, Sullivan received only one "A" at CCMS, but accumulated several "Ds" (Perry, 1982). This undistinguished performance was recorded at a school that may have been suspect in its time. Although Perry (1982) regarded CCMS as most likely average for its day, Chapman (1976) described it as one of many fly-by-night, physician factories that sprung up during the late 1890s and early 1900s. Sullivan called it a "diploma mill" (Chapman, 1976). It was defunct by 1917, leaving behind no record of Sullivan's graduation (his diploma was later found among his personal effects).

Do these aspersions cast upon CCMS and Sullivan's performance there mean he was mediocre as a scholar and intellect? To the contrary, he was a brilliant, original thinker who may well have "gone through the motions" during medical school to make himself eligible for what he really wanted to do, become a psychiatrist.

Rather than receiving formal psychiatric training, Sullivan became a staff physician at St. Elizabeth's Hospital in Washington, D.C. (Chapman, 1976). There he trained himself. The lack of formal training in psychiatry led him to make numerous erroneous statements about psychiatry and abnormal behavior, some of them in print (Chapman, 1976). Yet having learned about psychiatry from the patients, rather than from the dogmatic psychiatric professors of the day, may have permitted the creative ideas that made him famous.

Sullivan's most significant clinical work involved schizophrenic men, for whom he established a successful residential treatment program grounded in experiences of interpersonal trust. He believed in the principle "like cures like," which guided his selection of "sensitive, shy" ward staff.

Sullivan's reputation as "troubled" survived his death. In 1957 two people, one a graduate of the White Foundation and the other claiming to be a former Sullivan patient, established a colony bearing Sullivan's name (Hoban, 1989). They call themselves the "Sullivanians" and claim to practice Sullivan's brand of therapy on each other. In fact, the White Foundation has dissociated itself from them and has asserted that what they do is not in the Sullivanian tradition. The "cult" has been accused of breaking up families, promoting sexual interchanges across family lines, farming out children to boarding schools, and holding parents as virtual hostages both financially and physically. While Sullivan would never have approved of such behavior, it is conceivable that his disordered life may have been partly the inspiration for it.

Harry Stack Sullivan died under mysterious circumstances on January 14, 1949 (Perry, 1982). He was found in a Paris hotel room, sprawled on the floor, his heart medication scattered about him. Rumors of self-destruction circulated immediately, especially in the suicide-ridden rural community where he was reared. Perry dismissed speculations that Sullivan directly committed suicide. She was well acquainted with Sullivan's heart ailment and knew that the official cause of death, "meningeal hemorrhage," was entirely plausible in view of his medical condition. However, she wondered whether certain thoughts that may have occurred to him on the day of his death had not contributed to his demise, or even caused it.

When he arose on the day of the fatal attack, the fact that it was his deceased mother Ella's birthday must have been on his mind. It was also close to the anniversary of a dear friend's death, and he may have remembered that relative Leo Stack had died of a similar attack in a hotel room on a day in January. Finally, Sullivan's prediction, made in 1931, that he would die of a "rupture of the middle meningeal artery at the age of 57. . ." was astoundingly accurate. Perhaps memories of these four events came together to hasten what was already inevitable. No one will ever know, but had he lived on, personality psychology certainly would have benefited.

Sullivan's View of the Person

Significant Others and the Self

Sullivan's theory revolves around the idea that a person's needs and developmental tasks are met in a series of two-person relationships, beginning with "a mothering one" and culminating in the selection of a sexual partner. While Sullivan believed we have as many personalities as we have interpersonal relationships, he formally defined **personality** as "the relatively enduring pattern of recurrent interpersonal situations which characterize a human life" (1953, pp. 110-111).

This orientation is certainly different from that of Freud who emphasized biologically based instincts. Sullivan did see himself as a psychoanalyst. Further, he used many of Freud's methods. Nevertheless, he backed away from Freud's underlying assumptions revolving around instincts and psychosexuality. Sullivan's point of view is, however, in the spirit of Adler's "social interest." It also bears some similarity to the inclination Horney chose: she considered anxiety dating to infancy to be critically important and she also was very concerned about relationships. Little wonder they developed a friendly and cooperative relationship.

Significant others are those people who are most meaningful to us in our lives. In essence, personality does not exist in the absence of important other people. Without them, there can be no development of a **self-system**, "that part of personality which is born entirely out of the influences of significant others upon one's feeling of well-being" (Sullivan, 1954, p. 101). Even our level of self-esteem depends largely upon the positive and negative evaluations we receive from significant other people. Interestingly, our relationships with them may be fantasized as well as real, including imaginary playmates, literary characters, and idealized public figures with whom we have never had face-to-face contact. An example is John Hinckley's fantasized relationship with movie actress Jodie Foster, whom he tried to impress by attempting to assassinate President Ronald Reagan.

A Need for Tenderness

For Sullivan, personality is derived from human experiences, all of which involve the reduction of tensions. Tensions are of two kinds: in common with Freud, physical needs, and, in contrast with Freud, interpersonal anxiety. *Needs* seek *satisfactions* ". . . all those end states which are rather closely connected with the bodily organization" such as relief of deprivation for oxygen, water, food, body warmth, and so forth (Sullivan, 1947, p. 6). *Interpersonal anxiety* seeks alleviation in relationships with significant others or in feelings of well-being.

Like Horney, Sullivan saw infants as being totally powerless and at the mercy of other people for their security. However, Sullivan further theorized that the infant's nearly absolute dependency revolves around a **mothering one**—a ". . . significant, relatively adult personality whose cooperation is necessary to keep the infant alive" (1953, p. 54). This critically important individual addresses the infant's **need for tenderness** which, different from "love," refers to relief from various tensions (1953).

Observations of tension in the infant create a reciprocal tension in the mothering one, which is experienced as tenderness and leads to activities aimed at relieving the infant's needs (Sullivan, 1953). The externally oriented, social implications of this need set Sullivan apart from Freud, whose theory places greater emphasis on intrapsychic events occurring within the individual. One of Sullivan's "theorems" ties together *tension born of needs in the infant* with the *tenderness* reaction on the part of the mothering one: "The observed activity of the infant arising from the tension of needs induces tension in the mothering one, which . . . is experienced as tenderness and [leads] to activities [that provide] relief of the infant's needs" (1953, p. 39). This formal statement effectively captures the essence of the almost umbilical connection between the infant and the mothering one.

Basic Concepts: Sullivan

Empathy, Anxiety, and Security

Another of Sullivan's theorems is: "The tension of anxiety, when present in the mothering one, induces anxiety in the infant" (1953, p. 41). Anxiety may be transferred to the infant when it is subjected to certain unsympathetic behaviors by the mothering one that communicate something is "bad," "disapproved of," or "wrong." This occurs even though the origin of tension in the mothering one has no direct connection with the infant. It may be due to the caregiver's personality, uncertainty about the parenting role, or circumstances unrelated to the infant, such as parental illness, fatigue, or upset due to bad news. However, the infant has no way of knowing this. The infant simply participates in the other person's tension or discomfort, through **empathy**, "the term that we use to refer to the peculiar emotional linkage [that exists between the] infant [and] other significant people—the mother or the nurse" (1947, p. 8). Anxiety acquired by this and other means can interfere with the satisfaction of physical and tenderness needs. For example, the infant may cry or vomit, thereby disrupting critical behaviors such as feeding, which further increases both its own and the mothering one's anxiety. Since it has no effective means to remove, destroy, or escape from the anxiety, the infant is totally dependent on a cooperative other person for relief. Because of the infant's helpless condition, only the mothering one can provide relief in the form of **interpersonal security**, "relaxation of the tension of anxiety" which is the experience of return to a tranquil, untroubled state (1953, p. 42). This unique experience is different from the satisfaction that occurs when physical needs are met.

Six Stages of Development

Sullivan (1953) conceptualized personality development as consisting of six stages or developmental epochs, spanning infancy through late adolescence. Each stage centers on a unique kind of interpersonal relationship.

Modes of Experience

Three of Sullivan's six stages of development revolve around his rather abstract and complex "modes of experience." Because they are critical to Sullivan's thinking regarding the stages and are difficult to "put a finger on," the modes deserve separate treatment.

The **prototaxic** mode is the earliest (infancy), most primitive type of experience, a state of generalized sensation or feeling, in the absence of thought (Sullivan, 1953). The infant knows only what William James called a "big, blooming, buzzing confusion"—vague perceptions of momentary states having no "before" or "after." There is no awareness of self as separate from the world. Sullivan, who often avoided formal definitions, is helped by sympathetic colleague Patrick Mullahy who characterized the prototaxic mode as follows:

> *The infant vaguely feels or "prehends" earlier and later states without realizing any serial connection between them. . . . He has no awareness of himself as an entity separate from the rest of the world. In other words, his felt experience is all of a piece, undifferentiated, without definite limits. It is as if his experiences were "cosmic." (Mullahy, 1948; as quoted by the editors of Sullivan, 1953, p. 28)*

The **parataxic** mode is experienced as the infant becomes a child who begins to use speech, but still makes few logical connections within the sequence of its experiences (approximately the pre-school years; Sullivan, 1947; 1953). Thinking and speech are disorganized and disjunctive as in a dream, and understanding remains minimal. There is a sense of "magic" in which things "just happen," as in seeing colorful Christmas lights suddenly appear with the simple flip of a switch. In adults, parataxic experience may serve as a rough basis of generalized memory, related to habits. Examples include routine activities that often occur without conscious decision-making, such as dressing, walking to class, eating, or doing repetitive piecework. Again, Mullahy comes to Sullivan's aid:

> *As the infant develops and maturation proceeds, the original undifferentiated wholeness of experience is broken. However, the "parts," the diverse aspects, the various kinds of experience are not related or connected in a logical fashion. . . . The child cannot yet relate them to one another or make logical distinctions among them. . . . Since no connections or relations are established, there is no logical movement of "thought" from one idea to the next. The* parataxic mode *is not a step by step process. Experience is undergone as momentary, unconnected states of being. (Mullahy, 1948; as quoted by the editors of Sullivan, 1953, p. 28)*

In other words, the unbroken mass—like a glob of jelly—that was feeling and perception is now segmented into parts, like separate cubes of jelly. Nevertheless, the parts are disconnected and not logically related to one another.

The **syntaxic** mode becomes important during more mature childhood when the meaning of words becomes shared with most other people in society so that experience, judgments, and observations can be shared (approximately the early elementary school years; Sullivan, 1953). An individual becomes able to communicate syntaxic experiences with another because both parties define language symbols alike. This is the stage of "consensual validation" in which children learn to separate experiences they share with others from experiences peculiar to them, make their thoughts and feelings clear to others, and be clear on what others are thinking and feeling (Sullivan, 1953). Again, Mullahy is helpful:

> *The child gradually learns the . . . meaning of language—in the widest sense of language. These meanings have been acquired from group activities, interpersonal activities, social experience. Consensually validated symbol activity involves an appeal to principles which are accepted as true by the hearer. (Mullahy, 1948; as quoted by the editors of Sullivan, 1953, p. 28)*

When children acquire this mode, others have taught them the shared rules of organizing thoughts so that thoughts and speech are no longer disconnected and disjunctive. The undifferentiated mass that became the unsystematically linked assortment of pieces has now become an assemblage of separate parts each bearing some relationship to some of the others.

As you can see, the direction of development as reflected by the three modes is toward increased socialization. Over time, the social "majority" rules over personal interpretations. With this background, you can now turn your attention to Sullivan's six developmental stages.

Infancy: Prototaxic Feelings about "Good" and "Bad" Caregivers

The **infancy** stage starts at birth and continues until the appearance of speech (Sullivan, 1953). The development of personality begins with feeding. This is because the infant's initial interpersonal situation is the "nipple-in-lips" experience, which revolves around the infant's oral zone and the mother's mammary zone. The experience integrates the infant's need for water, food, and contact, and the caregiver's need to show tenderness. Notice that this period is much like the "oral stage" as conceived by Freud, but departs from the psychoanalytic view by including the interpersonal notion of "caretaker tenderness." The infant's accompanying hand and foot movements—touching, grasping, pulling, pushing, rubbing, patting, and cuddling—become an increasingly important part of this first interpersonal situation.

As the infant begins to accumulate experiences, it forms **personifications**, investments of human attributes in persons or objects that do not actually possess the assigned traits, at least not in the degree to which they are applied. For example, if the infant's need for nourishment is accommodated by the willing presentation of a satisfying nipple, it forms the early personification "good nipple." When the infant's interactions with mothering ones are experienced as satisfying, warm, and comforting, it forms the personification "good mother." This empathic sensory image is not of the real mother, but of the infant's vague, prototaxic sense of feeding experiences as good because they result in relaxations of tensions. If the same caregiver, or a substitute, interacts with the infant in ways that are "rough, sound unpleasant, hurt the baby, and generally discompose him," the infant will be led to form a second rudimentary personification, that of the "bad mother" who has the "nipple of anxiety" (Sullivan, 1953, pp. 116 & 87). Sullivan summarized these personifications: ". . . all relations with . . . people . . . [who] are a part of . . . satisfying . . . the infant's needs blend into a single personification which I call the good mother . . . all experience . . . which results in severe anxiety blends into a single personification which I call . . . the bad mother" (Sullivan, 1953, p. 120).

These personifications may endure in memory as "eidetic people"—"illusory people," "imaginary people," or "past people" who are sometimes dredged up and matched to people in adult life (boss as "bad mother"). Personal personifications develop as well. The individual comes to know "me," "good me," "bad me," and "not me" (Rychlak, 1981).

Despite understanding the difference between "rough" behavior and "tender" behavior, you may still wonder how the rather primitive prototaxic skills of the infant allow it to differentiate between "bad mother" and "good mother." The infant cannot understand what the mothering one says, nor can it interpret "appearances" (Sullivan, 1953). "Good" and "bad" mothers may look the same in basic physical appearance, including clothing. The "good nipple" and the "bad nipple" may be identical in appearance. The signs the infant must read to tell "good" from "bad" are more subtle. In the case of the "bad mother" they are **forbidding gestures**, negative, covert cues such as a wrinkled brow, a cold tone of voice, a too tight grasp, a hesitancy, reluctance, or even revulsion at having to interact with the infant. Sullivan put it this way:

> *The discrimination of heard differences in the mother's vocalization and seen differences in the postural tensions of the mother's face, and perhaps later of differences in speed and rhythm of her gross bodily movements in coming toward the infant, presenting the bottle, changing the diapers, or what not—all these rather refined discriminations [made] by the . . . receptors of vision and hearing . . . are frequently associated with the unpleasant experience of anxiety, including the nipple of anxiety instead of the good nipple. (Sullivan, 1953, pp. 86-87)*

At this and later stages Sullivan wrote of a process having the flavor of Freud's and Adler's "complex" but called **dynamisms**, "the relatively enduring energy [units] which [periodically] characterize the organism in its duration as a living organism" (Sullivan, 1953, p. 103). These energy systems are self-contained, intact entities that can operate on their own, but may function in relationship to other such systems. Think of them as packages of energy that wax and wane in their

---

BOX 6.1   What Were (and Are) Your Personifications?

Sullivan would argue that you have had many personal personifications as an infant, as a child, and on through the other stages into adulthood. Think back to your childhood and forward in time in an attempt to identify your personifications. It will help if you recall the "early experience" exercise from the Adler chapter. Also search your memory for incidents that reflected on you as a person. To help in this process some possible personifications are listed to stimulate your thinking or, if they apply, to be selected by you.

"good me"	"bad me"	"not me"
"clever me"	"mischievous me"	"worthless me"
"brilliant me"	"kind me"	"awkward me"
"helpless me"	"ingenious me"	"devious me"
"shy me"	"bold me"	"manipulative me"
"self-sacrificing me"	"altruistic me"	"martyred me"
"sensitive me"	"faithful me"	"uncertain me"

You may wish to share the choices you made with those of other members of the class. Note choices that are shared with other people and exchange recollections of what events inspired the coincidental personifications.

---

power and in their impact on the individual. They may develop at one or other of the stages, but can continue to crop up throughout life. Like tensions, dynamisms are of two kinds: (1) integrating, organizing, isolating tendencies; and (2) energy packages that involve certain "zones" or arenas of interaction. The self-system is a dynamism of the first kind. An example of the second kind that has it origins in the infancy stage is the *oral dynamism*, an energy system that encompasses interactions focusing on feeding or nourishment. Because dynamisms organize and channel physical energy, they have the power to dominate personality and cause it to follow one developmental direction rather than another.

It is from early experiences with others that the infant begins to differentiate its own self-system from the world around it. Experiences of positive satisfactions, in which the mothering one is pleased, are organized around a personification of "good me." In this case, interpersonal security prevails. On the other hand, experiences of anxiety in the parent/infant relationship are organized around a personification of "bad me." Insecurity is the prevailing tendency. In this way, the undifferentiated nature of early experience begins to break down into parts. The infant has learned to make some distinctions between itself and the world.

Sullivan (1947) was very concerned with child-rearing practices. He identified the kinds of early parental attitudes contributing to psychological maladjustment later in childhood: believing the infant must be clean and dry (achieve bowel and bladder control by 15 months); becoming upset when the infant tinkers with its genitals; treating an infant as if it were being willfully troublesome; and fancying that the infant "takes after" some other person in the family.

Childhood: Parataxic Learning Applicable to Social Habits and Self

The **childhood stage** emerges with articulate speech and ends with the appearance of the need for peers (pre-school years). A number of important developmental tasks are begun during this stage. First, there is rapid social acculturation in what is "proper." Children come to accept their parents' lessons in cleanliness, feeding habits, toilet training, obedience, oughts, and musts. Second, language is acquired as a communication tool for manipulating the outside social world into alleviating one's tensions. Third, there is continuing development of the self-system, the function of which becomes to avoid or minimize incidents of anxiety.

Through a maturing ability to learn, the child becomes more skillful at reading the forbidding gestures of significant others. In this sense, the self-system is somewhat parallel to Freud's concept of ego in seeking to secure necessary satisfactions without incurring much anxiety. The self-system maintains normal functioning by minimizing anxiety through *selective inattention* to threatening events and by anticipating, and thereby avoiding, experiences that are incompatible with its past development. It sinks into maladjustment when it resorts to *dissociation*, completely severing any connection of the threatening events or experiences to the self (Rychlak, 1981). More generally, it is through our self-systems that we psychologically carry our parents around with us throughout our lives, as a continuing frame of reference regarding what is "approved" and "disapproved." In this sense, the self-system is partly analogous to what Freud called "superego."

Fourth, there is learning of such negative emotions as disgust, shame, anger, and resentment. "Willie, I told you not to do that. Now say you are sorry" (Sullivan, 1953, p. 200). There also is learning of such negative forms of social interaction as malevolence, hatred, and isolation. Sullivan (1953) considers the learning of malevolence as "perhaps the greatest disaster" to happen during the childhood phase of personality development. Ironically the child may develop malevolence while seeking tenderness.

> . . . *many children have the experience that when they need tenderness, when they do that which once brought tender cooperation, they are not only denied tenderness, but they are treated in a fashion to provoke anxiety or even, in some cases, pain. A child may discover that manifesting the need for tenderness toward the potent figures around him leads frequently to his being disadvantaged, being made anxious, being made fun of, and so on. . . . Under those circumstances, the developmental course changes to the point that the perceived need for tenderness brings a foresight of anxiety or pain. The child learns . . . that it is highly disadvantageous to show any need for tender cooperation from the authoritative figures around him, in which case he shows something else . . . the basic malevolent attitude, the attitude that one really lives among enemies. . . . (Sullivan, 1953, p. 214)*

Sullivan had a strong interest in the processes by which children learn. He proposed five main avenues to acquiring new, useful information. Three of these are straightforward, common-sensical, and rather self-evident: (1) *trial and success* (behaviors that succeed are stamped into memory as habits); (2) *rewards and punishments*; and (3) *trial and error* (noting errors in order to avoid them). However, two of them are unique and innovative, thus, worth more extended consideration. Children may **learn by anxiety**—when anxiety is not severe, individuals may become acquainted with the situations in which it is present so that those circumstances may be avoided. Even early in life children can learn that some situation or object is "not-me" and not desirable, thus to be avoided. Later, with the arrival of language ability, such circumstances can be labeled as anxiety-provoking, thereby making them easier to shun. A still higher plane of learning by anxiety involves the **anxiety gradient**, "learning to discriminate increasing from diminishing anxiety and to alter activity in the direction of the latter" (Sullivan, 1953, p. 452). Here the child must be able to monitor sometimes subtle changes in its feelings and become aware of the situations in which the changes occur. Then when anxiety rises, they can move themselves to circumstances that will likely lower anxiety. For example, the child might learn that playing with the genitals when the mothering one is present causes steadily rising anxiety. To change the gradient, the child must in the presence of the mothering one, withdraw its hands from the genitals and apply them to a task that is associated with lowered anxiety. An example task would be grasping a pencil or crayon to make drawings that please the mothering one. "Acting like an artist" is an example of *sublimation*, avoiding anxiety by engaging in activities that meet some need, such as deriving pleasure from use of the hands, but are socially acceptable.

The second type of learning that is unique to Sullivan is **eductive**, learning relationships by "pulling them out" of the entities that contain them (this term is more related to induction/deduction than "education"; Sullivan, 1953, p. 156). This process of extracting a relationship from the concrete or abstract parts involved in it *does* imply the ability to appreciate "mechanical-geometric relations" that appear for some people at intellectual maturity (p. 156). However, it may be displayed earlier, in more primitive form. For example, very early in life the child learns to appreciate the relationship between the parts of its body.

By reference to three broad considerations, Sullivan wrote of the socialization of the child—becoming a functional citizen of society. First, the *frequency* with which the child behaves in specifiable ways can cue her or him, and those who train the child, as to which behaviors are being acquired. Attention to frequency may allow children and their parents to cultivate behaviors that are socially desirable and cull those that are undesirable. Second, and closely aligned with frequency, is *consistency*, the "repetition of particular patterns of events" as opposed to inconsistency represented by a "reduced frequency of a pattern of events or a greater variety of patterns of events" (p. 172). If the child behaves consistently, it can be assumed that he or she is learning or has learned the behaviors being performed. Consistency cues the child and his or her trainers that a certain course of behavioral acquisition is underway. Third, the parental contribution to socialization is emphasized in the notion of *sanity*, "parental modification of [training] efforts in accordance with the [child's] capacity for observation, analysis, and elaboration of experience at a given time" (p. 173). Sanity is shown by parents who fully understand the capabilities and deficiencies of their children so that educational demands are reasonable and appropriate to their children.

Juvenile Era: Syntaxic Experiences of Finding Playmates and Questioning Parents

The **juvenile era** is ushered in with the child's need for peer companions, or "playmates rather like oneself." It coincides with the early elementary school years, during which the child has many opportunities to learn the ways of other children and show social subordination to new authority figures such as teachers, coaches, and club leaders. During this time children gain *compeers*, playmates who teach them more about their social capabilities and shield them from loneliness.

BOX 6.2   What Learning Processes Were Involved in Your Childhood Training?

Four of Sullivan's learning processes are arranged into two categories and each is briefly defined for you (the eductive process is excluded as it emerges spontaneously and, therefore, is not highly trainable). For each of the four, pick a number between 0 and 100 to represent the percentage of your training—instituted by you or your parents—that employed the process in question.

Your four numbers should add up to one hundred. For example you might assign 10 to "learning by anxiety," 20 to "rewards and punishments," 40 to "trial and success," and 30 to "trial and error."

Positively Oriented Processes

Process	*Number out of 100*
Trial and success— attempting a behavior until it succeeds.	
Trial and error—observing own and other's behavior to profit by knowledge of mistakes.	

Negatively Oriented Processes

Process	*Number out of 100*
Learn by anxiety— individuals become acquainted with anxiety provoking situations so that these may be avoided.	
Rewards and punishments—arranging for pleasure to encourage a behavior and punishment to discourage its undesirable counterpart.	

Note which process you assigned the largest number. If its assigned number is 40 or greater, you are indicating that it was clearly the primary training procedure in your learning history. Tally by category: add the two numbers in the positive category and the two in the negative category. If one of these two subtotals is 60 or more you are indicating that you were primarily subjected to positively or negatively oriented processes, depending on the category to which the number applies.

The juvenile develops an appreciation of differences in living never conceived of before, some "right" and some "wrong." Ideas and social operations learned at home may be found not to apply at school or with friends, and are reformulated. Authorities, including one's parents, are reduced from godlike figures to people. Along with cooperation are experiences of competition, stereotyping, ostracism, and compromise. References are made to "our team" and "our teacher." Social accommodation is partly motivated by peer pressure. A personally meaningful orientation to living begins to take form, based on a growing understanding of one's needs and future goals. Sullivan likens the juvenile stage to what Freud called the "latency period."

Preadolescence: Collaborating Happily with a Chum

The period of **preadolescence** is brief, beginning with the need for interpersonal intimacy in the form of a close relationship with another person "of comparable status." Somewhere between the ages of 8½ and 10, the child "begins to develop a real sensitivity to what matters to another person" (Sullivan, 1953, p. 245). One's predominant interest is in establishing a relationship with a *chum*, a particular member of the same sex who becomes a close friend. Preadolescents contribute to the happiness of their friends through collaboration: making personal adjustments aimed at providing mutual satisfactions. When two young people become mutually important to each other, the personal worth of both is supported by the process of consensual validation, in this case, sharing attitudes. Preadolescents may spend hours with one another in mutual daydreaming. Participation in cliques or gangs may be traced to interlocking, two-person relationships in which pair members A and B also have individual relationships with pair members C and D, respectively. Loneliness resulting from the absence of close peer relationships may be overcome by an irresistible need for cooperative companionship that is so powerful people seek relations with others despite the fear of being rebuffed.

Early Adolescence: Experiencing Lust toward a Sexual Partner

Early adolescence erupts at puberty when the need for intimacy evolves toward lustful feelings of closeness and tenderness with a sexual partner. Interest in a member of one's own sex is replaced by interest in a member of the opposite sex. The object of interest is no longer a person quite like oneself, but one who is "very different." The epoch continues until patterns of behavior emerge that satisfy **lust**, Sullivan's term for "certain tensions of or pertaining to the genitals," culminating in orgasm (1953, p. 109). At this stage, a "lust" dynamism along with intimacy needs become important.

Sullivan classified the lust dynamism and intimacy needs into three categories: (1) orientation to others on the basis of intimacy needs; (2) orientation to others on the basis of partner's status (same or different gender, human or not, alive or dead); and (3) orientation to others on the basis of how the genitals are used during sexual interaction. As should be apparent, (1) refers to intimacy needs, while (2) and (3) refer to the lust dynamism.

Sullivan used the Greek root word "philos," meaning "loving" as the foundation for terms referring to expressions of intimacy needs. He postulated modes of *intimacy expression* that correspond to three kinds of people: each mode is chosen by a different type of person. First there is the **autophilic person**, one who manifests no preadolescent development, because it has not occurred or was attempted without success, causing the continuation of self-directed love. This kind of person's intimacy expressions have the flavor of "narcissism" as Freud would have applied the term. "An **isophilic person** has been unable to progress past preadolescence, and continues to regard as suitable for intimacy only people who are as like himself as possible . . . that is, members of his own sex" (Sullivan, 1953, p. 192; emphasis added). Finally "A **heterophilic person** has gone through the preadolescent period and made the early adolescent change in which he has become intensely interested in achieving intimacy with members of . . . the other sex" (Sullivan, 1953, p. 192; emphasis added).

The "orientation to others according to status" category, related to the lust dynamism (2), contains mostly familiar entries. *Homosexuals* orient to the same sex, *heterosexuals* orient to the opposite sex, and *autosexuals* orient to themselves. Less familiar is *katasexual* which refers to preference for non-humans such as animals or dead people.

The lust dynamism regarding use of the genitals (3) has six varieties. **Orthogenital** involves the integration of one's own genitals with the "natural receptor genitals" of the opposite sex, that is, heterosexual use of the genitals (p. 293). In **paragenital** use of the sex organs one acts as if to seek contact with genitals opposite one's own, but in such a way that impregnation will not occur. Rubbing one's own genitals against those of an opposite sexed person is an obvious example. **Metagenital** use does not involve one's own genitals, but another person's genitals are involved. Masturbating someone else is an example. **Amphigenital** refers to the case where one or both members of a pair, who both may be homosexual or heterosexual, take on a role that is different from their usual role. For example, a woman straps on a penis-like device and uses it in sex with her partner. The other two entries in this category are more straightforward: *mutual masturbation* which is self-explanatory or *onanism* which refers to heterosexual intercourse that is terminated before orgasm occurs.

In sum, Sullivan thought that one's sexual expressions exist on three planes: with regard to intimacy needs (heterophilic and so forth), with regard to sexual orientation to others (homosexual and so forth), and with regard to use of the genitals (paragenital and so forth), where the last two involve the lust dynamism. In this way Sullivan argued that sexuality has implications for both intimacy and physical gratification.

In terms of sexual attitudes, Sullivan identified Americans as the most "sex-ridden" people he knew. He related these unfortunate inclinations to two cultural conventions: discouraging early marriage and discouraging premarital sex. The effect of the sexual twilight zone we erect between the beginning of adolescence and adulthood is to widen the gap between the awakening of adolescent lust and the "proper" time in life for "appropriate" sexual expression (marriage).

TABLE 6.1   Sullivan's Six Developmental Epochs

Epochs	Characteristics	Capacities for
Infancy:	Need for contact with caregiver; Prototaxic experience	Beginning speech
Childhood:	Need for adult participation in activities; Parataxic experience	Language
Juvenile Era:	Need for acceptance by peers; Syntaxic experience	Peer or playmate relationships
Preadolescence:	Need for intimate exchange with a loved one	Close, same-sex relationship—chum
Early Adolescence		Close, opposite-sex relationship; Patterning of lustful or genital behavior
Late Adolescence		Mature and independent development of love relationships in which another person is as important as oneself

Late Adolescence: Establishing Love Relationships
What separates early and late adolescence is not biological maturation but an achievement. Here partially developed aspects of personality fall into place. The person is able to tolerate some previously avoided anxiety, which allows favorable changes to be made in the self-system. **Late adolescence** begins with the discovery of an orientation to genital behavior and how to fit that revelation into the rest of life and ends with "the establishment of a fully human or mature repertory of interpersonal relations" (Sullivan, 1953, p. 297). Freud would have seen his "genital stage" in Sullivan's writings about late adolescence. Being able to take first steps on adult legs, one can "establish relationships of love for some other person, in which relationship the other person is as significant, or nearly as significant, as one's self" (p. 34).

Table 6.1 summarizes the six stages along with the corresponding bench marks.

Evaluation

Contributions

Physical Contact and Peer Relationships
Sullivan's theory of personality development emphasizes the importance of physical contact between the infant and "a mothering one," as well as progressive involvement in peer relationships over time. His point of view stresses the role of

empathic, nonverbal communication in close, child-maternal relationships. These emphases are supported by independent lines of research.

Human infants do show a need to have intimate physical contact with a parental figure, termed "primary object-clinging" by John Bowlby (1969). In a 1951 report to the World Health Organization, Bowlby concluded that mental health in infants requires the experiencing of a warm, intimate, and continuous relationship with a maternal figure, not necessarily the biological mother. He indicated that infants placed in institutional settings, such as hospitals and orphanages, who do not receive physical contact from a nurturing figure soon show developmental and survival difficulties attributable to interpersonal deprivation.

To illustrate, Spitz (1946) observed symptoms of depression in 45 of 123 infants who had been placed in nursery homes following separation from their parents. Symptoms included loss of appetite, trouble sleeping, crying, slow motor movements, apathy, physical withdrawal such as turning toward a wall, vulnerability to infection, and slowed development. An extreme form of this reaction is *marasmus*, a "hospitalism" syndrome in infants who self-destructively "waste away" in the absence of any demonstrable physical cause (Bosselman, 1958). Fortunately, such symptoms in an infant can be counteracted by daily physical contact with a particular adult who consistently cares for the infant, such as a nurse. This important finding has been translated into international prevention programs involving routine, daily "cuddling" of all babies in institutions. As you may recall, after the fall of the communist regime in Rumania, many institutionalized infants and children were found to be suffering from a condition similar to that described by Spitz. During 1990 and 1991, many U.S. citizens traveled to Rumania and brought children back with them, or stayed and provided the kind of close and warm interaction that they needed for survival.

Researchers have also differentiated two patterns of infant behaviors in experiments involving limited separation and reunion with mothers. On the one hand, separation may elicit *attachment* behaviors, through which infants try to find the missing caregiver and reestablish physical contact. On the other hand, infants, especially those subjected to more prolonged separation, may show *detachment* behaviors of indifference, protest, or despair (Bowlby, 1969; Suomi, Collins, Harlow, & Ruppenthal, 1976). Ainsworth (1979) has linked personality adjustment at ages 4–6 to the type of attachment characteristic of infant/mothering-one interactions during infancy. In follow-up studies, infants who were "securely attached" at age 1 were not only socially more cooperative and emotionally positive in later years, but also less angry, aggressive, and avoidant, compared with "anxiously attached infants" (remember Shaver's research related to Horney's theory). Ainsworth noted that secure attachment is fostered more by *how* the caregiver holds the infant, close to the body and face to face, rather than how long the infant is held.

The research of Harry Harlow (1959) and his co-workers is relevant to Sullivan's theory. Harlow placed infant rhesus monkeys in individual cages containing two substitute or surrogate mothers (also see Harlow, 1958). One was constructed of wire mesh containing a milk-supplying nipple. The other was made of terry cloth and in some cases also contained a nipple. Observations revealed that infant monkeys spent far more time climbing and clinging on the cloth-covered surrogates, regardless of whether it was the source of milk or not. When frightening stimuli were introduced into the cages, such as a mechanical teddy bear beating a drum, the infants immediately sought security by running to the cloth mothers. Results pointed to the "overwhelming importance" of bodily contact and the comfort it supplies to infants, compared to the libidinous "oral sensations" of classical psychoanalysis.

Harlow and Harlow (1974) have stated that "the importance of peer relationships . . . cannot be overemphasized" (p. 199). Such social interactions provide critical opportunities for learning affection toward peers, control of fear and aggression, sex roles through play, sexual competence, and parental behavior. Many of these social functions are the same as may be served by Sullivan's "compeer" or "chum." There even may be an evolutionary advantage in having independent sources of affection, with parents and peers compensating for potential deficiencies in one another.

Suomi and Harlow (1972) reported fascinating use of younger-age peers as "therapists" in successfully rehabilitating monkeys who had been socially isolated for 6 months. Isolates were permitted to interact with socially normal monkeys. The approach reflected in the nonthreatening behaviors of the young monkey "therapists" may be analogous to the "trust" and the gradual "reeducation" dimensions characteristic of Sullivan's approaches to therapy with humans. It certainly is analogous to the benefits peers offer one another.

The "Psychiatric Interview": A Contribution to Helping People Achieve Psychological Adjustment

Sullivan's (1954) posthumous book *The Psychiatric Interview* is a classic text on the most widely used assessment technique, the interview of individuals with psychological problems. Sullivan saw the interview as an alternative to Freud's methods. The interview appears to work better with a wider range of patients, from the mildly to the seriously disturbed. Sullivan's three contributions to understanding people through interviewing encompass: (1) assumptions about the nature of interview data; (2) structural outlines for obtaining and organizing information; and (3) guidelines for interpreting the interview process and defining the roles of the participants.

Sullivan (1954) believed that two factors determine that "there are no purely objective data in psychiatry" (p. 3). First, a large degree of inference is required before the information people provide about themselves begins to make sense. Second, the interviewer directly influences the information people provide. In brief, *data* about the patient passes through the interviewer who operates as a *participant observer*:

> the psychiatrist cannot stand off to one side and apply his sense organs . . . to noticing what someone else does, without becoming personally implicated in the operation. His principal instrument of observation is his self—his personality,

him *as a person. The processes and the changes in processes that make up the data which can be subjected to scientific study occur, not in the subject person nor in the observer, but in the situation which is created between the observer and his subject. (Sullivan, 1954, p. 3)*

This statement indicates an ironic circumstance, not fully recognized by Freud. Attempts to assess the personality of another individual inevitably involve the intrusion of the assessor's personality. Once the assessor's personality intervenes, it contaminates the data bearing on the interviewee's personality. Then one is stuck with a dilemma: to what degree do the data tell us about the interviewee's personality and to what degree does it inform us about the interviewer's personality.

Sullivan makes several points concerning the organization of personality as it is revealed in the psychiatric interview. The heart and soul of the interview is:

a situation of primarily vocal *communication in a* two-person *group . . . [which involves] a progressively unfolding* expert-client *. . . [relationship that illuminates]* characteristic patterns of living. . . . *benefit [derives from learning about] . . . patterns he experiences as particularly troublesome or especially valuable. (Sullivan, 1954, p. 4)*

Sullivan identified four stages of the interview. First, the *inception* of the interview is the formal reception of the client and inquiry about why he or she has come to the interviewer. Second, the *reconnaissance* stage "consists in obtaining a rough outline of the social or personal history of the patient" (p. 40). In the critically important third phase, *detailed inquiry*, in-depth exploration occurs that involves many "subtleties and complexities" of technique all employed in the interest of examining "another person's life" (p. 410). In the fourth phase, *interruption* signals that a particular interview session has come to an end, but other sessions are expected to occur, and *termination* means no further sessions are expected.

The detailed inquiry is the core of the psychiatric interview. It begins with an attempt on the part of the therapist to gain an accurate impression of the patient. This pursuit is hindered by the patient's understandable concern about what the "doctor" thinks of him or her. Initially the patient attempts to avoid a bad impression if not create a good one. At this point the job of the therapist is to gain the patient's confidence so that honest disclosures about her or him will be made. This task may be accomplished by showing irritation-free tolerance for the patient's circuitous answers to questions, "walking around the obvious," as Sullivan put it (p. 98). Eventually, the patient will see that direct and forthright answers will be favorably received.

Beyond the initial game of cat and mouse played by interviewer and patient, there are two substantive issues addressed during the detailed inquiry phase. The interviewee may signal anxiety, the first issue, by abrupt changes or transitions in the course of the interview. The interviewer may take advantage of these changes to either lessen anxiety, for the comfort of the patient, or raise it, for the purpose of exploring it. Episodes of anxiety may be especially intense when the patient is concerned about the therapist's view of her or him. In any case, these episodes are uniformly unwanted. Unlike fear which may sometimes attract us—we may attend a scary movie or ride a roller coaster—anxiety is never wanted, according to Sullivan. Thus, in therapy, as in everyday life, when anxiety is on the rise, patients do whatever is necessary to lower it. They may even sometimes "act . . . like asses" (Sullivan, 1954, p. 101). As you might surmise, episodes of anxiety during therapeutic interviews cue interviewers that they have "hit a nerve" of the interpersonal kind.

The second substantive issue involves the *self-system*. During the later part of childhood, the individual refines **security operations**, skills that allow avoidance of forbidding gestures. When these skills are properly and successfully applied, the child can maintain a state of relative euphoria. Should these abilities fail—the self-system is unable to protect the person's feeling of well-being—a drop in euphoria occurs and is experienced as anxiety. Thus, protecting well-being or relative euphoria is a basic task of everyone from infant to adult and certainly is a major goal of the patient during the interview. The exercise of security operations gives the person better **foresight**, the capacity to look ahead in search of good experiences and in the interest of avoiding bad ones. Foresight is facilitated by looking constantly for signs of approval and disapproval in others.

What the patient needs from the interviewer are signals indicating that he or she is doing fine and is "approved." Absent or ambiguous signals from the therapist generate anxiety. Under these circumstances, the game of cat and mouse may begin again: "You are reading me and I look good . . . No! I'm coming across badly . . . I'll try to communicate another impression." All these signals, communications and miscommunications, are evidence that the self-system is "up and running." The job of the interviewer is then to help the patient *tune* the self-system, make it run right, so that she or he can receive euphoria-maintaining signals.

These are the therapeutic tasks of the psychological professional during the psychiatric interview, but what can patients do for themselves? Believing, like Adler, that troubled people must take action in their own behalf, Sullivan outlined three jobs to be done by patients (Sullivan, 1947). First, the patient, and everyone else, can learn to **notice changes in the body** that signal decreases or increases in the tension signifying anxiety. By monitoring their bodies, patients can recognize when anxiety is rising or falling and the situations in which these events occur. Being aware of the situations associated with increases or decreases of anxiety is a kind of *insight* that precedes coping with anxiety.

Second, the patient—and the rest of us—can learn to **notice marginal thoughts**, thoughts that monitor, critique, and alter speech in terms of formation, grammar, and so forth and in terms of errors that may cause incomplete or misunderstood communications to others. There are two kinds of "critics." The first is called I_1 and is merely concerned with the mechanics of speech. We are often aware of this "rather unfriendly critic" (Sullivan, 1954, p. 99). It is an irritant, that chastises us for our failures to speak correctly. By contrast, I_2, a "rather intelligent creature," is concerned with more central matters: how well we are presenting ourselves to other people. I_2 is a mirror that reflects the impression we are making on others back to us. We may pay attention to I_1 and, based on its feedback, correct ourselves as we go. However, I_2, because it deals with more threatening interpersonal matters, is likely to be beyond our conscious awareness and show up only in increased tensions. Should we be able to tune in to I_2, we would be taking the first step toward dealing with the interpersonal issues that face us, and, at the same time, move toward lowering tension.

The third action that all of us can take, patients or not, is to **make prompt statements of all that comes to mind**, a process that is enabled by trusting the "situation to the extent of expressing the thoughts that it provokes" (p. 100). Performing this feat is easier said than done, however, because of two inhibitory factors. First, in order for prompt statements to occur, parataxic processes must be fully developed and the individual must have insight into them. Second, people are likely to be plagued with thoughts of past behavioral disasters. They may wonder whether they are currently creating a bad impression in the mind of the interviewer and, therefore, may be reluctant to "speak their minds" about the current circumstances. Instead they may provide "a circumstantial account of some insignificant current event, or an extravagant report of the marvelous good results that have . . . been achieved by exposure to the psychiatrist" (p. 100). Only when they learn to speak straightforwardly about the current situation will they be able to provide the information the interviewer needs to help them.

The tasks of the interviewer, revolving around anxiety and the self-system, and the three actions by the patient jointly constitute the therapeutic benefits that are associated with the psychiatric interview. The psychiatric interview is a productive "two-person-group" partnership which exists for the benefit of the patient.

Limitations

Formal science was not well understood nor highly valued by Sullivan, who was trained as a physician and psychiatrist. Like Freud, Horney, and Jung, and to a lesser degree Adler, he was a clinician and theorist rather than a scientific researcher. In fact, as noted earlier, Sullivan declared the virtual impossibility of "doing science" with regard to personality. He placed greatest reliance on informal methods of study: his ideas were developed in offices, hospitals, and libraries, not in scientific laboratories. More generally, unlike psychologists of Sullivan's day, psychiatrists of his time did not make "doing science" a major priority. They were strictly therapists who were more apt to be guided by non-science concerns, such as addressing the psychological problems of persons who are struggling with their lives and in need of help.

In view of these circumstances, it is little wonder that, to this day, there is a virtual absence of direct scientific support for Sullivan's theory. Although consistent with Sullivan's ideas, even the results of the "monkey" studies by Harlow that were cited earlier were not directly inspired by Sullivanian theory. In fact, these studies support the ideas of Bowlby, as well as those of many other theorists including Horney, not just Sullivan. It seems that Sullivanians must look to other people for support of their ideas, as they have generated precious little of their own.

If Horney is the best writer among the theorists covered in this book, Sullivan is probably the worst. By any criteria, his written communications were poor, and he knew it (Chapman, 1976). After being frustrated in attempts to interpret writings concerning some of his major concepts, readers may wonder whether he was being purposefully evasive, or whether his alleged schizophrenic condition interfered with his ability to communicate. In any case, his writings were so obscure in places that his editors had to insert footnotes containing others' interpretations in order to alleviate reader frustration (see, for example, Sullivan, 1953, pp. 28–29). I was so stumped by certain passages regarding some of his central notions that I had to rummage through many adjacent pages before coming up with an interpretation. At these times, a haunting question came to my mind, "Does anyone fully understand Sullivan?"

While many of Sullivan's concepts approached profundity, others bordered on the trivial and still others appeared to be borrowed from someone else. For example, "rewards and punishments" is a common sense notion familiar to everybody's grandmother, and "trial and success" appears borrowed from E. L. Thorndike, without credit. Sullivan seemed to theorize about everything, but it mattered little to him whether others had already thoroughly "covered the subject."

Sullivan used virtually all of Freud's concepts, for example, free association, repression, and insight. This observation could make one wonder whether he was really a Freudian who developed a language that made him "sound" different. If he did not simply co-opt Freud, he may have gotten major ideas from other theorists. For example, did he originate the emphasis on anxiety, or did he get it from Horney, a theorist with whom he was personally familiar?

Conclusions

Sullivan may have borrowed from Freud and others. It has been argued, however, that some of what readers of Sullivan attribute to Freud is actually original Sullivanian thought that was not even inspired by Freud (Robbins, 1989). He may also have sometimes written about trivia, but he certainly introduced some highly original and useful ideas, including some that anticipated certain modern theorists. For example, "prototaxic, parataxic, and syntaxic" are ideas that originated with Sullivan and will always be associated with his name. Also, one may wonder, who "stole" from whom? Maybe Horney was heavily influenced by Sullivan. Finally, some of his ideas laid a solid foundation for future theory and research. "Foresight"—being pulled by the future rather than being pushed by the past—was one of his creative ideas that has several modern advocates. Perhaps he did not originate "looking ahead," but he certainly cast some new light on it. Forbidding gestures, subtle signs often communicated without words, was an early consideration of what has become the currently fascinating field of "nonverbal communication."

Some individuals question the credibility of a disturbed psychiatrist who tried to offer the rest of us advice concerning our problems. However, one must remember that many creative contributors to the human condition, scientists, artists, and entertainers, were individuals who had "brilliant lights in the attic that sometimes blinked erratically." The revered artist Van Gogh was considerably off-center. Relativity theorist Albert Einstein and "the father of the atomic bomb" Robert Oppenheimer were at least eccentric. Even extraordinary comedians, such as Lenny Bruce and Richard Pryor, led troubled lives (the Woody Allen you see on the screen could well be the real Woody). In fact, even profoundly disturbed people, such as schizophrenics, can be unusually creative (Carson & Butcher, 1992). Perhaps what some of us may view as "obscurity in Sullivan's writings" is creative thinking that is too unique and complex to be penetrated by less than deeply reflective contemplation. It may be time to reconsider Sullivan's works, this time with attention to what is "written between the lines."

Summary Points

1. Harry Stack Sullivan's family were recent Irish immigrants living in a small New York community. His achievements may have been spurred by a desire to rise above his background. The child and adolescent Sullivan was a loner with a confused sense of sexuality. As his time at Cornell was troubled, he soon left the university and disappeared, possibly because he suffered a schizophrenic episode. When he surfaced, it was to enter a medical school of uncertain reputation where he performed poorly. Without benefit of a formal residency, he became a psychiatrist interested in schizophrenia. In the middle of a distinguished career, Sullivan died under mysterious circumstances.

2. Sullivan's definition of personality highlighted his "two persons at a time" approach to personality. In fact, the core part of personality, the self-system, "is born entirely out of the influences of significant others upon one's feeling of well-being." Sullivan postulated that people experience two kinds of tensions: (1) physical needs and (2) interpersonal anxiety. He believed that tension in the infant induced tension in the mothering one which is experienced as tenderness and leads to meeting the infant's needs.

3. "Empathy" is the mode through which the infant participates in the other person's tension or discomfort. Anxiety aroused through the empathy mechanism can lead to disruptive behavior. Relief is provided by interpersonal security. Sullivan postulated three modes of experience. The prototaxic mode is manifested in the "booming, blooming, buzzing confusion" of infant reality. The parataxic mode involves speech, but little logical connectiveness within the sequence of experience. The syntaxic mode entails the advent of shared meanings so that individuals can communicate and relate to one another.

4. In infancy "nipple-to-lips" contact with a mothering one becomes central. Personifications first appear at this time. Also at this time, the infant learns to read "forbidding gestures." Dynamisms, self-contained energy packages, first develop during this period. The self-system is an example of the organizing, integrating kind of dynamism.

5. During the childhood stage, speech and the need for peers emerge. The self-system continues to develop in the direction of greater facility at avoiding anxiety. Manifestations of the need for tenderness become more complex: what once brought tenderness may now bring pain; since seeking tenderness may be disadvantageous, the child may develop a malevolent attitude. Sullivan posed five learning processes of which two are highly unique: (1) learn by anxiety: the child appreciates the anxiety gradient, discriminating increasing from diminishing anxiety, and may resort to sublimation, activities that avoid anxiety but meet some need; and (2) eductive: learning relationships by pulling them out of entities. Sullivan also pointed out the importance of frequency, consistency, and sanity in the training of the child.

6. During the juvenile era, the child's need for peers becomes central. Here what the child has learned at home about living may not apply to life among peers. Parents lose their godlike aura and children begin to see themselves as members of groups and connected to non-family. During preadolescence, the child becomes genuinely sensitive to the needs of others and seeks another person of comparable status for a close relationship. During early adolescence, lustful feelings arise and tenderness with a sexual partner is sought. Both intimacy needs and the lust dynamism become central.

7. Expression of the intimacy need takes several different forms: (1) autophilic, *intimacy need* directed to self; (2) isophilic, directed to people like oneself; (3) heterophilic, directed to opposite sex. The sexual orientations are autosexual, homosexual, or heterosexual (they may also be katasexual). Genital use forms are: (1) orthogenital, integration with opposite sex person; (2) paragenital, sex without the risk of pregnancy; (3) metagenital, one's own genitals not involved; (4) amphigenital, pair members switch roles; (5) mutual masturbation; and (6) onanism, termination of intercourse before orgasm.

8. Harlow's work with wire and cloth "monkey mothers" confirms the critical importance of close physical intimacy with a mothering one: infant monkeys prefer the cloth to the wire "mother" with a milk-supplying nipple. Spitz showed that infants without a mothering one develop severe depression. Other work indicates that separation from a mothering one may elicit attachment in some infants and detachment in others. "Monkey therapists" improved the condition of young monkeys that had suffered the despair of social isolation.

9. Sullivan noted two limitations of his psychiatric interview: (1) inference is required to interpret the information that people provide; (2) the interviewer may influence what the interviewee provides. The interview has four stages: (1) inception; (2) reconnaissance; (3) detailed inquiry; and (4) interruption or termination. Detailed inquiry begins with a game, in which patients are concerned with the impression they make. The self-system institutes security operations to maintain a state of relative euphoria. If these operations work well, the person gains better foresight. The patient can make three contributions to the success of her or his therapy: (1) notice changes in the body that herald tension changes; (2) notice marginal thoughts, especially I_2; and (3) make prompt statements of all that comes to mind.

10. Sullivan was a clinician, not a scientist. Not surprisingly, there has been very little scientific research in direct support of his theory. Readers may have to scramble for additional information to interpret a given one of Sullivan's passages. Sullivan was known to theorize about everything, even the trivial. He used so many of Freud's concepts that one wonders whether Sullivanian theory is actually Freudian. Nevertheless, many of Sullivan's ideas are highly original and extremely useful. Others, such as foresight and forbidding gestures, anticipated much modern theory and research. If he was a troubled person, disturbed individuals are often creative.

Running Comparison

Theorist	Sullivan in Comparison
Freud	He questioned Freud's sexual instincts and psychosexuality, but agreed on physical needs. He also talked about "oral gratification," but with emphasis on tenderness, not physical tension reduction. Used Freudian terms: free association, repression, and insight. "Dynamisms" are something like complexes, the self-system somewhat ego-like and a little superego-like. The juvenile era is somewhat equivalent to the latency period and the autophilic is somewhat narcissistic.
Adler	Some of his ideas had the flavor of social interest (preadolescence need for companionship) and he, like Adler, believed people must do for themselves. Adler's complexes are like his dynamisms.
Horney	They both showed interest in anxiety dating to infancy and in human relationships.
Fromm	The "katasexual" is somewhat like the narcrophilous character of Fromm.
Carl Rogers	Both sought to make patients feel approved and both thought that patients could do much for themselves.

Essay/Critical Thinking Questions

1. Sullivan had a life-long sexual identity problem. What factors led to this problem; what factors might lead to the problem in anyone?

2. Can a person's fears or perceptions that it is time to die hasten her or his death? Answer by using Sullivan as the case in point.

3. Sullivan thought that a person's world is made up of twosomes: the person coupled with each significant other in her or his life. Can you develop an argument against this central assumption?

4. What are the critical traits of a "mothering one?" Is gender an important factor? Why or why not?

5. Prototaxic, parataxic, and syntaxic are probably the best known of Sullivan's concepts. Are they really that central or does something else account for their familiarity? (If you argue that they are not really that central, tell what is. If you do see them as central, defend your position and forget the second half of the question.)

6. Can you fit Sullivan's six stages into the psychosexual stages (that is, collapse them into Freud's stages)?

7. Why is physical contact between infant and mothering one so important to primates, monkey and humans alike? What is the essential reason it is so important? An example answer is that the infant, being recently removed from fetal status, is accustomed to being physically close to a mother.

8. Sullivan's detailed stage of the psychiatric interview is complex. Can you break it up into at least three parts?

9. Sullivan outlines three actions that patients can take to contribute to the therapeutic aspect of the interview. Can you add two more that are consistent with his theory?

10. The text states that disturbed people, even schizophrenics, can be quite creative. How could that be? What is it about a disturbed person that may generate or promote creativity?

7

THE SEASONS OF OUR LIVES: ERIK ERIKSON

- Is it necessary to suffer a crisis of identity in order to fully appreciate the "identity crisis"?
- Does the development of human personality end with adolescence?
- At each stage of our lives, are we caught on the horns of a new dilemma?
- Does rebellion by youth have any redeeming social value?
- Are the major tasks of life over by retirement age?

Erik Erikson is quite different from the other theorists covered in this book. He is the only theorist who has no advanced degree. In fact, Erikson never went beyond high school. Yet he made it all the way up the academic ladder to a professorship at Harvard. Because he lacked formal training, he is not so devoted to the usual academic traditions in psychology. His point of view is quite universal, mixing Freudian language with anthropological considerations. Some may regard his orientation as more philosophy than science. But unlike others who have wandered away from psychological science toward philosophy, such as Erich Fromm, some of Erikson's concepts have received significant scientific support.

Despite his devotion to Freud, his basic concepts are highly original and drawn from the common language rather than psychological jargon. This inclination makes his ideas not well related to most of the other theorists' concepts. His most creative idea, one for which he will always be known, is the "identity crisis." It is the vehicle upon which he rode into a personality territory that was virtually unexplored by other theorists. Gordon Allport did write about the "mature personality," but it was Erikson more than anyone else who popularized the idea that personality development does not end with adolescence. It was also Erikson, in contrast to other theorists, who detailed personality development during the adult years. While Allport wrote of adult life without reference to stages, Erikson elaborated three stages of adult development. Just as he has expanded the horizons of personality psychology, he will broaden the scope through which you view the rest of your life.

Erikson, the Person

Erik Homburger Erikson was born (1902) of Danish parents in the German town of Frankfurt (Stevens, 1983). His name, sans Homburger, meant "Erik son of Erik," an appellation that was all he had left of his real father ("Erik Erikson," 1970). Abandoned by the senior Erik even before his birth, Erikson was reared and nurtured by the Jewish pediatrician who married his mother when he was only a few years old (Stevens, 1983).

A look at Erikson's childhood makes it easy to see where his interest in "identity crises" originated. He was a child with an identity dilemma. As most boys are, he was pressured to pin his identity to his biological father, but it is practically impossible to tack anything onto a virtual void. Thus, he turned to his adopted father, who loved him and treated him well (Hall, 1983). As a reflection of his esteem for his adopted father Erikson initially adopted "Homburger" as his surname. Even early in his career, including the period when he worked with Murray, he went by Erik Homburger. Yet his ambivalence showed when later he relegated Homburger to a middle initial. However, the confusion about his stepfather was only a rare outward sign of the identity crises that occurred to him repeatedly. An ideal Aryan in appearance—he was tall and blond—Erikson faced taunts served up by the children at his father's synagogue. At the same time he was shunned by some of his German schoolmates because of his stepfather's religion. Later he toyed with the idea of following in his stepfather's professional footsteps, but threw it aside, along with other aspirations for an advanced education. The lack of an advanced degree was itself a source of identity conflict. Was he a full-fledged academic or not? A former colleague thought that the lack of the academic "union card"—the Ph.D.—haunted Erikson when he joined the faculty at Harvard (Keniston, 1983). Later in life Erikson aptly expressed how vacillation between one kind of identity and another affected him during his youth, "I was," he recalled, "morbidly sensitive." ("Erik Erikson," 1970, p. 87).

Eschewing college, young Erikson took up painting (Roazen, 1976). In 1927 an old friend and director of a progressive school in Vienna invited Erikson to ply his trade in the Austrian capital. Sponsors of the friend's school included Dorthy Burlingham, a member of the immensely rich Tiffany family. This scion of the famous American family could well afford to commission portraits of her four children. It turned out that she also was undergoing psychoanalysis at the hands of the master himself, Freud. In addition, Burlingham was a friend of Freud's daughter Anna who counted the four Tiffany heirs among her first patients. Erikson experienced only brief interaction with the four children and short service as a replacement for the vacationing friend before Burlingham and Anna Freud asked him if he would be interested in becoming a child analyst. Though he was unfamiliar with this new specialty, Erikson was intrigued and agreed to undergo training analysis with Anna Freud. Soon he was drawn into the inner circle of the Vienna psychoanalytic society.

Owing to the oral cancer that already plagued Freud and Erikson's shyness, the two seldom conversed. Nevertheless, he became a devoted follower of Freud who reveled in the excitement of a secretive psychoanalytic movement that was forced underground by the disdain of the medical establishment. In the six

Erik Erikson

years that Erikson remained in Vienna, he delivered his first paper before the Vienna Psychoanalytic Society, pursued an education in the Montessori method of schooling, and met his bride to be, a Canadian-born, American student, Joan Serson.

A number of factors made Erikson view his time among the Vienna analysts as somewhat uncomfortable. Roazen (1976) thought that Erikson was "dissatisfied as one of Freud's younger disciples" (p. 4). As a newcomer, Erikson felt called upon to be a "servant for the master" (p. 4). He was even known to drive Freud around in Burlingham's car. Also, his status as a "lay" analyst may have bothered him. His lack of a medical degree probably was a shortcoming, but there were two reasons why he was at least reasonably well-respected, despite this deficiency. First, Freud was upset with the medical establishment for not openly accepting his point of view. Therefore, he could readily overlook Erikson's and others' lack of "proper credentials." Second, it was deemed less essential for child analysts to have medical qualifications. In fact, Freud welcomed lay analysts in the hope of attracting a variety of people with broad backgrounds. Erikson was also attractive because he was one of the few men willing to pursue the fledgling profession of child analysis. Thus, being highly sensitive, Erikson may have had concerns about his status, but they appear to be largely unfounded.

Another source of discomfort was the constitution of the Vienna group, especially the child analysts. Freud had lost his most famous and able male analysts and had surrounded himself with women, mostly recruited by daughter Anna. "Erikson felt stifled by what he described as the maternalistic overprotection of the women analysts" (p. 6). Further, he, like the males who had abandoned Freud, felt the pressure to conform. He wrote about "a growing conservatism and especially a subtle yet pervasive interdiction of certain trends of thought. This concerned primarily any idea which might be reminiscent of the deviations perpetrated by those earliest and most brilliant of Freud's co-workers . . ." (quoted in Roazen, 1976, pp. 6–7).

Perhaps his disaffection with Freudian thought, which he never openly admitted, accounted for his quick response to Hitler's assumption of power in Germany during 1933. Erikson and his new wife first tried to establish citizenship in Denmark. When that effort failed, they migrated to the United States where Erikson became the first child analyst in Boston (Stevens, 1983). There he was immediately accepted as a member of the American Association of Psychoanalysis, despite his lack of medical qualifications. Although lay analysts were rarely admitted, the American Association so revered the International Psychoanalytic Association to which Erikson belonged and was so in awe of anyone who had been close to Freud, they easily sidestepped the matter of credentials.

Erikson did try to do something about his deficient qualifications. He attempted a graduate course in the psychology program at nearby Harvard, but failed (Roazen, 1976). That apparently was his last effort at a formal, advanced education. His alliance with Harvard, however, did not end. Soon he was working on the research program that led to the book that made Murray famous. (You will learn that it was Erikson, then called Homburger, who likened Murray to Napoleon). During this period he had the opportunity to work with children of both the wealthy and the poor (Stevens, 1983).

After a stint at Yale's Institute of Human Relations, during which he made a side trip to a Sioux Indian Reservation, the Eriksons moved to California where, in 1939, Erik took a position at Cal Berkeley. After ten years on the west coast working on a longitudinal child development program, analyzing Hitler's speeches during the war, and studying life aboard submarines, he took a teaching post at the University of California. Unfortunately it was short-lived. When confronted with the demand that he sign an anti-communist loyalty oath, Erikson, who was not communist, refused and resigned. Returning to the east coast, he received an appointment to a psychoanalytic center specializing in child psychiatry. The appearance of *Childhood and Society* in 1950 was destined to bring him fame. By 1960, he was so well-known and respected that he was appointed Professor of Human Development and lecturer in psychiatry at Harvard, an extraordinary development in view of his nonexistent academic credentials. After his retirement, he and his wife returned to the San Francisco area. There he remains active as a spokesperson for the rights of children and the elderly and for an emphasis on people rather than nations.

Erikson's View of the Person

Freudian?

Erikson has been counted among the Freudians (or neo-Freudians). Little wonder: he has declared himself a Freudian more than once (Roazen, 1976). There is no question that he is devoted to Freud. Having read everything Freud wrote, including his correspondence, Erikson could not resist citing Freud at every possible opportunity.

His dedication to Freud seems to stem from his beliefs about "great leaders." During his study of Gandhi, his reflections on the Indian practitioner of non-violent protest revealed his conception of the dilemma that followers of giants must resolve. ". . . who is the true representative of revolutionary advance—he who modestly continues the work of a giant and adapts it to less heroic circumstances, or he who continues to flex his muscles to see whether he may prove to have gigantic measurements himself" (quoted in Roazen, 1976). It seems that Erikson came down on both sides, one explicitly and the other implicitly. Explicitly he was 100 percent devoted to Freud, often excusing the Master's personal weaknesses—his railroad phobia—and his theoretical vulnerabilities—his conception of women. Erikson waved his hand at Freud's bizarre middle-aged abandonment of sexual relations and overlooked his nearly neurotic correspondence with Wilhelm Fliess. He felt obligated to dig for a seemingly appropriate citation of Freud with each mention of his own original ideas. In fact, he was in the habit of giving Freud credit for some of his personal ideas that can be traced to Freud only with considerable stretch of the imagination. Even Erikson's most original and important idea was laid at Freud's door. "Erikson's many citations of Freud's single mention of the concept of inner identity is an instance of a disciple trying to foist off an original idea onto the founder of psychoanalysis" (p. 12). As late as 1967 he would declare, "I am primarily a psychoanalyst . . ." (quoted in Roazen, 1976, p. 3). In terms of his explicit pronouncements, there is little question that Erikson was Freudian.

Accepting credit for one's own ideas is to abandon humility. Taking credit is also accepting blame. Erikson tacitly acknowledged that it is difficult for creative people to achieve "the courage of their own originality" (quoted in Roazen, 1976, p. 12). "When I started to write extensively about twenty-five years ago, I really thought I was merely providing new illustrations for what I had learned from Sigmund and Anna Freud. I realized only gradually that any original observation already implies a change in theory. The scientific climate has changed so much that older and new theories cannot really be compared" (quoted in Evans, 1976, p. 292). Thus, Erikson implicitly acknowledges that his ideas are more his own than Freud's.

As you will see, though he often resorts to Freudian jargon when elaborating his ideas, his concepts are unique, common-language notions, not reducible to Freudian conceptions. He deemphasizes sexual motivation in favor of the quest for identity. The unconscious takes a backseat to the ego, which, in Erikson's hands, becomes molded into a form of the self. The superego becomes more the conventional conscience. At times he seems more like Jung than Freud, as his interest in anthropological issues and ancient cultures appears to exceed his concern for the obsessions of current, Western society. He was more concerned with people's mission in life as it evolves through the life span than their struggles with unresolved traumas of childhood. In short, despite the homage frequently paid Freud, Erikson's point view is highly original.

On Women

Erikson used masculine pronouns in writing about his ideas. He frequently couched his pronouncements in masculine terms: "Evolution has made man . . . ," "mature man," "Whatever chance man has to transcend the limitations of his self . . ." (Erikson, 1968a, p. 291). In writing about the sexuality of male and female children, he proclaimed, "In the boy, the sexual orientation is dominated by phallic-intrusion; in the girl, by inclusive modes of attractiveness and 'motherliness' " (p. 289). In Vienna, he felt "stifled" by the women with whom he worked (Roazen, 1976, p. 6).

Yet, being a sensitive person, he appears to have changed as he matured during the early stages of the women's movement. In almost no other area did he so closely approximate declaring that Freud was "wrong." In an interview he indicated,

> "Obviously [Freud and I] would not agree today with all the generalizations which have been made with regard to the Oedipus complex, least of all the female Oedipus complex" (Evans, 1976, p. 294). "My feeling is that Freud's general judgment of the identity of women was probably the weakest part of his theory. Exactly what is to blame for that I don't know, except that he was a Victorian man, a patriarchal man" (p. 299). "Freud's perception might also have been colored by the sexual mores of his time, which could not admit at first that an upper-class woman could have passionate and active sexual wishes and yet be refined and intelligent" (pp. 299–300). "At any rate, psychoanalytic literature tends to describe woman as an essentially passive and masochistic creature, who not only accepts the roles or identity assigned to her submissively, but needs all the masochism she can muster to appreciate the phallic male" (p. 299).

On the Tasks and Polarities of Life

The "tasks of life" theme is at the heart of Erikson's theory. At each succeeding stage of human development the person has new tasks to master. Thus, to Erikson, life and its challenges are constantly evolving. Contrary to the way Freud thought of it, or even the way Allport conceived of it, maturity to Erikson is not something most people achieve or not. It is instead a never-ending process.

How well people conquer the tasks of a given stage determines toward which of two poles they migrate. One of the two poles represents positive and the other negative development. The poles symbolize the horns of a dilemma. Parents, the society in which the individual is immersed, interactions with peers, and the person's own skills and talents determine how well the dilemma is resolved. Resolution promotes the development of a new **strength**, a virtue arising from dominant movement toward the positive pole. With resolution comes the ability to face the challenges of the next stage.

BOX 7.1   What Are Your Own Sources of Identity?

Before Erikson's unique view of "identity" is considered, exploring your own feelings of identity should help you appreciate the flavor of the concept. First, examine all of the "sources of identity" listed below. Then try to decide which are most important to you. It is a difficult task. Once, Barbara Jordan, famous former Congresswoman, now a professor, was asked to choose between two prominent sources of identity, being African-American and being a woman. This eloquent commentator on the Constitution paused to reflect for a moment. She did make a decision, but, fortunately, I do not recall what it was: it would not be proper to hold her to it.

After examining the sources, rank them in order, giving the most important source a rank of one ("1"), the second most important a two ("2"), and so forth until all sources are ranked. Force yourself to make choices; the result of the ranking will tell you much about yourself. The choices are listed alphabetically.

career (specify present or anticipated career)
child of my parents
ethnic group (specify African-American, white, or whatever applies)
friend to several people
gender (male or female)
hobbyist (specify sports, exercise, or whatever applies)
human being
parent
sibling (brother or sister)

Basic Concepts: Erikson

Erikson believes that people go through eight stages of psychosocial development. **Psychosocial** refers to a union of Freud's physical yearnings (id) and the cultural forces that act on the individual ("Erik Erikson," 1970). These phases include four childhood stages, one adolescent stage, and three adult stages. They are characterized by **epigenesis**—"epi" means "upon" and "genesis" means "emergence": the stages literally emerge "one on top of another in space and time" (quoted in Evans, 1976, p. 294). Each is built on the other like each upper-level math course is built on lower-level courses. His most basic concepts are tied to the eight stages.

Apparently, Erikson was strongly influenced by German philosopher Georg Hegel, who advocated a reality in which thesis and antithesis, the conflict of opposites, yielded synthesis, the resolution of conflict. Maturity and contentment result from synthesis; stagnation and maladjustment follow failure to resolve conflicts. The conflict at each stage is termed a "crisis." In effect, at each stage, the crisis that the individual experiences entails being stretched between the opposing positive and negative poles associated with the stage. Successful resolution of a crisis prepares the person for the next step in the struggle for identity. As you may have already surmised, the popular phrase "identity crisis" originates in Erikson's conception of the eight psychosocial crises.

Erikson makes it clear that resolution of the crisis is never absolute. To approximate resolution the person must experience a **favorable ratio**, the greater the magnitude of the pull to the positive pole relative to the pull to the negative pole the better (Erikson, 1968a). In turn, the more favorable the ratio, the more the individual manifests the strength or virtue available at a given stage.

Lest the reader think that Erikson's repeated references to "crises" makes a pessimist of him, it is important to note that resolution of conflicts is normal and expected, and "crises" are welcomed turning points, not threats of catastrophe (Erikson, 1968a). Each resolution of a crisis brings with it progress toward a full and rich identity.

Infancy

Infants arrive with basic physiological needs that parents must be willing and able to meet. Nearly always, parents satisfy those needs, at least to some degree. The opposite condition, the one that generates the first crisis, is the inevitable delay or neglect of satisfaction and the occurrence of weaning. **Basic trust** results from the infant's sense that it can count on satisfaction of its needs (Erikson, 1968a); the world takes on the aura of a "trustworthy realm." Its opposite is **basic mistrust**, the feeling of abandonment and helpless rage that accompanies uncertainty of satisfaction. Trust is injected into the infant in different ways by different mothers. Each mother is unique and, thus, conveys trust in a unique way. "Moreover, mothers in different cultures and classes and races must teach this trusting in different ways, so it will fit their cultural version of the universe" (quoted in Evans, 1976, p. 293).

Erikson makes a point of the observation that both trust and mistrust are learned. We all must learn trust if we are to be fully functional humans, "but to learn to mistrust is just as important" (quoted in Evans, 1976, p. 293). Mistrust is part of life also, and we must become familiar with it. We can hope, however, that trust will outweigh mistrust in the ratio of the two orientations.

Basic trust lays the foundation for the first of the strengths or virtues, **hope**, the enduring belief in the attainability of basic satisfactions. "You see, hope is a very basic human strength without which we couldn't stay alive" (quoted in Evans, 1976, p. 293). It is the foundation of faith, often manifested in adult religious practices (E. Hall, 1983). In fact, faith is protected by religion, its **institutional safeguard**, a cultural unit that protects and promotes products of crisis resolution. Failure to develop basic trust yields mistrust and hopelessness, conditions that can lead in adulthood to severe addiction or psychotic states.

Early Childhood

During this second stage, the child develops motor skills that open up the first possibilities of independence (Erikson, 1968a). Part of the trauma the child experiences at this time is in the transition from the first to this more mature second stage. Just when the child has learned to trust his mother and the world, it must become self-willed. It must change from being the one-sided trusting soul to being also worthy of others' trust. Only by calling on others to trust it, rather than just trusting in others, can it exercise its will.

Children can now move to desired objects and thereby possess them without the aid of parents. The dawning of grasping ability allows children to experience the power of imprisoning an object within fingers, hands, and arms. Power also comes from letting go, but so does conflict. To hold can be destructive, as in restraining, or it can be positive, as in cuddling. Letting go can have two additional meanings: giving up something desirable, or casually "letting it be." Aside from the Freudian anal implications of retaining and letting go, Erikson hints at the "dilemma of freedom" attributed to Fromm, to let go of something is to be free of it, but it is also to be without it.

With the newly acquired muscular skills, the child experiences doing for himself. Unfortunately, he also knows the frustration generated by needing the help of others who can do more for him than he can do for himself. For Erikson as well as Allport, self-esteem derives from doing for oneself.

Consistent with this orientation, the two poles of the crisis involve the themes of independence and the self-esteem that comes with it versus the self-estrangement that accompanies dependency. **Autonomy** is independence stemming from the reasonable self-control that allows children to hold rather than restrain, to let be rather than lose. **Shame and doubt** is the estrangement that results from the feeling of being controlled and of losing self-control. It is the precursor of *neurosis*, a desperate struggle for control of one's environment, and *paranoia*, a manifestation of feeling controlled by others.

The strength that emerges from resolution during early childhood is **will power**, "the unbroken determination to exercise free choice as well as self-restraint in spite of the unavoidable experience of shame, doubt, and a certain rage over being controlled by others" (Erikson, 1968a, p. 288). The exercise of free choice has its institutional safeguard—the principles of law and order and of justice. However, Erikson argues that "law and order" gone awry can rob people of the very choice it is supposed to protect.

Erikson acknowledges that infants go through a Freudian "anal stage," but "we have to consider that the anal musculature is part of musculature in general" (quoted in Evans, 1976, p. 293). The task of the infant is to learn management of all his musculature, including his sphincters. In contrast to Freud, culture is more emphasized than universal physiology in accomplishing the task of sphincter control. Erikson asserts, "It would, of course, only be in cultures in which cleanliness and punctuality are overemphasized for technological and sanitary reasons that the problem of anal control might develop into a major issue in childhood" (quoted in Evans, 1976, p. 293).

Play Age

In the third or fourth year, children become aware of the differences between the sexes. During this third stage, sex-role playing and sexual feelings occur for the boy. But to Erikson the girl plays the feminine role, trying to look attractive and to be nurturing, rather than being sexual. Conscience appears at this stage and forever places a restraint on actions, thoughts, and fantasies. One of the poles at this stage is **initiative**, acting on one's desires, urges, and potentials. The other is **guilt**, the harness that restrains pursuit of desires, urges, and potentials; the exercise of an overzealous conscience. The boy learns that competition for a favored position with his mother leads to the inevitable fear of damage to his genitals. The result is guilt at having taken the initiative well beyond that which is permissible (Evans, 1967). Erikson turns further from Freud when he suggests that it is only natural for the boy to fall in love with his mother, because she is everything to him. She is the center of his life and his caretaker. Any fantasies a person may have will tend to focus on what is crucial to her or his survival and prosperity. Therefore, any fantasies the boy has will likely center on his mother, including fantasies arising from his emerging genital urges. Presumably, the girl has analogous problems associated with pursuit of her father's attentions. For both genders, guilt can arise from a failure to demonstrate competence when the initiative is taken (Evans, 1967).

At first, children's play does not involve real purpose, but wish fulfillment and fantasy. Gradually, this begins to change. "The child begins to envisage goals for which his locomotion and cognition have prepared him. The child also begins to think of being big and to identify with people whose work or whose personality he can understand and appreciate" (quoted in Evans, 1967, p. 25). That is, children begin to display realistic, practical **purpose**, "the courage to envisage and pursue valued and tangible goals guided by conscience but not paralyzed by guilt and by fear of punishment" (Erikson, 1968a, p. 289). It is the strength that comes from resolution of the play-age crisis. Failure at resolution leads to general repression or inhibition and to adult pathology such as sexual impotence, overcompensation, exhibitionism, and psychopathic acting out. All of these are attempts to regain the lost initiative.

School Age

According to Erikson, at each stage, the child becomes a somewhat different person. At the school age, the fourth stage, children evolve into intellectually curious people. They want to know, to learn. During this time, children begin to lay the groundwork for becoming parents. They play at the parental role to prepare themselves for the real thing. For the first time, they relate to the larger society and one of its core elements, work. They learn to apply themselves to tasks that have practical outcomes, like salary for work. These tasks may be schoolwork for grades or housework for a monetary allowance.

In a show of homage to Freud, Erikson sometimes referred to the school age as the latency period (Evans, 1976). In so doing he acknowledges that sexual interest and activity is repressed during this phase. He is quick to add, however, that Freud missed all the cognitive development that blossoms during the school age "because he was only concerned with what happens to sexual energy during that time" (quoted in Evans, 1976, p. 295). This apology, issued on Freud's behalf, is a charitable way of saying that an overly narrow focus on sexuality caused his former mentor to miss the most important developments.

One of the poles of school age is **industry**, children's absorption in the "tool world" of their culture—the workaday world—thereby preparing them "for a hierarchy of learning experiences which [they] will undergo with the help of cooperative peers and instructive adults" (Erikson, 1968a, p. 289). Of course, school is the first productive situation that provides an inkling of the "tool culture." The other pole of the crisis, **inferiority**, occurs if children perceive their skills or status among peers to be inadequate. This perception arises because of failures at establishing competence in some specialized way, such as playing a sport or spelling well. Race or ethnic background may become barriers that prevent children from experiencing success and the accompanying actualization of the will to learn. Inferiority can yield regression to the hopelessness of the Oedipal rivalry that characterized the previous stage. The triumph of inferiority may lead to an obsession with work so that it becomes the sole source of identity. "If the overly conforming child accepts work as the only criterion of worthwhileness, sacrificing too readily his imagination and playfulness, he may [as an adult] submit to 'craft-idiocy' . . . [becoming] a slave of his technology . . ." (Erikson, 1968a, p. 289).

Resolution of the crisis at the school age gives children critical experiences, including working beside and with others and "division of labor." From this resolution emerges the strength of **competence**, "the free exercise (unimpaired by an infantile sense of inferiority) of dexterity and intelligence in the completion of serious tasks" (Erikson, 1968a, pp. 289–290). With competence, children are ready to become cooperative participants in some segment of the culture.

Adolescence

As Allport indicated and most theorists agree, the adolescent search for self represents the fulcrum upon which the lifelong struggle for identity is balanced. For Erikson, adolescence, the fifth stage, allows a synthesis of previous stages, but it is more than the mere sum of what developed earlier. It is also an extension into the future.

One pole of the adolescent crisis is **identity**, accumulated confidence that the sameness and continuity one has previously cultivated are now appreciated by others, allowing, in turn, the promise of careers and lifestyles to come. "Continuity" is an important term in the conception of identity. "Identity means an integration of all previous identifications and self-images, including the negative ones" (quoted in Evans, 1976, p. 297). The opposite of identity is **identity confusion**, the failure of previous identity developments to coalesce in such a way that it is clear what roles one is expected to play in the future. The victory of confusion predicts acute maladjustments due to a feeling of meaninglessness. These symptoms can lapse into psychotic episodes.

Adolescent identity is not merely obtaining genital maturity in the Freudian sense: an ability to be concerned about others, because one's own problems relating to previous periods have been largely solved (Evans, 1976). Identity problems for teens are in part related to their personal histories and in part arise from identity pitfalls peculiar to their historical era. For example, today's teenage boys may be torn between the macho orientation that so heavily influenced their fathers' identity and the more gender neutral identity that seems appropriate today.

In their struggle to answer the question "Who am I?" adolescents often form cliques. These clans bolster self-images and provide a mutual defense against "enemies" whose different characteristics challenge the "truth" of their own developing identities (E. Hall, 1983). If teens turn this condemnation of the "different" against society, delinquency can result. Antisocial behavior may also occur in "a person whose potentialities as a person have no place in the historical trends of his time . . ." (quoted in Evans, 1976, p. 297). However, adolescent rebellion is not seen by Erikson as a necessarily negative force, at least when the larger culture is considered (Erikson, 1968a). Societies must be flexible, and Erikson sees adolescent challenges as a source of cultural rejuvenation. Youth, in their quest for identity, question the norms of their society, vigorously supporting those that meet the challenge and contributing to the demise of rules that cannot bear close scrutiny. Times of unrest among the young attest to the sickness of a society failing to meet the promise of youth—that the best will rule and the rulers will bring out the best in people. During periods of upheaval, the mind of youth and that of society become one in the pursuit of ideological unification and return to coherent purpose.

The strength that comes from the adolescent period is **fidelity**, "the opportunity to fulfill personal potentialities . . . in a context which permits the young person to be true to himself and true to significant others . . . [and to] sustain loyalties . . . in spite of inevitable contradictions of value systems" (Erikson, 1968a, p. 290). For Erikson, fidelity is the cornerstone of identity. It is, however, not devotion to a particular ideology, but loyalty to ideologies that are appropriate to the individual. As Erikson put it, "I would go further and claim that we have almost an instinct for fidelity—meaning that when you reach a certain age you can and must learn to be faithful to some ideological view. Speaking psychiatrically, without the development of a capacity for fidelity the individual will either have what we call a weak ego, or look for a deviant group to be faithful to" (quoted in Evans, 1976, p. 296).

The need to adopt ideologies, particularly a focal ideology, can be a trap that ensnares the impulsive teen. Erikson believes that "adolescents are easily seduced by totalitarian regimes and all kinds of totalistic fads" (quoted in Evans, 1976, p. 297). Like Allport, he is especially concerned because youth are prone to succumb to the siren song of "nationalism." The allure of nationalism is in its ideological simplicity and resultant promise to answer all questions and solve all problems. Youth must somehow avoid impulsivity in responding to the almost instinctual demand of fidelity that one quickly adopt the most obvious ideology available. Only with restraint will the magnetic force of simplistic ideologies like nationalism be resisted until broader ideologies are considered.

Another danger posed by ideology is that it may become the basis of identity. An ideological framework, such as tribal norms, may be forced on youth in such a way as to become the foundation of identity. In so-called "primitive" societies, youth go through puberty rites that concretely and immediately define for them their place in their society. In such cases, the option to exercise choice in adopting identity is precluded. Of course, whether an identity so obtained is benevolent or malevolent depends on the nature of the society.

It is important to note that the imposition of "tribal norms" is not peculiar to "primitive" societies but can occur in "advanced" technological societies as well. When we thoughtlessly become what our parents are and what our grandparents were, an identity has been imposed upon us and we have passively accepted it.

Young Adulthood

During previous stages, strengths allowed the genders to merge in cooperation and fruitful communication. When "falling in love," teenagers attach themselves to another person in an attempt to arrive at self-definition. Teens "in love" see themselves reflected in an "idealized other," but do not actively attempt to differentiate themselves from the other. Now, during the sixth stage, the biological differences come to the fore, so that the genders, similar in consciousness and language, become different in the mature quest for love and procreation. The two poles of this sixth stage are tied to the themes of attachment to and alienation from others. **Intimacy** "is really the ability to fuse your identity with somebody else's without fear that you're going to lose something yourself" (quoted in Evans, 1967, p. 48). It is more than the mere physical intimacy that occurs in sexual exchanges (E. Hall, 1983). "Of course, I mean something more—I mean intimate relationships, such as friendship, love, sexual intimacy, even intimacy with oneself, one's inner resources, the range of one's excitements and commitments" (quoted in Evans, 1976, p. 300). With this broader definition of intimacy in mind, Erikson anticipates modern theories of marital success (Allen, 1990). He asserts that intimacy is what makes marriage possible; without it marriage is meaningless.

The other pole in the crisis for this stage is **isolation**, the failure to secure close and cooperative relationships with the same and especially the opposite gender such that partners' identities are important to, but distinct from, one's own. The triumph of isolation dooms the individual to infantile fixations and lasting immaturities that interfere with love and work. On the other hand, intimacy brings the strength of this period. **Love** "is the guardian of that elusive and yet all-pervasive power of cultural and personal style which binds . . . the affiliations of competition and cooperation, procreation and production" into a "way of life" (quoted in Evans, 1976, p. 291). Love is also the shared devotion that overcomes antagonisms caused by differences in functions assigned to partners in a relationship. "Love, then, is a mutuality of devotion greater than the antagonisms inherent in divided function" (p. 291).

Adulthood

"At this stage one begins to take one's place in society, and to help in the development and perfection of whatever [society] produces" (quoted in Evans, 1976, pp. 301–302). Humans are not only "learning animals" they are teachers as well. It is at the maturity of adulthood that the need to be needed and the accumulation of wisdom lead to assumption of the "teacher" role. Thus, during the seventh stage, people strive for **generativity** "the concern with establishing and guiding the next generation" (Erikson, 1968a, p. 291). Erikson admits that generativity is "not an elegant word" (Evans, 1976, p. 301). He indicates that he might have used "creativity" instead of generativity, but the substitution would put "too much emphasis on the particular creativity which we ascribe to particular people" (Evans, 1976, p. 301). Generativity has a broader meaning that is applicable to people in general: "everything that is generated from generation to generation: children, products, ideas, *and* works of art" (p. 301).

The failure of generativity leads to **stagnation**, the arrest of the ripening process that comes with inability to funnel previous development into the formation of the next generation. Boredom is the constant companion of stagnation, as is false intimacy and adult self-indulgence. Inevitably, the failure of generativity shows up in the next generation as the aggravation of estrangements in childhood, adolescence, and early adulthood.

Care, the strength of maturity, is "the broadening concern for what has been generated by love, necessity, or accident—a concern which must consistently overcome the ambivalence adhering to irreversible obligation and the narrowness of self-concern" (Erikson, 1968a, p. 291). Care is a major force behind utilization of "proven methods with which each generation meets the needs of the next" (Erikson, 1968a, p. 291).

Erikson was at first concerned about the selection of "care" because of its multitude of connotations, including "anxious solicitude" (Evans, 1976). However, he has been able to conclude that the word has evolved and now means " 'to care to do' something, to 'care for' somebody or something, to 'take care of' that which needs protection and attention, and 'to take care not to' do something destructive" (quoted in Evans, 1976, p. 301).

Old Age

Power in old age is wit in full bloom—a storehouse of knowledge, an inclusive understanding, and a maturity of judgment. These intellectual contributions provide a bridge to the next generation by reminding all that the knowledge of a given generation is not "truth," but a cog in the infinitely large and everturning wheel of human experience. Crisis at this time involves contributing to the continuity of the human condition versus distraction from that noble purpose by an obsession with death. The poles for this eighth stage revolve around wholeness and completeness versus disintegration and defeat. **Integrity** is "an emotional integration faithful to the image bearers of the past and ready to take (and eventually renounce) leadership in the present" (Erikson, 1968a, p. 291) Lack of resolution leads to **despair**, a feeling that time is too short for the achievement of integrity and the accompanying contribution to the connection between generations. Despair can result in bitterness at not being able to extend oneself into the future, a losing battle with death, rather than a calm acceptance of it. Despair yields psychological death before the physical counterpart. The symptoms of despair often include depression, hypochondria, and paranoia.

The strength that comes from resolution of the eighth crisis is **wisdom**, a "detached and yet active concern with life in the face of death," not magical access to "higher knowledge" (Erikson, 1968a, p. 292; E. Hall, 1983). With wisdom, death is accepted, and one's role in the human drama is assured.

Erikson is not entirely satisfied with "wisdom" "because to some people it seems to mean a too strenuous achievement for each and every old person" (quoted in Evans, p. 301). In fact, during old age people may show a renewal of infantile traits, even including senile childishness. Wisdom in any sense of the word is not a necessity during old age. "The main point is again a developmental one: only in old age can true wisdom develop in those who are thus gifted. And in old age, some wisdom must mature, if only in a sense that the old person comes to appreciate and to represent something of the wisdom of the ages, or plain old wit" (p. 301).

Table 7.1 summarizes Erikson's eight stages and the crisis of identity associated with each.

TABLE 7.1   Erikson's Eight Stages

Stage	Crisis	Resolution	Poor Resolution	Strength
Infancy	Basic trust vs. mistrust	Confidence in satisfaction of needs	Rage due to uncertainty of satisfaction	Hope
Early childhood	Autonomy vs. shame and doubt	Independence stemming from self-control	Estrangement due to being controlled	Will power
Play age	Initiative vs. guilt	Acting on desires, urges, potentials	Conscience restrains pursuits	Purpose
School age	Industry vs. inferiority	Absorbed in "tool world"	Skills and status inadequate	Competence
Adolescence	Identity vs. identity confusion	Confident one's sameness seen by others	Previous identity developments fail	Fidelity
Young adulthood	Intimacy vs. isolation	Fusing identity with another	No close relationships	Love
Adulthood	Generativity vs. stagnation	Guiding the next generation	Arrest of the ripening process	Care
Old age	Integrity vs. despair	Emotional integration	"Time is short"	Wisdom

---

BOX 7.2   Assessing Crisis Resolution

"Epigenesis" characterizes Erikson's stages: one builds on the other. Resolving crises at one stage can affect how well one does at subsequent stages. However, unlike Freud, Erikson felt that failure of resolution of a crisis at a given stage means neither failure at subsequent stages nor permanent failure at the stage in question (Ochse & Plug, 1986). Erikson was optimistic, believing that later crisis resolution might retroactively resolve earlier crises.

In view of Erikson's position, it should be interesting and encouraging for you to examine how well you did in resolving earlier crises. Look at Table 7.1 closely, starting at the top. Assess how well you have done at each succeeding stage by whether or not you show the presence of the characteristics under "Resolution," the absence of the traits under "Poor Resolution," and at least some evidence for the strength that is associated with the stage. Remember not to despair should you fail to show resolution at some early stage. At some later point you may experience resolution that retroactively resolves earlier crises.

Theoretical and Empirical Support for Erikson's Point of View

Daniel Levinson (1978) and Gail Sheehy (1977) developed theories about adult crises. Although their postulations are more elaborate than Erikson's, they were probably heavily influenced by the Danish psychologist's point of view. Erikson's theory predates their points of view and he pioneered the idea of the "crisis of identity." He also was their predecessor in writing about adulthood crises. In view of these circumstances, the widespread attention and acceptance of their theories can be considered support for Erikson's orientation regarding adult life.

Levinson: The Mid-life Crisis

Daniel Levinson was in his mid-forties when he conceived of a research project on mid-life (Levinson, 1978). He was in his late forties when the project began with a sample of adult men. Like Erikson, Levinson had been inspired by his own life experiences. His struggle for meaning at the mid-point of life resulted in a landmark study.

The *mid-life transition* is a bridge between young adulthood and middle age, a time at which individuals look back at their previous successes and failures and make assessments concerning their future prospects (Levinson, 1978). Part and parcel of this soul-searching is reappraising the past. Because of a heightened awareness of mortality at about forty, people begin to reevaluate the past in order to use the future more wisely. They raise questions about their contributions to spouses, children, and careers and the contributions of family and career to themselves. The consequence of this reassessment is almost always *de-illusionment*, a reduction of illusions, a recognition that assumptions and beliefs about self and the world are not true. Illusions have worked well in earlier life as fuel to drive ambitions and ideals. At mid-life it is time to cast them aside in favor of objective assessment.

With reappraisal comes restructuring, a change in the organization of one's life. It may take the form of major upheaval, the *mid-life crisis*, during which family and career may be replaced and an entirely new lifestyle adopted, or appear as a simple reordering of priorities. In any case, the process of *individuation* begins, a procedure by which a person's relationship between self and the external world is changed so that there is a clearer separation between self and the world. It is a reintroduction of the method for achieving maturity that operated during childhood. As an infant, as a child, and as an adolescent, people progressively see themselves as distinct from their parents, their homelife, and their peers. At mid-life, the distinction becomes sharper and includes differentiation from family, career, friends, and the expectations that restrict the behavior and thought of all adults. Levinson acknowledges that when individuation comes into play, the mind turns to Erikson's generativity (vs. stagnation).

Some people sail through the mid-life transition with little questioning and searching. Their lives may be sufficiently stable and satisfying that they need not experience severe crisis. Others come to terms with the loss of some dreams and are able to contemplate the future without much pain. However, Levinson contends that most people's struggles with the self and the external world reach crisis proportions (80 percent in his sample). They display anguish, show guilt and upset, and explore, even try, new lifestyles. Their impulsivity approaches that of adolescents. They may astound friends and family with changes in personality affected by variations in clothing, hair style, and use of language.

To realize that one has reached middle age is to realize that life is partly over, and, in turn, that death must be considered. According to Levinson, we all cling to the illusion of our own immortality. When certain declines in function occur at age 40 or so, such as a relative lack of vigor and intellectual quickness, people can no longer avoid thinking about the unthinkable. The possibility of death runs head on into the cherished assumption of immortality. The contradiction thus generated is not eliminated by giving up the illusion of immortality. Rather, in those who successfully pass through the transition of mid-life, immortality is seen in a new light. If one leaves behind a *legacy*, material goods, wisdom for others to use, and examples for others to follow, one lives on despite the demise of the body.

Sheehy: Women Are Different

Gail Sheehy (1977) was heavily influenced by exposure to an advanced copy of Levinson's manuscript on his study. She became even more concerned about the "mid-life" crisis, its variations and the paths out of it, than Levinson. However, her point of view is much less structured than his.

Unlike Levinson, Sheehy does not neglect women's crises. For Sheehy, age 35 begins a dangerous period for women. Thirty-five is usually the age at which the last child is sent off to school, ending the period of intense child-care. Now she has time to think and her thoughts may turn to her attractiveness. She may reason that she will lose her looks soon so she had better use them while she can. Alternatively, she may seek reassurances that she is still attractive. In either case, an affair may result.

The end of the intense child-care period is also a time when women enter the work force. Economic necessity as well as filling the child-care void is a reason for working outside the home. Whatever the reason, when she enters the work force, she is likely to stay. This highly significant event can be good or bad or a mixture of both. She may be well-educated and thereby equipped to enter the professional ranks. If so, she will be frustrated to find that competitors for advancement, often men, are way ahead of her by virtue of their greater experience. Yet eventually, she may obtain acceptance and the status that comes with it. If she is poorly educated, she will soon come to realize that advancement is unlikely for her. Frustration caused by being behind or despair due to being stuck at a low-level job may cause a crisis.

Age 35 may also signal the onset of other events that could precipitate a crisis. If she is divorced, she may take a new husband at about this time. If she is distraught for any of the reasons mentioned so far, she is at an age where running away is most probable. In addition, at this time she is likely to begin thinking about physical changes that hit at the heart of her identity: physiologically she will be able to bear children for only a few more years. To lead a productive mid-life and old age, she must come to grips with the changes in her social roles, such as those involved in work and child-care. She must also learn to accept the physical changes that will be more abrupt and visible than those associated with men's mid-life.

Empirical Support: Research Confirming Erikson's View

There have been few attempts to look at Erikson's stages as a whole, but one of the most recent is quite impressive. Ochse and Plug (1986) looked at the status of trust, autonomy, initiative, industry, intimacy, and generativity among white and black South Africans aged 15 to 50 (integrity was omitted due to the lack of elderly subjects). These researchers generally accepted Erikson's "epigenesis" and, therefore, expected that "one stage would build on another."

The seven positive poles of the first seven stages were represented by questionnaire items, along with measures of well-being and social desirability. As expected, subjects responses to the questionnaire indicated that the more the positive poles were manifested in their responses, the higher their senses of well-being. However, there was also a relatively strong correlation between manifestations of the positive poles and scores on social desirability, a measure of "faking good." If subjects responded as if they possessed the characteristics implied by the positive poles merely in order to show socially desirable traits, support for Erikson's theory would be invalidated. In reaction to this possibility, the researchers pointed out that subjects may not have been "faking good." Instead "perhaps they really believe good of themselves and their social image" (p. 1248).

Also as would be expected in view of the largely adult age of subjects, a factor analysis of results revealed factors corresponding only to adult poles: intimacy vs. isolation and generativity vs. stagnation. The lack of distinct factors relating to childhood, however, distracts from Erikson's theory. If the concepts relating to the childhood poles were distinct they would have been reflected in distinct factors. The researchers suggest that the lack of childhood factors "may reflect the overlap in Erikson's constructs, which has been noted by other researchers" (Ochse & Plug, 1986, p. 1245).

It was also expected that intercorrelations among the crisis poles for crises that had already been passed—those of childhood—would be relatively strong. Such was the case for white women and to some degree for white men, but not for blacks. In fact, the intercorrelations among the poles tended to be high regardless of whether subjects had yet passed crises. This result was taken to mean that "Erikson's personality components to some extent develop in parallel and are interdependent even before the relevant crises are resolved" (p. 1246). In some degree this outcome contradicts the "epigenesis" notion that earlier crises are resolved before later ones. Nevertheless, the researchers were quick to point out that Erikson "does suggest that all the components develop to some degree throughout life, even before their critical stages" (p. 1246).

According to the authors, Erikson contends that the "ego continues throughout life to reintegrate existing and newly forming components of the personality" (p. 1246). Thus, the mean correlations between poles should increase with age. In fact, the results reflected the expected increase.

It was expected that "intimacy" would be generally higher for women than for men. This prediction was confirmed, but only for whites. For blacks it was reversed: intimacy was higher for men than for women. This outcome was one of several cases in which results of blacks were different from those of whites, and, in some cases, less consistent with Erikson's point of view.

One would also expect that identity would become more highly related to intimacy in the early twenties than in the teens. Further, identity would become most highly related to generativity in middle age, when generativity becomes salient. This prediction was born out for white women. For white and black men, only the prediction regarding generativity was supported.

Other results showed that poles associated with already passed childhood stages showed declines with increases in age, but those associated with adult poles increased with age. Also men showed stronger autonomy, initiative, and industry, as sex-role adoption would predict. Finally, and very important, factor analysis revealed a strong and overriding factor. The researchers felt that it might be labeled "identity" in the global sense. This interpretation suggests that the various crises at the several stages are indeed "identity crises."

In a recent study, Kowaz and Marcia (1991) showed impressive support for Erikson's "industry" concept. First they developed a measure of industry that focused on three components: (1) cognitive (skills and knowledge); (2) behavioral (applications of skills and knowledge); and (3) affective (attitudes and experiences relating to the acquisition and application of skills and knowledge). Example items were the following: for component 1 (cognitive), "Some kids at my grade level really know the basics of spelling, arithmetic, reading, and science. BUT other kids don't really know the basics."; for component 2 (behavioral), "Some kids finish doing everything they start to do. BUT other kids don't get things finished."; for component 3 (affective), "Some kids feel there is at least one kind of thing they do really well. BUT other kids are average in everything they do." (p. 392). These components were developed into rating questionnaires for elementary school children, their parents, and their teachers.

Results showed that the children's self-ratings of industry were highly correlated with teachers' industry ratings of children and parents' ratings of children. That is, all three groups agreed on industry ratings of the children. Further, there was a general tendency toward high interrelations among the components of measures of industry. These results mean that industry can be measured highly reliably and shows high coherence.

Evidence for the validity of the concept "industry" was also strong. Component 1 industry scores were positively correlated with achievement scores, whether measured by children's subjective judgments of school achievement or grades. An overall score on industry was also related to achievement test scores. For teachers' judgments, being on- versus off-task was positively related to industry scores. "Level of reasoning" was also positively related to the overall measure of industry. In addition, average industry scores were positively related to a preference for reality work over fantasy.

The researchers developed a measure of concern for the process involved in a task, as opposed to interest only in the task outcome. This measure was positively related to the overall measure of industry: the more the industry, the more the interest in the process versus the outcome. Finally, overall contentment was positively related to industry.

The results showed that the concept "industry" strongly applies to the age group that should orient to this pole, according to Erikson. Children, teachers, and parents agreed on judgments of industry. Further, indexes of industry predicted scores on measures that should logically be related to industry, such as achievement, being on-task, and orienting to reality.

A couple of additional studies illustrate research in generativity, although neither is devoted exclusively to Erikson's theory. McAdams, Ruetzel, and Foley (1986) looked at a measure of generativity in relation to indexes of power and intimacy motivation as measured with use of the Thematic Apperception Test (TAT) developed by Murray. Subjects were adults between the ages of 35 and 49. The index of generativity was taken from an interview in which subjects explored plans for the future. Two independent decoders who were unfamiliar with research hypotheses examined condensed transcripts of the interview. They were looking for evidence indicating concern for guiding the next generation either *directly*—care giving, teaching, leading, mentoring—or *indirectly*—contributing in a literary, scientific, artistic, or altruistic sense. The transcripts were scored according to methods developed by other researchers.

Results showed that TAT scores indexing power and intimacy motivation were positively associated with the measure of generativity: the greater the generativity, the greater those motives. The researchers interpreted this result to mean "that generativity calls on an adult's fundamental needs to feel close and to feel strong vis-a-vis others" (p. 806).

Franz, McClelland, and Weinberger (1991) followed up research beginning in the early 1950s. Participants, now aged about 41, were 94 men and women who completed a questionnaire and submitted to an interview. The measure of generativity was taken from written details of "hopes and dreams for the future" submitted by subjects (p. 589). These plans were scored by two students using a method developed by McAdams. Results showed that *psychosocial* maturity—indexed by having close friends at mid-life, a long, happy marriage, and children—was positively related to generativity: the higher the generativity score the higher the psychosocial maturity score.

Evaluation

Contributions

Erikson's is a remarkable story. With only a high school education, he made it to the lofty status of Harvard professor. More important, despite the lack of "proper" academic credentials, he has written a theory that has heavily influenced not only academics, but also the public. Erikson was a hero during the 1960s because of his views regarding youth and rebellion. His assertion that people continue to grow and change in specifiable ways not only opened new vistas to millions of older people, it also revolutionized the study of personality. Prior to Erikson it was becoming a dogma that personality is set in stone by the end of the teens. Erikson's unique and creative thoughts opened the eyes of other theorists, such as Levinson and Sheehy, to the possibility of personality growth after youth has ripened into middle age. Never again will psychologists neglect older people or believe everything currently happening in their lives was predetermined by events in their youth.

Like a few other theorists covered in this book, such as Adler, Horney, Fromm, Rogers, and Allport, Erikson is important because of the person he is. Making it as an academic without academic credentials is somewhat akin to making it as a politician without the backing of the political power brokers. Similar to Adler and Murray, Erikson turned psychological deficiencies into ideas that not only helped him but are valuable to countless others as well. If we adopt his respect for the goals and aspirations of people of all ages, we will take an enormous stride in the direction of respecting all people everywhere.

While researchers have found little of interest in the concepts of certain theorists with the "right credentials," they have paid considerable attention to some of Erikson's notions. There is now up-to-date evidence that people pass through something at least akin to Erikson's epigenetic stages. Further, at least some of the ideas that he apparently took right off the top of his head have been supported by research. In particular, the concepts of "industry" and "generativity" have received appreciable support. Noting that these concepts cut across the life span, one can bet that other ideas by Erikson will eventually receive empirical support.

The overriding message in Erikson's writings is that identity is a dynamic process, not a static entity. "Who a person is" changes and evolves over time. Although stages are built on top of stages, what a person will become is not necessarily "better" than what that person currently is. Neither is it the case that we abandon what we currently are when we seek to be something else. Rather mastery of current pursuits signals the development of new capabilities that can be used to foster further accomplishments. According to Erikson, we are able to continually expand and broaden our horizons with much benefit to ourselves and to others.

Limitations

While it is admirable that someone could gain the respect of academics without obtaining the academic union card, a doctorate, Erikson's lack of advanced training showed up in his thinking. There is a certain lack of logical consistency in his ideas. For example, it is not entirely clear why he chose the labels "autonomy vs. shame and doubt" to characterize developments at early childhood. Likewise, why was "initiative vs. guilt" chosen for the play age? While "autonomy" makes some logical sense, why is "shame and doubt" the other side of the coin of the early childhood crisis? "Guilt" or "inferiority" or another label might fit just as well. The opposite of "autonomy" is "dependence" and the counterpart of "initiative" could be "dependence" as well, or it could be "passivity." "Competence" seems to fit as well at early childhood as "will power" which may be regarded as a cliche phrase that has been adopted by everyone from frustrated dieters to Adolf Hitler. Erikson was openly dissatisfied with "wisdom." Aside from the multiple meanings attached to the word, which he does mention, he might have added the fact that the word is so overused it has become trite.

"Fidelity" seems to be a particularly murky concept. The way Erikson defines it and the way he talks about it do not match well. If it is related to adoption of ideologies as Erikson indicates, one could wonder whether adolescence is the appropriate place for it. Perhaps the seeds of ideological flowering are planted during the teens, but the blossoming may well occur during young adulthood or even later.

Research on Erikson's point of view, while generally supportive, turned up some weaknesses. Ochse and Plug (1986) found some evidence that Erikson's poles of crises develop in parallel, as opposed to building one on another. These researchers try to save epigenesis by pointing out that Erikson had suggested that all poles develop to some degree throughout life. But can he have it both ways? From a scientific point of view, the answer is "no." It must be shown that various poles are obvious in their manifestations at the time when they are supposed to appear, but exist only in "trace amounts" at other stages.

These same researchers found that Erikson's theory worked much better for white than for black South Africans. This outcome raises the possibility that the theory is limited to people of European descent (white South Africans are mostly of Dutch and English stock). Further, there were gender differences that seem not to be predicted by Erikson's theory. Because men show stronger autonomy, initiative, and industry, the theory may be more applicable to them than to women.

The lack of factors relating to childhood poles reported by these same researchers indicates that those poles may not be distinct, one from the other. As the researchers put it, the concepts relating to these poles may overlap. Had they been non-overlapping, they would have been reflected in distinct factors. Ochse and Plug note that other researchers have also alluded to the overlap of Erikson's concepts. These interpretations certainly are consistent with my earlier suggestion that some of Erikson's concepts could fit stages other than the ones to which they were assigned.

While Erikson has inspired several researchers as well as many ordinary citizens, he has apparently failed to recruit notable followers to take up his cause. There are few if any Eriksonians around, at least among well-known psychologists. Perhaps it is because his theory has relatively little practical import compared to others. It has no therapy associated with it, and unlike other theories, such as that of Bandura, Erikson's theory has been little used to solve real world problems.

Conclusions

While Erikson's lack of academic training may be a fault that places limits on his theory, it may also be regarded as a virtue. One wonders whether he would have seen that personality development does not end at age 20 if he had been trained in the typical psychology department. As it is, his vision is more acute than most. He anticipated the "mid-life" crisis and reminded us all that elderly people can be productive. Not only does he provide us with the possibility of productivity during old age, he points out creative tasks appropriate to the golden years.

Erikson's example reminds us that creative thoughts applicable to the lives of people are not the sole province of the highly educated. Not being encumbered by academic dogmas and methodologies, he was able to focus on what others had neglected. He brought an end to the overemphasis on youth just at the right time. As we enter the era of the "graying of the population," the thoughts of Erik Erikson will become more and more relevant.

Summary Points

1. Erikson was born the son of Danish parents, but he was reared by a Jewish physician whose surname he adopted for awhile. As a young man he forsook college in favor of a career in art. A potential job as a children's portrait painter proved to be his passport into Vienna's secretive psychoanalytic society. There he developed an undying loyalty to Freud. Upon arriving in the United States, he made an abortive attempt to do graduate work and was employed by Murray for a time. After jobs at Yale and the University of California, he became a professor at Harvard.

2. Erikson was a Freudian in the sense that he felt he owed allegiance to Freud and he couched explanations of his own concepts in Freudian jargon. Most of his important concepts, however, are distinct from and independent of Freud's ideas. While he showed a rather stereotyped conception of women early in his career, later he began to reject Freud's unflattering view of women. He believed that life and its challenges were constantly evolving. At each successive phase of life, people find themselves on the horns of a new dilemma and confronted with new tasks.

3. Erikson believed that we pass through a series of eight psychosocial stages, each building on the earlier ones (epigenesis). Each stage brings with it a new crisis: people are caught between two conflicting poles with which they have not struggled before. The crisis thus represented is never fully resolved, but, hopefully, the ratio of orientation to the positive pole, relative to the negative pole, is favorable.

4. In the first stage, infancy, the poles are basic trust and basic mistrust. The strength of this period is hope. It is the foundation of faith which is protected by the institutional safeguard, religion. Early childhood presents the poles autonomy vs. shame and doubt. Its strength is will power, the determination to exercise free choice which is protected by law and justice. Erikson acknowledges that children go through an "anal stage," but it is more cultural in nature than physiological.

5. Stage Three involves initiative vs. guilt. The boy does fantasize about his mother even in a sexual way, but it is because she is central to his life, not solely because of genital urges. The strength of this period is purpose. At the school age, the horns of the dilemma are industry and inferiority. The child at this stage prepares for the workaday world and the "tool culture." The strength of this period is competence.

6. Adolescence is the phase during which identity itself comes into focus: the poles are identity vs. identity confusion. At this stage previous identity developments either come together or not. It is a time of rebellion against the rules and norms of society. Fidelity is the strength: loyalty to self, others, and to personal ideologies. Ideologies must be adopted, but the dangers are seduction of youth by totalitarian ideology and subordination of identity to ideology.

7. In young adulthood, intimacy is fusion of one's identity with another's without loss to self. Love binds together competition and cooperation, procreation and production. It overcomes antagonisms such as those related to differences in function between relationship partners. In adulthood, generativity is concern for guiding the next generation. Care, the strength of this period, is concern for others, as in "to take care of," "to do for," and "to care for" others.

8. In old age, integrity opposes despair: passing on the power and leadership to the next generation vs. failure to establish a connection between generations. The strength is wisdom in the sense of "wisdom of the ages," not strenuous accomplishment. Levinson's mid-life transition entails a show of de-illusionment and individuation. To prosper, we must give up our illusion of immortality and contemplate a legacy. To Sheehy, women's mid-life crisis begins at 35: children leave and attractiveness declines. At work, women face competition with men of greater seniority. Divorce and concern that their biological clocks are ticking also confront women.

9. The poles for young adulthood and adulthood were extracted from factor analysis, but the lack of appearance of the other poles suggest overlap among them. An overriding factor that may be labelled "identity" was also extracted. Several predictions from Eriksonian theory were supported, but usually for whites, not blacks. There were also some troublesome gender differences. In another study, teacher, parent, and child ratings of children's industry were closely related and measures of industry predicted achievement, grades, and being on- vs. off-task. Two other studies showed the viability of the concept "generativity."

10. Erikson's theoretical and career accomplishments are remarkable considering that he had no advanced education. He became a hero to youth during the 1960s and a champion of the elderly currently. He turned psychological difficulties into benefits for us all. Research support for his view has been mostly positive and he has taught us that "identity" is a dynamic process. Unfortunately his theory is in part illogical. Some concepts seem exchangeable across stages, some are trite in meaning, some, like "fidelity," are murky, and some have too many meanings. Research has turned up other problems.

Running Comparison

Theorist	Erikson in Comparison
Freud	He de-emphasized the unconscious in favor of psychosocial factors. Although he mentioned oral, anal, and phallic factors and the latency period, he played down their physical-sexual side in favor of psychosocial aspects. He came close to calling Freud "wrong" about women and disagreed with him that a stage's "problems" must be resolved before a more advanced stage can be approached.
Gordon Allport	He agreed with Allport that self-esteem derives from doing for oneself. Like Allport he wrote about maturity, but with subdivisions and in more detail. They both deplored nationalism.
Erich Fromm	He also considered the dilemma of freedom and was somewhat philosophical.

Essay/Critical Thinking Questions

1. Can you speculate on how Erikson's theory would have been different had he been born into a family of Danish intellectuals?

2. Had Erikson, like Jung and Adler, completed a doctorate, but worked with Freud, would he have clung so tenaciously to giving "the Master" credit for his own ideas?

3. What are the tasks of your life now and what do you expect them to be in ten years?

4. Other than for hope and will power, can you conjure up possible institutional safeguards for at least two other Eriksonian strengths?

5. Besides "guilt," what could you come up with that might be a better opposite to "initiative" for the play age, but still be true to Erikson's theory?

6. Of Erikson's concepts, why have "industry" and "generativity" been singled out for special research attention?

7. Why do "identity developments . . . coalesce" during adolescence? Why not at some other stage?

8. In young adulthood, how are you able to "fuse your identity with somebody else's without losing" it?

9. Erikson's "care," the strength at adulthood, is very much like the common notion of "being a caring person." Why is "being a caring person" so "in focus" during adulthood? Why not earlier or later?

10. Can you call upon Levinson's theory to indicate how one can beat the problem of mortality?

8

THE SOCIOPSYCHOLOGICAL APPROACH TO PERSONALITY: ERICH FROMM

- Does sociology have anything to say about personality?
- Are there basic needs rooted in the very essence of humans?
- Is it reasonable to assume that most people in a given society share a generalized "character"?
- Is there such a thing as a "warrior personality"?
- What can the study of life in a Mexican village tell us about personality?

Erich Fromm stood at the crossroads of modern personality psychology. Similar to Erikson, he came from the Freudian branch, but he took a turn away from the famous psychiatrist toward a more psychologically based approach to personality theory. Fromm, compared to theorists covered earlier, described Freud's scientific contributions in glowing words: "He is founder of a truly scientific psychology, and his discovery of unconscious processes of the dynamic nature of character traits is a unique contribution to the science of man which has altered the picture of man for all time" (Fromm, 1962, p. 12). Yet Fromm's lengthy criticisms of Freud center on the claim that psychoanalysis "can define man scientifically" (Funk, 1982, p. 13). Indeed, Fromm believed that Freud's most basic notions are not amenable to scientific consideration. Most of these critical ideas cannot be converted to forms that can be observed scientifically. As if to take back the words of praise just quoted, when he compared Freud with social theorist Karl Marx, as he often did, Marx was the clear winner. "I consider Marx, the thinker, as being of much greater depth and scope than Freud" (p. 12).

Another reason that Fromm is pivotal in the history of personality theory resides in his academic training and background. He is the first of the theorists covered in this book who was trained in a university graduate school. Like Erikson, he had no medical school training. Fromm studied psychology, philosophy, and sociology. He received his Ph.D. from Heidelberg in 1922 following completion of "a dissertation on the sociopsychological structure of three Jewish Diaspora communities . . . " (Funk, 1982, pp. 2–3). Quite naturally his orientation would be away from physiological matters toward a **sociopsychological orientation**, the sociological study of people that sheds light on their psychological nature. During his long career, Fromm held professorships in several departments of psychology, including those at Michigan, Michigan State, Yale, and New York University. Because his background was a mixture of sociology, political philosophy, and psychology, he was the prophet of things to come: personality research and theory was to be taken away from psychiatry and given over to psychology and allied sciences.

Fromm, the Person

Erich Fromm was born in Frankfurt, Germany, March 23, 1900, the only child of Orthodox Jewish parents. As a Jewish boy in a Christian community, he experienced feelings of "clannishness" on both sides, along with occasional episodes of anti-Semitism. He characterized his father, the owner of an independent business, and his mother, a homemaker, as "highly neurotic" and himself as an "unbearable, neurotic child" (Funk, 1982, p. 1). Fromm wrote that "an anxious and moody father and a depression-prone mother was enough to arouse my interest in the strange and mysterious reasons for human reactions" (Fromm, 1962, pp. 3–4).

Young Fromm, whose family was deeply religious, became engrossed in the teachings of the Old Testament "which touched me and exhilarated me more than anything else I was exposed to" (Fromm, 1962, p. 5). While he was bored by the biblical account of Canaan's conquest, the stories of Mordecai and Esther, and the Song of Songs, he was enthralled by the tale of Adam's and Eve's disobedience, by Abraham's plea for deliverance of Sodom and Gomorrah's inhabitants, and by Jonah's mission to Nineveh. Fromm's favorite biblical characters were Isaiah, Amos, and Hosea. They moved him not so much by their prophesies of disaster as by their visions of the "end of days" when nations "shall beat their swords into plowshares and their spears into pruning hooks: nation shall not lift sword against nation, neither shall they learn war any more" (p. 5). These words were adopted by the international peace movement to which the adult Fromm was to contribute substantially.

Fromm developed his concepts in large part by reflecting on the thoughts of Freud and Marx, whose ideas he tried to synthesize (Fromm, 1962). His interest in psychoanalysis was triggered by an incident that occurred during his adolescence.

A 25-year-old friend of the family, an artist, killed herself following the death of her widowed father, with whom she had spent nearly all of her time.

> *I had never heard of an Oedipus complex; or of incestuous fixations between daughter and father. But I was deeply touched. I had been quite attracted to the young woman; I had loathed the unattractive father; never before had I known anyone to commit suicide. I was hit by the thought "How is it possible?" How is it possible that a beautiful young woman should be so in love with her father, that she prefers to be buried with him to being alive to the pleasures of life and of painting. (Fromm, 1962, p. 4)*

Erich Fromm

In 1929 Fromm began psychoanalytic training at the Berlin Institute under the tutelage of Hans Sachs and Theodor Reik, primary Freudian figures of the day (Funk, 1982; Hausdorff, 1972). However, he never met Freud. Because he had no medical training, Fromm was suspect in some corners of the Freudian world. Although Freud's notions were rather simplistic from a biological perspective, even for the time, somehow many Freudians thought that one needed medical training to fully understand psychoanalytic concepts. These followers of Freud probably account for the belief that Fromm de-emphasized Freud's biological notions because his lack of medical training prevented him from pursuing them.

For awhile after his psychoanalytic training, Fromm appeared to be a devout Freudian (Hausdorff, 1972). *The Development of the Dogma of Christ*, published in 1931, supported Freud's idea that religion is an illusion adopted in the interest of infantile gratification. Fromm's Freudian period continued past his move to the United States in 1934. Late in his life, however, he was to say, "[I am] a psychoanalyst who is a very unorthodox Freudian" (Hausdorff, 1972, p. 3). It appears that Fromm became permanently "unorthodox" during the writing of his highly successful book, *Escape from Freedom*, published in 1941. This widely read book advanced Fromm's unique ideas concerning how a society and its ideology, including such totalitarian states as Nazi Germany, can shape the thinking of its citizens. Needless to say, this publication was the right book at the right time: the United States was entering World War II against Japan and Germany, models of the authoritarian societies to which Fromm had referred.

Fromm declared that World War I was "the event that determined more than anything else my development" (Fromm, 1962, p. 6). In this pronouncement, he joined Jung and Adler. Fromm was 14 when the war began and, at first, was confused by people's reactions to armed conflict. Prior to the outbreak of hostilities, his

Latin teacher, who seemed peace loving, proclaimed his favorite "law" to be "if you want peace, prepare for war" (p. 6). When the war began, however, the teacher was obviously delighted. "How was it possible that a man who always seemed to have been so concerned with the preservation of peace should now be so jubilant about the war?" (p. 6). The "armament preserves peace" dilemma began to be resolved for him by experiences in his English class. He and other students were told to learn the heart of the British national anthem over the summer. However, by the time they returned to school, the British had become "the enemy." The students proudly announced that they would not learn the anthem. Fromm's teacher answered their defiance with a calm, prophetic reminder, "Don't kid yourself; so far England has never lost a war" (p. 7). "Here was the voice of sanity and realism in the midst of insane hatred—and it was the voice of a respected and admired teacher!" (p. 7). Fromm would listen to such voices for the rest of his life. Never again would he think it merely odd that "arms could bring peace"; he would view it as insane.

Amidst Orwellian double-talk of "strategic retreats" and "victorious defenses," he found that a number of uncles, cousins, and schoolmates had been killed. He again asked himself "How is it possible?" Fromm puzzled over the justification of the war glaring from the headlines of German newspapers: "was Germany not fighting against the very embodiment of slavery and oppression—the Russian Czar?" (p. 7). When he read convincing evidence that Germanic nations were, in fact, responsible for the war, his consternation deepened. But confusion became mixed with horror when he realized that young men were buying their country's propaganda and paying dearly for it. They were not sacrificing life and limb for peace, freedom, and justice. They were being maimed and killed because their governments had declared the other side "evil," just as the other side had denounced them as "evil." He became "deeply suspicious of all official ideologies and declarations" (1962, p. 9).

Fromm was truly a citizen of the world. He received his academic training at the Universities of Heidelberg, Frankfurt, and Munich, Germany. While in the United States he lived in many different locations. Fromm established the Department of Psychoanalysis at the National Autonomous University of Mexico in Mexico City. Although he retired from his Mexican professorship in 1965, his productivity increased rather than declined. Fromm produced about 20 percent of his books after his retirement, including the report on his monumental study of Mexican villagers. The area surrounding beautiful Lake Maggiore, straddling the Swiss-Italian border, became the setting for Fromm's last years. He took up residence there in 1976, the year his last book appeared. Fromm died in the Swiss town of Muralto on March 18, 1980 (Funk, 1982).

Fromm's View of the Person

It was Fromm's continued search for answers to perplexing questions regarding the ills of society that led him to Marx and Freud. Yet in studying the theories of these 20th century giants he began to see flaws, defects in their attempts to be scientific and deficiencies in science itself. Eventually, he began "believing in the superior value of blending empirical observation with speculation (much of the trouble with modern social science is that it often contains empirical observations without speculations) . . . I have always tried to let my thinking be guided by the observation of facts and have striven to revise my theories when the observation seemed to warrant it" (pp. 9–10). With these words, he adopted the scientific principle of empirical observation, and also assigned heavy weight to speculation.

Fromm's socialist inclinations began in childhood when he talked politics with a socialist who worked with his father (Fromm, 1962). Although he considered himself at the time "not suited for political activity," after he settled in New York City, he became a member of the American Socialist Party (p. 10). During the Vietnam era, he was active in the peace movement and supported peace candidate Eugene McCarthy (Funk, 1982). Fromm was a co-founder of SANE (the Organization for a Sane Nuclear Policy).

Fromm was a lifetime socialist, like Adler, but he also had serious reservations about the Soviet brand of socialism (Funk, 1982). When Fromm was in his seventies, Hausdorff (1972) asked him to define himself. Fromm replied, "[I am] a socialist who is in opposition to most Socialist and Communist parties . . ." (p. 3). He saw socialism from a humanitarian perspective and was repelled by what he regarded as Communist attempts at subjugation of the human spirit in the interest of perpetuating the power of party officials. That he thought of Soviet Communism as a failed attempt at instituting the Marxist form of socialism is seen in his derisive reference to the "perversion of the Russian revolution" (Fromm, 1962, p. 11).

Despite these reservations, Fromm's continued devotion to socialism, even in its communist form, is seen in his solution to the confused social order that existed in his time. To solve social ills he offered **humanistic communitarian socialism**, a political system embracing economic, social, and moral functions wherein ordinary citizens interact cooperatively and are actively involved in the various functions (Fromm, 1955; 1976).With this process of governing, the governed would participate in all facets of society. In so doing each person would help to ensure that all people equally enjoy the products of society, and no one is exploited. The object would be "serve the people" not "make a profit."

Basic Concepts: Fromm

Fromm considered a broad spectrum of social factors. He discussed such cultural influences on personality as the feudal system of the Medieval Age, the Protestant Reformation, 19th-century industrialization, and 20th century Nazism, fascism, communism, and capitalism. Despite the diversity of his writings on social matters, his works remained within a psychoanalytic context. Nevertheless, he was a **humanistic psychoanalyst**, one who believes in the essential worth and dignity of each person, and in the importance of helping each person to do the most with what she or he has. Speaking from this perspective, he was quite comfortable talking about human values, ethics, and meaning. In his willingness to deal with these abstractions, he followed in the steps of Jung. Fromm was convinced that psychology cannot be divorced from philosophy, ethics, sociology, or economics. He saw psychology as having the potential to debunk false ethical judgments and build objective and valid rules of conduct.

Existential Needs

According to Fromm, people are alike in that they all experience the same inherently contradictory and troublesome actualities of human existence. These worrisome facts are grounded in opposites that are rooted in the very essence of humans—for example, freedom-subjugation (Fromm, 1973). Thus, all persons find themselves joined with others, yet alone; living, yet dying; free, yet responsible; conscious of their potentialities, yet powerless over their limitations. People also are alike in sharing **existential needs**, needs that must be met if one's *existence is to be meaningful*, one's inner being is to be developed, one's talents are to be fully exploited, and abnormality is to be avoided. Fromm emphasized eight such needs.

Frame of Orientation and Object of Devotion

People need a **frame of orientation**, a cognitive "map" of their natural and social worlds that enables them to organize and make sense of puzzling matters and allows them to operate in the arena of rational understanding. A frame of orientation is an important factor in a person's life whether or not it is "true" or "false." Thus, although they are falsehoods from an objective point of view, beliefs "in the power of a totem animal, in a rain god," or in the "superiority and destiny of [my] race" may function as frames of orientation (Fromm, 1959, p. 160). In fact, false or irrational ideologies may be particularly seductive when adopted as frames of orientation. Unlike rational or scientifically based frames of orientation, political and religious doctrines may seem to offer solutions to every important problem. "The more an ideology pretends to give answers to all questions, the more attractive it is" (Fromm, 1973, p. 231).

In addition, people need some **object of devotion**, a goal that gives meaning to their existence and position in the world. Such an "ultimate concern" provides direction in life, reduces isolation, and permits transcendence beyond one's immediate self. Fromm wrote:

> The objects of man's devotion vary. He can be devoted to an idol which requires him to kill his children or to an ideal that makes him protect children; he can be devoted to growth of life or to its destruction. He can be devoted to the goal of amassing a fortune, of acquiring power, of destruction, or to that of loving and of being productive and courageous. He can be devoted to the most diverse goals . . . yet . . . the need for devotion itself is a primary, existential need demanding fulfillment regardless of how this need is fulfilled. (Fromm, 1973, pp. 231–232)

Relatedness

Humans have an intense need for **relatedness**, "the necessity to unite with other living beings . . . [constitutes] an imperative need on the fulfillment of which man's sanity depends" (Fromm, 1955, p. 30). Among the ways that one can fulfill the relatedness need is by joining another person in a **symbiotic union**, a coupling of beings in which each meets the needs of the other while they "live 'together' " as "two, and yet one" (Fromm, 1956, p. 15). As birds feed on the pests that infest the crocodile and the rhinoceros, each member of a symbiotic pair serves the other.

There are two forms of the symbiotic union, both destructive. In the *passive* union, the person submits to the control of another person, institution, or substance that "directs him, guides him, protects him; . . . is his life and his oxygen . . ." (Fromm, 1956, p. 16). Submission takes the form of masochism in that the person is used and abused by the power to which he or she has submitted. If one becomes subservient to another person, that individual becomes an idol. Subjugation can involve the whole body, as in sexual submission. Submission can be "to fate, to sickness, to rhythmic music, to the orgiastic state produced by drugs or under hypnotic trance—in all these instances, the person renounced his integrity, makes himself the instrument of somebody or something outside of himself . . ." (p. 16). If submission is to a country or society, the subservient person may show **automaton conformity**, the condition that occurs when the person, out of fear of aloneness, gives up freedom for union with society, and she or he bends over backwards to maintain the union by strict adherence to social norms and conventions (Fromm, 1956).

In the *active* symbiotic fusion, the theme of the union is domination, "or to use the psychological term corresponding to masochism, sadism" (p. 16). The dominating individual seeks to escape from aloneness by making another person a part of him or her. He or she achieves self-inflation by incorporating another person who, in turn, masochistically worships the sadistic individual. Each is dependent on the other; neither can live without the other. "The difference is only that the sadistic person commands, exploits, hurts, humiliates, and that the masochistic person is commanded, exploited, hurt, humiliated" (p. 17). While the sadist and the masochist are different, they also are the same: they have fused with another at the sacrifice of their personal integrity. Not surprisingly, a given person can react both sadistically and masochistically, usually toward different objects. Hitler, for example, was sadistic toward the German people, who worshiped him as a god. But he was masochistic in regard to fate: he rode destiny wherever it carried him, from the glory of conquest to the ignominy of suicide.

In contrast to the tragedy of symbiotic union, **mature love** "is union under the condition of preserving one's integrity, one's individuality . . . [it] is an active power of man" (p. 17). The power of love demolishes the barriers that separate people. It overcomes isolation and separateness, yet it maintains personal integrity. Love is "becoming one and yet remaining two" (p. 17). In the case of love, there is no need to inflate either one's own or the other person's image. The need for illusions regarding the other person and oneself vanishes. Fromm believed that "in the act of loving, I am one with All, and yet I am myself, a unique, separate, limited, mortal human being" (Fromm, 1955, p. 32). When one truly loves another person, one loves all of humanity, and therefore, oneself.

Rootedness

Rootedness is a deep craving to maintain one's natural ties and not be "separated" (Fromm, 1973). Without roots we would have to stand alone, in isolation and helplessness, not knowing where or who we are. Most people show progress in life by substituting new roots for old. When biological separation occurs, through birth and maturation, substitute attachments are sought, both symbolically (God, country) and emotionally (love, community). The more complete the original separation, the greater the need to form new roots that approximate the paradise of security represented by envelopment in the womb. The intensity of the craving for roots as deep and secure as the original ones can be so overwhelming that the individual may regress to a near infantile state in which dependence on some symbolic substitute for mother occurs. Such substitutes include "the soil," "nature," or "God." The healthy opposite to this regression toward a primitive state is finding new roots in "the brotherhood of man, and by freeing [oneself] from the power of the past" (Fromm, 1973, p. 233). A destructive "symbiotic" regression was illustrated by the young woman discussed earlier who committed suicide after her father's death. The woman was unable to separate herself from her father. An example of mature love is provided by Fromm himself in his marriage to Annis Freeman in 1953 (Hausdorff, 1972). He was truly one with her, but he clearly maintained his integrity as reflected in the enormous productivity he showed during the years of their marriage. In sum, one can respond to the need for roots through love, or one can take the destructive route by seeking a symbiotic relationship.

Identity

Identity is the need to be aware of oneself as a separate entity, and to sense oneself as the subject of one's own actions (Fromm, 1955). The person is able to say and feel "I am I." This need also applies to seeing others as separate persons.

Members of ancient clans sometimes were unable to see themselves as existing separately from the group, expressing their identity as "I am we." Throughout history, individuals have identified themselves with social roles. Medieval roles included" I am a peasant" or "I am a lord." You may recognize these ideas as akin to "persona," the mask concept Jung developed. When the feudal system broke down, major uncertainties were created. Peasants and lords were unable to answer the questions "Who am I?" or "How do I know who I am?" They then turned to nation, class, religion, and occupation as substitutes for unique identity. People have sought to obtain a false sense of identity, security, or status by adhering to such social roles as "I am an American . . . a Protestant . . . an executive." Citizens living in the 20th century also have sought to *Escape from Freedom* (Fromm, 1941) by giving up their individuality to totalitarian governments.

Fromm maintained that we must discontinue these tragic and fruitless strivings for identity. We must abandon "being" the roles that we play or "being" as others desire us. Instead we must devote ourselves to "being" separate entities who can relate to others without dissolving into them.

Unity

Unity is a sense of inner oneness within one's self and with the "natural and human world outside" (Fromm, 1973, p. 233). Unity can be attempted through dressing in animal skins, in efforts to unite with the animal portion of nature. Unity can also be attempted by subordinating one's energies to an all-consuming passion for power, fame, or property. Failures to achieve unity can evade consciousness if one anesthetizes oneself through alcohol, drugs, sexual orgies, trances, or cultist rituals. These tricks played on consciousness are attempts to restore unity within oneself. Indeed when one is drugged or drunk one achieves a sense of unitary experience that is a kind of oneness. However, Fromm believed that this method has only temporary, positive effects and is counterproductive in the long run. It cripples those who use it, estranges them from others, twists their judgment, and makes them dependent on the substance or passion in which they have chosen to invest themselves.

The true and certain path to unity lies in developing human reason and love. Religion can be the light to illuminate that path, but only if one participates in it, rather than passively submits to it. All the great religions of the world have a common goal: "to arrive at the experience of oneness, not by regressing to animal existence but by becoming fully human—oneness with man, oneness between man and nature, and oneness between man and other men" (Fromm, 1973, p. 234).

Transcendence

Transcendence is the act of transforming one's accidental and passive role of "creature" into that of an active and purposeful "creator" (Fromm, 1955). As you will soon see, this idea is much like the humanistic notions of Carl Rogers and Abraham Maslow. It can be accomplished through various means, in as simple a process as planting seeds and producing material goods or in as complicated a manner as creating art and ideas, and loving others. By creative acts humans can rise above the "creature" in them and ascend to new heights where purposefulness and freedom dwell. But "how . . . does man solve the problem of transcending himself, if he is not capable of creating, if he cannot love? There is another answer to this need for transcendence: if I cannot create life, I can destroy it. To destroy life makes me transcend it" (Fromm, 1955, p. 37). Because humans must transcend themselves, they are compelled to create or to destroy, to love or to hate. Both the destructive and the creative paths lead to transcendence. "However, the satisfaction of the need to create leads to happiness; destructiveness to suffering, most of all, for the destroyer himself" (Fromm, 1955, p. 38). It follows from this position that we must do all we can to foster creativity, a potential that exists in all of us, so that happiness prevails rather than destructiveness. Later you will read about programs developed by Carl Rogers and B. F. Skinner that are designed to promote creativity.

Effectiveness

Effectiveness is the need to compensate for "being in a strange and overpowering world" by developing a sense of being able to do something that will "make a dent" in life (Fromm, 1973, p. 235). To be effective is to "get things done," "to accomplish," and to be a person "who has the capacity to do . . . something" (p. 235). It also offers some proof of one's existence and identity, based on the realization "I am, because I effect." People may experience joy by producing effects that are either positive or negative—making a noisy clatter, eliciting a smile from a loved one, doing what is forbidden, destroying property, or even causing terror in a victim. We first manifest effectiveness in child's play when we experience the "joy of being a cause" (p. 235). One of the earliest expressions of effectiveness is the child utterance "I do . . . I do." As you will see later in consideration of ideas developed by Gordon Allport, seeking to be effective, to do for oneself, is a landmark developmental event. According to Fromm, it arises in part from being overwhelmed by parental power: ". . . to rule when one had to obey; to beat when one was beaten; in to *do* what one was *forced* to *suffer*, or to do what was forbidden to do" become principle goals of the child (p. 236). As adults we are preoccupied with effects and are compelled to be the producer of those effects. We must "elicit an expression of satisfaction from the baby being nursed, a smile from the loved person, sexual response from the lover, interest from the partner in conversation" in order to feel "I am because I effect" (pp. 235 & 236). As with other concepts of Fromm, this one has its down side. If we cannot by our actions elicit loving feelings in others, we can cause them fear and suffering. The choice between construction and destruction is, as always, ours to make.

Excitation and Stimulation

Excitation and stimulation is the need for the nervous system to be "exercised," that is, to experience a certain amount of excitation (Fromm, 1973). The importance of this need is supported by research showing brain-generated dream activity during sleep, by the abnormal reactions of infants and monkeys reared in environments lacking varied sensory stimulation, and by studies of normal young adults exposed to environments lacking in sensory variation.

Consistent with Fromm's view, hundreds of studies on sleeping and dreaming demonstrate that the brain must be continuously stimulated, even during some phases of sleep (see Anch, Browman, Mitler & Walsh, 1988). Because sensory stimulation is shut off during sleep, the brain, in effect, self-stimulates. During rapid eye movements (REM) associated with dreaming, the senses act as if they are functioning, even though they are receiving no information. Beyond the eyes, ears, and other sense organs, the brain, even in terms of its electrical activity, operates almost as if it is awake and receiving sensory input. Thus, we can experience vivid, full-color dreams that are so real we may awake perspiring and in a state of terror (or ecstasy). When experimental subjects are deprived of dreams, by, for example, being awakened whenever their eyes move under their lids (REM), they appear to suffer difficulties in problem solving and may show at least short term emotional disturbances (see Anch et al., 1988, for a cautionary note). Stimulation and excitation are ever present needs.

The work of Canadian psychologist D. O. Hebb (1949) established that proper functioning of the brain requires continuously varied sensory stimulation. Primates, experimental monkeys or children in institutions, have been reared in stale environments in which what is seen or heard or felt does not change. Compared to monkeys and children reared amid everchanging sights and sounds, the deprived primates' brains, and thus their intellects and perceptual capabilities, failed to develop properly. Hebb's collaborators placed normal college students in an environment designed to eliminate variation in visual, auditory, and tactile stimulation (Heron, 1957). They wore diffusing goggles that let in light, but no pattern or form. Also, they were exposed to a fan that generated "white noise" (all the auditory frequencies humans can hear scrambled together), and had their hands covered. Living two to four days under these circumstances was enough to cause the students' brains to malfunction. Not only were their electrical brain waves abnormal, they showed bizarre hallucinations ("A tiny spaceship is firing pellets at my arm."), emotional disturbances ("The experimenter is out to get me."), and intellectual deficiencies (poor problem solving). Subjects were so starved for stimulation they would have cherished a phone book to read. Environmental conditions like these were a part of the "brainwashing" methods used on U.S. prisoners of war by the Chinese during the Korean War.

According to Fromm, the need for varied sensory input can be satisfied by two kinds of stimuli: simple or activating. **Simple stimuli** are like those that generate reflexes in that they call for reactions more than actions, particularly *surface reactions* that are immediate and passive in nature. Simple stimuli are often associated with "thrill" excitements: accidents, fires, crimes, wars, arguments, sex-related movies and advertisements, and television violence. These stimuli cause knee-jerk, automatic, gut reactions. Repeated presentation of them destroys their power.

Activating stimuli are more complicated than simple stimuli, in that they cause the person to become engaged in productive activity for longer periods of time. Examples include stimulation from generating ideas, reading novels, painting landscapes, enjoying musical works, and being with loved ones. Unlike simple stimuli, activating stimuli engage the "stimulee" to be a participate in the stimulation, not a passive pawn manipulated by it (Fromm, 1973, p. 240). Rather than losing their power with repetition, truly activating stimuli continue to be potent with repeated presentation. To Fromm, activating stimuli are healthier but require greater maturity because they do not lead as quickly to excitement. Activating stimuli require great effort, patience, discipline, concentration, tolerance, and practice at critical thinking. Rather than reacting, the person must bring these stimuli to life.

You will come across a further consideration of "needs" later in this book. The theory of Henry Murray revolves around needs to a great extent, as does that of Abraham Maslow.

BOX 8.1   Which Needs Are Most Prominent in Your Life?

Fromm believed that all of his existential needs must be met by all people. Nevertheless, he certainly wrote or spoke nothing to contradict the possibility that some needs may be more prominent in some people than in others. In fact, part of the uniqueness associated with a person's individual character may be associated with paying more attention to some needs as opposed to others. The current exercise will help you appreciate this point with regard to yourself in compari-son to other members of the class. Below each brief statement of the several needs is a scale. By placing an "X" nearer one end of the scale than the other you can indicate the degree of time and attention you devote to each need (for a given need, you can place your mark above any scale point that you deem appropri-ate). When you finish making the marks, you will have one more task to do before comparing your responses to those of other students.

Frame of orientation and *object of devotion* are a cognitive map to guide us in making sense of puzzling matters and a goal that gives meaning to our existence, respectively.

__:__:__:__:__:__:__:__:__

spend much time and
attention to this need

spend little time and
attention to this need

Relatedness is the necessity of uniting with other living beings, to relate to them; it is an imperative need upon the fulfillment of which rests our sanity.

__:__:__:__:__:__:__:__:__

spend much time and
attention to this need

spend little time and
attention to this need

Rootedness is a deep craving to maintain one's natural ties and not be "separated."

__:__:__:__:__:__:__:__:__

spend much time and
attention to this need

spend little time and
attention to this need

Identity is the need to be aware of oneself as a separate entity, and to sense oneself as the subject of one's own actions.

__:__:__:__:__:__:__:__:__

spend much time and
attention to this need

spend little time and
attention to this need

BOX 8.1   *Continued*

Unity is a sense of inner oneness within one's self and with the "natural and human world outside."

—__:__:__:__:__:__:__:__:__

spend much time and   spend little time and
attention to this need   attention to this need

Transcendence is the act of transforming one's accidental and passive role of "creature" into that of an active and purposeful "creator."

—__:__:__:__:__:__:__:__:__

spend much time and   spend little time and
attention to this need   attention to this need

Effectiveness is the need to compensate for "being in a strange and overpowering world" by developing a sense of being able to do something that will "make a dent" in life.

—__:__:__:__:__:__:__:__:__

spend much time and   spend little time and
attention to this need   attention to this need

Excitation and stimulation is the need for the nervous system to be "exercised," that is, to experience a certain amount of excitation.

—__:__:__:__:__:__:__:__:__

spend much time and   spend little time and
attention to this need   attention to this need

Now, draw a line from the mark on the first scale to the one on the second scale and so forth all the way down to the mark on the last scale. You have drawn your "need profile," analogous to the personality profile covered in Chapter 1. If all students simply hold up their books so they can see each other's profiles, you all can appreciate the unique-ness of individuals' profiles. Even though the number of need scales is small, it is likely that each student's profile line will be different from that of each other student (individual differences). That observation will confirm that people and their need patterns are unique; each person is an original, unduplicated by any other person in the world.

Individual and Social Character

Individual Differences among People

Although they share common existential problems and needs, people are also different from each other. This is seen in Fromm's definition of **personality**, "the totality of inherited and acquired psychic qualities which are characteristic of one individual and which make the individual unique" (1947, p. 50). Inherited differences, and differences among people in their developmental histories, lead them to experience the same environment in different ways. People also show uniqueness "in the specific way they solve their human problem" (1947, p. 50).

Fromm actually devotes much greater attention to the concept of character than to personality. *Character*, which is based not on Freud's libido, but on the individual's relatedness to the world, develops at two levels: individual and social.

Individual character is the pattern of behavior characteristic of a given person—"the relatively permanent system of all noninstinctual strivings through which man relates himself to the human and natural world" (Fromm, 1973, p. 226). Because character involves deeply rooted habits and opinions, it serves a decision-making function. It is a semiautomatic process of action and thought that saves an individual from having to make deliberate, conscious decisions every time choices must be made. Character is analogous to reflexes in that it becomes activated as soon as appropriate stimuli are present, without the intervention of thoughtfulness. Once energy is channeled in a certain way, action takes place "true to character."

Individual Differences among Societies

Thus far in this book, differences among people have been discussed. However, a contribution unique to Fromm is his interest in identifying character differences among entire societies.

Social character represents "the core of a character structure common to most people of a given culture . . . [and] shows the degree to which character is formed by social and cultural patterns" (1947, p. 60). Social character is clearly the product of one's society. In a sense, individual character becomes partly "lost" as it is subsumed by social character. Fromm put it this way: "the whole personality of the average individual is molded by the way people relate to each other, and it is determined by the socioeconomic and political structure of society to such an extent that . . . one can infer from the analysis of one individual the totality of the social structure in which he lives" (Fromm, 1947, p. 79).

Fromm (1947) has identified six types of social character: receptive, exploitative, hoarding, marketing, necrophilous, and productive. These social-character types express themselves in how individuals relate to things and to people (including themselves). Fromm classifies the first five as *nonproductive*, those that yield, at best, pseudo-connection to others and, at worse, destructive relations with others. They are distorted, incomplete, or ultimately unfulfilling. In contrast, the productive orientation is based on *love*, the mutual intimacy that preserves individual integrity. Although the types are "ideals," and usually blended in people, one type is likely to be dominant depending upon cultural values. Also, because of the interaction between individual and culture, it is always possible for individuals to affect their society.

Fromm cast each type in terms of **assimilation**, how people acquire things, and **socialization**, how people relate to others. Also, four of the five non-productive types were divided into two pairs. One pair was labeled *symbiotic* because persons partaking of these types are involved in relations where one member submits to the exploitation of the other. The second pair is dubbed *withdrawal*, as people of these types consider other people to be threats from whom they must maintain distance or to whom they must direct destructiveness. A fifth non-productive type is considered separately.

Persons of a **receptive** orientation experience the source of all good as being outside themselves (Fromm, 1947). According to Fromm, the receptive person". . . believes that the only way to get what he wants—be it something material, be it affection, love, knowledge, pleasure—is to receive it from that outside source" (p. 62). People of this type receive from others, and they show their oral nature by being fond of food and drink. Receptive people are dependent, favor saying "yes" rather than "no," listening to others rather than talking, and seeking to be loved and helped rather than giving love and help. Obviously Fromm was influenced by knowledge of Freud's oral receptive type.

If they are religious, they want and expect everything from God and nothing from their own efforts. If they are not religious, they may wish for a "magic helper," someone who will meet their every need and solve their every problem. Should they look to many people as sources of life's benefits, they will show a peculiar brand of loyalty: "gratitude for the hand that feeds them and fear of ever losing it" (p. 62). Because they are loyal to many people means that they will stretch their loyalty thin. As a result they frequently are caught between conflicting loyalties and promises. More generally, they tend to be optimistic and friendly. They exude confidence in life and what it has to offer, but they show extreme anxiety when they sense that a "source of supply" may be withdrawn. In terms of *assimilation*, people of this type passively receive (accepting). On the *socialization* side, they masochistically submit (loyalty).

The receptive orientation is found in societies that are stratified such that the lower classes depend on the upper classes. The "unfortunate members" are lead to assume that through "sacrifice, duty, and love" they will be "taken care of" by the "fortunate" (powerful) members of society (p. 108). They rationalize their masochism by arguing that it is their "lot in life" to submit to the care of others. Peasants in a feudal society may fit this model.

People of an **exploitative** orientation also experience the source of all good as outside themselves, but rather than expecting to receive from others, they take things through force or cunning. Their orientation is to grab, steal, and manipulate, while being suspicious, cynical, jealous, and hostile. They underrate what they have and overrate what others have. Their mottos are "I take what I need" and "Stolen fruits are sweetest." Therefore, in the realm of love, stolen affection is a jewel, love freely offered by an unattached other is a lump of coal. Not surprisingly, they find married or otherwise attached people very attractive. Expressions of love are reserved for "marks": people who are "promising objects of exploitation" (Fromm, 1947, p. 65). These people bear some resemblance to Freud's oral aggressive type.

Like the receptive type, exploitive individuals cannot do for themselves. They must take the fruits of others' labors, including their mental efforts. People of this type are intellectual bandits. Having no useful ideas of their own, they literally pick others' brains. More generally, they get no thrill from creating their own "goods," but they get a rush from taking others'.

In terms of traits, exploitive types are hostile and cynical. To them there are two kinds of people, those who get in the way and must be removed, and those who are useful for some selfish purpose. Instead of the optimistic, accepting attitude of the receptive type, these individuals are suspicious of others—what are they withholding? are they trying to do to me what I want to do to them? Instead of a friendly orientation to others, they are jealous —"whatever others have is better than what I have." As you might guess, they are masters of the cutting remark and the subtle put down. In terms of assimilation, people of this type are exploiting (taking). As to socialization, they relate to others in a sadistic fashion (authority). Like the receptive type, they relate to others in a symbiotic manner, but they are the takers, not the receivers.

This orientation is represented in societies dominated by feudal lords and 19th-century robber barons, who exploited human and natural resources through power, wealth, ruthless competition, authoritarianism, and the "right of might." In more modern times, it seems well-illustrated by the Soviet Union during the Stalinist era (1920s to the 1950s). Peasants were required to give what they produced to the "state" (actually Stalin and party members close to him). If they refused, they were allowed to starve; after all, they were useless. If they protested, they were "removed": sent to the infamous Soviet prisons, the gulags, or killed. Stalin was a true exploitive sadist who enjoyed sending warped communications to his victims. He would greet people warmly . . . just before having them killed (Fromm, 1973). He would assure representatives of a Soviet ethnic group that their favorite poets would not be arrested . . . they would be seized shortly thereafter.

Persons of a **hoarding** orientation differ from the two preceding types: they believe the "goods" come from the inside not the outside, themselves not others, so security is based on an attitude of saving, of letting out as little as possible (Fromm, 1947). Rather than seeking symbiotic relations with others, they *withdraw* from others. They set up "a protective wall, and their main aim is to bring as much as possible into this fortified position and to let as little as possible out of it" (p. 65). Their motto is "Mine is mine, and yours is yours." Though the motivational basis is more sociopsychological than libidinal, this kind of person is somewhat akin to Freud's anal retentive type.

People of this type are misers about everything: money, material things, the past, love. They do not give love, they get it by owning the "beloved." Everything they had in the past which is now only a memory is still cherished. They would keep everything they have grabbed since they were old enough to grasp, if they could. Thus, they are "sentimental": they ruminate endless about bygone feelings and experiences.

These people are sterile, "tight-lipped," even grim. Being prone to withdrawal, they are unpleasant to be around: they regard others as candidates for possession, not potential companions in a human relationship. Hoarding applies to information as well as everything else. They know much, but can do little with it, because they are rigid, bound by the extreme orderliness that is peculiar to them. Hoarding types are compulsively clean, obsessively punctual, and irritatingly obstinate. "No!" is their favorite exclamation. To say "yes" threatens them with the possibility of giving up something. They peer through the gates of their fortresses, beckoning to those who would enter and be counted among their possessions, but never venturing forth into others' world. In terms of assimilation, they are hoarding (preserving). As to socialization, they are destructive (assertiveness).

This orientation is represented by societies adopting a Puritan ethic of hard work and success, in which middle-class stability is provided through family and possession of property. North America during the late 1600s and the 1700s through the early 1800s may illustrate this kind of society. The Puritan religion was thriving during a great part of that period. Self-sufficient family farms were the most basic social units of that time. Farms produced almost all that a family needed and hard work in the family interest was necessary for survival. In so far as people had specialized professions, such as blacksmith and candle maker, they were even more literally defined by their jobs than we are today. The European tradition of naming people for their professions came to the "new world" with the first settlers. Thus, surnames such as "Butcher" and "Goldsmith" still exist today. Nevertheless, American society of this period did not wholly fit Fromm's "hoarding" notion: the spirit of cooperation among and within family units appears to have been much greater than Fromm would have expected.

The **marketing** orientation is unique to the modern historical era in which exchanging goods for money, other goods, or services became the backbone of a "supply and demand" economy (Fromm, 1947). In this contemporary economy, supply of a commodity determines its value, not its inherent usefulness. For example, fuel is essential for running industry and automobiles and for heating homes, but its value is determined by whether it is in short supply or there is plenty of it. Thus, although the usefulness of gasoline remains constant, it is relatively inexpensive when much is available, but expensive when some world crisis makes it in short supply.

By analogy, people of this orientation experience themselves as salable commodities whose "exchange value" depends on whether they are in short supply or not. They seek to package and sell themselves so that they seem unusual or rare and, thus, "in demand." Here is where "personality" enters the picture. While a minimum level of competence is necessary to be marketable at all, in a given profession, a great many people will possess that degree of skill. Further, in almost every profession, there will be many people with much more than minimum competence. With so many people being relatively indistinguishable in terms of skills, whether a given person stands out enough "to get hired" depends on such personality traits as " 'cheerful,' 'sound,' 'aggressive,' 'reliable,' 'ambitious' . . ." (Fromm, 1947, p. 70). People battle to distinguish themselves so that they will look like "one of a kind" and thereby appear to be in short supply. Ironically, "since success depends largely on how one sells one's personality, one experiences oneself as . . . simultaneously . . . the seller *and* the commodity to be sold" (p. 70).

Under these circumstances, people are not concerned with their lives or happiness, but with being salable. They begin to feel so much like commodities that Fromm analogized them to "handbags." Each handbag must make itself more attractive than its rivals if it is going to be sold. To demand a higher price, it must look more expensive than its rivals. If it "sells" it can "feel" elated because it has been proven more "valuable" than its rivals. Conversely, if it fails to sell it will "feel" dejected, worthless.

"Like the handbag, one has to be in fashion on the personality market, and in order to be in fashion one has to know what kind of personality is most in demand" (p. 71). Helpfully, the media supplies the raw materials one needs to construct a marketable personality. Personality traits that have sold are depicted on the TV, in the movies, and in popular magazines. "The young girl tries to emulate the facial expression, coiffure, [and] gestures of a high-priced star as the most promising way to success. The young man tries to look and be like a model he sees on the screen" (p. 71). Some people do well at this game, but, in a sense, all fail in the end. One can manipulate one's traits to form a hopefully marketable commodity, but one can never be sure whether the finished product will sell. Therefore, one's self-esteem is at the mercy of the market: it is high if one "sells," low if one does not, and one can never be sure of the sales outcome. Assimilation is represented here in "marketing" (exchanging) and socialization in "indifference" (fairness). Because Fromm believed that the modern capitalistic society of which you are a member clearly generates the marketing type, no further example is needed.

The **necrophilous character** is engrossed by death, dwells on it, and glories in it (Fromm, 1973). Fromm added this social character after the others. Contrary to the well-known clinical use of the term, desire to have sexual relations with corpses, in Fromm's use, "necrophilous" is *generalized* to mean a preoccupation with death. The origin of the term dates to an incident during a speech by a General Millan Astray delivered at the onset of the Spanish Civil War, 1936. When one of the General's followers shouted his favorite motto from the back of the room— "Viva la muerte!" ("Long live death!")—Spanish philosopher Miguel de Unamuno arose from the audience to express his disgust. In so doing he described "Long live death!" as a "*necrophilous* and senseless cry . . ." (p. 331). When Fromm reflected on this incident during the early 1960s he conceived of the new "death loving" character. The concept "necrophilous" certainly does have the flavor of the notion "Thanatos," that Freud contrived. However, while "necrophilous" and "Thanatos" are related, Fromm goes so far beyond Freud as to make the coincidence of their concepts minimal.

The necrophilous type gains meaning and identity by transforming life into death. Fromm wrote, "Necrophilia in the characterological sense can be described as the passionate attraction to all that is dead, decayed, putrid, sickly; it is the passion to transform that which is alive into something unalive; to destroy for the sake of destruction; the exclusive interest in all that is purely mechanical. It is the passion 'to tear apart living structures' " (p. 332; emphasis eliminated). The necrophilous person extracts a feeling of power and elation from vicariously or directly participating in the transformation of life into death. Although Fromm did not explicitly refer to assimilation and socialization for this type, it is possible to extrapolate from his writings: the assimilation term would be "necrophilous" (life to death) and the corresponding socialization concept could be "murderous" (war-like). In relation to "symbiosis" (receiving and exploiting) and "withdrawal" (hoarding and marketing), individuals of the necrophilous type might be labeled "unhumanizing" in testimony to their fascination with lifeless people.

Fromm saw the necrophilous inclination emerge from dreams and the subtle actions of people. Albert Speer, Adolf Hitler's personal architect, later his armaments minister, and possibly his only friend, had a dream that symbolically illustrated the Nazi leader's necrophilous tendencies (Fromm, 1973). In it Speer finds himself in Hitler's car. "Our drive ends at a large square surrounded by government buildings. On one side is a war memorial. Hitler approaches it and lays down a wreath" (Fromm, 1973, p. 333). And Hitler lays another wreath, and another and another. All the while he is chanting "Jesus Maria," possibly a remnant from his Catholic upbringing. By laying the wreaths on the memorials, Hitler pays homage to death, but does so in the typical, mechanical, unfeeling fashion of the necrophilous person. The chant may also be seen in symbolic terms: Hitler's religion had become death.

Other dreams of death on a grand scale are provided by Fromm to illustrate the destructive nature of the warlike, necrophilous person. One dreamer reported "I have made a great invention, the 'superdestroyer.' It is a machine which, if one secret button is pushed that I alone know, can destroy all life in North America within the first hour, and within the next hour, all life on earth" (p. 334). Referring to another scene, the dreamer said "I have pushed the button; I notice no more life, I am alone, I feel exuberant." In another dream, the mechanization of everything that so thrills the necrophilous person is well illustrated. The dreamer is at a party where young people are dancing, but their rhythm becomes slower and slower until everyone is immobile. At this moment two very large people enter the room carrying some equipment. One of them approaches a boy and bloodlessly cuts a hole in his back into which a box is inserted. The same is done to a girl by the other oversized person. Keys are inserted into the boxes and, when switched on, the boy and girl dance vigorously. The same "operation" is performed on all other persons present. People become machines whose aliveness can be switched on or off.

Illustrations of societies that spawn the necrophilous type are numerous and familiar. Some societies of this century include those that revolved around Hitler, Italian dictator Mussolini, Stalin, and the bloodthirsty Cambodian despot Pol Pot (who was still at large and in command of his troops in 1993 after slaughtering two million of his people). Unfortunately, certain leaders continue to set a necrophilous tone for their people even in the 1990s. Witness the works of Saddam Hussein.

Table 8.1 summarizes Fromm's social character types, including the only positive one, our next consideration. The **productive orientation** is an attitude of relatedness to the world and oneself that encompasses all realms of human experience: reasoning, loving, and working (Fromm, 1947). Productive people "comprehend the world, mentally and emotionally, through love and through reason" (p. 97). The productive orientation is not concerned with practical results or "success."

TABLE 8.1   Fromm's Social Character Types

Assimilation	Socialization	
Nonproductive Orientation		
Receiving (accepting)	Masochistic (loyalty)	symbiosis
Exploiting (taking)	Sadistic (authority)	
Hoarding (preserving)	Destructive (assertiveness)	withdrawal
Marketing (exchanging)	Indifferent (fairness)	
Necrophilous (life into death)	Murderous (war-like)	unhumanize
Productive Orientation		
Working (creating)	Loving & Reason (integrity)	humanize

Most important is the use of the potent powers to act and to express personal character that are possessed by all humans.

The human capacity for *productive reasoning* can be used to penetrate the surface of ideas, actions, and emotions, get into them, and, thereby, gain understanding of their essence. The power of *productive love* can break through walls that separate people, allowing each of us genuine understanding of other people's mental and emotional cores. Productive love is characterized by care, responsibility, respect, and knowledge (note the resemblance to Erikson's "care" at the adulthood stage). *Productive work* allows people to transform materials into other forms, using reason and imagination to visualize things not yet existing. It also promotes creativity and fruitful planning.

In essence, the productive orientation provides an answer to the basic contradictions of human existence. It suggests that a person's main task in life is to give birth to oneself, to become what one potentially is, a theme that is elaborated by the humanists covered next. The most important product of this effort is one's own "mature and integrated" personality. This is because Fromm, like Jung, believed that every person is more than "a blank sheet of paper on which culture can write its text" (1947, p. 23). A human nature exists. Therefore, what is ethically good in Fromm's humanistic framework is the unfolding of personal powers according to the laws of human nature. This view led Fromm (1959) to propose a positive concept of mental health that is not just the absence of sickness but the presence of "well-being." To manifest well-being one must be aware, responsive, independent, fully active, united with the world, and able to under-

---

> **BOX 8.2   Social Character Types Applied to Societies**
>
> Now that you have considered Fromm's "social character types" it will be interesting to see how they fit your own society. Go back to Table 8.1 and give a rank of "1" to the type that you feel fits your society best. Give a rank of "2" to the type that fits next best and so forth for all six types. If everyone in your class does this exercise, your professor might be willing to poll the class to see which type was ranked highest. Each student could announce the rank given to a particular type and the professor could determine the modal rank for each type (the most frequently used rank). This could be done for all types, thereby revealing which is ranked highest on average. It would be interesting to repeat this process for some other society, such as that represented by the former Soviet Union or India. Then your society could be compared with others as to which type fits best.

stand that only living creatively gives meaning to life. One must be joyful in the act of living—expressing joy throughout one's whole body—and concerned with being rather than having (Fromm, 1976). Failure to make use of one's innate, human powers results in unhappiness, psychological disturbance, and neurosis. It appears that Fromm saw no former or present major society able to reliably generate productive types.

Evaluation

Contributions

Many of Fromm's important contributions have been covered earlier: for example, his needs and types. Others revolve around reinterpretations of institutions and Freudian theory, his groundbreaking social character research in an actual society, and his influential books.

The Family Reconceived as the Agent of Society
Fromm (1973) saw the family as the psychological agency through which a child acquires the core of social character shared by most other children partaking of the same culture. Parents are the representatives of a society's atmosphere and spirit, which they transmit just by being the persons they are. An important developmental aim is for parents to help the child "desire to act" as it "has to act." This is best seen when social and individual character coincide. A person of the hoarding orientation who saves money, purchasing necessities only, gains psychological and social satisfactions by doing business in a society that values economic efficiency and thrift. An authoritarian, exploitative person who listens to ideological speeches about political forces so powerful that human submission is the only alternative, also achieves dual satisfactions. Thus, individual psychological traits cement the social structure.

The Sociocultural Reinterpretation of Freud

Regarding Freud's psychosexual stages of development, Fromm (1941) suggested that Freud had reversed the causal relationship between erogenous zones and personality traits. Thus, according to Fromm, Freud's "oral" personality is not due to physiologically pleasant oral sensations. Rather, personality in the form of a receptive character feeds back on physiology to create the "oral language of the body."

The personality originates as a reaction to social experiences with other people. Recognizing that parental care or affection is given only under conditions of surrender, the child becomes fearful and experiences a weakening of its strength and self-confidence. The child then gives up its natural self-initiative and learns to direct its energies toward "an outside source from which the fulfillment of all wishes will eventually come" (Fromm, 1941, p. 292).

Fromm (1947) also reinterpreted Freud's concept of the Oedipus complex. In Fromm's view, it represents the child's struggle for individual freedom from parental authority rather than an awakening of genital sensations. The child's fight is to minimize the effects of guilt or submission, which threaten to weaken the self, by seeking to become a full-fledged human being rather than a cultural robot.

Fromm maintained a lively interest in the Freudian therapeutic concepts of "free association," "transference," and "insight" (Bacciagaluppi, 1989). He also, however, had reservations about the strict Freudian interpretations of these concepts. In fact, there was almost nothing about Freud's theory that Fromm accepted without some qualification.

Social Character in Mexican Villagers

Fromm and Maccoby (1970) undertook a field study of social character in a Mexican village as a test of Fromm's (1947) theory. They wanted to demonstrate that the social character common to a group could be assessed and related to socioeconomic variables.

An open-ended "interpretative questionnaire" of about 90 items was given to 406 adults (95 percent of all residents) of a Mexican farming village. Social character among the villagers was found to be high in receptive orientation (44 percent) and low in exploitative (11 percent). Men were more receptive than women, who were more hoarding. Sociopolitically, villagers were most often submissive (49 percent) rather than democratic (7 percent) or rebellious (7 percent). Fixations involving parents were almost entirely directed toward the mother (96 percent). Fourteen percent of adult-male villagers were alcoholic. Of them, 80 percent were receptive in character, compared with only 37 percent of abstainers.

The results pointed to three main categories of social character mixtures: productive-hoarding, nonproductive-receptive, and productive-exploitative. These social adaptations corresponded to three distinct socioeconomic conditions: free landowner, landless day laborer, and a kind of business entrepreneur, respectively. The hoarding orientation was the one "best adapted" to the economic demands of peasant farming in the village. By contrast, the receptive peasant, who was seen as being "out of tune" with the world, was poorly adapted. Interestingly, even the type of crop landholders chose to plant was related to social character. Productive-hoarding landowners tended to plant rice, a crop requiring harder work but promising higher profit. Receptive landholders tended to plant sugarcane, a crop requiring less work but twice the time to grow, and promising less profit. Overall, support was provided for the general hypothesis that "social character is the result of the adaptation of human nature to given socioeconomic conditions" (p. 230).

Interesting Books on Popular Issues

Fromm dealt directly with sweeping societal, ethical, and political issues, including those of the great 20th-century socioeconomic systems. Countless people have been influenced by his best-selling books. *Escape from Freedom* (1941) introduced a novel idea that was alien to democratic people at the time. Contrary to the "universal human desire to be free," all people at some times, and some people all the time, may desire to relinquish their freedom to "the state" or to another person. *The Sane Society* (1955) discusses the insanity of many societies and offers some alternatives. *The Art of Loving* (1956), entitled like current self-help books, taught people that to be in love is not merely to desire another person. It is becoming one with another but remaining oneself. His 1973 book, *The Anatomy of Human Destructiveness*, is a cogent and provocative commentary on the forces promoting life and death in contemporary culture. It is a chronicle of the evil and sickness that characterized such necrophilous figures as Nazi leaders Hitler and Himmler, the architects of the holocaust. His 1976 book, *To Have or to Be?*, discusses humankind's critical need to control irrational social forces and proposes guidelines for a new society.

Limitations

Fromm may be regarded as more of a philosopher than a scientific theorist. His theory consists of rather isolated categories of concepts that are not systematically related to one another, for example, those under the category-labels "needs" and "character types." In fact, there appears to be no conceptual glue capable of sticking these distinct categories of concepts together. They deal with different domains, in the one case the psychological realm, in the other, the social arena. At best, Fromm writes about "needs" in the context of "social character." Even here he does not make a direct conceptual link between categories in the manner that Freud ties id, ego, and superego to the psychosexual stages.

Also troublesome is the apparent abandonment or redefinition of major concepts somewhere between 1955 (*The Sane Society*) and 1973 (*The Anatomy of Human Destructiveness*). The perfectly meaningful needs "relatedness," "identity," and "transcendence" are displaced by the equally important "unity," "effectiveness," and "excitation/stimulation." Fromm may have intended "unity" as a replacement for "identity" and "effectiveness" as a substitute for "transcendence" which, in 1973, he dismissed in a footnote. The newer concepts are unique and worthwhile, but they do seem to overlap with the earlier notions that they may have been intended to replace. While "excitation/stimulation" seems a reasonable addition in view of developments in neuroscience, the apparent abandonment of the useful notion "relatedness" is difficult to explain—and Fromm does not explain it.

A theory that changes for reasons other than in response to hard evidence belongs more in the realm of philosophical speculation than science.

Fromm's social character types, as interesting as they are, nevertheless involve serious shortcomings. To confirm that a person has a *trait*, a component of personality, one must be able to look at the person's behavior in a given situation and assume that it will *generalize* to many other different situations. Only then, it is assumed, can one say the person has a trait corresponding to the behavior. Personality psychologists have had major difficulties demonstrating that such a generalization is warranted (Allen, 1988a, 1988b; Allen & Potkay, 1981, 1983a). People show a tendency to vary in their behavioral performances from one situation to the next and from one occasion to the next. If making the critical generalization at the individual level involves considerable risk, how much more cautious must we be in generalizing a social character type to many if not most members of a society? Given that people vary within themselves from occasion to occasion, as total persons they certainly must differ one from the other to a large degree. In view of the great variability within and among individuals, it is tenuous to assume that many, much less most, members of a society are "marketing types," or "receptive types," or any other type. Without much firm evidence—and there is little available—it simply is unreasonable to believe that even a simple majority of any large society's population share the same type. Thus, *The Handbook of Social Psychology* through its first two editions alluded to this problem of generalization in its chapter on "national character," which was acknowledged to be equivalent to "social character" (Lindzey, 1954; Lindzey & Aronson, 1969). Apparently the problem became insurmountable. By the third edition, the chapter on "national character" was deleted (Lindzey & Aronson, 1985).

In regard to scientific backing for Fromm's theory, a computer search failed to turn up current, scientific research done to support "psychosocial psychoanalysis." Either Fromm's concepts are difficult to transform into concrete terms so they can be studied scientifically, or they are too alien to modern scientific thinking to be of interest to contemporary sociopsychological scientists. Only when and if Fromm's theory generates scientific data can it be legitimately called "scientific."

Fromm's overemphasis on the negative side of human nature and culture was determined, in part, by factors associated with the German militarism and anti-semitism present during his formative years. Other social and individual influences may have contributed as well, for example, the childhood experiences of isolation and disturbances noted in his biography. Whatever the reasons for this pessimistic outlook, one could certainly argue that it is not an accurate picture of reality. Perhaps Fromm, like Freud, was wrong in depicting humans as struggling to overcome the evil, misery, and conformity that, he thought, constitutes their basic nature.

Conclusions

Maybe Fromm *was* more of a philosopher than a scientific theorist. Nevertheless, he was an original thinker and one of our most helpful commentators on modern life. Perhaps his concepts have received little attention because they are complex and thus difficult to study, not because they are unimportant. Also, maybe he was realistic rather than pessimistic. In addition, the Mexican village study shows that even a small village can have many types and combinations of types; all members of a society do not necessarily fall under the same social character type.

Fromm had a talent for selecting the very topics that interest people the most. Further, he could get right to the heart of problems with human nature and with modern societies. As a person, Fromm inspired love and admiration from his friends and colleagues. "I can see his piercing blue eyes full of understanding, of love, expressive of his being. . . . They could cry with the pain of others or Fromm's own pain, but they also knew how to laugh to tears at some funny or jocular event. His tears or his laughter touched the heart of the other" (Silva-Garcia, 1989, p. 245).

He was also a pioneer. As an early psychological humanist he did much to shape current humanistic thought, the topic of the next two chapters. His conceptions of love, productivity, and union with other people and nature were nutrients added to the fertile soil out of which psychological humanism grew. Unfortunately, the humanistic theorists whose ideas you will consider next have made little effort to remind us of Fromm's contributions. Therefore, in beginning to read the chapters on humanism, you will need to actively recall his groundbreaking ideas.

Summary Points

1. Fromm praised Freud, but took a sociopsychological stance, a natural position for one whose training was academic rather than medical. Fromm was born into a "neurotic" German family of Jewish descent. The suicide of a young woman following the death of her father led Fromm to Freud. The massive destruction and governmental doubletalk associated with World War I shaped his humanistic and antiwar orientations.

2. Each of us has a "frame of orientation," a cognitive map of our worlds that helps us make sense of puzzling matters. We all also have "objects of devotion": goals that give meaning to our existence. Relatedness is the necessary need to unite with other living beings that can take on two symbiotic forms: (1) one person masochistically submits to another and (2) one person sadistically dominates another. The positive alternative is mature love in which there is union with another, but maintenance of one's personal integrity.

3. In rootedness, the alternatives are destructive pursuit of substitutes for that secure, dependent state represented by the womb or finding new roots in the brotherhood of man. Identity is the need to be aware of oneself as a separate entity. Tragically we tend to use nations, races, or religions as sources of identity. Unity is a sense of inner oneness. We can seek it through the quest for power, fame, and property. Having failed to achieve unity, we may turn to some drug or passion. The productive alternative is love and reason.

4. Transcendence is the act of transforming one's accidental and passive role of creature into that of an active and purposeful creator. The alternative to creativity is destruction. Effectiveness is the need to compensate for "being in a strange and overpowering world." To be effective is to accomplish and to resist parental domination. If we cannot be effective through love of others, we can effect others by causing them to suffer.

5. Excitation and stimulation is the nervous system's need to be "exercised." The brain must be stimulated even during sleep. Needed sensory input is of two kinds: (1) simple and (2) activating. People differ among themselves: the essence of "personality." However, character, based on the individual's relatedness to the world, was more emphasized by Fromm. Individual character is a personal pattern of behavior that is deeply rooted in habits and opinions.

6. Fromm postulated six social character types, five non-productive and one productive. Each is cast in terms of assimilation and socialization. The non-productive types are divided into two pairs and one isolated type. One of two symbiotic non-productive types is receptive—oriented to experience the source of all good as being outside oneself. People of this type take from and depend on others, they do not give. They show unusual loyalty to their providers and may display sacrifice, duty, and love regarding the powerful people who care for them.

7. A second symbiotic type is exploitive. This type grabs, steals, and manipulates and is cynical, suspicious, and jealous. One of two "withdrawal" types is hoarding. They build a fortress, take inside what is theirs, and allow others to enter only if they will become possessions. A second withdrawal type is marketing—oriented to an exchange of goods for objects of value or services. These people are overwhelmed by the supply and demand economies in which they are immersed. They seek to take on personality traits that will "sell."

8. The last non-productive type is necrophilous—engrossed by death. The necrophilous person extracts a feeling of power and elation from vicariously or directly participating in the transformation of life into death. Necrophilous themes show up in dreams in the form of mechanically paying homage to the dead, envisioning oneself in possession of the power to destroy the world, and seeing people as robots whose aliveness can be turned off or on. Societies ruled by the despots of World War II and present nations ruled by war lovers provide fertile ground for this type.

9. People of the productive orientation have an attitude of relatedness to the world, and themselves, that encompasses reasoning, loving, and working. They break down walls between people and relate to others in terms of care, responsibility, respect, and knowledge. Out of thoughts about the productive type came Fromm's ideas about well-being. Fromm saw the family as an institution headed by parents who transmit their society's atmosphere and spirit to children.

10. Oral personality is due to the personality entity of receptive character that feeds back on physiology to create an "oral language of the body." Likewise, the Oedipus complex arises from a struggle for freedom from parental authority. Fromm's research in a Mexican village produced evidence of three character mixtures. His books dealt with sweeping issues that were of interest to many people. However, his theory is more philosophical than scientific and lacks coherence. Further, concepts tended to drop out of his theory and new ones entered with little explanation. Fromm's social character types entail severe difficulties and his theory has received little scientific support. Nevertheless, he was a warm person, an original thinker, and a pioneer humanist.

Running Comparison

Theorist	Fromm in Comparison
Freud	He was ambivalent about Freud's scientific contributions, de-emphasized biological causation, thought the Oedipal complex was due to a struggle for freedom from parents, but talked about free association, transference, and insight and partially agreed that religion is an illusion. His social character types bore some resemblance to Freud's adult, fixated types and Thanatos. He thought that personality caused physiological reactions, rather than the other way round.
Jung	Like Jung (and Adler) he was heavily influenced by WWI, and willing to talk about abstractions such as value, ethics, and meaning. Identifying self with social roles was akin to Jung's personas. He also believed that people are born with something; they are not like blank tablets.
Erikson	His productive love is similar to Erikson's care of the adulthood stage.
Carl Rogers	Transcendence was akin to some of Rogers' humanistic ideas (and Maslow's). Like Rogers (and Skinner), he was concerned about creativity.
Abraham Maslow and Henry A. Murray	Like these two theorists, he was concerned about needs.

Essay/Critical Thinking Questions

1. How *might* Fromm have been affected by war in contrast to the way he was, in fact, affected? In answering, retrace Fromm's experiences, in his school days and at other times.

2. Fromm was a socialist. Can you see anything he did with his point of view that has concrete implications? If not, you might want to argue, and illustrate, that his political orientation was too poorly developed—or too ambiguous—to inspire any concrete applications.

3. Select one of Fromm's needs, the one that you think fits reality the best. Can you illustrate how it has been manifested in your own experience, direct or indirect?

4. Can you describe a symbiotic relationship from your experience? Select a couple from your experience who have such a relationship and describe the way they interact.

5. Which social character type fits your society best? Defend your decision with examples.

6. Could you argue that a certain historical figure was a necrophilous type? Select a figure—other than the ones listed in the text—and give examples that show this individual to be necrophilous.

7. Could you do number 6 over again, but this time select a figure who is a productive type? Be sure to use examples.

8. Look at your own community, the one you grew up in. What social character fits it best? If more than one type fits, what are the types? Give examples.

9. Can you defend the application of a social character type to an entire society? Argue that a type might be reasonably seen as fitting a whole society, or suggest why it will never fit everyone.

10. What was Fromm's most important contribution? Select a contribution and tell why it is likely to live on in the years to come.

9

EVERY PERSON IS TO BE PRIZED: CARL ROGERS

- Is it possible to regard everyone you encounter in an unconditionally positive manner?
- What happens when what you experience is out of tune with your self-concept?
- Is there anything psychologists can do to make world peace more likely?
- Are therapists doing their jobs if they refuse to offer the people they serve any advice?
- Should therapists and the people they serve be equal partners in the therapeutic process?

Psychologists often classify personality theories into four major categories: the psychoanalytic tradition begun by Freud; the behavioral tradition, represented by B.F. Skinner; the humanistic tradition, represented in this chapter by Carl Rogers and in the next chapter by Abraham Maslow; and the cognitive tradition covered in subsequent chapters. Rogers is one of the leading figures in modern psychology because of the impact he has had on so many psychologists, professionals from other disciplines, and laypeople. His ideas have also received more systematic research, study, and validation than those of any other humanistic psychologist, and possibly more than some other theorists covered in this book.

Rogers, the Person

Carl Ransom Rogers was born on January 8, 1902, in Oak Park, Illinois. The fourth of six children, he was "tender and easily hurt, yet feisty and even sarcastic in his own way," since this was necessary to survive in family give-and-take (Kirschenbaum, 1979, p. 5). His home atmosphere was marked by fundamentalist religious practices, little social mixing, and a firm belief in the virtue of hard work. Carl even recalled experiencing a slight feeling of "wickedness" while drinking his first bottle of soda pop.

Carl was a lonely, "solitary boy, who read incessantly, and went all through high school with only two dates" (Rogers, 1961, p. 6). An outstanding student, he was nicknamed "Mr. Absent-Minded Professor" by his practical, do-it-now family. He loved reading the Bible and adventure stories, as well as creating stories of his own. During adolescence, he became fascinated with night-flying moths, which he observed and bred year round, and he enjoyed reading advanced, scientific books on agriculture.

> *There was no one to tell me that Morison's* Feeds and Feeding *was not a book for a fourteen-year-old, so I ploughed through its hundreds of pages learning how experiments were conducted—how control groups were matched with experimental groups, how conditions were held constant by randomizing procedures, so that the influence of a given food on meat production or milk production could be established. I learned how difficult it is to test a hypothesis. I acquired a knowledge of and a respect for the methods of science in a field of practical endeavor. (Rogers, 1961, p. 6)*

As an undergraduate at the University of Wisconsin, Rogers majored in agriculture and history. Later he dropped these initial majors, became quite religious, and began a curriculum aimed at the ministry. He was one of 12 American students selected to travel to China for a World Student Christian Federation Conference. It proved "a most important experience" in stretching his thinking and teaching him that sincere and honest people could have very different beliefs. His newfound independence of thought caused "great pain and stress" in his relationship with his parents, but "looking back on it I believe that here, more than at any other one time, I became an independent person" (Rogers, 1961, p. 7).

In 1924, Rogers married Helen Elliott, a classmate of his in second grade and his first date in college. An art major, Helen was a gentle, straightforward person whose good sense and willingness to think openly about real issues appealed to Rogers. Her "steady and sustaining love and companionship during all the years since has been a most important and enriching factor in my life" (Rogers, 1961, p. 7). Carl credits their two children, David and Natalie, with "teaching me far more about individuals, their development, and their relationships than I could ever have learned professionally" (Rogers, 1961, p. 12). David later became an administrator in a medical setting, and Natalie worked with her father as a co-therapist in encounter groups.

Rogers studied religion at Union Theological Seminary, which had the most liberal such program in the country. However, Teachers College, Columbia University was right across the street. He enrolled there and soon drifted into child psychology, "just following the activities which interested me" (Rogers, 1961, p. 9). After receiving his Ph.D. in 1928, he worked for several years at a child-guid-

ance center in Rochester, N.Y. During these
early professional years, Rogers soaked up
the views of Freud and his followers. He
found these ideas to be in great conflict
with the rigorous, experimental aspects of
his academic training, and with his work as
a professional helper. Relying on his own
clinical experiences with people, he began
formulating a person-centered point of
view. He thought the person needing help
should choose the direction of personality
change. Unlike traditional psychoanalysts,
he would not adopt the role of authoritarian
doctor in relation to a patient, because "it is
the [person] who knows what hurts, what
directions to go, what problems are crucial, what
experiences have been deeply buried" (Rogers,
1961, pp. 11–12). In fact, he rejected the **medical**

Carl Rogers

model, the idea that people with psychological problems are sick and need some
sort of treatment, at least analogous to medication, that will make them normal
again (Rogers, 1987a). This orientation was reflected in his use of the word *client*
instead of patient. He did not want to bring clients back to normal, that is, back to
average. Instead he endorsed the **growth model**: he wanted to help people
"remove whatever blocks to growth exist" so they could move beyond being normal or average (p. 40).

In subsequent years, Rogers held teaching, therapy, and administrative positions at Ohio State University, the University of Chicago, and the University of
Wisconsin. In 1947, he served as president of the American Psychological Association. He was the first psychologist in the association's history to receive both the
Scientific Contribution Award and the Distinguished Professional Contribution
Award. His fellow psychologists recognize him as an innovative pioneer who has
made a lasting impression on psychology. References to Rogers as a "respected
gadfly" and a person willing "to stand up and be counted" reflect lifelong themes
of independence, openness to experience, and self-trust.

Rogers, in the years before he died, continued to work very actively in La Jolla,
California, at the Center for Studies of the Person, which he co-founded: "The days
are not long enough to accomplish my purposes" (communication to Charles R.
Potkay, May 9, 1985). Rosalind Cartwright, one of his former colleagues, has spoken of him as a living example of his own theory, "a man who has continued to
grow, to discover himself, to test himself, to be genuine, to review his experiences,
to learn from it, . . . to live honestly, fully, in the best human sense" (Kirschenbaum,
1979, p. 394).

*So, who am I? I am a psychologist whose primary interest, for many years, has
been in psychotherapy. . . . I rejoice at the privilege of being a midwife to a new*

personality—as I stand by with awe at the emergence of a self, a person, as I see a birth process in which I have had an important and facilitating part. (Rogers, 1961, pp. 4–5)

Carl Rogers died unexpectedly on February 4, 1987 following surgery for a broken hip (Gendlin, 1988). At the time he had been particularly energetic and effective. In his last years he traveled the world, from South Africa to the Soviet Union with a stop off in Northern Ireland, in order to promote world peace and an end to conflict between warring groups (see Rogers & Ryback, 1984; Rogers & Malcolm, 1987; Rogers & Sanford, 1987; Rogers, 1987b). Fortunately, he published a number of articles during these final years. Many of them are used in the pages that follow to help me help you better understand this extraordinary individual and his contributions to people everywhere.

BOX 9.1   The Real Rogers

Being a world famous person, a figure larger than life, Rogers came to be regarded in stereotypic fashion. Textbook writers and teachers of sophomores have come to view him as someone

1. who never became angry, much less directed verbal aggression to someone during therapy
2. who believed in absolute equality of therapist and client
3. who never showed strong emotion during therapy
4. who believed that empathy was a passive process in which the therapist merely listens to clients and simply becomes a mirror in which they can see their own emotions
5. who regarded himself as a counselor and was heavily identified with that area.

None of these perceptions of Rogers were true, at least not in the absolute terms they have been stated in written and oral communications.

While conducting conflict resolution groups composed of black and white South Africans, Rogers became enraged when a white psychologist claimed that

one of the young black revolutionaries was just trying to "get attention" (Hill-Hain & Rogers, 1988). "That was just grossly untrue . . . one white guy got up and was going to hit him and I exploded at him too" (p. 62). In the same interview Rogers said, "I draw the line when I feel that one person is hurting another person in the group" (p. 65). He also referred to this event when making the point that no one is always able to step into another person's emotional shoes, not even himself. "That's why I offered no apology for exploding at [the psychologist]" (p. 65).

Rogers agreed with a critic's condemnation of person-centered therapists who rigidly show unqualified commitment to equality between the therapist and client and absolute commitment to offering no guidance during therapy. "I totally agree with her . . . in deploring the inauthentic, mechanical, wooden, dogmatic, client-centered therapist. In fact, I probably feel worse about such therapists than they do, because I feel personally offended" (Rogers, 1987c). However, he went on to further address the issue of equality. He indicated that before sessions, he would wonder, " 'Can I be totally *present* to this client? Can I *be* with

BOX 9.1 *Continued*

him or her?' . . . It would never occur to me to ask myself, 'Can I make this relationship an equal one?' " (p. 38). In fact, relationships in Rogerian therapy sometimes are not equal; they are tilted in the direction of the client or person. If Rogers and an African-American person were in therapy, as was sometimes the case when he was at the University of Chicago, he would give himself over to being a student undergoing instruction in the African-American experience. Only when an African-American client communicated that Rogers was adequately schooled would he attempt to feel as one with him or her.

During one of his South African group sessions, Rogers was strongly affected when a key black participant left the group (Hill-Hain & Rogers, 1988). As he sat on the floor, in the middle of the group, feeling the pain of South African blacks, he began to cry. It was not because others were in tears. It was because he felt like *"one of the group* in every sense" (p. 68). This kind of reaction was rare for him—"I've been in enough groups that it takes quite a lot to really touch me personally" (p. 68)—but again, he had no apologies.

In an article published after his death, Rogers wrote of empathy: "It is regarded superficially; it is regarded as passive when you just sit back and listen. To be really empathic is one of the most active experiences I know. You have to really understand what it feels like to this person in this situation. . . . To really let oneself go into the inner world of this other person is one of the most active, difficult, and demanding things that I know" (Rogers, 1987a, p. 45).

Rogers is often identified with "counseling," a multidisciplinary pursuit often practiced by non-psychologists and persons without doctorates. Even the long-time colleague who wrote Rogers' obituary regarded Rogers as a founder of counseling as a discipline, and considered him highly identified with counseling (Gendlin, 1988). In response to Gendlin's "fine memorial," Donald E. Super (1989), who had known Rogers since 1935, acknowledged counseling's debt to Rogers as well as the fact that Rogers' therapy section was called the Chicago Counseling Center and that his 1942 book was entitled *Counseling and Psychotherapy.* Then he wrote, "But Carl remained a psychotherapist, out of the mainstream of counseling psychology, a member of the Clinical but not of the Counseling Division [of the American Psychological Association]" (Super, 1989, p. 1161).

Rogers' View of the Person

Rogers' point of view revolves around a subdiscipline of psychology he helped to found. **Humanistic psychology** emphasizes the present experience and essential worth of the whole person, promotes creativity, intentionalism, free choice, and spontaneity, and fosters the belief that people can solve their own psychological problems. It gained momentum during the 1950s and early 1960s with the publication of several important books (Maslow, 1954, 1959, 1962; Buhler, 1962; Rogers, 1961, 1970) and a flagship journal, the *Journal of Humanistic Psychology,* founded in 1961. Proponents of humanistic psychology proclaimed their movement a "major breakthrough," because of the primary importance it placed on understanding the entire person, "the functioning and experience of a whole human being" (Bugental, 1964, p. 25). This emphasis also characterizes psychology's holistic (Angyal, 1965), organismic (Goldstein, 1939), and Gestalt (Perls, 1969) points of view, in which every person is understood in a comprehensive and integrative manner as being more than the simple sum of his or her parts (Kohler, 1947).

Humanistic psychology emerged from two other philosophical orientations. **Existential psychology** is an approach to understanding each person's most immediate experience, the conditions of his or her existence, and the necessity of exercising freedom of choice in a chaotic world (Binswanger, 1963; Boss, 1963; Kierkegaard, 1954; May, Angel, & Ellenberger, 1958; Merleau-Ponty, 1963; van Kaam, 1963, 1965, 1969). The origin of humanistic psychology was closely tied to developments in existential psychology. Existentialists encourage psychologists to get inside each person's world, to understand how that person lives, moves, and experiences his or her "being-in-the-world" (Heidegger, 1949). The critical existential concept *being* refers to a condition that is unique to each entity, whether it is a person or a grain of sand, and that transcends the particular qualities of the entity (size, weight, color). Being can not be assessed by the usual scientific or psychoanalytic methods. It can only be intuitively grasped.

Existentialists also encourage psychologists to value consciousness and personal responsibility (Frankl, 1963). Human freedom is defined not as freedom *from* responsibility but freedom *to* accept responsibility. Thus, one cannot rely on upbringing, early experience, heredity, or present environment to shape oneself. One must make oneself. This rather total responsibility for oneself can be burdensome and even frightening (Sartre, 1957). For this reason, existentialists often write about nothingness, alienation, despair, absurdity, and anxiety.

Although humanistic psychologists have been influenced by the existential concept of personal responsibility, their outlook is typically more positive. Humanists stress the unique capacities of each individual for self-realization and personal growth, not their despair, alienation, and anxiety. They assign greater importance than other personality theories to the study of choice, joy, love, creativity, and authenticity. In contrast to proponents of classic or methodological behaviorism (Watson, 1930), humanistic psychologists do not believe that humans begin their lives as blank sheets of paper on which the environment writes its text. Instead, similar to Fromm and Jung, they see the aim of each person's life as an unfolding of inherent powers present in human nature. They stress the uniquely human aspects of experience, including personal choice, interpersonal relationships, intentions, purposes, and transcendental or spiritual experiences (Bugental, 1964).

The second source of humanistic psychology is a method of addressing reality. **Phenomenology** involves an attitude of discovery that encompasses a search for essential issues, an emphasis on consciousness, the necessity of describing experience, and a desire to grasp reality as each individual uniquely perceives it. This subjective approach to knowledge and understanding is a major characteristic of humanistic psychology (Husserl, 1961; Heidegger, 1949). "The only reality I can possibly know is the world as I perceive and experience it at this moment. The only reality you can possibly know is the world as YOU perceive and experience it

at this moment. And the only certainty is that those perceived realities are different. There are as many 'real worlds' as there are people!" (Rogers, 1980, p. 102).
This is not to say that there is no objective world, one we can all agree on. Rather
it acknowledges the subjective world and gives it at least equal status with the
objective world.

A person's experiences are real for that person at that particular moment in time.
This is why Rogers regularly included such qualifiers as "real for me" and "based
on my experience" in his writings and conversation. On the one hand, it is up to
each person to decide what he or she is to do or to be, based on an individualized
vantage point of perception and experience. On the other hand, a person should
leave how other persons behave and how they lead their lives up to them. Thus,
each person must assume personal responsibility for his or her own decisions and
no one else's. Some psychologists believe that Rogers is wrong to refuse the role of
expert therapist and the answering of clients' questions such as "What do you think
I should do?" Right up to the last year of his life, Rogers refused to accede to critics'
wishes that he tell others how to live their lives (Hill-Hain & Rogers, 1988).

Apart from questions of scientific truth, the phenomenological approach has
particular implications for studying persons. If we wish to understand a person,
we need to get inside his or her individual world of meaning. We do so by showing **empathy**, sensing and participating in the emotions of others. Thus, humanistic psychologists are less interested in studying behavior as a neurophysical event
than they are in investigating the meaning that each person attaches to what she or
he does.

As theorists and therapists, therefore, humanistic psychologists seek to
avoid "the sort of scientific detachment pretended to or achieved at great cost by
other orientations" (Bugental, 1964, p. 24). Rather they seek to validate their findings through subjective experience rather than relying solely on impersonal,
objective criteria such as statistical methods and experimental tests. This
approach has made it necessary to discover new methods for studying human
experience. Like Gordon Allport, humanistic psychologists typically emphasize
the *idiographic* approach: the belief that meaningful discoveries will come from
understanding one case at a time. As Rogers writes, "What is most personal is
most general" (1961, p. 26).

For Rogers, as well as other humanistic theorists, the most important matter
in the consideration of personality is the person as a whole, including the individual's conscious awareness, freedom to choose, self-determination, and quality of
experiences. His is an **organismic approach**, the human organism is viewed as a
total being whose physical, psychological, and spiritual aspects cannot be separated except by artificial means. In brief, it is the *person* who is placed first. This is
why Rogers' theory of therapy is now usually called the *person-centered* approach
(formerly it was "client-centered," a phrase still used by some therapists and
Rogers, even in his last articles; Rogers, 1987c; Super, 1989). The central hypothesis
of the person-centered orientation is that "individuals have within themselves vast
resources for self-understanding and for altering their self-concepts, basic attitudes, and self-directed behavior" (Rogers, 1980, p. 115). Further, these resources

can be tapped by providing "a definable climate of facilitative psychological attitudes" (p. 115).

Rogers thus differs from Freud in accenting the positive potentialities in human nature. The natural development of human beings is toward the "constructive fulfillment" of their inherent possibilities.

> *I am inclined to believe that fully to be a human being is to enter into the complex process of being one of the most widely sensitive, responsive, creative, and adaptive creatures on this planet.*
>
> *So when a Freudian such as Karl Menninger tells me (as he has, in a discussion of this issue) that he perceives man as "innately evil" or more precisely, "innately destructive," I can only shake my head in wonderment. (quoted in Kirschenbaum, 1979, p. 250)*

Rogers rejects the conception of learning he attributes to most universities. "A . . . unique element is that [my theory] is based on a learning that is experiential as well as cognitive. That is something that seems very hard for universities to accept. Most of the universities I know think that education goes on [only] from the neck up. . . . That is not so! Education may be limited to that, but learning is something else" (Rogers, 1987a, p. 39). This statement is another expression of the organismic approach.

Rogers recognized that his ideas have been heavily influenced by his relationships with clients in therapy. However, he believed that these experiences are representative of all human relationships. Psychotherapy relationships are only a special instance of interpersonal relationships in general, and "the same lawfulness" governs all such relationships (Rogers, 1961, p. 39). He has supported this belief by writing a number of popular books on such topics as freedom to learn in education (1969), encounter groups (1970), becoming marriage partners (1972), and the revolutionary impact of personal power (1977).

Basic Concepts: Rogers

Actualization

Concepts related to *actualization* are the foundation blocks of Rogers' humanistic approach. In its most general form, actualization is a biological phenomenon; in human beings, it becomes an active tendency toward actualization of the self.

The General Actualizing Tendency
All living things display the **general actualizing tendency**, an "inherent tendency of the organism to develop all its capacities in ways which serve to maintain or enhance the organism" (Rogers, 1959, p. 196). This constructive biological tendency is the "one central source of energy in the human organism," giving rise to all other motivations (Rogers, 1980, p. 123).

The actualizing tendency expresses itself through a wide range of behaviors, in response to a wide variety of needs. It has four significant characteristics:

1. It is *organismic*—a natural, biological, inborn predisposition reflected in the total functioning of every living being.
2. It is an *active* process. It accounts for the observation that organisms are always up to something, whether seeking food or sexual satisfaction, initiating, exploring, producing change in the environment, playing, or even creating.
3. It is *directional* rather than random or reactive; it inclines every form of life toward growth, self-regulation, fulfillment, reproduction, and independence from external control.
4. It is *selective*, meaning that not all of an organism's potentialities are necessarily developed (for example, the ability to bear pain).

Rogers illustrated the operation of the actualizing tendency using a boyhood observation. Recalling that his family stored its supply of winter potatoes in the basement, several feet below a window, he noted,

> *The conditions were unfavorable, but the potatoes would begin to sprout—pale white sprouts . . . these sad, spindly sprouts would grow . . . toward the distant light of the window. They were in . . . futile growth, a sort of desperate expression of the directional tendency. . . . They would . . . never mature, never fulfill their real potentiality. But under the most adverse circumstances they were striving to become. Life would not give up, even if it could not flourish. (Rogers, 1979/1983, p. 228)*

Self-Actualization

In addition to the general actualizing tendency, Rogers postulated a specifically human tendency. The tendency toward **self-actualization** is a person's lifelong process of realizing his or her potentialities to become a fully functioning person. The expression of self-fulfillment is the psychological entity that becomes actualized: "to be that self which one truly is" (Rogers, 1961, p. 166). The direction of self-actualization is toward "the good life," defined as whatever is *organismically valued* by the total person who is inwardly free to move in any direction.

Rogers (1961) associated the process of self-actualization with enhanced functioning in three areas. First, self-actualization involves an increased openness to **experience**, all the emotions, cognitions, and perceptions occurring to the organism at any given moment that potentially can be consciously considered. **Awareness** is the conscious apprehension of experience, which Rogers (1979/1983) sees as an important development in human evolution. Thus, a self-actualizing person is aware of and listens to inner feelings without being defensive.

Second, the self-actualizing person lives existentially, flowing spontaneously with each moment of life and participating fully in it. She or he is *time competent*, experiencing life in the "here and now," without rigid preconceptions that things must be the way they have been in the past and without needing to control how things should be in the future. Third, the self-actualizing person places greater trust in his or her organismic functions, intuitively doing what feels right after weighing all available information. She or he relies little on the past or on social conventions. In addition, the self-actualizing person shows an increased appreciation of free choice, creativity, the trustworthiness of human nature, and the richness of life.

The Importance of the Self

The concept of self-actualization suggests the central role played by the "self" in Rogers' theory. The existence of a self seems to be clearly implied by our everyday language: *"I* am in love." "Walking in the rain makes *me* feel good." "These clothes are not *me*." Belief in the importance of self is one of the distinguishing marks of humanistic psychologists. For Rogers (1947), the person's experience of self is a basic aspect of life. It forms and determines behavior. In fact, the construct of self is such an important part of Rogerian theory that some psychologists have designated it "self theory" (Patterson, 1961).

Rogers did not begin his theorizing by assuming the importance of the self in human experience. Rather, he started with a notion of the self as "a vague, ambiguous, scientifically meaningless term" no longer in vogue among respected psychologists (1959, p. 200). His ideas about the self emerged from his observations of therapy clients, who regularly expressed such ideas as "I wonder *who I am,"* "I don't want anyone to know the *real me,"* "I'm not being *my real self,"* "It feels good to let myself go and *just be myself.*"

Self as Self-Perceptions
Although Rogers has never formally defined personality, he did define **self**, the organized, consistent, conceptual whole composed of perceptions of the characteristics of the "I" or "me," the values attached to these perceptions, and the relationships of the "I" or "me" to various aspects of life (Rogers, 1959, p. 200). The definition reflects Rogers' basic commitment to the phenomenological approach. Its emphasis is clearly on the perceptual origins of self, in which one's *self* is a set of perceptions of one's self. Thus, for Rogers, the self was functionally equivalent to *self-concept.* It includes all of the individual's evaluations of his organismic functions and human relationships, "by which he tends to order and interpret his . . . experiences" (Shlien, 1970, p. 95). Also, relevant to *self* is how self-perceptions relate to other perceptions and to objects in the external world (Evans, 1975). To illustrate, a person may have the self-perception, "I am six feet tall." She may relate this to her perceptions of other people, as in "I am tall," and even place a value on her perception, as in "I am too tall."

The purpose of the exercise in Box 9.2 is to help you get closer to your own perceptions of your self.

**BOX 9.2   Adjective Descriptions of Your Actual
and Desired Self**

Instructions: On the left side of a sheet of paper, write down adjectives that best describe the self you are at the present time in your life (actual self). On the right side, write down adjectives that best describe the self you would like to be (ideal self). Work quickly, and be sure to write down single words that are found in the dictionary, not sentences, para- graphs, or words that you invent. Write down between 10 and 15 self-descriptive adjectives under each heading. Do not worry if some of your words seem con- tradictory; just write whatever adjectives best describe your actual and ideal self.

Your Actual Self   *Your Ideal Self*

Students in past research studies by Allen and Potkay typically wrote down about 10 adjectives when allowed to record as many as they wanted (see our 1983a book). How do you compare with them and how do your words compare with those of other students in class? In what ways are your descriptions of self *as you are* and self *as you would like to be* the same or different? What do you make of words that do and do not appear on both lists? Consider how you would go about transforming yourself from present self into ideal self.

Consistent with the implication that you are now a certain self (actual self) and may become another self (ideal self), Rogers believes that the self is best under- stood as a continuing process, not a fixed endpoint. Thus the self is very likely to be undergoing change. This is why a person may organize self-views in different ways at different points in time. You probably do not view yourself the same today as you did five years ago, and you likely have had the experience, "I used to think of myself that way, but now I think of myself in the opposite way."

Other people may not see you the same way you see yourself. A student at my university was quite surprised to learn of this discrepancy while doing a self-study as a term project. She had been asked to describe her true self with adjectives and then obtain adjective descriptions of her true self from her mother, father, boyfriend, and best girlfriend. The words she used to describe her own *self*—inse- cure, stubborn, impatient—were much more negative than those used by other persons in her life—intelligent, friendly, lovable. Her explanation was that "I failed to update my . . . self to match my true self of today" (Allen & Potkay, 1983a).

For Rogers, the **ideal self** is the self a person most values and desires to be. It is "the self-concept which the individual would most like to possess, upon which he places the highest value for himself" (Rogers, 1959, p. 100). Therefore, attaining the self-ideal is a major pre-condition for feelings of worth. Rogerians often have a person describe actual and ideal selves and then ask her or him to compare the two descriptions, just as you were asked to do. The closer the correspondence between a person's actual and ideal self, the greater the person's sense of self- acceptance and adjustment. You may regard the correspondence between your actual and ideal selves as indicating degree of self-acceptance and adjustment, but be cautious. Unless you know the typical degree of correspondence shown by many other people like yourself, you lack a good standard of comparison to use in evaluating your level of correspondence.

Congruence with Experience

Our self-concepts may be more or less in agreement with experiences related to self. When a person is in a state of **congruence** his or her self-concept and experiences relating to self are consistent. The actualizing tendency is then relatively whole and unified, and the person shows mature integration and psychological adjustment. By contrast, **incongruence** reflects an inconsistency between self-concept and experiences relating to self. Self-perceptions may be inaccurate, because of beliefs that are rigid, distorted, unrealistic, or overgeneralized. Inaccuracy may also result from the defensive tactic **denial** which involves the inability to recognize or accept the existence of an experience that has occurred. It is reflected in the reaction "No! It can't be!" to a rumor circulating among office workers that one has failed to receive a desperately sought-after promotion. **Distortion** involves a reinterpretation of an experience so as to make it consistent with how one wants things to be, as in the reaction "You are all wrong. Yesterday the boss was very friendly to me." You can see that Rogers, like Freud, believed that people have defenses against threatening experiences.

Inaccurate self-perceptions can contribute to experiences of inner confusion, tension, and maladaptive behavior. Rogers cites the example of a boy who had been observed lifting girls' skirts. When questioned, the boy denied what he had done, stating that it "couldn't" have been he. The boy was in a state of incongruence. His perceptions led him to maintain a self-concept inconsistent with his actual experience. Because his self-concept did not include sexual feelings or desires, his organismic experiences of sexual curiosity and desire were in conflict with his self-concept. He shut out of his awareness behaviors, feelings, or attitudes inconsistent with his self-concept. The boy's denial reflected *defensiveness* aimed at maintaining the current structure of the self in the face of contradictory information (Rogers, 1959). It is a typical response when one's self-concept is threatened. "In the strictly technical sense, his self-picture couldn't do it, and didn't do it" (Rogers quoted in Evans, 1975, p. 17).

Movement toward growth and improved adjustment in this boy would require him to revise his self-concept toward congruence. The process undoubtedly would be accompanied by anxiety as the boy became aware of the incongruence between his self-concept and his experiences. The reason for the discomfort is that "each of us seeks to preserve the concept or picture that he has of himself and that a sharp change in that picture is quite threatening. Any change destroys some of the security that we feel we need" (Rogers quoted in Evans, 1975, p. 17). If the boy were able to lower his defenses, the new information about himself then could be incorporated as part of his self-concept. If not, *maladjustment* could occur with the boy remaining unaware of what is going on in himself. His growth and self-actualization would stagnate.

Personality Development: Three Favorable Conditions

What determines whether a person's self-concept becomes congruent or incongruent with experience? Rogers points to external circumstances, particularly of an interpersonal nature, under which personal growth is facilitated or blocked. His boyhood observation of his family's potatoes highlights the importance of environmental conditions as influences on the actualizing tendency of living things. The potatoes failed to realize their fullest potentials because of unfavorable conditions outside themselves.

Similarly, the interactions between persons and interpersonal environments represent an important aspect of human development. The actualization tendency points all people in the direction of becoming the persons they truly are, regardless of the social environment. However, certain interpersonal conditions facilitate actualization strivings, whereas others do not. Rogers' work with clients in therapy led him to identify three "necessary and sufficient" conditions for growth and change in personality. These three conditions are interrelated and may be best understood as general attitudes toward a person that are held by other people. When these conditions are present, persons become fully functioning, showing optimal maturity and adjustment.

Unconditional Positive Regard

All people have needs that can be fulfilled only by other people in human relationships. Chief among these is a universally learned need for **positive regard**, the experiencing of oneself as making a positive difference in the lives of other persons and as receiving warmth, liking, respect, sympathy, acceptance, caring, and trust from others (Rogers, 1959; Standal, 1954). This need is met when other people in a person's life provide **unconditional positive regard**, these people communicate, with no strings attached, that one is accepted, valued, worthwhile, and trusted, simply for being who one is. The person experiences the other's acceptance without feeling that it depends on his or her doing some "right" thing or having to be the way the other person thinks the person "should" be. No aspect of the person is judged "more or less worthy of positive regard than any other" (Rogers, 1959, p. 208). There is no generalized labeling of the person as "bad" or "good." Rather, the person feels unconditionally "prized," valued, and accepted, simply for being whoever he or she is.

However, there is another, less preferred way for a person to feel valued. Under this circumstance, positive regard is received only when the person meets certain *conditions of worth* set up by significant others. Here the individual feels prized in some respects, but not in others. She or he then avoids certain experiences judged by other people to be relatively "unworthy" and seeks out certain other experiences judged relatively "worthy." This occurs even if the person was once attracted to the "unworthy" experiences and repelled by the "worthy" experiences. This second way is "conditional" because it involves contingencies stated in if-then terms. Significant others say, in effect, "If you say or do the things I like or want, then I will value you and consider you important. If you don't, then I won't."

BOX 9.3 Rogers Related to Adler, Freud, and Jung

People who knew the works of Rogers and Adler could see a similarity. Rogers wrote of an encounter with Adler:

I had the privilege of meeting, listening to, and observing Dr. Alfred Adler. This was the winter of 1927–28, when I was an intern. . . . Accustomed as I was to the rather rigid Freudian approach of the Institute [where he was interning]—seventy-five-page case histories, and exhaustive batteries of tests before even thinking of "treating" a child—I was shocked by Dr. Adler's very direct and deceptively simple manner of relating to the child and the parent. It took me some time to realize how much I learned from him. [Ansbacher, 1990, p. 47]

Rogers apparently learned two important lessons from Adler. First, exhaustive case histories may be regarded as mechanical, cold, and unnecessary methods for getting to know a person. More warm and informal techniques will work as well or better. Second, a therapist need not spend many sessions indirectly probing the past of a client in order to understand her or him. One can jump right in and relate to the person during her or his *here and now*.

The passage referring to Adler also makes a "backdoor" reference to Freud. Obviously, Freud was thrust down Rogers' throat during the internship, a period of neophyte status when thoughtless acceptance is likely. Before he could begin to think of the person-centered approach he eventually adopted, Rogers had to rid himself of Freudian notions. That he did in the 1940s. During this time he was accused of "destroying the unity of psychoanalysis" by founding his client-centered approach to therapy and

of "violating the sanctity of the analytic relationship" when he used an early electronic device to record therapy sessions (Gendlin, 1988, p. 127). Reactions to these "heresies" helped Rogers make a clean and total break with Freudianism.

Campbell Purton, a Jungian enthusiast as a teen, began to become aware of common ground between Jung and Rogers when he later became a therapist and studied Rogers' ideas (Purton, 1989). Purton makes a reference to a particular aspect of Jungian therapy that is quite Rogerian, one that you may recall from the chapter on Jung. Jung anticipated Rogers by rejecting the authoritarian relationship between therapist and "patient" that was popularized by Freud. He worked with clients on a one-on-one basis and regarded them as partners. Often Jung participated in whatever he had asked clients to do.

There are other coincidences between Jung and Rogers (Purton, 1989). Both believed that the techniques used in therapy were of secondary importance. Helping the client was the primary concern. Jung had his "persona," Rogers his "facade": a front behind which people suffering from incongruence would frequently hide. Jung wrote of "individuation," a process somewhat similar to Rogers' "self-actualization." Both concepts involve "wholeness," "uniqueness," and "becoming one's own self."

Although there is little evidence that Rogers was aware of a debt to Jung, a pioneer who pre-dated him, it is still interesting to note that their ideas overlap a great deal. Both showed a deep and abiding belief in the worth of people. By contrast, Rogers was very aware of his debt to Adler and his disagreement with Freud.

When conditional acceptance characterizes the social environment, a child learns to behave and think in ways approved by others, especially parents. The child learns, "If I do what my parents want, then I will be loved. If I don't do what they want, then I won't be loved." With this kind of lesson, incongruence between self-perception and "who one is" will tend to occur. Under these circumstances one's actualizing tendency is likely to become blocked. Then denials and distortions of personal experiences that are disapproved by others are likely to occur. Also, acceptance of experiences that are incongruent with "who one is" becomes probable.

A common misconception about unconditional positive regard is that people who provide it to a person must always approve of everything the person says or does. To combat this misinterpretation, Rogers carefully distinguishes between the individual as a person and the individual's freely chosen values and behaviors. For example, while parents may prize their child, it is possible for them to do so without valuing all of the child's behaviors equally. They may express pride when their child shares a candy bar with a friend, or displeasure when their child bites a friend. However, their approval and disapproval would be in relation to the child's specific acts, not in relation to the child as a person. It is the sharing that is approved and the biting that is disapproved, not the child. Even though the parents might wish the child not to bite, biting does not lead to rejection of the child as a whole person. The child continues to be prized, regardless of his or her behavior.

Accurate Empathy

If a person is to achieve congruence of self-concept with his or her experience, therapists and other people must correctly "hear" what the individual is experiencing and refrain from judging it. Rogers believed the ability to understand another person is of "enormous" value. He found it "enriching to open channels whereby others can communicate their feelings, their private perceptual worlds, to me" (1961, p. 19). **Accurate empathy** is Rogers' term for the ability to accurately perceive the client's internal world in a non-evaluative way. Such empathic understanding goes beneath the surface of another person's words and actions, to inner feelings, attitudes, meanings, and motives.

Congruence in Interpersonal Relationships

In order for a person to grow, the therapist and significant other people must naturally and openly demonstrate their willingness and ability to be themselves in relationships with that person. This state of genuineness on the part of one person toward another was regarded as a kind of *congruence*: the two people feel the same level of comfort or emotional involvement with the issue they are considering. In therapy, the therapist must exhibit an openness to inner experiences in such a way that it conveys congruence with the client. Even an experienced therapist might admit to the client, "I find myself frightened because you are touching on feelings I have never been able to resolve myself" (Rogers, 1959). A therapist uncomfortable with some aspect of the relationship with the client would be considered incongruent if she or he remained unaware of the discomfort, avoided dealing with it, or communicated reactions opposite to what is real for him or her. Incongruence retards progress in therapy, because the wholeness of the therapist is not present in the relationship.

Developing Positive Self-Regard

Important change may occur when favorable conditions of personality development are present. When individuals receive unconditional positive regard from others, particularly during the formative years, they will develop **positive self-regard**, a favorable attitude toward themselves. This, in turn, allows them to develop their own values in accordance with their real experiences, independently of "approving" others. Although they will be aware of expectations concerning what they "should" do, they will trust their own judgments instead of being bound by others' conventions. Positive self-regard unlocks actualizing tendencies and allows individuals to become fully functioning humans.

By contrast, when others impose conditions of worth on an individual, experiences of positive self-regard become less likely. In this case, people's **locus of evaluation**, the source of evidence about themselves, does not lie within them but outside, in others. The judgments of others form the standard for evaluating an experience or object. A young woman's letter to Rogers (1980) illustrates locus of evaluation in others, rather than in oneself:

> I think that I began to lose me when I was in high school. I always wanted to go into work that would be of help to people but my family resisted, and I thought they must be right. Things went along smoothly for everyone else for four or five years until about two years ago. I met a guy that I thought was ideal. Then nearly a year ago I took a good look at us, and realized that I was everything that he wanted me to be and nothing that I was. I have always been emotional. . . . My fiance would tell me that I was just mad or just happy and I would say okay. . . . Then when I took this good look at us I realized that I was angry because I wasn't following my true emotions.

Procedures for Changing Personality

Person-Centered Therapy

Rogers' ideas about personality development, when applied to person-centered therapy, involve the assumption that, if certain conditions exist, then a characteristic process of personality change will occur (Rogers, 1959). These conditions are positive regard, accurate empathic understanding, and congruence. They also include the client's anxiety and motivation to change. The specific techniques of person-centered therapy are designed to reflect these basic premises.

Research has shown that the direction of change for clients in Rogerian therapy is from a personality that is fixed, separated, and tied to the past to one that is spontaneous, integrated, and flowing toward experiences occurring in the present. Seven characteristic stages of this process unfold during therapy according to Rogers (1961). It is impossible to capture all aspects of these complex and comprehensive stages as experienced by the client, but the following observations are representative:

Stage 1. The client's communications are mostly about externals, not about self.

Stage 2. The client describes feelings but does not recognize or "own" them personally.

Stage 3. The client talks about self as an object, often in terms of past experiences.

Stage 4. The client experiences feelings in the present, but mainly just describes them, with distrust and fear, rather than expressing them directly.

Stage 5. The client experiences and expresses feelings freely in the present; feelings "bubble up" into awareness with some desire to experience them.

Stage 6. The client accepts his or her feelings in all their immediacy and richness.

Stage 7. The client trusts new experiences and relates to others openly and freely.

If this process occurs, then certain personality and behavioral changes will occur. These changes, the outcomes of therapy, lead the person toward greater self-actualization. They reflect increases in congruence, openness to experience, adjustment, correspondence between actual and ideal self, positive self-regard, and acceptance of self and others.

An example of a therapeutic session illustrates the course of person-centered therapy. Imagine a successful lawyer who works 60–70 hours a week but is unsatisfied with his life. In an early session, the client begins by talking about trivia not really related to his concerns. "I can't understand why my kids are so materialistic. They just want more junk . . . everything they see on TV. I'm just the 'horn of plenty,' satisfying their every whim."

The therapist replies, "So you feel that your kids just use you to satisfy their needs." The remark reflects the client's feeling and emotions back to him so they may be affirmed, a process that makes them more available for reconsideration.

The client continues in this vein for a time and then, in a later session, he begins to express his more central emotions, but acts as if they are not his own. "It's funny, today, how people end up with careers that are unrelated to what they want to do or are capable of doing. I know this guy who is selling insurance and making a fortune, but living for a camping trip on the weekend. He's an outdoor type . . . wanted to be a forest ranger." The therapist nods, indicating that the client is understood.

On a later date the client begins to talk about himself, really for the first time. However, he talks about the past as if to analyze another person rather than his present self. "I can remember trying to copy the Mona Lisa when I was a kid. How naive can you get! Here was this little kid trying to act like a great artist. I did some pretty good drawings on my own . . . my teachers said so, but they weren't good enough to satisfy me." The therapist listens intently and utters "uh huh" to communicate that the client's feelings are appreciated.

After several sessions, the client gets around to himself in the present, but he is merely descriptive rather than analytical. "I still paint, you know. Sometimes late at night . . . sometimes on weekends. Did you know that I have an arrangement with an art gallery? I've sold some of my paintings, but didn't get much . . . can't make a living that way. They want me to come in with them . . . invest, you know, in the gallery and help manage it. Small change that would be . . . but you know I'm really happy when I'm there among those paintings . . . get a bigger kick out of selling a painting for a hundred bucks than settling a case for a hundred thousand."

The therapists indicates, "You feel that painting is very enjoyable and that you have had some success at it." The client begins to recognize how important art is to him.

In subsequent sessions, the client comes back to art more and more and talks about his current feelings to a greater and greater extent. "Well today was something else. I took off from work early and went to the gallery. . . . I have a corner in a back room where I can paint. I'm working on something right now that really excites me. I'll have to show it to you. I know now that art is a part of me . . . heart and soul."

In the last sessions before termination of therapy the lawyer hardly mentions law. All he can talk about is his latest work of art and his plans to slowly substitute hours at the gallery for hours at the office. Here he shows awareness of courses of action that are more in tune with his actualizing self. "I have enough money saved to help make a go of the gallery. I find that my younger colleagues take care of the law practice quite nicely. You know I've never been happier. My kids don't seem so greedy anymore. Let them have what they want. . . . I'll give them all I can. They'll eventually find themselves."

BOX 9.4 Rogers Describes "Carl Rogers"

Earlier in this chapter, you were asked to write down adjectives that described your real self and your ideal self. How do you think Carl Rogers would describe himself if he were asked to check off adjectives that best represent his "self"?

A few years before Rogers died, Charles Potkay asked him if he would be willing to complete a standard measure of self-description, the Adjective Check List (ACL) (Gough & Heilbrun, 1980). The ACL is a respected personality measure characterized by theoretical neutrality, a large research base, widespread

use, and convenience of administration. It consists of 300 adjectives often used for purposes of individual description. The person is asked to read each word quickly and indicate "each one you would consider to be self-descriptive."

Although Rogers had "many reservations," he was "somewhat intrigued" by the project and filled out the ACL form (personal communication to Potkay, 1983). (Rogers believes that personality assessment techniques do not convey a sense of the real person and may interfere with the development of genuine therapy relationships.)

BOX 9.4 *Continued*

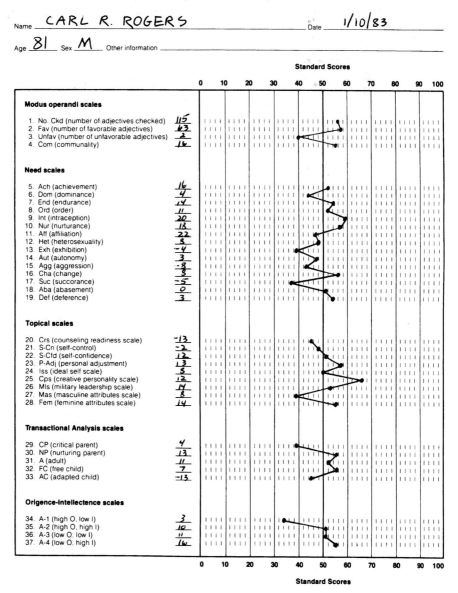

Profile Recording Sheet for the Adjective Check List

Name _CARL R. ROGERS_   Date _1/10/83_

Age _81_   Sex _M_   Other information _____

Standard Scores

Modus operandi scales

1. No. Ckd (number of adjectives checked) — 115
2. Fav (number of favorable adjectives) — 63
3. Unfav (number of unfavorable adjectives) — 2
4. Com (communality) — 16

Need scales

5. Ach (achievement) — 16
6. Dom (dominance) — 4
7. End (endurance) — 14
8. Ord (order) — 11
9. Int (intraception) — 20
10. Nur (nurturance) — 18
11. Aff (affiliation) — 22
12. Het (heterosexuality) — 8
13. Exh (exhibition) — -4
14. Aut (autonomy) — 3
15. Agg (aggression) — -8
16. Cha (change) — 8
17. Suc (succorance) — -5
18. Aba (abasement) — 0
19. Def (deference) — 3

Topical scales

20. Crs (counseling readiness scale) — -13
21. S-Cn (self-control) — -2
22. S-Cfd (self-confidence) — 12
23. P-Adj (personal adjustment) — 13
24. Iss (ideal self scale) — 8
25. Cps (creative personality scale) — 12
26. Mls (military leadership scale) — 14
27. Mas (masculine attributes scale) — 8
28. Fem (feminine attributes scale) — 14

Transactional Analysis scales

29. CP (critical parent) — 4
30. NP (nurturing parent) — 13
31. A (adult) — 11
32. FC (free child) — 7
33. AC (adapted child) — -13

Origence-Intellectence scales

34. A-1 (high O, low I) — 3
35. A-2 (high O, high I) — 10
36. A-3 (low O, low I) — 11
37. A-4 (low O, high I) — 16

Standard Scores

FIGURE 9.1   Rogers' Adjective Check List   *Continued*

BOX 9.4   *Continued*

A profile of Rogers' overall scores appears in Figure 9.1. The graph shows the pattern of Rogers' high and low scores on each of the 37 scales measured by the ACL. These dimensions are numbered and named in the column at the left of the figure. Using ACL guidelines for interpretation, "standard scores" of 50 are considered average, while scores of 60 or above and 40 or below are given more weight because they are one standard deviation above and below the mean, respectively. Thus, Rogers' highest score (scale #25) falls above the average, while his lowest score (scale #34) is below average. It should be noted that the meaningfulness of the profile is partially limited because the comparative norms used to plot it are derived from responses of 900 male students attending the University of California at Berkeley, not older adults or famous

psychologists. However, compared with the normative sample of college students, Carl Rogers' pattern of adjective descriptions reflects the following:

1. High creativity, intellectual quickness, and breadth of interests (scale #25)
2. Low impulsiveness and a firm stance on ethical issues (scale #34)
3. Emotional independence and effective goal-attainment (scale #17)
4. A relatively cautious approach to seeking public attention (scale #13)
5. Gentleness and high value placed on inner feelings (scale #27)
6. Tolerance of the fears and weaknesses of others, and a desire to bring people together (scale #29)
7. A low degree of unfavorable self-descriptions (scale #3)

Evaluation

General Contributions

Rogers has had great impact on personality psychology and psychotherapy. In particular, he has contributed to an understanding of persons, an appreciation of caring interpersonal relationships as factors in personality growth and therapeutic change, and demonstrations of scientific openness and theoretical flexibility.

Rogers phenomenological approach has had three major influences on understanding personality. First, it has allowed individual human beings to speak for themselves about the nature of their own personal experiences. Rogers has guided psychological professionals in suspending views as to what a person *should* be, in order to understand how a person actually *is*. He suggested that important information is likely to come less from authorities with professional training than from common people, during a democratic, grass-roots exchange.

Regarding scientific method, use of the Rogerian phenomenological approach has questioned psychology's so-called objective frameworks for understanding human behavior. These frameworks have sought to understand people from the outside: behaviorally, mechanistically, and impersonally. Rogers has doubted the existence of an absolute way of interpreting reality, and the desirability of even seeking such a narrow "truth" (Rogers, 1980). He paved the way for multiple inter-pretations of human experience, especially at the highest, most complete levels of self-actualization where individual differences seem greatest.

Second, Rogers has contributed to the understanding of personality by renewing interest in concepts of the *self*. New insights into the self have resulted from direct observations and therapeutic experiences with a broad spectrum of normal, maladjusted, and well-adjusted people. Installing concepts related to the self at the core of his theory makes it consistent with early philosophical traditions in U.S. psychology. William James (1890/1950), father of psychology in the United States, wrote of a "self of selves," a person's inner, conscious view of the sameness of his or her personality. However, under the influence of behaviorism, psychologists ignored early notions of the self (Jung), until the Rogers'-led humanists began to gain prominence.

Third, Rogers has tried to enhance our understanding of people by emphasiz-ing trust in them. Given sufficiently supportive psychological conditions, individ-uals can be trusted to actualize their biologically based resources and move in directions that are ultimately good for them and other people. This basic assump-tion is an outgrowth of Rogers' belief that all organisms have inherent, natural capacities for growth, understanding, change, and purposeful direction. This is not to say that positive motivations, strivings, or outcomes always occur. Histories of individuals and groups show that they do not.

Rogers has promoted the responsible use of personal freedom. This is why he was so perplexed by psychoanalytic conclusions about human destructiveness and irrationality (Freud, 1930/1961) and by behavioristic conclusions that human beings are under the control of highly structured external environments (Skinner, 1948). Rogers believed that rational solutions to human problems are possible without recourse to strict environmental controls.

Caring about the Person in Human Relationships

Rogers has stressed the role of caring, interpersonal relationships in the process of developing, maintaining, and changing personality. In person-centered therapy, the therapist is not a blank screen or expert technician, but a person, "a viable human being engaged in a terribly human endeavor" (Truax & Mitchell, 1971, p. 344). Under the influence of Rogers, even behavioral therapists, often criticized for ignoring interpersonal relationships, have modified procedures "which used to seem less than human to their critics" (Gendlin & Rychlak, 1970).

In fact, Rogers has done more to revise the concepts, practices, and research methods of personality change than any single psychologist since Freud, the founder of psychotherapy. He did so by demonstrating caring for others, even when such demonstrations violated traditional psychoanalytic "rules." For instance, early in his career he showed human responsiveness by departing from routine child-guidance procedures and answering "Yes" to a despairing mother's question, "Do you ever take adults for counseling here?" (Rogers, 1961). Later in a filmed therapy session, Rogers departed from traditional psychoanalytic taboos against communicating "countertransference" feelings to patients by saying to the client, Gloria, "I care about you right now, in this moment" (Shostrom, 1965). He even indicated he could see himself as a father to Gloria, who would make a fine daughter. Gloria continued to keep in occasional touch with Rogers, because of the closeness achieved during this half-hour interview.

Rogers' Scientific Contributions

Rogers has changed the field of psychotherapy through the value placed on subjecting his clinical observations to independent research investigation (Rogers, 1989a). His (1942) case of Herbert Bryan was the first complete series of therapy sessions to be electronically recorded and transcribed (800 78-rpm record sides and 170 book pages). Never before had such a wealth of information been made available to psychologists, word for word, complete with "uh-hum's" and pauses. Standard procedure, beginning with Freud, was for therapists to rely entirely on memory when summarizing sessions, often at the end of a full day's contact with six or eight patients. By exposing their practice to the scrutiny of other professionals and the public, Rogers and his students showed how psychotherapy could be demystified (Wexler & Rice, 1974). Their work "turned the field . . . upside down" and "made possible the empirical study of highly subjective phenomena" (Rogers, 1974, p. 116).

Rogers has also changed professionals' ideas about scientific procedures and theory by adopting flexible attitudes in his professional and personal relationships with others. His own theoretical formulation began with full recognition that every theory is fallible. Each theory is a "changing attempt" to construct a network of fragile threads containing an unknown amount of error and mistaken inference (1959). Rogers believed that science may begin anywhere, even away from the laboratory and computer. He has always been stimulated and excited by the new ideas of younger colleagues who seem "less stuffy, less defensive, more open in their criticism, and more creative in their suggestions" than his older colleagues (1974, p. 121). Following his example, Rogers' students and colleagues have shown a responsiveness to new ideas rather than orthodox, blind devotion (Wexler & Rice, 1974).

Unlike some theorists covered so far, such as Freud and Jung, many of Rogers' concepts can be translated into a form that can be quantified or expressed in numbers. An outstanding example of how readily certain of Rogers' ideas can be translated so that they become scientifically testable entities is provided by Harrington, Block, and Block (1987).

These researchers were interested in Rogers' theory about the process by which child-rearing practices determine level of creativity at adolescence. Their subject-sample was composed of individuals who had been followed and periodically tested beginning at approximate age three and continuing to approximate age 14. Subjects' parents were also involved in the testing.

Harrington, Block, and Block studied Rogers' writings about child-rearing and creativity. Then they translated his notions about that relationship into items on some instruments designed to measure child-rearing practices. One of these measures involved having parents report the practices they typically used. Some items that were judged most typical of Rogers' "creativity fostering environment" (CFE) included, "I respect my child's opinions and encourage him to express them."; "I let my child make many decisions for himself."; and "I encourage my child to be curious, to explore and question things." (p. 852). Some items judged least typical of Rogers' CFE included, "I do not allow my child to get angry with me."; "I believe that children should be seen and not heard."; and "I do not allow my child to question my decisions." (p. 852).

Other measures assessed parental teaching behavior during parent/child, task-completion sessions that were observed by raters. Resultant ratings were then transformed into items related to Rogers' CFE. Items judged to be most typical of CFE included, "Parent was warm and supportive."; "Child appeared to enjoy the situation."; and "Parent was supportive and encouraging of the child." Items judged to be least typical of CFE included, "Parent tended to control the tasks."; "The parent was hostile in the situation."; and "Parent appeared ashamed of child, lacked pride in child." (p. 852).

Creativity items were developed in an analogous fashion and used to assess creativity when subjects were teens. Items that were judged applicable to creative individuals included, "Tends to be proud of own accomplishments."; "Is curious, exploring, eager for new experiences."; "Has a wide range of interests."; and "Values own independence and autonomy." Items that were judged applicable to non-creative individuals included, "Is uncomfortable with uncertainty and complexities."; "Gives up and withdraws where possible in the face of adversity."; and "Is self-defeating." (p. 853).

Harrington, Block, and Block (1987) related the measures of CFE to those of creativity. They found statistically-significant, positive relationships between instruments with items that measured Rogers' CFE and instruments with items that measured creativity. These results convinced them that Rogers' ideas about creativity, and the environmental circumstances that foster it, are scientifically valid. Just looking at the items they used gives one a relatively clear impression concerning what creativity is and what parental practices promote it.

Limitations

Although emphasis on subjective experience and on the self is a major contribution, it creates limitations in regard to the scientific status of Rogers' personality theory and therapy. The major weaknesses thus generated are: (1) the lack of an explicit definition of personality; (2) difficulty in translating some concepts into testable form; (3) problems involved in accepting self-reports; and (4) the inadequacy of nondirective therapy for some individuals.

No Explicit Definition of Personality
Although references to personality appear in his writings, unlike others covered later, Rogers has failed to provide a clear definition of personality. He has pre-

BOX 9.5   Carl Rogers: Globe-trotting Peacemaker

Not all of Rogers' contributions were related to "psychotherapy," "personality theory," or "science." Rogers the person had great influence on individuals involved in some of the most disturbing and serious conflicts occurring in the world today.

His efforts to end disastrous conflicts took him to every quarter of the globe. On a trip to Northern Ireland he attempted to induce Protestants and Catholics to regard each other as human beings rather than mortal enemies (Rogers & Ryback, 1984). Using his client-centered method adapted to a group context, Rogers brought religious rivals together in close proximity. As you might expect, initial reactions were explosive. For example, Gilda, a Protestant, who Rogers described as young and pretty, said, "If I seen an IRA man lying on the ground . . . I would *step* on him, because to me he has just went out and taken the lives of innocent people" (p. 5). Yet, under Rogers' skillful guidance, individuals revealed themselves and, thereby, came to appreciate one another's humanity. After considerable interaction in the context of Rogers' group, Dennis, a Protestant, and Becky, a Catholic, spoke warmly of one another:

Dennis: The general impression back in Belfast is, if [Becky] is a Catholic . . . you just put her in a wee box and that is the end of it. But you just can't do that. She has communicated to me that she is in a worse position than what I am. . . . I feel that she feels the absolute despair that I would feel. I don't know how I would react if I were one of her lads. I would probably go out and get a gun . . . and end up dead.

Becky: Words couldn't describe what I feel towards Dennis from the discussion we had at dinner time. We spoke quietly for about ten minutes and I felt that here I have got a friend and that was it.

Dennis: We sat at dinner time and had a wee bit of yarn [storytelling] quietly when you were all away for your dinner . . .

Becky: I think he fully understands me as a person.

Dennis: I do, there is no question about that . . .

Becky: And for that reason I am very grateful and I think I have found a friend. (p. 5)

These same techniques were used in the encounter between black and white South Africans that reduced Rogers to tears (Hill-Hain & Rogers, 1988). Similar methods produced similar results in the former Soviet Union (Rogers, 1987b). This last adventure in group interaction, played out in Moscow and Tbilisi, was responsive to Rogers' larger concerns. He had in mind more than just settlement of local conflicts. For the last several years of his life, Rogers wrote passionately about the need to eliminate nuclear weapons, a concern that I share with him (Allen, 1985). He believed that social scientists could contribute much toward the end of the nuclear threat (Rogers & Malcolm, 1987). In fact, it was his fervent wish that his group interaction methods, used so successfully to alleviate local tensions, might be applied to international conflicts that have the potential to produce nuclear holocaust (Rogers, 1989b; Rogers, 1987c; Rogers and Ryback, 1984). I can picture a group composed of President Clinton, Yeltsin, and their underlings interacting under Rogers' guidance. If only he could be here to lead such a group. Because he cannot, the best we can do is to apply his wisdom and sensitivity, and we had better hurry.

ferred to use the concepts *person, self,* and *self-concept.* However, "person" and "self" are broader than personality and "self-concept" is more narrow. If self-concept is the personality of the individual from her or his own point of view (Allen, 1990), personality from the perspective of outside observers is not addressed from Rogers' position.

Problems of Translating Concepts

Despite the ease with which some of Rogers' concepts have been translated into measurable terms, many others defy straightforward translation. For example, some scales have been developed for measuring Rogerian concepts of *empathy, warmth,* and *genuineness.* The natural difficulty in measuring these notions is reflected in the fact that scales developed by Truax and Carkhuff (1967) differ somewhat from those developed later by Carkhuff (1969). In appraising the therapeutic effectiveness of these scales, Mitchell, Bozarth, and Krauft (1977) judged results to be inconclusive, and explained this unsatisfying outcome by reference to the possible low relevance of the measurement scales to the concepts. Efforts have also been made to develop measures of other Rogerian concepts. The Experiencing Scale, developed by Gendlin and Tomlinson (1967), is a refinement of Rogers' (1959) earlier Psychotherapy Process Scale (PPS). The PPS is aimed at evaluating the degree to which a client is in touch with or avoids important emotions. Although this measure does not rely on client self-reports, but on therapists' ratings, biases related to therapists' personal or professional expectations could influence ratings.

Acceptance of Conscious, Self-Reported Experience

In his classic text on personality, Gordon Allport (1937) alluded to the inclination of behaviorists and psychoanalysts "to distrust the evidence of immediate experience" and dismiss the self, ego, or "person" in psychology. While scientific evidence has shown that "self-concept" is amenable to measurement, these critics of self-notions make some telling points. First, self-perceptions may be incomplete or inaccurate representations, related to inability to see oneself realistically. Second, even accurate self-perceptions may not be reflected in self-statements if the individual is unwilling to communicate them. Third, both self-perceptions and self-statements may not correspond to what the person is doing, thinking, and feeling. While inability to measure concepts does not make them useless, it does put them beyond the realm of science.

The Nondirective Approach

Unlike most other psychotherapists, Rogers has accumulated considerable evidence supporting the effectiveness of his therapeutic procedures (see Kirschenbaum and Henderson, 1989). Nevertheless, these methods are apparently not for everyone. In the filmed psychotherapy session mentioned earlier, the client, Gloria, was rather obviously frustrated with Rogers' unwillingness to offer expert advice. Despite her continued contact with Rogers' later, at the time of the session, it seemed that Gloria preferred the other two therapists to Rogers. Recently I overheard some counselors expressing similar frustration. They were describing an observation of a Rogerian session in which the client was seeking advice and not getting any. It seemed obvious to them not only that the client needed advice but what advice he needed. Despite their observations, the therapist persisted in merely nodding and saying "uh-huh." Perhaps Rogers' predominantly intelligent and not-so-severely disturbed clients were better off left to their own devices. However, other clients, who may be more disturbed and less well-equipped, may need some suggestions as to how they might deal with their problems.

Conclusions

Carl Rogers' was many things to many people, but disliked was hardly ever one of them. He was a person who practiced what he preached. As a result, Rogers was the warm, accepting person that he hoped we would all become. In reading the various interviews with Rogers and tributes to him offered by his many disciples, it is evident that his followers were not just interested in his point of view. They were sincerely devoted to Rogers the person. These loving colleagues and friends comforted, protected, and nourished him, just as he did them.

Rogers exemplified the best of the human spirit. He could truly melt into another person so that he became one with her or him. In so doing, he surrendered himself in the interest of someone else, perhaps the most noble act a human can perform.

Summary Points

1. Rogers was a farm boy from Illinois who learned principles of science and growth from an agricultural book. He cut his teeth on Freud, but later abandoned psychoanalysis and the medical model in favor of the growth model. As an adult, Rogers became a warm person, but was somewhat different from his image. He could become angry and agitated, he thought equality in therapy was not an issue, he was sometimes overcome with emotion during therapy, he deplored the rigid use of the client-centered method, and he was not heavily identified with counseling.

2. Humanistic psychology emphasizes the present experience of the whole person. It has close ties to existential psychology. The more positive humanistic approach focuses on joy, love, and authenticity. The phenomenological approach, central to Rogers' view, assumes the reality that one knows is subjective and personal. However, we can participate in the private world of others through empathy.

3. "The person" is literally the center of Rogers' theory and therapy. People are viewed in a positive light and are seem as capable of solving their own problems. Relationships with people in therapy are only instances of those that occur everyday. People have an inherent "general actualizing tendency" that is organismic, active, directional, and selective. Self-actualization is a lifelong process of realizing one's potentialities that involves openness to experience, awareness, living existentially, and trust in one's organismic functions.

4. The existence of the self is verified by statements like "Who am I?" and "That is not me." The self is perceptions of the characteristics of "I" and is functionally equivalent to "self-concept." It can be related to an "ideal-self." Congruence occurs when our self-concepts are in agreement with the self we actually experience. Incongruence occurs when the opposite is the case. It entails denial and distortion.

5. Adler taught Rogers the error of rigid adherence to Freud's psychoanalysis and of dwelling on clients' past. Rogers came to oppose psychoanalytic principles, but his ideas sometimes coincided with Jung's: both rejected authoritarian relationships with clients, both believed using specific therapy techniques to be of secondary importance, both talked of a "facade," and both wrote of "wholeness," "uniqueness," and the self.

6. External factors, particularly interpersonal ones, often determine whether personal growth occurs: 1) unconditional positive regard, 2) accurate empathy, and 3) congruence. The first concerns being regarded with acceptance and trust just for who one is. When acceptance becomes conditional, problems result. Unconditional positive regard means accepting the person, no matter what, but not necessarily the person's behavior. Accurate empathy means correctly perceiving the client's world in a non-evaluative way. Congruence is applicable to therapist/client relationships.

7. Unconditional positive regard can lead to positive self-regard, but not if the locus of evaluation is in other people. Personality change flows from fixed, separated, and tied-to-the-past to spontaneous, integrated, and "in-the-present." Progress in therapy proceeds from talk about externals, to disowned descriptions of feelings, to self in the past, to feelings in the present that are merely described, to feelings freely expressed in the present, to full acceptance of feelings, to relating to others openly and freely and trusting in new experiences.

8. Rogers' self-description reflected the open, creative, accepting, tolerant, effective, and gentle person that he was. Rogers' contributions include allowing people to speak for themselves with regard to the nature of their feelings. His methods have lead to questioning the attempt to understand people from the outside. He has been the great promoter of the fruitful concept "self" and the investment of trust in people. He attributes positive motivations to people and honors their natural actualizing tendencies, while recognizing they do not always behave well.

9. Rogers, while humanizing other approaches, adopted the motto "do whatever is necessary to enhance the person." As a scientist he has demystified psychotherapy, opened it to the public eye, and revised mechanized approaches to therapy. Many of his concepts have been translated into measurable form as evidenced by Harrington, Block, and Block's verification of his proposed relationship between child-rearing practices and creativity. As a person, Rogers has attempted to do something about serious conflicts in various parts of the world. Further, he has suggested that his group method may be used to help save the world from nuclear conflict.

10. Limitations of Rogers point of view include lack of a specific definition of personality, problems of translation of some concepts, problems with the self-report method he used, and inadequacy of the nondirective therapy method for some people. Despite these shortcomings, Rogers the person stands as an example of human warmth and concern for the well-being of each person.

Running Comparison

Theorists	Rogers in Comparison
Freud	Optimistic and positive compared to Freud, rejected his involved probing into the past, but shared his belief in defenses.
Jung	He shared Jung's non-authoritarian, mutual participant orientation to therapy, belief that method was less important than helping client, "facade" (persona), individuation (self-actualization), interest in the self, and belief in wholeness and uniqueness of each person.
Adler	He learned to be direct and straightforward from Adler. Also he agreed with Adler on eschewing lengthy case histories and multiple tests to discover past problems.
Abraham Maslow	Shared many ideas with fellow humanistic psychologist Maslow, especially self-actualization.
Gordon Allport	Shared Allport's idiographic approach.
Harry S. Sullivan	Shared Sullivan's interest in significant others.

Essay/Critical Thinking Questions

1. Beyond the religious perspective, what is the meaning of death?

2. What was it about Rogers' early history—childhood through young adulthood—that lead to his scientific, anti-psychoanalytic, yet humanistic orientation?

3. Aside from a moral or philosophical point of view, what are the advantages of Rogers' assumption that people are basically good and worthy.

4. Picture yourself as a self-actualized person. How would you describe yourself?

5. Indicate the ways your self-concept is incongruent with your actual experience of yourself. How is self and self-ideal involved in this discrepancy?

6. Apparently there is overlap between the ideas of Jung and Rogers. Select some other theorist from previous chapters. How does Rogers' theory agree or disagree with that theorist?

7. Unconditional positive regard should apply to the person, not her or his every behavior. Despite this assumption, in practice, what problems might be encountered in applying unconditional positive regard to a person?

8. Phenomenology seems to make good sense. After all, aren't the person's own perceptions of his or her world most valid? However, what logical and psychological binds does one get into by simply accepting people's phenomenological reports?

9. It seems reasonable to "operationalize" concepts in order to study them scientifically. Nevertheless, what happens to concepts such as *warmth*, *empathy*, and *positive self-regard* when these notions are operationalized?

10. When someone begins to tell you about a minor or major problem that she or he has, begin to react to this person in good Rogerian fashion. How does the person react to your "uh-huh's," nods, and rephrasing, instead of advice?

10

ABRAHAM MASLOW: BECOMING ALL THAT ONE CAN BE

- Can a psychologist who despised his mother turn out right?
- Must we meet our basic physiological needs before we can address other kinds?
- Is it enough to have high self-esteem or must one be unfettered by society's demands and thus free to fully exploit one's talents and inclinations?
- Can people be all good who are unconcerned about what others' think, devoted to creativity and the pursuit of beauty, and fully accepting of themselves?
- If one achieves the highest level of personality attainment, is there still more to seek?

The two brightest stars in the humanistic firmament are certainly Carl Rogers and Abraham Maslow. Not surprisingly, they share much in common. Both are more concerned with the here and now and being all one can be, rather than with the past or even the future. Both flirted with the ideas of Sigmund Freud briefly, and both were influenced by Alfred Adler. Both also emphasized the importance of self-actualization in personality functioning and development, but here the similarities fade. For Rogers, self-actualization was one of several central concepts. For Maslow, it was the single most important concept. According to Rogers, self-actualization was within the grasp of most people. According to Maslow, it was reserved for a special few.

As people they were quite different. Rogers came from a warm and traditional family. Maslow considered himself an abused and neglected child and a victim of prejudice. Rogers was totally warm and accepting and always assumed the basic goodness of humans. Maslow could show the same traits, but he seethed with suppressed anger and was more than willing to acknowledge the sinister side of human nature. Yet in their own separate ways, both humanists sought to help people lay aside others' expectations and become what they were destined to be.

Maslow, the Person

When Samuel Maslow arrived in the United States from the Ukrainian city of Kiev, he brought little with him, except the ability to speak Russian and Yiddish, a language common among European Jews (Hoffman, 1988). After a brief sojourn in Philadelphia, he moved in with relatives in New York City. There he met and married his first cousin, Rose, a woman who would prove more devoted to religion than to her family. Abraham, the first of their seven children—one died in infancy—was born April fool's day, 1908. Fate had played a trick on him. It had given him parents who were part of a master plan to ensure his eternal torment.

Maslow claimed that his mother was cold, vicious, superstitiously religious, and dedicated to making him miserable (Hoffman, 1988). Even the most trivial of his youthful transgressions inspired her to declare that God would strike him down. Continual threats of divine retribution affected Maslow profoundly. For one thing, it nurtured the scientist in him: "I tested . . . that if you do such and such, God will strike you down. If I climbed through the window, [I was told that] I wouldn't grow. Well, I climbed through the window and then checked my growth" (p. 2). Finding that his torso continued to elongate, Maslow concluded that religion was a virulent form of superstition, a position he clung to with great tenacity.

The experiments saved his sanity, but they did not deliver him from continued religious harassment at the hands of his mother. While undergoing religious instruction forced on him by her, he was required to proclaim his love for mother Rose. When he choked on the words, dropped materials from which he was reading, and fled in tears, his ever "insightful" mother exclaimed, "You see! He loves me so much he can't even express the words!" (p. 11).

His mother's alleged cruelties were numerous and varied. She would see to it that he received less food than his siblings, an affront to his status as eldest son, and a not too subtle message: in so far as food means "love" he was unloved (Hoffman, 1988). One day young Maslow brought home some prized 78 RPM recordings, laid them and the rest of his collection on the living room floor for inspection, and absent-mindedly left the room without honoring her command to "Pick up your mess." When he returned she was screaming "What did I tell you?" and grinding her heels into his treasured recordings (p. 8). On another occasion he brought home two kittens and spirited them away to the basement, but Rose heard the meowing and confronted him. He had dared to bring stray cats into her house and feed them on her dishes. While Maslow watched in horror, she picked up each kitten in turn and smashed its head against the brick basement wall until it was dead. To the dismay of his siblings, Maslow publicly expressed his antagonism toward mother Rose several times during his life. When she died, he refused even to attend her funeral.

In contrast to mother Rose's cruelty, Maslow's father Samuel was merely absent. Probably owing to the sad state of his marriage, he left early in the morning for the long trek to his job and made it a point to stay late at work to chat with his cronies. When he finally arrived at home, his children were often already in bed. During childhood, Maslow basically had no relationship with Samuel. When Maslow grew to young adulthood, however, the elder Maslow's business failed, a victim of the depression, and the father became a ward of the son. They lived together for some time and became friends. Thus, like Adler, and unlike Freud or Sullivan, Maslow was a father's son, rather than a mother's boy.

Abraham Maslow

Like Julian Rotter, whose ideas will be covered soon, Maslow's fledgling intellect was nourished by the Brooklyn libraries. But life in Brooklyn for Jewish boys was harsh, and access to the libraries difficult. He learned to stay on Jewish turf lest he fall prey to ethnic youth gangs that controlled surrounding areas. When he ventured forth to visit the local library branch, he had to use special paths, ones with handy escape routes. In self-defense, Maslow tried to join a Jewish gang, but they wanted him to kill cats and throw stones at girls, acts that were against his nature. Instead he skillfully sneaked from home to the library with such high frequency that he soon finished the children's books and was awarded an adult's card.

At school, anti-semitism was also an everyday problem. Once when he won the class spelling bee, his bigoted teacher refused to accept the outcome. The "horrible bitch" pitched words at Abraham until he fumbled one: "parallel" (p. 4). Then she announced to the class that she knew all along he was just a fake. Still Maslow did well at school, so well he was dubbed "that smart Jew."

Added to these miseries was the problem of Maslow's appearance. Like Horney, he felt unattractive. Gangly and in possession of a prominent proboscis, he was sometimes subjected to ridicule. His own father declared before the whole family, "Isn't he the ugliest kid you've ever seen" (p. 6). Occasions like these gave Maslow a serious inferiority complex and led him to describe his childhood as "miserably unhappy" (p. 6).

After attending a select boy's high school where he performed reasonably well in all but a few key courses, Maslow began a career as an itinerant college student. He wanted to attend revered Cornell, one of the few universities in the Eastern United States that did not have strict quotas limiting the number of Jews admitted. His best friend, cousin Will, was accepted there, but Maslow lacked the confidence to apply.

Having given up on Cornell, in the winter of 1925, Maslow enrolled in City College where he found some joys and some sorrows. Trigonometry proved to be a major source of grief. Maslow hated it so much that he could not bear to attend class. Thus, he failed owing to poor attendance, despite having passed the tests. Unlike most of us, he could not grind through life's drudgeries. If Maslow could not bear to do something, he refused to do it, even if doing it was a practical necessity.

After working briefly as a busboy one summer—he felt mistreated and walked off the job—and a semester on academic probation, Maslow decided to try law. Enrolled in a less than prestigious school, he became immediately bored. True to character he quit, disappointing his father at whose behest he had tried law.

During this period Maslow flirted with socialism, but never became the activist that Adler and Fromm had been. Perhaps he was preoccupied with other matters, most especially his attraction to first cousin Bertha. Probably his desire to flee Bertha "who I couldn't get close to . . . anyhow" and his desire to join Will led to Maslow's transfer to Cornell in 1927 (p. 24).

Just as had been the case for Sullivan, Cornell was mainly a bad experience for Maslow. Despite its relative lack of exclusionary policies regarding Jews, anti-semitism was alive and well in Ithaca and on university grounds as well. Accordingly, Maslow located in Collegetown, a community that contained housing for "lesser-status . . . bohemians and those neither interested in nor acceptable to the Greek letter societies" (p. 25). Not only did the Greeks exclude Jews, many Ithaca landlords refused to rent to them and the *Cornell Sun,* a university sanctioned student newspaper, barred Jews from its staff.

Cornell also provided Maslow with his first exposure to psychology. Like George Kelly, whose theory is covered next, the beginning psychology class made the discipline look anything but inviting. Maslow had the bad luck to enroll in a class assigned to a pretentious dinosaur among professors by the name of Edward B. Titchener. A disciple of Wilhelm Wundt, psychology's founder, Titchener had come to Cornell in 1892 as the chief American proponent of Wundt's "structuralism." Some thirty-five years later Maslow witnessed the spectacle of Titchener, adorned in academic robes, parading to the lectern followed obediently by a entourage of his graduate students. There he espoused a point of view considered long dead by nearly everyone but himself. Structuralism was dull stuff indeed, and one of two important reasons why Maslow transferred back to City College after only one semester.

The other reason was missing Bertha. But when he called on her, inherent shyness prevented him from demonstrating his love. One day, in the presence of Bertha's assertive sister Anna, he was sitting beside his sweetheart longing to touch her. Seeing the timidity of Maslow and the passivity of Bertha, Anna became impatient and pushed the reluctant lovers together. "For the love of Pete, kiss her will ya!" declared Anna, and when he did, "life began" (p. 29).

By the spring of 1928, Maslow was restless again. He had learned about the liberal atmosphere at the University of Wisconsin and the esteemed professors who resided there, including Kurt Koffka, a founder of Gestalt psychology. So once again, he transferred. That summer, on a visit to City College, a former professor recommended *The Psychologies of 1925,* a book containing an essay by John B. Watson, the leading behaviorist of the time. Maslow later wrote, "The thing that really turned me on was Watson's chapter. . . . In the highest excitement, I suddenly saw unrolling before me into the future the possibility of a *science of psychology* . . ." (p. 33). How ironic it was that a future humanist would be beckoned to his academic destiny by a psychologist who wished to consider only stimuli and responses. But Maslow was stuck on psychology, despite the discovery that Koffka had been a visiting professor who had already left the Wisconsin campus.

John B. Watson

While his career had been launched, his personal life was still on the beach. Bertha was in his every thought. Finally, he could stand it no more. He proposed via telegram and she accepted. On the last day of 1928, they were married.

His disappointment at Koffka's departure was soon quelled. Wisconsin's small and not-yet-esteemed psychology department contained faculty and students who would eventually become famous. Professors were also congenial: students were treated more like colleagues than underlings. By 1930, when he had finished his B.A. degree, he had already taken many graduate courses. During his subsequent graduate school years, he was exposed to the likes of Clark Hull, soon to become the foremost learning theorist of the 1930s. However, he eventually migrated to the laboratory of Harry Harlow, whose research with monkeys was considered in the Sullivan chapter.

As time passed and Maslow achieved fame, the anger at the mistreatment he received as a child and the disgust at the anti-semitism he suffered began to fade. He became a warm and accepting person. However, there was still an undercurrent of bitterness that seemed to obstruct his best efforts on occasion. Alderfer (1989) noted that Maslow had trouble leading sensitivity training groups. "The man whose intellectual work played such an important role in the then rapidly growing humanistic psychology movement was unable to act in ways . . . consistent with his own theory" (p. 359). When the protest era of the 1960s emerged, Maslow was a natural for the role of Guru, the wise leader of soul-searching youth. However, Alderfer suggests that Maslow was uncomfortable with youth's questioning of authority. It can be said that Maslow courageously overcame a tragic childhood, but it left its indelible mark on him.

Maslow spent some time as an academic vagabond. He continued working at Wisconsin while leisurely finishing his dissertation—completed in 1934—then he took a temporary position at Teachers College, Columbia University. Finally Maslow landed a permanent position on the faculty of the brand new Brooklyn College (1937–1951). The rest of his academic career was spent at Brandeis University (1951–1969), where he chaired the psychology department for ten years. In 1968, he served as president of the American Psychological Association. After several bouts with poor health dating to early mid-life, Maslow died of a heart attack in 1970.

Maslow's View of the Person

The Evolution of a Theorist

Maslow's love of music and his attraction to free thinking politicians and academicians rested uneasily with his initial devotion to the study of invariable behaviors in animals (Hoffman, 1988). Yet success is a magnet that has pulled many researchers along, even against their wills. After early publications with Harlow, Maslow gained his own fame. He showed that what looked like sexual behavior in monkeys—the constant mounting of one monkey by another—was actually a display of dominance. "The higher a monkey's dominance position, the more likely it is to mount its subordinates; the lower its position, the more likely it is to be mounted by others" (p. 61). Although he helped to establish interest in primate "dominance hierarchies," Maslow eventually abandoned all aspects of his animal work.

Being concerned about earning a living during the depression era, Maslow entered medical school. As was usual when he did something for reasons other than intrinsic interest, Maslow became bored and dropped out. Because earlier attempts to work at the famous Yerkes primate facilities fell through, Maslow was getting desperate. Facing a poor job market and an "old gentile boy" network—he had already been denied a research grant because of anti-semitism—Maslow was ready to take anything. Much to his joy, famed learning psychologist Edward L. Thorndike became interested in his work. Thorndike of Columbia University Teachers College had been the author of the "law of effect," a basic principle of learning. By this time, however, he had become a generalist. Instead of watching cats learn to escape from boxes, he had grand plans for applying psychology and was awarded the unheard of amount of $100,000 to carry them out. Maslow could return to New York City, continue his research, and make a living while doing so.

Even as he was immersed in his animal studies at Wisconsin, Maslow had become interested in the Freud-Adler quarrel. Now he found himself in the middle of the most exciting place at the most fascinating time during the early history of personality psychology. New York City was sparkling with the brilliance of Horney, Fromm, Adler, and others, including Gestalt psychologist Koffka. Among these luminaries, Adler was singled out by Maslow as having special impact on him. When Maslow showed up for a series of lectures by the renegade ex-Freudian, he was pleasantly surprised to find a nearly empty classroom. Having few competitors for Adler's attention, the two became well-acquainted. Undoubtedly, Adler's notions of social interest, law of movement (directed free choice), striving for superiority, and the prehumanistic idea "creative power of the individual" influenced Maslow heavily.

The Gestalt Influence

However, it was the Gestalt psychologists who probably contributed the most to Maslow's intellectual evolution. The New School for Social Research in New York City had become the "University in Exile" for European scholars fleeing Hitler. Among them was the founder of Gestalt psychology, Max Wertheimer, an inspiring teacher, but not a prolific writer. Thus, it was left to Koffka, in whose class Maslow sat during 1938, to lay some important planks in the flooring of Maslow's theory.

Max Wertheimer

Gestalt psychology—initially concerned only with perception—held that simple perceptions were "wholes" made up of integrated parts (Matlin & Foley, 1992). One could consider the parts or the whole, but not both at once. Thus, a mosaic, the tiny tiles that form faces and figures in works of art (and in institutional flooring), could be appreciated as a whole, or its parts considered. More important, the parts and the whole were not separate entities, but were inextricably tied up together: a whole is an integration of parts such that the parts and the whole cannot exist separate from one another. Gestalt theory was largely composed of "laws of organization" that explained how parts are formed into wholes. Among these are: (1) grouping *similar* objects together to form a whole; (2) grouping *proximal* (near) objects; and (3) the *law of closure*, incomplete objects such as a circle with a section out are completed by "the mind's eye." Another is the familiar *figure-ground* rule that explains the "vase and the face" and the "old and young women" reversing pictures that appear in introductory psychology texts.

The idea of wholeness and of parts that are inextricably tied to the whole became fundamental to Maslow's thinking. In Maslow's words, "Our first proposition states that the individual is an integrated, organized whole" (1954, p. 63). To elucidate this point, he drew an analogy to the study of the stomach. It can be investigated by extracting a specimen from a cadaver and examining it as if it normally functioned independent of the body from which it was taken. Alternatively, the stomach can be studied in living, breathing organisms. To Maslow, the latter is much preferred, because the stomach cannot be fully understood apart from the living body into which it is integrated. At the level of motivation involving the stomach, it is not the stomach that "is hungry," it is the individual. "Furthermore, satisfaction of hunger comes to the whole individual, not just to a part of him" (p. 63).

The vase and the face—a well-known reversing picture

Motivation

To Maslow, motivational factors underlie personality. *Motivation* comes from the root word *motion* and refers to the process by which organisms are propelled toward goals. *Drives* are simple tensions that demand to be satisfied. Hunger is an example. While *drive* is a traditional psychological concept and seems easily understood, Maslow (1954) considered it to be inherently ambiguous. Looking at behavior that appears associated with a certain drive may mislead us. People apparently behaving at the behest of the hunger drive may find food and eat it. However, their ultimate goal may be security, not reduction of the hunger drive. Likewise, people engaging in sexual behavior may actually be seeking increased self-esteem. It is these end-goals—security and self-esteem in the examples—that hold the key to understanding people. Such goals transcend the particular life circumstances of the given person. Goals can be cast as **needs** for certain satisfactions that are sought by all humans, regardless of their culture, environment, or generation.

Maslow took the unique point of view, overlooked by most theorists, that a given behavior, thought, or feeling may occur at the behest of multiple motivations (Maslow, 1954). Henry A. Murray adopted a similar position. We are in the habit of attempting to find *the* reason for every significant action displayed by either ourselves or others. Actually, human behavior is extraordinarily complex. Anything a

---

BOX 10.1   Why Do We Do What We Do? Let Us Count the Reasons . . .

Nonprofessionals and psychological professionals alike can sometimes be quite simple-minded about human thought, behavior, and feeling. Even obviously complex actions like proposing marriage, committing suicide, and changing careers may be discussed as if only one motive is involved. "He proposed because he is in love"; "People commit suicide because they hate themselves"; "She changed careers to make more money." Rarely are single motives sufficient to explain such complex actions.

Below are several ordinary decisions, activities, or psychological conditions. Contemplate each and for each imagine that you are the person involved. Then write down as many reasons why you "did what you did" as you can conjure up. An example precedes the exercise items.

"I spent the afternoon cleaning out my cabinets and closets." I wanted to get organized. I couldn't find anything. I wanted to be neat like my sister. I felt the need to expend some energy. I wanted to take something apart and put it back together again. I was depressed and needed a distraction. I was bored and needed to fill some time.

"I went shopping all afternoon and didn't find a thing."

"I ate everything I could find in the house."

"I wrote my Mom a nasty letter."

"I told my best friend, 'I care for you more than anyone else.' "

"I took the afternoon off, started a novel, and read until 3 A.M."

person does is likely to be traced to many motivations. Not only do we perform sexually for physical gratification and increased self-esteem, we may also be seeking closeness, friendship, safety, love, and, perhaps, other important satisfactions. A person suffering from paralysis of the arm for which no physical basis can be found may experience many motivational benefits: pity, love, and attention to name a few. Only the rarest of thoughts, behaviors, or feelings are likely to stem from just one motivational source.

According to Maslow, while the needs a person experiences are universal, the methods used to satisfy them may be specific to the person's culture. Everyone needs to bolster and maintain self-esteem. Self-esteem may be boosted by being a good hunter, a superb athlete, an outstanding pottery maker, or a feared "witch doctor," depending on the culture. Likewise, environment may determine the particular form of need satisfaction, but Maslow was quick to point out that the role of environment is often overemphasized. Exactly how the urge to eat is satisfied will depend in some degree on whether we find ourselves in Chicago, New York, or Houston. It may also depend on whether we are on a camping trip, in a shopping mall, or stuck at Aunt Sue's house. However, an environmental circumstance does not force certain satisfactions on us. Rather our perceptions of that circumstance and operations on it shape need fulfillment. By making reference to "environmental barriers," Maslow explained that environments are what we make of them: "a child who is trying to attain a certain object of value to him, but who is restrained by a barrier of some sort, determines not only that the object has value, but that the barrier is a barrier. Psychologically there is no such thing as a barrier; there is only a barrier for a particular person who is trying to get something that he wants" (p. 74).

Finally, a motivation cannot be considered in isolation from other motivations. The satisfaction of a given need may depend on the prior, simultaneous, or subsequent satisfactions of other needs. Again, Henry A. Murray advocated a similar position. We can hardly be creative if our stomachs have been empty for days. During the process of supporting and comforting other people, we can expect to receive self-esteem bolstering comments from them. Only after we have secured a safe apartment in a big city can we expect to enjoy interactions with family at home. Motivations relate to other motivations in a multidimensional matrix of almost infinite complexity.

Basic Concepts: Maslow

Not by Bread Alone: Five Basic Human Needs

Maslow (1954, 1970) offers two answers to the question "Do people live by bread alone?" When people have no bread, the answer is "Yes." But, when bread is plentiful, the answer is "No." Consider the example of desperately hungry people who constantly think about food, dream about food, and have recollections only about food. All other interests are unimportant. Life itself is defined in terms of eating. To them, Utopia is a place where there is plenty of food. As ex-POWs and concentration camp inmates can testify, once a person has been severely deprived of food, food becomes all that matters.

However, the picture is quite different when bread is available and the person's belly is continuously filled. Gratification of hunger frees the person to pursue other needs. When these higher-order needs emerge, they begin to dominate the individual, taking the place of hunger. After these additional needs are satisfied, still higher-order needs emerge. Maslow places these needs in a hierarchy ranging from the most fundamental biologically based needs to the most abstract, uniquely human needs.

Physiological needs encompass specific biological requirements for water, oxygen, proteins, vitamins, proper body temperature, sleep, sex, exercise, and so on (Maslow, 1954). At this primitive level of the hierarchy, biological urges may be thought of as "needs" rather than "drives," because the satisfactions in question are the ultimate goals. For example, when food is scarce, seeking food is not a means to some other end.

Safety needs include security, protection, stability, structure, law and order, and freedom from fear and chaos. These needs are most readily inferred from negative reactions of children to sudden unpredictability and disruption in their lives. In fact, reactions to any stimulus that leads children or adults to feel psychologically endangered and threatened suggest that this need has been activated. You will note the similarity to "basic anxiety" proposed by Karen Horney. Veterans home from Vietnam had plenty in their stomachs. However, many spontaneously recoiled when a car backfired nearby or when the peculiar whirring, whipping sound of a helicopter occurred within hearing range.

Belongingness and love needs orient the person toward affectionate relations with people, and a sense of place in family and groups. During the course of his career, Maslow witnessed the rapidly expanding acceptance of participation in *sensitivity groups*, an assemblage of people who have come together to reveal their inner feelings and to achieve intimacy with others. He viewed this trend as an index of the widespread hunger for interpersonal contact, intimacy, and togetherness. Maslow noted that most theorists have stressed the "thwarting of love needs" as a fundamental cause of human maladjustment (Maslow, 1970).

Esteem needs are of two kinds: (1) there are personal desires for adequacy, mastery, competence, achievement, confidence, independence, and freedom; and (2) there are desires for respect from other people, including attention, recognition, appreciation, status, prestige, fame, dominance, importance, and dignity (Maslow, 1954). Satisfaction of esteem needs results in feelings of personal worth, self-confidence, psychological strength, capability, and a sense of being useful and necessary. "But thwarting of these needs produces feelings of inferiority, of weakness, and of helplessness" (p. 91). In turn, these feelings produce either discouragement, compensation, or neurosis.

The quintessential longing is the **need for self-actualization**, "the desire for self-fulfillment . . . the tendency for [one] to become actualized in what [one] is potentially" (Maslow, 1954, pp. 91–92). This powerful force can be cast as the desire to become more of what one is, to become everything that one is capable of being. What a person *can* be, that person feels compelled to *become*, whether athlete, parent, or community leader. Musicians experience a powerful need to make music, artists to paint, poets to write. Each person hears a voice from within that whispers, "Be true to your nature."

It is in the manifestations of self-actualization that people differ the most. Because each person is different from each other person, that which each person feels the need to becomes is unique. "At this level, individual differences are greatest" (Maslow, 1970, p. 46).

Maslow categorized the first four basic needs as **deficiency needs (D-needs)** because they require fulfillment involving the environment in order for the person to avoid physical sickness and psychological maladjustment (Goble, 1970; Maslow, 1968). Citing evidence from research studies, Maslow concluded that an individual's appetites or food preferences are a fairly clear indication of actual physiological needs or deficiencies of the body (P. T. Young, 1941, 1948). If the body is lacking a particular biochemical substance, the individual will attempt to satisfy the deficiency by developing a hunger for the missing nutritional element. Maslow (1970) also saw support for his concept of basic needs in Walter Cannon's (1932) theory of *homeostasis*, a process through which the body automatically attempts to maintain constant physiological balance. The acid/alkaline balance would be an example. D-needs meet the following criteria: (1) people yearn persistently for their gratification; (2) deprivation sickens people or stunts their growth; (3) gratification cures the deficiency illness; (4) steady supplies prevent these illnesses; and (5) healthy people do not demonstrate the deficiencies.

Although self-actualization needs tend not to emerge until there has been some prior satisfaction of the physiological, safety, love, and esteem needs, gratification of basic needs is not sufficient to guarantee self-actualization. Self-actualizing persons certainly show sufficient gratification of their basic needs. In addition, they demonstrate freedom from illness, positive use of their capacities, and motivation that is linked to a set of personal values. Further, while self-actualization implies the prior fulfillment of all lower-order needs, it is different from them. In contrast to the four other needs, its direction is positive or *growth-motivated* rather than negative or *deficiency-motivated*. Self-actualization is a *growth need*, not a D-need.

Maslow has arranged the basic needs into a hierarchy, in a first-things-first manner. Lower-order needs are *prepotent*, or stronger and more immediately demanding than higher-order needs. They occur earlier in the developmental process and require gratification prior to higher-order needs. A deficiency in a lower-order need dominates personality functioning until it is satisfied. Only then is the person freed to begin addressing the need that is a step up in the hierarchy. Safety is a "stronger, more pressing, earlier appearing, more vital need" than belongingness, and the need for food is prepotent to both (Maslow, 1959, p. 123). Figure 10.1 shows the hierarchical order of needs proposed by Maslow, with physiological needs prepotent to safety needs which, in turn, are prepotent to belongingness and love needs, and so on, up the steps.

Hierarchical needs are not met in all-or-none fashion, but are overlapping. The common pattern is for people to experience partial satisfaction or little satisfaction

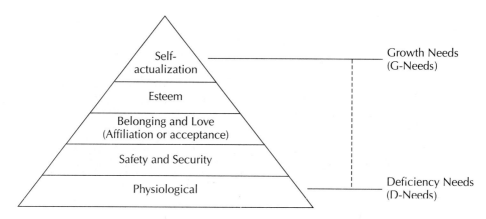

FIGURE 10.1   Maslow's Hierarchy of Needs

of their needs at the same time. Using arbitrary figures, Maslow (1970) speculated that, in this society, the satisfactions of an average person's five needs might be 85 percent physiological, 70 percent safety, 50 percent love, 40 percent self-esteem, and 10 percent self-actualization. Also, hierarchical needs are not met suddenly. People need not experience 100 percent satisfaction of a lower-order need before they can begin to pursue the next highest need on the hierarchy. The emergence of a new need occurs gradually as a lower need is satisfied. If belongingness and love needs are satisfied only 10 percent, esteem needs may not be visible at all. However, with 25 percent love satisfaction, the esteem need may emerge at the 5 percent level.

There are, of course, exceptions to the order of needs appearing in the hierarchy. Romeo and Juliet were willing to die for love. India's Mahatma Gandhi was willing to deny his own safety and physiological needs for self-actualization and higher-order values, including personal dignity, social equality, and political freedom. However, just as people do not realize complete satisfaction of lower-order needs and then *suddenly* experience the next highest need in full bloom, they cannot *suddenly* deny lower-order needs while continuing to pursue higher-order needs. Gandhi was able to *gradually* deny lower-order needs as he focused on higher order needs. Had he been abruptly placed in a Nazi concentration camp and *suddenly* reduced to an animalistic level via torture, starvation, and exhaustion, he might have been scratching for food and clinging to survival like other inmates (Allen, 1990). Abruptly take away the satisfaction of basic physiological needs and most people would slide down Maslow's hierarchy. The comfortable and secure can choose not to eat, sleep, or even breathe. People precipitously reduced to a basic survival level are usually compelled to eat if they can.

In the most typical reversal of needs, the relatively prepotent need for belongingness and love is satisfied along with esteem. The person who believes that satisfaction of the esteem need carries with it satisfaction of the love need may adopt the notion that love comes to those who are powerful, respected, feared, and aggressive. For this person, the need to be an object of affection is met by putting on a front of confidence (pseudo-esteem), thereby promoting the belief that this persona will elicit "love."

It is also possible to experience permanent loss of a need, as in the case of an antisocial (psychopathic) individual whose cravings for love during infancy were never met. By adulthood, desire and ability to give and receive affection has been lost. A critical period in this person's development was probably bypassed, similar to animals who lose their sucking or pecking reflexes when these are not exercised soon enough after birth. An individual's level of aspiration may also be permanently lowered. For example, someone who has experienced chronic poverty or unem-

Mahatma Gandhi

ployment may continue to seek only minimal satisfactions in life, such as just obtaining food or shelter.

Human Nature Is Born, Not Made

Although Maslow recognizes that external environments may be helpful to people in actualizing their inherent characteristics, he does not believe environments can teach people to be human or that environments shape humanness. Although culture, family, and parents may function as sun, food, and water to human actualization, they are not its seed. For Maslow (1970), human nature is inborn, not made. It has an essential, built-in structure comprised of potentialities and values that are intrinsic and common to all members of the species. Maslow considers all human needs and values **instinctoid**, or instinct-like, because of their biological, genetic, and universal characteristics. Thus, all basic and higher-order needs are "in the strictest sense" biological needs, "related to the fundamental structure of the human organism itself," with "some genetic basis" involved, however weak (Maslow, 1969, p. 734). Maslow used the term *instinctoid*, because *instinct* was fraught with problems. Instinct when applied to humans has traditionally placed them on the same plane with lower animals. Maslow strongly rejected the assumed strict continuity of humans and other creatures. *Sexual* when applied to human beings was not, in Maslow's thinking, the same thing as sexual in other beings. Further, the idea of instincts seems to imply that we are born only with lower-order needs. Higher-order needs, such as love, are developed after birth by associative learning. For example, while the infant is being fed, the mother "expresses love." Thus, love supposedly gains its power and, in fact, its very existence as a motivating force, through its association with feeding. Maslow clearly rejected this association account of higher-order needs, and asserted that these needs do not depend on lower-order needs for their existence. The only essential link of higher-order needs to lower-order needs is that humans' longing for esteem and self-actualization arises only after physiological, safety, and belongingness needs are addressed.

Self-Actualizing Persons: Superior Personalities

Maslow does not believe that all choices or choosers are equal. Consider an analogy to animal choosers. Chickens allowed to select their own diet showed great individual differences in ability to select beneficial foods (P. T. Young, 1941/1948). Some were "good choosers," and some were "bad choosers." Good choosers became stronger, larger, and more dominant than bad choosers, allowing them to get the best of everything. Later, when diets selected by good choosers were forced upon bad choosers, the latter did get stronger, bigger, healthier, and more dominant, although they never reached the level of good choosers. Thus, organisms who were good choosers could choose what was good for the bad choosers better than the bad choosers actually chose for themselves.

Human choosers operate similarly. Maslow attempted to understand the values embedded in human nature by observing the cream of the human crop. "Only the choices and tastes and judgments of healthy human beings will tell us much about what is good for the [entire] human species in the long run" (Maslow, 1959, p. 121). Maslow studied the "best" of human personalities,

TABLE 10.1   Characteristics of Self-Actualizing Persons

Clear, efficient perceptions of reality and comfortable relations with it
Acceptance of self, others, and nature
Spontaneity, simplicity, and naturalness
Problem centering (having something outside themselves they "must" do as a mission)
Detachment and need for privacy
A forceful will and relative independence from environment
Continued freshness of appreciation
Mystic experience, peak experience
Gemeinschaftsgefuhl, feeling of kinship and identification with the human race (the same German word used by Adler and later translated as *social interest*)
Personal relations with others (deep but limited in number)
Democratic character structure
Ethical discrimination between means and ends, between good and evil
Philosophical, unhostile sense of humor
Creativeness
Transcendence of any particular culture, resisting cultural molding
Imperfections: sometimes thoughtless, socially impolite, cold, boring, irritating, stubborn, ruthless, forgetful, humorless, silly, angered, superficially prideful, naively kind, anxious, guilty, and conflicted (without maladjustment)

defined as those he viewed as being the most psychologically healthy, mature, highly evolved, and fully human. He designated a few of these superior persons **self-actualizers**, people who fulfill themselves by making complete use of their potentialities, capacities, and talents, who do the best they are capable of doing, and who develop themselves to the most complete stature possible for them. Self-actualizers live Nietzsche's exhortation, "Become what thou art!"

Eleanor Roosevelt

One may wonder who are these "best personalities" and what are they like. A list of at least "potential" self-actualizers includes Abraham Lincoln, Thomas Jefferson, Albert Einstein, Eleanor Roosevelt, Harriet Tubman, Albert Schweitzer, Jane Addams, Frederick Douglass, Cesar Chavez, and Adlai Stevenson. Had Maslow lived longer, he might have added Martin Luther King and Mother Teresa. A number of the common characteristics of super-personalities are summarized in Table 10.1.

Do not feel too disappointed to learn that you probably are not a self-actualizer or that self-actualizers are not likely to be present among your college classmates. Maslow's (1970) initial screening of 3,000 students yielded only one immediately usable subject, partly related to limitations of youth and experience.

Even superior psychological health was defined by Maslow as applying to less than 1 percent of college students, those evaluated as "growing well." Any such disappointment may be tempered by learning that self-actualizers are not likely to be present among your college professors either, nor among your friends, family, or distant relatives and acquaintances. This is supported by the small number of persons Maslow has identified as meeting his criteria for self-actualization.

BOX 10.2   Where Are You on Maslow's Hierarchy Right Now?

Now that you have a preliminary understanding of the hierarchical needs, go back to Figure 10.1. Think of yourself as you are just now. Assuming that you are well fed and feel safe and secure, what need is in focus at this time? Is it belongingness and love? Esteem? (If Maslow is correct about the rareness of self-actualizers, it is probably not self-actualization.) Choose one and write a paragraph to verify your choice (list the kinds of experiences you long for right now).

Not by Basic Needs Alone: Meta-Needs and Peak Experiences

Accompanying self-actualization are certain special needs. These are **cognitive needs**, needs to know, to understand, to explain, and to satisfy curiosity, and a variety of **aesthetic needs** related to beauty, structure, and symmetry. Such needs have been identified collectively by Maslow (1967) as **meta-needs, or being values (B-values)**, terms used "to describe the motivations of self-actualizing people" (Maslow, 1970, p. 134).

The preferences, values, and motivations of superior personalities were of great interest to Maslow. A number of *specific* B-values of self-actualizers have been identified by Maslow (1967). They include truth, goodness, beauty, unity and wholeness, transcendence, aliveness, uniqueness, perfection, completion, justice, order, simplicity, richness, totality, effortlessness, playfulness, self-sufficiency, and meaningfulness. Again, all of these meta-needs, or B-values, are closely enmeshed with the overriding need for self-actualization and are not, strictly speaking, "motivated" but meta, or beyond motivation.

Maslow believed that self-actualizers are more likely than others to have **peak experiences**, intense, mystical experiences associated with simultaneous feelings of limitless horizons, powerfulness, and helplessness, a lost sense of time and place, and great ecstasy, wonder, and awe (Maslow, 1970). These experiences have a high degree of personal importance, strengthening or transforming the person. They come from love and sex, bursts of creativity, moments of insight and discovery, and times of fusion with nature. Peak experiences are natural phenomena, not supernatural, and were described by William James many years ago (1958).

Evaluation

Maslow's Contributions to Our View of Humans and Their Experience

Maslow's contributions are many and diverse. The emphasis here is on his beliefs that human values and needs are inherent and that humans are self-directing, his insightful criticisms of psychological science, his speculations about a psychological Utopia, and his contributions to diverse fields and disciplines.

Humans Have Inherent Needs and Values and Are Self-Directing

Unique among psychologists is Maslow's (1959, 1967, 1969) insistence that needs are as much a part of the human constitution as voice boxes and symbolic thought. He places emphasis on (1) the existence of universal human needs and values and (2) their biological origin. Like Rogers, Maslow believed that "the organism is more trustworthy, more self-protecting, self-directing, and self-governing than it is usually given credit for" (1970, p. 78). Also like Rogers, he believed strongly in a universal, inborn *organismic valuing process*, or "bodily wisdom." Maslow (1959) analogized to hundreds of free-choice experiments in which animals of all kinds behaved in ways that were "good" or "right" for them. For example, although some did better than others, animals were able to select adequate diets when offered a sufficient number of alternatives (P. T. Young, 1941, 1948). As for human infants, Maslow observed the evolution of psychologists toward increased confidence in "the internal wisdom of our babies" (Maslow, 1959, pp. 120–121). Infants can make good choices with regard to diet, time of weaning, amount of sleep, time of toilet training, need for activity, and so on. This point of view contrasts with that of behaviorists like B. F. Skinner who emphasize environmental control over infant behavior.

Insightful Criticisms of Psychological Science

Maslow has been especially critical of traditional approaches to determining standards for optimal personality functioning. Scientific approaches too readily assume that people are so similar to animals that results of animal studies can be generalized to humans. While useful analogies between humans and animals may be drawn, their essential natures differ.

Clinical approaches rely too heavily on samples of maladjusted people, thereby offering a warped view of human nature based on observations of disturbed and miserable lives. Other approaches adopt a statistical-averaging procedure in which findings from all people are thrown into a single hopper. With this methodology, individual differences are lost. More specifically, Maslow considers this technique of little use, because it mixes information from healthy and sick people equally, resulting in a concoction that is neither vintage champagne nor cheap wine.

Psychological Utopia: Eupsychia

Maslow, like Sullivan, believed that most basic human needs could be satisfied only through interpersonal relations. Although he developed no method of psychotherapy, he often saw therapeutic interactions as exemplifying "good human relationships." Quality relationships support human needs for security belongingness and self-esteem, on the way toward self-actualization (Maslow, 1970). Psychotherapy relationships dispense "psychological medicines" needed by all human beings: mutual frankness, trust, honesty, lack of defensiveness, emotional release, healthy passivity, relaxation, affection, love, and even childish silliness. Effective, democratic psychotherapists can do much to help individuals identify their inner needs and compensate for their deficiencies. These benefits then transfer to relationships outside the therapy setting.

Maslow (1970) firmly believed that self-actualization could be facilitated by a good environment which would include good people. Such an environment would (1) offer the individual all necessary raw materials; (2) get out of the way whenever appropriate; (3) allow the individual to pursue her or his own wishes, demands, and choices; (4) accept delays and abandonment of choices; and (5) respect the wishes, demands, and choices of individuals.

To make the criteria for the ideal environment more concrete, Maslow speculated about a future **Eupsychia** (Yew-sigh-key-ah), a utopian society characterized by psychological health among all its members. Its philosophical base would be anarchistic, meaning there would be no governmental imposition on individual liberty. Basic and meta-needs would be respected, much more than usual. There would be more free choice than people are used to, as well as less control, violence, and contempt. It also would be Taoistic in its philosophy, valuing what is simple, loving, and unselfish. Overall, the good environment would stress spiritual and psychological forces as well as material and economic ones. Eupsychia would not work for all, however. "When we speak of free choice in human beings, we refer to sound adults or children who are not yet twisted and distorted" (Maslow, 1970, p. 278). You may find it interesting to compare Maslow's conceptions of the Utopian society with those of B. F. Skinner, whose ideas have formed the basis of a real, functioning community.

Contributions to Many Fields and Concerns

Maslow's ideas, especially his hierarchy of needs, have been adapted to many different professional areas. The hierarchy has been especially useful to people concerned with personnel management, marketing, and organizational operations (Alderfer, 1989; Buttle, 1989). In organizational settings, relations among employees within and between management levels will not be smooth and efficient unless each employee recognizes the need satisfactions being sought by other employees. Only with such understanding will employees be able to facilitate one another's need satisfactions and integrate the pursuit of satisfactions with company goals. Creativity will be locked out of the executive board room unless high-level management personnel are encouraged and aided in attempts to approximate self-actualization. Finally, the marketing of products will be less than optimally effective if the needs that products address are not considered when decisions about product "packaging" are made. Maslow's book *Eupsychian Management* (1965) is in large part devoted to these issues.

The enormous variety of fields to which Maslow's ideas have been applied is illustrated by two additional examples. First, Maslow's hierarchy has been adapted as a tool to facilitate conferences between speech-language pathologists and their advisors (Houle, 1990). Prior to conferences, pathologists select one role expectation and one of Maslow's needs to be foci during the upcoming conference.

Second, self-actualization in athletes has been recently examined. A group of researchers compared blind and sighted athletes on scores derived from responses to Shostrom's Personality Orientation Inventory, or POI measure of self-actualization (Sherrill, Gench, Hinson, Gilstrap, Richir, & Mastro, 1990; Shostrom, 1966). The POI is a paper-and-pencil personality questionnaire made up of 150 pairs of items, in a forced-choice format. People respond to each item-pair by selecting the pair member that best applies to them. Examples similar to POI items are: "(a) I enjoy my life" or "(b) I do not enjoy my life"; and "(a) People should keep their feelings to themselves" or "(b) People should express their feelings to others."

Blind and sighted athletes were identical in self-actualization profiles, except that blind athletes scored lower on Existentiality and Self-acceptance. Athletes as a group scored lower than the general population on two major POI scales: Time Competency and Inner-Directedness. However, they were average or strong in Self-actualizing Value, Feeling Reactivity, Spontaneity, Self-Regard, and Acceptance of Aggression.

Supporting Evidence

Some fundamental concepts of Maslow's theory have received at least partial support, often of an indirect or philosophical nature. For example, the influence of an actualizing tendency has been affirmed by other theorists and some researchers, both within and outside psychology. More specifically, support for the universal striving to be all that it is possible to be (the formative tendency) and the tendency toward self-actualization has been reported, and evidence of a need hierarchy and of peak experiences has been provided.

Universal Formative Tendency

Some support for "the formative tendency" has come from disciplines outside psychology (Royce & Mos, 1981). Contemporary biological concepts encompass not only *entropy*, the organismic tendency toward disorder, but *syntropy*, the ever-operating trend toward increased order and interrelated complexity that is evident at both organic and inorganic levels. Albert Szent-Gyoergyi (1974), a Nobel Prize winning biologist, has written of an innate drive in all living matter to perfect itself. Work with sea-urchin larvae has demonstrated that each of the two cells formed after a fertilized egg divides has the capacity to develop into a whole sea-urchin larva, not just portions (see Rogers, 1979/1983). This is because the genetic code contains *rules* of growth, rather than specific, fixed information. This feature leaves room for information to be generated within the organism.

Self-Actualization

Maslow emphasized the idea of an inborn tendency toward actualization. Support for this emphasis comes from a number of other humanistic theories. Maslow credits a follower of Gestalt tradition, Kurt Goldstein (1939), with originating the concept "self-actualization." Goldstein saw "the drive of self-actualization" as the only human motive (Maslow, 1954). Although their positions were not identical, like Maslow, Goldstein believed that the organism's self-realization or "urge to perfection" is expressed through actual performance and preferred "choices" in life.

Shostrom's (1966) POI provides scores on a variety of humanistic dimensions, as described in the discussion of blind and sighted athletes. Use of the POI has yielded evidence for the validity of self-actualization. In a study cited by Shostrom (1966), the POI scores of two therapy-patient groups were compared. One group was predicted to be relatively high in self-actualizing tendency, because it was composed of patients averaging 27 months of therapy. The other group was expected to be less self-actualizing, because it was comprised of patients just beginning therapy. The differences between group scores were statistically significant on all dimensions. The two groups also differed on 7 of 9 maladjustment scales of an independent measure, the Minnesota Multiphasic Personality Inventory.

Hierarchy of Needs

Graham and Balloun (1973) have reported partial support for Maslow's hierarchy of needs, based on data from 37 San Francisco residents. First, participants responded to open-ended interview questions asking them to describe the most important things in their lives. Graduate students then rated these verbatim responses on a 5-point scale ranging from "very high" to "little or no" desire expressed for physiological, security, social (acceptance by others), and self-actualization needs. Results supported the hypothesis that comparisons of needs at different levels on the hierarchy would show greater satisfaction for lower-order needs than for higher-order needs. Second, participants made direct ratings of their present degree of satisfaction or dissatisfaction at each of the four need levels, and their desire for "none" to "very much" improvement at each level. Correlations between these ratings ranged between −.42 and −.72, with a median or middle value of −.62, which was statistically significant. This confirmed the hypothesis that the *level of satisfaction* of any given need would be negatively correlated with *desire for satisfaction* of that need: the less the satisfaction, the more the desire for satisfaction.

As just illustrated, until recently there has been a tendency for researchers to consider the hierarchy as a whole or concentrate on measurement of self-actualization. Williams and Page (1989) corrected that shortcoming by developing measures relevant to the safety, belonging, and esteem levels of the hierarchy. For each of these levels they assessed: (1) need gratification (perceptions of the degree to which a need is being gratified); (2) need importance; (3) need salience (the degree to which a need is "on one's mind and demands one's attention"); and (4) self-concept (as related to a given need level; for example, one could have a positive or negative self-concept regarding how much others are seen as caring for oneself).

Williams and Page made a number or predictions that clarify how their measures would pinpoint the level at which a person is functioning and whether the person is preparing to move to a higher level. A person's degree of need gratification at a given level should be negatively correlated with the salience of the need at that level. That is, the more a need has been gratified, the less it should be on one's mind (salience). As one is entering a new, higher level, one's self-concept should become attuned to the new level. For example, if one has accommodated belongingness needs and is moving to esteem needs, one's self-concept should be based more on feelings of adequacy, competence, achievement, and status in others' eyes (esteem) than on affectionate relations with others (belongingness).

Further, the self-concept should be in tune with need gratification for the level at which one currently dwells, but negatively related to need gratification for the level one has just transcended. Finally, it should be possible to ascertain at which level a person dwells and predict whether the person is primed to move up. Suppose a person indicates that all needs up to and including those relating to esteem are important, and the person's highest self-concept score is at the esteem level. Then it can be concluded that the person is operating at the esteem level. In addition, suppose the person is somewhat unsatisfied in terms of esteem, but all lower-order needs are satisfied. Under these conditions it is possible to predict that the person is not likely to move from esteem to self-actualization anytime soon.

Williams and Page used undergraduate psychology students in three studies designed to test their hypotheses. Generally, the students were found to be functioning at the esteem level.

Evidence supporting this conclusion included: (1) "importance" scores were highest for esteem needs and self-concept was most in tune with that level; (2) the needs at the two lower levels were rated as important, but not particularly "on the mind" (salient); and (3) need gratification was high for all levels, but of the three under investigation, it was lowest for esteem. In all, the researchers made 16 predictions. One such prediction was that the higher the safety need gratification, the lower the safety self-concept, because, having met safety needs, the individual would be pursuing needs at higher levels. Fourteen of the 16 predictions were confirmed. This outcome lends credence to the researchers' contention that their measure shows the level at which a person dwells and predicts where the person will go next in the pursuit of need satisfactions.

Peak Experiences

Research findings have contributed some support to Maslow's concept of "peak experience." Ravizza (1977) interviewed 20 athletes in 12 different sports who reported expanded views of themselves as fully functioning individuals. Their "greatest moment" in sports showed many similarities to Maslow's description of the peak experience: loss of fear (100 percent of sample), full attention or immersion (95 percent), perfect experience (95 percent), godlike feeling of control (95 percent), self-validation (95 percent), universe as integrated and unified (90 percent), and effortlessness (90 percent). Nevertheless, some aspects of Maslow's description were not met: the athletes' experiences were more narrow in focus than broad, more oriented to the body than to cognitive or spiritual reflection, and more important to immediate circumstances than to bringing about major changes in their lives. Thus, athletes' "greatest moments" were only partially equivalent to Maslow's peak experiences.

Mathes, Zevon, Roter, and Joerger (1982) reviewed the research literature on peak experiences and then developed a 70-item scale to measure peak-experience tendencies, the Peak Scale. An "empirical picture" of individuals reporting peak experiences, consistent with Maslow's theorizing, emerged after five studies using the scale. Individuals who scored high on the Peak Scale evidenced cognitive experiences of a transcendent and mystical nature, as well as feelings of intense happiness. High scorers reported living in terms of B-values such as truth, beauty, and justice. Women, but not men, tended to show slightly higher self-actualization scores on the POI compared with persons not reporting peak experiences.

Limitations

It will come as no surprise to you that criticisms of Maslow's work are most frequently lodged against ideas relating to self-actualization, and against the hierarchy of needs. "Peak experience" has received a measure of criticism as well. By and large, Maslow has been charged with arbitrariness and failure to consider alternatives. In addition, research relating to his ideas has generated contradictions.

Self-Actualization

To his credit, Maslow did not begin with the question of what human values *should* be, but with observations of what healthy people *do* when they are permitted to choose, and live their lives freely. Thus, he supported his ideas about self-actualization by observing "super-personalities," people operating at the highest levels of personality functioning (Maslow 1970). Seen from another perspective, however, these so-called "self-actualizers" are not professional experts on human behavior; they are expert human beings. Even they cannot allow us to get at self-actualization directly: we cannot ask them to tell us about self-actualization as if they were expert psychologists. As with Rogers, a further weakness is seen in Maslow's methodological approach to these superior personalities. It is based on a small, arbitrarily selected sample that was not objectively observed, rather than on systematic assessment.

Maslow's identifications of "self-actualizers" were based on his personal selections, resulted from inferential reviews of a variety of materials not publicly available, occurred after the fact, and were biased toward Western civilization. Maslow himself recognized some of these shortcomings (1959). Other commentators have acknowledged the shaky nature of identifying self-actualizers and the traits they are supposed to possess. While dismissing his own approval of Maslow's values as "beside the point," M. Brewster Smith (1973) declared that Maslow's values are too one-sided.

Phillips, Watkins, and Noll (1974) compared Maslow's "self-actualization" with existentialist Viktor Frankl's "self-transcendence." Based on writings by Maslow and Frankl, a contrast was made between measures of the two concepts: the POI (self-actualization; Shostrom, 1966) versus the Purpose in Life Test (PIL) (self-realization; Crumbaugh & Maholick, 1969). Although the two concepts should have been highly similar, Phillips and colleagues found differences as well as similarities. Regarding the ability to meaningfully assess "self-actualization," Tosi and Hoffman (1972) supported the POI only partially. It was validated mainly as a measure of "healthy personality" as indexed by three factors: (1) extraversion, (2) open-mindedness, and (3) existential nonconformity.

More than any other criticism of Maslow's central concept, the most damning has to be the charge that his conception of "self-actualization" is neither universal nor the "best" rendition of "human fulfillment." Ajit K. Das (1989) in a paper entitled "beyond self-actualization" has suggested that other notions of "fulfillment" exist in non-western societies and may, in some respects, be more attractive than "self-actualization." In contrast to self-actualization, Das offers "self-realization" extracted primarily from Buddhism. Compared to self-actualization, self-realization is a more active process. It does not just happen after lower needs are satisfied; one must work at self-realization. Further, the self-absorption that characterizes self-actualization is relatively de-emphasized in the case of self-realization in favor of concern for others. Box 10.3 contains some information about self-realization that, when compared with Table 10.1, will allow you to see the difference between it and self-actualization. Then you can draw your own conclusions about which is "best."

Buddha

The selfishness that taints the otherwise benevolent self-actualization, but not self-realization, is a problem for many individuals inside and outside of psychology (Das, 1989). For

---

BOX 10.3   Self-Realization

According to Buddha, the way to *Nirvana*, the ultimate state characterized by oblivion of care, pain, and external reality, is to first grasp the Four Noble Truths and then follow the Eightfold Path (see Das, 1989).

The Four Noble Truths

1. Dissatisfaction and suffering are inherent in the lives of humans.
2. Dissatisfaction and disappointment arise from people's desires and cravings. Most people are not able to accept life as it is. Instead they deny that craving creates tension and attempt to prolong pleasant experiences even as they try to shorten unpleasant experiences.
3. Suffering is abolished only by eliminating cravings. One need not deny all desires, but only the most demanding desires that dominate one's life.
4. The way to eliminate craving and dissatisfaction is to follow the Noble Eightfold Path.

The Eightfold Path

(broken down into three categories of behaviors)

1. Adhere to moral conduct—right speech, right action, right livelihood—which requires that no act harmful to self or others be committed and that one actively helps others. The mind must also be kept free of evil thoughts.
2. Maintain mental discipline—right effort, right alertness, and right concentration—which requires control of one's mind. After a rigorous period of training, one will be able to control one's thoughts and feelings and also empty one's mind of all contents so that perfect tranquility can be achieved.
3. Develop intuitive wisdom—right understanding and right purpose—which requires correct understanding of the Four Noble Truths, and the tendency to abide by them.

example, had Maslow applied his criteria for self-actualization to candidates for the annual *Mother Jones* magazine humanitarian awards, he would have rejected most of the actual recipients. The focus of actual recipients' lives is selfless concern for others, not "self-knowledge," "creative expression," or "having peak experiences." By looking again at the bottom part of Table 10.1, which contains some negative characteristics of self-actualizers, you will realize that these people have a minority of traits that are less than benevolent. To illustrate these traits, I had a personal, though remote, experience with a famous psychologist who claimed to be "self-actualized." As a member of an audience to which this individual spoke, I was less than favorably impressed when he declared that he would turn away his best friend if that person wished to speak with him "during the time of day I put aside for myself."

Peak Experiences
As already emphasized, scientific criteria usually demand that it be possible to translate important concepts into measurable terms. However, many of Maslow's concepts are difficult or impossible to translate. Concepts such as "truth," "joy," and "beauty" are examples. "Peak experiences" provide a prime illustration. Different researchers and theorists have used the phrase differently, lending a flavor of arbitrariness to it (Mathes, Zevon, Roter, & Joerger, 1982).

There are contradictions regarding peak experiences as well. Such experiences are supposed to be the province of high "self-actualizers." Yet, while Sherrill and colleagues (1990) found that athletes tended to be relatively low on self-actualization, Ravizza (1977) found that athletes are prone to having peak experiences, albeit limited ones.

The Hierarchy
The needs hierarchy itself has not escaped criticism. Alderfer (1989) saw enough deficiencies in the hierarchy that are relevant to business and industry to warrant replacing it with his own. With obvious disapproval, Buttle (1989) indicated that Maslow's hierarchy "is reified, if not deified, in the marketing literature" (p. 201). He went on to declare that "Maslow never explained why he selected the five basic needs, why they were ranked as they were, or why others were not included" (p. 202). Buttle concluded his criticism of Maslow's hierarchy by suggesting alternative conceptions of needs for use in marketing.

Conclusions

Many of the criticisms lodged against Maslow's work seem less telling in view of research evidence produced near the end of his life and after his death. The allegation that he relied on arbitrarily obtained "simple observations and descriptions" in conceiving of "self-actualization" is growing irrelevant as scientific data increasingly support his assumptions about the concept. The growth in the application of his hierarchy to various professional areas may some day obliterate the charge that the needs are not universal and are misapplied to some areas. Further, Williams' and Page's (1989) work seems destined to render the hierarchy's needs measurable and progress up the hierarchy predictable.

Maslow considered his most important educational experiences to be those that taught him what kind of a person he was: psychoanalysis, his marriage to Bertha, and the "thunderclap" of having a child. World War II also had a dramatic impact on him, making him want "to prove that human beings are capable of something grander than war and prejudice and hatred" (in M. Hall, 1968, p. 54). He advised his two daughters, "Learn to hate meanness." Thus, Maslow became a caring and wise person, if not the warm and untroubled individual that was Carl Rogers. One could dote on Rogers because of the fine person that his gentle upbringing allowed him to become. Also, one could be filled with admiration for Maslow, because he became an exemplary human being despite cruel treatment at the hands of his mother and the anti-Semites who abused him at every turn.

Maslow's unique approach to understanding human experience was to find "the best" humankind has to offer—that fraction of the population representing superior self-actualization, peak experiences, understanding, and creativity. Having discovered "the best," he used them to show us how to become better than we are. Although these superior personalities tell us much, none can better inform us about how to be than the example set by Maslow himself.

Summary Points

1. Abraham Maslow was the first of seven children born in 1908 to a neglectful father and an allegedly cruel mother. During childhood, Maslow's first love were the books of the Brooklyn Library, access to which was perilous due to neighboring anti-Semitic gangs. After undistinguished performance at a prestigious high school, Maslow enrolled in City College, Cornell, law school, and finally the University of Wisconsin. There he became a "monkey psychologist," a kind of fame that led to his first job.

2. After temporarily rejecting psychology because of exposure to the archaic Edward Titchener, and contemplating the Adler-Freud quarrel, Maslow landed a research position under Edward L. Thorndike. Thus, he returned to New York City where he fell under the influence of Adler and the Gestalt psychologists. Armed with Gestalt holism, Maslow turned his attention to motivation, the process by which people are propelled toward goals. These goals can be cast as "needs" for certain satisfactions that are sought by all humans, regardless of culture, environment, or generation.

3. While needs are universal, methods of satisfying them can be culturally or environmentally determined. Maslow believed that needs are formed into a hierarchy, with more primitive, lower-order needs demanding satisfaction before more complex and uniquely human needs are addressed. Physiological needs demand satisfaction first. Second, safety needs must be met. Third, belongingness and love needs demand attention. Fourth, esteem needs require consideration. These are the deficiency needs (D-needs).

4. "Self-actualization" is "the tendency for [one] to become actualized in what [one] is potentially." D-needs are prepotent, stronger, and demanding prior satisfaction before other needs can be addressed. Needs are not met in all-or-none fashion, but higher-order needs cannot be met until lower-order needs are largely satisfied. In exceptional cases, people may deny lower-order needs and still pursue higher-order needs as Gandhi did.

5. Although culture, family, and parents may function as sun, food, and water to human actualization, they are not its seeds. Human nature is inborn, not made. Thus, even self-actualization needs are instinctoid, because of their biological, genetic, and universal characteristics. Genuine self-actualizers, however, are quite rare. Self-actualizers are the good choosers who show the rest of us what is good for the human species. They are persons who fulfill themselves by making complete use of their potentialities.

6. Although self-actualizers possess such positive traits as spontaneity, autonomy, ethicality, and creativity, they may also be thoughtless, prideful, and socially impolite. Self-actualizers have their own sources of motivation, B-values. They may also have peak experiences—intense, mystical experiences associated with simultaneous feelings of powerfulness and helplessness.

7. Maslow believed that humans have universal, positive needs and values and are self-directing. In fact, organisms, whether they be lower-animals or human babies, if left to their own devices, can do well choosing what is best for them. His optimistic view of people led him to propose a psychological Utopia, called *Eupsychia*. This proposal assumes that environments can be contrived that will foster the satisfaction of higher-order needs.

8. The enormous variety of fields to which Maslow's ideas have been applied include business and speech pathology. Researchers have shown that blind athletes, and athletes in general, show a unique pattern of responses to the POI. Several theorists in others fields, such as biology, have supported ideas that, in turn, confirm Maslow's belief in the inherent striving of creatures to actualize their potential.

9. In support of "self-actualization," Shostrom has confirmed that people who would be expected to make a better approximation to self-actualization scored higher on all POI dimensions than others. Graham and Balloun showed that individuals display greater satisfaction of lower- than of higher-order needs. Williams and Page confirmed this result and demonstrated that self-concept is most in tune with the level of the hierarchy at which a person is currently operating. Further, needs gratification at a given level is negatively correlated with salience of needs at that level.

10. While there is some evidence for peak experiences, they may be realized only partially, and people not expected to have such experiences report them. The needs hierarchy has been replaced in some fields and Maslow's failure to explain its origins has been noted. Self-actualization deficiencies include Maslow's arbitrary selection of self-actualizers to study, the non-universality of self-actualization, the selfishness of self-actualizers, and the existence of an attractive alternative, self-realization. Nevertheless, current research is erasing many of the criticisms of self-actualization and the hierarchy. Maslow himself can be praised for the exemplary human that he was, despite a troubled upbringing.

Running Comparison

Theorists	Maslow in Comparison
Adler	Like Adler, he was a father's boy. Adler's concepts social interest (*Gemeinshaftsgefuhl*), law of movement, striving for superiority, and creative power of the individual probably influenced him.
Horney	Like her, he felt unattractive. Her "basic anxiety" is similar to his safety needs.
George Kelly	Like Kelly, his first experience with psychology was not positive.
Henry A. Murray	He agreed with Murray that a behavior is a function of many needs and the satisfaction of any need may be tied to the satisfaction of others needs.
Sullivan	They both believed that needs are satisfied through interpersonal relations.

Essay/Critical Thinking Questions

1. We often think of child abuse as physical. In fact, it can be verbal and "psychological." Could you put yourself in Maslow's shoes when he was a child? His mother apparently did not abuse him physically, but did mistreat him verbally. Write a short piece indicating other forms of such abuse that Maslow might have suffered.

2. There is much to do about quotas these days. In fact, as Maslow's case illustrates, quotas have always been with us: they have been used to exclude Jews and people of color. Until the 1960s, the quota for blacks at most major universities was zero. Nowadays, quotas still mean that members of the present majority are most likely to be hired or otherwise selected ("12 percent of new hires must be black; thus, 88 percent can be white"). But can you imagine yourself in a situation more similar to young Maslow's? Sometime during the next century people of color will be the majority. Imagine that you are white, its 2080, and the quotas seem designed to exclude you. Write a paragraph telling how you would feel.

3. Are there other meaningful hierarchies? How about a hierarchy of feelings, of rewards? Construct your own psychological hierarchy.

4. Has Maslow missed some meaningful needs? Write a brief argument supporting an addition to Maslow's hierarchy.

5. Does Maslow have needs in the right order? Write a brief argument for a reversal in his order. For example, could you argue that esteem really belongs ahead of belongingness and love?

6. Could you argue that the associative learning position is correct? That is, love, esteem, and so forth, are derived from lower-order needs. Show how some other higher-order need could be based on a lower-order need.

7. Could you elaborate on Maslow's Eupsychian society? Write a paragraph describing a society that would foster self-actualization.

8. Is Maslow's claim that he chose "super-personalities," observed them, and then conceived of "self-actualization" legitimate? Indicate how his preconceptions about "self-actualization" may have led him to choose certain "super personalities" rather than others. Hint: did his preconceptions cause him to exclude self-denying people (people more concerned about others than themselves)?

9. Could you compare at least two products and show how each appeals to a different need on Maslow's hierarchy?

10. Maslow would say it is highly unlikely that you and I are self-actualizers. Yet, in contradiction, we probably have had some peak experiences. Can you describe some peak experiences that you have had?

11

MARCHING TO A DIFFERENT DRUMMER: GEORGE KELLY

- What psychological dimensions do you use to conceive of your world and its people: good-bad? ambiguous-clear? sane-insane? other?
- Can you apply the principles of science to the solution of your own problems?
- Are your thinking processes complex or simple?
- Can you imagine you are a child again, relating to your mother?
- Who is the most pitied person in your life?

One of the issues running through most previous and subsequent chapters has been whether the "inside" or the "outside" of people is stressed by theorists. As you will see, the behaviorists look only outside. As you already know, the psychoanalysts are rather exclusively concerned with the inside. Other theorists to be covered later consider both perspectives. This chapter focuses on a theory of personality that emphasizes an internal aspect, cognition, while not neglecting the external world. It introduces an important figure in yet another break with the Freudian and behaviorist traditions—a break as profound as the rift created by the humanists. George Kelly is aptly described as in the vanguard of the "cognitive" revolution.

Kelly, the Person

George Kelly was the maverick son of a preacher, born in a small Kansas town (1905). A rugged individualist, quite literally of pioneer stock, he was skeptical concerning psychological principles from day-one of his first psychology class. Sitting in the back row of the introductory psychology classroom, Kelly tilted his

George Kelly

chair against the wall and waited for something interesting to occur (Kelly, 1969). Two to three weeks lapsed, during which he could state only one clear impression, his professor seemed nice. Then one day he was inspired to sit up and take notice. A capital "S" and a capital "R" were prominently displayed on the blackboard, connected by an arrow pointing from the former to the latter. Here, thought Kelly, is the meat of the matter. However, further lectures only disappointed him. Many years later he wrote of the experience:

Although I listened intently for several sessions, after that the most I could make of it was that the "S" was what you had to have in order to account for the "R" and the "R" was put there so the "S" would have something to account for. I never did find out what that arrow stood for—not to this day—and I have pretty well given up trying to figure it out. (1969, p. 47)

And he pretty well gave up on psychology, for the time being, choosing instead to pursue a career in engineering. Three years later he was out of engineering and back in school, forced by the Great Depression to learn something more practical. Being interested in sociology and labor relations, he thought it high time to have a look at Freud. "I don't remember which one of Freud's books I was trying to read," wrote Kelly (1969, p. 47) "but I do remember the mounting feeling of incredulity that anyone could write such nonsense, much less publish it."

Skepticism characterized his second encounter with psychology, which, ironically, may explain why he became a psychologist. Kelly needed to practice his considerable gift for healthy skepticism and psychology provided the perfect forum: one can argue that all psychological principles can be questioned.

Skepticism is sometimes accompanied by sarcasm, and indeed, Kelly provided several cases in point. When prompted to consider the process of salivation, he felt called upon to cast some aspersions Pavlov's way: "Salivation . . . takes place in a manner that suggests the anticipation of food, or perhaps hunger—I am not sure which. Perhaps what is anticipated is an activity we call eating. Whatever it indicates, Pavlov seems to have demonstrated it and there is no reason we should not be grateful even though we are not quite sure what it was he demonstrated" (Kelly, 1980, p. 29). When inspired to cite examples of people who fail to benefit from experience, he recalled a naval officer with "a vast and versatile ignorance," and a school administrator who "had one year of experience—repeated thirteen times" (Kelly, 1963, p. 171). He even took a swing at all of his colleagues. In observing that his fundamental assumptions apply to everyone, he wrote, "The same goes for psychologists, who are known to have human characteristics too" (p. 25).

Sometimes, however, he was more humorous than sarcastic. In making the point that people orient to the future, not the past, he described a friend's peculiar approach to driving: "A friend of mine, while driving her car, customarily closes her eyes when she gets caught in a tight spot. This is an anticipatory act; she suspects something may happen that she would prefer not to see. So far, it hasn't happened, though it is hard to understand why" (Kelly, 1980, p. 26).

If sarcasm was a characteristic of Kelly, it certainly was overridden by a more central feature of his personality. Kelly was a warm and accepting person. He practiced therapy to help people and to learn from them. In thirty years as a psychotherapist, he never collected a penny for his services. George Thompson, a former colleague, wrote of this preacher's son:

> At the 1963 Convention of the American Psychological Association, some 40 former students of George Kelly attended a dinner to pay tribute to their good teacher and warm friend. These professors, scientists, and therapists came from all parts of the United States. All of them knew that here was a man who had helped them find their ways to more productive lives. Many others who could not attend wrote letters of appreciation for his wise counsel and guidance. (1968, pp. 22–23)

Similarly, in the summer of 1965, Kelly's associates at Ohio State gathered to salute their colleague and friend who had just been granted an endowed chair at Brandeis University. Papers were read by three of Kelly's former doctoral students and by a visiting professor from England, who had spread Kelly's ideas through several of Britain's universities. At the end of these presentations, Kelly rose to invite the entire assembly to his house for dinner. Nearly 100 accepted the gracious offer. Thompson wrote of the occasion:

> There was good food for all and a characteristic abundance of warm fellowship. The dinner (was) only a token to a man who had contributed so much, but (it) did reflect in modest measure the affectionate humanity of George Alexander Kelly— scholar, teacher, and warm friend. (1968, pp. 22–23)

Above all, Kelly was open-minded. Perhaps this aspect of his personality stemmed from his extreme versatility (or perhaps his open-mindedness was the cause and his versatility the effect). That versatility is best appreciated by reference to Kelly's own words:

> I had taught soap-box oratory in a labor college for labor organizers, government in an . . . institute for prospective citizens, public speaking for the American Bankers Association, and dramatics in a junior college . . . I had taken a Master's degree with a study of workers' use of leisure time, and an advanced professional degree in education at the University of Edinburgh, and . . . I had dabbled . . . in education, sociology, economics, labor relations, biometrics, speech pathology, and

cultural anthropology, and had majored in psychology (the latter) for a grand total of nine months. (Kelly, 1969, p. 48)

Kelly's training in psychology yielded a Ph.D. from Iowa State University in 1931. While his early career was spent at Fort Hays State College in Kansas, Ohio State University claimed him for more years than any other academic institution.

His extraordinary versatility lead Kelly to a dozen or so universities, each for an appreciable period of time, and around the globe for the purpose of applying his theory to the problems of the world. Little wonder that he embraced the assumption, adopted by many philosophers of science and dismissed by none, that in the realm of science there are no truths (Hempel and Oppenheim, 1960). In psychology, as in other sciences, there are theories which are supported by evidence to varying degrees, but no truth. For a personality theorist, this was an unusual assumption, but then Kelly was an unusual theorist.

Unfortunately, Kelly died in his early 60s (1967), having produced relatively few writings. Fortunately he has had such strong impact on his students that his writings, as well as numerous speeches, lectures, and conversations, have been thoroughly mined. The psychological "gold" produced by several posthumous publications edited or written by his students contributed greatly to this chapter.

Kelly's View of the Person

As you recall, Freud thought of humans as helpless particles blown about by the hidden winds of hedonic impulse. Each human was seen as an effect of inaccessible and uncontrollable causes. Jung viewed humans from a broader perspective, but one might argue that he regarded them as captives of their ancestral past. Adler, Sullivan, Fromm, and Horney saw people as the products of their social environments. B. F. Skinner believed that consequences of behavior, provided by the environment, control human action. By contrast, Rogers and Maslow assumed that humans are capable of determining their own fates.

As usual, Kelly did not adopt the orientation of any of his predecessors or contemporaries. Rather, he declared that people are governed by an internal process: the way they construe events in their worlds. While this process is internal, it results from consequences of an external factor, social relations (Kelly, 1955). Kelly also thought that people had free will, in that they could choose from many alternative constructs that emerged from their relations with others.

Kelly's conception of time was different from that of the theorists covered so far, except possibly Adler. While he did not neglect the distant past, the recent past, or the present, he declared humans to be basically future-oriented (Kelly, 1980). He thought that the behavior of people was determined largely by their predictions of future events. Adler's "fictional finalism" does imply that people strive to meet a future goal, albeit a fictitious one.

It is interesting to speculate about how Kelly came to adopt such an intellectual, pragmatic, and "hard-nosed" point of view. He was an engineer, and a person made practical by the Great Depression. It was natural for him to orient to thinking rather than other psychological modes. As a victim of the Depression, little wonder that he looked more to the future than to the dismal present. As a person who was constantly changing not only physical location, but self as well, he had little inclination to the past. Perhaps Kelly's most important departure from the precepts of traditional, psychoanalytic psychology was that he saw himself as no different from those he studied and attempted to help in therapy (Kelly, 1969; for more about the inconsistency between researchers' views of themselves and of the people they study, see Allen, 1973, and Allen and Smith, 1980). Most psychologists, he charged, viewed themselves as objective, rational scientists who determine the causes of people's actions and suggest corrections for maladaptive behavior. On the other hand, their clients in therapy and their research subjects are seen as incapable of objective observation, unable to sort out the causes of their behavior, and inept at developing a systematic program for positive behavioral change. By contrast, Kelly saw himself as a scientist in his roles as research psychologist, psychotherapist, and just plain person. Thus, because he was no different from others, clients, research subjects, and people in general were viewed as scientists. The best way to understand Kelly's belief that all of us operate like scientists on a day-to-day basis is to consider Kelly's recollection of how he discovered "people as scientists."

> *A typical afternoon might find me talking to a graduate student at one o'clock, doing all those familiar things that thesis directors have to do: encouraging the student to pinpoint the issues, to observe, to become intimate with the problem, to form hypotheses . . . to make some preliminary test runs, to relate his data to his predictions, to control his experiments so that he will know what led to what, to generalize cautiously, and to revise his thinking in the light of experience. At two o'clock I might have an appointment with a client. During this interview I would not be taking the role of the scientist, but rather helping the distressed person work out some solutions to his life's problems. So what would I do? Why, I would try to get him to pinpoint the issues, to observe, to become intimate with the problem, to form hypotheses, to make test runs, to relate outcomes to anticipations, to control his ventures so that he will know what led to what, to generalize cautiously, and to revise his dogma in the light of experience. At three o'clock I would see [the] student again. Likely as not he was either dragging his feet, hoping to design some worldshaking experiment before looking at his first subject to see firsthand what he was dealing with, or plunging into some massive ill-considered data-chasing expedition. So I would try to get him to . . . [do] . . . all the things that I had [tried to get him] to do at one o'clock. At four o'clock another client! Guess what! He would be dragging his feet, hoping to design a completely new personality before venturing his first change in behavior, or plunging into some ill-considered acting-out escapade, etc., etc. (Kelly, 1969, pp. 60–61)*

Kelly had what the Freudians would call *insight*. Of course, he was acting as a scientist, and so was the student, when they were discussing the student's research. However, he was also a scientist when he was getting his distressed client to become a better scientist. Thus, students doing research, their advisors, clients in psychotherapy, their psychotherapists, and "people on the street" behave like scientists daily. Sometimes they do well at it and sometimes badly. Each tries to pinpoint the relevant issues related to his or her problem, make observations of the people involved in the problem, become intimate with the problem, form hypotheses, run "experiments," relate outcomes to predictions of the future, control pursuits so that it is clear what led to what, generalize cautiously, and revise strongly-held beliefs in the light of experience. For Kelly, people are scientists, all of them, all of the time.

Basic Concepts: Kelly

Personality as a System of Constructs

Underlying all of Kelly's thinking are the cognitive structures known as **constructs**, ways of construing events or "seeing the world" so that the future is anticipated (Kelly, 1980). Thus, his theory was called *"Personal Construct Theory"* (PCT). The individual's **personality** consists of an organized system of constructs that may be ranked as to importance. *Construct* became the foundation upon which Kelly built his most basic theoretical framework or postulate. A *postulate* is a basic assumption which is the starting point for a theory. It is a broad statement that is just accepted; it cannot be directly tested. Kelly's **fundamental postulate** is the assumption that a person's psychological processes are routed through various channels or pathways by the ways in which she or he anticipates events (Kelly, 1963). In a sense, these ways of "seeing the world" form the channels that are directed toward the future. Predictions *pull* the person along through life, as opposed to being *pushed* by unconscious impulses and drives or pricked into action by stimuli in the environment.

To set the stage for Kelly's other theoretical concepts, it is helpful to build on the notion of constructs by looking at how two individuals, Jim and Joan, go about a day in their lives. As you read, pay special attention to the words in italics.

Jim's Problem

"What's wrong now?" Joan inquired as she approached a figure who was slumped against the wall outside a classroom. Jim's reply was inaudible, partly because his hands covered his face and partly because he was too depressed to speak up.

Undeterred by the lack of a response to her question, Joan continued, "Let me guess . . . It's Professor Martindale again."

Jim's head sprang upright. Though his hair cascaded over his eyes, it failed to hide the fierce look that distorted his face. "Damn it," he was nearly screaming. "I've tried everything. I give up."

Joan looked around self-consciously, hoping that, somehow, students passing them in the hall had not noticed the outburst. Then she eased down next to her friend. Softly she entreated, "Tell me about it."

"It's the same thing . . . same old thing," he muttered.

Joan leaned back against the wall and exclaimed with a sigh, "OK then, tell me about your latest clash with Martindale."

"He hates me, I'm sure of it. The jerk said we could turn our papers in late, if we had a good excuse. Well, I had a good excuse . . . it was spring break . . . I was stuck in Florida . . . we were in somebody else's car. I mean, how could I get home . . ."

Joan's chin drew back and down. A familiar frown curled her lips. Martindale had looked the same when Jim had first related the "stuck in Florida" story. It was that incredulous look.

Jim's Constructs

"See there, see there" rasped Jim. "You're no different. I thought I could expect some sympathy from you . . . you're supposed to be a *good friend*, someone with a little *intelligence*. Go away . . . just get lost."

Joan moved closer and slipped her arm around Jim's shoulders, but he elbowed her away. "Jim, you know you can *trust* me . . . I am your *good friend*, but gimme a break. I know you believe that your excuse is OK . . . let me just put it this way . . . try it on some other people; I'll bet you that you'll get the same reaction."

There was silence for a minute, then Joan continued. "Look, let me make a suggestion. Why don't you . . ."

"That's not all . . ." Jim broke in. This time he was shouting. Joan was looking for a place to hide. "He laughed at me! . . . said he was just kidding about the excuse. 'I don't take excuses. The other students know that . . . it was just my way of making a joke . . . a little irony, you know.' Does he ever think I'm *stupid*! He probably thinks he couldn't *trust* me farther than he could throw me. And I thought *educated* people were my kind of people. Well, you live and learn. I'll know better next time."

Joan's Suggestions for Change

"That's what you said the last time you had it out with him," Joan could sense the taste of foot-in-the-mouth the minute she uttered the words. Jim climbed to his feet. He'd had enough of her, but before he could get away, Joan grabbed his shirt sleeve and dragged him back down. "Look, I'm sorry," she pleaded, "but it's just that . . . sometimes it seems like you don't learn from *experience*. I mean you just stick with an old idea, no matter what. Why is it so important that Martindale like you? I don't care whether he likes me or not."

After a time Jim settled down and he began to chatter amiably with his friend, which was usual for them. They talked about Jim's relationship with Martindale. "OK, you win," asserted Joan, "so you have some kind of fixation for Martindale—father figure is what my psych teacher would say—OK, I accept that. Now let me give you a suggestion . . . try this out. I mean you have had plenty of time to *evaluate* him. You think he's one of the '*good guys*,' right?" Jim shook his head in a vigorous "no" sign, but Joan ignored him. "What you have to do is let him know you think he belongs in select company. I mean . . . as I see it . . . you expect him to think you're a 'good guy,' but you won't put him in that same category. I know how you are. Surely you can understand that people like those who like them—it's sort of a law—but they can't read your mind. You have to communicate your feelings to people. If I know you, you've been very stiff and formal with Martindale. Am I right?"

Jim's head was hanging down, "Yeah," he mumbled, "you do know me."

"Actually, what it amounts to," Joan was talking rapidly now, "you think he's a *'good guy,'* you *admire* him and you want him to *admire* you. I know, because, if I like someone, I want that somebody to throw a little admiration my way."

"Admire?" You could almost see the question mark on Jim's face. "*Trust* maybe, but admire? I don't resort to hero worship."

"Well you had better consider *'admiration.'* If you like someone, admiration is a way to communicate it without saying anything . . . I mean, without using words . . . the sound of your voice will do."

"All right," said Jim, almost in a whisper, "I'll try it."

Joan's Constructs

Now Jim hopped up and offered Joan a hand. They left the building and strolled along leisurely, toward their dorms. Neither said anything for a while, then Jim remarked in a calm and collected voice, "You know, sometimes I wonder who I am. Who am I anyway?" he was smiling as he posed the question.

"Good ole Jim, that's who you are," came the reply. "A little weird, but fun to be around."

He shoved her playfully. "OK, who are you, smarty?"

"Is that a serious question?"

"Yeah," he mocked, "who are you?"

"Well I don't think about it all day, but I guess I'd answer in terms of who I'm *like* . . . you know, similar to."

"And who is that?" said Jim in a sober voice adopted to match her own suddenly serious tone.

"I guess I'm an *athlete* at heart," mused Joan who was a member of the varsity track team. "Steffi Graf, that's who I'm like . . . or uh . . . who I'd like to be."

"Tough break," kidded Jim. "You don't have her killer instinct."

Joan went along with the teasing and added, "Nor do I have the ability . . . but who knows, maybe I'll get better and maybe track will be as big as tennis some day."

They reached the crossing that split the paths to their dorms and paused for a moment. "Big bash at the 'Gin Mill' this Saturday, need a ride?"

"No thanks," responded Joan as she backed down the path to her dorm. "I'm going home . . . back to God's country . . . down on the farm . . . with the *good* neighbors and the wide open spaces . . ."

"And the horse manure," interjected Jim in a loud voice, as they were now many yards apart.

She lobbed a rock at him, "You can have your stinking old city, full of dopers and muggers. You love it . . . I'm going back where everything is small and people are concerned . . ." her voice trailed off.

Jim's and Joan's Personalities
It is instructive to analyze Jim's and Joan's conversation from Kelly's point of view. A look at Figure 11.1 will allow you to examine some concrete examples of constructs (Kelly disliked the concrete, but could not avoid it). The figure displays Jim's and Joan's construct systems. A **construct system** is an organization of many constructs with the more important, and often more abstract, at the top and the less important constructs at the bottom. The constructs at the top are called **superordinate** while the ones at the bottom are called **subordinate.**

The Construct System Is the Individual's Personality
Jim's most superordinate construct is represented by "trust-distrust," while Joan's most superordinate construct is "evaluative-descriptive." To *evaluate* is to pass judgment on, to *describe* is to label someone or something. As Kelly (1963) readily acknowledged, a construct can be thought of as a special kind of concept. Constructs have two opposite poles, like a magnet. The **emergent pole** is the primary and principle end, like "good" in good-bad and "intelligent" in intelligent-stupid (Kelly, 1955). The **implicit pole** is the contrasting end, like *uneducated* in educated-uneducated and *urban* in rural-urban. Normally, the emergent pole is formed first, but as soon as it develops, the implicit pole usually comes into existence. According to Kelly, people see the world in terms of contrasts; every thing or being has an opposite. The contrasts are there, even if

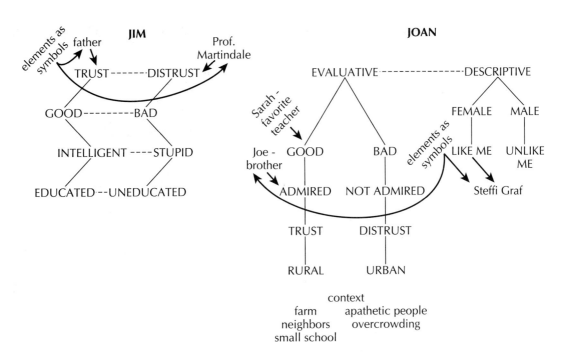

FIGURE 11.1   Joan's and Jim's construct systems

a person adopts a construct such as tolerant-intolerant and has never expressed or is unaware of the implicit pole, intolerant. Adopting *tolerant* automatically brings *intolerant* with it.

It may have occurred to you that examples of Kelly's constructs resemble traits. Figure 11.2 shows Jim's and Joan's constructs arranged like personality dimensions: behavioral dimensions corresponding to traits. You can see that Kelly's constructs are similar to dimensions. Kelly himself might balk at placing constructs in the trait category. However, its seems reasonable to point out that they bear some resemblance to traits, as long as one does not forget that Kelly's constructs are "ways of seeing the world" rather than internal dispositions that directly guide behavior.

Armed with these concepts, it is now possible to begin the analysis of Jim and Joan. It is easy to see that Jim is highly dependent on the construct "trust-distrust," his most superordinate construct. Like other constructs, it has what Kelly called a **range of convenience**, the extent and breadth of the event-category to which a construct applies. For example, trust-distrust is applicable to events involving people, such as the episodes of Jim's conflict with Professor Martindale. Because it is reasonable to assume that Jim experiences many events involving many different people, trust-distrust may be said to have a wide range of convenience. Nevertheless, it has its limits. Trust-distrust is scarcely applicable to solving mathematical problems or to viewing unique architecture. A superordinate construct's *range of convenience* may be thought of as including its subordinate constructs.

By contrast, a construct's **range of focus** refers to the events to which it is most readily applied. Trust-distrust is more readily applied to relations with people to whom Jim feels close, rather than to relations with more casual acquaintances.

Jim's construct, trust-distrust, can be characterized in yet another way. It is relatively **impermeable**, a reference to certain constructs that tend not to change in terms of range of convenience or place in the construct system. In fact, Joan noted

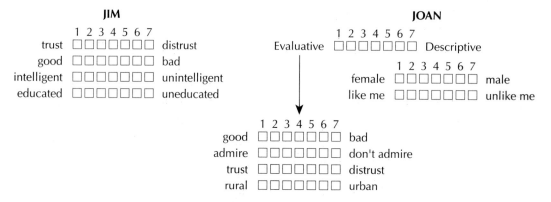

FIGURE 11.2 Jim's and Joan's construct systems adapted to dimensions.

that Jim's constructs are impermeable in general (remember she said that he fails to learn from experience). Trust-distrust is also part of Joan's system, but it is much more subordinate. Thus, the construct systems of Jim and Joan display common-ality, a reference to the sharing of constructs by two or more people whose experiences are similar. Jim and Joan are both students, thus, as you might expect, Figure 11.1 reveals that they do share constructs.

In comparison to commonality, **individuality** refers to differences among construct systems both in terms of the constructs comprising the system and in terms of how the constructs are organized. Such differences are due to differences in experiences. Joan is an athlete, Jim is not. Jim's problem, as Joan pointed out, is that he has failed to learn from **experience**, what one learns from the events of the past. Jim continues to try the same old strategies with Professor Martindale, and they are not getting him what he wants—mutual trust. Thus, Joan suggests a change in Jim's construct system. She thinks that Jim should embrace a new construct, "admire-not admire," and reorganize his construct system to be more like hers, with "trust-distrust" subordinated to "admire-not admire." Joan is trying to save Jim from **anxiety**, what a person experiences when his or her construct system does not apply to critical events, as Jim's fails to apply to events in his relationship with Professor Martindale. Joan should be cautious. In suggesting the new construct "admire-not admire" she may subject her friend to **fear**, the experience one has when a new construct appears to be entering the system, and may become dominant. On the other hand, she need not worry too much about subjecting Jim to **threat**, realization of the possibility that a person's entire construct system will be overhauled. Joan is suggesting a new construct and some reorganization, not a major upheaval.

Joan as Scientific Psychotherapist

Joan the psychotherapist acts like a scientist in attempting to make a better scientist of Jim. She pleads with him to make his constructs more permeable. More important, she suggests a hypothesis for Jim to test. She feels that expressing admiration will allow Jim to obtain the mutual trust that he wants to exist in his relationship with Professor Martindale. To test the hypothesis, Jim is told to try admiration out on Martindale. He then can observe to see how it works. If admiration has the intended effect, he should **replicate**, repeat a test in the hope the results will be the same as before. Replication provides the basis for anticipating future events. If one can repeat an observation of the successful application of a construct, one can be confident that the construct will apply again in the future, under similar circumstances. The greater the number of replications, the greater the confidence.

If Jim carries out Joan's suggestions, he will be acting according to one of Kelly's most basic principles, **constructive alternativism**, the assumption that a person's present interpretations of her or his life situation are subject to revision and replacement (Kelly, 1963). It is assumed that a construct system cannot remain the same, but must change with changes in the person's life situation.

BOX 11.1   Similarities of Kelly's Ideas to Those of
            Other Theorists

Kelly's relationship to other theorists warrants special attention, because he bears little resemblance to any of them, but shares assumptions with some of them. While Kelly chastised the behaviorists for their alleged obsession with minutia, such as "Ss and Rs," he shared some common assumptions with them. For example, like B. F. Skinner, who advocated the arrangement of environments to maximize positive reinforcements, Kelly believed that constructs could be changed by human intervention.

Similar to Albert Bandura and other social learning theorists, Kelly believed that anticipation of the future, rather than the accumulation of past events, governs human thought, feeling, and behavior. "I believe that everything [people do] follows lines laid down in [their] effort[s] to anticipate what will happen . . . . [People] never wait to see what will happen; [they] look to see what will happen. Even my motorist friend is looking for something, though she shuts her eyes to do it" (Kelly, 1980, pp. 26 & 27).

Kelly wrote, "The phenomenological psychologists, of whom I certainly am not one, usually take the view that it is only the experience of the passing instant that is of essential psychological significance" (Kelly, 1980, p. 22). Nevertheless, he shared some assumptions with the humanists and phenomenologists (Benesch & Page, 1989). Like Rogers, Kelly did not believe that one and only one set of procedures is effective in therapy: "Unlike most personality theories, the psychology of personal constructs does not limit itself to any pet psychotherapeutic technique" (Kelly, 1980, p. 35). Recall that Jung had similar feelings about therapeutic techniques. Like

Rogers and Jung, Kelly also held that therapy is an *experience* in which both therapist and client participate and contribute as partners: "Psychotherapy needs to be understood as an experience. . . . Psychotherapy takes place when one person makes constructive use of another who has offered himself for that purpose. The professional skills of the therapist, as well as much of his repertory as an experienced human being, are brought into the transaction" (p. 21). Further, like Rogers, Kelly thought of therapy as an opportunity to become one's own self, relatively free of the constraints imposed by society and other people: "Psychotherapeutic effort, . . . as well as any other worthwhile human undertaking, is not to conform to oneself, whole or fragment; or to society, lay or ordained . . . . [The] objective is for man continually to determine for himself what is worth the price he is going to end up paying . . . to keep moving toward what he is not . . . (Kelly, 1980, p. 20).

Like Skinner and Rogers, creativity was one of Kelly's concerns: "The creativity cycle we envision is one that employs both loosening and tightening in a coordinated fashion. The cycle starts with a loosened phase in which construction is vague, elastic, and wavering. Out of this fertile chaos shapes begin to emerge and one seeks patiently to give them definite form until they are tight enough to talk about and to test" (Kelly, 1980, p. 34). Because creative people are flexible, and Kelly was a creative person, despite his sarcasm, there was not much he dismissed out of hand. Even though his orientation was to conscious thought, Kelly acknowledged the psychoanalytic view that people have an unconscious (Jankowicz, 1987).

Relations among Constructs

Looking back at Figure 11.1, the different organizations of Jim's and Joan's construct systems can be appreciated. Jim's system is organized by **extension of the cleavage line**, a reference to the observation that the poles of Jim's subordinate constructs fall directly under the corresponding emergent and implicit poles of his superordinate construct. Thus, "good" falls under "trust," "bad" under "distrust" (Kelly, 1963). However, Joan's system begins at the top by **abstracting across the cleavage line**: whole constructs fall under superordinate emergent and under superordinate implicit poles. In Joan's case, all of her constructs fall under her most superordinate construct, "evaluative-descriptive." The whole construct "good-bad" falls under the emergent pole, "evaluative," while the whole construct, "female-male" falls under the implicit pole, "descriptive." This feature of Joan's system makes it more complex and flexible than Jim's. She can approach her life situation from an evaluative stance (there are good people and bad people) or from a purely descriptive stance (there are North Americans and Europeans).

Elements are objects, beings, or events. The **context** of a construct is composed of all those elements to which the construct applies. The context of Joan's construct, "urban-rural," includes the elements farm, neighbors, apathetic people, and overcrowding. Whereas "range of convenience" and "focus of convenience" refer to rather gross and abstract circumstances such as "relations with people" and "eating habits," context and elements refer to the actual, concrete things or people that exist in a person's life circumstance.

A **symbol** is one of the elements to which a construct applies that may be used as the name of the construct. Figure 11.1 indicates that, for Jim, "father" symbolizes the trust-distrust construct. For Joan "Steffi Graf" symbolizes the construct, like me-unlike me. Of course, the picture of Jim and Joan as indicated in their conversation and in Figure 11.1 is oversimplified. Kelly would argue that no one's personality could be neatly represented in a figure. For one thing, the figure would have to be as large as a house, and for another, many constructs are too abstract to be represented as concretely as in Figure 11.1. Also, people normally do not blurt out their constructs as cooperatively as did Joan and Jim. More sophisticated methods of getting at constructs are needed, such as those considered below.

Personality Development

You may have wondered how Jim and Joan acquired their construct systems. That is, how did Jim and Joan develop their personalities? Kelly's comments about the transition from childhood to adulthood complemented his theory nicely.

Predictability

Because "anticipation of future events" is a cornerstone of Kelly's PCT, it is not surprising that "forecasting the future" has a prominent place in his discussion of construct development in children. **Predictability** refers to the ability to predict the future. A construct is as useful as the degree of predictability it provides. Thus, parents, the major components of every child's environment, are well advised to provide predictability. If they fail to do so, their child's need for anticipation of the future may be reflected in some rather extreme behavior (Kelly, 1955).

For example, if "predictability" is a scarce commodity in certain children's lives, they may cling to instances of it, even if their resultant behavior has negative consequences. As an illustration, assume a child, Johnny, has parents who treat him in a consistent manner only with regard to a few issues, all involving punishment. Johnny cleans his room; sometimes it is noticed, sometimes not. Johnny helps fold clothes and sometimes he is praised. However, Johnny has noticed that should he stop up the bathroom sink while playing "laundry," the consequent overflow brings a highly reliable reaction from his parents. They apply the palm of a hand to his bottom. So, a naive behaviorist might assert that Johnny will avoid stopping up the sink. Not so, according to Kelly. Stopping up the sink is the best way to acquire the precious predictability that Johnny so badly needs.

Dependency Constructs

Even given a reasonable amount of predictability in a child's social environment, early construct systems will still be characterized by impermeability of the few simple constructs that compose them. Children are small, weak, and vulnerable. They must depend on others for survival. Thus, the bulk of a child's early construct system is constituted by **dependency constructs**, special constructs that revolve around the child's survival needs. A "mother" construct would be an example. For a young child the "mother" construct might have a context containing elements such as warmth, safety from frightening sounds, nourishment, and so forth. Notice the similarity to Jung's mother archetype and mother complex.

At first the child might see the world in terms of "like mother-not like mother." The construct is very global and mother is seen in a very restricted manner. The university classes she teaches and the Chamber of Commerce committees she chairs play no role in the child's conception of her. She is warmth, comfort, and food. However, with growth and development, the construct will become more permeable and she will be more than warmth and kindred elements. In time, the entire construct will likely disappear altogether and "mother" will become a symbol for some other construct or an element of several constructs. The general disposition to impermeability of constructs dissolves in the tide of ever increasing maturation.

Role Playing

The relationship with the mother is but the beginning of a long line of relationships that will extend throughout life. The extent to which one can appreciate the construct system of another person is the extent to which one can play a role in a relationship with the other person (Kelly, 1963). Playing a **role** involves behaving in ways that meet the expectations of important other people in one's life.

In turn, such behavior provides the predictability that one requires. Thus a six-year-old may assume that her role relative to her parents is that of the passive, compliant, "seen but not heard" child. If she behaves in a passive, compliant, quiet manner, she predicts that she will be fed, cuddled, provided with toys, and so forth. At least during childhood, the hypothetical child's assumed role might work out fine, provided she correctly perceives that her predictions are confirmed.

However, assume that all does not go so well. Assume that her observations are faulty and she is seeing confirmation of her predictions which, in fact, does not exist. Eventually, she will have to stop deluding herself. Sooner or later she will have to face up to the fact that her parents do not really want a passive, compliant, quiet child. Perhaps in "reality" they expect her to play the role of the assertive, active, independent child. The outcome of such a revelation would be **guilt**, the result of the person's perception that he or she is being dislodged from some critical role, one that was thought to be very important in relating to important people. In more common terms, guilt comes from not measuring up, not being one's parent's child, not fitting the mold that important others have sculptured for oneself. In the last analysis, guilt results from the failure of people to accurately "read" the construct systems of other people. Perhaps Kelly would admit that people need Roger's empathy (Beck, 1988).

Choices: The C-P-C Cycle

Whenever individuals face significant or dramatic change in their life situations, whether it is a shortterm variation or a longterm upheaval, they must search their systems of constructs for dimensions that will best accommodate the change. They must make an **elaborative choice**, a selection of an "alternative, aligned to one . . . construct dimension, which appears to provide the greater opportunity for the further elaboration of [one's] system" (Kelly, 1980, p. 32). "At a certain stage in one's development it may be more promising to choose to do something that will help . . . define [one's] position more clearly and thus consolidate . . . gains. . . . But at other times one will choose to extend his [or her] system so it will embrace more of the unknown and bring more of the future within [one's] grasp" (p. 32).

No matter which of the two directions we take in confronting life-change, the process is the same. We go through the C-P-C choice cycle. First we construe. "To do this we go through a **circumspection phase** . . . a period of 'trying on for size' the various constructs available in our personal repertory" (Kelly, 1980, p. 32; emphasis added). To illustrate the process, suppose, on short notice, a person receives a promotion. Now, for the first time, she is *boss* to several employees and must decide how to relate to them. If she does not have many constructs, this phase will not take long and she may look like "a person of action." If circumstances are changing too rapidly for her to keep up, she may race through this phase of the cycle and appear to be impulsive. Of course, she may take her time.

In any case, she next moves to the **preemption phase**, a period during which "one construct is allowed to preempt the situation and define the pair of alternatives between which the person must make his [or her] choice" (Kelly, 1980, p. 33). Henceforth, unless she backtracks, she will stick with the construct that has surfaced. Suppose that construct is "authoritarian-egalitarian." Finally, commitment occurs, the principle of elaborative choice takes over, and she makes a **choice**, a decision between the alternatives provided by the construct that has preempted the situation. She chooses to be authoritarian in her relations with her new subordinates. Thus, she completes the C-P-C cycle: circumspection, preemption, and choice.

Evaluation

Contributions: Supporting Evidence and Practical Applications

Support for some aspects of Kelly's PCT has been hard to come by. One reason is the nature of the theory: it is a tight logical system incorporating numerous abstract concepts, few of which are easy to translate into testable terms. Also the fact that each person's construct system is different from that of each other person creates a paradox. Researchers must resolve the dilemma of employing a sample of persons to make generalizations about construct systems that are different for different persons. Nevertheless, there are some studies that seem to support Kelly's theory, both in terms of verifying some of his concepts and in terms of supporting his assumptions.

Poles
Kelly (1963) indicated that a critical testable aspect of his theory is the assumption that people cast their worlds in terms of opposites. Kelly's theoretical structure is built on the supposition that each construct has two poles. If that supposition proved false, the structure might tumble. Predictions of the future would fail if a construct, for example, was represented by "all people are good," rather than "some people are good" and "some people are bad." In fact, if each construct had only one pole, there would be nothing to predict: all people would be treated in exactly the same manner. Life would be one certainty after another.

Accordingly, Kelly (1963) placed heavy emphasis on some work by William H. Lyle, a former student. Lyle first selected some words that appeared to belong to four categories "cheerful-sad," "broad-minded/narrow-minded," "refined-vulgar," and "sincere-insincere." A pilot sample of subjects then were told to place the words into the eight different classes represented by the eight words just listed. This procedure provided a basis for accuracy scores in the main study. Main study subjects were given the same words and told to place them into the eight classes (plus a ninth, "don't know" class). They were given a point for a "correct response" each time they placed a word in the same class as did the pilot subjects.

Thus, each main study subject had eight accuracy scores, one for each of the eight word classes. Then a method to be detailed later, factor analysis, was used on the accuracy scores to see what word classes grouped together. Results revealed five collections of words or factors, one for "general intelligence" and four others exactly matching the four categories "cheerful-sad," "sincere-insincere," and so forth. Subjects tended to lump together "cheerful" with "sad" words and "sincere" with "insincere" words. If they made classification mistakes with "refined" words, for example, they made mistakes with "vulgar" words as well. In short, they classed or organized the words into sets of opposites, just as Kelly believed constructs are organized.

Extension of Kelly's Theory

Kevin Benesch and Monte Page (1988) investigated the circumstances under which individuals are able to appreciate the important constructs of other people. To pursue that interest, subjects were recruited in triads, each consisting of three people who were close acquaintances. One triad member was designated the "target." The other two members, called "peers," reacted to the target in various ways that amounted to attempting to specify the target's critical constructs. Targets also indicated their critical constructs. Results showed that, under certain circumstances, there was good correspondence between targets' and peers' perceptions of targets' critical constructs. Peers tended to accurately perceive the target's critical constructs when personality dimensions related to constructs reflected high meaningfulness and high stability (consistent use of constructs across people and objects). That is, targets' conceptions of their critical constructs matched those of peers when the constructs in question reflected high meaningfulness and high stability. Commonality among the contents of these friends' construct systems may have helped them appreciate each other's critical constructs. These results extend Kelly's theory by indicating the circumstances under which individuals are able to "read" others' constructs.

Kelly's PCT was originally used as a way to conceptualize personality and as a basis for helping people in therapy. In more recent years it has been used with greater specificity. PCT is now employed to conceive of specific circumstances faced by a restricted category of people, for example, elderly people who have lost a spouse. Viney, Benjamin, and Preston (1989) found that elderly people who had suffered the loss of a spouse displayed "guilt" in Kelly's sense of the word: they felt dislodged from important roles. As an illustration, a woman whose husband had died felt dislodged from the roles of wife and homemaker, roles that involved core constructs. Viney and colleagues suggested that elderly persons who have lost spouses lack the means of validating their core constructs and need help in locating new sources of validation.

Cognitive Complexity

An additional source of supporting evidence was provided by another of Kelly's former students, James Bieri. Bieri (1955) defined a new dimension, cognitive complexity-cognitive simplicity. A **cognitively complex** person has a construct system containing constructs that are clearly differentiated, that is, sharply distinguished one from the other. Complex people, having a differentiated construction system, cast other people into many categories and thus see much variety in people. On the other hand, a **cognitively simple** person has a construction system for which distinctions among constructs are blurred—a poorly differentiated system. They cast other people into a few categories. A very cognitively simple person would, for example, use mainly one construct such as good-bad, lumping half of humanity into the "good" class, and the other into the "bad" class. Bieri (1955) showed that cognitively simple people have difficulty seeing the differences between themselves and others (they tend to assume that others are pretty much like themselves). By contrast, complex people can draw sharp distinctions between themselves and others.

Kelly (1955) has indicated that the more constructs one uses the better she or he will be at predicting future events, including the behavior of other persons. Bieri (1955) also confirmed this assumption. Complex subjects were better at predicting the behavior of others. If people use mainly one construct, say "good-bad," they are likely to put themselves in the "good" class. Given little information about other people—which were the conditions of Bieri's experiment—they will predict that others are good, like themselves. Complex persons use many constructs, some for application to themselves and some for application to the many other people in their lives. Table 11.1 summarizes the characteristics of cognitively complex and simple people.

Other researchers have over the years used the complex-simple dimension to provide strong support for Kelly's theory. For example, Signell (1966) reported that children tend to increase in cognitive complexity during the period 9–16 years of age. Also, Sechrest and Jackson (1961) found that social intelligence—an index of social effectiveness—was strongly related to cognitive complexity. In a more recent study Linville (1982) reported the following results: (1) college students showed more complexity in their descriptions of their own age group than of an older age group; (2) students who were more simple in their representations of older males were extreme in their evaluation of older males; (3) individuals who were induced to adopt a simple orientation toward food used in a study of taste gave more extreme evaluations than did those induced to adopt a more complex orientation; and (4) young males gave older males more extreme evaluations than they gave to members of their own age group.

TABLE 11.1   Comparison of Cognitively Complex and Simple People

Cognitively Complex Person	Cognitively Simple Person
Maintains a clear distinction among constructs	Distinction among constructs blurred
Casts others into many categories	Casts others into few categories
Can easily see differences between self and others	Has difficulty in seeing differences between self and others
Skilled at predicting behaviors of others	Inept at predicting behaviors of others

Current research continues to support the cognitively complex-cognitively simple dichotomy. For example, Uhlemann, Lee, and Hasse (1989) asked subjects to rate the expertness of a counselor depicted conducting a therapy-session on videotape. The expertness measure assessed subjects' sensitivity to nonverbal cues that were systematically displayed by the counselor. Subjects were categorized into four levels of cognitive complexity based on a test of complexity. Subjects were also subjected to one of three levels of arousals: (1) low—they were alone while viewing the video; (2) moderate—others were present; and (3) high—the others present were supposedly "observers" who would evaluate the subjects. Bieri's PCT-inspired theory of complexity would predict that a complex person would be more sensitive to the nonverbal cues: she or he would have higher social intelligence and would be more sensitive to the behaviors of other people that might allow discrimination among them. Results showed the expected effects, but were qualified by level of arousal. When arousal was moderate or high, high-complex subjects were more discriminating of nonverbal behaviors than low-complex subjects.

In another contemporary study, Engelhard (1990) attempted to explain why equality between the sexes on mathematical ability changes to an advantage for males as courses in math become more abstract. Subjects were teens in the United States and in Thailand. Results indicated that as the cognitive complexity required to solve math problems increases, boys began to display an advantage. However, gender differences were not great, especially in Thailand, and girls tended to do better in the less abstract forms of math (arithmetic and algebra as opposed to geometry).

Bieri's (1955) cognitive complexity continues to be popular. Its prospects for popularity in the future received a boost recently when a program for convenient computer scoring of complexity test responses was developed by Greene, Plank, and Fowler (1989). It is apparent that additional uses for this fruitful dimension will be discovered in the 1990s and beyond.

The REP Test

Among Kelly's most enduring contributions is the **Role Construct Repertory (REP) Test**, an assessment device designed to reveal an individual's construct system. It has not only been useful as a method for the assessment and study of personality, but has also been a helpful companion to the therapy process. As you will see, it is being even more broadly applied at present and promises to be applicable to an expanding variety of problems in the future.

The REP Test and PCT in Business and Industry

According to A. D. Jankowicz (1987), "A major stimulus for the broad application of personal construct psychology came with the early abandonment of the fixed set of role titles used as elements in Kelly's original [REP test]" (p. 484). In the place of Kelly traditional titles, self, mother, father, brother, sister, and so forth, applied researchers have inserted a variety of labels that are relevant to various situations in business and industry. For example, through the use of products' names in place of the usual role titles, researchers discovered the constructs applied by home testers to cosmetics and perfumes. They could then use the dimensions rep-

BOX 11.2   Joan's Responses to the REP Test

The best way to understand the REP test is to participate in the use of it. First, participate vicariously: follow Joan's use of the REP (she graciously volunteered to complete it). Read the instructions, beginning in the next paragraph, and then follow the responses Joan "wrote" into List A and Figure 11.3.

List A provides 15 role definitions. Read each definition carefully. In each blank, write the first name of the person who best fits that role in your life. It is essential to use the role definitions as given in List A. If you cannot remember the name of the person, put down a word or brief phrase that will bring the person to mind. Do *not* repeat any names; if some person has already been listed, simply make a second choice. Thus, next to the word "Self" write your own name. Then next to the word "Mother" put your mother's name (or the person who has played the part of a mother in your life), and so on, until all 15 roles have been designated with a specific individual.

List A: Definition of Roles for the Demonstration

1. *Self*: Yourself *Joan*
2. *Mother*: Your mother or the person who has played the part of a mother in your life. *Sandra*
3. *Father*: Your father or the person who has played the part of a father in your life. *Michael*
4. *Brother*: Your brother who is nearest your own age, or, if you do not have a brother, a boy near your own age who has been most like a brother to you. *Joe*
5. *Sister*: Your sister who is nearest your own age, or, if you do not have a sister, a girl near your own age who has been most like a sister to you. *Sue*

6. *Spouse*: Your wife (or husband), or, if you are not married, your closest present girl (boy) friend. *Ed*
7. *Pal*: Your closest present friend of the same sex as yourself. *Rowda*
8. *Ex-Pal*: A person of the same sex as yourself whom you once thought was a close friend of yours but in whom you were badly disappointed later. *Sharon*
9. *Rejecting Person*: A person with whom you have been associated, who, for some unexplained reason, appears to dislike you. *Howard*
10. *Pitied Person*: A person whom you would most like to help or for whom you feel most sorry. *Ronald*
11. *Threatening Person*: The person who threatens you the most or the person who makes you feel the most uncomfortable. *Sally*
12. *Attractive Person*: A person who you have recently met who you would like to know better. *Paula*
13. *Accepted Teacher*: The teacher who influenced you most. *Sarah*
14. *Rejected Teacher*: The teacher whose point of view you have found most objectionable. *Donald*
15. *Happy Person*: The happiest person who you know personally. *Al*

Now look at the first row of the matrix in Figure 11.3. Note that there are circles in the squares under columns 9, 10, and 12. These circles designate the three people who you are to consider in sort number 1 (Rejecting Person, Pitied Person, and Attractive Person). Think about these three people. In particular, how are *two of them alike* in some way that *differentiates them from the third person?* When you have decided the most important way that two of them are alike but different from the third person,

BOX 11.2   *Continued*

Sort Number	Self (1)	Mother (2)	Father (3)	Brother (4)	Sister (5)	Spouse (6)	Pal (7)	Ex-Pal (8)	Rejecting Person (9)	Pitied Person (10)	Threatened Person (11)	Attractive Person (12)	Accepted Teacher (13)	Rejected Teacher (14)	Happy Person (15)	EMERGENT POLE	IMPLICIT POLE
1								⊗	○		⊗					Admired	Not Admired
2		○	⊗	⊗												Trust	Distrust
3					○							⊗		⊗		Like Me	Not Like Me
4		○						⊗				⊗				Strong	Weak
5	⊗									○	⊗					Rural	Urban
6				○				⊗					⊗			Capable	Incapable
7			○					⊗			⊗					Female	Male
8						⊗				○				⊗		Cheerful	Sad
9						⊗	○					⊗				Interesting	Uninteresting
10	⊗			⊗	○											Good	Bad
11		⊗	○								⊗					Talkative	Quiet
12						⊗	○					⊗				Athletic	Unathletic
13	⊗					⊗	○									Calm	Anxious
14	⊗	○	⊗													Invulnerable	Vulnerable
15				⊗						○				⊗		Ambitious	Unambitious

FIGURE 11.3   Joan's REP Test responses.

put an X in the two circles that correspond to the two persons who are alike. Do not write anything in the third circle; leave it blank. Next, write a word or short phrase in the column marked "Emergent Pole" that tells how the two people are alike. Then, in the column marked "Implicit Pole," write a word or short phrase that explains the way the third person is different from the other two. Finally, consider the remaining 12 people and think about which of these, in addition to the ones you have already marked with an X, also have the characteristics you have designated under "Emergent Pole." Place an X in the

square corresponding to the name of each of the other persons who has this characteristic. When you have finished this procedure for the first row, go to the second row (sort number 2). The process should be repeated until the procedure has been carried out for each of the rows. In summary, the steps to be followed for each row (sort) are:

1. Consider the three people who are designated by circles under their names. Decide how two of them are

Continued

BOX 11.2 *Continued*

alike in some important way, and different from the third.

2. Put an *X* in the circles corresponding to the two people who are alike; leave the remaining circle blank.
3. In the "Emergent Pole" column, write a brief description of the way the two people are *alike*.
4. In the "Implicit Pole" column, write a brief description of the way the third person is *different* from the two who are alike.
5. Consider the remaining 12 people, and place an *X* in the squares corresponding to those who can also be characterized by the description in the "Emergent Pole" column.
6. Repeat steps 1 through 5 for each row of the matrix.

Briefly consider Joan's responses. First she completed Figure A. There Joan listed important persons in her life who fit such categories as Father, Pal, Rejecting Person, Attractive Person, and Accepting Teacher. Next, she completed the sorts indicated in the matrix shown in Figure 11.3. She used the circles marked in each row to compare the different individuals. In sort 1, Joan compared Rejecting Person, Pitied Person, and Attractive Person and indicated which two were most alike. Her "Xs"

show that she sees her Rejecting Person (Howard) and her Attractive Person (Paula) as more alike than other possible combinations of the three people. For each sort, Joan was asked to write a word or phase under "emergent pole" that describes how the two similar people are alike. Then she was to place a word or phrase under "implicit pole" to represent how the third person is different from the two similar individuals. Joan's entries for sort 1 demonstrate that, for her, Howard and Paula are alike in being admired, while Pitied Person (Ronald) is different from the other two in being "not admired." Similarly, in sort 4, Joan found that her Ex-pal (Sharon) and her Accepted Teacher (Sarah) were alike in being strong, while Mother was seen as weak. Any additional "Xs" Joan might have put on a given row would have indicated other persons who fit the label under the "emergent pole" for that row. Taken together, Joan's responses for all the sorts reveal her construct system.

Now that you've run through Joan's responses, complete the test yourself. An extra form has been included for that purpose (In Box 11.3). If you follow instructions carefully, you will master the test, and more important, gain some insight into your own construct system.

resented by the constructs—for example, poignant-bland—to rate the products. This method allowed the researchers to get at the heart of consumers' conceptions of the products, an achievement that might have alluded them had they tried to use dimensions *they* thought were relevant. In an analogous fashion, researchers discovered the beliefs, values, and items of knowledge used by senior managers so that this information could be used by new managerial employees to smooth the way into their novel positions of authority.

Jankowicz, who works in the banking industry, has concentrated on identifying the "constructs the effective loan agent used and to examine whether they are different in kind and extent from the constructs used by less effective loan agents,

BOX 11.3   Your Own Construction System

List A lists 15 role definitions. Read each definition carefully. In each blank, write the first name of the person who best fits that role in your life. It is essential to use the role definitions as given in List A. If you cannot remember the name of the person, put down a word or brief phrase that will bring the person to mind. Do *not* repeat any names; if some person has already been listed, simply make a second choice. Thus, next to the word "Self" write your own name. Then next to the word "Mother" put your mother's name (or the person who has played the part of a mother in your life), and so on, until all 15 roles have been designated with a specific individual.

List A: Definition of Roles for the Demonstration

1. *Self:* Yourself ———.
2. *Mother:* Your mother or the person who has played the part of a mother in your life. ———.
3. *Father:* Your father or the person who has played the part of a father in your life. ———.
4. *Brother:* Your brother who is nearest your own age, or, if you do not have a brother, a boy near your own age who has been most like a brother to you. ———.
5. *Sister:* Your sister who is nearest your own age, or, if you do not have a sister, a girl near your own age who has been most like a sister to you. ———.
6. *Spouse:* Your wife (or husband), or, if you are not married, your closest present girl (boy) friend. ———.
7. *Pal:* Your closest present friend of the same sex as yourself. ———.
8. *Ex-Pal:* A person of the same sex as yourself whom you once thought was a close friend of yours but in

whom you were badly disappointed later. ———.
9. *Rejecting Person:* A person with whom you have been associated, who, for some unexplained reason, appears to dislike you. ———.
10. *Pitied Person:* A person whom you would most like to help or for whom you feel most sorry. ———.
11. *Threatening Person:* The person who threatens you the most or the person who makes you feel the most uncomfortable. ———.
12. *Attractive Person:* A person who you have recently met who you would like to know better. ———.
13. *Accepted Teacher:* The teacher who influenced you most. ———.
14. *Rejected Teacher:* The teacher whose point of view you have found most objectionable. ———.
15. *Happy Person:* The happiest person who you know personally. ———.

Now look at the first row of the matrix in Figure 11.4. Note that there are circles in the squares under columns 9, 10, and 12. These circles designate the three people who you are to consider in sort number 1. (Rejecting Person, Pitied Person, and Attractive Person). Think about these three people. In particular, how are *two of them alike* in some way that *differentiates them from the third person*? When you have decided the most important way that two of them are alike but different from the third person, put an X in the two circles that correspond to the two persons who are alike. Do not write anything in the third circle; leave it blank. Next, write a word or short phrase in the column marked "Emergent Pole" that tells how the two people are alike. Then, in the column

Continued

BOX 11.3 Continued

Sort Number	1 (Self)	2 (Mother)	3 (Father)	4 (Brother)	5 (Sister)	6 (Spouse)	7 (Pal)	8 (Ex-Pal)	9 (Rejecting Person)	10 (Pitied Person)	11 (Threatened Person)	12 (Attractive Person)	13 (Accepted Teacher)	14 (Rejected Teacher)	15 (Happy Person)	EMERGENT POLE	IMPLICIT POLE
1								O	O		O						
2		O	O	O													
3					O								O	O			
4			O					O					O				
5	O										O	O					
6					O				O					O			
7				O					O		O						
8						O					O			O			
9							O	O				O					
10	O			O	O												
11		O	O								O						
12							O	O				O					
13	O						O	O									
14	O	O	O														
15				O					O				O				

FIGURE 11.4 Your Construct System

marked "Implicit Pole," write a word or short phrase that explains the way the third person is different from the other two. Finally, consider the remaining 12 persons and think about which of these, in addition to the ones you have already marked with an X, also have the characteristics you have designated under "Emergent Pole." Place an X in the square corresponding to the name of each of the other persons who has this characteristic. When you have finished this procedure for the first row, go to the second row (sort number 2). The process should be repeated until the procedure has been carried out for each of the rows.

In summary, the steps to be followed for each row (sort) are:

1. Consider the three people who are designated by circles under their names. Decide how two of them are alike in some important way, and different from the third.
2. Put an X in the circles corresponding to the two people who are alike; leave the remaining circle blank.
3. In the "Emergent Pole" column, write a brief description of the way the two people are *alike*.
4. In the "Implicit Pole" column, write a brief description of the way the

BOX 11.3   *Continued*

third person is *different* from the two who are alike.

5. Consider the remaining 12 persons, and place an X in the squares corresponding to those who can also be characterized by the description in the "Emergent Pole" column.

6. Repeat steps 1 through 5 for each row of the matrix.

effectiveness being defined objectively in terms of the relative size of loan defaults" (p. 485). Researchers have also used the REP technique to reveal the constructs that quality control inspectors use to separate defective from acceptable products. Apparently, in business/industry settings, the REP technique is applicable to an indefinite number of problems.

Fixed-Role Therapy

Though Kelly was not tied to a particular kind of therapy, he did develop a unique therapeutic method. In **fixed role therapy** a client plays the role of an imaginary character who possesses certain constructs that are in contrast to his or her actual constructs (Kelly, 1955). The therapist would use the client's actual constructs as a basis for creating the construct or constructs of the imaginary character.

The process would go something like this: (1) the client would describe himself in terms of central and troublesome constructs; (2) the therapist would, in the simplest case, write a fixed role for the imaginary character requiring the client to assume a construct that demands very different behavior than is usual for him (his verbally aggressive tendency to cut in when others are talking and talking over them is replaced with an orientation to "biting the tongue" and "letting others speak their piece"); (3) the client tries the role, then he and the therapist discuss reactions of others to the new character; and (4) the client does not necessarily adopt the new role, but gains some insight into what it is like to be on the other side of the role he normally plays.

Limitations

Like those of other theorists, Kelly's basic assumptions can be attacked. In addition, Kelly may be seen as concentrating too much on cognition and too little on other aspects of people. Also like other theorists, some of Kelly's ideas have not been strongly verified by research. Kelly himself is a possible reason why his ideas are not as popular today as they might have been. Finally, despite its usefulness for many purposes, the REP test has some limitations.

The Notion of Opposites

As indicated earlier, Kelly's theory is based on the notion of opposites as manifested in constructs. The most obvious attack on this central idea is that some candidates for "construct" do not involve opposites. Either the opposite is missing altogether, or it is not a true opposite. To illustrate the lack of a true opposite, for some candidates the only specifiable opposite to the emergent pole is the negation of that pole. For example, "admire-not admire" was purposely used in the Jim and Joan illustration (see Figure 11.1). "Admire-not admire" would certainly qualify as a construct (so would just about any set of two words which are apparent opposites). However, the implicit pole is the negation of the emergent pole; it is not something, but the absence of something. One can admire a person, but not to admire a person is rather ambiguous. It implies no definite relationship or action. Similarly, an examination of a list of words which were all generated during the process of self-description (that is, disclosure of constructs) reveals a large number of emergent poles the opposites of which are negations (Allen and Potkay, 1983a). For example, "awful" and "bizarre" seem to have no opposites except "not awful" and "not bizarre."

While, in some cases, implicit poles are merely negations of emergent poles, in others, they may be absent entirely. Kelly himself has acknowledged that his clients sometimes cannot articulate an implicit pole for a construct. He assumed that, in such cases, the implicit pole is submerged. A **submerged pole** has either never been put into word form, perhaps because the construct is new, or is being suppressed (a client insists "all people are good" in order to escape the perception that people are bad and out to get him; Kelly, 1963). Perhaps some people do submerge implicit poles, or it may be that they do not express an implicit pole because none exists for them.

One may say, "All well and good, but what about Lyle's support of Kelly's notion of opposites?" Examination of the word list mentioned previously reveals that all of the eight labels for the eight classes of words used in Lyle's study have extreme favorability values. For each of the four sets of words, one member of the pair refers to a characteristic that is highly valued and desired by people in our society, while the other word refers to a highly undesirable characteristic. Table 11.2 presents these words and accompanying values falling along a scale where 550 represents highest favorability and 50 lowest favorability. All eight emergent poles do have rather obvious opposites that are not just negations. However, one might question whether these words are representative of construct labels that are used by real people. Do the emergent poles of real people's constructs all have such clear opposites? Do the constructs of real people have poles that are so extremely different in favorability? It seems intuitively obvious that some real peo-

TABLE 11.2   Lyle's Word Categories and Associated Favorability Values*

Cheerful	475	Sad	213
Broad-minded	425	Narrow-minded	142
Refined	342	Vulgar	77
Sincere	504	Insincere	107
Average (mean)	437		135

* From Allen and Potkay (1983a)

ple would have constructs with no opposites to emergent poles and constructs with poles that are not extremely different in favorability. Thus, Lyle's study should be replicated with a more representative sample of potential constructs.

Where Are the Emotions?

You may have noticed that reference to emotions (roughly "feelings") is largely absent from Kelly's list of concepts. Anxiety, fear, threat, and guilt are mentioned but defined in rather unconventional and emotionally-bland cognitive terms. People are not just "thinkers"; they also have emotions. While Kelly did acknowledge "feelings," he was unable to say much about the constructs that would apply to them. He did indicate that "feeling" constructs would mainly be *preverbal*, constructs that have no words associated with the emergent and implicit poles. If "feeling" constructs are preverbal, they are forever relegated to the unconscious. Being in some sense unconscious, feelings or emotions are not substantially considered in Kelly's conception of personality, which is so clearly dominated by consciousness.

Some Concepts Not Verified

Like those of several other theorists, some of Kelly's concepts are too vague to verify empirically. Among these are some of Kelly's attempts to include emotionality in his theorizing. Excellent illustrations include the concepts: (1) *threat* that the system of constructs may be overhauled; (2) *anxiety* that the system does not apply to critical events; and (3) *fear* that new constructs may be dominating. Aside from these being strange definitions for words commonly used by other theorists, a recent attempt to verify them has failed. Beck (1988) investigated these concepts and found little support for hypotheses based on them. In fact, in some instances results were opposite of predictions.

Kelly Himself

Jankowicz (1987) noted that, ironically, Kelly is more popular elsewhere, especially in Britain, than he is in his native United States. Further, his general popularity, while growing, still lags behind that of most personality theorists covered in this book. One possible explanation is—how else can I put it—Kelly's personality. While many psychologists admired his wit and sense of humor, and some others found his sarcastic/skeptical view of psychology refreshing, some of his colleagues found him a bit abrasive. In addition, he was a rather reserved and private individual, not the public person that Rogers and others were. Perhaps a theorist's personality should have nothing to do with the way her or his ideas are received by the scientific community, but it does.

Shortcomings of the REP

One of the REP test's virtues is also a major limitation. It involves an idiographic approach, one person at a time. Each REP outcome is unique to the person who produced it. A given person's constructs, as revealed by her or his REP responses, may not be meaningfully compared with those of other persons, much less generalized to all other people. Such is the case even in industry/business applications. The REP outcomes produced by successful loan officers or product quality-control inspectors cannot be readily generalized to other loan officers or inspectors, whether successful or not. Just as a radiologist's method for reading an x-ray is unique to her or him, one's REP outcome is specific to oneself (Matlin & Foley, 1992). In fact, the REP reflects the PCT from which it is drawn. PCT itself is highly idiographic. Thus, it is alien to the most popular orientation in the United States: nomothetic—identifying universal characteristics and broad principles that can be generalized across all humans. Parity in popularity with other major theories will probably have to await a change in the major U.S. orientation.

Conclusions

George A. Kelly is certainly one of psychology's most original thinkers. In fact, there may be limited research support for his theory because it is so original researchers may not know how to approach it. Although some of his ideas resembled those of some other theorists, Kelly did not borrow from anybody. His theory is composed mainly of fresh, new ideas. Nothing resembling ids, archetypes, or needs exist in the theory. Little wonder that some psychologists have had trouble relating to PCT. However, that state of affairs seems to be changing. Examination of current personality texts and journals reveal that Kelly is resurgent. Because his theory was made public some 40 years ago, people have had time to get used to his very different and highly novel ideas.

If Kelly is to be criticized for having little to say about feelings, he is to be congratulated for emphasizing what others have ignored. Kelly more than any other psychologist has made cognition the primary basis for the study of personality. Also, Kelly's "one subject or client at a time" approach is not lacking in merit just because it is not often embraced, especially in the United States. My colleague, Charles Potkay, and I personally favor the idiographic approach (see Allen & Potkay, 1983a, and Potkay & Allen, 1988). Humans are just too complicated and each is too unique to readily generalize from what one displays to most others (also see Allen, 1988a and 1988b).

Finally, because Kelly has provided a cognitive basis for understanding personality at a time when the cognitive approach is burgeoning, many of his ideas are here to stay. The notion of "constructs," the dimension of complexity-simplicity, the REP test, and many other contributions will likely cement Kelly's name in the halls of psychology, evermore.

Summary Points

1. George Kelly was an individualistic, unconventional person whose background ranged from engineering to labor relations. He made a point of rejecting "stimulus-response" and Freudian psychology. Yet with all of his sarcasm and skepticism, he was a warm friend and mentor to colleagues and students. He believed that thought processes were the key to understanding people and that people, as well as therapists and researchers, acted like scientists in their pursuits.

2. *Constructs*, ways of construing events, were basic to Kelly. His fundamental postulate was that people's processes are routed by the ways they anticipate events. Jim's and Joan's conversation illustrates two different construct systems each having *superordinate* and *subordinate* constructs that have emergent or primary poles and implicit or contrasting poles. A construct's range of convenience is the extent of the event-category to which it applies and its range of focus is the events to which it most readily applies.

3. Some constructs are impermeable, while some are characterized by commonality and others by individuality traceable to differences in experience. Anxiety occurs when a construct system does not apply to critical events, fear when a new construct enters a system and may be dominant, and threat when a system appears to be facing overhaul.

4. When Joan tried to get Jim to change his system, she recommended that he adopt "admired-not admired," try it out, and then try it again (replicate). Joan was assuming *constructive alternativism*: that people's present interpretations of their life situations are subject to change. Though Kelly mimicked no other theorist, he shared assumptions with some. He believed in people's ability to change what controls them (Skinner), was future-oriented (Bandura), and was in agreement with the humanist (Rogers) on some issues, was not an advocate of a particular therapy (Rogers and Jung); he was interested in creativity (Skinner and Rogers).

5. Jim's construct system was organized by *extension of the cleavage line*, poles of subordinate constructs fall under emergent and implicit poles of superordinate constructs. Joan's system reflected *abstracting across the cleavage line*, whole constructs fell under superordinate emergent and under superordinate implicit poles. The context of a construct are all the *elements*—objects, beings, or events—to which it applies. A *symbol* is an element to which a construct applies that may serve as its name.

6. Children will do whatever is necessary to achieve predictability—including "misbehavior." Dependency constructs tend to dominant early systems ("mother construct"), but eventually they give way to more permeable constructs. Playing a role involves behaving in ways that meet expectations of important other people. However, if we misread others' expectations guilt results. The need for elaborative choice starts the C-P-C cycle: *circumspection* (trying on for size), *preemption* (a construct preempts the situation and defines alternatives), and *choice* (decision between alternatives).

7. Lyle provided some evidence that words referring to constructs are organized into pairs of opposites. Banesch and Page showed that friends are able to appreciate the critical constructs of one another. PCT has wide applicability: for example, it helps to understand the plight of elderly people who have lost a spouse. Bieri demonstrated that cognitively complex persons have constructs that are clearly differentiated, while the opposite is true of cognitively simple persons.

8. Signell showed that complexity increases with age and Linville reported that simple college males described older males in less complex terms and gave them more extreme evaluations. Uhlemann, Lee, and Hasse reported that complex subjects were more discriminating of nonverbal behavior when moderately or highly aroused. Engelhard showed that as the cognitive complexity required to solve math problems increases, boys began to display an advantage.

9. Kelly's increasingly popular REP test involves having individuals indicate the important people in their lives and, while considering them in threes, pick two who are alike in some way and different from the third. Jankowicz found that the REP procedure is useful in business and industry, when role titles are replaced by product names. In fixed role therapy, a client adopts the role of an imaginary person having a construct(s) that contrast with the client's.

10. Limitations of PCT include that some constructs have no real opposites to their emergent poles (perhaps they are *submerged*?), just the negation of that pole. Lyle's work in support of PCT suffers from non-representativeness of the words he used. Kelly has also been criticized for ignoring emotions which were written off as "preverbal." Some of his concepts have not been clearly verified by research, such as threat, anxiety, and fear. Kelly himself was a problem: his abrasiveness may have lowered the popularity of PCT. Finally the REP test suffers from being too "idiographic": applicable to only the particular persons who complete it. Yet Kelly's novel ideas and idiographic approach are beginning to catch on.

Running Comparison

Theorist	Kelly in Comparison
B. F. Skinner	Unlike Skinner, he was oriented to the future, but both believed that people could be changed by planned human interventions, and both were interested in creativity.
Rogers	Like Rogers, Kelly held that individuals have choices. They also agreed that one should not limit oneself in therapy to traditional methods. Both were concerned with creativity and both felt that clients were more like partners.
Maslow	"Becoming oneself" was a major goal in therapy for both, but Kelly was less concerned with the present moment.
Jung	Mother construct resembled Jung's mother archetype.

Essay/Critical Thinking Questions

1. Think of a problem that you have right now, one that is of a psychological or interpersonal nature. How would you go about solving it—locating the source of it and taking steps to eliminate it? (Hint: use the scientific approach.)

2. Based on your presumed earlier completion of the REP test, draw your construction system as in Figure 11.1 (if you have not completed the REP test, do so first).

3. Indicate the constructs of a close friend (could be a romantic partner). Then write a fixed role script for that friend.

4. Think of a situation in which you have suffered from "anxiety" as Kelly defines it. How would you conceive of the way that your construction system failed to apply to critical events and what did you do about it (or what would you have done knowing what you know now)?

5. Based on your answers to questions 2 and 3, how would you conceive of the commonality between your construction system and that of your friend?

6. Think back to your childhood. What dependency constructs characterized your immature construction system?

7. Think of a change in your life situation that occurred at some time in the past (a change in one or more of your interpersonal relationships would be a good example). What was the form of the resultant guilt—in Kelly's sense of the word— and what did you do about it?

8. Think of another past change in your life (high school to college change in friendships?). Use the C-P-C cycle to indicate how you arrived at an alternative provided by a construct that allowed you to deal with your new situation.

9. Concentrate on the complex-simple dichotomy. What evidence can you provide to support the argument that you are a complex individual?

10. How would you get Kelly out of the predicament involved with the observation that some implicit poles are merely negations of emergent poles? (Hint: come up with some example constructs that suffer from this problem and attempt to locate synonyms to the words referring to their poles such that negations become real opposites.)

12

THE SOCIAL SIDE OF PERSONALITY: JULIAN ROTTER AND WALTER MISCHEL

- Does it make any sense to talk about "personality" outside the social settings in which it unfolds?
- Do your expectations concerning whether or not you will be rewarded for performing a behavior affect the likelihood you will show that behavior?
- What determines your outcomes—your traits, values, and efforts or fate, luck, chance, and powerful others?
- Do your abilities have anything to do with your personality?
- Do you lay plans to regulate your behavior in advance of behaving in a social situation?

George Kelly's cognitive approach is continued in this chapter, but is expanded. The theorists covered here, Julian Rotter and Walter Mischel, emphasize our thinking about the *social situations* that we encounter. Their theories are relatively closely connected—Mischel was a student of Rotter. Both list among their basic concepts *expectancies*, what people expect will happen when they perform certain behaviors in a certain situation. Obviously, both believe that personality cannot be considered apart from the social situations in which it unfolds. Both have been rather skeptical about the basic assumption underlying *traits*: behavior is quite stable across social situations. Consequently, neither apply the label *trait* to any of their basic components of personality. Here, however, the similarities taper off. While the two theories do not contradict one another, and may even be seen as complementary each to the other, they are different in terms of details. Nevertheless, it is clear that the social learning orientation is part and parcel of both theories. Thus, it seems appropriate to provide a broad and general definition of the position common to Rotter and Mischel: **social learning** is acquiring useful information through interacting with (relating to) people and other elements of the environment (Phares, 1976).

Rotter, the Person

Like Maslow, Julian B. Rotter traces his roots to Brooklyn, New York, where he was born to Jewish parents in 1916. Noting the obligation to acknowledge the "teacher who most contributed to my intellect," Rotter (1982, p. 343) takes a page out of Maslow's book. He cites the Avenue J. Library in Brooklyn. As a high school student, he spent so much time with his "teacher" that he soon exhausted its wisdom, at least in the category of fictional works. Therefore, he searched the stacks for something new and stumbled onto books by Adler and Freud. By the time he was a senior in high school, he was interpreting other people's dreams. His senior thesis was entitled "Why We Make Mistakes."

Rotter pursued psychology while an undergraduate at Brooklyn College, but only as an elective. Just as with George Kelly, the background of the Great Depression caused Rotter to choose a practical major, namely chemistry. Nevertheless, he took more psychology than chemistry. This combination of a hard science and a psychology emphasis paid big dividends when Rotter later entered graduate school in psychology.

While pursuing his studies, Rotter was inspired by the lectures of social psychologist Solomon Asch, a student of Gestalt psychology famous for his conformity research. In turn, Asch got Rotter interested in the ideas of Kurt Lewin, a pioneer in the study of group dynamics who was strongly influenced by the Gestalt movement. These more socially oriented individuals must have had a great impact on Rotter, because, relative to other personality psychologists, he emphasized the importance of social situations over traits.

Part of Alfred Adler's importance was his influence on many young theorists of his day. Already you have seen that Rogers and Maslow acknowledge Adler's contribution to their thinking. During Rotter's college years, Adler arrived in Brooklyn. His almost evangelistic lectures further convinced young Julian that psychology was his destiny.

After Brooklyn College, Rotter arrived at the University of Iowa with empty pockets. Thanks to the chair of the psychology department, Lee Travis, he was able to earn enough to survive. Soon he was enrolled in a seminar run by Kurt Lewin, who convinced him that interactions between people and the social situations in which they find themselves are of central importance.

From there it was on to Worcester State Hospital where he met his wife to be, Clara Barnes, and where he participated in one of the first-ever clinical psychology internships. Determined to be among the first clinical psychologists, he then entered Indiana University to pursue a Ph.D. in clinical psychology. Having finished his work in 1941, Rotter looked at job prospects with some trepidation. Like

Maslow, he had learned that many academic doors were closed to Jewish people. Fortunately, he was able to land a clinical position in a state hospital where, for practical purposes, he taught for the first time. Unfortunately, World War II interrupted this first job. Rotter joined the Army, serving as a psychologist and personnel consultant. There, among other contributions, he devised a method for reducing the incidence of "absence without leave."

After World War II, Rotter found that a strong demand for still scarce clinical psychologists was more than enough to overcome anti-semitism. He had his choice of universities and he selected Ohio State where George Kelly was to be counted among his colleagues. After Kelly gave up the clinical directorship in 1951, Rotter took it over.

It was in the army and at Ohio State that Rotter began work on his social learning theory. While he was happy and productive at Ohio State, the fascist spirit of Communist-baiting Senator Joe McCarthy was all too alive and well in the Midwest. Accordingly, in 1963, Rotter moved east taking his current position at the University of Connecticut. There his thinking on social learning fully crystallized.

Rotter has served on the Education and Training Board of the American Psychological Association (APA), on the APA Council, and on the United States Public Health Service training committee. He has been president of the Eastern Psychological Association and of the APA divisions for Social/Personality and for Clinical Psychology.

Rotter's View of the Person

Up until this point, theorists have tended to place heavy reliance on explanations of behavior, thought, and feeling in terms of internal factors. Here the focus is on a point of view that considers the interplay between internal and external factors. Rotter (1966) does believe that people gripped by the forces of a powerful situation do show a general trend in behavior different from that shown under other circumstances. However, within such situations, persons still display individual differences in behavior.

Consider an example. Rotter (1966) writes of several studies in which some subjects were exposed to a *chance* or *skill* situation. In the chance situations, subjects were told that luck would determine how well they would do, but in the skill situations their own abilities would determine their performance. As an illustration, Phares (1962) presented subjects with a list of 12 nonsense syllables (such as ilo, pmn, rfv). First, he determined how long each subject had to view each syllable before she or he could correctly call out its letters (exposures were for fractions of a second). Then, the entire list of syllables was presented ten times, with the same six syllables always accompanied by the delivery of shock to subjects and the other six never associated with shock. During the ten presentations, the shock that accompanied six of the syllables could be terminated, if subjects learned which of several buttons was the one that stopped the shock. Subjects in a chance condition were told that sometimes a certain button would stop the shock accompanying a particular syllable and sometimes a different button would work, depending on chance. Skill condition subjects were informed they could terminate the shock by determining which of the buttons *always* stopped the shock associated with a particular syllable.

After these ten presentations, it was again determined how long each subject had to view each syllable before being able to correctly name its letters. If a subject required less viewing time to identify a shocked syllable after the presentations than before, it was assumed that the subject had learned the syllable during the presentations. A comparison of the exposure times before and after the ten presentations revealed that subjects in the *skill* condition *reduced* the exposure times needed to identify the nonsense syllables followed by shock more than did subjects in the *chance* condition. People do better in skill than in chance situations, because they experience control over circumstances.

However, individual differences in behavior among people assigned to the chance situation can be considerable. The same is true for the skill situation. For example, before each attempt at the chance or skill task, subjects are usually asked to indicate how well they expected to do. Regardless of whether they have been told that chance or skill would determine their outcomes, some subjects, but not others, tended to show the **gambler's fallacy**, the expectation that a failure on one attempt means that success on a subsequent attempt becomes more likely, whereas success means a greater likelihood of failure in the future. People who are prone to the gambler's fallacy think that a string of losses means they will surely soon be winners. They "reason" that luck determines their outcomes and luck is supposed to change. Other individuals show the opposite of the gambler's fallacy. They believe that skills determine outcomes. A string of successes means to them they have mastered the situation and will continue to experience success.

In sum, Rotter believes that environments can control behavior: "Behavior in different situations will be different . . ." (Rotter, 1990, p. 491). People in the *chance* condition, as a group, behaved differently than those in the *skill* condition. However, even within powerful situations, people may show individual differences in behavior. Some people are prone to the gambler's fallacy, others are not, and they show these trends across many different situations: ". . . there may be a gradient of generalization from one situation to another" (Rotter, 1990, p. 491).

Unlike some theorists, Rotter has laid out his basic assumptions in plain sight. They are seven in number.

1. "The unit of investigation for the study of personality is the interaction between the individual and his or her environment" (Rotter, 1982, p. 5).
2. "Personality constructs are not dependent for explanation on constructs in any other field" (p. 6). Simply put, personality constructs can stand on their own without being specified in terms of physiology or neurology.
3. "Behavior as described by personality constructs takes place in space and time" (p. 6). This assumption admits that personality constructs can also be specified in the terms of physics, chemistry, or neurology, but cautions against such dual specification. Dual specification leads to fruitless attempts to reduce

constructs to the lowest common denominator, for example, events at the connection between two nerve cells.

4. "Not all behavior of an organism may be usefully described with personality constructs. . . . This postulate simply recognizes that each construction system has a particular range of convenience" (p. 7). Notice that Rotter borrows language developed by George Kelly, his former colleague. Rotter continues, "Not all events can be usefully described in personality terms. Just as some events are not amenable to description in chemical terms, so too do some events resist psychological interpretation" (p. 7). Simple reflexes are examples as they are better described in physiological terms.

5. "A person's experiences (or a person's interactions with his or her meaningful environment) influence each other. In other words, personality has unity" (p. 8). Rotter believes that, with experience, the individual's personality begins to develop relative stability: there is some generalization of behavior across situations.

6. "Behavior as described by personality constructs has a directional aspect" (p. 8). It may be said to be goal-directed. Here Rotter's position coincides somewhat with that of Maslow. However, he is relatively more behavioristic, even showing some agreement with B. F. Skinner: "The preceding principle is based on the *empirical law of effect*" (p. 8). Thus, goals are achieved by behaviors that have been rewarded in the past for leading to goal attainment. The circularity inherent in this account is avoided by assuming, with good reason, that goals can be specified *before* behavior has been rewarded by goal attainment.

7. Finally, "The occurrences of a behavior of a person is determined not only by the nature or importance of goals or reinforcement, but also by the person's anticipation or expectancy that these goals will occur. Such expectations are determined by previous experience and can be quantified" (p. 10). According to Rotter, people are not merely pushed by past rewards, they are pulled by the anticipation of future goal attainment.

Basic Concepts: Rotter

Reinforcement Value, Psychological Situations, and Expectancy

For our purposes, Rotter's theory is based on three main concepts (Rotter, 1975; 1982; 1990). These are reinforcement value, psychological situation, and expectancy. In Rotter's social learning theory, **reinforcement** refers to anything that has an influence on the occurrence, direction, or kind of behavior (Phares, 1976). You may contrast this view with the narrow definition that B. F. Skinner has offered (covered in a subsequent chapter). Also, Rotter distinguishes between reinforcements on the basis of value. **Reinforcement value** is the degree of preference for any reinforcement to occur if the possibilities of many different reinforcements are all equal (Rotter, 1954). The value of a reinforcement depends on how much it is preferred by an individual, compared to other reinforcements that are equally available. Imagine a woman named Martha who sometimes dates a man named Fred. For Martha, going out with Fred has low reinforcement value, because, given a choice among several other dates, Fred would be just about the last selected.

A **psychological situation** is characterized in a way peculiar to a person, allowing the person to categorize it with certain other situations, as well as differentiate it from still others (Phares, 1976). Situations are in the "eye of the beholder." If a given situation is seen in a certain way by a particular individual, that is the way it is for that person, no matter how strange the categorization might seem to others. For some individuals an exhibition of classical music is entertainment, for others it is a scholarly endeavor, and for still others it is a waste of time. Further, a given person will see classical music as belonging in the same category as other forms of entertainment, such as baseball and movies. Others would place it in the same category as reading or researching library files, forms of scholarly pursuits. Martha plans to attend a rock concert, which she considers to be a social gathering. She believes one should take a companion to a concert, but it should be a person one would not be afraid to ignore when opportunities to mingle with others arise.

Expectancy is "the probability held by the individual that a particular reinforcement will occur as a function of a specific behavior on his part in a specific situation or situations." (Rotter, 1954, p. 107). Our hypothetical Martha has every reason to expect that should she pick up the phone and dial Fred's number he will be right over. Fred is madly in love with her, a feeling she does not reciprocate. That is, Martha has the specific expectancy that calling Fred will be reinforced by his presence with her at the concert—an outcome of high likelihood and, in and of itself, low reinforcement value. But she has another important expectancy as well. She expects opportunities to mingle with her friends at the concert, an outcome of high reinforcement value.

In addition, Martha has a relevant **generalized expectancy**, an expectancy that holds for a number of situations that are similar to one another to some degree (Rotter, 1966). The operation of generalized expectancies becomes more probable when individuals are faced with *new or ambiguous situations* that they characterize as bearing some resemblance to known situations (Rotter, 1966). Martha has been to relatively few rock concerts, but she expects that these will be like other social occasions. Her generalized expectancy is that whether she impresses her friends will depend upon chance rather than her social skills (whether her friends are "in a good mood," the concert goes well, and so forth). On the basis of these assumptions about Martha, we can predict that she will call Fred who will escort her to the concert where she will encounter friends who she will impress or not, depending on "what fate has in store."

Locus of Control: Internals and Externals

Arriving at the idea of "generalized expectancy" has been the goal all along. Rotter (1966; 1967) has identified two important generalized expectancies. One is the basis for as famous a personality measure as exists in psychology.

Locus of control refers to "the degree to which persons expect that . . . reinforcement [and other outcomes] of their behavior is [dependent on their] behavior or personal characteristics versus the degree to which [they expect it is due to] chance, luck, or fate, . . . powerful others, or is simply unpredictable" (Rotter, 1990, p. 489). That is, the control of outcomes can be perceived as located in one's own behaviors and skills, or as residing in luck and chance. According to Rotter, locus of control is "currently one of the most studied variables in psychology and the other social sciences" (1990, p. 489).

People who believe in **external locus of control** perceive that reinforcement of their behaviors is due more to luck, chance, fate, powerful others, or complex and unpredictable environmental forces, rather than determined by their own behaviors or characteristics (Rotter, 1966). Individuals believing in **internal locus of control** perceive that reinforcement is dependent on their own behavior or characteristics—not fate, luck, or chance. People who believe in internal locus of control are often called *internals*, while those who believe in external control are called *externals*.

Beliefs in external control or in internal control are certainly individual difference factors. However, Rotter (1975) is extremely careful to point out that calling a person an "external" or an "internal" is not a reference to a "trait" or a "type" (Rotter, 1990). In fact, he chastises researchers who apply factor analysis to his measure of locus of control and concludes that the measure has little generality across circumstances (Rotter, 1990; see Harper, Oei, Mendalgio and Evans, 1990, for an example of what he is talking about). He never indicated that external or internal loci of control would generalize strongly across situations. As illustrated in the **gambler's fallacy** study, situations can determine locus of control, just as people's beliefs about control can determine their behavior in a situation. Being a generalized expectancy, locus of control may determine outcomes if a situation is ambiguous. However, if a situation by its nature is associated with outcomes determined by chance or outcomes dependent on personal skills, the situation, not locus of control, will determine outcomes.

Although there are several measures of locus of control, the one most in use has been the Internal-External (I-E) Scale, developed by Rotter (1966). Rather than presenting it here verbatim, I have designed a measure that mimics the I-E Scale, but has items composed of common beliefs. By completing my version of the I-E Scale, you should easily get a flavor of what is involved with being an external or internal. The measure is presented in Box 12.1 for your use. Remember, the scale is for educational purposes. Do not use it in an attempt to classify yourself as an external or as an internal.

Characteristics of Internals and Externals

Conformity and Maladjustment

Because externals believe that they are hapless victims of their environments, one would expect that they would be more conformist. Indeed, Phares (1976) reports

BOX 12.1   An I-E Scale

Instructions. For each item, select the alternative that you more strongly believe to be true. You must select one and only one alternative for each item. Be sure that the alternative you select for a given item is the one you actually believe to be most clearly true, not the one you think that you *should* choose or the one you wish were true. Remember that this is a measure of your personal beliefs. There are no correct or incorrect answers and no high or low, good or bad scores.

   Do not spend much time on each item, but do make a choice for each item. In some cases, you will find that you believe both statements or neither one. Please make a decision anyway.

1. **a.** I often find myself saying something to the effect of "What will be will be."
   b. I believe that what happens to me is my own doing.
2. **a.** I deserve credit for most of my accomplishments.
   b. I've been fortunate to have done well on a number of occasions.
3. **a.** When your time comes, you pass away; that's just the way it is.
   b. I plan to live a long time, and I wouldn't be surprised if I made it to 100.
4. **a.** I'm a pretty confident person. I can make things happen.
   b. Sometimes I'm amazed at how things seem to happen to me all by themselves.
5. **a.** I feel like a Ping-Pong ball. Life just bounces me back and forth between happy and sad.
   b. If I want to be happy, I just choose a fun thing to do and go do it.
6. **a.** You get what you deserve and deserve what you get.

   b. I don't feel guilty about the good things that happen to me or moan about the bad things. It could just as well have happened to someone else.
7. **a.** I wish the world wasn't full of so many bullies.
   b. If people start to coerce me, I just stand up and look them in the eye.
8. **a.** People are good to me because I treat them right.
   b. I don't know when to expect that people are going to be nasty to me or nice.
9. **a.** I plan things, and they turn out as I expect.
   b. "Come what may," that's my motto. I'm a tumbleweed, caught in the wind.
10. **a.** I live my life one day at a time.
    b. I plan my day, my week, my month, and my year. I look ahead.
11. **a.** I'm not afraid to risk life and limb. What the heck, you could fall in the shower and break your back.
    b. I'm pretty careful at driving, sports, and so forth. I expect to keep this body a long, long time.
12. **a.** I feel pretty helpless when I'm with friends. I usually end up doing what they want.
    b. My friends and I are democratic about deciding what we'll do together, but my voice is always heard.
13. **a.** My voice is heard above the crowd.
    b. People just seem to drown me out.
14. **a.** When it comes to making love, if my partner wants to, fine; if not, that's OK too.
    b. I tend to decide when, where, and what my partner and I do in the love category.

BOX 12.1   *Continued*

15. **a.** I enter many lotteries, drawings, and things like that. I keep hoping I'll strike it rich.
    b. I steer clear of everything from bingo to poker. The odds are too long.
16. **a.** I'm always rooting for the underdog.
    b. Me, I stick with the winners.
17. **a.** In this country, anyone with some talent and some sweat is going to make it.
    b. If you're lucky, you're rich; if not, join the crowd.
18. **a.** Minorities are doing better, because they are getting more education and working harder.
    b. Minorities are doing better, because they are finally getting a few breaks.
19. **a.** Some people wander around under a black cloud, while the sun shines on others.
    b. Let's face it, some people have ability and use it; some have it and waste it; and some just don't have it.
20. **a.** Life is a great glob of complexity. It would take an Einstein to win at it.
    b. It's really quite simple: if you're good and work hard, you succeed.
21. **a.** I like to compete because if I win it's great, and if I lose I can say "the gods frowned on me."
    b. I like to compete because if I win, I can say "I did it."
22. **a.** I think we should help each other, because misfortune could strike any of us.
    b. I think people should help themselves. If something bad happens to them, they caused it, and they can fix it.
23. **a.** Sometimes I feel powerful, able to do whatever I want.
    b. Sometimes I feel powerless, the victim of mysterious forces.
24. **a.** Things happen that puzzle me. I just can't make sense of them.
    b. Give me enough time and enough information, and I can usually make sense of anything.
25. **a.** We are likely to be swept up in the ebb and flow of events.
    b. If we can get to the moon, we can change the course of mighty rivers and make the weather do our bidding.

Give yourself a point if you chose each of the following alternatives: 1.a.; 2.b.; 3.a.; 4.b.; 5.a.; 6.b.; 7.a.; 8.b.; 9.b.; 10.a.; 11.a.; 12.a.; 13.b.; 14.a.; 15.a.; 16.a.; 17.b.; 18.b.; 19.a.; 20.a.; 21.a.; 22.a.; 23.b.; 24.a.; 25.a. The higher the score, the more external you are.

If you scored from 20 to 25 on the I-E scale, you are in the *high external* range. A score of 0–5 makes you *high internal*. Most people fall between those extremes (whatever your score, remember the cautions mentioned above). If you are inclined toward one end of the scale or the other you are probably curious as to whether it is better to be an internal or an external. Originally Rotter (1966) thought that neither was "better" than the other in a practical sense. More recent evidence has caused him to reconsider.

that externals are more likely to conform in the standard conformity experiment. By the same token, internals react against attempts to influence them, even sometimes moving in a direction opposite of the influence attempt.

Rotter (1966) originally recognized a greater likelihood of *maladjustment* among externals. At the same time, he also hypothesized that there would be a curvilinear relationship between locus of control and psychological adjustment, with both extreme internals and extreme externals being maladjusted. However, more recently, he indicated that such is probably not the case (Rotter, 1975). It seems that externals are considerably more likely to be maladjusted, relative to internals.

Phares (1976) reported that externals are higher in anxiety and lower in self-esteem than internals. In terms of more serious maladjustment, schizophrenia may be related to externality. There is also preliminary and tentative evidence that it is associated with depression. More recent work supports the possibility that psychological problems are related to externality (Hermann, Whitman, Wyler, Anton, and others, 1990; Ormel & Schaufeli, 1991).

Substance Abuse

Perhaps surprisingly, internals may be more likely to abuse substances such as alcohol and heroin. It may be that high internality scores among substance abusers can be explained by the fact that such people are continually told "your cure is up to you." Alcoholics may therefore be using their I-E responses to reflect what they think is expected of them. If so, they may not be real internals. Alternatively, they may be internals who "self-medicate" to avoid externally imposed medications. Further, a recent study found no relationship between locus of control and parental alcoholism, a result contrary to the intuition that children of alcoholics would be relatively external (Churchill, Broida, & Nicholson, 1990). In any case, much more attention should be paid to the relationship between internal or external orientation and various psychological problems. At this point in time, the literature does not yet allow clear conclusions.

Achievement and "Race"

A sophisticated review of the literature on academic achievement and locus of control indicates the higher the internality the higher the achievement (Findley and Cooper, 1983). This same review raises another interesting question about the nature of locus of control. From the very beginning (Rotter, 1966), it has been reported that externality was greater among African Americans than Euro-Americans. This result seems to make intuitive sense, as relatively powerless persons should believe that they are at the mercy of their environments. However, the result seems to be due to culture rather than to "race," a suspect concept (see Allen & Adams, 1992, and Hirsch, 1981, for questions about the validity of "race"). Support for this contention comes from studies that find it is lower socioeconomic class African-Americans who are highly external, not their middle-class counterparts (Rotter, 1966). Thus, how well one is doing in life, both practically speaking and in terms of how one is regarded by others, may determine one's level of internality-externality.

Although the work of Findley and Cooper (1983) did not support the greater externality in African-Americans reported by Rotter (1966), the failure may be due to the small number of studies reviewed. Alternatively, perhaps African-Americans have changed in more recent years or it may be that middle-class subjects were used in most studies reviewed by Cooper. The change-over-time proposition would be consistent with the hypothesis that how well one is doing in life determines one's level of internality-externality. If African-Americans are doing better, they should become less external.

Divorce and Marital Adjustment

Although one may be said to have a generalized expectancy of internality or externality, change in expectancy may occur during the course of one's life, at least on a temporary basis. A study of divorce illustrates how internality-externality changes with the ebb and flow of life's fortunes. Doherty (1983) reported that women increased in externality following divorce, and then dropped back toward internality with the passage of time. Nevertheless, more recent work shows that externals and internals react to divorce differently. Via mailed questionnaire, Helen Barnet (1990) asked 107 divorced men and women about how long it took to decide on a divorce, their locus of control, stress due to divorce, and adjustment to divorce. Internals showed more pre-divorce decision distress and less post-decision distress than externals. They were also less distressed overall than externals. Because internals believe that they have control, they tend to display more distress-inducing lengthy deliberation over divorce, relative to externals. For the same reason, they adjust better to divorce, once a decision is made. Contrary to previous results, men were more external and experienced more post-divorce maladjustment.

Other work suggests that internals may be less likely to experience a divorce, because they are better at resolution of marital conflicts. Miller, Lefcourt, Holmes, Ware, and Saleh (1986) had married couples complete a special Marital Locus of Control (MLC) questionnaire and then resolve some conflicts. In an example of conflict resolution, husbands and wives were instructed in private. One was told to assume "you are resigned to visit in-laws" while the other was to assume "you have reservations about visiting in-laws and plans are not finalized." Then they got together in front of a video camera and resolved this and two other conflicts. Analyses of the MLC responses and the videotapes revealed that individuals who were internal for marital satisfaction were more active and direct in problem solving than externals. Also internals were more effective in communicating and achieving their desired goals and showed higher levels of marital satisfaction than externals.

Child-Rearing Practices and Personality Development

Researchers have studied how the processes of personality development differ for internals and externals. After reviewing the literature on locus of control and child-rearing practices, Phares (1976) concluded that internals are exposed to parental warmth, protectiveness, positivity, and nurturance. On the other side, externals tend to have cold, rejecting, and negative parents. Evidence also exists that parents may actually tutor their children to be internals or externals. Davis and Phares (1969) found that parents whose children's locus of control was similar to their own tended to be more indulgent and less disciplinarian than parents whose children's locus of control was dissimilar.

A child who believes in external locus of control is produced by a capricious, unpredictable world in which a given behavior is one day punished, the next rewarded, and the next ignored altogether. The degree to which the outcome of a behavior is stable, is the degree to which one has the possibility of claiming credit for that outcome. Following this logic, the literature reflects a definite connection between inconsistency of reinforcement within the family and tendency toward externality.

Whether an individual is a first or only child as opposed to a younger sibling may have an influence on internality-externality. The logic of locus of control and the evidence just reviewed would predict that the protective, demanding, but loving parents characteristic of only and first-born children should produce internal offspring. Phares (1976) reports some support for this line of reasoning, but adds that the birth order/locus of control relationship is clouded by a complex of variables beyond the two of interest. For example, sex and family size play a role in whether first and only children tend toward internality. In any case, the relationship between locus of control and birth order is not very strong. Recollection of the discussion of birth order in the chapter on Adler will leave you unsurprised about confusion in results relating this variable to locus of control.

Changing Externals

Because extreme externality, not extreme internality, is apparently a serious psychological handicap, changing externals has occupied a number of researchers and psychotherapists. Change appears possible because externality is not a trait and thus not assumed to be entirely stable. Examples of interventions into natural settings and psychotherapeutic interventions illustrate attempts to change externals.

DeCharms (1972) sought to change African-American teachers and students from "pawns" to "origins." **Pawns** are instruments of outside forces; **origins** are the locus of their own intentions and behaviors. Obviously pawns are essentially externals and origins are internals. DeCharms required the teachers to attend a week-long motivational training session and designed exercises for teachers to use throughout the school year. The training included: (1) encouragement of self-study and evaluation; (2) becoming familiar with the thought and behavior of people with affiliative, achievement, power, and other motives; (3) learning to appreciate the value of planning and of setting realistic goals for the fulfillment of some motive; and (4) general training to promote "origin" rather than "pawn" behavior. The in-class exercises included attempts to improve self-concept and achievement motivation as well as to make goals more realistic and to teach the origin-pawn concept. Results included greater professional advancement among trained compared to untrained teachers. Questionnaire results suggested that students of trained teachers saw them as encouraging the behavior of origins. Academic achievement by students of trained teachers also showed improvement.

More recently Ryan and Grolnick (1986) investigated whether a classroom environment perceived to be more "origin" than "pawn" would affect children's feelings and cognitions in a way that would promote academic success. Using the same measure employed by deCharms, these researchers assessed children's perceptions of the degree to which their teachers and classroom climates were "origin." They found that the more "origin" the classroom the higher the children's perceived self-worth, cognitive competence, internal control, and mastery motivation, and the lower their perceived control by unknown sources or powerful others. Child subjects also wrote projective stories about an ambiguous classroom scene. In terms of children's imaginations, ratings of these stories revealed that origin-like behavior of students was related to autonomy-oriented teachers and to low aggression. These results indicate that making the classroom environment more "origin" would help children both personally and academically.

Phares (1976) describes attempts to change externality in the context of psychotherapy. He reports greater decreases in externality by clients who seek psychotherapy because of acute problems as compared to those who enter therapy to treat more chronic difficulties. He also describes an adolescent who moved toward internality by adopting an active, success-oriented means of controlling his parents, rather than the shrinking, meek, and submissive techniques he had been using. Phares reports other work in which students became more internal after four half-hour therapy sessions centering on "personal growth experiences."

One problem in bringing about any change in a psychotherapeutic client is matching the client to the therapy. If the style and general orientation of the client and the psychotherapy do not match, the client might be resistant to attempts at change. In particular, an external may not change if the belief system he brings to therapy conflicts with the basic nature of the psychotherapy. For example, the therapy practiced by Albert Ellis is relatively controlling and structured, while the psychotherapy of Carl Rogers is relatively open and client-centered. Phares (1976) reports that college students who preferred the more directive approach of Ellis over Rogers' non-directive method were more external than their counterparts.

In a similar vein, psychotherapists were asked to evaluate the profiles of behavioristic and psychoanalytic colleagues. They rated the behaviorists as more overbearing and more likely to promote externality. The psychotherapists who served as raters also took the I-E Scale and imagined they had problems requiring psychotherapy. Those who were more internal indicated that their imagined problem would be better solved by psychoanalytic therapy, while externals chose behavioristic theory. Phares (1976) concluded that how clients perceive a psychotherapeutic method may partly determine how they respond to it.

Certain questions raised by I-E research remain unanswered. Are internals more likely to be depressed because they would be expected to attribute failure to their own internal processes, an orientation related to depression by other researchers? Are Asians, who are more collectivistic (rather than individualistic like North Americans), more external because of their dependence on the esteem accorded them by members of groups to which they belong? Answers to these and other intriguing questions await further activity by I-E researchers.

Other Generalized Expectancies

Internality and externality are not the only possibly generalized expectancies that might be specified. In fact, Rotter's theory allows for an indefinite number of generalized expectancies—expectations that show a gradient of generalization across situations. To illustrate, a couple of additional generalized expectancies are considered here.

Interpersonal Trust

A great deal of what one communicates to others and what others communicate to oneself is done without words. Facial expressions and posture tell other people about a person, just as those factors tell the person about them (Ekman and Friesen, 1974). Obviously the better one is at "reading" others' nonverbal signals, the better one is able to ascertain whether whatever behavior she or he is directing to another person is working to yield reinforcement. If a person is trying to fish for a compliment from someone, it is like casting a line into muddy waters if he or she cannot read from the face and body of the target whether the hook is close to sinking in.

The ability to intercept and correctly interpret nonverbal communications may be related to **interpersonal trust**, a generalized expectancy that people's verbal promises are reliable. That is, people who possess the generalized expectancy that they can rely on the word of other people are said to be high on interpersonal trust. Especially in view of the connection between successful detection of deception and ability to read nonverbal communications (DePaulo & Rosenthal, 1979), it seems reasonable to expect that people who trust others are people who have the ability to tell when others are being truthful. Conversely, people who are low in interpersonal trust are likely to be people who cannot tell when others are being straight with them. Applying this logic leads to the prediction that people who are high in interpersonal trust will be skilled at deciphering nonverbal communications. In fact, Sabatelli, Buck, and Dreyer (1983) found interpersonal trust higher in married people who were skilled at decoding nonverbal communications.

Generalized Expectancy for Negative Mood Regulation

Catanzaro and Mearns (1990) suggested that some people may develop a generalized expectancy for **negative mood regulation** (NMR), a belief that one can muster the cognitive and behavioral means to alleviate a negative-affective state or bring it under control. They reasoned that a measure of generalized expectancy for NMR should predict success at attempts to cope with negative moods. After developing and validating the NMR expectancy measure, they related scores on it to a measure of depression and to subjects' self-reports of sadness. As predicted, NMR scores were negatively related to depression and to self-reports of sadness: the higher the NMR scores the lower the depression scores and the reports of sadness. People high in negative mood regulation coped better with negative mood. Mearns (1991) also found that high expectancy for NMR yielded more active coping than low NMR expectancy. In this study NMR scores predicted level of depression in the first week after a romantic relationship ended.

Evaluation

Contributions to Controlling Our Lives

There seems to be little question that locus of control is here to stay. If anything, interest in it is increasing (Rotter, 1990). As long ago as 1975, Rotter was able to count at least 600 studies dealing with the I-E measure. Inspection of journals during the late 1980s and early 1990s indicates that the number has greatly increased and is going up at an accelerating rate. Interest is likely to continue increasing because locus of control is in tune with the current trend to focus on the interaction between personality factors and situations.

Rotter (1954, 1966, 1990) was a pioneer in recognizing that one can account for human behavior only by considering multiple determinants, including situational effects. He has always maintained that mindless use of just a personality measure is a fruitless approach to understanding people. In addition to expectancies like locus of control and factors like the situation, one must also consider values of reinforcements (Rotter, 1975). Further, internality-externality resembles a trait dimension only in that people can be distributed along the continuum. However, rather than being discrete, positions on the internality-externality dimension blend one into the other, more so than in the case of traits. Also, a person will vary her or his position at different points in time and under differing circumstances. This "sliding scale perspective" suggests that the meaning of internality-externality must be considered in the context of many other factors, and, relative to traits, cannot be interpreted meaningfully apart from that context. This kind of flexibility and openness characterizes Rotter and guarantees that his notions will contribute to psychology indefinitely.

Limitations

Locus of control is the centerpiece of Rotter's point of view. Evidence for and against this crucial notion in large part determines the validity of his theory. Rotter himself has noted some problems with locus of control. In 1966 he presented evidence that it overlaps with **social desirability**—the need to please others by displaying the characteristics that are valued in our society (for example, goodness, honesty, sincerity, and so forth). The implication of this association is obvious. In completing the I-E Scale, subjects and clients may be trying to favorably impress researchers or psychotherapists, rather than accurately reporting their actual characteristics. One could argue that the extent to which social desirability is manifested in I-E responses is the extent to which locus of control scores reflect response distortion rather than being an index of an actual personality factor.

Because so many people now go to college and learn about internals and externals, the perception that internals are the "good guys" and externals are the "bad guys" may be widespread. Also, the I-E items may be so transparent that respondents can easily see which refer to the "good guys" and which to the "bad guys," even if they have never heard of I-E. Some respondents, therefore, might actively and consciously try to make themselves look like "good guys" by endorsing as many of the "internal" items on the I-E Scale as they can identify.

Another perhaps more severe problem is the apparent existence of two kinds of externals, one of which contradicts very basic assumptions about externality (Rotter, 1975). **Defensive externals** are people who are highly competitive and do well on tests, but endorse external items for the apparent purpose of blaming others for their failures. **Passive externals** (also called "congruent") believe they are controlled by fate or chance. Whereas passive externals are consistent with Rotter's theory, defensive externals are not. According to Rotter's social learning theory, people who indicate that they are controlled by outside forces are not supposed to be competitive.

Rotter (1975) tried to skirt the problem by indicating that the theory and scale are still valid, but I-E scores simply identify two kinds of externals. Such an assertion does not explain the puzzling nature of defensive externals. Defensive externals may well be people who are using locus of control to provide an excuse for their failures, but the problem is that many other equally plausible explanations of their behavior are possible. For example, "defensive externals" may be subject to the widely known social condition of *alienation* as well as its accompanying feeling of powerlessness and estrangement from others, but fight it by being highly competitive. Adequately explaining how two types of externals can coexist in a theoretical domain that is constructed to account for only one remains to future researchers and theoreticians.

Conclusions

The key to being a personality theorist with lasting impact is to have a few continually useful concepts associated with one's name. Freud has his "psychosexual stages," Jung his "archetypes," Adler his "style of life," Rogers his "unconditional positive regard," and Maslow his "hierarchy of needs." Rotter has his "internals and externals." A hundred years from now when some theorists covered in this book are forgotten, "Rotter" probably will still be a name known to most psychologists. Aside from locus of control, Rotter should also be remembered for two other reasons: (1) his recognition that stability of personal attributes across social situations is limited and (2) his belief that the consideration of the interplay between personal and environmental factors is essential to understanding people.

Mischel: A Challenge to Traits

Rotter (1982) acknowledged the contributions of his many students and elected not to list them, lest some seem more prominent than others. Nevertheless, it is clear that his most accomplished student is Walter Mischel. Mischel expanded on Rotter's social learning ideas in two important ways. First, he went far beyond Rotter in denouncing *traits*—permanent, invariable, internal entities that determine stable behavior across many social situations. Beginning with his famous 1968 book, Mischel started a revolution that caused psychologists to rethink their assumptions about traits. Although the "bombing" of basic assumptions about traits has ended, some of those assumptions

Walter Mischel

lie smoldering in the ruins. Trait psychology will never be the same.

Second, in the place of *traits,* Mischel inserted cognitive facilities as the controllers of behavior. In so doing he originated some productive thinking about personality and, at the same time, opened up whole new research vistas. Mischel's work is living proof that personality may be conceptualized solely in terms of cognitive capacities, without reference to "traits" in the traditional sense.

As you recall, social learning theory emphasizes how people learn from other people. It is addressed to personality and, in some of its forms, amounts to an **interaction point of view**, the interplay between *internal entities*, or person factors, and *social situations* is emphasized, rather than either in isolation from the other. For Mischel, certain personal cognitive factors interact with situations to produce behavior. However, his point of view, called **cognitive social learning theory** proposes that important factors are cognitive facilities rather than traits. Specifically, Mischel's **personal cognitive factors** are memories of previous experiences, from the past history of an individual, that determine strategies the person employs for producing behavior at the present time. In interaction terms, Mischel's theory predicts that the history of rewards and punishments experienced in a given situation and skills and strategies developed in that situation will determine present behaviors.

Mischel, the Person

Like Adler—and Freud, in terms of his principle residence—Walter Mischel is Austrian (*American Psychologists* (*AP*), 1983). He was born on February 22, 1930 near Freud's office in Vienna. Also like Adler and Freud, Mischel and his family fled Vienna when the Nazis overran Austria in 1938. Following two years as refugees, Mischel's family settled in Brooklyn, the childhood home of Maslow and Rotter. Mischel attended primary and secondary school there and was the recipient of a college scholarship. Unfortunately, his father's illness required that he temporarily forgo postsecondary education in favor of employment. Later, while working as a stock boy, elevator operator, and assistant in a garment factory, young Mischel attended New York University where he pursued interests in painting, sculpture, and psychology. His passion for art was fueled in part by exposure to life in Greenwich Village, where a youthful B. F. Skinner also spent some time.

Just as Kelly had been turned off by S-R psychology studies in rat laboratories, so was Mischel. He much preferred reading Freud, the existentialists, and poetry. By 1951, Mischel had made a professional choice in favor of clinical psychology and entered the master of arts program at City College. There he studied with Gestalt-oriented Kurt Goldstein who had been one of Maslow's mentors. During this period he became a social worker, helping impoverished teens and elderly people. It was these real-life experiences that soured him on the usefulness of Freudian notions and projective testing as avenues to understanding people. Thus, he resolved to pursue a more research-oriented clinical program, leading to the pursuit of a doctorate at Ohio State during the Rotter-Kelly era.

From 1953 to 1956, Mischel soaked up the wisdom of Rotter and Kelly. Although Mischel may be considered a Rotter student—his theory is more like Rotter's than any other—he also gives Kelly heavy credit for shaping his thinking. Kelly's cognitive "constructs" and his belief that research subjects and clinical clients can be "scientists" had much impact on Mischel.

Armed with a solid cognitive background, Mischel spent 1956–1958 in a Trinidad village studying religious cult groups that practiced spirit possession. He assessed cult members' fantasy, cognition, and action both during possession and while in a normal state. Out of this work grew his interests in "choice preferences for delayed, more valued outcomes versus immediate, but less-valued outcomes" (p. 10). These experiences lead to his studies of delay of gratification and his determination to investigate people in their natural environments, not the laboratory.

Following two years at the University of Colorado, Mischel became an assistant professor at Harvard where he came under the influence of Gordon Allport and Henry A. Murray, among others. There he met and married Harriet Nerlove, a graduate student in cognitive development. In 1962, Walter, Harriet, and their three children moved to Stanford where he chaired the department in 1977–1978 and again beginning in 1982.

Mischel's View of the Person

Mischel's 1960s work in developing methods for identifying potentially successful Peace Corps volunteers led directly to the founding of his most useful thesis: "Under appropriate conditions people may be able to predict their own behavior as well as the best available indirect tests and inference methods" (p. 10). That is, he (1973) came to believe that people know themselves better than psychologists can come to know them by use of their best personality assessment techniques. Mischel's almost phenomenological attitude, "if you want to know about people, ask them about themselves," greatly influenced Charles Potkay and I in our own investigations of people's self-descriptions (Allen & Potkay, 1983a; Potkay & Allen, 1988).

Mischel stated this position even more clearly in his classic book *Personality and Assessment* (1968). There he challenged the basic assumption underlying notions of "traits": cross-situational consistency. He declared that objective observations indicate that people tend to discriminate between one situation and the next, leading to change in behavior from situation to situation. Such cross-situational inconsistency would predict that measures of traits would be poor predictors of corresponding behaviors. Indeed, Mischel showed that the correlations between measures of behaviors in various situations and measures of traits hover around .30, thus accounting for only about 9 percent of behavioral variation. When trait testers responded with attempts to improve their measures, Mischel suggested that they had missed the point. ". . . much of the personality assessment practiced at that time stereotyped individuals into categories that grossly oversimplified their complexity and that had limited predictive value for the individual case" (*AP*, 1983, p.10).

These proclamations left Mischel with a dilemma: people perceive cross-situational consistency in their own and other people's behavior, but scientific observations offer little confirmation of those perceptions. To account for the discrepancy between perceived and actual consistency, Mischel and his colleagues showed that certain *prototypical behaviors* do have *temporal stability* that is often mistaken for cross-situational consistency. For example, a prototype of aggressiveness is objecting to, arguing with, disputing, and "putting down" other people (verbal aggression). A student may see displays of this prototypical behavior by a classmate as stable, because the classmate may show it in the *same situation* (class) across many points in time (during most class sessions). The student's temporally stable aggressiveness may be mistaken for cross-situational consistency, because the observer fails to recognize that the aggressive behavior is occurring repeatedly in the same situation across time, not across different situations.

You may wonder how we may expect accurate reports from people about their own behavior when they mistake temporal consistency for cross-situational consistency. In fact, we should not expect accuracy unless we ask people the right questions. If one asks people, in effect, "are you consistent" or "is your friend consistent," they will say "yes, of course." In our society we value being consistent, which often means "reliable" (Cialdini, 1985). However, instead of this or other leading questions, one can ask people to describe themselves, in effect, describe what they have been doing, and also ask them to describe the situations in which they behaved. With this kind of questioning, people reveal that they vary from situation to situation (Allen & Potkay, 1983a; Potkay & Allen, 1988).

BOX 12.2   How Consistent Are You?

To demonstrate that you may vary more than you realize, you could repeat the "actual self/ideal self" exercise from the Rogers chapter, but with a twist. This time, on scratch paper, write down five self-descriptive adjectives each day for a week. Also, briefly record in long hand what happened to you each day. Do this in a spontaneous and uncritical manner, without any thoughts about being "consistent." After accumulating seven such self-descriptions, give them to a friend who is open and honest with you and have her or him place a plus (+) by each adjective that seems "favorable" when used to describe a person and a minus (–) next to "unfavorable" adjectives (tell the friend to put a zero next to adjectives that cannot be classified, but to use the zero very rarely). If you are a typical person, you will notice two characteristics of your descriptions. First, you will tend to mix favorable and unfavorable adjectives

in a single day's description and you will tend to record different adjectives on different days. This result occurs because you encounter many different situations during a day and different situations on different days. Second, notice the correspondence between what happens to you and the words you use to describe yourself. The words you use in self-descriptions may be thought of as labels for the behaviors you performed (Allen & Potkay, 1983a). They should correspond rather well with "what happened to you"—the situations you were in. For example, if you whispered tender sentiments to the love interest in your life (situation), you may have recorded "romantic" (behavioral label) in the description of yourself. Should you want further information about this "Adjective Generation Technique" (AGT), consult Allen & Potkay (1983a).

Basic Concepts: Mischel

Competency

Just what does a person acquire from her or his past history of operating in a situation that allows the person to perform effectively in the situation, on future occasions? For one thing, a person gains the perception of personal competence to perform effectively in the situation: operation in the situation teaches one how to behave effectively. **Competency** embraces both the cognitive ability to size up a situation so that one understands how to operate effectively in it and the capability of performing behaviors that will lead to success in the situation. It involves "knowing what to do" in a situation and being able to do it. Some people may not know that the ability to engage in "small talk" is critical to success at parties. Others may know the importance of small talk, but just cannot do it. Still others recognize the significance of small talk and do it well. Only this last set of people would have the competencies leading to success at parties.

Of course, people vary in how many competencies they possess. Some people have a large "bag full of tricks" they can use in a wide variety of situations. Others, unfortunately, have rather few competencies and can operate efficiently in a relatively small number of situations. However, the important factor in success is not so much the number of competencies that a person possesses, but the suitability of these competencies for the specific situations that she or he is likely to encounter. A generally effective person can size up a specific situation accurately, determine what behaviors are appropriate at each instance during the situation, and effectively perform those behaviors. Profiting from the experience of having previously operated in the situation is the key to personal effectiveness. Some people learn from experience in a situation. They come to understand its basic nature and they develop behaviors appropriate to it. Others do not.

Characterizing Events

"Sizing up" a situation is a more complicated process than you may have assumed it to be based on the previous section. It is an intricate and demanding process, because each situation tends to be complex: constituted by many components. A **component of a situation** is some part of the total situation, such as its physical characteristics, or, more important, factors associated with people who are present when the situation is unfolding. Components generate events. **Events** are simply occurrences that are produced by components of a situation. "Stuffiness" is an example of an event produced by a component of a possible college-class situation, a small poorly ventilated room. More potent events are the behaviors that are performed by people who operate in a situation.

    Characterizing events associated with a situation is placing them into meaningful categories. It is an early and critical step in sizing up a situation. A person may characterize events associated with an entire situation, or with individual components of it. For example, one student may place verbal events associated with the college class situation into the "silence is golden" category, signifying that speaking out is inappropriate. Another student may decide that the college class is the appropriate place for voicing any opinion that is relevant to the topic at hand. Obviously, these two people will behave quite differently in class. Which person is most successful will depend on which "reads" the dominant component of the situation—the professor—most accurately. Does the professor prefer "silence is golden" to "free expression of opinions?"

    In addition to such global characterization, or instead of it, a person may place specific events associated with a situation into several separate categories. These specific events are often behaviors of critical persons who are found in the situation. For example, a student may characterize instances of rapid and enthusiastic professorial speech as attempts to "impart important information," the stuff tests are made of. Such a characterization could lead to some frantic notetaking. The same student may interpret a dramatic pause following the presentation of a "main point" as a signal that it is time for students wishing to express their vital interest in the professor's lecture to pose questions.

    One of the most usual ways that people characterize the behaviors of other individuals operating in a situation is to attribute traits to them. The process involves placing people in such categories as "introverted," "dishonest," "sincere," "humorous," and so forth, based on their behaviors. In the person's perceptions, placement of an individual into a trait category is helpful in deciding on what behaviors to use in interacting with that individual. While Mischel continues to believe that placing people in trait categories is not the best strategy for understanding them, he has acknowledged that people do use traits to characterize themselves and others, a fact that psychologists must consider (Mischel and Peake, 1982a; 1982b).

Special note should be taken of the observation, made from the point of view of a given individual, that others' actions are not the only important behavioral events in a situation (Mischel, 1973). A particular person who is trying to size up a situation is also one of its components. That person's own behaviors are important events associated with the situation. One of the most valuable cognitive competencies that a person can possess is the realization that there are certain behaviors the person can perform that will change a situation, making it one in which he or she can operate more effectively. According to Mischel, people do not just passively respond to situations, they actively shape them. For example, suppose hypothetical person Sue finds herself at a business meeting during which the participants are all talking loudly and all at once. In this setting, she is not able to "do her thing," which is to apply precise logic to practical problems. Being somewhat soft-spoken, Sue feels the need to change the situation to better suit her capabilities. Thus, she makes her way to the front row, waves her hand so that the presiding official cannot miss it, and raises a "point of information." This action causes the official to pound her gavel until there is silence in the room and then to turn the floor over to Sue. Now Sue has transformed the situation into one in which she has a long past history of effective operation.

Expectancies

An extensive past history in a situation is likely to give a person a good grasp of what to expect when certain stimuli are present and when certain behaviors are performed. For Mischel, a **stimulus** is a very definite, well-defined component or event associated with a situation and can be either physical or behavioral. Anybody who has spent years as a lawyer will likely believe that certain stimuli lead to predictable outcomes in the courtroom. When the person dressed in black robes emerges from an adjoining room and steps behind the bench, lawyers have the expectancy that everyone will rise. For Mischel, an **expectancy** is a belief based on past experience that provides a prediction of future outcomes. In our courtroom example, the stimulus can be a component of the situation—the judge—or a behavior—the bailiff's verbalization "all rise." In either case, the stimulus gives rise to the expectancy of certain outcomes, often behaviors.

People also have beliefs with regard to what will occur should they or others behave in a certain way in a given situation. That is, people have expectancies concerning the outcome of particular behavioral performances. Knowing the rules of the court, lawyers can easily predict what will happen if their clients continually interrupt the proceedings by shouting at the judge.

In sum, knowing a situation is, in part, knowing what will result from the performance of a given behavior in the situation. It is also knowing what will happen when a certain stimulus is present.

Values of Outcomes

In sizing up a situation so that successful behaviors can be performed, it is not enough to know what to do and to be capable of doing it. If ones fails to accurately characterize the situation, its components and its events, one will not know *when* to do whatever will lead to success. However, accurate characterization is still not enough. One must know what to expect when specific stimuli emerge from the situation and when specific behaviors are performed in the situation. Additionally, the definition of success itself may depend on values one attaches to outcomes associated with the situation.

To take an example from Mischel (1973), people familiar with a particular form of psychotherapy will know that clients who make favorable references to themselves experience a definite outcome, approval from the therapist. Among those people are some who, when acting as clients, will greatly value the approval that results from favorable self-reference. Other clients, however, will not value approval or will value it less. It is a good bet that the frequency of favorable self-reference will be very different for the two groups of knowledgeable clients. The **value of an outcome**, be it a behavioral outcome or the outcome of some stimulus, is a powerful part of "sizing up" a situation. Knowing the outcomes that are typical of a situation, a person will adopt strategies and perform behaviors that will increase the likelihood of valued outcomes. In fact, **success** may be defined as effectively performing the behaviors which yield the outcomes that are valued by the performer.

Self-Regulatory Plans

A final aspect of sizing up a situation is one's own **self-regulatory plans**, rules, established in advance of opportunities for behavioral performance, that act as guides for determining what behavior would be appropriate under particular conditions. Self-regulatory plans involve more than rules covering a kind of situation, such as being at a party. People are aware that situations do not stay the same from one point in time to the next. A given situation will tend to vary even on a single occasion during which it is in effect. Have you attended a party where everyone engaged in the same activities throughout the entire duration of the affair? Probably not. Parties often start with "feeling each other out," figuratively speaking, until people are acquainted or reacquainted with one another, and thus, feel comfortable with one another. Then the merrymakers loosen up, and the fun really begins. Although one may have plans for parties in general, such as how to dress, whether to approach others or wait for them to approach oneself, and so forth, one must also have plans concerning what to do at different phases of the party. For example, what to do if somebody has too much to drink; what to do when "things are dragging a little." People generally have answers to these and other questions worked out in advance, in the form of plans.

Supporting Evidence

Delay of Gratification

Self-regulatory plans tend to be different for different people, because each person has a unique past history. Furthermore, plans are flexible. They may change permanently due to experience or may be altered temporarily due to the demands of the situation in which one finds oneself. Much of Mischel's and colleagues' research efforts have gone into determining how children accomplish the self-regulatory task of **delaying gratification**, postponing some pleasure so that it can be enjoyed to the maximum degree or in its most optimal form. In a recent review of their work, Mischel, Shoda, and Rodriguez (1989) report that enduring individual differences in this variety of self-control have been found as early as the preschool years. Further, children of preschool age who delayed gratification longer than others in certain laboratory situations, developed into adolescents who were more competent, showed higher scholastic performance, and coped better with frustration/stress.

Shoda, Mischel, and Peake (1990) described the procedures they have used in demonstrating that preschool delay-ability is positively related to adolescent competence. They also revealed the personality factors associated with the ability to delay. In these studies, an experimenter first asked children to identify which of several objects they found most desirable (for example, marshmallows or pretzels). Then they are placed in a room stripped of distracters and asked whether they would *prefer* a little or much of the desired object (for example, one versus two marshmallows). Then the experimenter said she had to leave and indicated, "if you wait until I come back . . . then you can have this one [points to two marshmallows]. If you don't want to wait you can ring the bell and bring me back any time you want to. But if you ring the bell then you can't have this one [points to two marshmallows], but you can have that one [points to one marshmallow]" (p. 980).

Children use different strategies to accomplish delay. Rodriguez, Mischel, and Shoda (1989) provide examples of strategies children use: (1) covering up the preference (for example, M&Ms) or leaving them in the open; (2) thinking of the preference abstractly or concretely (M&Ms are "round buttons" rather than "yummy and chewy"); and (3) thinking of the task or the enjoyability of the preference ("I'm waiting for the M&Ms" or "The M&Ms taste yummy and chewy"; p. 360). Overall Shoda, Mischel, and Peake (1990) found positive correlations between preschool seconds-of-delay-time and adolescent cognitive/academic competence as well as the ability to cope with stress/frustration. They also found that coping strategies used in preschool were related to certain adolescent personality factors as revealed by parents. For example, leaving the preference (M&Ms) exposed was negatively (inversely) related to "How likely is your child to be sidetracked by minor setbacks?"; "How likely is your child to yield to temptation?"; and "When trying to concentrate, how distractible is your son or daughter?" (p. 983). Leaving the preference exposed was positively (directly) related to "How likely is your child to exhibit self-control in frustrating situations?"; "How well does your child cope with important problems?"; and "How capable is your child of exhibiting self-control when frustrated?" (p. 983).

People Are Interactionists, Not Trait Theorists

A number of years ago, Gene Smith and I showed that, contrary to popular belief among many psychologists, when asked the "right" questions, ordinary people reveal themselves to be interactionists, not trait theorists (Allen & Smith, 1980). Usually people are asked to "observe" someone's behavior and then asked whether the other person's behavior was caused by her or his "traits" or the situation he or she was operating in. If, instead, people are asked to choose the most plausible explanation of behavior from definitions of several such explanations, including a definition of *trait* and one of *interaction*, they choose *interaction*. Mischel and his colleagues have gone beyond this beginning effort by showing that specifying the situation in which a behavior occurs or qualifying a trait explanation of behavior improves people's predictions of behavior. Shoda, Mischel, and Wright (1989) investigated adults' impressions of children's aggressive behavior. When situations were specified ("child hits when provoked") rather than unspecified ("child hits"), impressions (for example, "is an odd child") were more accurate in predicting differences among children in overall, actual aggression. Other work by Wright and Mischel (1988) took a closer look at the "trait" statements children and adults used to explain behavior. This more careful observation revealed the use of *qualifiers* (the target person *sometimes* is aggressive) and *conditional statements* (the target person is aggressive *when* teased by others). These outcomes indicate ordinary people recognize that behavior is not altogether cross-situationally consistent (*sometimes*) and its performance often depends on the existence of certain situations (*when*).

BOX 12.3   Uncovering Natural Interactionism

You can discover for yourself that people are natural interactionists, rather than naive trait theorists, if you ask the right questions. Ask a friend to describe someone he or she knows well by using the AGT method employed in Box 12.2 ("Write down five adjectives to describe [so-and-so]"). Pick one of the words generated by your friend and probe deeper. "You say that so-and-so is [for example] kind. Is that always true?" When the answer almost inevitably comes back "No," ask "How often?" The answer is practically certain to be words to the effect of "*sometimes.*" Then ask, "*When* is so-and-so kind?" Repeat this process with another target (a new so-and-so) and, perhaps, with another friend. You will likely become convinced that people are aware at some level of consciousness that behavior varies across situations and is often tied to particular situations.

Summing Up the Mischelian Principles

To tie together Mischel's principles in one small package that shows how these cognitive rules are manifested differently in different people, consider an example that involves all of them. Assume that Diane and Don are participating in a sand-lot softball game (from Allen & Potkay, 1983a). Their competencies are quite different. Whereas Diane is an excellent ballplayer, Don is just average. Their characterizations of events associated with the game situation are also different. Don sees softball on the sandlot as an occasion for "having fun and cutting up," while Diane is dead serious. Their views of stimulus and behavioral outcomes are different. While both might recognize that a solid hit is an exciting event, only Don sees the behavioral outcome, hitting the ball, as an occasion for backslapping and cheering. Further, the values they assign to outcomes are different. Diane finds the praise that follows a long hit to be better than "money in the bank," while Don could not care less. Finally, their self-regulatory plans are also different. Don plays with abandon, trying to turn every hit into a home run, whereas Diane is careful not to stretch a hit too far and risk being thrown out.

Evaluation

Mischel's Contributions

Walter Mischel started an intellectual revolution in personality psychology. He opened up minds with his declaration that the notion of trait, and the assumption of behavioral stability that lies behind it, is of limited utility for understanding and predicting behavior. Personologists who had previously just accepted "trait" were forced to dredge up the assumptions underlying the concept and support them. The result was more incisive thinking and greater caution in using the concept. Trait theorists sharpened their definitions and honed their research techniques.

Further, the intuitively reasonable position "interactionism" that was unsuccessfully championed by Rotter suddenly became the "position of choice." Faced with undeniable evidence that behavior varies considerably across situations, rather than remaining stable, many trait theorists found it expedient to call themselves "interactionists." Unfortunately, many of them continued to operate as if behavior is rigidly stable across situations. The net result was mainly lip service to the observation that certain behaviors occur mostly in particular situations that call them forth, not in all situations. The fact that "lip service" very often is followed by real change virtually ensures that interactionism will actually catch on in the future. Then the point of view of personologists will be more in tune with that of the people they study.

In addition, Mischel's work on delay of gratification has numerous important implications (Mischel, Shoda, & Rodriguez, 1989). Early ability to delay gratification has been solidly related to later academic achievement and emotional stability. It follows that techniques useful in enhancing delay should be developed and taught to children. Examination of the procedures used by Mischel and colleagues and the results they have obtained indicates that such techniques could be readily developed. These methods for enhancing delay may be especially beneficial to "children at risk," a growing constituency of our public schools.

Limitations

The importance of Mischel's challenge to "traits" is undeniable and his theory is intriguing. Despite these significant contributions, he has not yet developed an enduring and useful concept, like "locus of control," that will ensure his continued presence among recognized major contributors to personality psychology. Only "self-regulatory plans" have been significantly researched, and only one of them, methods for delaying gratification, has received considerable attention. Further, most of the research concerning Mischel's theory has been done by himself and his colleagues. Other researchers have infrequently focused on his ideas, compared to the heavy attention paid to the concepts of other theorists covered in this book.

The rejection of traits and the complete absence of them from his theory has not been well received in some quarters. Certain theorists and researchers think that Mischel has overstated his case (for example, Bem & Allen, 1974). Others reject his position outright (for example, Epstein, 1977). In fact, the debate over traits has become so acrimonious that Mischel has been in danger of isolation from his colleagues. This circumstance may explain why Mischel has considerably softened his earlier rejection of traits (Mischel, 1984).

Conclusions

Mischel's challenge to "traits" is one of the most important events in the modern history of personality research. However, a contribution of possibly greater importance has been largely ignored. Personologists should take another look at his theory with an eye to what it tells them about alternatives to understanding personality. For too long it has been assumed that personality cannot exist without the behavioral consistency assumed by trait theorists. To the contrary, Mischel's work has shown there are other ways to cast personality that are not burdened by trait assumptions (Allen, 1988a; 1988b). In fact, quietly Mischel has demonstrated that personality can be constructed in non-trait terms. His cognitive approach that eschews traits accounts for personality development and functioning without making tenuous and limiting assumptions about behavioral consistency. If Walter Mischel has taught us nothing more than to consider alternative conceptions of personality free from trait assumptions of behavioral consistency, we have learned a profound lesson indeed.

Summary Points

1. Rotter was born in Brooklyn and was nurtured by the Brooklyn Library. As a high school student he read Freud and Adler. When he entered Brooklyn College during the depression, he chose chemistry as a major, but took more psychology. After training at the University of Iowa, and an internship in clinical psychology, he completed a clinical Ph.D. at Indiana University. Following service in World War II, he chose Ohio State. Rotter focused on situations, but acknowledged individual differences in behavior. It was shown that subjects in a "skill" condition performed better than subjects in a "chance" condition, but there were individual differences within the chance and skill conditions.

2. Rotter emphasizes the interaction between the person and the environment. He asserts that personality has unity and its constructs are not always the best way to describe behavior, and he holds that behavior is directional and is guided by expectancies. Reinforcement value is the degree of preference for any reinforcement to occur if the possibilities of different reinforcements are equal. In turn, an expectancy is the probability held by the individual that a particular reinforcement will occur.

3. By contrast, a generalized expectancy is one that holds for a number of similar situations. Rotter's most emphasized generalized expectancy is locus of control. It led to the development of the internal-external dichotomy and the I-E Scale. Research has shown that externals are more conformist and more maladjusted, but less prone to substance abuse than internals who are higher in academic achievement. "Race" may also be related to locus of control. Also, internality/externality may change during the divorce process, but individual differences in I-E explain diverse reactions to different stages of the divorce process.

4. Research on I-E and child-rearing practices indicates that only internals' parents are warm, protective, positive, and nurturing. Teachers trained to be "origins" did better at teaching "origin behavior" and their students showed improved academic performance. Creating an "origin" climate in the classroom promotes self-worth, cognitive competence, and internal control in students. Whether externals change may depend partly on the beliefs they bring to therapy. Ellis' and the behaviorists' points of view are favored by external clients, while internal psychotherapists favor psychoanalysis.

5. Other generalized expectancies that have emerged through research include interpersonal trust. Another is negative mood regulation. Locus of control is such a solid concept that Rotter's name is sure to be known many years from now. Internality/externality is on a "sliding scale" in that a person will vary her or his position on the I-E continuum at different points in time. Unfortunately, social desirability contamination of the I-E dimension and the existence of passive externals raise unresolved dilemmas about locus of control.

6. Born in Austria, Mischel was reared in Brooklyn. His undergraduate days were spent at New York University where he studied art and psychology. Turned off by S-R psychology, he embraced clinical psychology at City College and eventually earned a Ph.D. in that area at Ohio State University. There he was influenced by Rotter and Kelly. His studies in Trinidad launched his interest in delay of gratification.

7. Mischel asserts, "If you want to know about people, ask them about themselves." His challenge to traits took the form of finding little relationship between measures of traits and behavior. This position created a dilemma: people perceive stronger cross-situational consistency than exists. The dilemma is resolved by recognizing that prototypical behavior displays temporal stability that is mistaken for cross-situational stability. Competency is the cognitive ability to size up a situation and to perform behaviors that will lead to success. The important factor in success is the suitability of these competencies for the situations that the person is likely to encounter.

8. Situations have components, including physical ones and people. In turn, events are occurrences that are produced by components. Characterizing events associated with a situation is placing them into meaningful categories. People may characterize the behaviors of other people by attributing traits to them. From the person's point of view, one of the most important components of a situation is herself or himself. A stimulus is a definite component or event associated with a situation. An expectancy is a belief based on past experience that provides a prediction of future outcomes.

9. Sizing up situations also involves establishing values for outcomes. Success is effectively performing the behaviors that yield the outcomes valued by the performer. Self-regulatory plans are rules that act as guides for determining what behavior would be appropriate under particular conditions. One kind of self-regulatory plan involves methods used to delay gratification. In experiments, children used various methods for delaying, such as covering the preferred object. Leaving the object exposed was related to a number of personality factors, such as resisting temptation.

10. Mischel has shown that people are intuitive interactionists. He has demonstrated that adults are more accurate in predicting aggression in children if the setting of aggression is specified. Also, prediction is better when qualifiers and conditional statements are used. Mischel's work on delay of gratification is noteworthy, especially since it has many practical implications. However, he has no powerful idea such as I-E associated with his name and the bulk of the work on his theory has been done by his research group. Instead of just being acknowledged for challenging traits, we should applaud Mischel for showing us that there are alternatives to traits for conceiving of personality.

Running Comparison

Theorist	Rotter in Comparison
Maslow	Like Maslow, he was a "student" of the Brooklyn Library and, like Maslow, he thought behavior to be "goal directed."
Adler	Adler turned him on to psychology. Birth order is roughly related to locus of control.

Kelly	He took over Kelly's clinical directorship and used some of his language.
Albert Bandura	Like Bandura, he believed that people are pulled by the future.
B.F. Skinner	They both talked about "reinforcement," but Rotter had a broader definition.

Theorist	*Mischel in Comparison*
Kelly	Like Kelly, he rejected S-R psychology. He was impacted by Kelly's cognitive constructs and "people can be scientists."

Essay/Critical Thinking Questions

1. Does the gambler's fallacy occur in reality with reasonably likelihood? Attempt to come up with a scenario in which someone is guilty of the gambler's fallacy though not actually gambling (investing in the market rather than visiting Las Vegas).

2. What we call "reinforcing" or "rewarding" is somewhat in the eye of the beholder. Can you provide three examples of outcomes that are reinforcing to you, but not to one of your friends?

3. What are you, an internal or an external? Decide which and give examples verifying that you are what you claim to be.

4. How were you reared? You should be able to describe your upbringing so that the way your parents reared you fits the choice you made in question number 3.

5. Let us suppose that you are an external and do not want to be. Design a program that has a chance of changing you in the internal direction.

6. Can you provide two examples of what looks like "cross-situational consistency," but is actually cross-time (temporal) consistency.

7. Briefly describe a situation (for example, a fraternity party), giving its critical components, including events, and characterize those events. What expectancies would you have for that situation and what self-regulatory plans might be successful in the situation?

8. How good were you at delaying gratification as a child? Think back on your ability to resist temptation. Give a couple of examples to show it was strong or weak. Now relate your ability to delay in childhood to your characteristics now.

9. Analyze a friend's behavior along some dimension, such as aggression, conscientiousness, or helpfulness. Can you show that whether the friend displays behavior belonging at one extreme or another on the chosen dimension depends on the nature of the situation the friend is operating in?

10. Can you describe a situation, other than a softball game, that allows you to contrast the behavior of two different people according to Mischelian principles? Look at the example under the title *Summing Up the Mischelian Principles,* and then create a new situation that serves the same summary function.

13

THINKING AHEAD AND LEARNING MASTERY OF ONE'S CIRCUMSTANCES: ALBERT BANDURA

- Which is the most important source of our learning, rewards and punishments or the models whose behaviors we imitate?

- Are we pushed by our past histories or pulled by our anticipation of future rewards?

- Does *biology, cognition* and *other internal events,* or the *environment* drive behavior or do each of these three factors feedback on the others so that each is involved in the cause of the others?

- Is it possible to be totally "self-confident" or is it more reasonable and possible to be confident concerning specific pursuits in life?

- Can a personality theory have anything meaningful to say about the cognitive processes that allow humans to do evil to other humans?

Learning theories take many forms. The variety considered here is sandwiched between a chapter concerned with two related kinds of social learning theory and a chapter on behavioristic ideas that B. F. Skinner promoted. Albert Bandura's account of how we acquire new behavior, thoughts, and feelings is also in the "social learning" category. It is, however, broader than the theories of Rotter and Mischel and, one could argue, the notions of Skinner. In fact, you are now embarking on an odyssey into one of the most comprehensive theories covered in this book, and the one that is probably more applicable to the full range of human problems than any other. Bandura's ideas help explain how we acquire everything from motor behaviors—how to swing a tennis racket properly—to how we overcome irrational emotions, such as fear of snakes. In addition, his concepts not only

Albert Bandura

explain how we have gained mastery over critical aspects of our environments, they also lay out procedures for achieving and maintaining new competencies. Bandura and his colleagues have studied and elucidated human pursuits ranging from aggression to the cognitive processes that allow humans to oppress other humans. Here is an opportunity for you to acquire knowledge that will be truly useful to you in your life.

Bandura, the Person

Albert Bandura, one of the greatest of contemporary psychologists, was born on the fourth day of December, 1925, in the Canadian village, Mundare, Alberta (*American Psychologist*, 1981). After experiencing the climate in the area, his answer to the common question, "Where do cold fronts come from?" is sure and certain: his birthplace. Bandura attended the typical small town school of the day, elementary through high school in one facility. It was, however, not devoid of virtues. Due to a shortage of teachers and resources, pupils were forced to learn on their own initiative. Perhaps his school days were the source of Bandura's faith in the power of personal initiative.

The path to a more hospitable environment, and a college degree, lay through the forbidding Yukon. Young Bandura took a job patching the Alaskan Highway which was slowly sinking into its muskeg foundation. There he encountered a variety of individuals, ranging from parole violators and debtors to divorced men avoiding alimony payments. The experience may have been the origin of his interest in the psychological problems of everyday life.

After obtaining an undergraduate degree at the University of British Columbia, he enrolled at the University of Iowa where Kenneth Spence, a famous learning psychologist of the day, had the psychology department under his spell. Because of Spence's prominence, and Iowa's ties to Yale and Neal Miller, the furor over learning theories that raged at the time consumed Bandura and his classmates.

Having received his doctorate in 1952, and finished an internship at the Wichita Guidance Center, Bandura was appointed instructor at Stanford University. Working his way up through the ranks, he became a full professor in 1964 and occupied an endowed chair in 1974. Because he loves the area, in particular San Francisco's fine restaurants and Napa valley's quaint wineries, it seems that he is unlikely to leave.

In 1980 he received the American Psychological Association's award for Distinguished Scientific Contributions. He was cited "for masterful modeling as researcher, teacher, and theoretician" and for "innovative experiments on a host of topics including moral development, observational learning, fear acquisition, treatment strategies, self-control . . . and cognitive regulation of behavior. . . . His vigor, warmth, and humane example have inspired his many students . . ." (*AP*, 1981).

Bandura's View of the Person

Observational Learning and Reciprocal Determination

Observational Learning
Upon coming to Stanford, Bandura fell under the benevolent influence of Robert Sears who was studying familial antecedents of social behavior and identification learning. Branching off from this work, he and his first doctoral student, Richard Walters, launched a series of studies on aggression in children that are still being cited today. Their investigations into **observational learning**, learning by observing models as they perform useful behavior, demonstrated that "modeling is not merely a process of behavioral mimicry" (Bandura, 1989a, p. 18). People who observe a model learn the value of a behavioral performance in terms of what it will achieve.

Inside/Outside and Reciprocal Causation
A major issue in the area of personality has been whether forces inside or outside of individuals control their behavior. Bandura's theory relates behavioral consistency to the inside/outside question. Advocates of determination by factors outside of individuals emphasize the variability of behavior, due to the dynamic action of the environment. Those who believe that control of behavior comes from within indicate that stable processes from inside individuals give rise to stable behavior. By contrast, Bandura is concerned with the interplay of inside and outside factors and, thus, **social cognitive theory** focuses on both the variability and consistency of behavior and is

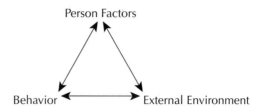

FIGURE 13.1   Reciprocity in the relationship between Person Factors, Behavior, and the External environment.

concerned with the interplay of factors inside and outside of people (Bandura, 1977; 1989a). "In *social cognitive theory* people . . . function as contributors to their own motivation, behavior, and development within a network of reciprocally interacting influences" (Bandura, 1989a, p. 6; emphasis added). To Bandura, *behavior, person factors*, such as cognition, biological variables, and internal events, and the *external environment* have reciprocal influences on one another: each influences the other and is influenced by the other. Figure 13.1 displays these relationships.

Person Factors, Behavior, and the External Environment

Behavior Can Affect Cognition, Feelings, and Even Neurobiology

Figure 13.1 implies some rather remarkable and even surprising assumptions. It is not so amazing that behavior could affect certain person factors, such as those in the cognitive category. If you do a thing well the first time you attempt it, you may change your thinking about your ability to do that thing. Should a person attempt to approach a porpoise upon a visit to a marina and succeed in repeatedly touching it on the first try, she or he may come to view "making friends with seagoing mammals" as a thing "I can do." Likewise, success on a first attempt may change certain internal events, such as one's feelings about the circumstances involved with the success. A person may develop positive feelings about close encounters with our ocean-dwelling relatives. However, that a person's behavior may affect his or her neurobiological functions may come as a surprise. If, over several years, one repeatedly reads, talks about, and writes about seagoing mammals, one will develop a "neurological network" for processing information about such mammals. In turn, it will make learning more about whales and porpoises easier in the future.

Environments May Also Affect Neurobiology

A woman who moves in with other women—takes up residence in a suite occupied by several women—adopts a new environment that may affect hormonal cycling. In time, the onset and ending of her menstral cycle may come to match that of her suitemates (Matlin & Foley, 1992). Cognitions, such as beliefs and expectations, can also impact on hormonal cycling and its accompaniments. If the woman, because of religious indoctrination, believes that "the curse" will strike her every 28 days, she will more regularly experience depression and physical discomfort premenstrually than other women (Paige, 1973). Regardless of her religious beliefs, if she comes to expect that she is about to start her "period," whether or not she really is, she may experience certain physiological changes, such as increased water retention (Ruble, 1977).

Behavior Affects Environment and Vice Versa

It is obvious that humans' behaviors can affect their physical environment: witness the tragic increase in pollution, due to thoughtless human behavior. Influence in the other direction is equally obvious: because of pollution-driven ozone depletion, people may avoid sunny beaches in the future.

Cognition and Feeling Affect Behavior and Environments

According to Bandura's model in Figure 13.1, cognitions and internal events, such as feelings, influence both behavior and environments (Bandura, 1989a). If certain people believe that their behavior will not succeed in a given setting, it will fail. If they feel frightened when entering a given situation, they will avoid it. If their feelings and beliefs about forested lands are indifferent or negative—"turn them into commercial properties"—they will allow the forests to vanish.

Free Will, Personal Agency, and the Power of Forethought

More recently, Bandura has turned his attention to what people can contribute to their own fruitful motivation and effective action. Unlike B. F. Skinner, who admonished us to abandon the "false" assumption of free will, Bandura (1989b) believes that people can, through their own cognitive mechanisms, gain a significant measure of control over their environments. People can develop a sense of **personal agency**, a condition in which they come to believe that they can make things happen that will be of benefit to themselves and to others.

Consistent with the contention that people have "free will" to a meaningful degree, Bandura believes that people not only select the situations in which they will operate, they create many of those situations. One may feel forced to go to class or work, but one may chose to attend a concert or drop in on a friend. People may insert themselves into ready-made situations, or they may create their own: "throw a party" or start a debate.

Learning

In contradiction to some others who theorize about learning, Bandura believes that learning occurs because people are aware of the consequences to their responses. They can and do think about what these consequences will be. In support of these assumptions, Bandura (1977) reports considerable evidence that learning is difficult for humans, if there is little or no awareness of the link between behavior and consequences. Further, it is nearly certain that learning is *facilitated* by awareness. Being aware makes people capable of **forethought**, anticipation of "likely consequences of . . . [future] actions" (Bandura, 1989a, p. 27). Forethought frees people from the tyranny of past rewards or reinforcements. People behave in anticipation of future consequences; they do not exclusively behave in the presence of circumstances associated with reinforcement in the past. "The eye to the future," as opposed to "eyes in the back of the head," is a philosophical position that Bandura shares with Kelly. Behaviorists prefer animal research subjects; Bandura prefers humans. Animals do not have symbolic thought; people do. People can record consequences of actions as sentence structures or sets of symbols and thereby form hypotheses concerning what will happen in the future. If one observes that smiling at waiters yields efficient and prompt service, she or he will store that observation in words and construct the hypothesis that smiling works with waiters. This hypothesis operates as a motivator for smiling behavior in the presence of waiters and will, therefore, increase the likelihood of smiling at waiters on subsequent occasions.

"Social" and "Cognitive" in "Social Cognitive Theory"

Another principle underlying social cognitive theory is tied up in the term "social." People learn as much vicariously, through observing the behavior of others, as they learn through direct experience. Further, the terms "cognition" and "social" are close associates, because cognition is the vehicle by which people learn from people. If an individual watches another person receive a reward as a consequence of a behavioral performance, the observer will likely think (cognition), "If I behave in the same way, I'll receive the same reward." Observing another person model some behavior that results in reward is enough for learning to occur; rewards need not be directly received. In fact, individuals may learn even if their observations in no way include rewards.

Basic Concepts: Bandura

Models and Modeling

Learning by Others' Example
There are two fundamental concepts associated with observational learning. A **model** is a person who performs some behavior for an audience, showing how it is done and what benefits accrue from it. **Modeling** refers to the act of performing a behavior before one or more observers.

When people learn from observing others, they do not simply soak up whatever models have to offer. They begin observations of others with certain predispositions that determine what they learn from what they see. People want to master aspects of their own particular environments. Thus they look for those behaviors, among the many displayed by available models, that will allow mastery.

Symbolic Representation
People do not passively adopt a model's behavior (Bandura, 1989a). They "turn it over" in their minds, relating it to information they already have, rehearsing it, criticizing it, and thereby remembering it, if it is useful. In addition, people may transform information learned from a model into symbolic form so that it may be quickly and easily turned into action in the future. For example, one may ask, "Which way to the psychology building?" and hear in reply, "Follow me." If the

questioner is a psychology major, and thus will frequently use the directions, the model's movements might at first be visualized as a series of right and left turns, then as "right(r), left(l), r,l,l,r." In this way information provided by the model may be represented symbolically, after it has been initially accepted in more concrete form.

Turning Observations into Behavior

Of course, people do not stop with accepting models' behavior and transforming it into symbolic form. They will attempt to turn their observations into behaviors. The extent to which they are successful will depend in part on whether they have the skills to execute the modeled behaviors. Success will also depend on whether people have gleaned all the relevant elements of the modeled behavior from observations, before they try to behave. Given these conditions are met, observers create an *internal representation* of the behavior and then hone and refine it, along with the behavior, to suit their particular needs. This "polishing" is accomplished by an interplay between behavioral performances and the internal representation. For example, baseball players who have watched an expert hitter will have a mental representation of the hitter's swing. When they practice the swing, they will compare their attempt to their mental image and change the swing to coincide with the image. At the same time, as the swing evolves so that it becomes successful, the mental representation will change to accommodate peculiarities of the newly effective swing.

Attractive Models

Characteristics of models and observers are also important in determining what is learned, or even whether anything is learned. People do not observe whoever happens to be present. Attractive, successful models, those who have done well both generally and on specific tasks, are the ones whose behaviors are adopted. On the other hand, what people learn from models is in part determined by their own capabilities that existed prior to observations. If observers are unschooled in chemistry, they are unlikely to benefit from a laboratory demonstration in that field, no matter how effective the model.

Incentives

Reinforcements or rewards for the performance of behaviors enter the learning sequence in three different ways. First, a person may observe a model being rewarded for performing a behavior. Such an observation would produce an **incentive**, anything, concrete or abstract, that creates an anticipation of a positive outcome following the performance of a behavior (Bandura, 1989a). For example, a child observes another child receive lavish praise for preventing an altercation between some younger children. In the future the development of another conflict situation between younger children will act as an incentive for the observer to intervene in anticipation of praise. Second, the model, for example, a parent trying to teach a child to pronounce a word, may reward efforts of the observer to reproduce the behaviors previously modeled. Third, and perhaps most important, the observer may reward himself or herself for a good approximation to correct performance of a response. So if some children are trying to learn the utterance "arithmetic," they may "pat themselves on the back" when they come close to the proper pronunciation.

Other Things We Learn from Models, Besides Behavior

Expectancies

Behavior is not all that is learned from models. In **vicarious expectancy learning** people adopt other peoples' expectancies concerning future events, especially expectancies of those with whom they share relevant experiences (Bandura, 1977; 1989a). For example, people who have lived through a hurricane, but suffered little from its devastating winds, still have witnessed the suffering of people like themselves who are victims. Accordingly they adopt the victims' expectations. Thus, their vicarious expectancy of disaster may be almost as strong as that of actual victims, as reflected in their willingness to join with others in preparing for future storms. In general, vicarious expectancy learning is most likely to be transmitted to people from models with whom they share many experiences.

Creativity, Facilitation, and Innovation

An individual first accepts the behaviors of a model and then may creatively branch out from there. Thus, Beethoven adopted the forms of Haydn and Mozart, later going well beyond those artistic styles into his own greater emotional expressiveness (Bandura, 1977).

By contrast, in **response facilitation** nothing new is learned, but some old responses may be disinhibited as a result of watching a model's performance (Bandura, 1977; 1989a). In this case, the model's behavior acts like a social prompt, communicating that it is "OK" to perform the behavior which was inhibited. For example, a person who is fearful of dancing because religious training made the practice seem "evil," may experience disinhibition of dancing by watching a "good" person dance, with no ill effects.

Diffusion of innovation occurs when prestigious models try something new and thereby display its benefits and advantages to others. Once people have accepted an innovative behavior, its longevity will be partially determined by the permanence of the incentives associated with its adoption. The more permanent the incentives for adopting something new, the longer the innovation will stay around. Fads are short-lived, because adoption results only in fleeting social recognition. Hula hoops are an example. By comparison, the automobile illustrates a novelty that has become permanent. People who drive desirable cars are afforded continuous social recognition and also needed transportation.

There are some definite restraints on the adoption of novelties, however. These include lack of the skills needed to perform behaviors associated with the novelty. Soccer is finally catching on in this country, thanks to the super model, Pele, but adoption has been limited to those with adequate athletic skills. Financial limitations also interfere with adoption of innovations. The Japanese auto *Lexus* was recently introduced into this country. Already Detroit is copying its major features, but only a few can afford the genuine article.

Rewards

While behavior is often acquired vicariously, it is primarily maintained by rewards. There has been much debate concerning the relative importance of **extrinsic rewards**, rewards originating outside the individual—money, and **intrinsic rewards**, rewards from within the individual—self-satisfaction (Bandura, 1977). Extrinsically rewarded behaviors appear to be done for tangible payoffs. By contrast, intrinsically rewarded behaviors seem to be "done for their own sake." From Bandura's vantage point, both are necessary for a full account of human action. External rewards are needed to direct a person's attention to a behavior and to institute initial performance. Nevertheless, long-term maintenance of the behavior depends largely on development of intrinsic rewards. For instance, in order to begin the task of teaching a child to write, tangible rewards, privileges, or even money, will likely be needed to generate beginning attempts. Such rewards may have to be presented even on a sentence by sentence basis. The child may then progress to performing for less tangible rewards, such as praise from parents for a job well done, though the payoff is still external. Finally, if writing behavior is to be maintained, the child must learn what constitutes good writing behavior so that she can praise herself "under her breath" for writing a grammatically correct sentence. If she does so, intrinsic rewards have come into play.

Intrinsic motivation refers to the desire for intrinsic rewards, leading to the pursuit of the same. One of the problems with the notion of intrinsic motivation is that its presence is often inferred from the persistence of a behavior in the absence of any obvious external rewards. As Bandura (1977) notes, such an inference is unwarranted. To support his skepticism by example, if a person watches TV for many hours a day, one would be hard pressed to invoke "intrinsic motivation." More than likely, the lack of behavioral alternatives explains persistent glaring at the tube. To be sure that intrinsic motivation is at work, more information is needed. One must observe the persistence of behavior in the absence of appropriate external rewards, but in the presence of other behavioral alternatives. Alternatives would include some that could lead to external rewards. This problem can be avoided if support for the operation of intrinsic motivation comes from observation of **self-evaluation**, a process that involves assessing one's performance at various points along the way to task completion and issuing a vocal or "under the breath" judgment of its value. Thus, a clarinetist who repeatedly sounds a note, sometimes pausing to frown and shake her head, is engaging in self-evaluation. When a smile follows an attempt at the note, observers can conclude that the clarinetist has positively reinforced herself. Most forms of "practice" are intrinsically motivated, and, therefore, under the control of intrinsic reward.

It has been suggested that extrinsic rewards are somehow antagonistic to intrinsic motivation (Deci, 1975). Supposedly, "being paid" for performance of behaviors implies external rather than self-control of behavior, with accompanying feelings of lost self-determination and competence. Although support for the notion that external reward destroys intrinsic motivation is mixed at best, belief in the idea persists (Bandura, 1977). Such is the case, despite numerous contradictions existing in everyday reality. Artists, professors, athletes, and many others are more than happy to receive money for what they love to do.

Intrinsic reward is not the only way that one's behavior may be maintained in the absence of immediate, external rewards available to oneself. **Vicarious reinforcement** occurs when one observes another person being rewarded for performing a behavior. In order to appreciate this kind of reinforcement, one needs to first consider what determines the value of one's own external rewards. Then a discussion of the effects attributable to observing other people being rewarded becomes more meaningful.

BOX 13.1   What Is Rewarding to You?

Different events or outcomes are rewarding to different people. What you may view as a treasured reward, may inspire only a yawn from one of your friends. Below is a list of events or outcomes that are rewarding to some people, but not others. Check off what is rewarding to you and then get some friends to do the same. Even though you will be similar to your friends, notice the differences in what each of you regard as rewarding.

Listening to classical music

Eating ice cream

Looking at the stars

Debating politics

Sitting very still and thinking of nothing

Taking a walk in the woods

Having had a novel thought

Thinking through a problem

Eating at an exotic restaurant

Having a satisfying sexual experience

Throwing a frisbee

Resisting the lure of a favorite candy

Saying something nice about someone

Thanking a friend for being nice to me

Writing home

Picking flowers

Gossiping

Sleeping late

Watching airplanes land

Being alone

Telling somebody "I love you"

Flying a kite

Hugging my pet

Facing a challenge

Being really scared

Attending a committee meeting

Having snow fall on my face

Griping

Watching soaps

External rewards, of course, do not have any inherent absolute value. Value of rewards is relative, established by the process of **social comparison**, determining how well one is doing in life by comparing oneself to those who share one's life situation (Festinger, 1954). A factory worker does not determine how well he is doing in life by comparing himself with the plant manager. Instead he compares himself to people doing the same job. If, for example, he is earning as much, or a little more than people who share the same job, he can conclude that he is doing fine. "X" number of dollars earned per month is valued or not valued, depending on its standing, relative to what comparable others are earning.

Modeling alone works to initiate a behavior, but if models are rewarded for performances of the behavior, the impact on learning is greatly increased. If a model exhibits a behavior that is frightening or repugnant to an observer and is rewarded for the performance, the observer may be induced to try the formerly shunned behavior (Bandura, 1989a). According to Bandura, vicarious reward can induce people to try an undesired food, give up a valued object, and disclose personal matters, any of which could be beneficial (Bandura, 1977). In addition, vicarious punishment can be efficient. Bandura (1977) cites a study in which observers of models who were punished for performance of a prohibited behavior, later were just as unlikely to perform the behavior as were the models.

Defensive Behaviors

Defensive behaviors are adopted in order to cope with unpleasant events that are anticipated on future occasions (Bandura, 1977). If "sitting in the front row" becomes associated with embarrassment because of failure to answer the professor's questions, the defensive behavior "sitting in the back" may be adopted. The adoption occurs and persists because it allows anticipation of comfort, not because it is motivated by anxiety. If the latter were the case, people would always show anxiety when they perform defensive behavior. Instead, they show relief, once they become confident that their defensive strategy is effective.

Thus, anxiety is an associate of early defensive behavior, not the cause of it (Leventhal, 1970). Initially the unpleasant event is accompanied by both anxiety and defensive behavior. An anxious child takes a big stuffed bear to bed "to scare the wolves away." But after the defensive behavior is seen as a way to avoid the unpleasant event, it is performed in the absence of anxiety. Because defensive behavior is due to anticipating the avoidance of unpleasant events in the future, rather than for the purpose of coping with present anxiety, it is very difficult to eliminate. The absence of the unpleasant event is "proof" to the performer that his or her defensive behavior is "working." Therefore, if a child is asked, "Why do you take that huge stuffed bear to bed?" the now calm child replies, "Because it keeps the wolves away." When the response is, "But there are no wolves around here," the retort is, "See how well it works." "The way out" may be through modeling. If a trusted model can be observed operating in the context of the unpleasant event without performing the defensive behavior, and the unpleasant event fails to occur, the defensive behavior may be discarded. "See me in bed? No bear, but no wolves ever get me."

Self-Efficacy: Avenue to the Correction of Harmful Behavior

One route to a sense of personal agency is through the self-regulatory processes considered by both Mischel and Bandura (Wood & Bandura, 1989; Ozer & Bandura, 1990). One of the most powerful of these processes is **self-efficacy**, a belief concerning one's ability to perform behaviors yielding an expected outcome that is desirable (Bandura, 1989a; 1989b). When self-efficacy is high, one has confidence that she or he can perform behaviors allowing control of a difficult circumstance that might otherwise generate defensive behavior. Self-efficacy may be thought of as a specific form of confidence. While no one can be confident about everything he or she does, every person can develop beliefs in abilities to perform certain behaviors, each of which will yield a desirable outcome in a particular context.

As an illustration of the relationship between self-efficacy level and outcome expectancy, consider a contrast between Sarah and Sam on the matter of public speaking. Both individuals expect that making an effective public speech will be met with applause and other positive social outcomes. However, Sarah has strong feelings of self-efficacy with regard to critical behaviors involved in public speaking. She feels that she can obtain the relevant information that will go into her speech, organize it properly, memorize it, and present it in a clear and articulate manner. On the other hand, Sam has a different conviction with respect to self-efficacy. He feels that he cannot adequately perform any of the behaviors that will lead to the desired outcome.

Self-efficacy influences not only whether a person will attempt a behavior, but also determines the quality of performance once an attempt is made. High efficacy, entailing expectations of success, will generate persistence in the face of obstacles and frustrations. Persistence eventually leading to success will yield further bolstering of self-efficacy. Low efficacy will lower effort, thereby increasing the probability of failure and the likelihood of further decreases in efficacy.

The single most efficient method for boosting self-efficacy is *performance accomplishment*. Doing is believing. If a person with low self-efficacy can somehow be induced to perform a feared or repugnant behavior, self-efficacy may be dramatically bolstered. However, vicarious experience can also be effective, especially if people with low self-efficacy can view persons who share their fears perform the inhibited behaviors. **Participant modeling** in which the person with low self-efficacy imitates a model's efficacious behavior can be very beneficial, even where persuasion and other influence attempts have failed. Because people read their state of efficacy by reference to their level of emotional arousal in the face of a threatening situation, any methods that will lower arousal, will increase feelings of efficacy. Successful actual performance or positive vicarious experience are methods of lowering arousal.

Finally, consideration of self-efficacy brings us about as close to a trait as social cognitive theory comes. Actually, like Mischel, Bandura does not often use the word *trait*. However, self-efficacy has some characteristics in common with traits, though it deviates sharply from trait notions in some ways. Like traits are supposed to be, self-efficacy tends to be relatively stable over time. If no events relevant to a person's self-efficacy occur, the person is likely to maintain a constant level of the factor. On the other hand, self-efficacy is unlike a trait in that it is very specific to social or other external circumstances. Self-efficacy has reference to specific situations like "public speaking," "handling snakes," "parachuting," "writing a book," and "swimming." It is not the general, cross-situational phenomenon that traits are supposed to be.

Evaluation

Bandura's Theory Compared with Others

Learning Theory

Bandura's social cognitive theory can be contrasted with learning theories that emphasize internal drives and motives, as well as those that consider only external stimuli and responses. A *drive* is a physiological tension that forces an organism to perform tension-reducing behaviors. A *motive* is a reason to perform some behavior, such as "to quench a thirst." Being predicated on past histories of tension reductions, both drives and motives push individuals "from out of the past" toward certain goals, by instituting goal-directed behavior (motive as in motor and drive as in driven). Because they are "backward-looking" by nature, past events must be examined to confirm their operation. Drives and motives provide ready explanations after the fact, but not predictions. By contrast, forward-looking points of view, like social cognitive theory, provide predictions of future events.

In the last analysis, the worth of a theory is in its practical applications. Bandura maintains that theories stressing motives, drives, and similar internal processes have not been highly applicable, at least not relative to social cognitive theory and other contributors to methods for modifying behavior.

Bandura's social cognitive theory has generated support for certain of its predictions which directly conflict with behavioristic learning theories, most of which ignore cognitive factors. Many learning theories postulate that one must perform a response and then, rather immediately, experience reinforcement. According to social cognitive theory, organisms, especially people, learn through observing. It follows that people need not perform the behavior they have witnessed when it is observed. Likewise, they need not experience reinforcement either directly or vicariously in order to learn. They can observe a behavior, such as a method of approaching an attractive, potential date, and note "this method works." Then, sometime later, they can try out the approach with the expectation that their efforts will be reinforced. In this case, the cognitive factor, expectation of reinforcement, is the determinant of the future behavior, not previous experiences of reinforcement.

In sum, contrary to common learning theories, social cognitive theory holds that people learn a behavior when they view it, before they have a chance to perform it, and even if neither they nor the model have been reinforced for it.

Stage Theories of Development

Bandura asserts that social cognitive theory is partially inconsistent with stage theories such as the notions of Jean Piaget (1948) about cognitive development and postulations of Lawrence Kohlberg concerning moral development (1969). With moral reasoning as a case in point, stage theory hypothesizes that children at a given stage learn only what the skills available to them at the time allow them to learn. Thus, children of two, whose stage of moral reasoning is primitive, think only of punishments in evaluating the "goodness" of an act. If they are punished for the act, it is "bad," if not, it is "good." They cannot reason otherwise, because they lack the necessary cognitive skills. Only later will they be able to reason at a more abstract and complex level, judging an act as "good" if other people approve of it.

Bandura (1977) indicates that the evidence does not support the stage point of view. Individuals' level of moral reasoning is a function of the moral models available to them, not just their stage of cognitive development (Bandura, 1989a; 1990). Also, people, adults as well as children, reason at various levels or stages, depending on the circumstances (Bandura and McDonald, 1963). Bandura's theory has no trouble with variability in moral reasoning. If a 15-year-old on one occasion refuses an award from the John Birch Society, because he disapproves of its lack of concern for oppressed people, and on another occasion, cheats on a test because, "everyone else is doing it," social learning theorists would not be puzzled. They would look for differing circumstances under which the judgments were made as the source of the very different moral decisions. A long-standing family concern for the well-being of oppressed people may explain the refusal of the award, while the immediate press of the need to perform as well as peers may explain the cheating.

Humanistic Theories: Unconditional Positive Regard and Self-Actualization

Social cognitive theory also is not completely compatible with the idea of "unconditional positive regard," as espoused by Rogers. According to Bandura, not only must there be dependency between behavioral performance and outcomes for learning to occur and be maintained, learners must be highly aware of the dependency. The very label "unconditional positive regard" indicates no contingency between behaviors and outcomes. "Unconditional love," writes Bandura "were it possible, would make children directionless and quite unlovable" (1977, p. 102). While Rogers might have contended that love should not be used as a reward, in fact it often is. Further, young children have trouble discovering the relationship between behaviors and outcomes, which makes them relatively dependent on immediate external reward. Such being the case, they would be totally doomed to confusion if they received affection no matter what they did.

Unconditional positive regard is critical to the theories of Rogers, Maslow, and other humanists. As you recall, self-actualization is a person's lifelong process of realizing his or her potentialities; it is to become "that self which one truly is" (Rogers, 1961). Also, remember that unconditional positive regard administered during childhood is supposed to promote self-actualization in adulthood. Bandura, however, contends there is a contradiction in the connection between unconditional positive regard and self-actualization. If self-actualization involves discovering one's potentialities, how is the revelation to be made if one has been told during childhood, "Whatever you do that doesn't hurt anyone is approved"? Discrimination between worthwhile and not worthwhile pursuits are made as a result of appreciating that certain behaviors produce worthwhile outcomes, and certain others do not, not that most behaviors result in valuable outcomes.

Supporting Evidence

Self-Efficacy

Self-efficacy is the most researched of the self-regulatory mechanisms proposed by Bandura. In fact, it is one of the hottest research topics of the 1980s and 1990s. In view of the enormous number of studies on this self-regulatory mechanism—many more than could be reviewed here—a couple of research projects have been selected for detailed presentation because they aptly demonstrate the power of self-efficacy.

Bandura, Reese, and Adams (1982) conducted research in which subjects were recruited through a newspaper advertisement aimed at people with severe spider phobias. A *phobia* is an intense, irrational fear of an object that is not particularly dangerous. In one of their studies, subjects were 16 spider phobics, ranging in age from 16 to 61 years. Their fear of spiders was extreme, to say the least. One had difficulty taking a bath, because she had once encountered a spider in the tub. Another leaped from an auto she was driving, upon noticing a spider inside the car. One had difficulty reading or watching TV, because she was fearful that a spider would happen by, and catch her unawares. At the mere sight of a spider, even a picture of the insect, she would react with compulsive shivers, pounding of the heart, shortness of breath, and, on occasion, vomiting for hours.

Another subject indicated that whenever she even thought of a spider, she would picture herself being eaten by the creature. She had trouble sleeping at night, because she would wake up to inspect the ceiling for the presence of a spider. If she did detect one, she would stand on a stool, and kill it with insect spray. But sleep was still not forthcoming. Wide-eyed, she would lie awake staring at the ceiling lest the spider revive and climb back to its previous perch. Obviously these people had an incapacitating problem and sorely needed help.

Subjects first were administered a behavioral avoidance test, consisting of 18 items, each progressively more threatening than its predecessor. The test involved interactions with a large Wolf spider, previously shown to be especially frightening to spider phobics. Table 13.1 provides examples of the behaviors included on the test.

TABLE 13.1   Example Items for the Behavioral Avoidance Test

Approach plastic bowl containing spider
   Look down at the spider
   Place bare hands in the bowl
Let spider crawl freely in a chair placed in front of [yourself]
Let spider crawl over gloved hands
Let spider crawl over bare forearm
Handle spider with bare hands
Allow spider to crawl on lap

As you can see, interaction with the spider ranged from remote, viewing it from a distance, to intimate, allowing the spider to crawl on subjects' laps. At the beginning of the experiment, the best a subject could do was to view the spider at a considerable and safe distance, a near zero level of efficacy.

Self-efficacy judgments were made quite simply. Subjects were presented with the 18 performances listed on the behavioral test, and for each, were asked to indicate on a 100-point scale the degree of efficacy that they felt; that is, the degree to which they felt confident that they could perform the behavior. A "1" indicated no efficacy for a given behavior, and "100" meant complete mastery of the behavior in question. A subject's efficacy score was the number of behaviors for which the efficacy rating was at least 20 on the 100 point scale.

Next subjects were randomly assigned to low or medium efficacy-treatment condition. The induction of either a high or a low level of efficacy was administered by a female experimenter who employed two large Wolf spiders, different in color and shape from the one that had been used in the initial behavioral test. Two spiders were used because treatment sessions took several hours, enough to exhaust only one spider.

Subjects were treated individually. As a warm-up, a spider was placed in a vial and each subject was merely asked to inspect it. The experimenter then modeled several threatening behaviors as subjects watched. Demonstrations were initially made with the experimenter and the subject separated by considerable distance. Later the experimenter modeled very near the subject. First, the experimenter placed the spider in a plastic bowl and poked it with her finger as it scurried about. Next she modeled handling the insect and controlling its movements. She removed the spider from the container and handled the creature as it crawled over her arms, hands, and upper body. The model indicated how to control a freely moving spider by placing it on a towel draped over a chair and herding it about on the piece of furniture.

To expand on control of spiders, the experimenter released the spider onto the floor and allowed it to run about in search of a hiding place. She captured it by trapping it under a cup and sliding a thin card under the container. In this way she showed how it could be confined and easily transported from a house. Then she took the subject into a nearby lobby to inspect a Wolf spider's web, thereby modeling inquisitiveness regarding the insect's habitat. At regular intervals during the treatment each subject took the efficacy test. These administrations of the test were

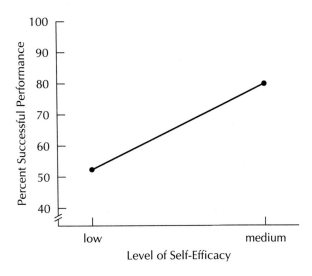

FIGURE 13.2 Relationship between self-efficacy and behavioral performance after treatment for low- compared to medium-efficacy.

repeated until each subject reached the level of efficacy corresponding to her assigned treatment condition (low or medium efficacy). Low efficacy was defined as being able to allow the spider to roam over a chair placed near the subject and being able to place a hand in the bowl containing the spider, near the creature. Subjects in the medium efficacy condition continued in treatment until they could endure physical contact with the spider by holding it in a gloved or a bare hand. After subjects had reached the assigned level of efficacy, the behavioral test, performed earlier, was repeated.

At the completion of major procedures, subjects in the low efficacy condition were raised to the medium level by further modeling, then their behavior and fear were again measured. Finally, at the end of the experiment, all subjects worked until they had achieved maximum efficacy.

As Figure 13.2 indicates, there was a very direct relationship between subjects' assigned level of self-efficacy and their behavioral performance after the treatment. Subjects assigned to the low efficacy condition achieved low performance on the behavioral test, after treatment, while those in the medium efficacy condition achieved medium behavioral performance, after treatment. Also low-efficacy subjects' behavioral performance was measured when they were at low efficacy and when their efficacy was raised to a medium level. As Figure 13.3 indicates, there was again a direct relationship between efficacy level and performance. If a subject indicated that she felt she could at most place her hands on the inverted bowl with the spider inside, she was unable to go beyond that performance. Self-efficacy predicted performance almost perfectly.

FIGURE 13.3   Relationship between self-efficacy and behavioral performance for subjects
when at the low-efficacy level and when at the
medium-efficacy level.

This remarkable study showed that in the time it takes to run a single experimental session, lifelong spider phobics acquired the ability to touch a creature previously so frightening that the mere thought of its presence had provoked spasms
of anxiety. Although permanency of their newly developed self-efficacy is in question, there is no doubt that a few additional sessions would have completely eliminated their irrational fears. Social cognitive theory is so powerful in a practical
sense it can transform lives.

In a similar study, Wiedenfeld, O'Leary, Bandura, Brown, Levine, and Raska
(1990) again attempted to show that phobics' performance in the presence of a
threatening creature corresponds directly to their perceived self-efficacy. In addition they wanted to measure effects on the immune system during self-efficacy
acquisition and the relationship of those effects to certain physiological responses
and endocrine (hormone) secretions. Subjects were snake phobics who had agreed
to participate in a training session designed to help them overcome their fears.

The behavior avoidance test used by the researchers was virtually identical to
that employed by Bandura, Reese, and Adams (1982), but a harmless corn snake
was substituted for the spider (see Table 13.1). The procedure was also similar to
that of Bandura, Reese, and Adams, except that all subjects went through all
phases of self-efficacy enhancement, from a pre-test/baseline phase, through a
efficacy-growth phase, finishing with a maximal efficacy phase. During the pre-
test/baseline phase, subjects' perceived self-efficacy was measured (it uniformly

was found to be very low) and indexes of endocrine, physiological, and immuno-logical functioning were obtained. During the efficacy growth phase, subjects were exposed to the corn snake in much the same way that Bandura, Reese, and Adams exposed subjects to spiders. An experimenter modeled progressively more threatening interactions with the snake, and invited subjects to emulate her behavior. This two-hour session was later followed by an additional two-hour treatment during which subjects were brought up to and maintained at maximal self-efficacy and performance attainment.

Self-efficacy showed the same course of development reported by Bandura, Reese, and Adams—it stayed at rock bottom levels during pre-test assessments, rose dramatically during efficacy-growth phase assessments, and stayed near the maximum strength "100" level during maximal-efficacy phase assessments. Levels of immune-system components, such as blood lymphocytes, helper T cells, and suppressor T cells, were assessed during the three phases. Indexes of these components showed dramatic changes from the baseline in the direction of immune-system enhancement during the efficacy-growth phase, and a slight drop-off in immune-system functioning during the maximal efficacy phase.

Cortisol elevations are often associated with immune-system suppression and heart rate acceleration typically accompanies stress enhancement. "In accordance with prediction, the findings generally showed that slow growth of perceived self-efficacy, high cortisol activation, and heart rate acceleration were associated with lower immunological status during the efficacy acquisition phase" (p. 1089). The slower was acquisition of self-efficacy, the greater were cortisol levels and heart rate acceleration, and the more sluggish was immune-system functioning. By contrast, rapid acquisition of self-efficacy was associated with relatively high immunological status.

Not all subjects experienced immune-system enhancement during the self-efficacy growth phase. About one-third of the subjects showed immuno-suppression during the growth phase and a recovery back toward baseline during the maximum-efficacy phase. Apparently for some phobics, at least initially, what was therapeutic exposure to snakes for other subjects was debilitating for them. Perhaps with additional sessions, they too might have experienced immune-system enhancement.

Wiedenfeld and colleagues' extraordinary study goes a step beyond Bandura, Reese, and Adams. Not only was self-efficacy enhanced resulting in close contact with a previously feared creature, for most subjects, immune-system functioning was enhanced during such exposure. These results lay open the exciting possibility that social cognitive theory will yield methods for eliminating the multiple suppressions of phobics' immune-systems that may accompany periodic thoughts of and real life exposures to feared objects.

Other Self-Regulatory Factors: Social Cognitive Theory in the Business Sector

Bandura and his colleague Robert Wood have applied social cognitive theory to problems regarding management of employees, decision making, and productivity. In one of their studies, 24 business graduate students participated in a managerial decision-making project (Wood & Bandura, 1989). Their job was to fill 18 orders for furniture, which constituted 18 trials in a production-simulation game (the trials were grouped into three blocks of six). The critical task in filling the orders was to allocate five employees optimally so that production was fast and efficient. To aid in their allocation decisions, grad-student subjects received a personnel file on each employee containing information about level of effort and skill, as well as experience, motivational level, and preference for routine versus challenging job assignments. Subjects also received information concerning the effort and skill required for each production subfunction (milling the wood, assembling the furniture, finishing the surface of each unit).

The manipulated factor in this experiment was whether or not decision-making skill was presented to subjects as a *stable entity* or an *acquirable skill*. Subjects assigned to the stable entity condition were told that decision-making ability is a "cognitive-processing capacity" revealed by performance. That is, it is something that one has or does not have. Subjects in the acquirable skill condition were informed that decision making is developed during practice. Here, the more one works at developing decision-making skills, the better one becomes. Social cognitive theory predicts that self-regulatory mechanisms and productivity will be enhanced by the acquirable skill condition, because it promotes personal agency in decision making.

Factors indexing several self-regulatory mechanisms were measured. Strength of self-efficacy was assessed in a manner similar to methods described earlier. *Assessing self-goals* was measured by the level of goals subjects set with each succeeding trial. Subjects could set production goals that ranged from 40 percent below to 30 percent above an established standard. *Analytic strategies* were assessed in terms of whether subjects changed *only one* or *several* motivational arrangement factors in arriving at decisions—examples of these factors included instructive feedback to employees and social rewards meted out to employees. The more decisions a subject could make in a block of trials while changing just one factor, the better were his or her analytic strategies. Such was the case because genuine "hypothesis testing" requires the change of only one factor at a time. Changing more than one factor at a time makes it uncertain which changed factor yielded any changed outcome. Performance was measured in terms of the number of simulated hours required to fill each order. "The fewer the production hours, the better the subject's managerial decision-making" (p. 410).

Results showed that self-efficacy was very high in the acquirable skills condition, relative to the stable entity condition, and increased over blocks of trials. By contrast, self-efficacy declined over blocks of trials in the stable entity condition. Exactly the same trend was found for self-set goals, analytic strategies, and performance productivity. These factors were at a generally high level in the "acquirable skills" condition and increasing across blocks of trials, but were at a generally low level in the "stable entity" condition and decreasing across blocks of trials. Telling acquirable skills subjects that "practice makes perfect" in regard to decision-making skills enhanced their feeling of agency, and in turn, boosted three self-regulatory mechanisms. The result was increased productivity.

Bandura and Wood (1989) conducted a nearly identical decision-making study, but this time they manipulated *controllability* and *performance standards*. The procedure was virtually the same as before, but some subjects were told that business organizations are controllable, predictable entities (controllability condition) and others were told that organizations are uncontrollable (uncontrollability condition). Some subjects in the controllable condition were told that they were to get employees to surpass customary productivity by 20% to 25% (high standards condition), while others were told that "they should try to get their employees to perform at least at a level that does not take them 20%-25% longer than the customary productivity" (p. 808; low-standards condition). Subjects in the uncontrollability condition were similarly subdivided. Thus, there were four groups of subjects: (1) high controllability—high standards; (2) high controllability—low standards; (3) low controllability—high standards; (4) low controllability—low standards.

Results showed that self-efficacy was generally highest in the high controllability compared to low controllability condition. Further, within those conditions, high standards tended to increase self-efficacy across blocks of trials, but low standards decreased it. The results for analytic strategies were somewhat different. The low standards, high controllability subjects showed superior analytic strategies that increased in superiority across blocks of trials. High standards, high controllability subjects also increased in analytic strategies across blocks of trials, but as a group they showed the poorest overall level of analytic strategies. This group was slightly below the low controllability subjects in overall level of analytic strategies. These results show that high standards under conditions of high controllability may be quite threatening to individuals. The high control along with high standards implied that subjects were personally responsible for high production, a burden that may have been too much for them. By contrast, high controllability and low standards is the "right mix" to produce good analytic strategies.

Goal setting and productivity were affected by controllability and standards in a way that was analogous to results of the previous study by Wood and Bandura. Goal setting and productivity were generally elevated and increased across blocks of trials under conditions of controllability versus uncontrollability. Standards had a somewhat different effect on goal setting. In the first block of trials, high standards did enhance goal setting relative to low standards, but there was no difference between the two conditions on the last two blocks of trials. It seems that high standards has its effects on goal setting quickly, and then it fades.

Results overall show that several self-regulatory mechanisms are enhanced by controllability, and effects show up in increased productivity. However, setting high standards can sometimes be counterproductive. If high standards are set in the context of high controllability, individuals may be overwhelmed by the implication that high productivity is expected and they will be held accountable for whether it actually happens.

BOX 13.2   Learning to Be More Efficacious

People with serious problems, such as phobias, probably ought to try vicarious expectancy learning, vicarious reinforcement, participant modeling, and other procedures derived from social cognitive theory, but only under supervision. Other people, however, may wish to master skills that have alluded them without resorting to formal training. It is possible to develop numerous, valuable, everyday skills, some of which each of us lack. The *general* procedure is straightforward: Be highly conscious and thoughtful in observing a model who possesses some ability you lack.

Pick a skill that you lack or one that you possess but would like to sharpen. Then find a model who has that skill and displays it in public under circumstances that allow you to watch. It always helps to obtain the cooperation of the model. Nevertheless, you can learn if the model frequently displays the desired behavior so that you can watch, even if you have not or cannot approach the model with a request for cooperation (the model may be a gourmet cook on TV or the president of your company and, thus, beyond your access).

To illustrate how you might proceed, consider this skill: learning to speak well in public. Assume that you have a good model's cooperation. The model could be anyone who speaks in public often, for example, an officer in your fraternity or sorority or a member of student government who you know. First, identify "problem areas," such as beginning a speech—a critical and often frightening part of public speaking. Ascertain how your model begins a speech. It may be "telling a funny story" or "talking off-the-cuff, without notes, about reasons why what is said is important" or "beginning with what is easiest to say, so that the start is smooth." Next, preferably in the context of an actual speech, have your model demonstrate her or his method of beginning a speech. When you have seen enough to feel reasonably efficacious, try beginning a speech in a non-threatening setting with your model in attendance for post-presentation consultation. Repeat this process for ending a speech, keeping an audience interested during a speech, or for other facets of speech making that you deem important. By repeating the cycle of asking pertinent questions of your model, having her or him demonstrate the answer, and practicing in the presence of your model, you can raise your self-efficacy with regard to some crucial behavioral performance. Then you will be able to perform regularly, and effectively, on your own.

To give you an idea of areas where you might benefit from cooperative associations with expert models, study the list of everyday skills that seem most amenable to mastery under circumstances that commonly exist.

Selling a product

Asking a meaningful question of a speaker (for example, a professor)

Starting a conversation with a stranger

Gaining the confidence of a child

Breaking off a conversation

Complimenting a friend

Tactfully saying no to an unreasonable request

Asking a favor of a friend

Carrying on a conversation with a member of the opposite gender

Asking a person for a date

Tactfully telling someone close to you that he or she has mistreated you

Keeping an argument civil

Implications of Social Cognitive Theory for Moral Functioning

Crime

Beyond these many and varied contributions, social cognitive theory has implications for the well-being and prosperity of humans in the future. For example, social cognitive theory has something important to say about a common concern in our society—crime.

Why do people steal and commit other crimes despite the threat of arrest and imprisonment? A look inside the prisons suggests an answer. Poor people and people of color are greatly overrepresented in our penal institutions. People will survive, and in so doing, they will choose methods of survival from whatever is available to them. Two factors govern selection of criminal behavior as a means of survival. First, it is one of the few behavioral alternatives open to those relegated to the bottom of the social ladder. Second, compared to other available alternatives, the incentives are great, relative to the likelihood of negative future outcomes (that is, being caught and imprisoned). One could work at a demeaning job, for low pay, and suffer certain humiliation and failure to prosper, or one could resort to crime. (Perhaps you will be able to imagine that making thousands weekly selling crack cocaine is more alluring than working for minimum wage at a fast food outlet, if these are among the few alternatives available to you.) In the case of many crimes, effort is minimal, likelihood of being caught and imprisoned minimal, and the outcome highly positive, relative to investment. It follows from these conjectures that public pronouncements to the effect "people are imprisoned for criminal behavior" will have little impact.

The middle class and above have more numerous and better behavioral alternatives available, relative to the poor and victims of social discrimination. The solution to many social ills, most especially crime, lies in making the full range of behavioral alternatives available to all the people, not just the relatively privileged.

Doing Evil and Avoiding the Cognitive and Emotional Consequences

Social cognitive theory has implications for the understanding of other troubling behaviors (Bandura, 1989a; 1990). As Bandura observes, "Over the years, much cruelty has been perpetrated by decent, moral people in the name of religious principles, righteous ideology, and social order" (1977, p. 156). Yet, "character flaws" do not adequately explain humans' inhumanity to humans. Instead the culprit is an intricate game of mental gymnastics. "People do not ordinarily engage in reprehensible conduct until they have justified to themselves the morality of their actions" (Bandura, 1990).

Social cognitive theory helps to explain how individuals perform inhumane behaviors without suffering severe psychological consequences. **Self-exonerative processes** is the general name given to cognitive activities that allow people to dissociate themselves from the consequences of their actions. Religion, ideology, and "order," all noble in concept, are abused in practice when they are invoked to justify doing evil. In social cognitive terms, "noble causes" such as those mentioned above, can be invoked to break the connection between behaviors and real consequences. Actual outcomes of behaviors that would otherwise be considered immoral and unforgivable are covered up, shoved aside and, thereby, effectually replaced by acceptable outcomes. For example, Klansmen adopt a religious facade, including the cross symbol, to cloak their vicious behavior in an aura of purity (see *Klanwatch*, a publication of Southern Poverty Law, 1001 South Hull St., Montgomery, Alabama 36101).

However, Klan behavior is sometimes so savage it is difficult to justify, even "with God on our side." In order to support murder and torture, it also becomes necessary for Klan members to dehumanize their victims. **Dehumanization** is a cognitive process that involves lowering the status of certain people from "human being" to "lesser being." It is difficult to perform, much less justify, torture of human beings, but it can be done to beings that are declared "not human" (Bandura, 1990). Thus, labeling people "gooks," "hymies," "spicks," "niggers," or "injuns" makes them fair targets for the slings and arrows of cruelty.

Other cognitive activities are helpful in setting the stage for the performance of reprehensible behavior. **Advantageous comparison** is a cognitive mechanism by which ". . . deplored acts can be made to appear righteous by contrasting them with flagrant inhumanities" (Bandura, 1990, p. 171). When confronted with accusations that the Nazis mistreated the Jews, Hitler was in the habit of citing the subjugation of Native Americans and the oppression of Indians and other "colonials" by the British (Speer, 1970).

Euphemistic labeling is the cognitive process of assigning a name to deplorable behavior that makes it seem innocuous or even laudable (Bandura, 1990). The "Vietnam experience" included many such labels. Destroying crops and jungle habitats was called "defoliation." Disenfranchising and physically relocating whole villages of people was called "pacification." Killing as many as possible and collecting their bodies like trophies was called "body count." These labels, produced by the military hierarchy, were responsible for the atrocities in Vietnam, not the soldiers to whom they were supplied. If one could replace the entire set of soldiers who served in Vietnam with another group, the result would be the same (Allen, 1978). The Nazis, of course, were masters of euphemistic labeling. "Euthanasia Program" was the fancy name given to gassing retarded and physically handicapped people (Dawidowicz, 1975). "The Final Solution of the Jewish Question" was the official title of the human tragedy now known as the "Holocaust."

Blaming victims for their own fate is all too common a cognitive exercise (Bandura, 1990; Wheeler et al., 1978). The Irish Republican Army (IRA) seems to specialize in this mental mechanism. When, during a war memorial ceremony, many innocent British sympathizers fell victim to a large IRA bomb exploded prematurely by a British scanning device, the IRA blamed the British. One must remember, though, the IRA does what it does partly because, historically, the British have done it to them.

Displacement and diffusion of responsibility involves placing the blame for one's deplorable acts onto others, and spreading the responsibility for reprehensible behavior to others who are present, respectively. Terrorists are prone to displacement. These mass murderers "warn officials of targeted nations that if they take retaliatory action they will be held accountable for the lives of the hostages" (Bandura, 1990, p. 175). Diffusion of responsibility allows one to walk right by a person who is suffering a calamity and hardly notice, so long as there are many others present to whom one may spread the responsibility for helping (Latané & Darley, 1970).

In **moral justification** individuals invoke religious or other moral bases to support their inhuman behavior (Bandura, 1990). Hitler constructed a peculiar moral code to which he referred whenever his savage acts seemed to require justification: the "destiny of the German people" justified any and every act in its own interest. Famed World War I marksman Sergeant York never could have done his many heroic deeds had he not been able to reconcile his behavior with his religious beliefs. He registered as a conscientious objector, but that status was denied. Unconvinced by his battalion commander's Bible citations of conditions under which Christians are permitted to kill, York retired to a mountainside for marathon prayers. He emerged dedicated to killing "the enemy."

Gradualistic moral disengagement, a process during which people slowly slip unawares into what was normally unacceptable behavior, has made monsters of everyday people. Terrorists are trained in a step-by-step process taking many months. With each step a mental wave swells and pounds against the belief that taking human life is wrong. By the end of training, abhorrence of killing is fully eroded. "Development of the capability to kill usually evolves through a process in which recruits may not fully recognize the transformation they are undergoing" (Bandura, 1990, p. 186). In the famous "obedience to authority" studies by Stanley Milgram (1974), subjects were gradually sucked into ostensibly harming another human by the graduated procedure of escalating electric-shock punishments with each error on a learning task.

While certain immoral behaviors can be predicted and explained by social cognitive theory, so can some forms of self-sacrifice and altruism. *Self-evaluation*, the primary source of intrinsic reward, can be so dominant that it becomes more important than external rewards and punishments. Mother Teresa, winner of the 1979 Nobel Peace Prize, has such strong convictions concerning the elimination of human suffering, that she worked for years in obscurity and deprivation to bring comfort to the poor, ill, and lame of Calcutta, India. During the early 1980s a young man rushed to the aid of a woman who was being raped on a public street, thereby totally ignoring the punishments for such behavior that were implied by the inaction of many bystanders. Similarly, Lenny Skutnik stood among several people as he watched a woman flounder in the Potomac following the crash of her plane. Seeing the helpless victim slowly disappear into the icy water, Skutnik dove in and hauled her to shore. His efforts received national acclaim, including introduction to the Congress by the President of the United States (*LIFE*, January, 1983). During the early 1980s, a crowd formed beneath a ninth floor window where a man was poised to jump (Mann, 1981). It happened in Los Angeles, city of notables, one of whom was on the scene. Muhammad Ali

Martin Luther King, Jr.   **Susan B. Anthony**

talked the man from his perch. The crowd cheered. Altruism well modeled is well appreciated.

Other models of noble behavior include Martin Luther King and Susan B. Anthony, a pioneer warrior in the battle for women's rights. King "had a dream" the fulfillment of which was more important to him than life itself. Assassination haunted him wherever he went, but he refused to be silent or to cease his travels. Dr. King faithfully continued his mission until the end. Anthony was a respected educator whose life could be described as very comfortable and secure. She readily jeopardized these advantages because she could not abide the absurdity and insensitivity of beliefs and practices to which the women of her day were subjected. The humane exploits of these and many other individuals remind us that people are capable of compassion and kindness, attributes that will more strongly dominate cruelty and indifference when more is known about social learning processes.

Limitations

With all its virtues, a serious fault of social cognitive theory appears to be that it attempts to explain too much of human behavior. It is too broad. Many of the all-encompassing theories which seem to explain everything, may actually explain very little. Such is the case, because these universal theories mainly provide explanations after observations of behavior are made. Although social cognitive theory does make legitimate predictions, it is open to explanation after-the-fact (explaining away unconditional positive regard and self-actualization might be considered examples). A scientific theory explains behavior before it occurs, rather than after-the-fact (Allen, 1978).

As once was the case with cognitive dissonance theory in social psychology, social cognitive theory has no clear boundaries (Collins and Hoyt, 1972; Linder, Cooper, and Jones, 1967). It is incumbent on psychological theories without limits to explain such varied psychological problems as chronic anxiety, severe depression, and schizophrenia. It must also explain socially destructive behaviors like prejudice and deindividuation (harmful behavior that results from losing one's sense of self, as when "lost in a crowd"). Yet the theory provides no concrete explanations of these behaviors. Sadness and shyness, joy and jealousy are not addressed meaningfully by social cognitive theory. Perhaps social cognitive theory was not intended to provide explanations of these diverse behaviors. If such is the case, it should be publicly stated. In the meantime the theory awaits the construction of borders about it. Like cognitive dissonance theory, which now has definite boundaries, social cognitive theory would benefit from a proclamation concerning when it applies and when it does not apply (Wheeler et al., 1978). If it is known when a theory can predict and when it cannot, its percentage of accurate predictions will go up. Also, given boundaries, there will be no attempts to explain after-the-fact what the theory cannot predict.

Conclusions

The breadth of social cognitive theory is certainly not entirely illusory. The theory makes powerful predictions and generates useful applications in a large number of arenas for human behavior. You have already seen how the theory suggested techniques that, in a matter of hours, eliminated phobias that had plagued individuals for years. Further, it is reasonable to argue that social cognitive theory has more research support and greater practical applicability than other theories covered in this book.

Social cognitive theory also has filled a void in other learning theories. It alone systematically accounts for the fact humans can learn simply by observing. More generally, the theory can explain many differences between humans and lower animals, especially in the area of learning, differences that other theories have ignored or failed to explain.

Social cognitive theory is on the cutting edge of the cognitive movement in psychology. As such it represents an orientation that will guarantee continued growth of psychology's scientific prominence. Decades from now when the contributions of cognitive psychology are reviewed, the name *Albert Bandura* will be spoken and written many times. By then Bandura's social cognitive theory may make some of the theories reviewed in this and other books seem like historical curiosities.

Summary Points

1. Bandura, Canadian born and bred, was educated in the best tradition of the country school: few teachers and facilities led to much individual initiative.

After graduation, he worked in the forbidding Yukon where he encountered fellow workers so unusual as to stimulate an interest in psychology. Following undergraduate work, he enrolled at the University of Iowa where he came under the spell of learning psychologist Kenneth Spence. Upon completion of his doctorate he was hired at Stanford, where he remains today.

2. At Stanford, Bandura was influenced by Robert Sears, but his unique contributions began with his and Walters' work on observational learning showing that "modeling is not merely a process of behavioral mimicry." His social cognitive theory acknowledges both the variability and the stability of behavior. It holds that person factors—including biological ones—behavior, and the external environment reciprocally influence one another. To Bandura, learning is difficult or impossible without awareness, especially in the form of "forethought."

3. A model performs some behavior for an audience. "Modeling" refers to the act of performing a behavior before an audience. People are active when they learn vicariously from a model. They take information from models, "turn it over" in their minds, and put it into symbolic form. Then they hone and sharpen what they have learned, translate it into behavior, and compare their performance with an internal representation. Rewards enter the sequence first in the form of incentives for future performance learned from models, second as benefits bestowed by models for good performance, and third as self-reward.

4. In vicarious expectancy learning other peoples' expectancies concerning future events are adopted. In response facilitation, old responses may be disinhibited by watching a model's performance. Diffusion of innovation occurs when prestigious models try something new and thereby display its benefits. Extrinsic rewards originate outside the person and intrinsic rewards come from within. Intrinsic motivation involves self-evaluation, a process that entails assessing performance repeatedly on the way to task completion. Vicarious reinforcement occurs when one person observes another being rewarded for performing a behavior. Reward value is established by social comparison.

5. Defensive behaviors are adopted in order to cope with anticipated unpleasant events. Self-efficacy may be thought of as a specific form of confidence that influences not only whether a person will attempt a behavior, but also the quality of performance once an attempt is made. Doing is believing. Thus, managing to perform a feared or repugnant behavior will likely boost self-efficacy. In participant modeling a person performs such behavior in imitation of an efficacious model. Unlike a trait, self-efficacy is tied to particular social situations.

6. Bandura has criticized learning theories because they hold that behavior is pushed by the past, and must be performed and reinforced, not just observed, if it is to be learned. Stage theory is criticized because cognitive development is more a function of models available than phase in life. Unconditional positive regard (UPR) is self-defeating because it eliminates the tie between performance and reward, and self-actualization is problematic because it is predicated on UPR.

7. In a spider phobic study, after observation of a model, subjects in a medium efficacy condition exceeded the performance of low efficacy subjects. Low efficacy subjects were then raised to medium efficacy. A second study dealt with snake phobics whose self-efficacy was enhanced through modeling, resulting in close contact with a snake and enhancement of the immune system. In a study of other self-regulatory factors, subjects in a decision-making simulation managed five "employees." Those in an acquirable skill condition showed relatively enhanced self-efficacy, self-goals, and analytic strategies. In a similar study, controllability generated results like those in the previous study, but performance standards had sometimes counterproductive effects.

8. Crime is generated in part by limited behavioral alternatives available to the poor and oppressed. When the incentives for crime are great, the effort required small, and the likelihood of negative outcomes small, individuals with few other alternatives will adopt criminal behavior. Most people cannot do evil to other humans unless they engage in self-exonerative processes in order to dissociate themselves from the consequences of their actions. *Dehumanization* is one of the mechanisms they can use. Others include *advantageous comparison* and *euphemistic labeling*.

9. Blaming victims for their own fate is also a common self-exonerative process as is displacement and diffusion of responsibility. Moral justification involves invoking religious or other moral bases to support one's inhuman behavior. In gradualistic moral disengagement people slowly slip unawares into what was normally unacceptable behavior. However, cognitive processes may also allow self-sacrifice and altruism. Through the process of self-evaluation, people like Mother Teresa, Martin Luther King, and Susan B. Anthony risk life and security for the sake of human rights.

10. With all of its virtues, social cognitive theory can be faulted for being too broad, having no clearly defined boundaries. So long as it remains without boundaries, it must explain an extraordinary diversity of phenomena and is open to explanations after the fact. Still, the breadth of the theory is not entirely illusory. Further, it is reasonable to argue that social cognitive theory has the greatest research support and practical applicability. Decades from now social cognitive theory may make many other current theories seem like historical curiosities.

Running Comparison

Theorist	Bandura in Comparison
Mischel	Both deal with self-regulatory mechanisms, but neither is concerned with traits.
Rotter	Like Rotter, he is concerned with expectancies.
Rogers	He differs with Rogers on "unconditional positive regard."
B.F. Skinner	He differs from Skinner in emphasizing anticipation of reward, rather that past history of reward.

Essay/Critical Thinking Questions

1. Can you cite an example, experienced by you directly or indirectly, in which a child learned aggressive acts without reinforcement or practice entering the learning sequence?

2. How might environmental conditions affect your neurobiology differently than illustrated by examples in the text?

3. If reinforcement or reward does enter the learning sequence at some point, at which two points in the sequence involving a model and an observer might it have the greatest facilitative impact on observers' likelihood of adopting modeled behavior?

4. The notion of "social comparison" has many implications. How does it play a role in friendship? Do you compare with friends? If so, how do you hope to come out in the comparison? What do the answers to these questions have to say about friendship and rivalry?

5. What defensive behavior do you show that might be addressed with self-efficacy training employing participant modeling?

6. Could you paint a picture of a person reared during childhood with unconditional positive regard who turned out with characteristics contradictory to "self-actualization"?

7. Could you briefly design an experiment in which the self-efficacy and other relevant self-regulatory mechanisms of workers in a child mental health facility would be raised resulting in better care for the children? Hint: you could manipulate controllability and attempt to raise self-goal setting along with self-efficacy.

8. How could you raise your self-efficacy with regard to performing exercise behaviors that have the potential of making you a healthier person?

9. Could you pick one of the self-exonerative processes and illustrate how it has led to undesirable social behavior on your part or on the part of someone you know well?

10. Supposedly, social cognitive theory has no boundaries and, thus, is too broad. In turn, its lack of boundaries forces it to address all kinds of phenomena. To counter this argument, could you use the theory to explain chronic anxiety or severe depression?

14

IT'S ALL A MATTER OF CONSEQUENCES: SKINNER'S BEHAVIORISM

- Is there any real difference between the principles dog trainers use to teach animals and those that explain how human beings acquire personality?
- Does environment determine behavior? language? creativity?
- Is it possible to build a personality so that it turns out in some desired way?
- Is it necessary to consider thoughts and feelings in attempts to understand people?
- Is one point of view sufficient to completely explain the psychological side of humans?

The theories reviewed so far all have been concerned with "what is inside," or a combination of "what is inside" and "what is outside." By contrast, **behaviorism** is a school of psychology for which the basic subject matter is "outside"; it is, overt (observable) behavior. In order to identify with the other sciences, behaviorists believe that the science of psychology should deal only with phenomena that can be verified by the senses. They eschew entities that are buried away in the "mind," such as private thoughts, feelings, or motivations.

Classic or methodological behaviorists have confined themselves to events that are *currently* observable—they focus on the here and now. B. F. Skinner developed a broader point of view, called **radical behaviorism**, which considers currently observable events and also potential, future events that can be observed and measured (Salzinger, 1990). Therefore, Skinner contemplated future environments that can be arranged so that desirable behaviors are promoted. He believed we can design environments that select behaviors—pick some behaviors to be strengthened rather than others—which are likely to be good for the people who behave, as well as for others. This point of view may sound utopian. In fact it is. Skinner designed a utopian society when he wrote *Walden Two* (1948), a book about a community in which punishment is shunned and rewards guide people in the full exploitation of all their natural skills and characteristics. Skinner wished to make this a better world.

Skinner, the Person

Burrhus Frederic Skinner, born in 1904, spent his formative years in Susquehanna, Pennsylvania. He remembers becoming intrigued with psychology at a very early age. As with most people, his first interest was in the more mystical phenomena. As a third grader, he recalls, he had an "extrasensory experience": He excitedly raised his hand to report that he had read a word just at the same moment his teacher spoke it. As an older child, he was fascinated by performing pigeons at a country fair, and during his college years, he wrote a play on "glands that change personality" and a term paper analyzing Hamlet's madness. As a young man, Skinner recalls thinking about thinking while paddling a canoe. However, he later regretted his sojourn into "mentalism."

After having received his undergraduate degree in English from a small New York school, Hamilton College (1926), Skinner drifted for a while. He very much wanted to be a writer, even receiving encouragement from Robert Frost, but he settled for an ordinary job and ordinary daydreams. Then, as if he had stumbled onto the "truth," he discovered behaviorism from books by Bertrand Russell, a begrudging fan of early behaviorist John B. Watson and H. G. Wells. Wells pondered what to do with a single life jacket if he were standing alone on a pier, with George Bernard Shaw floundering in the water on one side and "Pavloff" slowly disappearing from sight on the other (the reference was to I. P. Pavlov [1927] the famous Russian who taught dogs to salivate at the sound of a bell). The jacket was awarded to "Pavloff"—by implication, behaviorism—and so were Skinner's intellectual loyalties.

Soon thereafter, Skinner enrolled in the psychology graduate program at Harvard. During this period he spent some time in Greenwich Village, sampling the Bohemian lifestyle. There, in a night club, he noticed an attractive young woman, and, as was often the case when he found a woman interesting, he boldly introduced himself. When it was discovered that he was to be a psychology student, hypnotism became the topic. She professed a desire to be hypnotized and he accommodated her. It was an important experience for him, for two reasons. It cemented his identity as a psychologist and it was the beginning of an affair.

Skinner took up residence with the woman and thereby revealed a willingness to defy danger. The woman was married and often received visits from her husband, who was away on military duty. This unsettling arrangement eventually led Skinner to decide that the lifestyle of Greenwich Village was not for him.

B. F. Skinner   **I. P. Pavlov**

Other aspects of Skinner's personality are revealed in *Walden Two* (1948). It is no accident that a main character and obvious alter ego, "Professor Burris," is a straightforward, typical academic who resorts to his intellect rather than his emotions when trying to make sense of life. However, paradoxically, Skinner was capable of being frivolous and, on occasion, could even be the prankster. At his college graduation ceremony, he delivered an oration in Latin that was designed to satirize the school administration. When a school official loudly queried, "Why don't students bow when given a diploma?" Skinner made a point of bowing grandly upon receiving his diploma. The "cheap joke," as he put it, inspired laughter from the audience.

If one takes seriously what Skinner (1976b) says about Skinner, he has a personality that is difficult to pin down (Skinner, 1983a). Skinner himself has offered little help. In preparation for an earlier personality text by Charles Potkay and me, Potkay asked Skinner to complete a personality questionnaire. Skinner replied that he hated to be "crotchety," but he did not believe in such measures.

Skinner did not show a well-defined personality. That is, for every trait that can be inferred from his self-reports of behavior, he has also indicated behavior associated with the opposite trait. As a young man, Skinner was shy but outgoing, cautious but adventurous, intellectual yet sometimes quite silly. His personal life was rather conservative, but he occasionally violated sexual conventions. Perhaps it is all by design. It would not do for a person to have a clearly evident personality if he wishes to deny the existence of personality (Skinner, 1989). Despite these disclaimers, one can read a great deal about personality between the lines of Skinner's writings. In any case, Skinner has proven that a person can be interesting, even if he does not clearly manifest a large number of consistent traits.

Skinner's advanced degrees were both from Harvard, an M.A. in 1930 and a Ph.D. in 1931. After two fellowships, he was affiliated with the University of Minnesota from 1936–1945, during which time he conducted military research sponsored by General Mills, Inc., and served as a Guggenheim Fellow. From Minnesota, he moved to the University of Indiana, where he chaired the department of psychology from 1945 until he departed for Harvard in 1947. There he was William James Lecturer until 1948, when he joined the psychology department. At the beginning of 1958, he became Edgar Pierce Professor of Psychology, a position he continued to hold until his retirement.

Among Skinner's many honors are election to the National Academy of Sciences, the Warren Medal from the Society of Experimental Psychologists (1942), the Gold Medal for Distinguished Scientific Contributions from the American Psychological Association (1958), and the National Medal of Science. In 1990 he received both the American Psychological Society's William James Fellow Award and the American Psychological Association's Presidential Citation for Lifetime Contributions to Psychology (Salzinger, 1990). He died on August 18, 1990 near the Harvard facilities where he did much of his research and writing.

Skinner's View of the Person

Environmentalism: The Importance of Consequences

Skinner (1972g) rejects the repeated accusation that he is an "S-R," or stimulus-response, psychologist (Salzinger, 1990). According to the S-R conception, a stimulus in the environment, such as "the door within the door" that constitutes the dog's entrance into the house, absolutely demands a response from the dog—namely, entering the house. Not so, says Skinner. The dog's door sets the occasion for the response "enter," but it does so with some probability, not absolutely. Further, to understand behavior, a dog's or a person's, one needs a concept that is missing from the S-R account. A **consequence** is an event that occurs after a response has been performed and changes the probability that the response will occur again. For the dog, gaining entrance to the house is the consequence that will increase the likelihood it will poke its nose through its door in the future. Consequences are so central to Skinner's point of view that it is in the title of one autobiographical volume (Skinner, 1983b).

While not an S-R psychologist, Skinner stands "guilty" to the charge of being an environmentalist (Skinner, 1983a). For him (1971), the environment is everything, explains everything. He often referred to parallels between the environment-behavior relationship and "natural selection," the process developed by Charles Darwin to explain how humans and other animals evolved to their present state (Salzinger, 1990). Natural selection can be illustrated by example. Assume that certain birds live on an island made up of tightly packed rocks. They must catch the bugs that constitute their food by pecking among the rocks. Under these conditions, the island environment will select for survival those birds with the thinnest, longest bills—bills best suited for pecking among the rocks for food. Ultimately, only the thin-long-billed birds will survive to pass along their thin-long-billed genes through reproduction.

Likewise, humans over thousands of generations have become able to effectively perform certain behaviors. The environment has selected certain human, physical characteristics, such as agile fingers and hands, because these traits permit the performance of critical behaviors that have survival value. Thus, the environment selects traits that permit behaviors having survival-promoting consequences, such as the provision of food. Survival, in turn, allows reproduction and, thereby, propagation of the genes controlling the traits.

Further, Skinner points to individual differences in the kinds of consequences that are likely to generate behavior (Skinner, 1948). Only some people are genetically disposed to effectively build novel objects from available materials. These people are likely to emit many responses that involve construction. Because typical environments provide numerous important consequences of such responses, chances are that "building" behavior will often be selected and will increase in likelihood.

However, Skinner emphasizes that genetic input, determined by the environment through natural selection, predisposes individuals to certain behaviors rather than others, but it only defines the potential for behavioral development. The particular environment into which each of us is born determines our own peculiar repertoire of behaviors. An individual born with artistic potential will show artistic behaviors only if the opportunities relating to artistic behavior are available in her or his particular environment (Skinner, 1972c). An environment cannot select artistic behaviors if it does not provide important consequences for such behavior. In sum, the actual behaviors a person develops depend upon the characteristics of his or her environment.

"Beyond Freedom and Dignity"

If a stimulus has some probability of giving rise to a response, if genetic disposition defines the potential for behavioral development, and if our particular environments determine the actual behaviors we will develop, we are all slaves to our environments. That is, we lack freedom (Skinner, 1948, 1971, 1983). According to Skinner, **freedom** refers to our belief that we can choose from various behaviors, rather than having our actions controlled by the environment (Skinner, 1972f). Obviously, Skinner does not accept the belief that he attributes to us. To him, it is a fact that we are controlled by the environment (1983a, 1983b, 1989). To deny environmental control is to risk being controlled by subtle and malignant circumstances and by malicious people. Governments and particular people sometimes control human beings for the benefit of the controller, not those controlled (Skinner, 1987a). Often we do not detect the harm done to us by this control, because there may be immediate positive consequences, while negative consequences are deferred until a later time. For example, we may stand aside while our government is lax in regulating the level of pollutants that are allowed to escape into our waterways and air. We fail to react because "jobs are preserved" and "the economy is stimulated"—immediate, positive benefits for us all. However, we should realize that this leniency in regulating pollutants has negative consequences in the long run (Skinner, 1983a).

Skinner (1971) asked, why not decide for ourselves what will determine our behaviors? The alternative is to leave the control of behavior up to chance, or worse, leave it up to people who would control us for their own gains. Radical behaviorism is well illustrated by the belief that we can create control of our behavior by manipulating our environments to increase the likelihood of beneficial consequences (Salzinger, 1990). When we demand freedom, what we really mean is freedom from negative or aversive consequences and access to positive consequences. We can have that freedom only by arranging our own consequences, not by assuming we can control our behavior directly or by leaving consequences to "government" or "fate." Thus, Skinner does concede that we have freedom, but in a highly qualified sense. We can arrange our environment so that the consequences we desire become likely, but having done so, we are under the control of our creation (Skinner, 1983).

While some measure of freedom can be achieved, dignity is unobtainable. "We recognize a person's **dignity** or worth when we give him credit for what he has done" (emphasis added; Skinner, 1971, p. 58). When, in our everyday lives, we cannot readily identify the consequences that control an individual's behavior, we attribute the behavior to the individual, rather than to the environment. Thus, when a person makes an anonymous donation to a worthy cause, we assume it was done because of something inside the person, called altruism. In so doing, we ignore the consequences in the person's early environment that have determined his or her behavior. For example, the person may have been exposed to a culture that "honors" (consequence) selfless giving. To credit people when they "do good" is to ignore the consequences that gave rise to "doing good" (Skinner, 1983a). Skinner (1971) suggests that we should identify those consequences and bring them under control so that more people can "do good" more often. To accept his suggestion is to give up taking credit for what we do, to give up "dignity." In return, he assures us that crediting the environment instead of ourselves will lead us to seek out some benevolent consequences that control behavior. The net result of that search will be a behavioral technology that will ensure "doing good" is a frequent occurrence and "doing bad" a rarity.

Skinner practices what he preaches. In *Walden Two* (1948), his main character, Frazier, who designed the utopia described in the book, repeatedly denies that people are to be credited with what they do. Skinner himself once ended a speech with the following:

> *And now my labor is over. I have had my lecture. I have no sense of fatherhood. If my genetic and personal histories had been different, I should have come into possession of a different lecture. If I deserve any credit at all, it is simply for having served as a place in which certain processes could take place. I shall interpret your polite applause in that light. (Skinner, 1972g)*

BOX 14.1   Descriptive Words Once Referred to Behavior, But No More

Among the threats to his position that have bedeviled Skinner throughout his career is **mentalism**, the belief that thoughts and feelings determine behavior, not external consequences (Skinner, 1983b). More recently he has lamented the birth and development of the "cognitive revolution," a movement that stresses the importance of thinking processes in determing behavior (Skinner, 1989).

Many of the words that we use seem to support the cognitive orientation in that they refer to internal conditions. Our language is replete with words that refer to thoughts or states of mind: experience, attitude, comprehension, need, will, worry, and intention. Nevertheless, Skinner (1989) believed that these terms originally referred to behavior, not internal conditions. In earlier times, people were more behavioristic, but something happened between then and now to change that orientation. Partly because people like to take credit for what they do and partly because people are unable to see the often subtle consequences of their behaviors, the meanings of words changed. One of the mechanisms by which these terms became converted into mentalistic words relates to the observation that feelings and thoughts occur after or at about the same time as behaviors. However, rather than cause behaviors, these clearly evident thoughts and feelings are mistaken for causes because of their close proximity to behavior. The real "causes," consequences of behavior, are less often evident and fre-

quently less proximal.

"*Experience* is a good example. . . . the word was not used to refer to anything felt or introspectively observed until the 19th century. Before that time, it meant, quite literally, something a person had `gone through' (from the Latin *expiriri*). . . ." (Skinner, 1989, p. 13). Skinner provides many other examples. *Intention* came from the Latin word *tendere* and originally meant to physically stretch or extend, a reference to behavior. *Image*, which we now take to mean an internal copy of something, originally meant a colored sculpture of a head and shoulders—from the Latin word *imago*. Later it meant ghost but in neither case was it something inside the head. The words *anxious* and *worry* originally meant choke as in "the dog worries the rat that it caught" (p. 15). *Aware* once meant to be cautious, to *comprehend* meant to seize or to grasp and to *solve* used to mean to dissolve, as sugar is dissolved in water.

Consistent with his beliefs, the terms he used when he wrote or spoke in public referred to behavior. Even when caught "off-stage" Skinner could be the behaviorist he recommended that everyone should be. When my wife and I encountered him outside the site of a psychological convention, we could not resist introducing ourselves. Skinner responded simply, "I'm waiting for friends." He made reference to what he was doing, not to anything he might have been thinking or feeling.

Basic Concepts: Skinner

Skinner claims not to have a theory (Skinner, 1983a), and is viewed by some people as anti-theory (Kendler, 1988). In any case, Skinner's point of view has all the trappings of a theory, including numerous concepts. Here only part of Skinner's position will be considered, the part that is most relevant to personality.

Operant Conditioning

Skinner's approach to psychology focuses on the kind of conditioning that many psychologists call "instrumental" (see Kimble, 1961). Skinner's term is **operant conditioning**, a process by which an organism operates on its environment with consequences that influence the likelihood that the operation, or behavior, will be repeated. Because respondent conditioning, Skinner's equivalent to the kind of conditioning done by Pavlov, is of less importance to the study of personality, it is not covered here.

Contingent is a close second to *consequence* as the key word in Skinnerian terminology. If event B is **contingent** on event A, the occurrence of B depends upon the prior occurrence of A (Holland & Skinner, 1961). If the singing of birds is contingent on the rising of the sun, the occurrence of singing depends upon the prior appearance of the sun. In *operant conditioning*, consequences are contingent on the prior performance of some response, often a very discrete and concrete behavior, such as the "handshake" of a trained dog. Three kinds of consequences can be involved in operant conditioning: positive reinforcement, negative reinforcement, and punishment.

Positive Reinforcement

Reinforcement occurs when some event is contingent on the prior performance of some response, such as the meowing of a cat that alerts its master to its hunger. **Positive reinforcement** is a process whereby some event, usually a stimulus, *increases the likelihood* of a response upon which its presentation is contingent. It is easy to see why the word *reinforcement* was chosen. *Reinforce* generally means strengthen, and to *positively* reinforce a response means to strengthen it, in the sense of increasing its likelihood of occurrence.

With this background, we can take some examples. Skinner (1983a) often placed a pigeon in a cage that bears the technical name "free-operant chamber" but has become popularly known as the *Skinner Box*. As Figure 14.1 reveals, it looks like any other cage for housing animals, except that it has a panel that the pigeon can peck (A). Pecking the panel activates a food magazine (B) that releases grain down a tube (C) into a cup (D) inside the cage. In the simplest case, every peck of the panel is followed by the presentation of some grain. That is, the response "panel peck" is followed by reinforcement in the form of grain.

Notice the kind of response that occurs in operant conditioning. Unlike sweating or change of heart rate, operant responses are not automatic. The kind of response that occurs in operant conditioning is initiated by the animal, rather than occurring automatically. The pigeon can peck many times, or none at all. It can peck forcefully or softly. Further, it is the pigeon that gets things going in operant conditioning. Nothing happens until the pigeon starts pecking the panel, and it must perform the response itself. You may recognize that operant responses are controlled by the somatic nervous system, which operates the somatic or voluntary musculature (arms and so forth). Responses of this kind are said to be *emitted* because they are initiated by the organism, rather than being automatic.

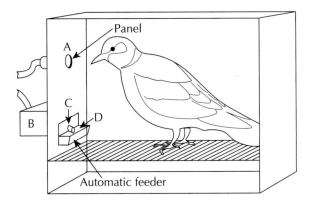

**FIGURE 14.1   Skinner box: pigeon pecks A,
which activates food magazine at B, causing food
to be delivered through tube C to cup D.**

Operant conditioning often begins when an animal starts responding more or less at random. A pigeon pecks quite a lot, for no apparent reason. Placed in a Skinner box, it will peck all around, eventually peck the panel, and grain will come down the tube into the cup. The pigeon will eat the grain and then wander around some more. Sooner or later, it will peck the panel again, with the same result as before. If one watches closely, it is evident that the time between pecks becomes less and less, until the pigeon is pecking at a fairly high rate. When the **rate of responding** becomes stable, conditioning is said to have been completed and a new response acquired. Rate of responding is also an index of strength of conditioning. In general, the higher the rate, the stronger the conditioning. **Extinction** occurs when a previously reinforced response is no longer followed by the same reinforcement and the response eventually decreases in frequency.

Operantly conditioning more complex responses than panel pecks requires special procedures. Suppose one wishes to teach a dog to turn in a circle. It will be necessary to use **shaping**—a process by which natural variability in behavior is exploited so that a new behavior is acquired by reinforcing *successive approximations* to it (Epstein, 1991). A hungry dog will often turn right and left in seemingly random fashion as it anxiously waits to be fed. When it makes a pronounced turn to the right or left, give it a bit of food (reinforcement). Wait for an even more pronounced turn in the same direction—a closer approximation—before providing more food. By reinforcing more and more complete turns—successive approximation—a full turn will soon be shaped. In shaping turning, it is usually best to allow the dog to initiate turns. However, some dogs may need *prompting*: they may have to be coaxed into performing at least an approximation of the desired response (Skinner, 1983b).

Positive reinforcement occurs every day in the life of every person, including a typical college student. Events occur during a student's day that include behaviors that have been reinforced many times in the past. At noon, the student makes his way to the cafeteria in his dorm, where he presents his student ID, picks up a tray, and fills it with food. These behaviors are positively reinforced by the food, although, admittedly, positive reinforcement may occur infrequently in some college cafeterias. The student proceeds to class, where his "class attendance" behavior is reinforced, as usual, by the stimulating lecture emanating from one of his several outstanding professors (hopefully this episode will not make the student seem atypical). Next, the student retires to the library for an afternoon of study, the reinforcement for which will be partially delayed until test day. For now, studying is followed by an abstract reinforcement event, the joy of learning. Leaving the library, the student reports to work where it happens to be payday. His work on that day, and several preceding it, is reinforced with a paycheck.

Negative Reinforcement and Punishment

Positive reinforcement is not the only means by which behaviors are learned. **Negative reinforcement** is a process whereby the likelihood of a response *increases* when it is followed by the *termination, reduction,* or *absence* of a stimulus (Holland & Skinner, 1961). Negative reinforcement involves aversive stimuli, such as electric shock. Such stimuli are called negative reinforcers. Behaviors that lead to success in escaping or avoiding negative reinforcers will increase in probability of occurrence in the future.

Escape and avoidance behaviors are illustrated by use of a shuttle box, as depicted in Figure 14.2. The box, actually a cage, has an electric-grid floor and a partition down the middle. The animal is placed in the box on one side of the partition, and electricity is activated on that side only. The shock is enough to be uncomfortable, but not harmful. The animal **escapes** by simply jumping to the side without shock. The jump is reinforced by the termination of the shock.

Avoidance learning becomes possible when a light is placed at each end of the box (see Figure 14.2). First, the animal learns to escape. Then, the light on the side containing the animal is illuminated a short time before the shock is activated. At first, the light has no influence on behavior. However, after a number of presentations of the light followed by the shock, the animal will begin to jump when the light is illuminated, before the shock is delivered. In this way the animal avoids the shock, or negative reinforcer.

Both positive and negative reinforcement involve increases in the likelihood of responses. By contrast, in the case of **punishment**, responses that are followed by the *presentation* of aversive stimuli *decrease* in likelihood of being performed in the future (Skinner, 1971). A moment of thought will reveal how negative reinforcement and punishment differ. In the case of negative reinforcement, responses *increase* in likelihood when followed by the *absence* (or termination or reduction) of aversive stimulation. By contrast, punishment involves a *decrease* in the likelihood of responses that are followed by the *presentation* of aversive stimuli. (This process is technically known as *positive punishment. Negative punishment* is omission of a positive reinforcer following the performance of a response.) If studying avoids

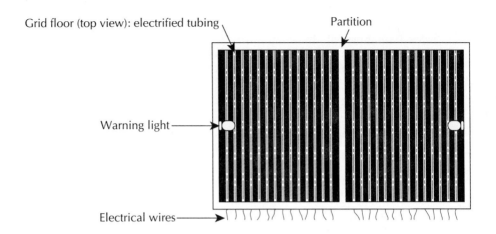

Grid floor (top view): electrified tubing

Partition

Warning light

Electrical wires

FIGURE 14.2   A top view of the shuttle box.

housework, parents are using negative reinforcement to increase studying. If a child's hand is spanked for getting into the cookie jar, punishment is being used to decrease pilfering of cookies.

Skinner has long maintained that punishment is not an efficient way to control behavior (Skinner, 1948). Later, laboratory research evidence forced him to admit that punishment can be very effective, although it rarely works well in practice. For example, if very strong shock emanates from the panel with each peck by a pigeon, the animal will stop pecking and may never resume again. Nevertheless, Skinner (1971) has a point when he maintains that punishment may have only temporary effects and may be accompanied by unfortunate byproducts. In some cases, punishment may lead to only temporary suppression of a behavior that is not desired by whoever administers the punishment. An organism may inhibit an undesirable behavior until the punishing agent is no longer present. Then the behavior may be performed at a high rate, making up for responses that were suppressed when the punishing agent was present. In addition, punishment may be accompanied by fear, anxiety, aggression, failure to perform beneficial responses, and, in humans, loss of self-esteem, confidence, and initiative.

As with positive reinforcement, it is easy to recognize many everyday examples of negative reinforcement and punishment. Some students avoid class the day after a test when grades are posted. Their behavior is reinforced by the absence of bad news about their test performance. Sometimes students fall asleep in class. Professors occasionally punish this behavior by a rude awakening.

Schedules of Reinforcement

To this point it has been assumed that every response an organism makes is reinforced. It is easy to recognize that such is often not the case in reality. Also it may be apparent that reinforcing every response, **continuous reinforcement**, is not even the most efficient way to proceed.

Suppose a traveling carnival has come to town. You attend and play a game where contestants use a bow and arrow. Every time you hit a balloon with an arrow you get a token that entitles you to a chance at winning a giant, stuffed animal. Assume that you are very good or that the game is very easy and you hit a balloon with each shot (trial). You would probably begin to respond slowly and would likely have difficulty persisting. In this case you would have been on a continuous schedule: each bow and arrow response was reinforced with a token-winning hit.

Suppose instead that you hit a balloon about every three tries rather than each time you shoot. Your rate of shooting would become much greater than in the previous example, and would likely be highly persistent. You would persist at a high rate because, rather than being continuously reinforced, your behavior would be subject to **intermittent reinforcement**, where responses are reinforced every so often, or after some number of responses has occurred (Holland & Skinner, 1961).

As a general rule, intermittently reinforced responses are performed at a higher rate and are more resistant to extinction than continuously reinforced responses. Thus, intermittent reinforcement generates stronger conditioning or learning. For this reason it is of more practical importance than continuous reinforcement. (Note, however, that a response is more easily acquired with continuous reinforcement.)

A **schedule of reinforcement** determines whether reinforcement is to be delivered either every so often or after some number of responses has occurred (Holland & Skinner, 1961). Some schedules are based on the amount of time since the last reinforcement, while others are founded on the number of responses performed since the last reinforced response.

In the case of a **temporal schedule** there must be an elapse of some amount of time between one reinforced response and the next. With a **ratio schedule** some number of responses must be performed between one reinforced response and the next. These two kinds of schedules can each be fixed or variable.

Fixed Schedules of Reinforcement

In a **fixed schedule**, a response is reinforced after a constant amount of time has elapsed or after a constant number of responses have been performed. In a **fixed-interval (FI) schedule**, the amount of time between one reinforced response and the next is constant (Holland & Skinner, 1961). It may be 25 seconds or 5 seconds, but it is always the same, or fixed.

Figure 14.3 provides a record of behavior that is reinforced on a fixed-interval schedule. The graph in this Figure and in Figures 14.4, 14.5, and 14.6 are called **cumulative records**, graphs of responses that are accumulated and plotted against time (Holland & Skinner, 1961). The cumulative records shown here all assume that learning has already occurred.

Notice that the record for the fixed-interval schedule (Figure 14.3) looks a little like a bunch of scallops, all interconnected. The organism begins responding

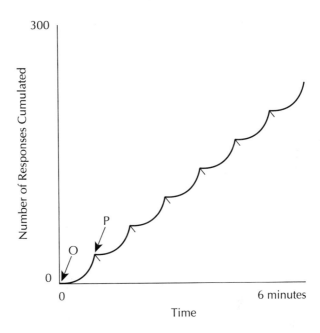

FIGURE 14.3   Cumulative record for a fixed-interval schedule (hatch marks indicate reinforcement).

slowly at the point in time labeled O. Because reinforcement does not occur until point in time P, the animal is in no hurry to produce responses. However, as the time for a response to be reinforced draws near, the rate of responding increases, as indicated by the steeper curve near the hatch mark at point P. When point P is reached, reinforcement occurs, and assuming it involves food, the organism stops to eat. Then it begins responding slowly once again. This pattern of responding generates the scallops.

For some students, studying is on a fixed-interval schedule. Just after a test, the rate of studying is near zero. Then, as the time for another test approaches, studying is performed at a higher and higher rate, until a very steep curve occurs the night before the test, which is just before students are sometimes reinforced by high grades. After the test, these students pause (often over refreshment), savoring reinforcement (assuming they are aware of having done well). Then the same old scallops begin again.

In a **fixed-ratio (FR) schedule** the number of responses occurring between one reinforced response and the next is constant. For example, on a FR(5) schedule, every fifth response is reinforced. As Figure 14.4 indicates, a FR schedule generates a record that looks like stair steps. The organism responds at a high and steady rate until reinforcement occurs, then it pauses for a moment. The pay of

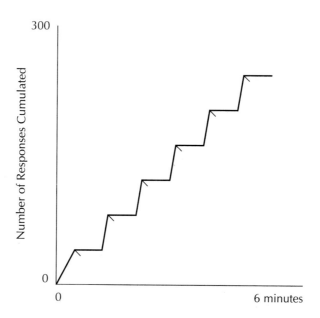

FIGURE 14.4   Cumulative record for a fixed-ratio schedule (hatch marks indicate reinforcement).

farm workers is sometimes on an FR schedule. Every so many bags of vegetables collected yields some predetermined amount of money.

Variable Schedules of Reinforcement
Variable schedules are more frequently encountered in real life. In a **variable schedule** reinforcement is delivered after some X amount of time has elapsed, *on the average*, or after some Y number of responses have been performed, *on the average*. That is, instead of a response being reinforced after exactly X units of time have elapsed, or after exactly Y number of responses have been performed, it occurs after X units, on the average, or after Y responses, on the average.

A **variable-interval (VI) schedule** requires that a given amount of time elapses between one reinforced response and the next, on the average. On a VI(5 seconds) schedule, sometimes the organism waits only 1 second before a response is reinforced; at other times, it waits 9 seconds; occasionally, it waits exactly 5 seconds. Overall, the intervals average out to a 5-second wait.

Note that the record for the VI schedule, depicted in Figure 14.5, is more irregular than its fixed-interval counterpart, shown in Figure 14.3. Also, notice that the curve is steeper than for the fixed interval. That is, the curve goes up at an angle that is closer to 90 degrees than is the curve for a fixed-interval schedule. The steeper curve is indicative of a higher rate of responding. A moment of thought will reveal why variable schedules tend to generate higher rates of responding

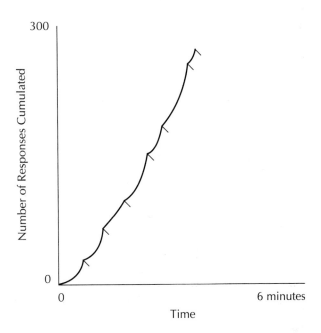

FIGURE 14.5   Cumulative record for a variable-interval schedule (hatch marks indicate reinforcement).

than fixed schedules. If a pigeon cannot anticipate exactly when a reinforcement is going to be delivered, it pecks away rapidly. After all, a response may be reinforced only a second after the last reinforcement. People act the same way. Not knowing when reinforcement will be delivered, people leave little time between responses, because only moments later a response might be reinforced. Contrast this situation with that of a fixed schedule. If one knows for sure that it is going to be 1 minute until a reinforcer is delivered, why work hard responding? Why not start responding in earnest about the time a response will be reinforced?

Variable schedules are also more resistant to extinction than fixed schedules. During extinction, reinforcement never occurs. However, organisms that have been on a variable schedule will continue to respond because past experience makes them used to long periods with no reinforcement.

Fishing seems to provide a real-life example of VI scheduling. As any person who fishes can tell you, there may be an hour between the initial cast and the one that lands the first fish, but, moments later, a cast may land another fish. However, the next cast that lands a fish may come two hours later. It may average out so that a cast is reinforced after a forty-five minute wait. Consequently, fishing behavior may be quite resistant to extinction despite relatively long periods without reinforcement.

A **variable-ratio (VR) schedule** requires that, on the average, a given number of responses be performed before a response is reinforced. As a general rule,

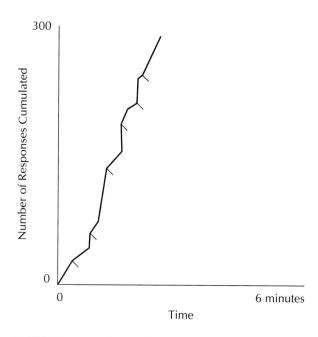

FIGURE 14.6   Cumulative record for a variable-ratio schedule (hatch marks indicate reinforcement).

a variable-ratio schedule will generate the highest rate of responding and the strongest resistance to extinction (see Figure 14.6). A VR(10) schedule designates a procedure by which every 10th response is reinforced, on the average. Sometimes the organism must respond 19 times before the reinforcer is delivered; sometimes, 1 response is sufficient. The schedule averages out to reinforcement after 10 responses.

Shooting basketballs is on a VR schedule, as is selling merchandise, but the clearest example is gambling. A person diligently working at a slot machine does not experience reinforcement after a fixed number of coins are placed in the slot. Nor does reinforcement occur on a per-unit-of-time basis. Rather, on the average, every so many responses of placing a coin in the slot is followed by reinforcement—the machine yielding up some of its monetary contents. Casual observation in casinos confirms that gambling behavior is highly resistant to extinction.

To sum up, schedules of reinforcement determine delivery of reinforcement based on the amount of time that has elapsed since the last reinforced response, or on the number of responses since the last reinforced response. A fixed schedule requires that an exact amount of time must elapse or an exact number of responses must be performed before reinforcement is delivered. With variable schedules, the amount of time or the number of responses required for reinforcement to occur is not exact, but variable. On the average, X elapse of time or Y number of responses is required for reinforcement to occur. As a rule, variable schedules generate higher rates of responding and greater resistance to extinction.

Personality Development

Although Skinner rejects "personality," his responses to questions about how behavior is acquired relate to the concept. For example, does speech develop according to an inherited script, is it acquired by mimicry, or do notions of environmental consequences to verbal responses apply? Of course, Skinner prefers the last alternative. In this section, Skinner's explanation of language learning is examined, as are some of his notions about rearing children, and the broader implications of his ideas for the design and construction of personality.

Development of Speech

Skinner (1957, 1972e) contends that learning to use words orally is a relatively simple matter. When a child of age two is confronted with the stimulus "red light" and utters the word "red," his response is reinforced by the "verbal community" (Mom, Dad, and siblings) with everything from praise to candy. When the child puts two words together, for example, "That red," his response is reinforced by the verbal community. Correct insertion of a verb ("That is red") is reinforced in a similar way, leading to the use of complete sentences that are grammatically correct. To put it more technically, use of oral language is learned by a process involving the formation of contingencies between verbal responses and reinforcements delivered by the verbal community. So-called "rules of language" are learned by the same principles as single words are learned. If the child says "I am five years old" instead of "I are five years old," praise by Mom and Dad will follow (Skinner, 1976a). Thus, in Skinner's view, the acquisition of language in children can be explained by reference to operant conditioning.

Building a Personality

Skinner wastes no opportunity to dismiss personality from the realm of science. In Chapter 1 of *Beyond Freedom and Dignity* (1971), he mocks the notion of "disturbed personality" (pp. 8 and 16) and flatly states, "We do not need to try to discover what personalities, states of mind, feelings, traits of character . . . or the other perquisites of autonomous man really are in order to get on with scientific analysis of behavior" (p. 15). Yet in that book, and in *Walden Two* (1948), he subtly, and perhaps unwittingly, indicates that people do have personalities, at least in the sense of showing individual differences in behaviors that are relatively constant across time and situations.

In *Walden Two*, the person one might think would be given even less personality than Professor Burris is "blessed" with a rich and full repertoire of behaviors that distinguish him from others. Frazier, the founder and leader of Walden Two, is an impulsive individual whose temper flares on many occasions. He shows a great deal of self-confidence, but seems rather vulnerable underneath all the bravado. At one point, Frazier bursts forth:

BOX 14.2 Baby in a Box

Skinner has been controversial at least since his wartime attempts to use pigeons to guide missiles (Skinner, 1972d). However, nothing he has done has caused more comment than rearing his infant daughter Deborah in a box. The apparatus used to house the child has been described by Skinner (1972a), along with the behaviorist's rationale for the unusual procedure. He writes that his wife Eve decided it was time to apply science to the nursery, in the interest of saving labor—presumably her own. The first consideration, quite properly, was the physical and psychological well-being of the child. As the description of Deborah's living quarters indicates, the box was spacious, providing ample room for the child and her toys. An open area in front was normally covered by a removable pane of safety glass. Notably the floor of the compartment was covered with a sheet that could be replaced instantly by means of a *roller* device. Also, it was no accident that the child was depicted in only a diaper. In fact, she was kept quite comfortable with no clothes, as her "home" featured temperature and humidity control.

Unconfined by clothes, Deborah was free to move her limbs in any way she wished. Compared with some babies who are restrained by clothes, she joyously exercised with all her might. The result was the development of strong back, leg, and abdominal muscles. Byproducts of the exercise were unusual agility of the feet and excellent hand/foot coordination. Deborah often played for hours with toys suspended from the ceiling of the box. Manipulating a music maker with her feet, the baby was able to compose her own tunes, much to the amusement of the family.

Feeding and changing the child took only about one and a half hours a day, but this was only a small portion of the time devoted to her. If she wanted to play, she was entertained in her habitat or removed for interaction with the family. Far from being neglected, Deborah was the center of attention. Neighborhood children were continually parading past the box for a chance to see and play with the "baby in the box." Instead of receiving less affection than children housed in the usual way, Deborah may have received more affection of higher quality. Freed from much of the drudgery associated with caretaking, her parents had more time for affection and a stronger inclination to display it.

Some of Skinner's techniques and "suggestions for a better society" were viewed by critics as mechanical and even tyrannical (Haney, 1990). Skinner himself was seen by some as a cold, unfeeling scientist. Putting his baby in apparent isolation only confirmed these perceptions of the famous behaviorist. In fact, Skinner was a warm and responsive father to Deborah and to his other daughter Julie. They often exchanged poems and touching notes. There are many examples of tenderness and concern for his daughters in the last volume of his autobiography (Skinner, 1983b). For example, when Debs, as he called Deborah, broke a leg on a ski trip to the Deux Alpes, Skinner flew to Geneva and then drove to Grenoble under dangerous winter conditions so he could care for her. When she arrived home, being confined to crutches, she was understandably cranky. A day after being somewhat unpleasant, Deborah wrote her father the following note: "Dear Pop, How are things? This is just a note to tell you I love you. Love, Debs. P.S. & that I apologize for my poor behavior of yesterday . . ." (Skinner, 1983b, p. 234). A later note to Debs contains an

---

BOX 14.2   *Continued*

astounding passage for a radical behaviorist to write: "I'm not embarrassed by any supposed shortcomings of yours or afraid you will prove to the world that I am a bad psychologist. Live your own life, not mine. Be yourself. I like your

Self" (p. 235). Self psychologists of the Rogers mold may take note.

And how did Debs turn out? She became an accomplished and successful artist. Julie is a professor married to a professor.

You think I'm conceited, aggressive, tactless, selfish. You're convinced that I'm completely insensitive to my effect upon others. . . . You can't see in me any of the personal warmth or the straightforward natural strength which are responsible for the success of Walden Two. My motives are ulterior and devious, my emotions warped. (pp. 236–237)

It seems that the author who condemns personality provides excellent examples of "lots of" (Frazier) and "little" personality (Burris) in his only novel. In *Beyond Freedom and Dignity* (1971), not only is it implied that people have personality, but Skinner alludes to the possibility of developing and changing personality by design.

In commemoration of the year 1984 Skinner wrote a new episode in which a resurrected George Orwell seeks admittance to Walden Two (Skinner, 1987a). Burris and Frazier appear to be their same old selves, despite the elapse of considerable time. Thus, Skinner provides testimony to the stability of personality.

Despite providing clear examples of traditional personality principles, Skinner continued to reinterpret personality concepts in behavioral terms. Table 14.1, which is adapted from *Beyond Freedom and Dignity* (1971), contains the description of a young man whose life has suddenly been dramatically transformed. As is evident, each standard trait that is assigned to the man is translated into the language of behavior. If the young man's behavior is weak and inappropriate and often has unavoidable consequences, rather than assuming that he is "insecure" and "anxious," Skinner sees him as a victim of transitory environmental circumstances. That is, he shows some behaviors that are performed rather consistently over time, but his actions are not the product of something that is permanently embedded within him—the traditional notion of traits. Instead, his behavior is due to something that is external to him—an environment that has changed naturally, but, by implication, could be changed through human intervention.

Whether or not one finds Skinner's attempt to dismiss internal entities (traits) convincing, it still must be granted that his notions implicitly include individual differences in behaviors that are constant across time and situations, the popular assumption underlying personality. If the relatively constant behaviors that signify *personality* can be changed through environmental intervention, it should also be possible to develop a personality by design.

In fact, Skinner wrote of "Creating the Creative Artist" (1972c). In that essay he implies that the predispostion for creating art may be inborn, but will not be

TABLE 14.1   Trait versus Behavioral Description of a Disturbed Man

Trait Description	Behavioral Description
Insecure, unsure	His behavior is weak and inappropriate.
Dissatisfied, discouraged	He is seldom reinforced; therefore, his behavior undergoes extinction.
Frustrated	Extinction is accompanied by emotional responses.
Anxious	His behavior frequently has unavoidable aversive consequences which have emotional effects.
Lack of purposefulness or sense of accomplishment	He is rarely reinforced for doing anything.
Guiltiness, shamefulness	He has previously been punished for idleness or failure, which now evoke emotional responses.
Disappointed, disgusted	He is no longer reinforced by the admiration of others, and the extinction that follows has emotional effects.
Hypochondriacal	He concludes that he is ill.
Neurotic	He engages in a variety of ineffective modes of escape.
Has an identity crisis	He does not recognize the person he once called "I."

manifested without the development of contingencies between artistic endeavor and reinforcement. But what exactly is reinforcing in a work of art, such as a painting? It has been argued that the content of a painting is somehow rewarding in and of itself, "intrinsically rewarding." However, if one examines popular subjects for paintings, Skinner asserts, common objects with survival value predominate (Skinner, 1983a)—"extrinsically rewarding" objects according to Bandura. For example, the human hand, a form of great strength and capability, is a very frequent subject. Pictures of food are also common in paintings. More abstract are portraits depicting family and loved ones, themes that have been associated with survival throughout the evolutionary history of humans. Paintings are reinforcing because of their content, but it is not some intrinsic value invested in a picture as such. Rather, the content, food and the human form, has value because of the evolutionary history of human beings and factors from the history of the particular artist. You may find these ideas reminiscent of Jung's beliefs.

During the lifetime of each artist, there are themes embedded in his or her works that especially appeal to people in the artist's community. When depicted on canvas, these themes result in a form of reinforcement that is familiar to us all, praise. Needless to say, the artist in question will represent in her or his works those themes that are repeatedly followed by reinforcement. Thus, the artist's own history of reinforcement, as well as the history of human beings, shapes her or his behavior when confronting the canvas.

However, creativity, in the sense of an idea that no one has ever had before, is an illusion (Skinner, 1972c). True, a successful artist does not merely copy the works of other artists, but does "copy" from her or his own experience. The resultant work of art may be unique in that no one has ever expressed the experience exactly as has our hypothetical artist. However, the work is not wholly original in that it represents an experience common to many people. Again, Skinner sounds somewhat like Jung. Further, once an artist has arrived at a form of expression that is at least an unusual rendition of some experience, and therefore it is reinforced, he or she is likely to repeat that expression throughout his or her career. To support this contention, Skinner points to Picasso. Supposedly, only the first of Picasso's paintings was not derivative. All the works that followed stemmed from the first effort.

How might a community encourage the pursuit of art in general, rather than just promoting a single artist? Skinner would supply a simple answer: mass exposure to art. Widespread display of art would help to develop artists in two ways. First, there would be an increase in the number of people who would appreciate art, and thus be able to reinforce artists' efforts with praise and attention to their works. Second, Skinner seems to be suggesting that large scale exposure to art would uncover most of those people who are genetically disposed to create works of art. You cannot produce great athletes in a society where sports are not played. If the opportunity to reinforce athletic prowess is not available, athletes will not develop, even though the genetic potential is present in members of the society. Proportional to population, the former East Germany won far more Olympic medals than any other country (in absolute numbers they were often second only to the former USSR). Skinner would explain this phenomenal success by reference to the interplay of genetics and reinforcement. Rather than simply working with the same material that other countries possess and doing a better job of developing it, East Germany thoroughly exploited excellent material by constructing contingencies between athletic performance and reinforcement.

Remaining to be specified is the kind of society that would promote such development by design. On the surface, it might seem to be a society in which "talent scouts" go on frequent quests for those characteristics that are needed by the society. To the contrary, in *Walden Two* the greatest number and variety of pursuits and accompanying reinforcements imaginable are made available to all members of the community. People receive credits for the jobs they perform daily, and, with some flexibility, they have to earn a certain number of credits per week in order to continue in the community. In contrast to real societies, Walden Two offers the most credits for tasks that are tiresome, difficult, and uninteresting (for example, collecting garbage) and the fewest credits for tasks that are enjoyable and interesting (for example, giving a lecture on a favorite topic). Under this system, medical doctors of Walden Two might receive fewer credits per unit time than laborers. Therefore, doctors would have to work longer hours than laborers to earn the same number of credits.

The net result of the Walden Two credit system is that most people try a wide variety of pursuits, but eventually migrate to those that they are genetically disposed to perform well. "Planners," such as Frazier, presumably because of their inherited disposition to "leadership," spend much of their time planning life in the imaginary society, but sometimes they tend the garden or chop wood. Other members of the community may work at mending fences, repairing the barns, and feeding the animals on many more occasions than they are employed at teaching or serving on committees. Walden Two is an efficient society because experiences rich in number and variety are arranged, creating an environment that selects behaviors the performers are best equipped to enact. It is not necessary to search for talent. Because the society offers the opportunity for performance and reinforcement of almost any conceivable behavior, talent simply emerges.

By the way, Walden Two is not entirely hypothetical. Some young people built a replica of Skinner's utopia near Richmond, Virginia (Kinkade, 1973). It has been successful, but might benefit from changes that Skinner would make in Walden Two, if he could do it over (see Skinner, 1983a).

Evaluation

Contributions

The number of studies that stem directly or indirectly from Skinner's research and ideas is impossible to estimate. There must be thousands. The *Journal of the Experimental Analysis of Behavior* has been, since its founding in 1958, devoted entirely to research in the Skinnerian tradition. Therefore, there is only room for a close-up look at a representative study, an investigation of superstitious behavior. In addition, a bit of supporting evidence for Skinner's view of the relationship between experiences of reinforcement and genetic disposition is considered.

Skinnerian Research Illustrated: A Study of Superstitious Behavior

According to Skinner, a **superstitious behavior** is a response that is accidentally reinforced, as there is no prearranged contingency between the response and reinforcement. That is, with superstitious behavior, reinforcement occurs periodically, regardless of what the organism does. However, because a given behavior and reinforcement accidentally occur together, the behavior is repeated and, by chance, is again followed by reinforcement.

In Skinner's (1972k) study of pigeon behavior, each of eight animals was deprived of food and then placed in a Skinner box, where a food cup was presented to the bird for five seconds at regular intervals. The cup was made available to the animal no matter what it did. One bird happened to be turning counterclockwise when the cup was presented early in the experiment. After a number of accidental coincidences of counterclockwise turns and cup presentations, the bird would reliably turn two or three times in a counterclockwise direction between food deliveries. Following several accidental coincidences of head thrusting and reinforcement another bird would thrust its head into one of the upper corners of the cage. Two additional pigeons learned to reliably swing their heads and upper bodies in a pendulum motion. Still another animal developed a tossing response, as if it were lifting up an invisible lever, and a sixth bird began to peck or brush at the floor without touching it.

Of course, superstitious behavior is common among humans. A former colleague of mine, who, ironically, was well schooled in Skinnerian behaviorism, once seriously refused to relinquish his seat at a poker table. He was sure his position at the table had everything to do with winning several hands and a good deal of money. It seems that few people are immune to superstitious behavior. It is common among athletes. You may know of some who refuse to part with old shoes or worn gear because they see a connection between use of these items and winning.

Superstitious behaviors are quickly extinguished if it is easy to appreciate that there is no connection between the behavior and reinforcement. A former coach of the Houston Oilers football team wore the same cheap suit for each of seven victorious pre-season games and through two winning regular season games. Then the Oilers lost a contest. Into the rag bag went the suit. If each instance of a superstitious behavior has been accidentally followed by the same clearly defined reinforcement, the behavior is likely to disappear the first time it is not reinforced.

Superstitious behaviors, however, are often learned on intermittent schedules. Take the case of astrology. A person who reads the astrological charts will only rarely experience any kind of reinforcement. Nevertheless, on some occasions, reading will be followed by reinforcement not too long after the charts are consulted. For example, an individual may read, "Good fortune will soon come your way." Two days later the individual finds $35. The find may be regarded as the predicted "good fortune"—that is, reinforcement for use of astrological charts. Lack of "good fortune" on the previous two days is ignored. Under these circumstances, the superstitious behavior may be difficult to extinguish. Superstitious people may need help: someone must point out to them that there is no contingency between their behavior and reinforcement.

The Interrelationship of Genetic Disposition and Reinforcement

Gromly (1982) reports an attempt to investigate the interrelationship between the genetic disposition of individuals and the history of reinforcement during their lives. He states:

> *Although learning theory and biological viewpoints are sometimes presented as competing explanations for behavior, they are more likely complementary. This appears to be so in the development of personality traits. One direction this complementary process might take is that, within the limits of their particular environment, people tend to select experiences that suit their biological dispositions. In this way, the selection of preferred experiences by individuals acts as an amplifier of differences that already exist. (p. 255)*

Skinner would likely agree with Gromly's statement, with one exception: people do not select experiences from their environment, the environment selects individuals' behavior and thus it selects the experiences that accompany the behavior.

People who are genetically disposed to be articulate may end up on the debating team where their ability to articulate will be amplified, provided only that a team is available to them.

To illustrate the possible link between genetic disposition and experiences, Gromly had university fraternity men keep a log of their experiences. Essentially, "logging experiences" amounted to recording the situations encountered and the corresponding behaviors performed. A sample log entry would be "played basketball today." They also rated themselves on scales designed to assess the possibly inherited dispositions "energetic-physically active" and "sociable-extraverted, socially outgoing." Results showed a close relationship between what the men reported doing and scores on "energetic" and "sociable." Thus, measures of genetic dispositions, "energetic" and "sociable," were closely related to behaviors and accompanying experiences consistent with those dispositions. In Skinner's terms, the *environment selected* energetic behaviors for those people who were genetically inclined to be energetic. It is important to note that the behaviors of "energetic" people in one environment are not likely to be the same as those of energetic people in another environment. A given environment does not simply extend and refine genetic disposition. It leads to specific and concrete behaviors that go far beyond the global and abstract genetic disposition (Skinner, 1972e).

Behavior Therapy

The phrase **behavior therapy**, psychological therapy employing behavioral techniques, first appeared in print in an article by Skinner and a colleague that described their use of the then new methods (Skinner, 1983b). Almost all of the vast number of techniques that fall under behavior therapy were directly suggested by behavioristic research or have been validated by that research (Skinner, 1972j). These methods include positive reinforcement, negative reinforcement, and punishment. Behavior therapy has been successfully used for everything from treatment of obesity, heavy smoking, and alcoholism to treatment of children who do not talk or relate to adults (autistic children) and treatment of psychotic adults (people who have withdrawn from reality; see Ullmann & Krasner, 1965).

It is beyond the scope of this book to consider even a small sample from the massive psychotherapeutic tool chest of behavior therapy. However, to get a flavor of behavior therapy and to see how it relates to Skinner's ideas, consider a hypothetical example suggested by Skinner (1972l). Imagine a child of five who is not psychotic or autistic, but who is so shy and withdrawn that he almost never talks or relates in any way to adult strangers. Such a child would have difficulty attending school and relating to teachers.

Behavior therapy can be beneficial. The child is placed in a room on one of two chairs positioned side by side in front of a vending machine. It has been established that candy is a good reinforcer for the child, and the machine is capable of vending the child's favorite confection. The machine is operated by an observer who is hidden behind a one-way mirror (the observer can see the child, but the child sees only his reflection). After a few minutes, an adult stranger enters the room and takes a seat next to the child. Nothing happens for a long while, and the adult leaves, returning shortly. Each entry is a trial. Several trials occur before the child finally utters a word to the stranger. Immediately, the vending machine operator presses a button, and out of the machine comes the child's favorite treat. Several more trials may occur before the child speaks again, but each episode of speech is reinforced by candy. Soon the child is talking regularly to the stranger, and the schedule is then changed to a VR(5). Later, the schedule is changed to deliver even fewer reinforcements per speech episode, and other strangers take the place of the original adult in order to spread the response to adults in general.

Whenever the child speaks to the stranger, the stranger replies. The replies occur at the same time as the candy reinforcer is being delivered. Thus, the stranger's replies become **secondary reinforcers**, stimuli that come to have all the properties of primary reinforcers (such as candy) through association with primary reinforcers (Kimble, 1961). Thereafter, replies can reinforce the child's utterances. Now the child can go out into the real world and talk to people, with each string of utterances being reinforced by people's replies: people respond to others' remarks. This feature makes it likely that the conquest of the child's shyness will generalize beyond the laboratory. If "shyness" is a trait, then the child will have undergone a "personality change."

Limitations

Perhaps Skinner has been most severely criticized for discounting thought, feeling, and other phenomena that exist "in the head" and thus cannot be directly observed (Skinner, 1971). He admits that individuals, including himself, do have thoughts and feelings, but he argues that there is no need to consider these internal entities in order to understand people (Skinner, 1983a). He believes that feelings or emotions are byproducts of behavior, not its determinants or predecessors (Skinner, 1971). According to this point of view, one flees (behavior), then is afraid (emotion). Assuming this sequence of events, emotions cannot be determinants of behavior. His easy adoption of the behavior-emotion sequence and rejection of its opposite (people are afraid and then flee) seems unwarranted. According to J. Jung (1978), the position that Skinner endorses is not amenable to testing by experimental procedures and has been subjected to severe criticism.

If Skinner's view of language development is correct, cognition is unimportant, and environment determines everything—a conclusion that many language experts and cognitive psychologists are loathe to accept. However, Skinnerian notions of language development and verbal ability have also come under heavy attack, beginning with review of Skinner's book *Verbal Behavior* (1957) by Noam Chomsky (1959).

As we have seen, Skinner argues that language is developed by the reinforcement of the child's utterances that is delivered by the verbal community, initially parents and siblings. Supposedly there is no such thing as Chomsky's inborn disposition to grasp the "rules" of language. To Skinner (1976a), "rules" are simply statements of contingencies between behaviors and reinforcements (if a child says "It hurt me," rather than "It hurted me." its utterance is reinforced). Thus, rules develop during the lifetime of the child and are not programmed into the brain at birth. But Skinner's position seems unable to account for the tremendous explosion of language development between the ages of 18 months and 3 years (Mussen, Conger, & Kagan, 1979). Language develops so rapidly during this period that a lengthy and painstaking process of primitive utterances being reinforced seems unable to account for it. Further, during this early period and later, children produce utterances that they are very unlikely to have encountered in their environment. More important, these unique utterances indicate that children do grasp the rules with no training. For example, a child might say, "Look, deers. They runned across the road." "Deers" and "runned" are incorrect usages that would rarely be employed or reinforced by adults. Yet, "deers" indicates a grasp of the rule "Plurals are formed by adding an 's.'" Similarly, "runned" represents a recognition of the rule "The past tense is formed by adding 'ed.'" Because these incorrect utterances would not have been reinforced in the past by the verbal community, the child's behavior might best be explained by reference to an innate disposition for grasping rules, rather than to environmental contingencies.

Most of us have solved a never-before-encountered mathematical problem in private. By a reasoning process, we have come up with an answer that had never occurred to us before, and thus could not have been the object of reinforcement in the past. Neither is it currently subject to reinforcement by the verbal community. This common experience, and others like it, constitute evidence that thoughts unrelated to behavior are important to everyday functioning (J. Hayes, 1978).

Feelings are important too. A few years before his recent death, famed British actor Sir Laurence Olivier was interviewed on TV (60 Minutes, January 2, 1983). He recounted that at one point in his career, he had developed severe stage fright. While portraying Shakespeare's Othello, Olivier was so overcome with fear and thoughts of inadequacy that he had difficulty catching his breath and wondered if he could continue. Yet somehow he finished. His portrayal of the troubled Moor was shown on 60 Minutes. Nothing in his performance revealed even a trace of his internal agony. The critics had also noticed nothing unusual; as always, they had praised Olivier's performance. There were no external consequences to his stage fright. However, the solely internal terror suffered by the actor was recalled as one of the most notable experiences of his life. Thoughts and feelings can be extremely important in the lives of people, even when unaccompanied by any external manifestations, behavioral or otherwise.

By his own admission, Skinner's (1989) behaviorism cannot account for the process by which we take in information through our senses and give meaning to it. Skinner and his works are virtually absent from the pages of books on sensation and perception (see comments by Matlin & Foley, 1992).

Conclusions

Skinner's ideas have certainly inspired numerous researchers and theorists to discover many new ways to predict and control behavior. His concepts have directed attention to specific aspects of human behavior and have stimulated a formidable

BOX 14.3   Skinner Criticizes His Critics . . . And They Respond

After years of being fairly polite to his critics, Skinner struck back with a vengeance in 1987(b). The title of his paper—"Whatever happened to psychology as the science of behavior?"—posed what, for him, was the critical question facing modern psychology. He answered his own interrogative by charging that humanistic psychology, psychotherapy, and cognitive psychology had virtually conspired to lure psychologists away from the study of behavior and back to mentalism.

To Skinner (1987b) humanistic psychologists are a band of revisionists who are threatened by the "fact" that environmental selection, rather than internal determinants such as the need for growth and self-fulfillment, accounts for the way we behave. He suggested that they are anti-scientific and even lumped them together with the controversial "creationists" who believe that the world is only a few thousand years old.

In response, a group of humanistic psychologists indicated astonishment at being called anti-scientific and at being grouped with the creationists (Krippner et al., 1988). They professed not to be threatened by the assumptions of behaviorism; in fact, for some purposes they found behaviorism reasonable. Further, they disclaimed any association with creationism and pointed out that their graduate programs embrace the scientific method. The humanists closed by inviting Skinner to visit their institution and, thereby, cure his ignorances of humanistic psychology.

Psychotherapists, according to Skinner, dwell on subjective, mentalistic phenomenon such as feelings and needs, and rely on memories of how people behaved, rather than observing them directly. To the contrary, Bornstein (1988) argues that psychotherapy researchers sometimes observe the behavior that occurs during therapy, rather than dealing with feelings and

remembered behavior. In contrast to Skinner's belief that there is something incompatible about psychotherapy and behaviorism, these researchers produce results that are, on the one hand, behavioristic in nature, and on the other hand, serve to relate behaviorism to psychotherapy.

Skinner (1987b) saved his harshest words for the cognitive psychologists. He argued that they are the chief culprits in the plot to return psychology to mentalism. To him cognitive psychologists are uninterested in behavior and do research that is irrelevant to behavior. Kendler (1988) replied that several schools of psychology focus on behavior and that some of them are cognitive in nature. More generally, "behavior can be interpreted as a function of (a) a theoretical network involving hypothetical or abstract structures and processes [cognitive approach]; (b) neurophysiological events; or (c) environmental events [behavioristic approach]" (p. 822). All are legitimate, and they are not mutually exclusive: there is no contradiction in taking all three approaches to understanding behavior.

It was during 1987 that Skinner lodged these accusations against his colleagues who endorse a non-behaviorist position. By the summer of 1990 he knew that he would soon die. In his last speech, given at the American Psychological Association convention only eight days before he died, he had the opportunity to recant his condemnation of the colleagues he would leave behind. But instead of repenting, he expanded the "creationist" label so that not only humanistic psychologists, but also cognitive psychologists, would fall under it (Bales, 1990). Noting the departure of cognitive psychologists from APA to the new American Psychological Society, he commented that it is "not a secession, but an improvement" (p. 1).

amount of research, commentary, and criticism. When he died, newspapers and popular magazines were filled with acknowledgments of his contributions. Psychologist Eric Ward, who worked with Skinner, characterized Skinner's impact as so great that it has profoundly affected school teachers and parents, not just other psychologists (Hopkins, 1990). As an example, he mentioned "time out," a method now known to most teachers and parents. Originally, "time out" meant an interruption in the schedule of reinforcements while a pigeon pecked a panel other than the one connected to the food cup (that is, pecks went unreinforced). "Time out" when applied to children "involves briefly interrupting the rewards inadvertently stemming from bad behavior" (p. A9) by ignoring misbehaving children or placing them where their "bad behavior" cannot be reinforced.

As proof Skinner has continued to have great impact right up to the present time, just months before his death, articles written in praise of his position appeared in several publications, even in some that are apparently alien to behaviorism. For example, a month before his death, an article extolling his position was published in the *Humanist* (Bennett, 1990).

Two years after his death, the American Psychological Association devoted an entire issue of its principal organ, *The American Psychologist,* to Skinner and his works. Skinner's ideas were related to diverse issues ranging from existentialism to literacy/numercy and all the way to child development and self-interpretative behavior.

Even if the criticisms noted above are valid in some degree, it is still probably true that Skinner's point of view is one of the most general in all of psychology. It is difficult to find an introductory psychology book that does not consider Skinner in several different chapters. Likewise, social psychology, developmental psychology, personality, and psychotherapy texts typically devote considerable space to Skinnerianism. More important, through his contributions to child rearing and behavior therapy, he has had an important and positive influence on literally thousands and thousands of lives. There are those who would argue that Skinner's contributions have had more positive impact on more people than those of any other psychologist.

Summary Points

1. Skinner (1904–1990) was born in Susquehanna, PA. His Ph.D. was from Harvard where he spent most of his career. As a youngster Skinner dabbled in psychology, even flirting with mentalism. However, after college, a failed attempt to be a writer, and a sojourn in Greenwich Village, he was converted to radical behaviorism. Skinner, like "Professor Burris," his alter-ego in *Walden Two,* was a straightforward academic in many respects. However, he showed a variety of behaviors and was hard to pin down in terms of personality.

2. Rather than being an S-R psychologist, Skinner emphasized environmental consequences of responses and the process of environmental selection of behavior to be parallel to "natural selection." In his book *Beyond Freedom and Dignity* he asserted that freedom is possible in a limited sense, but dignity is an illusion. He also indicated that we can arrange our environments so that desirable consequences to our behaviors will occur. Skinner acknowledges that currently our language is replete with words that refer to internal states and cognitions, but has shown that many of these words originally referred to behavior.

3. In operant conditioning the organism operates on its environment with consequences that increase the likelihood of the operation. In positive reinforcement, a stimulus increases the likelihood of a response upon which its presentation is contingent. Indexes of conditioning and the termination of it are "rate of responding" and "extinction," respectively. In negative reinforcement the likelihood of a response increases when it is followed by the absence of an aversive stimulus. By contrast, in punishment, responses that are followed by the presentation of aversive stimuli decrease in likelihood.

4. In intermittent reinforcement, responses are reinforced (1) every so often, or (2) after some number of responses has occurred. A temporal schedule of reinforcement is based on the amount of time between reinforced responses. Ratio schedules are based on number of responses between reinforced responses. In fixed schedules, the amount of time or number of responses is constant. Variable schedules can be temporal or ratio, but the amount of time or number of responses varies around some average, rather than being constant.

5. Skinner believes that language develops via a process through which crude utterances are reinforced by the verbal community. Similarly, rules of language are learned because incorrect constructions are not reinforced, but correct ones are. Amid much controversy, Skinner reared his daughter Deborah in a "box." Among the advantages of this technique are freedom from child care drudgery, more time for affection, and more opportunities for creative child play. Despite all the controversy, Deborah, and her sister Julie, turned out well and have had a warm and close relationship with their father.

6. Skinner explicitly rejects the notion "personality," but he often supported ideas that are consistent with popular conceptions of personality. For example, some of Skinner's characters in *Walden Two* wear their personalities on their sleeves. Frazier is an illustration. On the one hand, he dismisses personality terms as readily translatable into behavioristic concepts. On the other hand, he has striven to show how society can promote the development of traits such as "creativity" and "leadership" by providing opportunities for reinforcement of "creative" and "leader" behaviors.

7. Skinner's research on *superstitious behavior*, behavior that is accidently reinforced, shows that pigeons can easily be induced to produce numerous superstitious behaviors. Further, the understanding of superstitious behavior obtained from the study of pigeons can be readily translated into explanations of human superstitious behavior.

8. Gromly's work with fraternity men who kept logs that recorded "energetic-physically active" and "sociable-extraverted, socially outgoing" behaviors supports Skinner's ideas regarding the interplay of genetic disposition and reinforcement. Men presumedly disposed to these traits, as indicated by their scores on some scales, tended to show behaviors and accompanying experiences corresponding to the traits. Skinner was a pioneer in the area of behavior therapy. Methods consistent with his work are illustrated by the case of the shy child who learns to speak with adults and who receives secondary reinforcement in the form of their replies.

9. Skinner's belief that feelings accompany or follow behavior has been criticized as scientifically untestable. His ideas about language development have been rejected by some critics because reinforcement cannot account for rule learning, reinforcement cannot explain solutions to problems that have never before been used by the problem solver, and feelings that remain entirely internal, but still have a profound impact on our lives. Skinner countered his critics by calling humanists creationists, accusing psychotherapists of being subjective and dependent on people's memories of behavior, and claiming that cognitive theorists are not interested in behavior. In rebuttal, humanists disavowed creationism, psychotherapists do research that includes direct behavioral observation, and cognitive theorists point to three non-mutually exclusive approaches to understanding behavior.

10. Despite the criticisms of his point of view, Skinner has inspired many fruitful theoretical and practical approaches to understanding and controlling behavior. His recent death was followed with an outpouring of testimonials to his many contributions, some from unexpected sources. Skinner's work has influenced virtually every branch of psychology and has even touched rank and file citizens through such notions as "time out."

Running Comparison

Theorist	Skinner in Comparison
Freud	Unlike Freud, he believed in external causation and condemned "mentalism."
Rogers	In private he acknowledged a self not unlike Rogers would. Also, like Rogers, he was concerned with creativity.
Jung	Like Jung, he alluded to symbols in art that reflect humans' evolutionary past.

Essay/Critical Thinking Questions

1. What was it about Skinner's early life and "character" that made a behaviorist of him, despite his early flirtation with mentalism?

2. Build an argument that suggests that freedom and dignity, as we commonly define them, are consistent with behaviorism after all, despite Skinner's belief to the contrary.

3. Write a list of common terms that refer to mental events—a different one than found in the book—and translate them into behavioristic terms.

4. Describe an operant conditioning experiment in which positive reinforcement is used to condition an animal to *eventually* press a bar on a VI(10) schedule.

5. Could punishment be used to eliminate the self-mutilative behavior of an autistic child? Would such use be ethical? How would you go about it?

6. Imagine a *Walden Three*. In it create a personality that is characterized by leadership capability. How would you find people who might turn out to be fine leaders and how would you select their leadership behaviors?

7. How would you extinguish the gambling behavior of a compulsive gambler? Describe the schedule of reinforcement such a person would be on and then indicate an ideal way to extinguish their troublesome behavior.

8. Pick a superstitious behavior of either yourself of a friend. How did it come to be? How would you extinguish it?

9. Describe how you might improve Skinner's "baby box." How would you make it more attractive to the public so that it might be used by them?

10. Illustrate how a disruptive child's aggressive behavior might be extinguished, and cooperative behavior shaped.

15

HUMAN NEEDS AND ENVIRONMENTAL PRESS: HENRY A. MURRAY

- Can a man who does not respect his father and is alienated from his mother turn out right?
- What kind of theorist would acknowledge a debt to Freud, then indicate that Freud's Oedipus complex does not apply to himself?
- Which is more important, a person's needs, her or his environment, or some combination of the two factors?
- What happens when more than one need arises at the same time?
- Can dreams predict real life outcomes?

You have now come round the full circle—well almost. Unconscious processes, emphasized by Freud, have been considered, as well as reactions to Freudian thought. The interpersonal approach of Sullivan and the sociopsychological orientation of Fromm have been covered. Rogers and Maslow have proposed their humanistic concepts of empathy and self-actualization. You have contemplated the cognitive constructs of Kelly and the interplay of the social environment with cognitive processes offered by Rotter, Mischel, and Bandura. Finally, the radical behaviorism of Skinner provided you with a stark contrast to the others. Next the thinking of Henry A. Murray establishes the cables and pillars for the required bridge from these several basic points of view to the orientation that has dominated modern personality research, personality traits.

In one way or another, Murray's thinking resembles that of most theorists covered so far, but, at the same time, it remains unique. Jung stimulated Murray's interest in psychology. Murray acknowledged a debt to Freud, but, like Horney, used Freudian thought as a point of departure from which he launched his own theory. While Murray rarely mentioned Adler, he, like Sullivan, clearly was interpersonally oriented: relations among people are critical in his theory. He was also sociopsychological: though he neglected Fromm, he borrowed heavily from social psychologist Kurt Lewin. Murray was definitely also cognitive and the interplay between internal needs and the external environment was prominent in his thinking. He even showed some affinity for the ideas of his contemporary B. F. Skinner, despite his disdain for experimental psychology. Murray states, "We may see . . . that certain effects are more fundamental to life and occur more regularly than any observed action patterns. This agrees with Skinner's conclusions" (Murray, 1981a, p. 140). Like Skinner, Murray believed it is the end effect of an action that is unique and relatively important. The action itself could be any number of behaviors, each equivalent in terms of its effects. Also similar to Skinner, but unlike the social learning theorists, Murray believed that behavior is more "pushed from the rear" than "pulled from the future" (Murray, 1981a).

Murray had an intellect for all seasons. You can travel across his broad mind from the first part of this book to the last part.

Murray, the Person

Henry A. Murray was born in 1893 to well-to-do parents who occupied a brownstone house on the present site of Rockefeller Center, New York City (Anderson, 1988). Unlike the other theorists, he never developed a meaningful relationship with either his father or his mother. Although he did not reject his mother as did Maslow, like Maslow he felt his mother favored his older and his younger siblings. She was an emotionally bland, prim and proper socialite who rarely showed affection or concern for her middle child. Once he said to her, "You make my feelings hurt me" (p. 141). On and off throughout his life, Murray attempted, sometimes lamely, to establish a relationship with her. He once even tried to administer his Thematic Apperception Test to her. Finally he gave up and declared them "dead to each other" (p. 141). Although his overt reactions to maternal rejection were mild, as a child, and later as an adult, he must have been seething inside. Even in his late sixties, Murray still spoke of the "marrow of misery and melancholy" that plagued him through the years (p. 141). In addition he stuttered most of his life, an affliction that was more "psychological" than physiological: it diminished to a mild stammer by the 1930s and largely disappeared later in life when time lessened the hurt.

Murray described his father as "a nice guy" (p. 142), a code for amiable dolt. Anyone he found mediocre was described similarly. The elder Murray was a disappointment for a number of reasons: he was not bright (he could not follow conversations between his physician sons); he was not self-sufficient (he married the boss's daughter); he lacked ambition; he was predictable (a conservative banker by profession); his values and way of life were commonplace and unimaginative. In fact, Murray came to see himself as the opposite of his father.

One might wonder what sort of father would have gained Murray's respect and affection. Murray had trouble sustaining admiration for anyone. He wrote James Anderson during 1981, "I'd admire someone for a while, and then it would fade, and it would be someone else. These were all tentative things" (p. 143). According to Anderson, Murray was imbued with a certain "specialness." Perhaps it was a fault, but it may have also been a virtue. Believing that his ideas had truth value and that he was the natural leader of any group to which he belonged drove Murray to conceive of original ideas and to inspire creative thinking in others. He was narcissistic by his own declaration, and sometimes joked about it. Erik Erikson, Murray's former research associate, "imagined what Murray's fantasy would be: to put a statue of himself in place of Napoleon's on the column in the Place Vendome in Paris" (p. 169). The leader of the team that produced the timeless research reported in Murray's *Explorations in Personality* (1938) might be cast as the benevolent dictator.

While this sense of specialness was not equivalent to arrogance, it did give him a feeling of privilege. Like many "great people," one intimate, romantic relationship was not enough. His wife, the former Josephine L. Rantoul, whom he married in 1916, was a traditional woman—a "good wife and mother"—but was insufficiently intellectual to fully satisfy Murray. To fill the void, he became involved with Christiana Drummond Morgan, a research collaborator, confidant, friend, and more. But in his day and time, maintaining two romantic relationships was very difficult, yet he could not give up either woman. When he became enthralled with Jungian thought, partly because of Morgan's enthusiasm for the Swiss psychiatrist, he acceded to her insistence that he visit Zurich to speak with the architect of the collective unconscious. There he found a solution to his dilemma. Jung, it turned out, had a similar problem . . . and adopted the usual solution: he arranged for his lover, Toni Wolff, to occupy a house near his own. Despite Jung's attempts to discourage him—it was very touchy business—Murray emulated his new-found Swiss colleague. He remained devoted to his wife and Morgan for the rest of their days.

Anderson (1988), through numerous communications over several years, made an in-depth analysis of Murray's personality. Besides the sense of specialness, and the narcissism that went with it, Murray had a clear recognition of his intellectual gifts. He also had a powerful need for achievement and a sense of independence that was forced on him by the lack of parental connections. While his desire for intimacy was strong, he was wary of closeness. Nevertheless, he achieved intimacy, especially with women. With men his orientation was different. Murray searched for weaknesses in his male associates and used his findings to assert his superiority. At the same time, he had a need for heroes, but quickly found all candidates for that role to have clay feet.

Despite his sometimes bubbly enthusiasm, he had an inner core of melancholy. Depression enveloped him at several points in his life. His gloominess even affected his literary preferences: Murray's interest in the doleful classic *Moby Dick* was so intense that he became a leading authority on it. Yet his belief in himself was undying and his intellect was towering. Henry A. Murray was destined to make major contributions.

Murray's academic credentials were as illustrious as they were unusual. After graduating from one of the most exclusive Eastern boy's schools, Groton, he enrolled at Harvard during 1911, where he was granted an undergraduate degree in 1915. Following medical training at Columbia University leading to the M.D. degree, Murray completed a 20-month internship in surgery (Smith & Anderson, 1989). During this period he helped care for future-president Franklin D. Roosevelt, who was beginning his struggle against polio, and he launched a successful career as a medical researcher (Smith & Anderson, 1989). For four years Murray studied the development of the chicken embryo at the Rockefeller Institute. Twenty-one articles reporting his research appeared in the leading medical and biochemical journals (Anderson, 1988). So intense was his interest in biochemistry that Murray went to study in England at Cambridge University where he received a Ph.D. in the field during 1927. By this date, he had become a respected pioneer in the fledgling field of biochemistry, but, as you will see, he was not satisfied with himself.

Murray's View of the Person

Early Exposure to Psychology

While an undergraduate, Murray, like Kelly and Maslow, found his first encounter with psychology anything but inspiring. Murray said of his German-trained professor of experimental psychology, "A bud of interest in psychology . . . was nipped by the chill of Professor Munsterberg's approach" (quoted in Anderson, 1988, p. 146). Later he wrote to Anderson of his dismay with Munsterberg's denial that "psychology had anything to do with people" (p. 146). Thus began a lifelong quarrel with experimental psychologists.

Even during his training as a medical researcher and biochemist, Murray was undergoing a "profound affectional upheaval" (Anderson, 1988, p. 146). "He suddenly and unexpectedly found himself 'in a blaze,' a blaze which would go on for three years and eventually pressure him to embrace psychiatry and psychology" (pp. 146–147). But just as his exposure to experimental psychology brought him no comfort, neither did his first inquiries into Freudian thought. Having overheard some students talking about Freud, Murray consulted W. Courtney, a neurologist on the faculty of his medical school and the revered father of a classmate. This academic compared Freud's ideas to vomit. In an attempt at Freudian humor, Courtney punned, "I regard [Freud's ideas] . . . as the greatest phallusy of the age" (quoted in Anderson, 1988, p. 146). Despite this rude introduction, Murray eventually gained some respect for Freud and his notions. However, Courtney's response was of little help at a time when Murray needed to embrace some psychological point of view.

It was in 1923 that Murray stumbled onto Jung's just translated *Psychological Types* (reprinted in 1961). The experience was a revelation to him and may have been a case of predestination, because he met the Jung enthusiast Morgan about the same time. It was in 1925 that Murray succumbed to Morgan's persistent urging and traveled to Zurich for three intense weeks with Jung (Smith & Anderson, 1989). Murray wrote of the experience,

> *Dr. Jung was the first full-blooded, all-encompassing, spherical human being I had ever met. . . . I had only the touchstone of my own peculiar tribulation to apply to his intelligence with the importunate demand that he interpret what I presumably knew best—myself. He proved more than equal to this exacting test and within an hour my life was permanently set on a new course. In the next few days "the great flood-gates of the wonder-world swung open" and I experienced the unconscious in that immediate and moving way that cannot be drawn out of books. . . . All this and more I owe to Dr. Jung. (Murray, 1981b, pp. 80–81)*

Consistent with his personality, Murray's admiration for Jung faded—"he wasn't good with his concepts . . . he'd believe anything I told him that was along the lines that he liked . . . but he would overlook what did not fit his theories" (Anderson, 1988, p. 155). Nevertheless, Murray credited Jung with "starting me off in earnest toward psychology" (p. 147).

In 1927 Morton Prince, recently commissioned to establish the Psychology Clinic at Harvard, wanted to hire an assistant. It was to be a psychology-faculty appointment that included lecturing and duties in the clinic. Because he was absent from the United States, a friend and professor of physiology interceded on Murray's behalf, declaring to Prince, "Here's this brilliant chemist in England. You want a scientist, don't you?" (p. 149). Despite "being entirely inadequate" Murray was offered the job and accepted. Within two years Prince was dead and Murray was director of the clinic. Needless to say, his education in psychology was even more abbreviated than that of Kelly, his companion in skepticism about experimental psychology. Murray was the featured lecturer in the first psychology courses he regularly attended.

Why Did Murray Become a Psychologist?

Jung was part of the answer. Murray's disaffection with his medical and biochemical work, which he found to be rote and lifeless, was another (Anderson, 1988). His work with medical patients did give him some intimate contact with other human beings, but he described it as "necessarily brief and superficial" (p. 149). More important, work in medical science allowed Murray no contact "with the deeper wellsprings of his personality . . . with his own inner life" (p. 149). In the end it was the "marrow of misery and melancholy" that became the strongest magnet drawing him to psychology. Murray fit the stereotype of the maladjusted individual who becomes a psychologist to solve personal problems. But it worked. Despite not being profoundly influenced by others' theories, as Murray developed his own point of view, he grew stronger and stronger until he could be accurately described as a well-adjusted person.

Developing a Unique Approach to Understanding People

Murray at first flirted with orthodox psychoanalysis. As a leader of the Boston Psychoanalytic Society he was instrumental in recruiting Franz Alexander, a favorite of Freud's among graduates of the Berlin Psychoanalytic Institute. At the beginning of the 1930s, Alexander arrived in Boston as resident psychoanalyst and engaged Murray in training analysis. Analysis lasted 9 months, 6 in Boston and 3 after Alexander moved to Chicago.

It is safe to say that Murray was not terribly impressed with psychoanalysis, at least not favorably (Anderson, 1988). He, in effect, laughed his way through analysis, never being serious about it—"I was too busy, otherwise-attached" (p. 158). Though he liked Alexander, they were never really in sync with one another. Among the few comments Murray made to Anderson about the experience was in regard to Alexander's wife: she was a blond, flamboyant, race-car driver who seemed incompatible with the stout, unemotional, former student of Freud. Murray imagined that she was attracted to him.

He did not speak to Alexander about his wife, nor did he speak to the psychiatrist about matters of substance, including his own love life. Later he was to regard the period of analysis as time not especially well spent. Learning about the contents of his unconscious did not cure his stuttering, nor did Freudianism help him understand his relationship with his parents. Because he thought of his father as a "nice guy," he was certain that the Oedipal situation did not apply to him. In the end, he dismissed Alexander as another "nice guy" and declared himself disillusioned with psychoanalysis.

Despite his overt reaction to psychoanalysis, there were some subtle signs that Murray was affected by the 9 months with Alexander. First, there were covert signs that an underlying current of hostility flowing deep within Murray was whipped into waves. Not only was Alexander described as fat and bland, his office was said to be "very depressing, the color of feces" (p. 159). Second, Murray must have been influenced, because thereafter he felt obligated to address Freud's notions in his own writings, though it was sometimes done in a sort of offhand manner (Murray, 1981a). He also practiced psychoanalysis, though sparingly (Anderson, 1988).

Freud's influence on Murray was evident in other ways. Murray believed in unconscious processes and often mentioned sexuality. More important, he liked the global, philosophical orientation of Freud, especially certain basic psychoanalytic assumptions. Prominent among these was the belief that there are complex internal processes going on which cannot be illuminated by scientific experiments. Experiments treat people like machines, cut from the same mold, with components that can be considered apart from the whole. Murray, like Maslow, came to believe that humans are dynamic wholes, not meaningfully divisible into parts and pieces.

In fact, Murray believed that his most important contribution was an insistence that the whole person always be considered; this may be his way of saying that he originated the "holistic" approach.

Needless to say, Murray's Harvard colleagues did not care for his complaint that subdividing psychology into the disciplines of the senses, perception, learning, and so forth fragmented the person and thus was a serious error. He fought with them like he claimed the members of the Boston Psychoanalytic Society fought with each other, like dragonflies (Anderson, 1988, p. 157). When famed neuropsychologist Karl Lashley arrived at Harvard in 1935, he tried to oust Murray. Department chair E. G. Boring warned Murray that he would be ostracized from the American Psychological Association for life if he published a paper containing comments such as "[John] Watson's proposal [is] naive, juvenile perversity" and "A budding psychologist . . . could scarcely have been disposed to adopt with zest the dogmas of those whose avowed conscious purpose was to convince us that consciousness and purpose were nonexistent . . ." (quoted in Anderson, 1988). Further, he persisted in opposing what he called the "scientism" of academic psychology. To him psychologists were playing at real science—of which biochemistry was an example—for the purpose of basking in the reflected glory of physical scientists. In so doing they were failing to understand that psychology not only could not but *should not* be like the other sciences. It should be designed to study whole people and whole people cannot be fitted into test tubes or under microscopes. Only Gordon Allport was clearly sympathetic to Murray. Allport was a social psychologist and personality theorist who spoke of studying "the individual" and of "personality traits." In preference to his colleagues' concern with "sensory elements" and "conditioned responses," Allport's ideas should have appealed to Murray. Allport did make friendly overtures to Murray, even acting with gentlemanly restraint when the two faced off in a student-arranged debate. But it was to no avail. Allport, like most other male associates of Murray, was dismissed with, "He thought of consciousness as large . . . and the unconscious as a little bit of a thing down there" (p. 154). Actually, this was narcissism at work again: everyone else's ideas were seriously flawed. Murray emerged from his years at Harvard with the perception of himself as a lone hero, fighting for the truth. With the dry wit that characterized him, he commented, "At departmental meetings there were five votes in favor of psychophysics and one vote in favor of psychoanalysis" (p. 153).

As his ideas about personality developed, Murray offered several basic "propositions" upon which personality is founded (Murray, 1981a). Among the most crucial was the assumption that the object of study should be individual organisms, not aggregations of organisms. This premise is consistent with an even more fundamental principle: holism. Another proposition was that rhythms of activity and rest are inherent in the organism and stem from internal factors. This assumption stresses that people are not just inert bodies passively responding to external stimulation. He also believed that one cannot get to know a human being by studying even a rather extended episode in her or his existence. One must study the **long unit** of the organism, its life cycle. "The history of the organism *is* the organism" (p. 127).

While the person is not just a tool of the environment, Murray contended that "an organism is within an environment which largely determines its behavior" (p. 127). In fact, much of what is now inside the organism was once outside—a present need for security may have originated in past threats arising in the environment. Because the internal and the external are so intimately connected, it is necessary to view the organism as a product of "creature-environment" interactions. These interactions may be considered the "short unit" of psychological inquiry. Thus, the long unit, an individual life, may be thought of as a succession of related short units or episodes.

The organism usually responds to patterns of meaningful wholes, not discrete "sense impressions." "In turn the reactions of the organism to its environment usually exhibit a **unitary trend**," activity that is organized and directional in nature, not willy nilly, trial and error (p. 128). An activity itself can be cast as an **actone**, a pattern of bodily movements in and of itself, divorced from its effect. Therefore, a certain condition of the organism, hunger, can be followed by several different actones, picking fruit, buying a meal, begging for food, each of which yields the same end effect, food in the stomach. The connection among the sub-effects associated with simple actones constitutes a trend toward some overall effect.

"Though the psychologist is unable to find identities among the episodes of an organism's life, he can perceive uniformities. For an individual displays a tendency to react in a similar way to similar situations. . . . Thus there is sameness (consistency) as well as change (variability) . . ." (p. 130). In these comments, Murray recognizes that *temporal consistencies* exist—people may react similarly to similar situations encountered across time. Such consistencies are one argument for the existence of traits. Nevertheless, Murray also acknowledges that behavioral variability is a fact of the organism's life (Allen & Potkay, 1983a).

Internal representations occurring early in the chain of events that end in an effect are neurologically based. "Since, by definition, it [internal representation] is a process which follows a stimulus and precedes an actonal response, it must be located in the brain" (p. 131). **Regnant** is the name given to "dominant configurations in the brain" that correspond to internal representations. **Regnancy** is the label for the "totality of such [brain] processes occurring during a single moment (a unitary temporal segment of brain processes)" (p. 131). These concepts were proposed by Murray to recognize the fact that everything we call "psychological" ultimately arises out of brain action. However, Murray made it clear that while "activities of nerve cells and muscle-cells are necessary conditions of the whole action . . . they are not in any full sense its cause" (p. 131). Brain action enables the chain of events leading to some effect; it is not the final cause of that sequence. "Cause" lies in a complex of interrelated external and internal events that is too intricate and vast to be encompassed by a simple statement.

". . . the constituents of regnancies in man are capable of achieving consciousness (self-consciousness) . . ." (p. 132). There are brain processes that correspond to what we call consciousness; humans are able to reflect on themselves as a result of these regnancies. On the other hand, there are unconscious regnant processes. "An unconscious process is something that must be conceptualized as regnant even though the [person] is unable to report its occurrence" (p. 132). This declaration is Murray's way of legitimizing unconsciousness by linking it to brain processes.

To further show that "nerve cells" do not cause effects at the end of the
environmental event > internal processes > actone

chain, Murray boldly suggested that the personality can affect the brain. Personality processes may even alter the autonomic nervous system, as in cases of neuroses that affect such vital functions as heart rate and blood pressure. Personality is not the slave of neurology; it is somewhat the other way round.

Basic Concepts: Murray

Definition of Needs

Like Maslow, Murray's most central concept is **need**, "a [hypothetical] construct which stands for a force ([of unknown] . . . physiochemical nature) in the brain . . . , [that] organizes perception, . . . intellection, . . . and action in such a way as to transform . . . an . . . unsatisfying situation [into a more satisfying one]" (Murray, 1981a, p. 189). Beyond this formal definition, Murray characterized a *need* as equivalent to a *drive* (he often used them interchangeably, as in the section title of his 1981a article "The Concept of Need or Drive"). Here Murray and Maslow differed greatly. The proposer of the "hierarchy of needs" took great pains to distinguish between "drives," which he thought to be of secondary importance, and "needs" which he emphasized.

Murray also alluded to another equation relevant to the organization of this text. His ideas provide a bridge to the later discussion of "traits," because a need can sometimes be thought of as "a more or less consistent trait of personality" (p. 142). He hastened to add that it can at times be considered a "temporary happening" (a state). Other evidence that Murray's needs are traitlike is seen in the fact that they have been transformed into one of the most frequently used personality-trait measures currently available (Paunonen, Jackson, & Keinonen, 1990).

At different points, Murray wrote of "need" in different, though not necessarily contradictory, terms (Murray, 1981a). At one point he conceived of a given need as aiming the organism toward a unique effect, different from the direction assumed by it when it is being influenced by other needs. At another point, in tune with Skinner he indicated that "a need is a . . . 'push from the rear' rather than a 'pull from the future' " (p. 148). In still another context he "loosely" referred to "need" as "an organic . . . readiness to respond in a certain way under given conditions" (p. 142). One may conclude that a need is a (1) drivelike, and (2) sometimes traitlike, entity that is (3) associated with brain functioning and (4) arises to transform an unsatisfactory situation through (5) readying the organism's mental and behavioral faculties to respond to "a push from the rear."

Varieties of Needs

Murray (1981a) divides needs into basic categories. The **viscerogenic needs** involve basic physiological drives, and, as such, are relatively straightforward and self-explanatory. *Positive* viscerogenic needs—characterized by approach orientation to objects—include n Inspiration (need for oxygen), n Water, n Food, n Sentience (need to experience sensory gratification, for example, sucking and bodily contact with another person), n Sex, and n Lactation. *Negative* viscerogenic needs—characterized by avoidant orientation to objects—are n Expiration (need to exhale carbon dioxide), n Urination, n Defecation, n Noxavoidance (need to get rid of noxious stimulation), n Heatavoidance, n Coldavoidance, and n Harmavoidance.

Psychogenic needs are secondary to viscerogenic needs and may be derived from them, but, being one step away from the biological side of the organism, are psychological in nature. Like the viscerogenic needs, psychogenic needs can be typed as positive or negative. Each type is associated with a vector which is a force with directional properties. **Adience** refers to the positive-need-promoting vectors that describe movement toward objects and people. There are several examples, many of them well-known to professionals, and some even known to the public. The term **n Achievement** indicates the drive to "overcome obstacles, to exercise power, to strive to do something difficult as well as [and as] quickly as possible" (Murray, 1981a, p. 157). The term **n Affiliation** refers to the desire for friendships and associations; "To greet, join, and live with others. To co-operate and converse sociably with others. To love. To join groups" (p. 159). The term **n Succorance** is the dependent attitude of seeking aid, protection, and sympathy by crying for mercy and help from affectionate, nurturant caretakers. This need has the flavor of unresolved basic anxiety, Horney's central notion. The term **n Order** involves arranging, organizing, and putting away objects; to be tidy, clean, and scrupulously precise; **n Dominance** is the drive to influence, control, persuade, prohibit, dictate, lead, direct, restrain others, and to organize the behavior of a group; **n Exhibition** is desiring to attract attention to one's person by exciting, amusing, stirring, shocking, or thrilling others; **n Aggression** refers to an assaultive or injurious orientation to others, including to belittle, harm, blame, accuse, ridicule, punish severely, react sadistically toward, or even murder; and **n Abasement** involves surrendering, complying, accepting punishment, apologizing, confessing, atoning, and generally being masochistic. This last need brings to mind Horney's portrayal of people with the masochistic need for submission to a lover (Claire). The terms n Sex and n Sentience are viscerogenic needs associated with adience vectors.

Abience is the name given to the negative-need-promoting vectors that describe movements away from objects and people. There are fewer clear examples in this category, but some of them will be familiar. The term **n Autonomy** is the drive to resist influence or coercion, to defy authority, seek freedom, and strive for independence; **n Inviolacy** is an attitude of attempting to prevent depreciation of self-respect, to preserve one's good name, to avoid criticism, and to maintain psychological distance; **n Blamavoidance** refers to avoiding blame, punishment, and ostracism by inhibiting asocial or even unconventional impulses; being a well-behaved, law abiding citizen; **n Infavoidance** is an orientation to avoiding failure, shame, humiliation, or ridicule by concealing disfigurement and refraining from attempts at anything seen as beyond one's powers; and **n Contrarience** is the drive to act differently from others, to be unique, to take the opposite side, and to hold unconventional views. The viscerogenic needs **n Noxavoidance** and **n Harmavoidance** fit the abience category. Table 15.1 contains a summary of Murray's needs.

TABLE 15.1   Summary of Murray's Needs

Adience Vectors (positive needs)		Abience Vectors (negative needs)
	Viscerogenic	
n Inspiration		n Expiration
n Water		n Urination
n Food		n Defecation
n Sentience		*n Noxavoidance*
n Sex		n Heatavoidance
n Lactation		n Coldavoidance
		n Harmavoidance
	Psychogenic	
n Achievement		n Autonomy
n Affiliation		n Inviolacy
n Succorance		n Blamavoidance
n Order		n Infavoidance
n Dominance		n Contrarience
n Exhibition		
n Aggression		
n Abasement		

BOX 15.1   Are You Avoidant/Withdrawn or Approaching/Attached?

Murray's needs may be cast into two broad categories: *avoidant/withdrawn (abience)*, avoiding objects and people or withdrawing from them, and *approaching/attached (adience)*, approaching objects and people or submissively/controllingly attaching oneself to them. Examine all of the psychogenic needs and the italicized viscerogenic needs in Table 15.1: 9 Adience and 7 Abience. Honestly decide which are prominent among the needs that typically drive you. Check off all of the ones you choose. Where does the balance lie? If 66 percent or more of your choices fit in the Adience category you may score yourself as approaching/attaching. For example, if you checked 10 needs, and 7 of them (6.6 rounded up) were in the Adience category, you may be regarded as approaching/attached. On the other hand, if 55 percent or more of your choices fall in the Abience category, you are better characterized as avoidant/withdrawn (for example, if you made 11 choices and 6 were in the Abience category). If you fail to meet either percentage criterion, you fit in neither the approaching/attached nor the avoidant/withdrawn categories. Of course, this is an exercise. Attach no special meaning to being in either category; neither is necessarily good or bad. However, if you are at one extreme or the other, you may examine your behavior in the future and decide that a better balance would be better for you.

Periodicity, Strength of Needs, and Interactions among Them

Strength

The **strength** of a need is measured in terms of its frequency, intensity, and duration (Murray, 1981a). A need may be considered strong because it occurs under given conditions with great regularly: high frequency. It may also be considered strong if it occurs occasionally with great intensity. Of course, a need is strong if it is persistent—when it is aroused, it continues to endure for a long time in the absence of satisfaction.

Periodicity

Periodicity refers to rhythms of activity and rest. There are periods during which certain needs are aroused and demand satisfaction, and periods during which those needs are quiescent. Viscerogenic needs are quite prone to periodicity. Everyone is familiar with the rise and fall of needs for food and sex. Psychogenic needs also show some tendency to periodicity. A person may alternate between "sociability and solitude, talking and listening, leading and following, helping and being helped, giving and getting, work and play" (p. 161).

The cycles of arousal and quiescence are divided into three phases. After satisfaction of a need, there is a **refractory period** during which no incentive will arouse the need. Following some time lapse, there is an **inducible period** during which the need is inactive but susceptible to excitation by appropriate stimulation. Finally, there is an **active period** during which the need is aroused and determining behavior of the organism.

If a need is somewhat vaguely perceived by a person, it may perseverate for some time after it is aroused. In this case, the need will be in a state of high inducibility or readiness and will be characterized by a low threshold to stimulation. Suppose the individual has feelings of anger (n Aggression) the source of which is unclear. These feelings may persist for as long as it takes to find some target against whom the pent up anger may be vented. The person in question is the proverbial "ticking time bomb." He or she will "go off" on the first individual who is so unlucky as to cross his or her path. That unfortunate individual will be a *substitute* for the real source of the anger.

Interrelation of Needs

During everyday life, an individual may experience the arousal of several needs, either all at once or in succession. Consequently, it is common to observe a person take a particular course of action that is designed to satisfy several needs. Like Maslow, Murray believed that people are complicated; they rarely do anything for just one reason.

Fusion of needs is Murray's name for a single "action pattern that satisfies two or more needs at the same time" (p. 161). An example would be an individual who gets paid to sing a solo in public (F n AcqExh). The person is satisfying n Acquisition—making money—while also taking care of n Exhibition—getting attention from others.

Subsidiation of needs occurs "when one or more needs are activated in the service of [one or more other needs]" (p. 161). In the following sequence, each need is subsidiary to the succeeding need, with the last mentioned need (n Achievement) being the most prominent: the one served by all the rest.

> *A politician removes a spot from his suit (n Noxavoidance) because he does not wish to make a bad impression (n Infavoidance), and thus diminish his chances of winning the approval and friendship of Mr. X (n Affiliation), from whom he hopes to obtain some slanderous facts (n Cognizance) relating to the private life of his political rival, Mr. Y, information which he plans to publish (n Exposition) in order to damage the reputation of Mr. Y (n Aggression) and thus assure his own election of office (n Achievement): (n Nox S n Inf S n Aff S n Cog S n Exp S n Agg S n Ach). [The need preceding the "S" is subsidiary to the one following the "S."] (p. 162)*

Contrafactions of Needs
Contrafactions of needs are cases where needs are related to their opposites in alternating phases. For example, "A phase of Dominance is succeeded by a phase of Deference. A wave of Aggression is followed by a wave of Nurturance . . . Abstinence follows Indulgence. . . etc." (p. 163). A person who is a Napoleon at work, is a groveling serf at home.

Conflicts of Needs
Conflicts of needs occur when needs oppose each other "within the personality, giving rise when prolonged to harassing spiritual dilemmas" (p. 163). "A woman hesitates to satisfy her passion because of the disapproval of her family (n Sex-C-n Blamavoidance) . . . A man hesitates to satisfy his desire to fly an airplane because of fear (n Achievement-C-n Harmavoidance)" (p. 163; "C" = "conflict"). These oppositions balance needs so that one or the other does not get out of hand.

Need Integrates (Complexes)

Needs may form the core of structures that, in turn, are central components of the personality. A critical predecessor to the formation of these core structures is **cathexis**, a process by which an object evokes a need. The object may be "cathected" by the need or the person with the need (Murray borrowed this concept from Freud). If the object is present, the need is likely to be aroused. "Objects" can be either inanimate entities or people. Common cathexes, with objects listed first and the cathected (c) needs second, are: garbage (c Noxavoidance); lighting (c Harmavoidance); doctor (c Succorance); sobbing child (c Nurturance); hero (c Deference); autocrat (c Autonomy).

A **need integrate** or **complex** is formed when "traces (images) of cathected objects in familiar settings become integrated in the mind with the needs and emotions which they customarily excite, as well as with the images of preferred modes" (actones or other means of creating satisfaction; p. 179). Integrates are much more abstract than needs, and thus harder to put into words. They are recurrent phenomena that fill our dreams, hallucinations, illusions, and delusions. A complex may come to consciousness (or unconsciousness) because of an encounter with an object that resembles the images with which it is integrated. For example, a bird floating effortlessly in the air may be cathected by the need to be free (n Automony). If so, the person with the complex would be expected to dream of birds flying and to see them as illusions when they are not actually present (in wallpaper; in the tree leaves; in sidewalk cracks). Complexes differ one from the other mainly in regard to the needs, modes (actones), and stimuli that compose them. The personality might be thought of as a "hierarchical system of . . . need complexes" were it not for Murray's belief that such a picture of personality is incomplete without an account of environmental influences (p. 183).

Need integrates or complexes manifest themselves in various forms, not just in dreams. For example, complexes show up in artistic expression and creation, drama, ritual, religion, fantasies, desires and temptations, fiction, fairy tales, plays and movies, art objects, and even child (or adult) play. At a more global rather than individual level, cultures can be sources of complexes. One may see complexes manifested in the art objects, stories, and religious practices that are part and parcel of a culture. Notice that need integrates appear to be more like the archetypes of Jung than Freud's "complexes."

Environmental Press

Unlike some theorists, Murray neglects nothing inside or outside the person. Thus, he devotes considerable space to the environment in which the person is embedded, although more is reserved for needs and other internal entities.

The environmental factors that influence the person are called **press**, which designate a directional tendency in the object or situation ("press" is also plural). Unlike the cathexis of an object, which *makes the individual do* something or other, ". . . *press* of an object is what it can *do to the subject* [person] or *for the subject*—the power that it has to affect the well-being of the subject in one way or another" (Murray, 1981a, p. 187). "Everything that can supposedly harm or benefit the well-being of an organism may be considered *pressive*, everything else is *inert*" (p. 185).

A press may be a sign of things to come. Individuals often actually perceive the pressive object, but they infrequently think of the object in the present tense: the object is now "doing this or that to me." Rather, the individual anticipates: "The object may do this or that to me (if I remain passive) or I may use the object in this or that way (if I become active)" (p. 185). However, Murray is quick to point out that press are not entirely anticipatory. Very often aspects of the present situation excite images of past pressive situations. These images allow the individual to operate smoothly and effectively relative to present press, because the person has past experience to act as a guide.

Press may be *mobile* or *immobile* and *positive* or *negative*. Positive press are enjoyable and beneficial. Negative press are distasteful or harmful or both. Mobile

BOX 15.2   Are Dreams Clairvoyant?

If complexes are at all like archetypes, they may relate to themes repeated over and over in human history. This repetition suggests that "history repeats itself." Should such be the case, manifestations of complexes, as may occur in dreams, might predict future events. Thus, past events of a certain nature that are reflected in complexes and manifested in dreams may foretell future events of the same nature. Conceivably, a case in point may be instances of kidnapping/murders. Because kidnapping/murders have occurred many times in human history, they are a part of human lore. Therefore, they may become the basis for complexes shared by people. Given this line of reasoning, people's dreams may predict the details of an actual kidnapping/murder.

Murray (1981c) capitalized on a much publicized event in order to ascertain whether dreams are clairvoyant, that is, able to predict future events. A few days after the baby of famous aviator Charles Lindbergh was kidnapped, but before any details of the crime were known to the public, Murray placed an ad in a newspaper to solicit descriptions of dreams relating to the crime. Some 1300 people responded.

The facts of the case were that the baby had *died* instantly after suffering blows to the head resulting in *three fractures of the skull.* Its *naked body* was found in a *shallow grave* in some *woods* near a *road* several miles from the Lindbergh home. An ex-convict of German extraction was later convicted of the crime.

Of the 1300 dreams many did contain references to "foreigners" or "foreign accents." This outcome was probably due to suspicion of foreigners that was rampant in the United States at the time of the crime (1932). However, in only about 5 percent of the dreams did the baby appear dead. Further, only 10 dreams were at all accurate in predicting the details of the crime when those became known. Seven dreams referred to the baby as deceased, and two others implied as much. Five of the 10 dreams made definite references to the wooded locale where the body was found. Five referred to a grave, two of them indicating that it was shallow. Three dreams referred to a road near where the baby was found, and another implied that a road was nearby. One dream indicated explicitly that the baby was naked, another implied nakedness, and in a third, the baby was clothed only in a diaper. Of the 10 dreamers, 3 claimed they had their dreams before the kidnaping had even occurred. Two of the three included mention of the Lindberghs, one also referred to "woods," and the one without mention of the Lindberghs did refer to a "roadside" and "diaper only." Only 3 of the 10 dreams included death, a grave, and a wooded locale.

The very fact that the dreams were collected argues that Murray endorsed the *possibility* that dreams are clairvoyant. Therefore, it is a tribute to his objectivity that he drew negative conclusions regarding the ability of dreams to predict the future. He correctly interpreted results as due to happenstance: by chance one would expect 10 (or more) of 1300 dreams to contain some accurate information relating to the facts of the crime as revealed later.

press are moving forces that may have beneficial or detrimental effects on the person. Examples are animals or people. Mobile press may be *autonomous,* meaning the object initiates an activity. A positive, mobile press in the autonomous category would be a sympathetic mother. A positive mobile press can also be *docile,* meaning regulated by the person. A servant is an example. "A *negative mobile* press would be exemplified by lightning, a storm at sea, a carnivorous beast . . ." (p. 186).

By contrast, "immobile press can have no effect unless the [person] approaches, manipulates, or influences them in some way (. . . a glass of water)" (p. 186). *Positive immobile* press are often inorganic objects such as nourishing food, or shelter, or toys, or money. *Negative immobile* press include quicksand, a barrier or poison ivy, any inert object about which the person might say, "It is dangerous . . . it cannot be used" (p. 186). Figure 15.1 illustrates this facet of press.

Press may also be distinguished in another important way. They may be **alpha**, press that actually exist, that is, are objectively verifiable. Alternatively, they may be **beta**, press that are determined by the person's own interpretation, that is, subjectively determined. A press (alpha) may, in fact, be favorably disposed toward a person. It may, however, be viewed (beta) by the person as detrimental. An example would be an objectively friendly person who is seen as belittling. When there is a great discrepancy between alpha and beta, the person is said to be laboring under a delusion.

Table 15.2 contains some examples of press. Notice that some of the same names applied to needs are also used for press.

Thema

Needs and press are internal and external entities, respectively. In view of Murray's holistic position and his inclination to see all factors relating to the individual as integrated, one would expect that he would see a way to merge needs and press. Indeed he did. A **thema** is a combination of a particular need and a particular press or pressive object. In the case of thema, some object is present that holds promise to do something to the person or for the person thereby generating a need

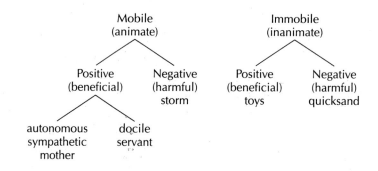

FIGURE 15.1   Properties of Press

TABLE 15.2   Press

p Affiliation	object is a friendly, sociable companion
p Nurturance	object is a protective, sympathetic ally
p Aggression	object is a combative person, one who censures, or one who belittles
p Rival(recognition of)	object is a competitor
p Lack(economic)	object is the condition of poverty
p Dominance	object is a restraining, prohibiting, or imprisoning person

consistent with it. Examples include: a friendly, sociable companion is present, resulting in the activation of n Affiliation (p Affiliation > n Affiliation); a combative, belittling person is present evoking n Aggression (p Aggression > n Aggression); a restraining, prohibiting person is present giving rise to n Dominance (p Dominance > n Dominance). Often a press leads to the activation of a need that reciprocates it, opposes it, or compensates for it: a rejecting person may inspire the rise of n Rejection resulting in reciprocity of rejection; a dominating person initiates n Autonomy; a belittling person initiates n Achievement.

Evaluation

Contributions

Needs
One of Murray's two lasting contributions to the field of personality is definitely his needs. A description of the uses to which Murray's needs have been put by numerous researchers and theorists would fill an entire, separate book. Here there is space to mention only a long-term use and a current research example.

Douglas N. Jackson's Personality Research Form (PRF) is a personality-trait measure based on Murray's needs (Jackson, 1984). Twenty of those needs are translated rather directly into 20 trait scales. After three revisions of the PRF manual, Jackson's measure ranks "as the fourth most frequently cited personality test in the psychological research literature" (Paunonen, Jackson, & Keinonen, 1990). Such a high level of use virtually guarantees that Murray's needs will remain in the mainstream of personality research and theory for an indefinite period of time.

Sampo Paunonen, Jackson, and Mirja Keinonen (1990) have recently expanded the PRF in a very interesting and useful fashion. They translated the 20 trait scales into a nonverbal form consisting of stick-figure illustrations depicting some trait and accompanied by the instruction, "Estimate the likelihood that [you] would engage in the type of behavior shown" (p. 486). Research subjects respond to the instruction by marking a scale with points representing different degrees of likelihood that they would perform the behavior depicted. For example, one illustration shows a frowning tennis player breaking a tennis racket after having missed a return. It is intended to measure the trait "aggression" (based on n Aggression). Subjects look at the illustration and mark a scale point that represents the likelihood they would perform the behavior depicted, breaking the racket.

Paunonen and colleagues (1990) showed that the nonverbal version correlated acceptably with the verbal form of the PRF in both Canadian and Finnish subjects. This and other evidence points to the validity of the new nonverbal PRF. Other evidence indicates that it is also reliable. The nonverbal PRF should be invaluable in the study of personality functioning in a variety of cultures, because it can be administered in the same form to people of each culture without loss and distortion due to translation into various languages. It will also be useful with children who are too young to respond to the verbal form and people who cannot read.

A study by Jefferson Singer (1990) illustrates the flexibility of Murray's needs. While the work of Jackson and his colleagues shows how the needs can be translated into "traits," Singer's work demonstrates how they can be re-conceived as "life goals." In Singer's study, 16 of Murray's needs were interpreted as "life goals" (the 16 needs were covered in 15 statements, because two needs were combined into one statement). For example, one goal statement was, "I would like to be a leader and sway others to my opinion" (based on n Dominance; p. 541). Another was, "I would like to have as sensual and erotic a life as possible" (based on n Sentience and n Sex combined; p. 541).

Subjects looked at each of the 15 statements and for each recalled a personal memory suggested by it. Each memory thus elicited was rated on the affect (feelings) it evoked using a 20-point scale where +10 was maximum positive affect and −10 was maximum negative affect. Each memory was also rated on a similar scale concerning its relevance in attaining the goal represented by the statement that evoked it. For example, in response to "I would like to be watched and marvelled at by others"—based on n Exhibition—a subject might recall, "At age 11, I went to church in a new dress Grammy made me and it seemed like everyone was watching me." In turn this memory might have received a +8 for positive affect and a +9 indicating it greatly facilitated attaining the life goal "exhibition."

Results showed that affective responses to memories (feelings evoked by memories) were substantially correlated with memories' relevance to goal attainment (achieving life goals, each of which corresponds to one of Murray's needs). Singer concluded, "The more relevant the subjects' memories were to the attainment of the goals that cued them, the more positive their affective responses to those memories were" (p. 545). A memory that is seen as facilitating the attainment of a life goal is likely to be associated with positive feelings.

The Thematic Apperception Test (TAT)

Murray's second timeless contribution was development of a much-used projective test, the **Thematic Apperception Test (TAT),** an instrument for assessing a person's self-reflective perceptions (apperceptions) revealing thema that are evoked by some ambiguous pictures (Murray, 1981d). With use of the TAT, research subjects or clinical clients are told that they are participating in a "test of creative imagination" (p.

A photo of a TAT being administered.

391). Then, one at a time, they are shown each of 20 (or more) pictures mounted on cards, such as a boy with a violin, a woman holding a man, and a girl with a doll. Subjects or clients are asked to "make up a plot or story" about each picture (p. 391). To assist them, they are asked some questions: "What is the relation of the individuals in the picture? What has happened to them? What are their present thoughts and feelings? What will be the outcome?" (p. 391).

The advantages of the TAT revolve around the claim that the subject/client can interpret the pictures in innumerable ways, because they are inherently ambiguous. Thus, whatever the subject/client says about the pictures comes from his or her own unique mind (usually assumed to be the unconscious mind). These advantages include extraction of responses from subjects/clients that are spontaneous and relatively uncontaminated by any cues provided by researcher or clinician. Such responses are rich with information, can be mined to great depths, and may provide a glimpse of the unconscious that cannot be achieved otherwise.

The narratives provided by subjects/clients have been scored in various ways. In early uses, these stories were analyzed informally and subjectively by the test administrator (Murray, 1981d). Analysis of a card usually involved the card as a whole, rather than each individual human figure on the card (Allen & Potkay, 1983a). Beginning around 1949 researchers began to obtain data that allowed more concrete, less subjective means of analyzing narratives inspired by pictures. The most frequent responses were catalogued so that future users of the TAT could check to determine whether a client or subject was providing a typical or atypical response to a given card. Cards were rated using various scales and scaling techniques to determine the degree to which they suggested achievement, aggression, sex, and other needs or thema.

While these efforts helped to objectify TAT analysis, scoring was still somewhat haphazard and unsystematic. To begin improvement, Charles R. Potkay listed major problems: (1) total cards are typically considered despite the fact that a given card may contain two figures that contribute to stories in different, even opposite, ways; (2) when objective methods are used to aid analysis, scales are employed that may limit subjects' or clients' responses or suggest to them how they should respond; and (3) when more objective methods are used, they usually involve only a few needs/thema achievement and aggression, for example, rather than the many needs/thema subjects/clients may have had in mind while making responses (Allen & Potkay, 1983a).

To remedy these deficiencies, Potkay and his colleagues had subjects generate any words that came to their minds when they looked at single figures, rather than whole cards (see Potkay, Merrens, & Allen, 1979, in Allen & Potkay, 1983a). With this method, called the Adjective Generation Technique (AGT), (1) single figures are considered, (2) problems with scaling techniques are avoided, and (3) subjects can use any terms contained in their vast repertoires of words.

Sixty male and 60 female subjects viewed 17 male and 17 female figures featured on 22 cards and then described each with three words. The instruction "write down [some number of] words" defines the AGT (Allen & Potkay, 1983a; Potkay & Allen, 1988). Table 15.3 contains a sampling of the figures investigated, and, for each, the three words used most frequently.

TABLE 15.3   Descriptions of Figures and Words Most Frequently Used in Description of Them (% of Subjects Using Word in Brackets)

TAT Figure	Three Most Used Adjectives
Boy with violin	bored [42], tired [32], sleepy [25]
Woman with books	pretty [18], young [18], intelligent [11]
Man working in fields	strong [43], hardworking [30], muscular [28]
Woman downcast	sad [25], upset [17], depressed [14]
Man holding woman	angry [34], mad [12], determined [10]
Woman holding man	loving [26], pleading [14], concerned [8]
Woman with back turned	old [31], sad [16], hurt [11]
Man looking down	worried [20], young [16], sad [11]
Man with pipe	angry [12], mean [8], domineering [8]
Man with gray hair	old [38], wise [22], understanding [13]
Girl with doll	young [28], bored [25], uninterested [9]
Woman daydreaming	thoughtful [19], thinking [10], wondering [10]
Woman on beach	scared [18], hurried [17], frightened [12]
Man embracing woman	loving [45], happy [14], old [10]
Boy sitting	lonely [45], young [21], poor [18]
Woman nude	dead [37], tired [13], exhausted [12]
Man silhouetted	lonely [15], searching [14], alone [13]
Man at lamp post	lonely [25], alone [18], old [10]

BOX 15.3   Clinical Analysis Using the TAT

Murray (1981d), with the assistance of Christiana Morgan, wrote an article illustrating the use of the TAT by reference to narratives produced by an undergraduate in response to cards. The student, called "B," was emphasizing music in his studies. The young man tended to be deferential and submissive to those he respected. B constantly squinted his eyes as if a photographer's flashbulb had just been triggered in his presence, giving him the appearance of puzzled anxiety. His overall demeanor was that of an "unobtrusive, banal" individual (p. 402). B came to the clinic because certain images were intruding on his reading. These unsettling visions would prevent him from retaining the meaning of the words he was reading, but not the impressions of the printed page. Thus, he lost the sense of what he was reading, but his unfailing recollection of the printed pages allowed him to get high marks on exams.

These images seemed at first glance to be as bland as the individual they tormented. He saw scenes from his distant past, such as pastures and brooks, buildings, and woods, and some from his recent past, including Harvard Square and the Boston State House. Nothing from B's autobiography, or the information he provided during the intake interview, hinted at an explanation of his symptoms. He had been brought up in a proper, Southern Methodist family by parents he regarded with equal favor. However, he tended to be more like his morally "right" father in general disposition if not in emotional intensity: the father had an explosive temper. His mother apparently nagged him often, but also showed him lavish affection. There was a younger sibling, a sister with whom he frequently quarreled. As a

child he was quite timid and prone to numerous fears. B shied away from water and animals. He was fearful of automobile accidents, and periodically dreamed of being chased by a bull.

B's self-description confirmed his timidity and included sensitivity, reticence, avoidance of athletics, and feelings of inferiority. The disclosure of frequent doll-play sessions with his sister until age 9, unusual neatness, and extreme sensitivity to smells seemed an unconscious effort to portray an effeminate nature.

Thoughts of death often plagued him, particularly after seeing a man killed in a fall from a hayrick. These fears were reinforced when he was comforted at his grandmother's funeral upon breaking into tears. Sex was alien to him: he did not masturbate until age 18, had still not experienced intercourse, and was appalled upon contemplating that his parents had done what a cousin described that farm animals do to produce offspring. According to Murray, "He held a theory of anal intercourse. He told of several experiences of fellatio occurring at about the age of 10, but said that there had been none since" (p. 403). As a child he slept with his father while his mother slept with his sister on the same porch.

In response to the card "the nude figure of a man clinging to a pole", B called the figure a "sailor" who scaled his ship's mast in an escape attempt made after having been chased from his cabin because of "some morbid . . . homosexual crime" (p. 403). He is shot down by a fellow sailor. Four months later, after psychoanalysis, he altered the story by indicating that the sailor climbed the

Continued

BOX 15.3   *Continued*

mast in an insane effort to escape the horror of his unsuccessful attempt at homosexual relations. His face "distorted and
carnal" he hurled himself into the sea (p.
403). The card "man clinging to a rope"
inspired similar fears of being trapped on
a precariously high perch, but no allu-
sions to homosexuality. Murray noted the
"obvious" homosexual themes of the first
two stories, and manifestations of B's
admitted fear of heights in all three.

To the "boy with violin," B responded with a tale of musical triumph
at a recital, but spoils the achievement by
declaring that the boy subsequently loses
"hands or fingers" and has to abandon
music. Murray depicted this latter
tragedy in his thema notation: p Injury >
n Achievement [failure] theme. After
psychoanalysis, B gave a more neutral
description of the boy with violin.

When confronted with "boy hud-
dled against a couch," B said the youngster had flown into a rage and shot a
horse or dog, thus his current state of
remorse. He related that, as a child, he
had directly participated in brutality to
animals (beatings) as well as vicariously
participated (decapitation). After psychoanalysis, the emphasis in his story
was less on brutality and more on the figure being remorseful and having learned
a lesson. Murray saw themes of self-pun-
ishment, castration anxiety, sadism, and
bestiality in B's narrative.

To the card "girl standing alone," B
responded, "Girl about to be attacked by
a demented person. She has gone on a
picnic with him. A coming storm
increases the carnal instincts of the boy.
He attacks the girl" (p. 404). To the card
"malicious-looking man grasping the
arm of a young girl [who recoils in ter-
ror]," B offered, "When the time comes
he takes her to attack her . . ." (p. 404).
Based on this story, as well as a remem-

bered movie in which a scientist fills a
woman's veins with ossifying material,
and a recollection of a movie hero's wife
dying in childbirth, Murray suggested
that B was prone to fantasies of women
being killed during intercourse or childbirth. These stories of girls being
attacked also hinted at a sadistic heterosexual orientation.

B was also given some of the
Rorschach Inkblots. In one he saw a man
looking at a medical book in which there
is an illustration of a dissected male or
female. In another, a man is seen engaging in a sexual act in which the object
addressed sexually is an embryo or a
part of a miscarriage. Murray indicated
that necrophilia is implied. B also was
asked to write a story and responded
with a tale of a minister who returns
home to find his brother in "compromis-
ing circumstances" with a woman (p.
405).

Murray's overall conclusion regarding B was that the young man felt guilt
over and fear of homosexuality. He also
showed evidence of anal sadism,
masochism, and a castration complex.
His castration anxiety may have
stemmed from having had his first nocturnal emission while sleeping in contact
with his enormous, temperamental
father, possibly the bull of his dreams.
He also showed womb fantasies, sadistic
trends, and necrophilia. B fantasied
about pregnancy and tried to picture
himself in his mother's womb. Once he
dreamed of opening a woman up and
filling her womb with straw. Another
time he fantasized that he was pregnant.
To build in masochism, just after the
pregnancy fantasy, he became constipated and lay doubled up on the floor
groaning with abdominal pain. The
necrophilic and anal themes were manifested in his "most exciting fantasy" dur-

BOX 15.3   *Continued*

ing which he opened one grave after another performing anal intercourse with each corpse in turn (p. 407). It seemed to Murray that birth, death, and sexual intercourse were closely linked in B's mind.

Table 15.3 entries will give you a good idea of the pictures contained in the TAT and their nature as defined by the most frequently used descriptive words. Note that because gender made no difference, percentages are for all 120 subjects.

Considering that subjects could choose any words from the many hundreds available to each of them, agreement among them on descriptions is remarkable. Averaged across figures, the percent of subjects who agreed on most frequently used words was 28. For second most used words it was 16 and for words used third most it was 12. For eight of the 34 figures agreement for most frequent words was greater than 40 percent to just less than 50 percent (in one case it was 52 percent). Obviously subjects were seeing much the same thing in these figures, indicating that they have definite meaning to people.

There were certain themes running through the figures. They tended to be old, and sad, but if they were male, they were angry and lonely, and if female, loving and nurturing (for example, motherly and concerned; remember not all the figures are included in Table 15.3). The adjectives that subjects generated were also scored on FAVorability, ANXiety, and FEMininity. "Man embracing woman" came out on top in terms of FAV. The figure reflecting the highest ANX was "woman on beach." "Woman holding man" was most FEM. Another analysis indicated that FAV and ANX were inversely related. AGT research has tended to find that the higher the FAV, the lower the ANX (Allen & Potkay, 1983a; Potkay & Allen, 1988).

Because the TAT was developed during a time characterized by more open sexism than exists today, male and female figures were compared statistically on FAV. Contrary to expectations based on sexism, results showed that females were more favorably described.

It is interesting to note the emotional tone that emerges from the figures included on the TAT cards: they are melancholy, sad and depressed, reflective, and lonely as a whole, just as their chief selector, Murray, was afflicted by a "marrow of misery and melancholy." Once again it is clear that the TAT cards are not entirely neutral with regard to the kinds of emotions and themes that they suggest.

Box 15.3 describes an actual, clinical use of the TAT cards. It will provide you with further insight into the nature of the TAT, as well as some examples of cards, figures, and responses to them, along with Murray's analysis. You may also find the individual who is analyzed to be quite interesting.

Limitations

Shortcomings of Murray's point of view and methods fall into four categories: (1) he pulled many of his critical concepts off the top of his head without input from previous research or theory; (2) he failed to differentiate his concepts from other similar notions; (3) he attempted to explain everything; and (4) his methodologies, most especially those associated with the TAT, were loose, informal, and intuitive, rather than scientific.

Murray's narcissism apparently affected his thinking. He imbued his ideas with an aura of self-evident truth as soon as he conceived of them, even though they often seemed not to have been inspired by scientific theory or data that pre-existed them. As soon as ideas occurred to him, he wrote of them as fact, without evoking other sources in support, except as after-the-fact citations to confirm what he already believed (Murray, 1981a). The lone, possible exception was the case of Freud. Although often evoked after-the-fact, Freud is so frequently mentioned in regard to Murray's ideas that have a clear psychoanalytic flavor, one can readily believe Freud was the source of those notions. Excluding Freud's influence, one is left with the impression that some of Murray's important concepts came "out of the blue," or out of his self-proclaimed intuitive genius, not from scientific data or theory. Ideas treated as if they stem from scientific thought, but in fact do not, may be more appropriately placed in the realm of philosophy.

At some points in his writings, Murray seems almost confused about the nature of his ideas. Are needs actually drives? Are they really traits of personality? If Murray could not decide, he was not alone. Indecision may have also character-ized his followers who used his needs. As indicated earlier, Jackson (1984) thinks of needs as "traits" and Singer (1990) conceives of them as "goals." Concepts are scientifically useful only in so far as they are clearly distinct from other concepts (Allen & Potkay, 1981; 1983b). Consistent with this lack of clear differentiation among concepts, some of his ideas do not fit well into appropriate categories. For example, n Play, to relax, amuse oneself, seek diversion and entertainment, was not included in Table 15.1, because it does not clearly fit under Adience or Abience vectors. What exactly Murray was talking about remains unclear.

Murray felt obligated to explain everything and reconcile his point of view with everyone else's position (1981a). He mentioned many of the popular concepts of his day, either rejecting them and asserting that his ideas were better or squaring them with his own. Thus, he attempted to reconcile some of his ideas with those of Skinner, but he rejected Watson's position out of hand. No theory can handle everything. Those that try almost always explain nothing very precisely.

Murray made so much of his disdain for scientism in psychology that he alien-ated his colleagues in experimental psychology. So thorough was his rejection of them and their methods that one wonders whether the former biochemist aban-doned science altogether. The TAT is a good case in point. Murray guided his col-leagues in more or less arbitrarily selecting TAT pictures. What he finally decided on were hardly the ambiguous figures appropriate to a projective test. Potkay and colleagues have shown them to be gender biased, females favored over males, and invested with definite meaning that is shared by subjects (See Allen & Potkay, 1983a; Potkay & Allen, 1988). Further, for many years, scoring of the TAT was unsystematic to the point that the quantitative methods so dear to science could not be used. Murray himself (1981d) tended to ramble in analyzing TAT narratives, revealing no particular system and often drawing unclear conclusions. Later more systematic methods were developed, but as Potkay indicates, these fall short of providing for fully valid and reliable interpretations.

Conclusions

Despite his much celebrated narcissism—and it probably was real—Murray was a warm and kind person who inspired the love and admiration of countless psychologists. As a measure of his impact, tributes to him began *before* he died. It is obvious from reading them that he touched the professional and personal lives of many colleagues. True, many of his ideas may have been off the top of the head, and his needs may not have been well differentiated from other concepts. However, the measure of a theorist's contribution is often more in how much he or she inspires others to new professional heights than whether the theorist's ideas as originally proposed were without flaws. As for the TAT, no one can deny its historical significance: it is one of the most cited and used tests ever. Rather than a fault, some would consider it a virtue that TAT output might be understood mainly by intuition. Clinical intuition may be a better tool for helping real people than all the products of scientific methodology in the world.

Summary Points

1. Henry A. Murray was the child of wealthy parents who sent him to the best preparatory school and to Harvard. His life was shaped by his lack of respect for his father and alienation from his mother: throughout his life he fought stuttering and a "marrow of misery and melancholy." As an adult he developed a sense of "specialness" and a distinct narcissistic orientation. These inclinations led him to distrust male colleagues, dismiss others' points of view, and find one woman insufficient.

2. After graduating with an M.D. and a Ph.D. in biochemistry, and spending several weeks with Jung in the interim, he assisted the head of the Harvard Psychological Clinic and immediately ran afoul of his "scientistic" colleagues. Drawn to psychology because of his personal problems, he pursued his own brand of "psychoanalysis." He became a primary mover in the Boston Psychoanalytic Society and underwent psychotherapy, but got little from it except reinforcement for his belief in the unconscious.

3. Murray believed that internal representations are regnant, related to "dominant configuration in the brain." To him, a need is a force in the brain that transforms an unsatisfying situation into a more satisfying one. He considered need to be nearly synonymous with drive and also overlapping with trait. One need category is called viscerogenic, and is further segmented into positive, for example, n Water, n Sentience, and negative, for example, n Expiration, n Noxavoidance. The other category is psychogenic, which is segmented into positive (the adience vector), for example, n Achievement and n Affiliation, and negative (the abience vector), for example, n Autonomy and n Contrarience.

4. Needs can be specified in terms of strength and periodicity. They have refractory periods during which they cannot be aroused, inducible periods during which they can, and active periods during which they determine behavior. In fusion of needs there is an "action pattern that satisfies two or more needs at the same time." Subsidiation of needs occurs "when one or more needs are activated in the service of another need" and contrafactions of needs are cases where needs alternate with their opposites. Conflicts of needs are cases where needs oppose each other.

5. A need integrate or complex is formed when images of cathected objects become mentally integrated with needs, emotions, and modes (actones) that they typically excite. Complexes are recurrent phenomena that fill our dreams, hallucinations, illusions, and delusions. They may also be manifested in artistic expression, drama, religion, fantasies, plays, and movies. While they may seem to allow clairvoyance through dreams, Murray found no evidence to support that connection.

6. Press "do to the subject" or "for the subject" and often are referred to in the future tense: "It may do this or that to me." Press may be mobile or immobile and positive or negative. In addition, positive mobile press may be autonomous or docile. Finally, press may be alpha, objectively verifiable, or beta, a product of subjective interpretation. A thema is a combination of a particular need and a particular press or pressive object.

7. Jackson's much used Personality Research Form (PRF) is a trait measure based on Murray's needs. Recently it has been translated into a nonverbal form that will be useful for cross-cultural research. Murray's needs have also been profitably translated into "life goals" in Singer's research. He showed that memories seen as facilitating the attainment of life goals are likely to be associated with positive feelings.

8. The Thematic Apperception Test (TAT) consists of one or more human figures mounted on cards. Research subjects/clients are asked to look at each card and then tell a story about it. Potkay and colleagues advanced previous attempts to discover information that would aid analysis of responses to the TAT cards. They used the AGT and showed that figures had definite, shared meaning for subjects: females were more favorably depicted, and the tone of the figures was melancholy.

9. Using the TAT, Murray analyzed B, a student who came from an upright, Southern Methodist family ruled by his large, temperamental father with whom he slept as a boy. As a child B was plagued by thoughts of death, portrayed himself as effeminate and fearful, and reported what were regarded as homosexual experiences. Themes in B's narratives evoked by TAT cards included homosexuality, anality, heterosexual sadism, masochism, and necrophilia. Murray concluded that birth, death, and sexual intercourse were closely linked in B's mind.

10. Limitations of Murray's point of view include: (1) his tendency to pull concepts off the top of his head; (2) his failure to differentiate his concepts from other similar notions; (3) his attempts to explain everything; and his (4) intuitive methodologies, especially regarding the TAT. Despite these shortcomings, Murray, the subject of several tributes even before his death, inspired many psychologists to develop his concepts in meaningful ways. The TAT and his needs stand as monuments to his intuitive genius.

Running Comparison

Theorist	Murray in Comparison
Freud	He used Freudian language and was a defender of psychoanalysis. He believed in the unconscious and the importance of sexuality.
Skinner	Like Skinner, he emphasized the "push from the rear" and the importance of the effect of an action, not its particular form.
Horney	n Succorance is like her unresolved basic anxiety and n Abasement is like her masochistic submission.
Sullivan	Like Sullivan, he was interpersonally oriented.
Maslow	Like Maslow, he believed humans to be dynamic wholes who rarely respond to one need at a time. Need was also central to Maslow, but only Murray said need is equivalent to drive.
Jung	Need integrates were like Jung's archetypes.
Gordon Allport	Like Allport, Murray also studied individuals rather than groups and ignored sensory elements and conditioned responses in favor of personality characteristics.

Essay/Critical Thinking Questions

1. How was Murray different from Maslow in the way he reacted to his mother? How were they the same in that reaction?

2. Can you argue that one can solve her or his own problems by becoming a psychologist? What is the counterargument?

3. Could you argue that studying the "long unit," the entire life history of the "organism," is the best way to understand people in general? Why is it better than "taking snapshots"—working piecemeal?

4. Did Maslow borrow from Murray? His major works did follow Murray's. What is it about the viscerogenic and psychogenic needs that might have given Maslow his idea about the "hierarchy of needs?"

5. Can you choose a couple of Murray's needs and join them by fusion (fusion of needs)? In so doing, use real life examples.

6. Can you identify a need integrate or complex that is shared by so many people in our society that it shows up in books and movies? Give some examples of its manifestations in the entertainment media.

7. Can you list some press that affect us regularly? Try to list some in addition to those in Table 15.2.

8. Can you give some examples of thema that regularly are seen in your interactions with other people? Use Murray's notation.

9. What else is wrong with the TAT in addition to those problems uncovered by Potkay and his colleagues? Look at Table 15.3 to see what you can discover.

10. Look again at B's reactions to TAT picture-cards. Can you come up with different interpretations of B's narratives than those provided by Murray?

16

THE FACTOR ANALYTIC APPROACH TO PERSONALITY TRAITS: RAYMOND CATTELL AND HANS EYSENCK

- Can people with "hard science" training do better psychological research than those whose backgrounds are entirely in psychology?
- In building a theory, should one collect data first, allow hypotheses to emerge from the data, and test the hypotheses with more data, or start with theory, derive hypotheses, and then test them through data collection?
- Do your genes determine your personality and your intelligence?
- Can how strongly you salivate to lemon juice say anything about your personality?
- Can personality be reduced to just three dimensions?

As you have seen, Murray's needs were used as if they were traits. In fact, Murray was regarded as a trait theorist by many colleagues in personality psychology. He was, however, not nearly as dedicated a trait theorist as the two covered in this chapter. Raymond Cattell and Hans Eysenck conceive of personality rather exclusively in terms of traits or traitlike entities.

While it is largely confined to traits, Cattell's point of view is perhaps the most complicated of all those covered in this book. He believes in isolating and reducing the raw material of personality to a manageable data pool, collecting massive amounts of data from the pool, and using intricate statistical methods to tease facts about personality from the data. Thus, he proceeds in a manner opposite to that of all the theorists considered so far, except for Skinner.

Eysenck shares many interests with Cattell. They both use the statistical technique "factor analysis" to discover a few central traits. Nevertheless, he differs from Cattell in embracing experimental psychology. Eysenck believes that researchers should take the principles developed in the psychology laboratory and relate them to personality by use of experimental procedures. Because of their differences, it is not surprising that the two personality psychologists arrive at different sets of traits to characterize personality.

Cattell, the Person

Raymond B. Cattell was born, 1905, in Staffordshire, England, the son of middle class parents. He labelled his father's career "design engineer," apparently in reference to the elder Cattell's role in Grandfather Field's manufacturing business (Cattell, 1974a). Raymond's father was congenial and inclined to deliver dinnertime lectures on history and current topics. The son has little more to say about the father, except to show veiled disappointment at the discovery, following the administration of IQ tests, that the "design engineer" was the intellectual inferior of his mother. She also is only briefly mentioned, but he implies a warm relationship with her and hints that the high intelligence he attributes to himself came mostly from her family. This judgment, made soon after he became a psychologist, is interesting because it shows an early orientation to conceiving of intelligence as mostly inherited.

Cattell describes his childhood as basically happy, but he is quick to add that it was "not easy" (Cattell, 1974b, p. 88). He described his parents and teachers as "exacting." One gets the feeling that the symptoms of stress Cattell showed later in his life were born of the strong drive to achieve instilled in him by the circumstances of his family's middle-class standing and the pressure exerted on him by his parents (Cattell, 1974a). Still, the claim to happiness appears to be genuine.

Three years before World War I started, he moved from England's midlands to the magnificent coast of Devonshire. There he and his brothers and friends "sailed, swam, fought group battles, explored caves, landed on rocky islands . . ." and generally enjoyed an idyllic childhood (p. 62). Even the War, when it arrived, became something of a plaything. Cattell was appointed a "sea scout" and charged with watching the coast for enemy ships. Like Fromm, Adler, and Jung, he was impressed with the destructiveness of modern warfare. "I enjoyed [the scouting] though awestricken to see the holes as big as a house that torpedo and mines could blow in steel plates. And then came the long trainloads of wounded from the Flanders . . . still in their bloodstained bandages" (p. 63). Young Cattell helped care for these stricken soldiers.

Schooling at the "selective secondary school" where Cattell was on scholarship continued despite the sacrifice of the best teachers to the war effort (p. 63). However, the headmaster at the school kept his position throughout the war. This "very intelligent and hard-driving man, a cousin of Kipling, whom he closely resembled" provided Cattell with a first scholastic role model (p. 63). The intellect and motivation of the man was not all that impressed Cattell: "He divided his time between giving me personal sessions in science and mathematics, and thrashing me for various original deviations from school regulations" (p. 63).

Cattell's connection to Freud—reflected in some of the traits he later identified—is mentioned in relation to his older brother and father. "A fine Freudian Oedipus situation [developed] between my older brother—the first born—and Father" (p. 63). The brother, one of two, is remembered fondly by Cattell. He recalls tagging along behind the older sibling during their daily treks to school. They were in the same grade, owing to Cattell's advanced status and the brother's modest intellectual skills. Yet the specter of sibling rivalry was also present. He wrote, "If I admit to scars of distrustful independence . . . they . . . come from the severe stresses of maintaining my freedom of development

Raymond B. Cattell

under a powerful brother three years older, who could be outwitted, but not overcome" (p. 63).

"At fifteen, I passed the Cambridge University entrance examination (. . . in which I was granted first-class honors), but since my scientific interest indicated London University, and my parents were loath to leave me on my own in London at that age, I did not go until sixteen" (p. 64). This proclamation is interesting in that Cambridge, not London University, is world famous and especially known for its excellence in science. It seems that every institute with which Cattell was associated was a haven for intellectual giants. It may have been a way for him to say that he was himself extraordinarily brilliant. In his writings he sometimes draws analogies between his own work and that of famous scientists.

While he may be a bit of a braggart with regard to his intellectual powers, his beliefs about himself are not exactly delusions. After distinguishing himself in secondary school, Cattell graduated *Magna cum Laude* in chemistry at the ripe old age of nineteen. But almost immediately he decided to apply his intellectual acumen to the pursuit of psychology. Just before he received his degree, he was enchanted by a speech concerning the work of Sir Francis Galton, a pioneer in mental testing. The speaker, Sir Cyril Burt, was soon to be one of his mentors and later to be involved in a scandal over I.Q. data. Immediately he was fascinated with psychological assessment. Despite protests from friends that he would go unemployed— there were only a handful of psychology chairs in all of England—he, like Murray, deserted his test tubes in favor of working with some of the most notable figures in the world of psychological measurement. In 1929 he received his Ph.D. in psychology and entered the field.

After a series of " 'fringe jobs' in psychology" during which there was time for research planning, but little research, Cattell spent five years gaining clinical experience (1974b, p. 90; Cattell, 1974a). He became director of a school psychological ser-

Institutions recognize achievement by giving honorary degrees. Here Senator Margaret Chase Smith receives such a degree from Rutgers. Cattell was convinced that such accomplishment and intelligence were largely inherited.

vice in Leicester, Devonshire, England, his home territory. There he successfully fought the dominance of psychiatry over psychology in the realm of explanation and treatment of psychological problems. During this time he became convinced that intelligence is mostly inherited. In 1936 he wrote an article for the *Eugenics Review* in which he answered "Yes" to the question, "Is national intelligence declining?" (Loehlin, 1984). The argument began with the assumption that the higher the social class the higher the intelligence. It proceeded with the observations that lower social classes were having more children. The conclusion was that more children among the less intelligent lower classes was driving the average national intelligence down. Further, subsequent work showed that the greater the family size, the lower the intelligence. Out of these efforts and Cattell's book *The Fight for Our National Intelligence* (1937) came the bold prediction that England's intelligence was in for a fall.

But, alas, it did not happen. Fifteen years later, there was, if anything, a slight increase in national intelligence (Loehlin, 1984). This disappointment did not deter Cattell from continuing his membership in the controversial Eugenics Society (Cattell, 1974a). **Eugenics** is the application of genetics to the improvement of human biological and psychological characteristics. In its most benevolent form, it was dedicated to exhorting people to choose spouses and monitor number of children carefully with an eye to promoting positive traits and discouraging negative traits.

In its more malevolent form, it advocates "species improvement by controlled breeding" (McGuire & Hirsch, 1977, p. 61) even to the point of calling for government programs to control human breeding. As late as 1984 Cattell was still defending the general eugenics position (Cattell, 1984).

This period between graduation with the Ph.D. and his first secure job in a real academic setting was a time of frustration and stress. Probably owing to long hours and laborious administrative duties, Cattell developed a "functional stomach disorder" from which "I have ever since suffered" (Cattell, 1974a, p. 68). The hard work, the stress, the stomach problem, and the low pay also took a toll on his marriage. Finally, his wife, who was accustomed to better, could stand the annual salary of $1200 and the "dark damp basement flat" no more (p. 68). She left and he yearned for a fresh start. Being frustrated with his job, and having severed his closest ties, he considered life in the United States.

Fortunately, at about this time, Edward L. Thorndike, who had been the salvation of Maslow, came to Cattell's rescue (Cattell, 1974a). The author of the "law of effect" had read *The Fight for Our National Intelligence* (1937) and was so impressed that he offered Cattell a position at Columbia University Teachers College in New York City. From there he moved to the G. Stanley Hall Professorship at Clark University and then to a lectureship at Harvard. After a time at Duke University, he accepted a Research Professorship at the University of Illinois where he prospered from 1945 until his retirement in 1973. He is now settled on Oahu where he is associated with the University of Hawaii at Manoa. Retirement to some is a perpetual vacation, but, like Fromm, Cattell saw it as an opportunity to produce a torrent of papers and books, guaranteeing a place for himself in the history of personality psychology.

Cattell's View of the Person

Cattell's Approach to Understanding the Person

One of the great virtues of Cattell's position is that he makes a refreshingly different basic, philosophical assumption. Unlike some other theorists, Cattell did not begin with "ideas off the top of the head" based on nothing more than simple intuition or subjective clinical observation. As an empiricist he believes that one collects data first then filters and sifts it through various statistical techniques until the facts emerge. These facts then generate hypotheses that can be tested. Thus, the proper mode of reasoning, according to Cattell, is first *inductive*, reasoning from particular observations to a more general statement of position. *Then* it becomes *deductive*, reasoning from a general statement to particular observations. He operates along the **inductive-hypothetico-deductive spiral**, "the detecting of regularities in observational data leads to a hypothesis from which experimental consequences are deduced, [leading] to further data from which new regularities are induced, and so on in an ever-expanding spiral" (Wiggins, 1984, p. 189). This approach is the method of astronomy, and often physics and chemistry, but rarely psychology, especially personality psychology. Personologists should note Cattell's strategy: eschew "off the top of the head" theorizing in favor of careful data collection from which meaningful hypotheses will arise.

Personality Defined

Through judicious use of the inductive-hypothetico-deductive spiral, eventually a complete picture of the human personality can be painted. In straightforward fashion Cattell defines **personality** "as that which tells what a [person] will do when placed in a particular situation" (Cattell, 1966, p. 25). It is expressed in a simple formula: **R = f(S.P)** where R stands for the "nature and magnitude of a person's behavioral response, . . . what he [or she] says, thinks, or does," which is some function (f) of S the "stimulus situation in which [the person] is placed," and P the nature of her or his personality (p. 25). While these conceptions seem delightfully simple, in fact, getting from P to R is a complicated matter.

Nature and Nurture

Cattell is noted for coming down on the nature side of the nature/nurture debate (Hirsch, 1975). Based on his own and others' research, he has argued that a number of human characteristics, most especially intelligence, are controlled to a great extent by the genes (Loehlin, 1984). Therefore, Cattell believes that the person is in large part shaped by genetic influences.

The Econetic Model

The relative emphasis on genetic influences should not be taken to mean that Cattell neglects the environment (Cattell, 1979, V. 1). R = f(S.P) is testimony to his attention to the environment. To express these sentiments more emphatically, Cattell has proposed the **econetic model**, a framework that integrates environmental situations with characteristics of the person—including personality components—in attempts to understand the person. When he discusses the various personality traits he has uncovered through research, he very often indicates the approximate degree to which each is controlled by the genes and how much each is controlled by the environment.

Factor Analysis

One of the ways one can isolate and verify traits is by seeking quantitative support for them in patterns of statistical correlations. To uncover these patterns, Cattell uses **factor analysis**, a statistical procedure for determining the number and nature of factors underlying larger numbers of measures (Kerlinger, 1973). The basic assumption is that certain simple responses correlate, or vary together, and thus may be grouped together to define a separate psychological dimension or factor. By determining "what goes with what," factor analysis is able to reduce large amounts of data from a complex to a simpler form (Spearman, 1927).

To help gain a concrete conception of factor analysis, imagine that a psychological test made up of many questions is administered to a group of 100 people. If one of the test items is answered in a certain way by 40 people, it is possible that these same 40 people will answer other items in systematically related ways. Suppose that they answer "Yes" to test item #1. They might also answer "Yes" to other, related items, let's say #26, #45, and #37, and "No" to others, say #17 and #82. At the same time, another subgroup of 40 people may answer the same items in the opposite way from the first group. And, the remaining 20 people may show no definite pattern. Obviously certain items are related to certain other items or subgroups of the entire sample would not be answering them in the same way. Factor analysis identifies such sets of items and determines that the items of each set share some common denominator. The **factor** in factor analysis refers to a hypothetical construct that is applied to a data cluster (set of items) and suggests what it is measuring.

The *analysis* in factor analysis refers to the procedures used to identify factors. These methods involve computations of many intercorrelations: Each item is correlated with each other item and each with the item clusters that are identified. Once a factor has been identified, it is assigned a label, based on the researcher's best judgment about the psychological dimension the cluster of items seems to measure. Judgments are guided by the content of items making the greatest contribution to a cluster identified as a factor. In turn, contributions of items to a factor are determined by statistical **loadings**, correlations of particular items with a given factor.

Factors resulting from factor analysis are not all of the same order of comprehensiveness or generality. Some are **primary factors**, which are relatively pure and narrow in scope. It can be arranged statistically that primary factors are independent (Cattell, 1966; Eysenck, 1984). Others are **secondary factors**, which encompass several primary factors and are called "superfactors" or "second-order factors" (Cattell, 1966; Eysenck, 1984). Cattell (1966) and others believe that extraversion-introversion is a secondary factor that subsumes certain primary factors.

In sum, Cattell approaches understanding the person by first observing simple responses, often reactions to questionnaire items. Through the use of factor analysis, certain clusters of these items are isolated as factors. These factors may allow the development of certain theoretical statements, which, in turn, may suggest further research to refine the previously discovered factors and associated statements. Eventually, after many reiterations of this inductive-deductive cycle, a picture of human personality may emerge.

Basic Concepts: Cattell

"There are no constructs in Cattell's theory that are not related to quantitative measuring procedures" (Wiggins, 1984, p. 177). Thus, Cattell does not have "concepts" in the usual sense: theoretical statements that are somewhat removed from the research procedures used to derive or confirm them. Many of the notions covered in the preceding section are shared with other researchers, and in all cases are related to research procedures. However, the two ideas that are covered next are unique to Cattell. They also refer to research procedures.

Data Types

Various kinds of data can be subjected to factor analysis, including *answers to test questions, ratings made by external observers,* and *measures of behavior.* In **Q-data** where Q is for questionnaire, people are their own observers, describing their behavior and feelings through paper-and-pencil inventories, self-reports, or interviews. "I have a toothache" is a sample response. Thus, with Q-data, observations are made by posing questions "which are answered by the person . . . from his [or her] own self-observations and introspection" (Cattell, 1966, p. 61). In **L-data** or *life-records,* ratings are "made by observers on the frequency and intensity with which specific kinds of behavior occur in the people they observe" (p. 61). Ratings are often made in everyday situations. An example observation would be "Maria is studious." **T-data** involves an observer's recordings of a person's behavior in some standard, contrived, laboratory-test situation. "Akeem reacts to a light by pressing a button in .34 seconds, on average" would be an example. T-data comes from "*objective* tests . . . miniature situations set up for a person to react to, in which he does not really know on what aspect of behaviour he is being scored (hence 'objective')" (p. 61). Factor analysis may involve any of the three data types.

Data Collection Techniques

Only three data collection techniques are covered here because the others "appear rarely if at all in Cattell's empirical work" (Cronbach, 1984, p. 229). The method most used by Cattell is called the **R-technique**, a "process of correlating behaviour measures across some hundreds of people [*tested on a single occasion*] and factoring them" (Cattell, 1966, p. 153). Thus, hundreds of people respond to all of many measures with the goal of discovering which of the measures cluster together. The R-technique is task or measurement centered. It is the most straightforward method to use in conjunction with factor analysis and often involves Q-data.

The *differential* R or **dR-technique** is the same as the R method, except that each of the hundreds of people responding to the several measures does so two times, usually after only a short delay, and each person's score on each measure is the second response minus the first. The differential R technique is useful in looking at change effects. In an example provided by Cattell, a psychologist is interested in the effect of a tranquillizer drug on people under stress. The psychologist decides to measure 200 hundred people on 40 measures relating to various aspects of anxiety and stress responses, some psychological and some physiological. After they have responded to the measures the first time, half of them are given the drug, and the other half get no drug, then they all respond to the same measures again. Second minus first scores are computed next. The forty change scores for each subject "are then correlated to see what goes with what, and factored to see how many independent influences are needed to account for the changes" (Cattell, 1966, p. 153). Thus, factors extracted from the data are used to help explain the change that has occurred. To facilitate accounting for change, the data of the subjects who took the drug may be factored separately from the data of those who did not. Then a comparison of the two factor structures might illuminate the change effects.

P-technique is "a factor analytic design which measures a single person on the same set of variables repeatedly over a number of different occasions" (Cattell, 1966, p. 372). This person-centered technique is the prime method for looking at change. With it the data matrix for 8 variables or measures and 20 days would be filled by having one subject respond to the eight measures on each of the 20 days. The matrix could then be factor analyzed for the purpose of extracting factors in the category **state** or mood, a psychological entity that fluctuates or varies over time and thus is "transitory," as distinguished from traits which are "permanent" (Cattell, 1977, p. 220). Cattell has done a considerable amount of work with states, often involving his *Eight State Questionnaire*. Unfortunately, most of it has employed the dR-technique, rather than the more appropriate P-technique. In fact, one of his best known and most accomplished students, John Nesselroade (1984), writes ."... it is the case that Cattell has never conducted a major longitudinal study" (a study in which subjects respond to measures on each of many days, not just two; p. 270).

Traits

Trait Subsidiation
A **trait** is a permanent entity that does not fade in and out like a state; it is inborn or develops during the life course and regularly directs behavior. Cattell has developed quite an elaborate method for classifying traits. It springs from *subsidiation*, the idea, borrowed from Murray, that some psychological entities are subsumed under others. Thus, traits are arranged in a hierarchy, from the most general and fewest in number, to the most specific and greatest in number. The **common trait** is "a trait which can be measured for all people by the same battery [of tests] and on which [the people] differ in degree rather than in form" (Cattell, 1966, p. 368). Thus, almost everyone can be given a position on a common trait dimension, varying, for example, from "extraverted" to "introverted." By contrast the **unique trait** is "so specific to an individual that no one else could be scored on [its dimension]" (p. 28). An example would be the ability to recall the names of flowers indigenous to a Brazilian jungle. Cattell paid very little attention to unique traits.

Second-Order Traits
At the top of the hierarchy are the most all-embracing or **second-order traits**, "superfactors" that subsume the other traits (identified earlier by the more generic label "secondary factors"). Cattell has dealt extensively with two of these higher order factors. One is **exvia-invia**, "a factorially established broad dimension within the area of behavior popularly referred to as extraversion-introversion" (p. 369). The other second-order trait is equally familiar: **anxiety**, the feelings of tension and upset, the source of which may be difficult to identify.

Source Traits
The **source trait** is "a [primary] factor-dimension, stressing the proposition that variations in value along it are determined by a single unitary influence or source"

(Cattell, 1966, p. 374). As the definition indicates, source traits are homogeneous: each controls a set of behaviors that resemble each other. They are inferred from primary factors.

Source traits are further broken down into three categories. An **ability trait** is reflected in "the manner of response to the complexity of a situation, [selected after] the individual is clear on what goals he wants to achieve in that situation" (p. 28).

The second category is the **temperament trait**, "a general personality trait [that] is usually stylistic, in the sense that it deals with tempo, persistence, [and so forth] covering a large variety of specific responses" (p. 28). A good example of a temperament dimension is "emotional vs. stable" (Wiggins, 1984).

Compared to the other two categories of source traits, Cattell devotes relatively more attention to the **dynamic trait**, which refers to motivations and interests (Cattell, 1966). This subcategory may receive more attention because it is complex, composed of three interrelated subordinate categories. Like Maslow's motives, dynamic traits are goal directed. The most basic is the **erg**, "An innate source of reactivity, such as is often described as a drive [or instinct], directed to a certain goal and accompanied by a certain quality . . ." (p. 369). The term comes from the Greek *ergon* for work or energy. There are many examples of ergs, but a couple of representative cases will suffice to illustrate the concept. The operation of the *sex erg* is signified by expression of such attitudes as "I want to satisfy my sexual need" (p. 190). An illustration of the *fear erg* is seen in "I want to see any formidable militaristic power that actively threatens us attacked and destroyed" (p. 189).

The second dynamic trait relates to the first. An erg is manifested in an **attitude**, an expression of an ergic goal that is generally subsidiated to an erg(s). The third dynamic trait category is **sentiment**, "a set of attitudes the strength of which has become correlated through their being all learnt by contact with a particular social institution [such as] sentiment to school, to home, to country" (p. 374). Immediately it is quite evident that attitudes are subsidiated to sentiments. Therefore, sentiments fall under ergs and, in turn, attitudes are subsidiated to sentiments. Sentiments organize and coordinate attitudes in the service of ergs. Illustrative sentiments are (1) *sentiment to religion*: "I want to see the standards of organized religion maintained or increased throughout our lives"; (2) *sentiment to career*: "I want to make my career in the Air Force" (pp. 191–192). Note the reference to society's institutions in both expressions.

The relationship among attitudes, sentiments, and ergs is reflected in the **dynamic lattice**, "the tracing of the subsidiation of attitudes, one to another, ending in the satisfaction of a number of primary ergic goals" (p. 369). A partial illustration of the dynamic lattice shows the nature of the relationship among attitudes, sentiments, and ergs (Figure 16.1).

Surface Traits
Surface traits are "a set of personality characteristics which are correlated but do not form a factor, hence are believed to be determined by more than one influence or source" (p. 375). They are the most subordinate traits, responses to the individual test items or the specific behaviors with which the researcher begins factor analysis.

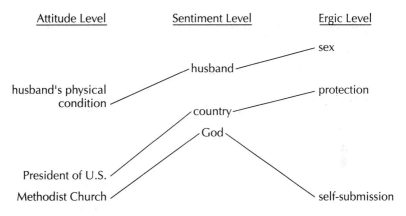

FIGURE 16.1 The Dynamic Lattice

Surface traits are gut level feelings, thoughts, and actions, the atoms of the personality molecule (the quarks may be neurological events, as Murray believed). Examples are "I laugh at other people's jokes" and "When I get mad, I throw things."

It will be helpful to look at Cattell's entire schema for classifying traits. See Figure 16.2 for trait type, factor analytic level (parenthetical statement), and examples.

It should be noted that the three main subcategories, ability, temperament, and dynamic, are not intended to be limited to source traits. Second-order traits can also be classified in the tripartite schema. For example, Cattell has referred to exvia-invia as a temperament trait dimension (Cattell, 1966). However, since Cattell has concentrated so heavily on source traits and these can be subsumed under second-order

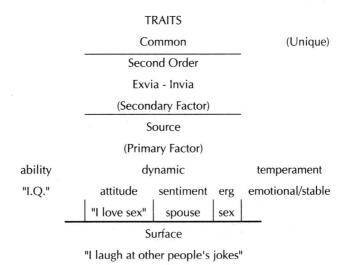

FIGURE 16.2 Cattell's Trait Classification System

traits, it makes sense to view the three categories as associated with source traits. Also worth noting is that states may be classified in much the same way as traits.

Learning

Cattell conceived of two varieties of learning in addition to those that concerned Skinner. One of these, **confluence learning**, is the acquisition of behaviors and attitudes which simultaneously subsidiate to two or more different goals. For example, a salesperson might learn a foreign language to serve both the career sentiment (she can now do business abroad) and the religious sentiment (the church is doing missionary work in the country where the language is spoken). Of course, in turn, these sentiments might serve the security erg and the self-submission erg, respectively.

In order to understand Cattell's second type of learning one must appreciate the **self-sentiment**, "The sentiment structure centred (sic) upon the individual's conception of himself and his desire to maintain this self-concept, in the eyes of himself and others, intact and acceptable" (p. 374). Obviously the self-sentiment is what other theorists mean by "self-concept" or one's conception of oneself. **Integration learning** is "learning consisting of a re-arrangement of satisfactions among a number of conflicting, independent drives [ergs]" (p. 370). The protection erg may conflict with the security erg, for example. A person may be conflicted who "believes in building weapons to destroy the enemy" (attitude associated with the "country" sentiment; protection erg) and also believes in the church doctrine, "it is wrong to kill" (attitude associated with the "God" sentiment; self-submission erg). This conflict may be cast as a confrontation of the self-sentiment with the Superego. These conflicts must be resolved through learning to rearrange satisfactions. Resolution would occur if the example person abandoned "building weapons" for some other way to satisfy the protection erg ("I believe that my country can negotiate the elimination of weapons."). Now the individual can say, "I am safe and can follow my conscience's dictates: 'Thou shalt not kill.' "

Cattell did not believe that learning is simply a matter of a single response satisfying a single need, as he thought Skinner and Pavlov believed. Each unitary activity we learn tends to serve several ergic motives. Learning may also resolve conflicts. In order to reflect the complexity of learning as it relates to personality, Cattell proposed the **dynamic calculus**, a set of equations that predict the course of learning, adjustments to environmental change, and the nature of ergic tension reduction (Cattell, 1984a).

Intelligence

Cattell endorsed the conception of intelligence fostered by his mentor Charles Spearman, an early mental tester. Spearman promoted "g" that supposedly subsumes the so-called primary mental abilities and forms a common core of general intelligence (McGuire & Hirsch, 1977). Cattell assumes that this general factor of intelligence is largely genetic. He argued that "g" fell into two categories (Cattell,

1984b. (**Fluid general ability** (g_f) is "that form of general intelligence which is largely innate and which adapts itself to all kinds of material, regardless of previous experience with it" (Cattell, 1966, p. 369). Whereas he reports that early evidence indicated "g" was 80 percent inherited, he claims that g_f is nearly 100 percent inherited. Only pre-birth accidents and post-birth events, such as head injury, prevent g_f from being fully inherited. By contrast **crystallized general ability** (g_c) is "a general factor, largely . . . abilities learned at school, representing . . . applications of [g_f], and amount and intensity of schooling; it appears in vocabulary and numerical ability [tests]" (p. 369). g_c is acquired intelligence that is little affected by the genes. The quality of schooling largely determines the magnitude of this ability.

The Personality of Nations

Syntality is national personality "equivalent to personality in an individual and capable of (a) predicting many behaviors and (b) by profile similarity measures permitting nations to be classified in a dozen types" (1984, p. 99). In one study, 18 families of nations were isolated from a pool of 100 nations (Cattell & Brennan, 1984). One family was composed of Canada and Australia and another of Britain, Sweden, and Switzerland. Thus, some nations form a family because their personalities are similar and different from the those of other families.

Evaluation

Contributions

For decades, Cattell has been among the most prolific of test developers, devoted to the process of constructing, refining, and extending his measurement techniques. His work has been programmatic, undertaken systematically rather than piecemeal. His firm belief is that individuals differ in relative locations on "permanent" trait dimensions as well as on "transitory" state dimensions and that these dimensions are assessable by means of personality questionnaires.

Assessing Personality with the 16 PF

True to his empiricist nature and his inductive-hypothetico-deductive orientation, Cattell began with the most basic, elemental reflections of personality, trait-descriptive words of the English language (Wiggins, 1984). He reduced 4500 trait words from the comprehensive list produced by Gordon Allport and his colleague Odbert (1936) to 160 synonym groups. These groups were regarded as "surface clusters" and eventually reduced to 171 terms by eliminating synonyms. The 171 *trait elements* were intercorrelated and 36 clusters of correlations were isolated. These clusters were called *surface traits*. Ten more were later added to make a total of 46 surface traits. This set was the grist for Cattell's factor analytic mill. Eventually, much refinement yielded the 16 primary factors of the now famous *16 Personality Factors* test or **16 PF**, a 16-scale test of adult personality measured in terms of

---

BOX 16.1   Your Own 16 PF Profile

Create your own 16 PF profile by simply placing an "X" in the scale interval (Figure 16.3) that you think represents your level on each factor and then drawing a line through the "Xs." Be honest with yourself; ignore the line for "John Skyman" while you are creating your own profile. After you have completed your profile, then you can compare it with "Skyman's."

Of course, you should recognize that your perceptions of your positions on the scales would not necessarily coincide with your actual positions if you took the 16 PF. In the actual test, for each factor there are several items over which a score is computed to represent the final factor score. You would not know your positions on the factors with confidence until you responded to all of the items.

---

16 source traits (Cattell, Eber, and Tatsuoka 1970). The final 16 PF was based on responses of 10,000 people. Later versions were developed for use at elementary, junior, and early high school levels.

In business and industry, the 16 PF has served as an aid to decision making about employee selection, efficiency, turnover, and promotion. In education, it has aided the planning of individualized programs for students and the prediction of school achievement. Cattell, Eber, and Tatsuoka's (1970) handbook for the 16 PF contains 125 profiles depicting ideal trait levels for various jobs, including sales personnel, airline pilots, mechanics, teachers, school counselors, nurses, and electricians. In clinical settings, the 16 PF has aided the diagnosis of people with behavior problems, anxiety, neurosis, alcoholism, drug addiction, and delinquency. It also has been used to understand similarities and differences in personalities of married couples seeking counseling. Figure 16.3 contains the popular and technical names for the scales of the 16 PF. Study them to get a feel for the different scales.

Notice the zigzag line through the middle of the scales. It represents the personality profile of a hypothetical pilot, "John Skyman." By following the line you can see how "John" scored on each scale. "John's" profile conforms well with data derived from 360 real airline pilots. The pattern reflected in the profile is an excellent combination of high reality contact and emotional stability under stress (Cattell, Eber, and Tatsuoka 1970).

Identifying Developmental Trends

Another of Cattell's contributions involves the identification of trends in personality development, from childhood through adulthood. Knowledge of age trends permits the plotting of standardized growth curves. Comparisons can then be made between individuals within a given age group, and between groups of persons of different ages and gender. Results are analogous to guidelines represented by the height and weight charts used by pediatricians in assessing patterns of children's physical growth. An example personality trend is found in 16 PF measures

Label	Low Score Description		High Score Description
A	Reserved (Sizothymia)		Outgoing (Affectothymia)
B	Less Intelligent (Low "g")		More Intelligent (High "g")
C	Emotional (Low ego strength)		Stable (High ego strength)
E	Humble (Submissiveness)		Assertive (Dominance)
F	Sober (Desurgency)		Happy-go-lucky (Surgency)
G	Expedient (Low super-ego)		Conscientious (High super-ego)
H	Shy (Threctia)		Venturesome (Parmia)
I	Tough-minded (Harria)		Tender-minded (Premesia)
L	Trusting (Alaxia)		Suspicious (Protension)
M	Practical (Praxernia)		Imaginative (Autia)
N	Forthright (Artlessness)		Shrewd (Shrewdness)
O	Placid (Assurance)		Apprehensive (Guilt-proneness)
Q_1	Conservative (Conservatism)		Experiencing (Radicalism)
Q_2	Group-tied (Group adherence)		Self-sufficient (Self-sufficiency)
Q_3	Casual (Low integration)		Controlled (High Self-concept)
Q_4	Relaxed (Low Ergic tension)		Tense (Ergic tension)

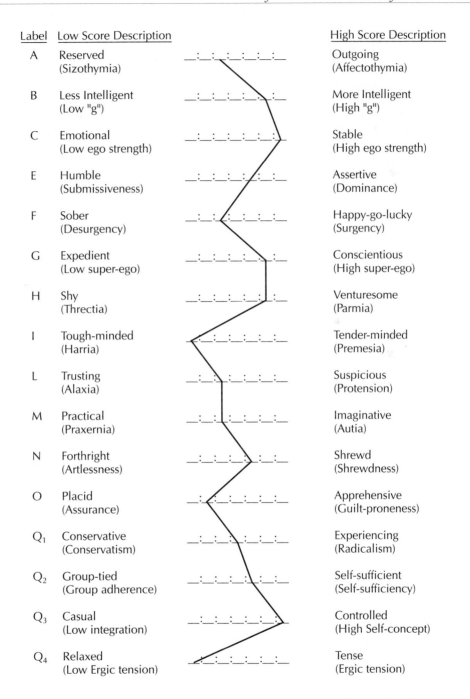

FIGURE 16.3 Technical (in parentheses) and Popular Labels for the 16 PF Factors A to Q_4

indicating that *superego strength*, or conscientiousness, generally shows a moderate but decelerating increase with age.

Classifying Tests

A third contribution involves a classification of tests. In 1967, Cattell and Warburton organized a detailed compendium of 612 objective tests of personality and motivation, covering 2364 variables. The purpose was to provide an index of specific tests so that interested psychologists would be able to choose one or more tests "suitable for some practical application or for testing some theory" (p. 13).

Cattell's Definition of Personality: Bringing the Strands of Psychology Together

Cattell's definition of personality is, perhaps, the most direct of those encountered in this book: "that which tells [predicts] what a [person] will do when placed in a given situation" (1966, p. 25). It supports his adherence to psychology's scientific aim of *predicting* behavior and it brings together different fields of psychology. His definition also suggests a balance of biological and environmental influences on behavior: the person brings the biological influences to the environmental situation.

Limitations

Because he depended on it so heavily, much of Cattell's theoretical, structural, and research interpretations rest on the validity and meaningfulness of factor analysis. Unfortunately, it is commonly said of factor analysis that researchers never get anything out of it they did not put there in the first place. This is because the results of factor analysis are extremely dependent on several biasing influences.

No Single Method
Controversy continues over which specific method of factor analysis should be used (Eysenck, 1984). Eysenck points out that one of the methods used in conjunction with factor analysis can force factors to be independent of one another. Another method can force factors to agree with theory. Cattell's 16 PF work involved a third method that allows factors to be dependent or correlated with one another. This procedure makes the factors "impure," according to Eysenck, and classifiable under second order factors. He queried "Why not use the second order factors as they are fewer in number and more inclusive?" Regarding who is correct, Cronbach (1970) wrote, "There is no one 'right' way to do a factor analysis any more than there is a 'right' way to photograph Waikiki Beach" (p. 315).

Subjective Judgments Remain
Factor analysis only partially reduces the amount of subjective judgment involved in answering questions about "what" and "how many" dimensions are present in personality. Arbitrariness on the part of researchers enters into the picture at three

points. First, they promote certain factor-analytic solutions rather than others not only by preselecting data likely to be "relevant" to their biases, but by later estimating how many factors are likely to be present in the data. Cattell (1973) and the Eysencks (1969) refer to this as "the number of factors problem." Different decisions by each theorist regarding the number of constructs underlying personality partly explains why different numbers of traits have been proposed to account for personality. Goldberg (1981) observes:

> *The number of primary personality factors in Cattell's system is in the 20-to-30 range, . . . the 16 most famous [constituting the] 16 PF. When his data were made available to others, however, virtually everyone who factored those data found only 5. (pp. 156–159)*

Second, once factors have been identified, cutoff values are required to establish whether an item makes a meaningful contribution to a factor. Statistical loadings of .60 and .40 on a factor are likely to be judged quite acceptable by most factor analysts. But what about .30, .20, and .10? There is another criterion available to help decision-making, but it is also a number for which some arbitrary cutoff point must be established.

The third source of subjectivity is perhaps the most serious. Although statistical programs are able to identify various factors present in a set of data, it is the factor analyst who interprets and labels all factors. By looking at the items contained in a factor, the analyst must subjectively decide what to call it. She or he assigns labels that are consistent with his or her own theory. Other analysts might label the factors differently, according to their own theoretical biases. This helps explain why one researcher's "neuroticism" and "extraversion" (Eysenck) are another's "anxiety" and "exvia" (Cattell).

Nature-Nurture: Heritability

Cattell cast almost everything he studied according to how much of its variability is determined by the genes and how much by the environment. For example, as you recall, nearly 100 percent of the variation (individual differences) in fluid intelligence is supposedly accounted for by the genes, but the figure is much smaller for crystallized intelligence (Cattell, 1966). Among 16 PF factors some are thought to be more controlled by the genes than by the environment—for example, self-sentiment; and some more environmentally controlled, super-ego strength (Cattell, Schuerger, and Klein, 1982).

Heritability popularly refers to the proportion of the variability in a trait that is accounted for by the genes. (See McGuire and Hirsch, 1977, for a discussion of the different indexes of heritability.) Heritability has been estimated in various ways, sometimes rather directly by use of correlations between the I.Q.s of identical twins reared apart (they are rightly assumed to be genetically identical, and perhaps wrongly assumed to be reared in entirely different environments). Cattell has adopted a seemingly more complex method for estimating heritability, one that he regards as among his major achievements. It is **Multiple Abstract Variance**

Analysis (MAVA), "a research design for discovering relative proportions of environmental vs. hereditary determination for personality traits (nature-nurture ratio)" (Cattell, 1966, p. 372). For those of you who enjoy mathematics, it involves writing a series of equations, each with one unknown, either relating to heredity or environment, and solving the set of equations simultaneously for the unknowns (Loehlin, 1984). To his credit, Cattell has used MAVA to go beyond the limited twins method. MAVA considers not only identical or fraternal twins but also brothers and sisters and unrelated people. Although the method may seem complex, actually Cattell has kept it relatively simple by ignoring certain important considerations (Loehlin, 1984).

In an example study, heritability was estimated using MAVA for the 16 PF factors ego-strength, super-ego strength, and self-sentiment (Cattell, Rao, & Schuerger, 1985). Results indicated that self-sentiment is more genetically determined and super-ego strength more environmentally determined, with ego-strength falling between the two. However, heritability estimates varied markedly depending on the method of estimation used. Also, results were not entirely in line with those of a highly similar study reported by Cattell, Schuerger, and Klein (1982). Further, Cattell's attempts at heritability estimation have come under fire for technical shortcomings. Esteemed statistician H. W. Norton wrote about one such attempt, "In conclusion, the statistical analyses reported by Cattell et al. are incorrect, and the 'results' they report should be ignored" (Norton, 1972, p. 225).

Again, to his credit, Cattell notes the variations in estimations with variation in technique, but he attempts to strongly interpret results anyway. This double-think about heritability results highlights a fact that is often ignored by Cattell and others: Heritability estimates are good only for the population used, at the time it is used (McGuire & Hirsch, 1977; Hirsch, 1975; Weizmann, Wiener, Wiesenthal, & Ziegler, 1990). They do not generalize to other populations or to another sample taken from the same population at another time. Further they are population measures; they do not apply to individuals from the populations: it is "an average statistic and *population* measure, [and] provides no information about how a given *individual* might have developed under . . . [different] conditions . . ." (Hirsch, 1975). Just as a species of tree develops differently on the top of a mountain than down in a valley, a given individual might turn out differently if reared under different conditions than those that actually existed for her or him. It is important to note that, because heritability is a population statistic, it is interpretable for the single population contributing the data from which it is estimated. For example, heritability estimates made using "whites" are meaningless when applied to "blacks."

The notion of heritability itself is suspect when used as Cattell and others have employed it. It was originally developed to estimate how successful animal breeders would be in their efforts to breed for certain desirable traits (McGuire & Hirsch, 1977; Weizmann, Wiener, Wiesenthal, & Ziegler, 1990). It was never intended to be used as a means to partition the variance in a trait into that accounted for by the genes and that accounted for by the environment. In fact, the very act of dividing up variation in a trait, whether intelligence or personality is considered, is suspect from a genetic point of view. Consider an analogy. The question, "In computing the area of a rectangle, which is more important, its length or its height?" makes no sense. Likewise, asking, "Which is more important, heredity or environment?" may be meaningless (Hirsch, 1975). Every genetic disposition unfolds in an environment. Likewise, one could argue that no environmental influence exerts itself apart from genetic input. Separating the genetic contribution to a trait from that of the environment in which it is expressed may be seen as artificial.

It seems clear that Cattell's work with heritability is at best controversial. While this possibility does not distract from his other contributions, it does suggest that his research and theory regarding heritability be viewed with considerable caution.

Other Criticisms

Cattell refuses to use common terms for factors (personality traits), claiming that these popular labels have surplus and confused meaning (Cattell, 1966). Thus, we are left with "exvia-invia" instead of the familiar extraversion and introversion, as well as other odd and difficult-to-pronounce labels. Further, certain symbols, such as R, T, and Q, are given different meaning in different parts of Cattell's theory. The scientific dictum of parsimony—make the inherently complex as simple as possible—is ignored.

Cattell, like others, declares that state and trait are distinct (Allen & Potkay, 1981). The index of his 1966 book refers to the distinction between state and trait. However, upon turning to the indicated page, all that one finds is a declaration that they are distinct. To his credit, in a later publication (1977) he, unlike others, acknowledges the lack of a clear distinction by referring to "the fact of there being no absolute distinction between traits and states" (p. 220). Yet, like others, he has always and continues to refer to traits as "stable" and states as "transitory" without saying how "stable" a personality entity must be before it is considered "trait" rather than "state."

Cattell is famous for the g_c / g_f distinction, but did he originate it? By his own admission, famed physiological psychologist Donald O. Hebb presented the same ideas at the same 1940 convention (Cattell, 1984b). It could be that they arrived at these ideas independently. If so, Hebb deserved some of the credit. Incidentally, "g", or general intelligence from which g_c and g_f are derived, has itself come under fire by those who believe that intelligence is multi-faceted (McGuire & Hirsch, 1977).

Cattell repeatedly refers to what he does as "experimental" and to where he works as "the laboratory" (e.g., 1984). Experiments are done in the laboratory, but Cattell rarely does experiments (as you recall, an experiment involves manipulating some variable). In an experiment, different subjects are treated differently and the emphasis is on how those different treatments *affect them* in ways that reveal something about the treatments. In the typical Cattell study, even if T data is collected, subjects are often treated the same and the emphasis is on how *they react to* contrived situations in ways that reveal their personalities. Even if experiments are done, as Eysenck (1984) points out, laboratory experiments produce data that are "essentially unsuitable" for analysis with the multivariate techniques that Cattell typically uses, including factor analysis (p. 328).

Conclusions

Even if one ignores his heritability work and the fact that his research techniques have been criticized, there is much to be admired among Cattell's many contributions. His empiricist stance is in stark contrast to the "off the top of the head" theorizing of many theorists covered in this book. Perhaps personality psychologists should be more like astronomers than chemists. Because what psychologists study is complex and difficult to "get the hands on," or even "the eyeballs," they should be cautious in forming hypotheses until after many observations are made. If they consider this advice, they are following Cattell's capable lead.

As mentioned several times before, the worth of a scientific contributor is often determined as much by whether he or she inspires others to think new and useful thoughts as by his or her own ideas. Cattell has literally trained dozens of personality psychologists. Some of them, such as Jerry Wiggins and John Nesselroade, have gone on to prominence.

If one had to point to a personality measure that taps personality more completely and meaningfully than all the others, one could well vote for the 16 PF. It is perhaps the most carefully developed by use of the most sophisticated methods. It also was not "done in a day" as are some measures. It evolved over many years of careful research.

Finally, the model of scientific contribution is not to "make your mark" with a few publications based on a few studies, each done in a short time, early in a career. Cattell is still producing research. He is a contributor for life.

Eysenck: 16=3—Conceiving of Personality in Three Dimensions

Eysenck and Cattell are often linked, perhaps because they both are pioneer factor analysts and both were trained in Britain. Both are associated with heavy use of complicated statistical methods. Both believe that personality and intelligence are strongly determined by the genes. Both have spent a professional lifetime trying to reduce personality to only a few dimensions. They even had the same mentor, Sir Cyril Burt. However, there are differences. In fact, in recent years they have been carrying on quite a debate. The issue? How many dimensions must one consider in order to account for personality, 16 or 3? Eysenck's argument for just "3" occupies most of the remaining pages of this chapter.

Eysenck, the Person

Hans Jurgen Eysenck was born in Germany on March 4, 1916 to a moderately known actor, Eduard Eysenck, and an aspiring actress, Ruth Werner (Gibson, 1981). He came of age during the deprivations of the period following World War I. After his parents' marriage was dissolved, Eysenck lived with his maternal grandmother who raised him in a permissive atmosphere. Consequently, he was a self-willed boy, well accustomed to having his own way. For example, at age 8, he bit the finger of a teacher who was trying to punish him for his adamant refusal to sing. Later, in high school, he proved a teacher wrong in his claim that Jews were lacking in military valor. Interestingly he did it with statistics: Jewish soldiers received a disproportionate number of German medals for valor during the war. In another incident, he refused to attend the lectures of a teacher who had given him less than the highest grade on an essay. This kind of behavior inspired Gibson (1981) to indicate, "Eysenck appears to have . . . a very good opinion of his own abilities" and ". . . of himself . . ." (p. 18).

Hans J. Eysenck

In fact Eysenck's hard-head and tough mind has raised the ire of many people during his life. By the time he was a teenager, the Nazis were in the process of taking over Germany. It was inevitable that Eysenck would continue his education elsewhere, because, to him, Nazism was absurd. He would have had to leave in any case, because his stepfather, Max Glass, was a Jewish movie producer-director who was no longer welcome in Germany. Thus, in the summer of 1934, Hans, Max, and Ruth departed for France where Max successfully resumed his career. There Eysenck briefly pursued an advanced education, until a visit to Exeter, England in 1933 led to a love affair with Britain. At age eighteen, in the autumn of 1934, the affinity for England was still so strong that it lured him to London. There he entered University College with the intention of pursuing a science curriculum. Unfortunately, he had a deficiency in science that would have required time and money to correct. Accordingly, he enrolled in psychology, which was just beginning to be recognized as a "science."

As fate would have it, Eysenck entered what then was the most scientific psychology department in England. It was the site of intense activity in *psychometrics*, the measurement movement in psychology. Even as an undergraduate, he did research with Sir Cyril Burt, and Burt helped him collect the data that went into his first publication. Sir Cyril also edited the article, and, without Eysenck's permission, altered it to fit his own theories. Undismayed, Eysenck took only three years to finish his psychology doctorate with honors. The topic was experimental aesthetics.

In the same year, 1940, Britain declared war on Germany and Eysenck was labeled an enemy alien. Barred from the armed forces, he did research at the Mill Emergency Hospital which was associated with the Maudsley Hospital, later his lifelong research center. During this period and later Eysenck was accused of being a "fascist," probably because he was a German who seemed to espouse "heredity is everything"—and thus traits cannot be changed. This position was in defiance of social programs that assumed "environment is everything"—traits can be changed. Despite these handicaps, Eysenck moved up the academic ladder. In 1950 he was granted the position of reader at the University of London. In 1955 he became a professor, despite the opposition of Cyril Burt, who had since turned against him. At the same time he was becoming a dominant figure at Maudsley. From these positions of power he defied the psychological establishment and began the long campaign for acceptance of his "Big 3" factors.

Eysenck's View of the Person

Eysenck is apparently not a warm and accepting person like Rogers (Gibson, 1981). While he is a supportive friend and colleague, his condemnation of psychotherapy, for which he narrowly escaped physical assault, may have emerged from his inability to be a therapist sympathizing with neurotic clients.

Like Cattell, he believes a continuous program of research conducted over many years is the proper approach to understanding the person. But, he advocates a different research program.

> *Thus, Cattell starts from the generation of hypotheses about the major factors involved, stays [with] factor analysis . . . and assigns . . . low importance to the fact that his primary factors are intercorrelated, and give rise to superfactors. . . . At each stage I follow exactly the opposite line. Starting out with a theoretical model . . . I use factor analysis to test theories rather than to originate them. I tried to use [theory] from . . . psychology and physiology to link the factors . . . with causal hypotheses which led outside factor analysis altogether" (Eysenck, 1984, p. 335; emphasis added).*

Eysenck added, "Cattell has been opposed to the current theories emerging from experimental laboratories, and has openly criticized 'brass-instruments' psychology. As a consequence his own work has little relation to the concepts which concern the classical experimentalists, or the psychophysiologists" (p. 329). By contrast, Eysenck does real experiments and relies on evidence and hypotheses from experimental psychology. Also he alternates between experimental procedures and factor analysis until he feels that he has honed and refined the construct he is working with.

Central to the difference between Eysenck and Cattell, and critical to Eysenck's uniqueness relative to other personality theorists, is the question, "At what level does one find the traits that are necessary and sufficient in number and nature to account for personality?" Contrary to Cattell and his 16 factors, Eysenck believes personality can be parsimoniously understood, with no loss of thoroughness or depth, by reference to only 3 second order factors. But neither has given an inch, as is evident in Cattell's (1986) response to Eysenck.

Basic Concepts and Contributions: Eysenck

Traits and Types in Eysenck's Theory

As with Cattell, the essence of Eysenck's theory is that personality can be described in terms of **traits** represented as statistical factors and defined as "theoretical constructs based on observed intercorrelations between a number of different habitual responses" (Eysenck & Eysenck, 1969, p. 41). Examples of traits relevant to Eysenck's theory include physical activity, impulsiveness, risk-taking, responsibility, worrisomeness, carefreeness, and sociability, all dating to the ancient Greeks.

Traits, in turn, are often grouped in categories called **types**, second-order dimensions made up of statistically intercorrelated primary traits. They can be thought of as superfactors, but Eysenck prefers "second-order" (1984). He has identified three such factors, reporting that they "or others remarkably similar to them" have been found repeatedly in different studies (1981, p. 6). Eysenck's three second-order factors or types are: *E, Extraversion-introversion; N, Neuroticism-stability; P, Psychoticism-superego functioning.* These types essentially are the same as Cattell's second-order factors exvia-invia and anxiety and his primary factor "super-ego strength," respectively (Eysenck, 1984).

Eysenck does not believe each person is either E or not-E, 100 percent N or not at all, totally P or totally not P. This means that all people show some degree of all three types. One person may show much extraversion, some neuroticism, and a little psychoticism. A second person may show little extraversion (much introversion), some neuroticism, and some psychoticism. For most people, values fall within the average range. Since very few people fall at such extreme degrees as 0 percent or 100 percent, pure types are hard to find. When it comes to extraversion-introversion, most of us are **ambiverts**, people who show medium degrees of this type, with behaviors characteristic of both aspects. Nevertheless, we tend to *perceive* people as falling at the extremes. If a person is induced to be introverted, he or she will see a partner as extroverted (Alicke & Klotz, 1993).

Biological Origins of Traits and Types

Eysenck has always maintained there is a "substantial" hereditary basis to personality (Eysenck, 1990). He complains that psychologists pay too little attention to hereditary influences on behavior, especially those in the United States, whom he views as overemphasizing environment and learning. Psychology's purpose is to study the behavior of organisms, but psychologists have failed to appreciate the degree to which organisms respond differently to the same environmental stimuli, independent of learning.

> *Personality is determined to a large extent by a person's genes; . . . while environment can do something to redress the balance, its influence is severely limited.*

[For] personality [and] intelligence . . . genetic influence is overwhelmingly strong, and the role of environment . . . is reduced to effecting slight changes. . . . (Eysenck, 1976, p. 20)

E, N, and P have "a strong genetic basis" (1981, p. 6). He estimates that, across all trait dimensions, including E, N, and P, about 60 percent of individual differences in personality is determined by the genes (Eysenck, 1990).

Eysenck also indicates that E, N, and P are closely tied to physiology (Eysenck, 1967; Eysenck & Eysenck, 1969, 1976). To illustrate, extraversion (E) has been linked with the brain's **ascending reticular activating system (ARAS)**, which acts as an arousal mechanism. The core of the system is the reticular formation of the brain stem. When stimulated by sensory input, it sends messages through ascending nerve fibers to arouse the cerebral cortex, the brain's upper crust that coordinates lower brain areas. In turn, the entire organism is activated. If the sensory input originates in environmental events having survival value, the cortex sends messages back down to the reticular telling it to continue promoting arousal. This feedback loop determines whether we continue to *attend to* given environmental events or not.

Eysenck links Neuroticism (N) to the limbic system, the brain's emotional center that regulates such functions as sex, fear, and aggression. Psychoticism (P) has been linked with the endocrine glands, specifically the ones that secrete sex hormones. One source of support for Eysenck's (1990) genetic position is research involving genetically identical twins and fraternal twins, who bear no more genetic similarity to one another than any two siblings. Because they are genetically identical, any differences between identical twins must be due to the environment. By contrast differences between fraternal twins may be due to either the genes or to the environment (Eysenck, 1967).

Eysenck (1967; 1990) points to empirical findings that show identical twins to be much more alike in personality than fraternal twins, even when identical twins have been separated early in childhood and raised by different parents, in different environments. Also, he contends that identical twins are more alike in criminal and neurotic behavior than fraternal twins. Further, adopted children are more similar to their biological parents than to their adoptive parents on a number of trait dimensions. Loehlin, Horn, and Willerman (1990) report partial support for Eysenck's position.

Toward a Scientific Model of Personality

Eysenck's (1981) **scientific model for studying personality** involves two interlocking components: (1) *description*, which seeks to answer questions about "what" personality is, for example, what are the identifiable individual differences in traits and types?; and (2) *explanation*, which seeks to answer questions about "why" personality is the way it is, "What are the causes of those individual differences?" In Eysenck's model, concepts are sought that will help reduce human behavior to a small number of variables that are tied together by rules or laws. Ideally, laws should enable psychologists to explain past events and to predict future events.

**BOX 16.2   The Maudsley Personality Inventory,
Short Form**

Instructions

The following questions pertain to the way people behave, feel, and act. Decide whether the items represent your *usual* way of acting or feeling, and circle either a "Yes" or "No" answer for each. If you find it absolutely impossible to decide, circle the "?," but use this answer sparingly.

1. Do you sometimes feel happy, sometimes depressed, without any apparent reason? YES ? NO
2. Do you have frequent ups and downs in mood, either with or without apparent cause? YES ? NO
3. Are you inclined to be moody? YES ? NO
4. Does your mind often wander while you are trying to concentrate? YES ? NO
5. Are you frequently "lost in thought" even when supposed to be taking part in a conversation? YES ? NO
6. Are you sometimes bubbling over with energy and sometimes very sluggish? YES ? NO
7. Do you prefer action to planning for action? YES ? NO
8. Are you happiest when you get involved in some project that calls for rapid action? YES ? NO
9. Do you usually take the initiative in making new friends? YES ? NO
10. Are you inclined to be quick and sure in your actions? YES ? NO
11. Would you rate yourself as a lively individual? YES ? NO
12. Would you be very unhappy if you were prevented from making numerous social contacts? YES ? NO

(Adapted From Eysenck & S. Eysenck, 1969; used with permission of Hans Eysenck.)

Now try to group the items into two categories: put together the six items that seem to go together, and then look at the other six items to see if they go together. If not, then categorize again until you come up with two sets of six items that seem to measure two different types. When you finish, you have performed a crude factor analysis. Categorize now before going on.

If you grouped the first six items together and labeled them as N and the last six as E, you have done well. Obviously, if you said "yes" to most of the first six items, especially numbers 1 and 2 which are loaded .75 and .74 on neuroticism, you are "high on neuroticism" (but do not take it too seriously; a six-item test result is not to be trusted without further evidence). Just as obviously if you indicated "yes" to most of the last six items, especially numbers 11 and 12 which are loaded .68 and .64 on extroversion, you are extroverted.

Researching Traits and Types

Eysenck's model of personality is closely linked to **psychometrics**, a quantitative approach to psychological measurement. Box 16.2 will introduce you to psychometrics.

Objective Personality Tests

Over the years, Eysenck has authored or coauthored a number of personality tests, each of which has been associated with the development of a different personality factor. The Maudsley Medical Questionnaire (MMQ) introduced the concept of neuroticism (N), the Maudsley Personality Inventory (MPI) added extraversion-introversion (E), and the Eysenck Personality Questionnaire (EPQ) added psychoticism (P) (Eysenck, 1952; Eysenck, 1959; S. Eysenck & H. Eysenck, 1968, 1976).

Reducing Observable Events to a Few Variables: E, N, and P

Like Cattell, Eysenck adheres to *subsidiation*, the Murray concept. Imagine a pyramid that has four levels representing the personality traits and responses falling under "extraversion." At the base of the pyramid are **specific responses (SR)**, everyday behaviors or experiences that may or may not be characteristic of an individual, such as saying "Hi" to a neighbor. At the next level up are **habitual responses (HR)**, specific responses (Cattell's surface traits) that recur under similar circumstances, such as *regularly* saying "Hi" to a neighbor. At the third level, habitual responses are organized into *primary factors*, or traits. For our extraversion example, these are sociability, impulsiveness, activity, liveliness, and excitability. Extraversion is at the top of the pyramid, the level of *secondary factors* or types. Thus, "[the four primary traits] would form a constellation of traits intercorrelating amongst themselves and giving rise to a higher order construct, the type" (H. Eysenck & S. Eysenck, 1969, p. 41). Obviously Cattell and Eysenck are very close on what is subsidiated to what; but Cattell emphasizes primary factors and Eysenck second-order factors.

The MMQ, MPI, and EPQ

Eysenck began his work by investigating N as a dimension of personality. Using the MMQ he found that 1000 neurotic soldiers scored twice as high on N as 1000 normal soldiers. N scores tend to decrease with age, to be higher for women than for men, and for persons in lower socioeconomic classes. High Ns are emotionally overresponsive and unstable, anxious, worrisome, moody, restless, touchy, complaining of bodily symptoms, and prone to break down under stress. Persons with low N are emotionally stable, calm, carefree, even-tempered, and reliable.

Eysenck revised the MMQ and gave it to 400 British men and women. Ultimately, 24 neuroticism items (N) and 24 extraversion items (E) were selected to form two scales for the new MPI. In general, E scores tend to be higher for men than for women, to decrease with age, and to be unrelated to socioeconomic class. Persons with high E scores tend to be sociable, popular, talkative, craving excitement, taking chances, impulsive, practical jokers, easygoing, optimistic, on the move, short-tempered, lacking control of feelings, and unreliable. Persons with low E scores tend to be retiring, fond of books, distant except with close friends, organized, reserved, pessimistic, ethical, imperturbable, controlling of feelings, and reliable.

In developing the measure of P, the EPQ, Eysenck (1952) was particularly interested in the theoretical question of whether psychotic and normal persons differ "in kind" or "in degree." Contrary to psychiatric classification systems, he expected most people would have at least a little "psychotic" or "criminalistic" tendency as part of their genetic makeup: there is no clear-cut separation between "psychotic" and "normal."People show more or less P and P is independent of N and E (S. Eysenck & H. Eysenck, 1976, pp. 17–18). In subsequent validity studies, the highest P scores were found among persons labeled "psychotic," especially schizophrenics, and among criminals and others showing antisocial behavior. Improvement of psychotic disorders through treatment results in lower P scores. P scores tend to be higher for men than for women, to be lower for persons in the middle socioeconomic class, and to decrease with age. Persons with high P scores are solitary, troublesome, uncooperative, hostile, cruel, unempathetic, sensation-seeking, liking odd things, liking films of war and horror, undervaluing people, socially withdrawn, sexually impersonal, deficient in thought and memory, distractible, devaluing education, suspicious, having mood disturbances, showing motor disturbances, suicidal, having psychotic relatives, delusional, hallucinatory, and creative. Since men show higher P scores than women, Eysenck believes that P may be physiologically linked with hormonal balance between androgen (male) and estrogen (female). The flavor of P is conveyed in Eysenck's (1970) description of a 21-year-old man who scored high on P. When asked to explain his endorsement of the EPQ "liking parties" item, he answered, "Well, at parties you get free grub, free likker and a chance to screw some bird, don't you?" Then, with an angelic smile, he added, "And sometimes you can break up the place, too" (p. 427).

Supporting Evidence

The Lemon-Juice Test for Extraversion-Introversion
Eysenck contends the more people's scores show them to be introverts (Is hereafter), the more strongly they should salivate to lemon juice, because Is have a higher level of cortical arousal through the ARAS than extraverts (Es hereafter; Corcoran, 1964; S. Eysenck and H. Eysenck, 1967). Thus, "under conditions of equal stimulation, [the reaction of nerves in the muscles and glands] would be greater for introverts" (p. 1047). In fact, Is do salivate more than Es when pure lemon juice is placed on their tongues.

Predicting Difference in Eye-Blink Conditioning
Eysenck (1957) believes that, compared to Es, Is learn (condition) more rapidly and more strongly in the "classical" dog-salivates-to-meat-powder set-up, because the two types differ physiologically. He got this idea from Russian physiologist Pavlov, who observed individual differences in the rates at which his dogs learn. Some had "strong" nervous systems and some had "weak" systems (Teplov, 1964). These "strong" and "weak" types resemble Eysenck's Es and Is. Because cortical arousal is greater in Is than Es, and "cortical excitation facilitates conditioning . . . ," Eysenck

assumes that Is condition more readily (1967, p. 117). Thus, Is have weak systems; they are easily aroused and greatly affected by strong stimulation. Maybe they turn inward to avoid it. By contrast, Es have strong systems that inhibit arousal. Maybe they turn outward to seek it.

Eysenck and Levey (1972) used classical eyeblink-conditioning. Regardless of conditions, a puff directed at the eye makes it blink. Thus, the puff is the unconditional stimulus (US). The conditional stimulus (CS) is a tone delivered to the ear just before the US is presented. Only *under the condition* of being associated with the puff will the tone make the eye blink. The unconditional response (UR) and the conditional response (CR) are the blinking of the eyelid.

Before the experiment, 144 male subjects were administered the MPI and were categorized as Es, Is, or ambiverted (As). For some subjects the time interval between the CS and US was 400 msec (thousands of a second). For others it was 800 msec. Also, for some subjects the strength of the puff US was 3 pounds per square inch. For others it was 6 pounds per square inch. It was expected that lower values would promote conditioning in Is and high values in Es. Results showed that, after 48 trials, conditioning tended to be greater for Is than for Es. More important, Is were more conditionable with the weak US, Es with the strong US, and As were intermediate. The shorter CS-US interval also favored conditioning in Is.

Loud Commercials More Appealing to Es

As everybody knows, commercials on TV and radio are played at a louder volume than the programs surrounding them. This strategy is assumed to overwhelm resistance to persuasion, thereby increasing the likelihood that listeners will purchase the advertised products. Cetola and Prinkey (1986) found that high volume works, but only Es favored commercials played at a louder volume than the preceding program; louder volume did not matter for Is.

Bad Exam News Is Worse for Is

Based on completion of the MPI by 200 college students, Fremont, Means, and Means (1970) isolated the 30 highest scoring (Es) and the 30 lowest scoring (Is) students. Each student was then given a brief written task requiring the learning of a digit-symbol code. Some Es and some Is were told they scored "higher than average," or told they scored "lower than average," or were given no information about their performance. An anxiety test was administered to all students immediately following the feedback session. When feedback was negative, Is clearly showed greater anxiety than Es. Is and Es differed under no other condition.

Drugs, Liquor, Coffee, and Tobacco

Eysenck believes that "depressant drugs [alcohol] change behavior in an extraverted direction while stimulant drugs [coffee, cigarettes] change behavior in an introverted direction" (1962, p. 14). In partial support of the hypothesis, Jones (1974) reported that although the detrimental effect of alcohol applied to Is and Es alike, it was significantly worse for Es. Gupta and Kaur (1978) showed that a stimulant, dextroamphetamine, improved the efficiency of Es but interfered with Is' performance on a perceptual judgment task. The hypothesis also helps to resolve a dilemma: *Hyperactive* children are given the *stimulant* Ritalin. If they are "cortically underaroused" like Es, the paradox is resolved (Powell, 1981). Stimulants function to make them more physiologically like Is, allowing them to become more attentive, responsive to social stimulation, and less impulsive.

Explaining Real-Life Behavior: Mass Hysteria

In 1965 a polio epidemic dominated press coverage of a town where a British secondary school was located, causing outsiders to avoid the "polio town." Later that year, an outbreak of physical symptoms occurred among girls attending the school (Moss & McEvedy, 1966). On day 1, students attended a lengthy church ceremony, during which 20 girls fainted. The next day, new fainting began to occur during school assemblies. Fainters rested on the floor, where the sight of them generated excitement and fear, resulting in overbreathing, dizziness, headache, feeling cold or hot, shivering, nausea, and faintness. Soon the behavior resumed spontaneously at school assemblies. Medical lab findings were negative. All 25 girls who fainted on day 1 and went to school on day 2 were affected, while none of the girls absent on day 1 were affected on day 2. Also, those still suffering on later days had been among those affected on early days. Consistent with the "mass hysteria" label, the number of new occurrences was higher during school assemblies than classroom sessions. The EPI was given to 535 of the students and results showed that affected students displayed a combination of high E and high N scores.

Limitations

Although he is less dependent on factor analysis than Cattell, Eysenck's factor analytic studies are subject to some of the same problems as Cattell's. Also, his work in behavior genetics is as suspect as Cattell's. Like Cattell, he has been scalded by some critics for applying heritability to differences between groups, such as blacks and whites (Hirsch, 1975).

Furthermore, Eysenck's suggestion that personality factors are largely genetically determined is sometimes given no support or only qualified support by other researchers. For example, Loehlin, Horn, and Willerman (1990) found that the primary source of change in some personality factors, including extraversion, was *individual experience*, not the genes. However, they did report some support for the genetic hypothesis: in the case of adopted and natural children, with increased age the children were tending to change in the direction of their real parents' personalities.

It should be noted that Eysenck and Cattell are not being criticized for studying the genetics of behavior, personality, and intelligence. It would be absurd to suggest that the genes have nothing to do with these psychological entities (Hirsch, 1981). The problem is with the heritability method favored by psychologists that artificially partitions the variation in psychological traits into the portion accounted for by heredity and the portion accounted for by environment. Psychologists need to become real geneticists trained in biological laboratories so they can do genetics as it traditionally has been done, with populations, not behaviors or cognitions (Hirsch, 1964). Properly trained psychologists could directly assess the genetic underpinnings of psychological traits rather than relying solely on statistical approximations. In fact, such work is currently being done (VandeWoude, Richt, Zink, Rott, Narayan, & Clements, 1990).

Probably Eysenck's best known experimental contribution is wrapped up in the link between E-I and the ARAS. While there seems to be general agreement that Is are, on average, more sensitive to stimulation and react more negatively to it, this difference is being laid at the door of newly specified brain mechanisms, not the ARAS (Stelmack, 1990). Despite this development, some researchers continue to support Eysenck's ARAS theory (Bullock & Gilliland, 1993).

Further, work by Gerald Matthews and his colleagues shows that the effect of extraversion on task performance is extremely complicated (Matthews, Davies, & Lees, 1990; Matthews, Jones, & Chamberlain, 1989). It is a complex function of the type of task, and surprisingly, the time of day at which the task is completed. Es and Is react differently to level of arousal in the AM, but in the PM only Is are affected by arousal level. Also it appears that arousal may be only indirectly related to the effect of extraversion on reactions to tasks. Es may have more resources available to them for use on certain kinds of tasks and "these resources are more reliably increased in subjects . . ." exposed to high arousal (Mathews, Davies, & Lees, 1990, p. 167). Thus, arousal may only facilitate what Es already have, rather than change the character of their reactions to tasks.

Finally, Eysenck, in effect, has reduced personality to just three dimensions. While many trait theorists have reduced personality to just five dimensions, virtually no one agrees with Eysenck's smaller number. Just three dimensions does not do justice to the extraordinary complexity of personality.

Conclusions

Hans Eysenck should be a model for other trait psychologists in that he is one of the few who uses the experimental method consistently, and the only major theorist to do so. It is almost as if others are afraid to use experimentation lest they find that their "stable" traits do not remain stable when subjected to experimental manipulations. While Eysenck's work with extraversion has been severely qualified, it has made the concept one of the most important in the personality field. Jung conceived of extraversion, but it was Eysenck who showed that it intrudes upon many aspects of human functioning.

Summary Points

1. Cattell was English born, the son of middle class parents. Always sold on himself, he won scholarships and honors and turned down a chance at Cambridge University. After graduating with honors from London University, he chose psychology over chemistry. Following some "fringe jobs" and stressful administrative duties, he finally ended up with E. L. Thorndike in the United States. From there he went to several prestigious professorships.

2. Cattell follows the inductive-hypothetico-deductive spiral. Consistent with the econetic model, R = f(S.P) expresses his belief that both personality and environment contribute to responses. He gives nature more weight than nurture. Factor analysis, his technique of choice, extracts primary and secondary factors and specifies loadings of items on these factors.

3. Cattell deals with three kinds of data: Q-data (questionnaire), L-data (ratings), and T-data (objective measures in lab situations). His data collection techniques are R-technique (correlating measures taken once from hundreds of people and then factored), dR-technique (same as R but with two responses), and P-technique (single person responds to same measures repeatedly). He emphasizes common traits and also studies transitory states.

4. Traits are subsidiated under one another as follows: Second-order traits; source or primary traits (ability, temperament, dynamic: attitudes, sentiments, ergs); and surface traits. Cattell conceived of confluence learning and integration learning which involves self-sentiment and the super-ego. Intelligence is believed to be largely inherited and is subdivided into fluid and crystallized. Nations have personalities too: syntality.

5. Cattell's lifelong project, the 16 PF, includes emotional-stable, expedient-conscientious, trusting-suspicious, conservative-experiencing, casual-controlled. Its uses range from personnel selection, through academic achievement to clinical diagnosis. Cattell has classified tests and pulled the strands of psychology together through his simple definition of personality. Factor analysis involves often arbitrary choices between several different procedures. Data sources are subjectively selected and so are criteria for deciding magnitude of loadings and factor labeling.

6. Cattell assumes the validity of "heritability" can be assessed by several methods each yielding different values. In fact, these are population statistics not applicable to other populations, or the same one at a different time, or to group differences. Heritability itself is suspect because it tries to separate genetic and environmental input. Other criticisms are duplication and unfamiliarity of terms, no clear distinction between state and trait, and falsely claiming to be experimental.

7. Eysenck was born in Germany to an actor and an aspiring actress. Reared by his grandmother, he was strong-willed. After fleeing the Nazis, Eysenck earned a Ph.D. and did research at Maudsley Hospital and as a Professor at the University of London. He believes that personality is more than adequately encapsulated by three second-order factors and that factor analysis should be used to confirm theory, not generate it. He does real experiments and uses concepts from experimental psychology and physiology.

8. His "Big 3" are extraversion-introversion (E), neuroticism-stability (N), and psychoticism-superego functioning (P). Extraversion is linked to the ARAS. His scientific model for studying personality has two components: description and explanation. So does his psychometrics: sophisticated statistical techniques and objective questionnaires.

9. Eysenck's hierarchy of traits produced through subsidiation is much like Cattell's except that specific responses are added at the bottom and surface traits are called "habitual responses." People who score high on E are impulsive, optimistic, sociable, and rather unreliable. High Is are the opposite. High Ns are unstable, anxious, worrisome, moody, and overresponsive. High Ps are solitary, troublesome, hostile, cruel, sensation-seeking, liking of oddities, sexually impersonal, and distractible.

10. Es have strong nervous systems and Is weak. Is react to stimulation more readily than Es. Is salivate more to lemon juice, condition more readily, react with more anxiety to bad news about test results, are deterred by stimulants, and react less strongly to alcohol. Hyperactive children may be changed in the I direction by the stimulant ritalin and mass hysteria may be explained by reference to high E and N scores. Some of Eysenck's postulations about heredity have been, at best, partially supported, and his assumptions about the ARAS have not been supported: the relation of E-I and arousal is complicated and indirect.

Running Comparison

Theorist	Cattell in Comparison
Freud	He used many Freudian concepts.
Skinner	Like Skinner, he begins with raw observations, the empirical approach. He conceived of two varieties of learning in addition to those that concerned Skinner.
Murray	He borrows Murray's subsidiation.
Maslow	Dynamic traits are like Maslow's goal direction. Also like Maslow, a given psychological process, for example, learning, serves not one but many functions.

Theorist	Eysenck in Comparison
Cattell	Both concerned about the number of traits accounting for personality, but Eysenck used experimentation. Both subsidiated traits.
Skinner	Both did lab research.
Jung	He revised Jung's extraversion.

Essay/Critical Thinking Questions

1. Is there something about Cattell's background that influenced his belief that traits and intelligence are primarily inherited?

2. Can you come up with another way to collect data in addition to the three defined in the text?

3. How would you draw the line between common and unique traits? That is, how unusual must a person's unique trait be before one can say that no one else can be placed on the trait's dimension? (Hint: think of the problem of differentiating trait and state or mood.)

4. Can you come up with an example of confluence learning from your own learning experience?

5. Take another look at the 16 PF. Can you categorize the factors into temperament, ability, and dynamic trait categories? Better still, further break down the dynamic category into ergs and sentiments. Note: there appears to be no "right or wrong" answer to this question.

6. If genetic research is done with populations, not traits, how would you go about attempting to locate a possible genetic basis for *Tourette's Syndrome* (nervous tics, uncontrollable, bizarre sounds, and cursing)? Just the first thing you would do is all that is needed here.

7. What was it about Eysenck's personality, revealed in his youth, that may account for his tendency to defy the establishment and postulate unpopular points of view?

8. Could you design a simple experiment to look at the relationship between introversion-extraversion and tolerance for pain?

9. Look at the list of traits attributed to high E, N, and P individuals. Can you see any overlap? Specify what you see.

10. How do you feel about reducing personality to only 3 dimensions? Argue that it is good for our understanding of personality or argue that it is bad.

17

PERSONALITY DEVELOPMENT AND PREJUDICE: GORDON ALLPORT

- Should a prominent personality theorist have unbounded confidence bordering on arrogance or a sense of true humility?
- Which should be emphasized, the unique traits that each person has and does not share with others or the universal traits that we all share?
- Does personality spring suddenly to life at some point during childhood, or does it develop piece by piece, little by little?
- Which is the clearer sign of a mature personality, a place in life, a major role to play, or insight into oneself and a genuine sense of humor?
- What is the personality of the prejudiced person like?

Gordon Allport is at least the equal of trait theorists Murray, Cattell, and Eysenck, but he is a different person with a different style. While Murray was a self-proclaimed narcissist, and Cattell as well as Eysenck are known for their hubris, Allport preached and practiced humility (Allport, 1967). His point of view was broad and open, encompassing the ideas of other theorists and including room for change. Further, Allport, like Kelly, took the hard road to understanding personality. Rather than assume that all persons can be fitted to a small number of trait dimensions, he believed that each person is unique, distinguished from others by her or his own peculiar traits.

The breadth of Allport's theoretical interests exceeded that of most theorists covered in this book. His concern for social problems led him to the study of diverse topics ranging from the psychology of rumors to personal maturity. He was a pioneer in the study of prejudice. By careful consideration of his groundbreaking work, you will be able to gain significant insight into personality development, maturity, and prejudiced thinking.

Allport, the Person

Gordon Willard Allport was born on November 11, 1897 in Montezuma, Indiana, the last of three sons (Allport, 1967). While Allport's father was "pure English," his mother was a mixture of German and Scottish (p. 4). Both were well educated: the father was a physician and the mother a school teacher. Allport's versatile father was in business before becoming a doctor and eventually combined medicine with business.

Like the atmosphere in which Rogers was reared, Allport's home life was characterized by warmth as well as "Protestant piety and hard work" (p. 4). His father set the philosophical tone for the entire family: "If every person worked as hard as he could and took only the minimum financial return required by his family's needs, then there would be just enough wealth to go around." This "broad humanitarian outlook" dictated a philanthropic orientation that was adopted by the entire family. Because his father lacked adequate hospital facilities, the Allport house became a hospital and family members its staff. Gordon recalled tending to office work, washing bottles, and interacting with patients. Just as his family's interactions were virtually free of strife, Allport's relations with others were unburdened by conflict. He was able to work successfully with a wide variety of people, including students who relished the friendly exchange of ideas that occurred in his graduate seminars. Just as he refused to engage in verbal combat with Murray—choosing instead to emphasize their similarities—he sought common ground when interacting with others.

As a young adult Allport tried to replace his more fundamental religious beliefs with a broader humanitarian religion. In the midst of trying on one religious garb or another, and failing to find a good fit, he remarked on the essentials of any global view that he might adopt: "Humility . . . [was] indispensable for me" (p. 7). His status as baby of the family also contributed to a humble outlook. His older brothers were largely successful, especially Floyd, a Harvard educated experimental psychologist in whose footsteps Gordon was destined to tread. Throughout his life, humility was manifested in frequent self-effacing remarks. In reference to his standing as second in his high school class of 100, he commented, "Apparently I was a good routine student, but definitely uninspired . . ." (p. 5). When he first had the opportunity to perform volunteer social service, he found it "deeply satisfying, partly because it gave me a feeling of competence (to offset a generalized inferiority feeling)" (pp. 6–7). Just before his death in 1967 as he was ruminating about his possible contributions, he expressed surprise at the numerous honors he received. Only one, his favorite, was deemed worthy of mention: his former students presented him with two volumes of their own writings inscribed "From his students—in appreciation of his respect for their individuality" (p. 24).

After Gordon graduated from high school in 1915, older brother Floyd suggested his own school, Harvard, from which he had graduated in 1913. With characteristic modesty, Gordon remembered "squeezing through the entrance tests" (p. 5). Almost immediately, he was attracted to psychology. Unfortunately, his first experiences were no better than Murray's, Kelly's, and Maslow's. Like Murray, his first psychology teacher was Munsterberg, whose appearance reminded Allport of Wotan, the god of war to whom Jung had alluded. He got no more out of the beginning class than the other three, but, like the others, he was not discouraged. Neither did he falter when hostilely confronted by the professor who nearly turned Maslow away from psychology. E. B. Titchener glared at him as he briefly described his dissertation project and later groused to one of his advisors, "Why did you let him work on [a personality] problem?" (p. 9).

Gordon W. Allport

During his undergraduate years, Allport took courses from many of the famous psychologists of the day. But psychology was not his only interest. Sociology and social ethics fascinated him. After a brief hitch in the Students' Army Training Corps during World War I, he returned to his classes full-time and began to pursue social ethics by volunteering to work in various social service capacities, such as for the Humane Society.

After finishing his undergraduate studies in 1919, Allport took a one year job teaching English and sociology at Robert College in Constantinople. Near the end of his stay in the ancient Turkish city, he received notice that he had been accepted into the psychology graduate program at Harvard. On the way back to Harvard he stopped off in Vienna to visit with Freud. With youthful audacity that later would embarrass him, Allport announced "that I was in Vienna and implied that no doubt he [Freud] would be glad to make my acquaintance" (p. 7).

Freud sent a reply "in his own handwriting inviting me to come to his office at a certain time" (p. 7). Arriving at Freud's office, Allport looked in wonder at the "famous red burlap room with pictures of dreams on the wall" (pp. 7–8). Once in Freud's inner office, the "master" remained mute, waiting for young Allport to state his business. Finding the silence awkward, Allport began to comment on the apparent dirt phobia of a boy he encountered on the tram that transported him to Freud's office. The child repeatedly complained to his mother about the "dirty man" beside whom he was forced to sit. One look at the stern and dominant mother and Allport thought he had the explanation for the boy's problems. True to form, "Freud fixed his kindly therapeutic eyes" on young Allport and queried, "And was that little boy you?" (p. 8). Allport was "flabbergasted" but at the same time was "guilty" and "amused" that Freud had "misunderstood" his reasons for telling the story. He believed that the therapist in Freud was probing for defenses to overcome and completely missed the "rude curiosity and youthful ambition" that was the actual motivation behind the story (p. 8).

The actual couch used by Freud in the psychoanalysis of many notables.

Allport apparently did very well in Harvard's psychology graduate program. Nevertheless, he managed to find some chinks in his academic armor. Though he lamented his imagined academic shortcomings, paradoxically he found graduate school easy. After only two years of course work he received his doctorate in 1922 at the age of 24. His dissertation was entitled "An Experimental Study of the Traits of Personality: With Special Reference to the Problem of Social Diagnosis." It almost certainly was one of the first major projects on personality done in the United States. Later he was to teach one of the first courses on personality.

After a fellowship in Europe, including exposure to the Gestalt view, and a lectureship in social ethics at Harvard (1924), he took a short-lived position at Dartmouth. When there was an opening in social psychology at his Alma Mater, he was offered the job and accepted without hesitation. By the end of the 1930s, Allport had become a permanent member of the staff, wrote his first book on personality (1937), and was elected President of the American Psychological Association (1939). World War II provided the opportunity to advise the government on the issue of morale and on the problem of rumors. He also became involved in attempts to understand the causes of war and to establish a lasting peace. In 1946 he participated in successful efforts to establish a multidisciplinary department, combining sociology, social psychology, clinical psychology, and social anthropology. In 1954 he wrote his famous book on prejudice. A year and a half before his death, he was awarded an endowed chair in social ethics.

With appropriate modesty, Allport devoted considerable space to detailing his many efforts in the interest of charities and social welfare. A self-proclaimed "political liberal" and "social reformer," he never missed an opportunity to condemn oppression and to praise social consciousness. In addition he was the epitome of the Renaissance man. No other theorist covered in this book was on the cutting edge of so many new movements or involved in such a diversity of academic pursuits.

Allport's View of the Person

Humanism?

Allport's personal warmth and social consciousness suggest a humanistic orienta-tion. Indeed, he even occasionally referred to himself as a humanist (DeCarvalho, 1991). Consequently it is clear that he was a humanist at least at the personal level. Less clear is whether he was a humanistic theorist, though he has been credited with coining the phrase "humanistic psychology" (DeCarvalho, 1991). In addition, he wrote a book partially entitled *Becoming* (1955). However, humanism is not even entered in the book's index, much less made the focus of a chapter. He *was* concerned about the self, but "self-actualization," "peak experiences," and "empa-thy" were not terms he often used. Further, the sociologist in him fostered an inter-est in groups for groups' sake, not a matter of great concern among typical humanists. Thus, it can be said that his point of view had the flavor of humanism, but was not mainstream humanism.

Emphasis on Unique Traits and Behavioral Variability

Allport was a pioneer in the study of personality traits, but he was a maverick among trait theorists (Allport, 1966; Zuroff, 1986). Whereas Cattell (and Eysenck) emphasized common traits at the expense of unique traits, Allport was the other way round (Allport, 1966, 1967). Like Kelly, he preferred to look at people one at a time and found that a given person's traits were generally not applicable to other people. This orientation contrasted with that of typical trait theorists. Cattell and Eysenck are **nomothetic theorists**, inclined to derive general laws concerning how a relative few traits apply to all people. By contrast, Allport was more an **idio-graphic theorist**, inclined to study each individual's unique traits without attempting to find a place for each along a relative few trait dimensions.

Cross-situational behavioral consistency, so dear to the hearts of typical trait theorists, was a matter of less concern to Allport (Allport, 1966; Zuroff, 1986). He would have agreed with Aldous Huxley that "the only completely consistent peo-ple are dead." He believed that "behavior in different situations was often incon-sistent, even contradictory, because different traits are aroused to different degrees in different situations" (Zuroff, 1986, p. 993). Zuroff believed that Allport was ahead of his time in being an interactionist. By the 1960s, Allport was writing about vari-ability of behavior from situation to situation and the possibility that a given trait is activated only in a certain situation or class of situations (Zuroff, 1986).

De-Emphasizing the Freudian Unconscious

The conversation with Freud helped to convince Allport that "depth psychology . . . may plunge too deep" (Allport, 1967, p. 8). He felt then and continued to

BOX 17.1   The Adjective Generation Technique: A Method Inspired by Allport

Several exercises in this book involve asking you to produce adjectives, or other words, to describe someone, usually yourself. This method, formally known as the Adjective Generation Technique (AGT), was first used by the author in 1969 and was developed by Charles Potkay and me from that year to the present (Allen & Potkay, 1983a; Potkay & Allen, 1988). The original idea for the AGT came from a demonstration performed by Allport and reported in his 1961 book. A stranger simply walked into a college classroom, gave a short ambiguous speech, and left. The professor then asked students to describe the stranger. "Allport's approach was to just look at the words to get a general qualitative idea of the kind of impression the visitor had made on class members" (Allen & Potkay, 1983a, p. 3). He apparently made no attempt to attach numbers to words relating to some psychological dimensions. True to Allport's open and eclectic approach, students produced the words, rather than checking words on a list or points on a dimension, either of which would be reflections of the assessor's orientation, not the students'. They could use any descriptive words in their vocabularies. Further, they were unlikely to paint an ingratiating picture of themselves, because they performed anonymously and had no idea whether their words would be scored in any way.

Unlike Allport, Potkay and I have often scored the words in some way. Words could simply be counted to see how many are produced when people generate as many as they desire. This method tells assessors how prominent the target of description was in the minds of describers: the more words, the more prominent. Words also might be categorized and their frequency in each category compiled. In one study, words most used to describe "good teachers" vs. "poor teachers" were compared: good teachers were "intelligent," "clear," and "humorous," while poor teachers were "boring," "dull," but "knowledgeable" (see M. Ward in Allen & Potkay, 1983a). In addition, each of nearly 2200 words has been assigned a value indicating degree of FAVorability, ANXiety, and FEMininity. When people describe themselves, one can assess how FAVorable their descriptions are, how much ANXiety descriptions reflect, and how FEMinine are the describers.

DAILY LOG SHEET

Date:_____

Write down five (5) words to describe yourself. Use only single words that can be found in the dictionary, no sentences or phrases.

——————
——————
——————
——————
——————

Briefly write down what happened to you that you regard as significant.

_____

_____

Charles Potkay and I believe that the AGT can be used to increase self-understanding. Get to know yourself a little better: make about 30 copies of the Daily Log Sheet and describe yourself for thirty days. It should be done at the end of the day and will take only about 5–10 minutes. For each day, just record self-descriptive words and briefly indicate what happened to you on that day. Just looking at the words will show you

BOX 17.1   *Continued*

how you are evolving over days and how "what happens to you" affects your view of yourself. If you want, you can get a copy of Allen and Potkay (1983a) from your library and look up FAV, ANX, and FEM values. Notice that on a single day you will frequently use both desirable words, reflecting high FAV, low ANX, and FEM appropriate to your gen-

der, and undesirable words. Further, you will find that the words you use differ day to day. This is quite normal and consistent with Allport's belief that different "traits"—your words may be considered trait labels—are aroused in the different situations you encounter on different days.

believe that psychologists would do well to look for and recognize open and obvious motivations, rather than immediately probe the dark depths of the unconscious. It was this "underemphasis" on the unconscious that irritated Murray. More generally, Allport was often critical of psychoanalysis, even parting company with his own brother when one of Floyd's books was deemed "too psychoanalytic for my taste" (p. 8).

The Eclectic View

Allport wrote, "Much of my writing is critical of prevailing psychological idols. At times I have crossed swords with learning theory, . . . dimensionalism in personality research . . . and simplified theories of motivations" (Allport, 1967, p. 22). Instead of adopting one of the popular schools of thought, Allport believed in using any approach, any philosophical position, any method of data collection that would shed light on the person (DeCarvalho, 1990). Allport was *eclectic*: he used whatever would help him understand the person. However, he did not randomly apply any and every method. Instead he employed a **systematic eclecticism**, taking the best and most effective methods and orientations from each school of thought and binding them into a comprehensive approach to understanding the person (DeCarvalho, 1990). With systematic eclecticism, subjective and objective data were used, the conscious and the unconscious were explored, mechanistic and holistic approaches were utilized, and the social as well as the personal orientations were considered. Using systematic eclecticism, Allport analyzed Jenny (1965) from the point of view of the "Jungian, Adlerian, [and] Freudian . . . [and] in the perspective of humanist and the existentialist." Allport argued that "the true understanding of Jenny was a synthesis of the partial truths stated by each system" (DeCarvalho, 1990, p. 269). All of these points of view were considered "true" in a qualified sense, because each uncovered some "human aspect of Jenny."

Basic Concepts: Allport

Personality Defined

According to Allport, **personality** "is the dynamic organization within the individual of those psychophysical systems that determine his characteristic behavior and thought" (1961, p. 29). For Allport, short definitions could not capture the complexity of personality; elaboration was needed. A *system* is a "complex of elements" that have the potential for mutual interactive activity (p. 28). *Dynamic organization* referred to the interplay of forces within an integrated system with tightly connected components. Activation of one component of the system activates others in an orderly fashion. A personality springs into integrated activity much like an orchestra: the conductor waves his baton signalling the violinists to play; when they sound a certain note, the drums begin to roll and so forth until all the components of the orchestra are active. "*Psychophysical*" simply "reminds us that personality is neither exclusively mental nor . . . neural (physical)." Its organization entails "the functioning of both 'mind' and 'body' in some inextricable unity" (p. 28). "*Determine*" refers to the fact that the "Personality is something that does something" (p. 29). In "*his characteristic behavior and thought*," use of the singular pronoun and the word "characteristic" in reference to "behavior and thought" reminds us that action and cognition are unique to a particular person.

Allport was careful to differentiate personality from other, ostensibly similar psychological entities. *Character* is sometimes used interchangeably with *personality*. In the Europe of Allport's youth, it was preferred to personality. There, however, character referred to something inborn or innate and subject to mainly "inside influences." In the United States, what is "out there" in the environment, namely behaviors, may reflect something inside, but is influenced by environment. Therefore, "personality" is the U.S. choice.

Personality is preferred to character for another reason. When people in the United States refer to character, they are often indicating something about someone's moral standing. "A person with character" is a person who is morally upright. Because science and morality are viewed as no more compatible than oil and water, character is avoided in favor of personality which has no moral connotations. Allport does note that character, moral functioning, is a legitimate concern in the study of personality. But, when morality in the form of character is considered, it is as a *part of* personality not as a *substitute for* personality.

Traits

Definition of Traits

In Allport's view, **trait** "is a neuropsychic structure having the capacity to render many stimuli functionally equivalent, and to initiate and guide equivalent (meaningfully consistent) forms of adaptive and expressive behavior" (p. 347). In more straightforward terms, a trait "guides" a person to respond to similar but not identical elements of the environment (stimuli) in much the same way. "Hostile person" defines a category of stimuli which has members that may take on different forms—different people are hostile in different ways. But whatever the forms, similar responses are called for within a given environmental context. If the context is a formal party and the hostile person is a guest, the appropriate response would be to calm the person whoever she or he happens to be. On the other hand, Allport would be the first to say that a different environmental context would call forth a different response to functionally equivalent stimuli: in a nursery school context, regardless of which child is hostile to other children, physical restraint may be called for.

Allport proposed the following criteria for traits:

1. *Has more than nominal existence*
2. *Is more generalized than a habit*
3. *Is dynamic, or at least determinative, in behavior*
4. *May be established empirically*
5. *Is only relatively independent of other traits*
6. *Is not synonymous with moral or social judgment*
7. *May be viewed either in the light of the personality which contains it, on in the light of its distribution in the population at large*
8. *Acts, and even habits, that are inconsistent with a trait are not proof of the nonexistence of the trait (p. 1)*

There are several implications of these criteria. First, it is obvious that Allport believes that people do have traits. Second, traits of personality are not matters of moral functioning. Third, traits may determine behavior. Fourth, inconsistencies are real, but do not mean traits are nonexistent. Behavior related to "kindness" may be inconsistent across situations because only some situations call forth "kindness." Inconsistency may also be apparent because different behaviors may manifest "kindness" under different circumstances even within the same environmental context (sometimes you have to be cruel to be kind). Fifth, traits are more generalized than habits. A habit is quite specific, like the habit of not talking while one is eating (talking "with a mouth full"). A trait, by contrast, is more broad, general, and variable. "Politeness" is a trait which would subsume "not talking while one is eating." Because it is subordinate, "not talking while one is eating" may be suspended in the greater interest of "politeness": if guests talk while eating, one would suspend one's habit in the interest of being polite to guests.

Sixth, and critical to Allport's theory, "trait" may refer to different but similar phenomena. **Common traits** "are . . . those aspects of personality in respect to which most people within a given culture can be profitably compared" (Allport, 1961, p. 340). Obviously, Cattell and Allport agree on what a "common trait" is, but Allport deemphasized common traits. He was referring to them when he derogated "dimensionalism": distributing everyone along each of a few common trait dimensions.

To Allport, a **personal disposition (p.d.)** is a trait that is unique to a particular individual. P.d. means approximately the same thing as Cattell's "unique trait." In his 1961 book, Allport is careful to use "common traits" in reference to traits that all people have, but possess in varying degrees and p.d. when referring to traits that are unique to particular persons. Oddly, by the time he wrote his seminal 1966 paper, he had lapsed into using "trait" to refer to both. Perhaps by the latter date, he assumed that readers were familiar with his theory and knew that he most often meant p.d. when he used "trait." Still, even in 1966 he periodically reminded readers about the distinction.

These reminders notwithstanding, using "trait" in reference to both "common traits" and "p.d." raises a perplexing question: How can "trait" be two things at once? The puzzle becomes more of an enigma when Allport acknowledges that the same labels may be used for both common traits and p.ds. A person can somehow be uniquely "conscientious" and, yet, all people can be placed on the "conscientiousness" dimension. Allport attempted to clear up this paradox by indicating that a trait label has a different *flavor* when referring to a particular person than when the reference is to people generally. For example, while most people can be cast as reflecting some degree of anxiousness, "Little Susan has a peculiar anxious helpfulness all her own" (Allport, 1961, p. 359). Notice that more words are needed to describe "Susan's" trait than the single word "anxious" which suffices to describe what most people show a degree of. "Anxiousness" must be qualified when applied to a particular person. Not surprisingly, Allport believed that trait labels fit common traits more readily than p.ds.

Cardinal, Central, and Secondary P.D.s

P.d.s can vary in terms of how close they are to the core of an individual's personality. A **cardinal p.d.** is pervasive and outstanding in the life of a person. A word referring to a cardinal p.d. that a person possesses is often our choice as the sole description of him or her. Names of historical or fictional characters are often used in reference to cardinal traits: quixotic, narcissistic, sadistic, Emersonian, Falstaffian, Faustian, Christlike, Don Juan, or Beau Brummell. More common terms may also refer to cardinal p.d.s: flaky, sober, realistic, immoral, superficial, and obnoxious.

A **central p.d.** is one of the entries on the relatively large list of traits we use to summarize an individual's personality. We list central p.d.s when we write a person a letter of recommendation. So-and-so is meticulous, thoughtful, even-tempered, and generous, but shy and moody.

Even farther removed from the core of personality are **secondary p.d.s**, dispositions that are "less conspicuous, less generalized, less consistent, . . . less often called into play . . . [and] more peripheral" (Allport, 1961, p. 365). Therefore, a person may be sporadically helpful, intermittently humorous, and occa-

BOX 17.2   Are Traits Specific to Situations?

Norman Endler and his colleagues' hold a position that is very close to Allport's in one important way (Endler, 1983; Endler, Parker, Bagby, & Cox 1991). Consistent with Allport's view, Endler's group has scientifically demonstrated that a given trait may be activated only in certain situations (the rule seems to apply to either common traits or p.ds.). With anxiety as the sample trait, the Endler group isolated four different classes of situations that evoke anxiety. In each class, a variation of anxiety is activated that is in tune with the nature of the situation and different from the form of anxiety elicited by the other three situations. In *social evaluation* situations, something a person does may be evaluated by other people. "Making a speech" is a good example, because it arouses social evaluation anxiety. *Physical danger* situations involve a potential for physical injury, but it is blown out of proportion. Driving on a narrow mountain road would evoke physical danger anxiety. In *ambiguous* situations, it is unclear how one should behave. Trying a new sport is an example, because anxiety due to ambiguity is likely to be aroused. The fourth kind of situation is dubbed *daily routine*, anxiety exhibited in mundane, everyday situations such as working or attending class. This last category was added as a baseline against which anxiety in the others could be compared.

Rather than a person being generally anxious, she or he would have, say, very high social evaluation anxiety, high physical danger anxiety, and low anxiety in the other two situations. This person would be anxious in all the situations in the social evaluation category, somewhat anxious in those situations in the physical danger category, and not anxious in the other two. There would be "behavioral consistency" in that the individual would be anxious in all the members of the social evaluations class of situations: for example, going to a costume ball and singing in front of a group. However, there would be little consistency across classes of situations: anxiety would peak then drop dramatically with movement from social evaluation to ambiguity situations.

You could learn more about yourself, and confirm Allport/Endler in your own mind, if you kept track of the kinds of situations in which you are anxious. The index of anxiety might be heart rate. Place the index and middle finger of the left hand just under the right chin, in the hollow next to the Adam's Apple. Count how many pulses occur in ten seconds and multiply by six (6). The result will be number of beats per minute.

Carry a log with a listing of the four classes of situations. When you are in a certain situation, classify it into one of the four categories and take your pulse. For most people who have been sitting somewhere for 10 minutes, a heart rate of 120 would be quite high and indicative of anxiety. (You will have to become familiar with your normal heart rate, to decide what is "high" and what is "low" for you.) Taking a sample of ten situations in each of the four classes should be sufficient. Average the heart rate numbers within each class for an idea of what makes you anxious and what does not.

sionally melodramatic, thereby displaying secondary p.d.s Unfortunately, any term might be used in reference to any of the three types of p.d.s Allport was quick to point out that there is no distinct dividing line between one kind of p.d. and the next.

Personality Development

Allport devoted a greater proportion of his writings to personality development than most theorists. In particular, he valued the notion of "self" and wished to show how it evolves during development. Like most theorists of personality development—Freud and Sullivan—Allport is a stage theorist.

The Proprium and the Seven Stages of the Developing Self

In one of his most important written works, Allport (1961) devotes a chapter to what he calls "sense of self," formally labelled the **proprium**, "me as felt and known . . . the self as 'object' of knowledge and feeling" (p. 127). But "why not simply [use] the term *self* . . ." and define it in the conventional way? (p. 127). He answered, "This chapter [in the 1961 book] has been devoted to the *sense of* selfhood, not the *nature* of selfhood. Our discussion . . . is primarily psychological, not philosophical, in nature . . . it is much easier to *feel* the self than to *define* [it]. Final definitions we leave to philosophy" (p. 137).

Early Infancy
Early infancy, the first stage, involves no sense of self. Infants initially are unable to separate themselves from their environment. They are conscious, but not self-conscious. If an infant picks up an object, the fingers and the object are one and the same. If she hurts her own foot she has no idea that it is *she* who inflicted the pain. She melts into Mother and they become fused. Later, as motor skills help the infant work out of this early phase, she crawls about and bumps into objects. In this way, she learns there are "things" that are apart from her body; she becomes aware of objects "out there" in another world. However, she does not yet know she is apart and distinct from that other world.

Bodily Self
The most primitive predecessor of selfhood emerges during the second part of the first year. Infants display signs of **bodily self**, sensations that emanate from the muscles, joints, tendons, eyes, ears, and so on. Frustrations relating to the body, such as a stubbed toe or an unsatisfied hunger, also contribute to appreciation of the bodily self. The bodily self becomes the foundation of selfhood and remains with us forever. However, it is noticed only under unusual conditions. Allport (1961) suggests a way of appreciating how all your bodily parts and elements are "you": contrast swallowing your own saliva with spitting it into a cup and drinking it. Your saliva is a part of you that you take for granted, until it becomes physically separated from your body; then it is alien.

Self-Identity
The bodily self is only the first chapter in the story of the self. Emerging during the second year of life, Allport's third stage, is **self-identity**, the continuity of self over

past, present, and future that results from the operation of memory. "Today I remember some of my thoughts of yesterday, and tomorrow I shall remember some of my thoughts of both yesterday and today; and I am certain that they are the thoughts of the same person—of myself" (p. 114). Because we all are changing over time, even as adults, this feeling of continuity is essential to a sense of self. The learning of language underlies the ability to appreciate continuity. Words are what one remembers that assure him he is the same person today as yesterday. The most important of these is the child's name, a word that serves as an anchor to which the ship of self-identity is tied. Each time "Johnny" hears his name—as in "Good Johnny!" "Johnny! Do that on the toilet!"—his feeling of self-identity is strengthened.

Self-Esteem
If bodily self is the cornerstone of selfhood, and self-identity its framework, some walls and a roof must yet go up. *Self-esteem* has been translated literally as "the esteem in which one holds oneself." Allport is more specific: **self-esteem** is pride in one's pursuits and accomplishments. During the third year, Allport's fourth stage, one of the child's favorite exclamations is "Let me!" "Me" has evolved beyond just a body and a sense of continuity to a feeling of instrumentality—the ability to successfully manipulate the environment. "I can do it" implies "I am what I am able to do; don't diminish me by doing for me." This prideful insistence on doing for oneself is matched by shame at having others do for one. Born with self-esteem is its fraternal twin, negativism. Allport writes of a child whose first words upon arriving at his grandmother's were "Grandmother, I won't." "Reverse psychology" may well have been inspired originally by this negativism. For example, some mother may have exclaimed, "I don't want you to eat your broccoli, it's bad for you" in the hope of getting her child to eat the "gross green stuff." (Perhaps that mother's son was George Bush.)

Extension of Self
A sense of body, of continuity, and of pride is a great part of our self structure, but does not include the most important element of the environment, other people. During Allport's fifth stage, bounded by the years 4 to 6, the child develops a fourth aspect of selfhood, an egocentric component. Children think that Santa Claus and even God are there to serve them. However, this self-focus contains an advancement. "He" becomes not merely himself, but is extended to include all that he "possesses." It is "his dog, his house, his sister." This **extension of self** is expanding oneself to include all those significant aspects of one's environment, including people. Now, the family and the self are one. They are like an external conscience that may turn on the child should he fail.

Self-Image
Related to this fledgling relationship to others is a fugitive fifth aspect of self that also emerges during the fifth stage. The **self-image** is composed of the hopes and aspirations that develop from the perceptions and expectations that others have of

oneself. Parents say the child is "good" or "naughty." Peers say that she is "smart" or "fat." She must do this, do that, be this, be that—whatever others expect. To discover whether she is living up to her developing self-image, she will compare others' expectations of how she should behave with her actual behavior.

Rational Coper

During the sixth stage (6 to 12) the self-image continues to develop, and a new aspect emerges: **rational coper**, the sense of selfhood that is not merely able to solve problems, but also can reason them through "in the head" and come up with logical solutions. The rational coper is much like Freud's "ego." It tries to efficiently satisfy the demands of the body (id), the external environment, and society (superego). As the rational coper develops, children become able to think about thinking.

Propriate Striving

During the seventh stage, adolescence, the individual continues to develop the self-image and experiences a renewed search for self-identity. Now self-identity focuses on tying together the teenager and the would-be adult. A teen may ask, "How can I be an adult and still be me?" Continuity must be maintained in the face of a major transition from one phase of life to the next. Society does little to solve teenagers' dilemma. They can join the army, but cannot legally drink. They can vote, but hold office almost nowhere. So teens experiment by rebelling. They stay out late, drink, and are sexually active—all the while hoping that their parents' restrictions on these activities will help define them. They want to become adults, but simultaneously be faithful to themselves as they were.

When thoughts turn to adult pursuits another component of selfhood comes into play, **propriate striving**, planning for the future by setting long-range goals. During adolescence, people come to realize that success in life will depend on planning ahead. To involve effective propriate striving, goals must be reasonably, narrowly focused and in tune with people's abilities. Earlier, there may have been thoughts of being a movie star or a famous athlete. Now, to be mature, goals must be realistic and married to a step-by-step plan for attainment.

TABLE 17.1   Allport's Evolving Sense of Self, Proprium (the self as felt and known)

Stage	Aspect of selfhood	Definition
1	Early infancy	No sense of self
2	Bodily self	Awareness of bodily sensations
3	Self-identity	Continuity of self
4	Self-esteem	Pride in one's pursuits
5	Extension of self	Self includes significant aspects of environment
	Self-image	Hopes and aspirations based on others' expectations
6	Rational coper	Reasoning and solving problems "in the head"
7	Propriate striving	Planning for the future

By adolescence, individuals are in an "identity crisis," a phrase borrowed from Erikson. They are trying to find their own identities apart from their parents. Adolescents try to cast off the conscience that parents, peers, and society have forced upon them and build their own. At this point, conscience shifts from outside the self to within. Now, self-esteem is bolstered by doing what is "right." The self-image includes aspiring to do what ought to be done, and propriate striving encompasses plans to be a fair, kind, and otherwise worthwhile person. As adolescence passes into adulthood, people no longer perform good deeds to avoid a vengeful conscience, but to strive actively for worthy goals that will support a mature self-image. Table 17.1 summarizes Allport's theory of personality development.

The Mature Personality

Individuals continue to evolve. Progress toward a *mature personality* is measured in terms of how well adults meet six criteria.

Extension of the Sense of Self

Extension of self is not fully formed even in the first ten years of life. At adolescence, it reaches out like the tentacles of a confused octopus. It does not know what experiences and roles to grasp for the self, and which to cast aside. With the advent of "puppy love," however, "The boundaries of self are rapidly extended" (1961, p. 283). The welfare of someone else becomes important to one's own, in fact, identical to one's own. Beyond adolescent love, "loneliness" is reflected in "new ambitions, new memberships, new ideas, new friends, . . . new hobbies, and above all one's vocation" (p. 283). All of these new pursuits become incorporated into the self.

Not only does the self take on the new, but it transforms the old. One may continue to do what one did, but the original reasons for doing those things fade. Old pursuits may become detached from original motivations. Allport's name for this transformation is **functional autonomy**, a process by which a new system of motivation evolves from an older one, but stems from tensions different from those of the original.

Allport illustrates this transformation by reference to "Hosea," the son of a famous politician who initially goes into politics so that he may "follow in his father's footsteps." Later he becomes fascinated by and enmeshed in the political process; being "his father's son" no longer matters. He pursues politics for love of the process and for the power and glory of it. Allport argues that much of what we do that is important to the self has become functionally autonomous from the original motivations. The new motivations are more abstract than the old. They include "aesthetics," "intrinsic interest," and "human well-being."

One problem of maturity is to extend oneself into the spheres of one's life. Allport provides an example, Sam, whose life's pursuits are typical. He works in a factory, knows many people, pays union dues, drinks at the local tavern, and finds movies to be significant diversions. However, he is constantly *task-involved* and rarely *ego-involved*. "He has not extended his sense of self into any of the significant areas of his life . . . the economic, educational, recreational, political, domestic, and religious. Sam passes them all by, incorporating none into his self" (p. 284). To be mature one must detach oneself from the "clamorous immediacy of the body" and find self-related reasons for doing whatever one has been doing (p. 285). Sam could become involved in his union for reasons of "fair and equitable treatment of workers," or local politics in the interest of "cleaning up the neighborhood."

Warm Relating of Self to Others

By extending the self, a person of warmth is capable of great *intimacy*. Warm relationships reflect a genuine capacity for love involving family, friends, and lovers. But mature warmth also entails *compassion*, a form of detachment. Gossip and possessiveness are avoided. Others are allowed to lead their own lives free of intrusions. "Both intimacy and compassion require that one not be a burden or nuisance to others, nor impede their freedom in finding their own identity" (p. 285).

Emotional Security (Self-Acceptance)

To Allport *self-acceptance* includes avoidance of overreaction to "drives" or gut tissue needs. Mature people are neither constantly seeking sexual gratification nor prudish and repressed about sex. They accept sexual urges as a part of themselves. Mature people do have fears and well they should: there are real dangers "out there." However, they do not recoil in terror at the thought of roaming a large city or at the prospect of confronting hostile protesters. Self-acceptance assures mature people that the exercise of reasonable prudence will allow them to successfully cope with dangers.

Self-accepting persons have high **frustration tolerance**—when things go wrong, they do not pitch a tantrum, blame others, or wallow in self-pity. Instead they accept some of the blame and find a way around the obstacle, or, failing that, resign themselves to some unpleasantness and bide their time until things get better. Part of self-acceptance is to know one is fallible, but to believe one is capable of compensating for faults.

Realistic Perceptions and Skills

"Maturity does not bend reality to fit one's needs and fantasies" (p. 289). The mature person seems to "see things" more clearly than others and, thus, has more wisdom than others. But does this mean one has to have high intelligence to be mature? Allport answers that intelligence helps in the achievement of maturity, but does not guarantee it.

Mature people are problem-solvers. "Although we often find skillful people who are immature, we never find mature people without problem-pointed skills" (pp. 289–290). Not only are mature people capable of solving task-related problems, they are capable of losing themselves in the task. They are problem-centered. "In short a mature person will be in close touch with what we call `the real world.' He will see objects, people, and situations for what they are. And he will have important work to do" (p. 290).

Self-Objectification: Insight and Humor

Imagine someone who announces, "I'm a master of the English language and a person who knows himself well." Immediately the person apologetically adds, "I don't mean to infer that I'm more smarter than others." Allport believed that most of us are like this individual in that we believe we have insight into ourselves, but we really do not. Can we obtain what we falsely claim? We can, of course, never know the "true person." Even if we assume there is a single, stable "true person"—thereby ignoring the possibility that a person is always in a state of flux—we could never know that "true person." No one is privy to all the complexities and subtleties that constitute a person, not even the person. Thus, the best we can do is to look at the discrepancy between what a person believes about her or himself and what other people believe about him or her. The less the discrepancy, the greater the insight.

In a study where subjects rated each other, the correlation between ratings of insight and sense of humor was .88. What makes a sense of humor such a close associate of insight? A **genuine sense of humor**, as opposed to an appreciation of sexual and aggressive jokes, is being able "to laugh at the things one loves (including, of course, oneself and all that pertains to oneself), and still to love them" (p. 292). Insightful people communicate that they know and accept their own limitations and deficiencies by laughing at their shortcomings. Such people are good judges of others and are accepted by them.

Perhaps the key to the close correlation between insight and humor is that a person with a good "sense of humor" communicates a match between perceptions of self by self and by others. Friends know a person's faults and find evidence for insight in the match between their knowledge of the person's deficiencies and the person's acknowledgment of those shortcomings.

The Unifying Philosophy of Life

One primary element in a unifying philosophy of life is **directedness**, having a goal or goals in life toward which one strives. The goals may change as one's life circumstances change, but they must be in place if one is to claim a mature personality. For example, goals may change after a series of "bad luck" incidents. Goals also evolve and become more realistic. For example, as a post-adolescent may have to admit, some earlier goals, becoming a corporate executive, are unlikely to be obtained. Allport points especially to the late twenties as a time of goal-shattering disillusionment with the early phases of marriage and career.

Some coherent value orientation is also necessary for a unifying philosophy to take shape. Allport believed that six ideal types, pure values not actual people, express value options best.

1. *The theoretical.* Here the dominant interest is discovery of the "truth." The inclination is toward the cognitive. People adopting this orientation are empirical, critical, and rational.
2. *The economic.* The dominant orientation is toward what is useful and what is practical. Individuals who embrace this orientation are like the "marketing type" that Fromm popularized. Their view may clash with other sets of val-

ues. The economic individual will denude the forest and pollute the rivers for present economic gain.

3. *The esthetic.* The esthetic orientation focuses on form and harmony. These values are diametrically opposed to theoretical values. Events in life are enjoyed for their own sake; truth is beauty. The interest is in people rather than the welfare of people; the trend is toward individualism and self-sufficiency.

4. *The social.* In the social orientation, the emphasis is on love of people. Being friendly, philanthropic, kind, and unselfish is valued. Power is repudiated in favor of love and selflessness.

5. *The political.* The political orientation is to seek power. The desire is for personal power, influence, and renown. The interest is narrow, confined to politics, because power is concentrated there.

6. *The religious orientation.* Unity is the magnet of the religious orientation. The quest is to become one with the cosmos, to relate to an all-embracing totality. People of this inclination "find their religious experience in the affirmation of life and in active participation therein" (Allport, 1961, p. 299).

Allport believed that a coherent *religious sentiment* is central to maturity of personality. He was not heavily invested in organized religion, but he seemed fascinated with the possibility of a higher power that is the center of human experience. He saw religious orientation as the most comprehensive and integrative of the six value orientations and believed some form of religious sentiment to be essential to the mature personality.

Religious sentiment can be immature: a deity is adopted who favors the person's immediate interests much as did Santa Claus during childhood. Another form of immature sentiment is the tribal type: "God favors my people to your people" (p. 300). In both cases the motivation is *extrinsic*, utilitarian and in the service of self-esteem maintenance.

By contrast a mature religious sentiment is *intrinsically* motivated: it is an end-in-itself, something that one surrenders to, not something to use. Religious sentiment, like humor, transports life's troubles from the routine context to a perspective that is more universal and generally meaningful. Like humor, religious sentiment allows one to avoid taking things too seriously: whatever is currently happening in life is trivial relative to the universal scheme of things.

Although rational thought is not excluded from religious sentiment, faith is the basic cognitive mode. Religious faith is unique and more comprehensive than other forms of faith. It represents a theory of life rather than being a collection of beliefs in specifics, such as that one will succeed in business. Religious faith is all engrossing and all encompassing.

Generic conscience is central to the development of personality. Allport also regarded conscience as a unifying force in personality: it lays down comprehensive guidelines for nearly all of a person's conduct. Ultimately it is the source of accepting responsibility for oneself and the wellspring of one's responsibilities to others.

Allport distinguishes the generic conscience of maturity from the "must sayer" of childhood. The child feels guilty for failure to live up to any of the immature conscience's commandments. The mature, generic conscience is not troubled by a knee-jerk need to avoid any transgression. Minor slips and sins are not the mature person's concern. Only adherence to personally selected moral standards is relevant to the self of the mature person. These standards will include some of the moral strictures of the mature person's society, but are not limited to them.

The extrinsically religious have a "spotty and inconsistent conscience readily soothed by self-justification" (p. 304). By contrast, conscience in the intrinsically religious person is a fully developed guide to behavior. Religious sentiment, therefore, is often closely tied to the generic conscious.

Personality and Prejudice

There are three reasons why Allport's book *The Nature of Prejudice* (1954) is perhaps the single most important work ever done on the subject of prejudice. First, it was the earliest comprehensive discussion of prejudice that was based on a significant body of scientific research. Second, it was extremely influential in shaping social scientists' thinking concerning prejudice. Third, because Allport has had so much influence on prejudice research done since 1954, it is relatively easy to fit some of today's findings regarding prejudice into his theoretical framework.

Prejudice Defined

According to Allport (1954), **prejudice** is felt or expressed antipathy based upon a faulty and inflexible generalization and may be directed toward a group as a whole, or toward an individual because he is a member of the group. Thus, prejudice is negative feelings regarding members of some group that are sometimes just felt internally and sometimes expressed openly. It is based on the faulty generalization that all, or almost all, members of some group, such as Native Americans, possess certain negative traits, such as drunkenness. Obviously such a generalization is always inflexible, because no trait will apply to almost all, much less all, members of a large group (even skin color varies greatly among people who are called "black").

While prejudice involves feelings, *discrimination* refers to behavior directed against a group or its members. Allport thought of discrimination as acting out prejudice. Many measures of prejudice amount to asking people—usually via questionnaire—how much they discriminate so their level of prejudice can be inferred. For this reason, it is possible to offer a more empirical definition of prejudice than is consistent with Allport's theoretical definition. Because *prejudice* measures often ask about *self-perceptions of discrimination*, it may be seen as "the degree to which people believe that they discriminate against members of some group, as indicated by what they say or write" (Allen, 1990, p. 325). As prejudice is most often assessed with the use of questionnaires completed anonymously, people's pronouncements about their level of discrimination probably represent what they really believe.

Social Distance

Given this empirical definition, it is immediately obvious that what people believe about their level of discrimination may not be accurate. Because nobody has total insight, some people who honestly claim not to discriminate against others may do so anyway. To explore this logical conclusion, it is necessary to consider **Social Distance (SD)**, a measure of discrimination that requires individuals to indicate how close to themselves they would allow members of some group to come. Allport (1954, p. 39) listed the items of the SD scale as follows:

I would admit (members of some group)

1. To close kin by marriage
2. To my club as personal chums
3. To my street as neighbors
4. To employment in my occupation
5. To citizenship in my country
6. As visitors only to my country
7. Would exclude from my country

Notice that the social relations to which the members of some group can be admitted vary from those involving a great deal of *intimacy* with group members, *commitment* to them, and *permanency* of relationships involving them (top of list) to those involving no intimacy, commitment, and permanency (bottom of list; Allen, 1975).

Not only do people who strongly claim not to discriminate against some often-disparaged group really believe themselves, these self-proclaimed "unprejudiced" people probably do not discriminate under most circumstances. Nevertheless, would they discriminate when asked to accept that same group for social relations that entail high intimacy, commitment, and permanency? An answer to the question may tell us whether what people believe about their level of discrimination is accurate.

A number of years ago, I gave some white college students a test to determine the degree to which they were prejudiced against African-Americans (Allen, 1975). Based on their scores, some students were classified as "unprejudiced," some as "prejudiced," and some as "ambivalent" with regard to prejudice (gave mixed signals about their level of discrimination). All of these subjects were then asked to indicate the degree of closeness they would allow African-Americans by use of an SD scale composed of items 1 and 3 (Triandis, Loh, & Levine, 1966). Results showed that all categories of these white subjects, even those who claimed they did not discriminate according to race, in fact did so. When it comes to relations involving intimacy, commitment, and permanency, even "unprejudiced" subjects show racial discrimination.

Although unprejudiced white subjects did discriminate on the SD scale, when it came to indicating who they admire, another part of my same study showed that they did not discriminate by race. In fact, they actually expressed more admira-

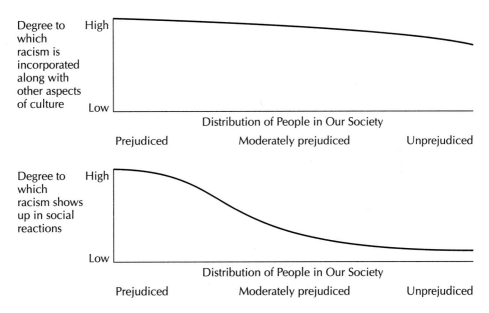

FIGURE 17.1   **The relationship between racism and prejudice**

tions for African-Americans than for whites. (This so-called "reverse discrimination" effect reverted to no discrimination when subjects thought they were hooked up to a lie detector machine.)

But why do self-proclaimed non-discriminators in fact discriminate when it comes to choices for intimate, committed, permanent social relations? Results of the administration of prejudice measures indicate that there are great individual differences in prejudice. Perhaps there is some underlying dimension for which individual differences are not great that explains why most people sometimes discriminate by race, even those who claim not to.

In the case of discrimination against African-Americans, such a dimension appears to exist. *Racism* is widespread negative sentiment directed toward African-Americans (and other people of color; Allen, 1975; 1990). It has been argued that racism is a part of the mainstream culture in this country. When people incorporate their culture, largely through the process of identification, they swallow it whole. They ingest not only the good aspects of their culture, of which there are many, they also consume the bad . . . racism. Because most people adopt their culture, most people in the majority would incorporate racism within themselves. This may be the reason that even unprejudiced people show discrimination in some areas: racism rears it ugly head when it comes to choices of others for intimate, committed, permanent relations, although it fails to show up in other realms (deciding who to admire). By contrast, racism is reflected often in a wide spectrum of prejudiced people's expressions and behaviors. Figure 17.1 displays the relationship between racism and prejudice.

Consistent with this consideration of racism, Allport found that racial animosity is very widespread. After examining the polls assessing antagonism toward various groups—most frequently African-Americans—Allport concluded, "These . . . studies tempt us to estimate that four-fifths of the American population harbors enough antagonism toward minority groups to influence their daily conduct" (p. 78). Although his statement was based on polls taken many years ago, there is reason to believe that it is still accurate today. While animosity was very open in the early fifties, today, for most of us, it has become limited to a few social relations and it has evolved to be more underground and subtle. The reluctance of white Americans to engage in intimate, committed, permanent relations with African-Americans is reflected in the still exceedingly low interracial marital rate (Allen, 1990). Also, many studies over the years have shown that careful investigation of subtle behaviors reveals definite traces of racial animosity (Allen, 1978; 1990).

"Race" Differences

Allport (1954) traces continued interest in alleged racial differences to arguments that subcategories of humans exist and can be arranged in a hierarchy from best to worst. It made thinking and life itself simpler to believe that there are big differences between one race and the next, and few differences among people of a given racial designation. It was also gratifying: one could declare one's own race "best" and view the members of other races as uniformly inferior.

Allport asserted that gender bias mirrors how we react to the races. "Only a small part of our human nature is differentiated by sex. . . . the vast proportion of human physical, physiological, psychological traits are not sex linked" (p. 109). Yet, despite the evidence of no difference on critical traits such as I.Q., "women are regarded as inferior, kept in the home . . . [and] denied many of the rights and privileges of men. The special roles assigned to them are far in excess of what sexual genetic difference would justify. So it is with race" (p. 109).

Allport, a pioneer in questioning "race," makes two important points about the concept. First, most of the world's people are of "mixed stock"; thus most do not fit any racial category. Second, "Most human characteristics ascribed to race are . . . [actually] ethnic, not racial" (p. 113). Today, the validity of "race" is again being challenged (Allen and Adams, 1992; Weizmann, Wiener, Wiesenthal, & Ziegler, 1990; Zuckerman, 1990). It now appears that three criteria must be met before "race" is applicable to humans: (1) consensually accepted criteria for differentiation among races must be developed and shown to actually erect clear boundaries between one "race" and the next; (2) variability within "races" must be adequately reconciled with assumptions of intraracial uniformity; and (3) overlap among races must be reconciled with the assumption that "races" are meaningfully distinct (Allen & Adams, 1992).

Stereotypes

According to Allport, prejudice affects our thinking as well as our feelings. It is associated with the development of beliefs concerning the traits supposedly possessed by all or most members of a group. A belief of this sort is called a **stereotype**, an exaggerated belief that members of a group possess a certain trait; "Its function is to justify (rationalize) our conduct in relation to that [group]" (p. 191). Such beliefs may have a "grain of truth" to them. In centuries past, Jews were "money handlers" in Europe, simply because they were allowed few alternatives for making a living. The problem is that this veridical observation evolved to become "most [or all] Jews are obsessed with making money." Though there may be a "grain of truth" to a stereotype, it is almost always false to assume that most of any large group possess any trait one can conjure up.

Stereotypes do tend to change in content over time, although the overall valence of their emotional tone may be relatively constant. Before World War II, the tone of our stereotypes of the Japanese was negative, but not strongly so. As soon as Pearl Harbor was bombed, stereotypes of the Japanese became viciously negative. As the Japanese wrought their economic miracle following the war, stereotypes became more positive. Currently, because they are viewed as beating us economically and "buying up America," stereotypes of the Japanese have become more negative.

What of the tone and content of stereotypes about African-Americans? Allport lists the following stereotypes of African-Americans that were held by white Americans at the time he was writing his 1954 book: unintelligent, morally primitive, emotionally unstable, overassertive, lazy, boisterous, fanatically religious, gamblers, flashy dressers, criminal, violent, reproductively prolific, occupationally unstable, superstitious, happy-go-lucky, ignorant, musical. To find out how these stereotypes might have changed I asked 81 white undergraduate students to each write down five words to describe African-Americans (they used the Adjective Generation Technique, Allen & Potkay, 1983a). Sixty-three African-American students were given the same instruction. Next I tallied the words most frequently used to describe African-Americans. The results are presented in Table 17.2.

You can see that whites' stereotypes of African-Americans are still negative. Though some content remains the same—"musical" and "loud" (boisterous)—there have been some changes. African-Americans are now seen as "humorous" and "athletic." Notice also that African-Americans' self-descriptions agree with whites on "independent," but mention "athletic" much less often and include "intelligent," omitted by whites.

Unlike in the vast majority of other stereotype studies, I asked African-Americans to indicate stereotypes of whites. (Usually African-Americans are not asked, or stereotypes of various white ethnic groups are assessed, not whites in general.) Table 17.3 displays the stereotypes of whites.

Again, African-Americans and whites show limited agreement. African-Americans are more negative about whites than whites are about themselves.

TABLE 17.2   African-Americans Described by Themselves and by Euro-pean-Americans (% of each sample using each word)

By Themselves		By European Americans	
6	misunderstood	6	boastful
6	emotional	6	moody
6	poor	6	poor
6	funny	6	strong
6	humorous	7	musical
6	inventive	7	obnoxious
6	powerful	7	prejudiced
8	corrupt	9	black
8	determined	9	mean
8	educated	9	smart
10	independent	10	arrogant
10	friendly	10	funny
11	athletic	10	independent
13	intelligent	11	corrupt
14	beautiful	11	friendly
14	oppressed	21	humorous
27	strong	25	loud
27	smart	40	athletic

Though both agree that whites are "greedy" and "smart," whites see themselves as "lazy" and "intelligent," but African-Americans do not. Whites now ascribe "lazy" to themselves, not African-Americans.

Neither these results nor those reported by Allport were produced by large, representative samples of U.S. citizens. My survey, however, does have some advantages. One plus is that subjects produced the words from their own vocabularies, rather than being forced to choose from some limited, possibly biased list. This fact probably accounts for results not predicted by previous surveys, like whites being seen as "corrupt," "prejudiced," and "greedy" and African-Americans as "friendly," "funny," and "humorous."

Painting the Picture of the Prejudiced Personality

The traits that highly prejudiced people share can be summarized in the phrase "threat oriented." The reference is partly due to viewing the world as a threatening place. However, some of the threat comes from within. The prejudiced person "seems fearful of himself, of his own instincts, of his own consciousness, of change, and of his social environment" (p. 396). To put it another way, very prejudiced people suffer from "crippled egos." By promoting oppression of other groups, they can ensure that their own status in society is not threatened.

Beyond this general description, Allport offers some specific traits that prejudiced people tend to have in common.

TABLE 17.3   European-Americans Described by Themselves and by African-Americans (% of each sample using each word)

By Themselves		By African Americans	
6	corrupt	6	inventive
6	free	6	competitive
6	happy	6	powerful
6	kind	6	wealthy
7	conceited	8	educated
7	educated	10	racist
7	egotistical	11	selfish
10	intelligent	11	greedy
10	prejudiced	13	rich
10	rich	16	mean
12	humorous	19	smart
12	independent	24	prejudiced
12	inventive	41	corrupt
12	lazy		
15	arrogant		
15	friendly		
19	competitive		
19	greedy		
32	smart		

Ambivalence about Parents

In a study of anti-Semitic women students that Allport relies on repeatedly, ambivalence toward parents is clearly evident. While they openly praised their parents, on projective tests these women showed hostility toward their parents. Tolerant subjects were the opposite: they were openly critical of their parents, but the projective tests revealed no underlying hostility toward parents. Prejudiced students' hostility toward their parents may stem from child-rearing themes of obedience, punishment, and actual or threatened rejection.

Moralism

Allport reports that very prejudiced people tend to be highly moralistic as reflected in high attention to cleanliness and good manners. When the anti-Semitic students were asked what would embarrass them the most, they "responded in terms of violations of mores and conventions in public. Whereas [the] non-prejudiced spoke more often of inadequacy in personal relations" (p. 398). Again child-rearing practices are implicated. The prejudiced had parents who punished them severely for any show of interest in their genitals and for aggression against the parents. The result is children who are guilt-ridden and full of self-hatred due to repeatedly being reminded of their wickedness. As adults their repressed hostility explodes onto members of other groups and their rigid morality is the source of a rationale for rejecting those individuals.

Dichotomization

Highly prejudiced people literally see in black and white. There is good and there is bad; there is right and there is wrong. This orientation was forced on them by parents who dished out approval and disapproval categorically: everything the child did was either right or it was wrong; there was no middle ground. Little wonder that as adults they see only two classes of people: those who are acceptable and those who are not.

Need for Definiteness

Allport believed that very prejudiced people are distinguished by their unique cognitive processes. Consistent with their tendency to classify everything into two categories, they show another critical characteristic. They have little *tolerance for ambiguity*: their cognitive orientation requires that everything be clearly distinguished from everything else, questions have definite answers, and problems have simple solutions. In short, prejudiced people want everything to be clear-cut, no gray areas. Shown an illusion involving a stationary point of light presented in darkness that appears to move, prejudiced people "reported the light as moving in a constant direction from trial to trial and to [move] a constant number of inches" (p. 401). By contrast unprejudiced people saw movement in all directions and to a variable extent. Prejudiced people imposed clarity and order on an inherently ambiguous situation, while unprejudiced people tolerated the ambiguity.

Externalization

Allport saw very prejudiced people as lacking in self-insight. They do not see their own faults; they project them onto other people. Further, "things seem to happen 'out there.'" (p. 404). Rather than believing that they control what happens to them by use of their own resources, they believe that fate controls them. Rotter would class these people as externals. Allport explained, "It is better and safer for a person in inner conflict to avoid self-reference. It is better to think of things happening to him rather than as caused by him" (p. 404). Also, prejudiced people externalize punishment: "It is not *I* who hates and injures others; it is *they* who hate and injure me" (p. 404).

Institutionalization

Allport believed the highly prejudiced person prefers order, especially social order. He finds safety and definiteness in his institutional memberships. "Lodges, schools, churches, the nation, may serve as a defense against disquiet in his personal life. To lean on them saves him from leaning on himself" (p. 404). Also, the prejudiced are more devoted to institutions than the unprejudiced. The anti-Semitic college women were more wrapped up in their sororities and more patriotic. While patriotic people are not necessarily prejudiced, Allport referred to evidence that very prejudiced people are almost always super-patriots. He cites an investigation in which club members completed a lengthy belief-questionnaire in return for a monetary contribution to their clubs. The large number of variables examined were reduced to only one trait held in common: *nationalism.* Allport is quick to point out that "the nation" to these people is not what it is to most people. When most people think of "the nation," it is the people, the principles of the constitution, and the lands that come to mind. Instead, prejudiced people view "the nation" as something that will protect them from people seen as unlike themselves and preserve the *status quo.*

Authoritarianism

Allport believed that very prejudiced people are uncomfortable with democracy. "The consequences of personal freedom they find unpredictable. Individuality makes for indefiniteness, disorderliness, and change" (p. 406). It is easier to live in a power hierarchy where everyone has a place and the top spot is occupied by an all-powerful person. In a word, prejudiced people are **authoritarian,** they show high deference for authority figures, submission to the power of authority, and a need to command those seen as lower in power than themselves. Allport cites a study in which prejudiced people listed dictators like Napoleon when asked who they admired most, while unprejudiced people listed figures such as Lincoln.

Authoritarianism is seen in prejudiced people's mistrust of others. Authority embedded in a strong nation can save oneself from suspected others. "To the prejudiced person the best way to control these suspicions is to have an orderly, authoritative, powerful society. Strong nationalism is a good thing. Hitler [wasn't] so wrong. . . . America needs . . . a strong leader" (p. 407). This crucial concept is still receiving attention from researchers (Peterson, Doty, & Winter, 1993).

Lessening the Effects of Prejudice

Table 17.4 lists conditions that research has shown to be effective in attenuating the effects of prejudice.

Allport's influence is clearly seen in the coincidence of his principles, derived by Green (1981), with the prejudice reduction methods. Principles and relations to items of Table 17.4 follow.

1. The interdependence of groups [2 & 3 in Table 17.4]
2. Perceptions of supportive organizational norms [3 & 5]
3. Intergroup associations and interactions [2 & 3]
4. The criterion of equal status [1]
5. Those once seen as different are accepted as peers [6]

A number of researchers have confirmed Allport's ideas on prejudice reduction. For example, Damico and Scott (1984) developed a questionnaire based on Allport's principles 1, 2, 3, and 4. Using it, they found that frequency of cross-race contact while in high school is a predictor of frequency of cross-race contact during college. Finchilescu (1988) investigated South African nurses'

TABLE 17.4   Contact between Majority and Minority Group Members as a Means of Reducing the Effects of Prejudice

Ideal Conditions for Contact	*Positive Effects of Contact*
1. The participants have equal status (majority are not more likely to be leaders than minority)	1. Learning about similarities in beliefs and values
2. Cooperation among participants leads to positive outcomes	2. Learning that minority are not all alike and neither are majority
3. Organizational officials create social rules that promote friendly inter-action (first names are used and officials model concern and affection for participants regard-less of majority/minority standing)	3. Cooperation between minority and majority is reinforced by officials
4. Participants are chosen so that they do not possess characteristics that are part of negative stereotypes ("loud" minority and "arrogant" majority are excluded from participation)	4. Negative stereotypes are destroyed by the observation that "other race" members do not possess characteristics associated with them
5. Organizational officials point to the positive effects of participation that would occur in other contexts thus leading to generalization of effects	5. Conflicts between old beliefs and new more fair-minded beliefs are reduced by reinforcement of new beliefs and non-reinforcement of old beliefs
	6. As participants get to know "other group" members, the importance of identity with their own group decreases, leading to less distinction between groups

Based on information in Brigham (1986). Used with permission.

reactions to interracial nurse training. Nurses in integrated training programs were much more favorable to interracial training than those in segregated programs.

Evaluation

Contributions

Allport's more general ideas seem to have had more impact than his specific concepts or his theory as a whole. His idiographic approach is periodically mentioned to remind us that seeking general principles applicable to all people may not be the best way to understand humans.

Personality writers have considered Allport to be the voice of moderation with regard to the matter of behavioral consistency (for example, Zuroff, 1986). While Allport did not see evidence for a high level of cross-situational behavioral consistency, he was quick to argue that there is sufficient repetition of behavior to support the existence of p.d.s. The idea of p.d.s itself is important, because it suggests that each person is even more unique than is generally recognized. Unlike many other theorists, Allport appreciated that understanding humans is very difficult, because each is so different from the others and each is extremely complex. Reading Allport reminds us that there are no easy solutions to the human puzzle. Further, Allport's notions about personality development have been highly influential. His chronicle of how the self (proprium) unfolds has provided many insights into how people come to be who they are.

The timely publication of *Nature of Prejudice* in 1954, the year of the Supreme Court's school desegregation ruling, was the most important event in the history of studying prejudice up to that time and for years after. Despite its age, the book continues to be cited and to inspire research. Allport's belief that prejudice can be reduced by interracial contact supported by organizational officials and occurring in an atmosphere of cooperation is still accepted today.

While not many of Allport's specific terms are often on the lips of typical personologists, there are exceptions. "Cardinal, central, and secondary dispositions" have been given more than lip service because they point to a crucial consideration: the centrality of dispositions (traits) to the life of the individual. "Functional autonomy" represents an insight on Allport's part. It suggests how certain relatively-temporary behaviors that may be of no special importance to a person can evolve into long-standing behaviors that come to characterize the individual.

Limitations

Allport's "theory" may be regarded as several mini-theories that are, at best, loosely tied together. In a sense, he seems to have jumped on his horse and ridden off in all directions at once. He does have a theory of traits and a personality development theory, but the connection between the two was not made explicit. Because he was both a personologist and a social psychologist, he wrote on diverse topics such as the proprium and prejudice. Little wonder that he was not able to tie things together very well.

Allport's emphasis on unique rather than common traits has put him out of the mainstream. The primary thrust of personality theory has been to state general principles that apply to all people and to specify traits that most people possess to some degree. Allport's insistence on the extreme uniqueness of each person makes the task of understanding humans look very daunting.

The boundaries between some of Allport's concepts are so indistinct as to be exceedingly hazy. The outstanding example is "cardinal, central, and secondary" p.ds. Within a single person, there seems to be no concrete basis for deciding why one p.d. is "cardinal," another "central," and still another "secondary." Also troublesome is that a given trait can be both a common trait and a p.d. It does not help much to indicate that a trait such as "kind" has a different "flavor" when found in one person as opposed to another. How is it the same trait if it is different when possessed by different people? In a sense Allport argues for a lack of continuity between people. Each person is an island unto herself or himself and must be understood using principles unique to him or her. Such conceptions make the study of people very costly.

Conclusions

Some people find fault with Allport's idiographic approach. Others, including myself, believe that he has correctly understood the complexity of people and the "fact" that their uniqueness makes the writing of general principles applicable to all a very arduous task. Many personologists have acted as if understanding people is easier than understanding chemistry or physics. In fact, people are the most complicated entities on this earth. Facing up to the difficulty of explaining them is the first step in the grueling task of sorting out all that complexity.

While Allport may be criticized for creating a series of mini-theories rather than one coherent theory, does writing a grand, all-encompassing theory make sense? After all, even Einstein failed when he tried to compose a theory unifying the major physical forces. In view of human complexity, it may be naive to attempt a theory, such as Freud's, that explains most things that are psychological in nature. Even theories restricted to explaining personality may be too ambitious. Given the present "state of the art" methods we have in personality, mini-theories may be the best we can do.

A few of the theorists covered in this book are notable not just for their theories, but also for the persons they were. Like Kelly, Allport received a warm, genuine tribute from his students. Like Rogers, he seemed undistracted by the pursuit of fame and fortune; his concern was for the well-being of people. Allport's life is a reminder that truly meaningful psychological theorizing provides many benefits for human beings.

Summary Points

1. Allport was born into a warm and philanthropic home headed by a school teacher and a physician. Always humble, he dismissed his academic feats in high school and later. The baby of the family, he followed older brother Floyd to Harvard. There, like others, his first experience with psychology was less than positive. Still he adopted the area and received a doctorate from Harvard, where he spent most of his years as a professor.

2. While Allport was a personal humanist, his theory was not humanistic. Unlike others, he was idiographic, inclined to study each person's unique traits.

He was also a forerunner of the interactionists. The Freudian unconscious was, to Allport, just as overemphasized as behavioral consistency. Instead he embraced a more modest assumption about the possibility of confirming traits.

3. Allport's eclectic view allowed him to use any ideas of other theorists that he deemed helpful. The Adjective Generation Technique came from his tendency to abandon typical methods in favor of what works to understand people. Personality is the dynamic organization of psychophysical systems that determine characteristic behavior and thought. A trait has the capacity to render many stimuli equivalent and to guide adaptive behavior.

4. Traits are not habits or character, but can be common or p.ds. Traits have a different flavor when attributed to a particular person rather than to people in general. Cardinal, central, and secondary p.ds. refer to centrality of traits within the personality. Allport's stage theory of personality development is founded on the proprium, "me as felt and known, the self as 'object' of knowledge and feeling."

5. The "bodily self" refers to sensations of the body. Self-identity is continuity of the self over time. Self-esteem is pride in one's pursuits and accomplishments. In extension of self, the self expands to include important elements of the environment. Self-image is composed of hopes developing from others' expectations. The rational coper can solve problems in the head. Propriate striving involves laying plans for the future.

6. Extension of the self in the mature personality is based on functional autonomy. Warm relating to others in maturity is founded on intimacy and compassion. Self-acceptance entails reasonable handling of urges and high frustration tolerance. Realistic perceptions of useful skills, insight, and humor are essential for maturity. Laughing at ourselves tells others that we have insight. A unifying philosophy of life involves directedness. Value orientations take six different forms.

7. Mature, intrinsically-motivated, religious sentiment is also essential to maturity. Generic conscience is concerned with self-selected principles, not with sins. Prejudice is felt antipathy based on faulty generalizations directed to most members of a group. More empirically, it is what people say and write about their discrimination. Even whites who claim not to discriminate by race, do so when making choices that entail high intimacy, commitment, and permanency. Underlying racism may be the reason why such people discriminate.

8. Race differences may be reduced to ethnic differences since "race" is a questionable concept. A stereotype, belief that most members of a group possess a certain trait, may contain a grain of truth, but is false when applied to most of a large group. Stereotypes of African-Americans are still negative, but have changed in content. A study of African-American's stereotypes of whites reveals several negative stereotypes.

9. The prejudiced personality is "threat-oriented." Prejudiced people have underlying feelings of hostility toward their parents and are highly moralistic. They dichotomize everything, show a high need for definiteness, tend to externalize their own hostility, and are devoted to their institutions, most especially "the nation." They also show high deference for and willingness to submit to authority.

Lessening prejudice is largely a matter of arranging cooperative, equal status inter-action between majority and minority that is supported by organizational officials.

10. Allport has been the voice of moderation on "behavioral consistency" and his "personality development" has been influential. *The Nature of Prejudice* was a landmark contribution to understanding prejudice. Certain of his specific concepts have been useful, but his theory is really some mini-theories. His emphasis on p.ds. puts him out of the mainstream and the borders between the three kinds of p.ds. are murky. Also, the distinction between p.ds. and common traits is not clear. Still, his emphasis on the uniqueness and complexity of people may be realistic.

Running Comparison

Theorist	Allport in Comparison
Freud	He thought that Freud dug too deep too often, but saw these coincidences: id (body), ego (environment), superego (society).
Fromm	His economic orientation and the marketing type of Fromm are similar.
Murray	He disagreed with Murray on the importance of the unconscious.
Maslow	They both alluded to multiple motivations.
Kelly	Like Kelly, he adopted the "one person at a time" approach.
Cattell & Eysenck	He disagreed with them on emphasizing common traits.
Erikson	He found Erikson's "identity crisis" useful.
Rotter	His prejudiced people were like Rotter's externals.
Sullivan	Both were stage theorists.

Essay/Critical Thinking Questions

1. Sometimes children turn out just like their parents. How was Allport like his parents?

2. Can you trace Allport's greater interest in p.ds. than in common traits to a deeper philosophical orientation?

3. How does Allport's generic conscience of adulthood differ from Freud's superego?

4. Could laughing at oneself be carried too far? Indicate a couple of reasons why making fun of oneself might sometimes be a mistake.

5. Besides the social relations specified on the Social Distance scale, what other intimate, committed, permanent relations can you name?

6. Might the "change" in stereotypes of African-Americans shown with recent use of the Adjective Generation Technique have something to do with the method used?

7. Can you make explicit the connection between how prejudiced people are reared and their attitudes toward their parents?

8. How does the need for "definiteness" in prejudiced people link to their prejudice?

9. Why does contact between minority and majority sometimes not lead to reduction in prejudice?

10. Why is a mini-theory better than an all encompassing theory?

GLOSSARY

Abience is the name given to the negative-need-promoting vectors that describe movements away from objects and people.

Ability trait is reflected in "the manner of response to the complexity of a situation, [selected after] the individual is clear on what goals he wants to achieve in that situation."

Abstracting across the cleavage line occurs when whole constructs fall under superordinate emergent and under superordinate implicit poles.

Accurate empathy is Rogers' term for the ability to accurately perceive the client's internal world in a non-evaluative way.

Active imagination is a method through which patients are encouraged to simulate dream experiences by actively engaging in imagination while fully awake.

Active period is the period during which the need is aroused and determines the behavior of the organism.

Actone is a pattern of bodily movements in and of itself, divorced from its effect.

Adience refers to the positive-need-promoting vectors that describe movement toward objects and people.

Advantageous comparison is a cognitive mechanism by which ". . . deplored acts can be made to appear righteous by contrasting them with flagrant inhumanities."

Aesthetic needs are related to beauty, structure, and symmetry.

Alpha is press that actually exist, that is, are objectively verifiable.

Ambiverts show medium degrees of exvia-invia, with behaviors characteristic of both aspects.

Amphigenital refers to the case where one or both members of a pair, who both may be homosexual or heterosexual, take on a role that is different from their usual role.

Amplification is broadening and enriching dream or other image content through a process of directed association.

Anal stage is a period in which sexual gratification occurs when defecation relieves the tension of a full bowel and simultaneously stimulates the anus.

Anal-expulsive is an adult type that involves a "diarrhetic" orientation. Anal-expulsive people react against others' attempts to restrict them by doing whatever they want.

Anal-retentive is an adult type which is characterized by delay of final satisfactions to the last possible moment; these people save and retain.

Anima is the representation of woman in man.

Animus is man in woman.

Anxiety (Cattell) is the feelings of tension and upset, the source of which may be difficult to identify.

Anxiety (Freud) is a state of extremely unpleasant emotional discomfort.

Anxiety (Kelly) is what a person experiences when his or her construction system does not apply to critical events.

Anxiety gradient refers to "learning to discriminate increasing from diminishing anxiety and to alter activity in the direction of the latter."

Arbitrary rightness is the strategy of people who see life as a merciless battle and, therefore, feel they must be definite and "right" about everything lest "foreign influence" control them.

Archetypes or ancient types are pre-existent forms that are innate and represent psychic predispositions that lead people to apprehend, experience, and respond to the world in certain ways.

Ascending reticular activating system (ARAS) acts as an arousal mechanism. The core of the system is the reticular formation of the brain stem.

Assimilation is how people acquire things.

Attitude (Cattell) is an expression of an ergic goal that is generally subsidiated to an erg(s).

Attitude (Jung) is a readiness of the psyche to act or react in a certain way to experience.

Authoritarians show high deference for authority figures, submission to the power of authority, and a need to command those seen as lower in power than themselves.

Automaton conformity is the condition that occurs when the person, out of fear of aloneness, gives up freedom for union with society, and she or he bends over backwards to maintain the union by strict adherence to social norms and conventions.

Autonomy is independence stemming from the reasonable self-control that allows children to hold rather than restrain, to let be rather than lose.

Autophilic person is one who manifests no preadolescent development, because it has not occurred or was attempted without success, causing the continuation of self-directed love.

Awareness is the conscious apprehension of experience.

Basic anxiety is "an insidiously increasing, all-pervading feeling of being lonely and helpless in a hostile world."

Basic conflict involves contradictory orientations to move toward, away from, and against others all existing within a neurotic.

Basic mistrust is the feeling of abandonment and helpless rage that accompanies uncertainty of satisfaction.

Basic trust results from the infant's sense that it can count on satisfaction of its needs; the world takes on the aura of a "trustworthy realm."

Behavior therapy is psychological therapy employing behavioral techniques.

Behavioral dimension is a continuum of behavior analogous to a yardstick.

Behaviorism is a school of psychology for which the basic subject matter is "outside"; it is overt (observable) behavior.

Belongingness and love needs orient the person toward affectionate relations with people, and a sense of place in family and groups.

Beta is press that are determined by the person's own interpretation, that is, subjectively determined.

Birth order is the child's position relative to other siblings.

Blaming victims for their own fate is a self-exonerative process for escaping self-blame.

Blind spot is an area of contradiction about which the individual manages to remain unaware.

Bodily self is sensations that emanate from the muscles, joints, tendons, eyes, ears, and so on.

Brief therapy approach involves techniques that are able to address and solve clients' problems in a specifiable and relatively small number of sessions.

Cardinal p.d.s are pervasion and outstanding in the life of a person.

Care is the strength of maturity, is "the broadening concern for what has been generated by love, necessity, or accident—a concern which must consistently overcome the ambivalence adhering to irreversible obligation and the narrowness of self-concern."

Case study method involves collecting background data about and making intensive observations on a single individual in order to discover how to treat that person or to obtain information that may apply to other people.

Castration anxiety is a generalized fear on the part of boys that they might lose their highly prized organs of pleasure (father may cut it off).

Catharsis is a process by which inner feelings are openly expressed in words or behaviors.

Cathexes (Freud) are investments or attachments of the personality's libidinous energy either to real objects in the external world or to fantasized images in the inner world.

Cathexis (Murray) is a process by which an object evokes a need.

Central p.d. is one of the entries on the relatively large list of traits we use to summarize an individual's personality.

Characterizing events associated with a situation is placing them into meaningful categories.

Childhood (birth to adolescence) is a relatively problem-free period dominated by instincts, dependency, and a psychological atmosphere provided by parents.

Childhood stage emerges with articulate speech and ends with the appearance of the need for peers (pre-school years).

Choice is a decision between the alternatives provided by the construct that has preempted the situation.

Circumspection phase refers to a period of 'trying on for size' the various constructs available in our personal repertory.

Cognitive needs are needs to know, to understand, to explain, and to satisfy curiosity.

Cognitive social learning theory proposes that important factors are cognitive facilities rather than traits.

Cognitively complex persons have construction systems containing constructs that are clearly differentiated, that is, distinguished one from the other.

Cognitively simple persons have construction systems for which distinctions among constructs are blurred—a poorly differentiated system.

Collective unconscious is a storehouse of ancestral experiences dating to the dawn of humankind and common to all humans.

Common trait (Cattell) is "a trait which can be measured for all people by the same battery [of tests] and on which [the people] differ in degree rather than in form."

Common traits (Allport) "are . . . those aspects of personality in respect to which most people within a given culture can be profitably compared."

Commonality is a reference to the sharing of constructs by two or more people whose experiences are similar.

Compartmentalization is a mechanism by which individuals separate key aspects of themselves and their life situations into "logic-tight" compartments.

Compensate is to overcome weaknesses by striving to become superior in some way.

Compensation is a basic law of the psyche referring to observations that a dream's meaning is often just the opposite of the person's conscious experience.

Competence is "the free exercise (unimpaired by an infantile sense of inferiority) of dexterity and intelligence in the completion of serious tasks."

Competency embraces both the cognitive ability to size-up a situation so that one understands how to operate effectively in it and the capability of performing behaviors that will lead to success in the situation.

Complexes are mental contents in the psyche that agglutinate or stick together like the clumping of red blood cells and eventually take up residence in the personal unconscious.

Component of a situation is some part of the total situation, such as physical characteristic, or, more important, factors associated with people who are present when the situation is unfolding.

Conflicts of needs occur when needs oppose each other "within the personality, giving rise when prolonged to harassing spiritual dilemmas."

Confluence learning is the acquisition of behaviors and attitudes which simultaneously subsidiate to two or more different goals.

Congruence is a state in which a person's self-concept and actual experiences relating to self are consistent.

Conscience is the internal agent that punishes us when we do wrong.

Consequence is an event that occurs after a response has been performed and changes the probability that the response will occur again.

Construction system is an organization of many constructs with the more important, and often more abstract, constructs at the top and the less important at the bottom.

Constructive alternativism is the assumption that a person's present interpretations of her or his life situation are subject to revision and replacement.

Constructs are ways of construing events or "seeing the world" so that the future is anticipated.

Context of a construct is composed of all those elements to which the construct applies.

Contingent refers to a relationship in which the occurrence of event B depends on the prior occurrence of event A.

Continuous reinforcement involves a reinforcement of every response.

Contrafactions of needs are cases where needs are related to their opposites in alternating phases.

Correlated refers to a condition that exists if variations in one variable correspond closely with variations in another.

Correlation coefficient is an index, represented by the letter "r," of the degree to which a relationship is linear.

Creative power of the individual is the process by which we each make original conceptions of ourselves and our world as we develop a style of life for solving the three great problems of life.

Crystallized general ability (g_c) is "a general factor, largely . . . abilities learned at school, representing . . . applications of [g_f], and amount and intensity of schooling; it appears in vocabulary and numerical ability [tests]."

Cumulative records are graphs for which responses are accumulated and plotted against time.

Cynicism is "the denying or deriding of moral values" because of a deep-seated uncertainty with regard to moral values.

Defense mechanisms are internal, unconscious, and automatic psychological strategies for coping with or regaining control over threatening id instincts.

Defensive behaviors are adopted in order to cope with unpleasant events that are anticipated on future occasions.

Defensive externals are people who are highly competitive and do well on tests, but endorse external items for the apparent purpose of blaming others for their failures.

Deficiency needs (D-needs) require fulfillment involving the environment in order for the person to avoid physical sickness and psychological maladjustment.

Dehumanization is a cognitive process that involves lowering the status of certain people from "human being" to "lesser being."

Delaying gratification is postponing some pleasure so that it can be enjoyed to the maximum degree or in its most optimal form.

Denial (Freud) is the process by which we refuse to think about or address whatever is too hard to bear.

Denial (Rogers) involves the inability to recognize or accept the existence of an experience that has occurred.

Dependency constructs are special constructs that revolve around the child's survival needs. A "mother" construct would be an example.

Dependent variables have values that are free to vary so that they are open to influence by the independent variables.

Despair is a feeling that time is too short for the achievement of integrity and the accompanying contribution to the connection between generations.

Diffusion of innovation occurs when prestigious models try something new and thereby display its benefits and advantages to others.

Dignity or worth is what we refer to when we give people credit for what they have done.

Directedness is having a goal or goals in life toward which one strives.

Displacement and diffusion of responsibility involves placing the blame for one's deplorable acts onto others, and spreading the responsibility for reprehensible behavior to others who are present, respectively.

Displacement is finding a new target for some feelings, one that is less threatening than the original.

Distortion involves a reinterpretation of an experience so as to make it consistent with how one wants things to be.

dR-technique is the same as the R method, except that each of the hundreds of people responding to the several measures does so two times, usually after only a short delay, and each person's score on each measure is the second response minus the first.

Dream series analysis involves large numbers of dreams in succession, because Jung believed that one or a few dreams did not tell the whole story.

Dream symbol is dream content that represents some person, thing, or activity involved in unconscious processes.

Dynamic calculus is a set of equations that predict the course of learning, adjustments to environmental change, and the nature of ergic tension reduction.

Dynamic lattice is "the tracing of the subsidiation of attitudes, one to another, ending in the satisfaction of a number of primary ergic goals."

Dynamic trait refers to motivations and interests.

Dynamisms refer to "the relatively enduring energy [units] which [periodically] characterize the organism in its duration as a living organism."

Early adolescence erupts at puberty when the need for intimacy evolves toward lustful feelings of closeness and tenderness with a sexual partner.

Early infancy is the first stage and involves no sense of self.

Early recollections (ERs) indicate how a person views her or himself and other people and reveal what the person strives for in life, what he or she anticipates, and, more generally, his or her conception of life itself.

Econetic model is a framework that integrates environmental situations with characteristics of the person—including personality components—in attempts to understand the person.

Eductive refers to learning relationships by "pulling them out" of the entities that contain them.

Effectiveness is the need to compensate for "being in a strange and overpowering world" by developing a sense of being able to do something that will "make a dent" in life.

Ego (Freud) is a coherent organization of mental processes that develops out of id energy, has access to consciousness, and is devoted to contacting reality for the purpose of satisfying id needs.

Ego (Jung) is what we think of as ourselves, the genuine us, and is the "centre of the total field of consciousness."

Ego ideal is positive standards in the form of internal representations of idealized parental figures that can result in feelings of pride and self-respect.

Ego-strength refers to the ability of the ego to successfully interact with reality on behalf of the id and inhibit id impulses until "safe" satisfactions are found.

Elaborative choice is a selection of an alternative, aligned to a single construct dimension, which appears to provide the greatest opportunity for the further elaboration of a system.

Electra complex is the dynamic corresponding to the Oedipal complex involving girls' love of father and hatred of mother.

Elements are objects, beings, or events.

Emergent pole is the primary and principle end of a construct, like "good" in good-bad and "intelligent" in intelligent-stupid.

Empathy (Rogers) is sensing and participating in the emotions of others.

Empathy (Sullivan) is "the term that we use to refer to the peculiar emotional linkage [that exists between the] infant [and] other significant people . . ."

Entropy is the equalization of differences in order to bring about a balance or equilibrium.

Epigenesis ("epi" means "upon" and "genesis" means "emergence") refers to the way stages literally emerge "one on top of another in space and time."

Equivalence is the circumstance in which energy consumed to accommodate one intention, "say something nice," is balanced by energy fueling an opposite intention, "say something nasty."

Erg is "an innate source of reactivity, such as is often described as a drive [or instinct], directed to a certain goal and accompanied by a certain quality . . ."

Erogenous zones are sensitive areas of the body from which instinctual satisfactions can be obtained.

Eros represents energy for preserving oneself (love of self) and one's species (love of others).

Escape simply involves jumping to the side of the shuttle box without shock.

Esteem needs are of two kinds: 1) there are personal desires for adequacy, mastery, competence, achievement, confidence, independence, and freedom; and 2) there are desires for respect from other people, including attention, recognition, appreciation, status, prestige, fame, dominance, importance, and dignity.

Eugenics is the application of genetics to the improvement of human biological and psychological characteristics.

Euphemistic labeling is the cognitive process of assigning a name to deplorable behavior that makes it seem innocuous or even laudable.

Eupsychia (Yew-sigh-key-ah) is a utopian society characterized by psychological health among all its members.

Events are simply occurrences that are produced by components of a situation.

Excessive self-control arises in reaction to a flood of contradictory emotions and involves holding feelings and behavior in a vice-grip.

Excitation and stimulation is the need for the nervous system to be "exercised," that is, to experience a certain amount of excitation.

Existential needs are needs that must be met if one's existence is to be meaningful, one's inner being is to be developed, one's talents are to be fully exploited, and abnormality is to be avoided.

Existential psychology is a philosophically based approach to understanding each person's most immediate experience and the conditions of his or her existence.

Expectancy (Mischel) is a belief based on past experience that provides a prediction of future outcomes.

Expectancy (Rotter) is "the probability held by the individual that a particular reinforcement will occur as a function of a specific behavior on his part in a specific situation or situations."

Experience (Kelly) is what one learns from the events of the past.

Experience (Rogers) is all that is going on within the organism at any given moment that is potentially available to awareness.

Experiment is a procedure whereby an experimenter first sets the variation in some independent variable(s) and then ascertains whether variation in some dependent variable(s) is influenced.

Exploitative orientation involves experiencing the source of all good as outside of oneself, and taking things through force or cunning, rather than expecting to receive from others.

Extension of self is expanding oneself to include all those significant aspects of one's environment, including people.

Extension of the cleavage line is a reference to the observation that the poles of a person's subordinate constructs fall directly under the corresponding emergent and implicit poles of his or her superordinate constructs.

External locus of control refers to people's belief that reinforcement of their behaviors is due more to luck, chance, fate, powerful others, or complex and unpredictable environmental forces, rather than determined by their own behaviors or characteristics.

Externalization is the tendency to experience internal processes as if they occurred outside oneself and to hold these "exterior" factors responsible for one's difficulties.

Extinction occurs when a previously reinforced response is no longer followed by the same reinforcement and the response eventually decreases in frequency.

Extraversion is an "outward-turning" of libido that involves a positive movement of interest away from one's inner experience toward outer experience.

Extrinsic rewards are rewards originating outside the individual (money).

Exvia-invia is "a factorially established broad dimension within the area of behaviour popularly referred to as extraversion introversion."

Factor analysis is a statistical procedure for determining the number and nature of factors underlying larger numbers of measures.

Factor in factor analysis refers to a hypothetical construct that is applied to a data cluster (set of items) and suggests what it is measuring.

Favorable ratio is the greater the magnitude of the pull to the positive pole relative to the pull of the negative pole the better.

Fear is the experience one has when a new construct appears to be entering the system, and may become dominant.

Feeling evaluates how experiences strike us, whether they are suitable to us or not; it is a kind of judgment that is an entirely subjective process.

Fictional finalism is a fictional goal toward which all psychological currents flow, thereby unifying the personality.

Fidelity is "the opportunity to fulfill personal potentialities . . . in a context which permits the young person to be true to himself and true to significant others . . . [and to] sustain loyalties . . . in spite of inevitable contradictions of value systems."

Fixation is the impairment of development at a particular stage because satisfactions appropriate for the stage are frustrated, resulting in permanent investment of libidinal energy in the stage.

Fixed role therapy involves a client playing the role of an imaginary character who possesses constructs that are in contrast to his or her actual constructs.

Fixed schedules are procedures for which a response is reinforced after a constant amount of time has elapsed or after a constant number of responses have been performed.

Fixed-interval (FI) schedules are schedules for which the amount of time between one reinforced response and the next is constant.

Fixed-ratio (FR) schedules are procedures for which the number of responses occurring between one reinforced response and the next is constant.

Fluid general ability (g_f) is "that form of general intelligence which is largely innate and which adapts itself to all kinds of material, regardless of previous experience with it."

Forbidding gestures are negative, covert cues such as a wrinkled brow, a cold tone of voice, a too tight grasp, a hesitancy, reluctance, or even revulsion at having to interact with the infant.

Foresight is the capacity to look ahead in search of good experiences and in the interest of avoiding bad ones.

Forethought is anticipation of "likely consequences of . . . [future] actions."

Frame of orientation is a cognitive "map" of people's natural and social worlds that enables them to organize and make sense of puzzling matters and allows them to operate in the arena of rational understanding.

Free association is a process in which the person adopts a mental orientation that allows ideas, images, memories, and feelings to flow spontaneously, without external guidance or suppression.

Freedom refers to our belief that we can choose from various behaviors, rather than having our actions controlled by an external force, the environment.

Frustration tolerance is exhibited when things go wrong; people who have it do not pitch a tantrum, blame others, or wallow in self-pity.

Functional autonomy is a process by which a new system of motivation evolves from an older one, but stems from tensions different from those of the original.

Fundamental postulate is the assumption that a person's psychological processes are routed through various channels or pathways by the ways in which she or he anticipates events.

Fusion of needs is the name Murray gave to a single "action pattern that satisfies two or more needs at the same time."

g supposedly subsumes the so-called primary mental abilities and forms a common core of general intelligence.

Gambler's fallacy is the expectation that a failure on one attempt means that success on a subsequent attempt becomes more likely, whereas success means greater likelihood of failure in the future.

General actualizing tendency is an inherent tendency of the organism to develop all its capacities in ways which serve to maintain or enhance the organism.

Generalized expectancy is an expectancy that holds for a number of situations that are similar to one another.

Generativity is "the concern with establishing and guiding the next generation."

Genital stage is the stage of mature sexual love, including both feelings of lust and of affection directed toward another person, that begins at puberty.

Genuine sense of humor, as opposed to an appreciation of sexual and aggressive jokes, is being able "to laugh at the things one loves (including, of course, oneself and all that pertains to oneself), and still to love them."

Gradualistic moral disengagement is a process during which people slowly slip unawares into what was normally unacceptable behavior.

Growth model emphasizes helping people to "remove whatever blocks to growth exist" so they could move beyond being normal or average.

Guilt (Erikson) is the harness that restrains pursuit of desires, urges, and potentials; the exercise of an overzealous conscience.

Guilt (Freud) is an intense feeling of regret over having done something wrong or evaluations of oneself as an undeserving, inadequate person.

Guilt (Kelly) is the result of the person's perception that he or she is being dislodged from some critical role.

Habitual responses (HR) are specific responses (Cattell's surface traits) that recur under similar circumstances, such as regularly saying "Hi" to a neighbor.

Heritability popularly refers to the proportion of the variability in a trait that is accounted for by the genes.

Heterophilic person is one who "has gone through the preadolescent period and made the early adolescent change in which he has become intensely interested in achieving intimacy with members of . . . the other sex."

Hoarding orientation is embraced by people who believe the "goods" come from the inside not the outside, themselves not others, so security is based on an attitude of saving, of letting out as little as possible.

Hope is the enduring belief in the attainability of basic satisfactions.

Humanistic communitarian socialism is a political system embracing economic, social, and moral functions wherein ordinary citizens interact cooperatively and are actively involved in the various functions.

Humanistic psychoanalyst is one who believes in the essential worth and dignity of each person, and in the importance of helping each person to do the most with what she or he has.

Humanistic psychology is the school of psychology that emphasizes the present experience of the whole person, assumes the essential worth of the person, and fosters the belief that the person can solve his or her own psychological problems.

Hysterical neurosis is a condition in which, for example, a person who feels angry may develop a "paralyzed" arm to lessen the chances of hitting someone.

Id is beyond conscious awareness and comprises whatever is present at birth, including everything that relates to the satisfaction of physical drives, such as sex and hunger, or primitive psychological needs, such as for comfort and for protection from danger.

Ideal self is the self a person most values and desires to be.

Identity (Erikson) is accumulated confidence that the sameness and continuity one has previously cultivated are now appreciated by others, allowing, in turn, the promise of careers and lifestyles to come.

Identity (Fromm) is the need to be aware of oneself as a separate entity, and to sense oneself as the subject of one's own actions.

Identity confusion is the failure of previous identity developments to coalesce in such a way that it is clear what roles one is expected to play in the future.

Idiographic theorists are inclined to study each individual's unique traits without attempting to find a place for each along a relative few trait dimensions.

Impermeable is a reference to certain constructs that tend not to change in terms of range of convenience or place in the construction system.

Implicit pole is the contrasting end of a construct, like "uneducated" in educated-uneducated and "urban" in rural-urban.

Incentive is any thing, concrete or abstract, that creates an anticipation of positive outcome following the performance of a behavior.

Incongruence reflects an inconsistency between self-concept and experiences relating to self.

Independent variables have variation that is arranged by the person who uses the experimental method, called the experimenter.

Individual character is the pattern of behavior characteristic of a given person, "the relatively permanent system of all noninstinctual strivings through which man relates himself to the human and natural world."

Individual differences is a key psychological phrase generally referring to the observation that people differ in a variety of ways. See Introduction

Individual psychology is an attempt to conceive of a unique human being as an interconnected whole, biologically, philosophically, and psychologically.

Individuality refers to differences among construct systems both in terms of the constructs comprising the systems and in terms of how the constructs are organized.

Individuation is the process by which a person becomes a psychological 'in-divid-ual,' that is, a separate, indivisible unity or 'whole.'

Inducible period is a period during which the need is inactive but susceptible to excitation by appropriate stimulation.

Inductive-hypothetico-deductive spiral is "the detecting of regularities in observational data [that] leads to a hypothesis from which experimental consequences are deduced, [leading] to further data from which new regularities are induced, and so on in an ever-expanding spiral."

Industry is children's absorption in the "tool world" of their culture—the workaday world—thereby preparing them "for a hierarchy of learning experiences which [they] will undergo with the help of cooperative peers and instructive adults."

Infancy stage starts at birth and continues until the appearance of speech.

Inferiority (Adler) is the persistent feeling that one does not measure up to society's ideals or to one's own fictional standards.

Inferiority (Erikson) occurs if children perceive their skills or status among peers to be inadequate.

Inferiority complex is Adler's term for the consequences of an exaggerated, persistent form of inadequacy that is partly explained by a deficiency in social interest.

Initiative is acting on one's desires, urges, and potentials.

Insight is a method through which personally unacceptable and socially "taboo" experiences buried in the person's unconscious can be made conscious.

Instinctoid is a reference to the instinct-like nature of needs, because of their biological, genetic, and universal characteristics.

Instincts are inborn forces whose characteristics are both physical (bodily needs) and psychological (wishes).

Institutional safeguard is a cultural unit that protects and promotes products of crisis resolution.

Integration learning is "learning consisting of a re-arrangement of satisfactions among a number of conflicting, independent drives [ergs]."

Integrity is "an emotional integration faithful to the image bearers of the past and ready to take (and eventually renounce) leadership in the present."

Intellectualization involves talking and thinking at an intellectual rather than an emotional level about what we do or contemplate that is threatening to us (smoker says "The link between cancer and smoking is unproven—I've seen the studies.").

Interaction point of view is a position that emphasizes the interplay between *internal entities* or person factors and *social situations*, rather than either in isolation from the other.

Intermittent reinforcement is a process in which responses are reinforced every so often, or after some number of responses has occurred.

Internal locus of control is the belief that reinforcement is dependent on one's own behavior or characteristics—not on fate, luck, or chance.

Interpersonal relations are the relationships between a person and each other important person in his or her life.

Interpersonal security is "relaxation of the tension of anxiety," which is the experience of return to a tranquil, untroubled state.

Interpersonal trust is a generalized expectancy that people's verbal promises are reliable.

Intimacy "is really the ability to fuse your identity with somebody else's without fear that you're going to lose something yourself."

Intolerance for ambiguity is the cognitive orientation requiring that everything be clearly distinguished from everything else, questions have definite answers, and problems have simple solutions.

Intrinsic motivation refers to the desire for intrinsic rewards, leading to the pursuit of the same.

Intrinsic rewards are rewards from within the individual (self praise).

Introjection is a process by which personality incorporates the norms and standards of its culture through identification with parents or other admired persons in society, such as clergy and teachers.

Introversion is an "inward-turning" of psychic energy and involves a negative movement or withdrawal of subjective interest away from outer objects and toward one's inner experience.

Intuition suggests where something seems to have come from and where it may be going; it is a kind of "instinctive apprehension," of unconscious origin, with no tangible basis.

Isolation is the failure to secure close and cooperative relationships with the same and especially the opposite gender such that partners' identities are important to, but distinct from, one's own.

Isophilic person is one who has been unable to progress past preadolescence, and continues to regard as suitable for intimacy only people who are as like himself as possible . . . that is, members of his own sex."

Jealousy is the fear of losing a relationship that is seen as the best available means of satisfying an insatiable concern for affection and incessant demands for unconditional love.

Juvenile era is ushered in with the child's need for peer companions, or "playmates rather like oneself."

L-data or life-records are "made by observers on the frequency and intensity with which specific kinds of behavior occur in the people they observe."

Late adolescence begins with the discovery of an orientation regarding genital behavior and how to fit that revelation into the rest of life and ends with "the establishment of a fully human or mature repertory of interpersonal relations."

Latency is a quiet period between ages 6 and 12 during which children repress their attraction to parents and become sexually disinterested.

Latent content is the underlying meaning of each dream.

Law of movement is the direction taken by the person that originates in his or her ability to exercise free choice in fully exploiting personal capabilities and resources.

Learn by anxiety is a process that occurs when anxiety is not severe; individuals may become acquainted with the situations in which it is present so that those circumstances may be avoided.

Libido is an energy variously described as "psychical desire," "erotic tendencies," "sexual desire in the broadest sense," and the "motive forces of sexual life."

Libido is psychic energy.

Loadings are correlations of particular items with a given factor.

Locus of control refers to "the degree to which persons expect that . . . reinforcement [and other outcomes] of their behavior is [dependent on their] behavior or personal characteristics versus the degree to which [they expect it is due to] chance, luck, or fate, . . . powerful others, or is simply unpredictable."

Locus of evaluation refers to the source of evidence about values, whether it is inside oneself or outside, in others.

Long unit is the life cycle of the individual.

Love "is the guardian of that elusive and yet all-pervasive power of cultural and personal style which binds . . . . the affiliations of competition and cooperation, procreation and production" into a "way of life."

Lust is Sullivan's term for "certain tensions of or pertaining to the genitals," culminating in orgasm.

Make prompt statements of all that comes to mind is a task of the patient during the interview that is enabled by trusting the "situation to the extent of expressing the thoughts that it provokes."

Mandala or magic circle is a round object often including an inner spiral that draws the eyes to the center of its surface.

Manifest content is what the dreamer remembers about the dream when awakened.

Marketing orientation is unique to the modern historical era in which exchanging goods for money, other goods, or services became the backbone of a "supply and demand" economy.

Mature love "is union under the condition of preserving one's integrity, one's individuality . . . [it] is an active power of man."

Medical model refers to the idea that people with psychological problems are sick and need some sort of treatment, at least analogous to medication, that will make them normal again.

Mentalism is the belief that thoughts and feelings determine behavior, not external consequences.

Meta-needs or *being values (B-values)* refer "to . . . the motivations of self-actualizing people."

Metagenital use does not involve one's own genitals, but another person's genitals are involved.

Middle age (age 40 to old age) brings with it the task of building a whole personality.

Model refers to a person who performs some behavior for an audience, showing how it is done and what benefits accrue from it.

Modeling refers to the act of performing a behavior before one or more observers.

Moral justification occurs when individuals invoke religious or other moral bases to support their inhuman behavior.

Morality principle is the code that concerns society's values regarding right and wrong.

Moving against people reflects compulsive cravings for power and prestige, as well as personal ambition.

Moving away from people reflects a person's concern with self, as seen in needs for admiration and perfectionism.

Moving toward people reflects neurotic needs for a partner and for affection; it also involves compulsive modesty.

Multiple Abstract Variance Analysis (MAVA) is "a research design for discovering relative proportions of environmental vs. hereditary determination for personality traits (nature-nurture ratio)."

n Abasement involves surrendering, complying, accepting punishment, apologizing, confessing, atoning, and generally being masochistic.

n Achievement indicates the drive to "overcome obstacles, to exercise power, to strive to do something difficult as well [and] as quickly as possible."

n Affiliation refers to the desire for friendships and associations; "to greet, join, and live with others."

n Aggression refers to an assaultive or injurious orientation to others, including to belittle, harm, blame, accuse, ridicule, punish severely, react sadistically toward, or even murder.

n Autonomy is the drive to resist influence or coercion, to defy authority, seek freedom, and strive for independence.

n Blamavoidance refers to avoiding blame, punishment, and ostracism by inhibiting asocial or even unconventional impulses; being a well-behaved, law abiding citizen.

n Contrarience is the drive to act differently from others, to be unique, to take the opposite side, and to hold unconventional views.

n Dominance is the drive to influence, control, persuade, prohibit, dictate, lead, direct, and restrain others and to organize the behavior of a group.

n Exhibition is desiring to attract attention to one's person by exciting, amusing, stirring, shocking, or thrilling others.

n Infavoidance is an orientation to avoiding failure, shame, humiliation, or ridicule by concealing disfigurement and refraining from attempts at anything seen as beyond one's powers.

n Inviolacy is an attitude of attempting to prevent depreciation of self-respect, to preserve one's good name, to avoid criticism, and to maintain psychological distance.

n Order involves arranging, organizing, and putting away objects; to be tidy, clean, and scrupulously precise.

n Succorance is the dependent attitude of seeking aid, protection, and sympathy by crying for mercy and help from affectionate, nurturant parents.

Necrophilous character is engrossed by death, dwells on it, and glories in it.

Need (Murray) refers to "a [hypothetical] construct which stands for a force ([of unknown] . . . physiochemical nature) in the brain . . . , [that] organizes perception, . . . intellection, . . . and action in such a way as to transform . . . an . . . unsatisfying situation [into a more satisfying one]."

Need for self-actualization is "the desire for self-fulfillment . . . the tendency for [one] to become actualized in what [one] is potentially."

Need for tenderness which, different from "love," refers to relief from various tensions.

Need integrate or complex is formed when "traces (images) of cathected objects in familiar settings become integrated in the mind with the needs and emotions which they customarily excite, as well as with the images of preferred modes" (actones or other means of creating satisfaction).

Needs (Maslow) are desires for certain satisfactions that are sought by all humans, regardless of their culture, environment, or generation.

Negative correlation refers to high values on one variable corresponding to low values on the other variable.

Negative mood regulation (NMR) is a belief that one can muster the cognitive and behavioral means to alleviate a negative-affective state or bring it under control.

Negative reinforcement is a process whereby the likelihood of a response increases when it is followed by the termination, reduction, or absence of a stimulus.

Neuroses (Freud) are patterns of abnormal behavior related to an over-control of instincts.

Neurosis (Adler) is an extreme form of reaction to shock, "a person's automatic, unknowing exploitation of the symptoms resulting from the effects of a shock."

Neurosis (Horney) is "a psychic disturbance brought about by fears and defenses against these fears, and by attempts to find compromise solutions for conflicting tendencies."

Neurotic needs are the coping techniques that are initiated in childhood—excessive, insatiable, and unrealistic demands developed in response to the basic anxiety that dominates the person.

Nomothetic theorists are inclined to derive general laws concerning how a relative few traits apply to all people.

Non-productive types are those who yield at best pseudo connection to others and at worst destructive relations with others.

Notice marginal thoughts is paying attention to thoughts that monitor, critique, and alter speech in terms of formation, grammar, and so forth and in terms of errors that may cause incomplete or misunderstood communications to others (patient task during interview).

Noticing changes in the body that signal decreases or increases in the tension signifying anxiety is one of the interview tasks of the patient.

Object of devotion is a goal that gives meaning to people's existence and position in the world.

Objective tests are highly structured paper-and-pencil questionnaires such as true/false or multiple-choice, each of which can be scored with a key so that scorers all agree on the scores.

Observational learning is learning by observing models as they perform useful behavior.

Oedipus complex is the constellation of feelings, desires, and strivings revolving around the boy's desires for his mother and his fearful/hateful orientation to his father.

Old age parallels childhood because of a return to submersion in the unconscious.

Operant conditioning is a process by which an organism operates on its environment with consequences that influence the likelihood that the operation, or behavior, will be repeated.

Operationalized refers to translation of concepts into a form that can be quantified or expressed in numbers.

Oral or *Narcissistic (self-centered) stage* is a phase which begins at birth and in which the organism's psychic activity focuses on satisfying the needs of the mouth and digestive tract, including the tongue and lips.

Oral-aggressive is an adult type that is derived from childhood pleasures associated with the mouth, food, and eating, but with greater chewing, biting, and use of teeth.

Oral-receptive is a personality type that is derived from childhood pleasures of receiving food in the mouth and ingesting it; it is associated with adult dependency and suggestibility.

Organismic refers to a natural, biological, inborn predisposition reflected in the total functioning of every living being.

Origins are the locus of their own intentions and behaviors.

Orthogenital involves the integration of one's own genitals with the "natural receptor genitals" of the opposite sex, that is, heterosexual use of the genitals.

Overcompensate is to bend over backwards to do or become whatever people's weaknesses have denied them.

P-technique is "a factor analytic design which measures a single person on the same set of variables repeatedly over a number of different occasions."

Paragenital involves use of the sex organs in which one acts as if to seek contact with genitals opposite one's own, but in such a way that impregnation will not occur.

Parataxic mode is experienced as the infant becomes a child who begins to use speech, but still makes few logical connections within the sequence of its experiences (approximately the pre-school years).

Participant modeling occurs when a person with low self-efficacy imitates a model's efficacious behavior.

Passive externals (also called "congruent") believe they are controlled by fate or chance.

Pawns are instruments of outside forces which control them.

Peak experiences are intense, mystical experiences associated with simultaneous feelings of limitless horizons, powerfulness and helplessness, a lost sense of time and place, and great ecstasy, wonder and awe.

Penis envy refers to girls' feelings of inferiority over not having the male organ and compensatory wishes to someday obtain one of their own.

Periodicity refers to rhythms of activity and rest.

Persona or mask is the identities we assume because of the socially prescribed roles we play.

Personal agency is a condition in which people come to believe that they can make things happen that will be of benefit to themselves and to others.

Personal cognitive factors are memories of previous experiences, from the past history of an individual, that determine strategies the person employs for producing behavior at the present time.

Personal disposition (P.d.) is a trait that is unique to a particular individual.

Personal unconscious "is made up essentially of contents [that] have at one time been conscious but which have disappeared from consciousness through having been forgotten or repressed . . ."

Personality (Allport) "is the dynamic organization within the individual of those psychophysical systems that determine his characteristic behavior and thought."

Personality (Cattell) "[is] that which tells what a [person] will do when placed in a particular situation."

Personality (Fromm) is "the totality of inherited and acquired psychic qualities which are characteristic of one individual and which make the individual unique."

Personality (Introduction) is a set of degrees falling along many behavioral dimensions, each degree corresponding to a trait, resulting in a unique profile, different from that of other individuals. See introduction.

Personality (Kelly) consists of an organized system of constructs that may be ranked as to importance.

Personality (Sullivan) is "the relatively enduring pattern of recurrent interpersonal situations which characterize a human life."

Personality profile is represented by the line that connects the degrees on the behavioral dimensions associated with various traits that a person possesses.

Personality traits are internally based psychological characteristics that often correspond to adjectival labels such as "shy," "kind," "mean," "outgoing," "dominant," and so forth. See Introduction.

Personifications are investments of human attributes in persons or objects that do not actually possess the assigned traits, at least not in the degree to which they are applied.

Phallic stage is a phase in which satisfaction is gained primarily by stimulation of the penis or clitoris, through masturbation.

Phenomenology is concerned with grasping reality as individuals perceive it, in a "fresh" manner that is free of preconceptions.

Physiological needs encompass specific biological requirements for water, oxygen, proteins, vitamins, proper body temperature, sleep, sex, exercise, and so on.

Pleasure principle refers to the achievement of pleasurable feelings as quickly and immediately as possible through the reduction of discomfort, pain, or tension.

Positive regard is experiencing oneself as making a positive difference in the life of another person and as receiving warmth, liking, respect, sympathy, acceptance, caring, and trust from others.

Positive reinforcement is a process whereby some event, usually a stimulus, increases the likelihood of a response upon which its presentation is contingent.

Positive self-regard is a favorable attitude toward oneself.

Positively correlated refers to a condition in which high values on one variable correspond to high values on the other, and low values correspond with low values.

Preadolescence is brief, beginning with the need for interpersonal intimacy in the form of a close relationship with another person "of comparable status."

Predictability refers to the ability to predict the future.

Preemption phase is a period during which one construct is allowed to preempt the situation and define the pair of alternatives between which the person must make his or her choice.

Prejudice is felt or expressed antipathy based upon a faulty and inflexible generalization and may be directed toward a group as a whole, or toward an individual because he is a member of the group.

Press designates a directional tendency in the object or situation ("press" is also plural).

Primary factors are relatively pure and narrow in scope, and it can be arranged statistically that they are independent.

Primary process is a continual flow of events involving infantile images and wishes that demand immediate and direct satisfaction.

Productive orientation is an attitude of relatedness to the world and oneself that encompasses all realms of human experience: reasoning, loving, and working.

Projection protects us from threat by allowing us to literally project our own unacceptable traits onto other people.

Projective tests present people with test items that are unstructured, ambiguous, or open-ended, thus allowing them a wide range of freedom in making responses. See Introduction.

Propriate striving is planning for the future by setting long-range goals.

Proprium is "me as felt and known . . . the self as 'object' of knowledge and feeling.

Prospective or "anticipatory" refers to a process through which dreams may "foretell" future events and outcomes.

Prototaxic mode is the earliest (infancy), most primitive type of experience, a state of generalized sensation or feeling, in the absence of thought.

Prototype is the "complete goal" of the style of life that is a fiction conceived as a means of adapting to life and includes a strategy for its achievement.

Psyche is total mentality, all of consciousness and unconsciousness.

Psychoanalysis refers to Freud's systematic procedures for providing a patient with the insight necessary to rid the personality of its neurotic conflicts.

Psychogenic needs are secondary to viscerogenic needs and may be derived from them, but, being one step away from the biological side of the organism, are psychological in nature.

Psychological determinism is a belief that nothing about human behavior occurs by accident or chance, everything about personality "is determined" or has a psychological cause.

Psychological situation is characterized in a way peculiar to a person, allowing the person to categorize it with certain other situations, as well as differentiate it from still others.

Psychometrics is a quantitative approach to psychological measurement.

Psychosexual refers to stages conceived of as "sexual" only in the broadest sense of the word, because some stages involve organs ordinarily seen as "sexual" and others organs not popularly regarded as "sexual."

Psychosocial refers to a union of Freud's physical yearnings (id) and the cultural forces that act on the individual.

Punishment is a process wherein responses that are followed by the presentation of aversive stimuli decrease in likelihood of being performed in the future.

Purpose is "the courage to envisage and pursue valued and tangible goals guided by conscience but not paralyzed by guilt and by fear of punishment."

Q-data are a kind of data, where Q is for questionnaire, and people are their own observers, describing their behavior and feelings through paper-and-pencil inventories, self-reports, or interviews.

$R = f(S.P)$ where R stands for the "nature and magnitude of a person's behavioural response, . . . what he [or she] says, thinks, or does," which is some function (f) of S the "stimulus situation in which [the person] is placed," and P the nature of her or his personality.

R-technique is a "process of correlating behaviour measures across some hundreds of people [tested on a single occasion] and factoring them."

Radical behaviorism considers currently observable events and also potential, future events that can be observed and measured.

Range of convenience refers to the extent and breadth of the event-category to which a construct applies.

Range of focus refers to the events to which a construct is most readily applied.

Rate of responding when it becomes stable, indicates that conditioning is completed and a new response acquired.

Ratio schedules are procedures for which some number of responses must be performed between one reinforced response and the next.

Rational coper is the sense of selfhood that is not merely able to solve problems, but also can reason them through "in the head" and come up with logical solutions.

Rationalization allows us to excuse our threatening and unacceptable behavior and thoughts (So I lost the money. Money is not what's important in life.).

Rationalization "may be defined as self-deception by reasoning."

Real self is the potential for growth beyond the artificial idealized image of self.

Reality principle refers to ego's capacity to delay satisfaction of id's demands until an appropriate object is found that will allow gratification without harmful side-effects.

Receptive refers to an orientation of people who experience the source of all good as being outside themselves.

Recognition of unconscious contents leads to synthesizing archetypes to consciousness, a process of blending conscious and unconscious into a whole, resulting in self-knowledge.

Refractory period is a time during which no incentive will arouse the need.

Regnancy is the label for the "totality of such [brain] processes occurring during a single moment (a unitary temporal segment of brain processes)."

Regnant was the name given to "dominant configurations in the brain" that correspond to internal representations.

Reinforcement occurs when some event is contingent on the prior performance of some response, such as the meowing of a cat that alerts its master to its hunger.

Reinforcement refers to anything that has an influence on the occurrence, direction, or kind of behavior.

Reinforcement value is the degree of preference for any reinforcement to occur if the possibilities of many different reinforcements are all equal.

Relatedness is "the necessity to unite with other living beings . . . [that constitutes] an imperative need on the fulfillment of which man's sanity depends."

Reliability is the degree to which test results are repeatable.

Replicate refers to repeating a test in the hope the results will be the same as before.

Repression refers to a selective type of memory in which threatening material is unavailable for recall, because it has been pressed down into the unconscious.

Response facilitation is a process in which nothing new is learned, but some old responses may be disinhibited as a result of watching a model's performance.

Role Construct Repertory (REP) Test is an assessment device designed to reveal an individual's construct system.

Roles involve behaving in ways that meet the expectations of important other people in one's life.

Rootedness is a deep craving to maintain one's natural ties and not be "separated."

Safety needs include security, protection, stability, structure, law and order, and freedom from fear and chaos.

Schedules of reinforcement determine whether reinforcement is to be delivered either every so often or after some number of responses has occurred.

Scientific model for studying personality involves two interlocking components: (1) description, which seeks to answer questions about "what" personality is—for example, what are the identifiable individual differences in traits and types?; and (2) explanation, which seeks to answer questions about "why" personality is the way it is—"What are the causes of those individual differences?"

Scientific refers to unbiased observations that are quantified so that systematic analyses can be performed.

Second-order traits are the "superfactors" that subsume the other traits (identified also by the more generic label "secondary factors").

Secondary factors encompass several primary factors and are called "superfactors" or "second-order" factors.

Secondary p.d.s are dispositions that are "less conspicuous, less generalized, less consistent, . . . less often called into play . . . [and] more peripheral."

Secondary process refers to the intellectual operations such as thinking, evaluating, planning, and decision-making that test reality to determine whether certain behaviors would be beneficial.

Secondary reinforcers are stimuli that come to have all the properties of primary reinforcers (such as food) through association with primary reinforcers.

Security operations involve skills that allow avoidance of forbidding gestures.

Seduction thesis refers to Freud's belief that his early female patients actually had been sexually molested by their fathers, as they claimed, and these traumas were the source of their adult hysterical neuroses.

Self (Jung) is the "total personality," the unifying core of the psyche that ensures a balance of conscious and unconscious forces.

Self (Rogers) is the organized, consistent, conceptual whole composed of perceptions of the characteristics of the 'I' or 'me,' the values attached to these perceptions, and the relationships of the 'I' or 'me' to various aspects of life.

Self-actualization (Rogers) is a person's lifelong process of realizing his or her potentialities to become a fully functioning person.

Self-actualizers (Maslow) are persons who fulfill themselves by making complete use of their potentialities, capacities, and talents, who do the best they are capable of doing, and who develop themselves to the most complete stature possible for them.

Self-evaluation is a process that involves assessing one's performance at various points along the way to task completion and issuing a vocal or "under the breath" judgment of its value.

Self-analysis is a process whereby people come to understand themselves better through their own efforts, often outside the context of psychotherapy.

Self-efficacy is a belief concerning one's ability to perform behaviors yielding an expected outcome that is desirable.

Self-esteem is pride in one's pursuits and accomplishments.

Self-exonerative processes is the general name given to cognitive activities that allow people to dissociate themselves from the consequences of their actions.

Self-identity is the continuity of self over past, present, and future that results from the operation of memory.

Self-image is composed of the hopes and aspirations that develop from the perceptions and expectations that others have of oneself.

Self-recognition is coming to know one's neuroses, idealized self-image, and real self, including positive and negative attributes.

Self-regulatory plans are rules, established in advance of opportunity for behavioral performance, that act as guides for determining what behavior would be appropriate under particular conditions.

Self-sentiment is "the sentiment structure centred (sic) upon the individual's conception of himself and his desire to maintain this self-concept, in the eyes of himself and others, intact and acceptable."

Self-system is "that part of personality which is born entirely out of the influences of significant others upon one's feeling of well-being."

Sensation determines that something is present; it is the same as sensory perceptions of sight, sound, smell, taste, and touch.

Sentiment is "a set of attitudes the strength of which has become correlated through their being all learnt by contact with a particular social institution [such as] sentiment to school, to home, to country."

Shadow is the dark side of the personality, the inferiorities of the person that are emotional in nature and too unpleasant to willingly reveal.

Shame and doubt is the estrangement that results from the feeling of being controlled and of losing self-control.

Shaping is a process by which natural variability in behavior is exploited so that a new behavior is acquired by reinforcing successive approximations to it.

Shock may be experienced when a person's fiction runs head-on into reality.

Significant others are those people who are most meaningful to us in our lives.

Simple stimuli are like those that generate reflexes in that they call for reactions more than actions, particularly surface reactions that are immediate and passive in nature.

Sixteen or *16 PF* is a 16 scale test of adult personality in terms of 16 source traits.

Slips of the tongue are verbal errors that seem to replace neutral words with ones that supposedly emanate from the unconscious.

Social character represents "the core of a character structure common to most people of a given culture . . . [and] shows the degree to which character is formed by social and cultural patterns."

Social comparison is determining how well one is doing in life by comparing oneself to those who share one's life situation.

Social desirability refers to the need to please others by displaying the characteristics that are valued in our society (for example, goodness, honesty, sincerity, and so forth).

Social Distance (SD) is a measure of discrimination that requires individuals to indicate how close to themselves they would allow members of some group to come.

Social feeling is a concern for the community of other human beings and a need to associate and cooperate with them.

Social interest is individuals' efforts to develop social feeling.

Social learning entails acquiring useful information through interactions with people and other elements of the environment.

Socialization is how people relate to others.

Sociopsychological orientation is the sociological study of people that sheds light on their psychological nature.

Source trait is "a [primary] factor-dimension, stressing the proposition that variations in value along it are determined by a single unitary influence or source."

Specific responses (SR) are everyday behaviors or experiences that may or may not be characteristic of an individual, such as saying "Hi" to a neighbor.

Stagnation is the arrest of the ripening process that comes with inability to funnel previous development into the formation of the next generation.

State or mood is a psychological entity that fluctuates or varies over time and thus is "transitory," as distinguished from traits which are "permanent."

Statistically significant is a condition that is reflected in a difference between conditions that is so large it is very unlikely to occur solely by chance.

Stereotype is an exaggerated belief that members of a group possess a certain trait; "its function is to justify (rationalize) our conduct in relation to that [group]."

Stimulus is a very definite, well-defined component or event associated with a situation and can be either physical or behavioral.

Strength (Erikson) is a virtue arising from dominant movement toward the positive pole.

Strength (Murray) of a need is measured in terms of its frequency, intensity, and duration.

Striving for superiority is a universal psychological phenomenon that parallels physical growth and involves the goal of bringing about perfection, security, and strength.

Style of life is the individual's unique but consistent movement toward self-created goals and ideals developed beginning in childhood.

Sublimation is a process that reorients instinctual aims in new directions that are more personally and culturally acceptable.

Submerged pole is an implicit pole that has either never been put into word form, perhaps because the construct is new, or is being suppressed.

Subordinate refers to constructs that are at the bottom of the construction system.

Subsidiation of needs occurs "when one or more needs are activated in the service of [one or more other needs]."

Success may be defined as effectively performing the behaviors which yield the outcomes that are valued by the performer.

Superego is the representation of society in personality that incorporates the norms and standards of the surrounding culture.

Superiority complex is Adler's term for an exaggerated, abnormal form of striving for superiority that involves "overcompensation" for personal weakness.

Superordinate refers to constructs that are at the top of the construction system.

Superstitious behavior is a response that is accidentally reinforced, as there is no prearranged contingency between the response and reinforcement.

Surface traits are "a set of personality characteristics which are correlated but do not form a factor, hence are believed to be determined by more than one influence or source."

Symbiotic union is a coupling of beings in which each meets the needs of the other while they "live 'together'" as "two, and yet one."

Symbol is one of the emergent elements to which a construct applies that is used as the name of the construct.

Synchronicity is the simultaneous occurrence of two happenings that are correlated but have no direct cause-and-effect connection.

Syntality is national personality "equivalent to personality in an individual and capable of (a) predicting many behaviors and (b) by profile similarity measures permitting nations to be classified in a dozen types."

Syntaxic mode becomes important during more mature childhood when the meaning of ords becomes shared with most other people in society so that experiences, judgments, and observations can be shared (approximately the early elementary school years).

Systematic eclecticism takes the best and most effective methods and orientations from each school of thought and binds them into a comprehensive approach to understanding the person.

T-data involves an observer's recordings of a person's behavior in some standard, contrived, laboratory-test situation.

Teaching machines are devices that run a program that teaches a topic through a step by step process involving positive reinforcement.

Teleological means to perform with a purpose.

Temperament trait is "a general personality trait [that] is usually stylistic, in the sense that it deals with tempo, persistence, [and so forth] covering a large variety of specific responses."

Temporal schedules are procedures for which there must be an elapse of some amount of time between one reinforced response and the next.

Thanatos is a class of instincts that is aimed at returning living things to their original non-living state.

Thema is a combination of a particular need and a particular press or pressive object.

Thematic Apperception Test (TAT) is an instrument for assessing a person's self-reflective perceptions (apperceptions) revealing thema that are evoked by some ambiguous pictures.

Thinking determines *what is present* and interprets its meaning; it brings ideas into connection with one another to form concepts or reach solutions.

Threat is realization of the possibility that a person's entire construction system will be overhauled.

Trait (Cattell) is a permanent entity that does not fade in and out like a state; it is inborn or develops during the life course and regularly directs behavior.

Trait (Allport) "is a neuropsychic structure having the capacity to render many stimuli functionally equivalent, and to initiate and guide equivalent (meaningfully consistent) forms of adaptive and expressive behavior."

Traits (Eysenck) are represented as statistical factors and defined as "theoretical constructs based on observed intercorrelations between a number of different habitual responses."

Transcendence is the act of transforming one's accidental and passive role of "creature" into that of an active and purposeful "creator."

Transference occurs when patients relate to the psychoanalyst as if he or she were some other person from their past with whom they were continuing to experience psychological conflict.

Type (Jung) is a habitual attitude, or a person's characteristic way.

Types (Eysenck) are second-order dimensions made up of statistically intercorrelated primary traits. They can be thought of as superfactors, but Eysenck prefers "second-order."

Tyranny of the shoulds is the belief that one should do this and that, whatever a good person should do, whatever is expected by others, rather than whatever one feels it is his or her nature to do.

Unconditional positive regard is provided when other people communicate, with no strings attached, that one is accepted, valued, worthwhile, and trusted, simply for being who one is.

Undoing is erasing "bad" behavior by displaying behavior designed to reverse the effects of the undesirable behavior ("Forgive me for hitting you! Let me grovel at your feet, and proclaim my undying love for you, and buy you flowers").

Unique trait is "so specific to an individual that no one else could be scored on [its dimension]."

Unitary trend is activity that is organized and directional in nature, not willy nilly, trial and error.

Unity is a sense of inner oneness within one's self and with the "natural and human world outside."

Validity is the degree to which a test measures what it was designed to measure. See Introduction.

Value of an outcome, be it a behavioral outcome or the outcome of some stimulus, is a powerful part of "sizing-up" a situation.

Variable refers to variation in quantity specified by numbers.

Variable schedules are procedures for which reinforcement is delivered after some X amount of time has elapsed, on the average, or after some Y number of responses have been performed, on the average.

Variable-interval (VI) schedule requires that a given amount of time elapses between one reinforced response and the next, on the average.

Variable-ratio (VR) schedules require that, on the average, a given number of responses be performed before a response is reinforced.

Vector is a force with directional properties.

Vicarious expectancy learning involves people adopting other persons' expectancies concerning future events, especially expectancies of those with whom they share relevant experiences.

Vicarious reinforcement occurs when one observes another person being rewarded for performing a behavior.

Viscerogenic needs involve basic physiological drives, and, as such, are relatively straightforward and self-explanatory.

Will power is "the unbroken determination to exercise free choice as well as self-restraint in spite of the unavoidable experience of shame, doubt, and a certain rage over being controlled by others."

Wisdom is a "detached and yet active concern with life in the face of death," not magical access to "higher knowledge."

Word Association Test (WAT) is a Jungian method in which persons are instructed to say the first word that comes to mind after hearing each of 100 words from a standardized list.

Youth (adolescence through young adulthood) begins at puberty, at which time physiological changes are accompanied by "psychic revolution."

REFERENCES

Abramson, L., Seligman, M. & Teasdale, J. Learned helplessness in humans: critique and reformulation. JOURNAL OF ABNORMAL PSYCHOLOGY, 1978, 87, 49-74.

Abt, L.E., & Bellak, L. (Eds.) PROJECTIVE PSYCHOLOGY, CLINICAL APPROACHES TO THE TOTAL PERSONALITY. New York: Grove Press, 1950.

Achterberg, J., and Lawlis, G.F. IMAGERY OF CANCER. Champaign, Illinois: Institute for Personality and Ability Testing, 1978.

Adler, A. STUDY OF ORGAN INFERIORITY AND ITS PSYCHICAL COMPENSATION; A CONTRIBUTION TO CLINICAL MEDICINE. New York: Nervous and Mental Diseases Publishing Company, 1907/1917.

Adler, A. Individual psychology. In C. Murchison. (Ed.) PSYCHOLOGIES OF 1930. Worcester: Clark University Press, 1930.

Adler, A. The structure of neurosis. In Ansbacher, H.L. and Ansbacher, R.R. (Eds.), ALFRED ADLER: SUPERIORITY AND SOCIAL INTEREST. Evanston, IL: Northwestern University Press (1964), 1932.

Adler, A. Advantages and disadvantages of the inferiority feeling. In Ansbacher, H.L. and Ansbacher, R.R. (Eds.), ALFRED ADLER: SUPERIORITY AND SOCIAL INTEREST. Evanston, IL: Northwestern University Press (1964), 1933a.

Adler, A. Religion and individual psychology. In Ansbacher, H.L. and Ansbacher, R.R. (Eds.), ALFRED ADLER: SUPERIORITY AND SOCIAL INTEREST. Evanston, IL: Northwestern University Press (1964), 1933b.

Adler, A. In H.L. Ansbacher & R.R. Ansbacher (Eds.), THE INDIVIDUAL PSYCHOLOGY OF ALFRED ADLER. New York: Basic Books, 1956.

Adler, A. SOCIAL INTEREST: A CHALLENGE TO MANKIND. New York: Capricorn Books, 1964.

Adler, A. THE PRACTICE AND THEORY OF INDIVIDUAL PSYCHOLOGY (Trans. by P. Radin). London: Routledge & Kagan Paul LTD, 1971/1929.

Adler, A. In H.L. Ansbacher & R.R. Ansbacher (Eds.), CO-OPERATION BETWEEN THE SEXES. New York: Norton, 1982.

Ainsworth, M.D.S. Infant-mother attachment. AMERICAN PSYCHOLOGIST, 1979, 34, 932-937.

Alderfer, C.P. Theories reflecting my personal experience and life development. THE JOURNAL OF APPLIED BEHAVIORAL SCIENCE, 1989, 25, 351-365.

Alicke, M. D. & Klotz, M. L. Social roles and social judgment: How an impression conveyed influences an impression formed. PERSONALITY AND SOCIAL PSYCHOLOGY BUL-

LETIN, 1993, 19, 185-194.

Alexander, F.G. PSYCHOSOMATIC MEDICINE, ITS PRINCIPLES AND APPLICATIONS. New York: Norton, 1950.

Alexander, F.G., and Selesnick, S.T. THE HISTORY OF PSYCHIATRY. New York: Harper & Row, 1966.

Allen, B.P. Perceived trustworthiness of attitudinal and behavioral expressions. JOURNAL OF SOCIAL PSYCHOLOGY, 1973, 89, 211-218.

Allen, B.P. Social distance and admiration reactions of "unprejudiced" whites. JOURNAL OF PERSONALITY, 1975, 43, 709-726.

Allen, B.P. Race and physical attractiveness as criteria for white subjects' dating choices. SOCIAL BEHAVIOR AND PERSONALITY, 1976, 4, 289-296.

Allen, B.P. SOCIAL BEHAVIOR: FACT AND FALSEHOOD. Chicago: Nelson-Hall, 1978.

Allen, B.P. Harrower's and Miale-Selzer's use of Hjalmar Schacht in their characterizations of the Nazi leaders. JOURNAL OF PERSONALITY ASSESSMENT, 1984, 48, 257-258.

Allen, B.P. After the missiles: Sociopsychological effects of nuclear war. AMERICAN PSYCHOLOGIST, 1985, 40, 927-937.

Allen, B.P. Dramaturgical quality. JOURNAL OF SOCIAL PSYCHOLOGY, 1988a, 128, 181-190.

Allen, B. P. Beyond consistency in the definition of personality: Dramaturgical quality and value. IMAGINATION, COGNITION AND PERSONALITY, 1988b, 7, 201-213.

Allen, B.P. PERSONAL ADJUSTMENT. Pacific Grove, CA: Brooks/Cole, 1990.

Allen, B.P. & Adams, J.Q. The concept "race": Let's go back to the beginning. JOURNAL OF SOCIAL BEHAVIOR AND PERSONALITY, 1992, 7, 163-168.

Allen, B. P. & Potkay, C.R. Variability of self-description on a day-to-day basis: Longitudinal use of the adjective generation technique. JOURNAL OF PERSONALITY, 1973, 41, 638-652.

Allen, B.P. & Potkay, C.R. The relationship between AGT self-description and significant life events: A longitudinal study. JOURNAL OF PERSONALITY, 1977a, 45, 207-219.

Allen, B.P. & Potkay, C.R. Misunderstanding the Adjective Generation Technique (AGT): Comments on Bem's rejoinder. JOURNAL OF PERSONALITY, 1977b, 45, 207-219.

Allen, B.P. & Potkay, C.R. On the arbitrary distinction between states and traits. JOURNAL OF PERSONALITY AND SOCIAL PSYCHOLOGY, 1981, 41, 916-928.

Allen, B.P. & Potkay, C.R. ADJECTIVE GENERATION TECHNIQUE (AGT): RESEARCH AND APPLICATIONS. New York: Irvington, 1983a.

Allen, B.P. & Potkay, C.R. Just as arbitrary as ever: Comments on Zuckerman's rejoinder. JOURNAL OF PERSONALITY AND SOCIAL PSYCHOLOGY, 1983b, 44, 1046-1087.

Allen, B.P. & Smith, G. Traits, situations and their interaction as alternative "causes" of behavior. JOURNAL OF SOCIAL PSYCHOLOGY, 1980, 111, 99-104.

Allport, G.W. THE USE OF PERSONAL DOCUMENTS IN PSYCHOLOGICAL SCIENCE. New York: Social Science Research Council, 1942.

Allport, G.W. THE NATURE OF PREJUDICE. Reading, MA.: Addison-Wesley, 1954.

Allport, G.W. PERSONALITY, A PSYCHOLOGICAL INTERPRETATION. New York: Henry Holt, 1937.

Allport, G.W. BECOMING, BASIC CONSIDERATIONS FOR A PSYCHOLOGY OF PERSONALITY. New Haven: Yale University Press, 1955.

Allport, G.W. PATTERN AND GROWTH IN PERSONALITY. New York: Holt, Rinehart and Winston, 1961.

Allport, G.W. Traits revisited. AMERICAN PSYCHOLOGIST, 1966, 21, 1-10.

Allport, G.W. In E. G. Boring & G. Lindzey (Eds.). A HISTORY OF PSYCHOLOGY IN AUTOBIOGRAPHY (Vol. 5). New York: Appleton-Century Crofts, 1967.

Allport, G.W. THE PERSON IN PSYCHOLOGY, SELECTED ESSAYS. Boston: Beacon Press, 1968.

Allport, G.W. & Odbert, H. Trait-names: A psycho-lexical study. PSYCHOLOGICAL MONOGRAPHS, 1936, 47, Whole No. 211, 1-171.

Alpher, V. S. Comment on Skinner. AMERICAN PSYCHOLOGIST, 1988, 43, 824-825.

AMERICAN PSYCHOLOGIST. 1958 award for distinguished scientific contributions to B. F. Skinner, 1958, 13, 735-738.

AMERICAN PSYCHOLOGIST. 1980 award for distinguished scientific contributions to Albert Bandura, 1981, 36, 27-42.

AMERICAN PSYCHOLOGIST, 1982 award for distinguished scientific contributions to Walter Mischel, 1983, 38, 9-14.

American Psychiatric Association. DIAGNOSTIC AND STATISTICAL MANUAL OF MENTAL DISORDERS. (Third edition) Washington, D.C., 1980.

American Psychological Association. A CAREER IN PSYCHOLOGY. Washington, D.C.: American Psychological Association, 1980.

American Psychological Association. STANDARDS FOR EDUCATIONAL AND PSYCHOLOGICAL TESTS. Washington, D.C.: American Psychological Association, 1974.

Ames, L.B., Learned, J., Metraux, R.W. & Walker, R.N. CHILD RORSCHACH RESPONSES, DEVELOPMENTAL TRENDS FROM TWO TO TEN YEARS. New York: Harper & Row, 1952.

Anastasi, A. PSYCHOLOGICAL TESTING. (Fifth edition) New York: Macmillan, 1982.

Anch, A.M., Browman, Carl P., Mitler, M. M. & Walsh, J. K. SLEEP: A SCIENTIFIC PERSPECTIVE. Englewood Cliffs, N.J.: Prentice-Hall, 1988.

Anderson, J.W. Henry A. Murray's early career: A psychobiographical exploration. JOURNAL OF PERSONALITY, 1988, 56, 137-171.

Angyal, A. FOUNDATIONS FOR A SCIENCE OF PERSONALITY. Cambridge: Harvard University Press, 1941.

Angyal, A. NEUROSIS AND TREATMENT, A HOLISTIC THEORY. New York: Wiley, 1965.

Ansbacher, H.L. In A. Adler, PROBLEMS OF NEUROSIS, A BOOK OF CASE HISTORIES. P. Mairet (Ed.) New York: Harper & Row Torchbooks, 1964.

Ansbacher, H.L. & Ansbacher, R.R. THE INDIVIDUAL PSYCHOLOGY OF ALFRED ADLER. New York: Basic Books, 1956.

Ansbacher, H.L. & Ansbacher, R.R. (Eds.). ALFRED ADLER: SUPERIORITY AND SOCIAL INTEREST. Evanston, IL: Northwestern University Press, 1964.

Ansbacher, H.L. Alfred Adler's influence on the three leading cofounders of humanistic psychology. JOURNAL OF HUMANISTIC PSYCHOLOGY, 1990, 30, 45-53.

Asch, S.E. SOCIAL PSYCHOLOGY. New York: Prentice-Hall, 1952.

Astin, A.W. Productivity of undergraduate institutions. SCIENCE, 1962, 136, 129-135.

Backteman, G., & Magnusson, D. Longitudinal stability of personality characteristics. JOURNAL OF PERSONALITY, 1981, 49, 148-160.

Bacciagaluppi, M. Eric Fromm's views on psychoanalytic "technique." CONTEMPORARY PYSCHOANALYSIS, 1989, 25, 226-243.

Baillargeon, J., and Danis, C. Barnum meets the computer: A critical test. JOURNAL OF PERSONALITY ASSESSMENT, 1984, 48,415-419.

Bales, J. Skinner gets award, ovations at APA talk. THE APA MONITOR, 1990, 21(10), 1 & 6.

Bandura, A. AGGRESSION: A SOCIAL LEARNING ANALYSIS. Englewood Cliffs, N. J.: Prentice-Hall, 1973.

Bandura, A. SOCIAL LEARNING THEORY. Englewood Cliffs, N. J.: Prentice-Hall, 1977.

Bandura, A. The psychology of chance encounters and life paths. AMERICAN PSYCHOLOGIST, 1982, 37, 747-755.

Bandura, A. Social cogntive theory. ANNALS OF CHILD DEVELOPMENT, New York: Jai Press, Inc., 1989a, Vol. 6, 1-60.

Bandura, A. Human agency in social cognitive theory. AMERICAN PSYCHOLOGIST, 1989b, 44, 1175-1184.

Bandura, A. Effect of perceived controllability and performance standards of self-regulation of complex decision making. JOURNAL OF PERSONALITY AND SOCIAL PSYCHOLOGY, 1989c, 56, 805-814.

Bandura, A. Mechanisms of moral disengagement. In W. Reich (Ed.), ORIGINS OF TERRORISM: PSYCHOLOGIES, IDEOLOGIES, STATES OF MIND (pp. 161-191). Cambridge, England: Cambridge University Press, 1990.

Bandura, A. & McDonald , F. The influence of social reinforcement and the behavior of models in shaping children's moral judgments. JOURNAL OF ABNORMAL AND SOCIAL PSYCHOLOGY, 1963, 67, 274-281.

Bandura, A., Reese, L. & Adams, N. Microanalysis of action and fear arousal as a function of differential levels of perceived self-efficacy. JOURNAL OF PERSONALITY AND SOCIAL PSYCHOLOGY, 1982, 43, 5-21.

Bandura, A., Ross, D., & Ross, S. Imitation of film-mediated aggressive models. JOURNAL OF ABNORMAL AND SOCIAL PSYCHOLOGY, 1963, 66, 3-11.

Bandura, A. & Wood, R. Effect of perceived controllability and performance standards on self-regulation of complex decision making. JOURNAL OF PERSONALITY AND SOCIAL PSYCHOLOGY, 1989, 56, 805-814.

Barber, T. X. "Hypnosis," suggestions, and psychosomatic phenomena: new look from the standpoint of recent experimental studies. In J. Fosshage and P. Olsen (Eds.), HEALING: IMPLICATIONS FOR PSYCHOTHERAPY (p. 269-297). New York: Human Sciences Press, 1978.

Barnes, H.E. Translator's introduction. In J-P. Sartre. BEING AND NOTHINGNESS. New York: Philosophical Library, 1953, viii-xiii.

Barnet, H. S. Divorce stress and adjustment model: Locus of control and demographic predictors. JOURNAL OF DIVORCE, 1990, 13, 93-109.

Barry, H., Child, I., & Bacon, M. Relation of child rearing to subsistence economy. AMERICAN ANTHROPOLOGIST, 1959, 61, 51-64.

Beck, J. E. Testing a personal construct theory model of the experiential learning process — A. The impact of invalidation on the construing processes of participants in sensitivity training groups. SMALL GROUP BEHAVIOR, 1988, 19, 79-102.

Bell, P.A., and Byrne, D. Repression-Sensitization. In H. London and J.E. Exner, Jr., (Eds.), DIMENSIONS OF PERSONALITY. New York: Wiley, 1978, 449-485.

Bem, D.J. Predicting more of the people more of the time: Some thoughts on the Allen-Potkay studies of intraindividual variability. JOURNAL OF PERSONALITY, 1977, 45, 327-332.

Bem D.J. & Allen, A. On predicting some of the people some of the time: The search for cross-situational consistencies in behavior. PSYCHOLOGICAL REVIEW, 1974, 81, 506-520.

Bem, D.J. & Funder, D.C. Predicting more of the people more of the time: Assessing the personality of situations. PSYCHOLOGICAL REVIEW, 1978, 85, 485-501.

Bem, S.L. The measurment of psychological androgeny. JOURNAL OF CONSULTING AND CLINICAL PSYCHOLOGY, 1974, 42, 155-162.

Bender, L. A VISUAL MOTOR GESTALT TEST AND ITS CLINICAL USE. New York: American Orthopsychiatric Association, 1938.

Benesch, K. F. & Page, M. M. Self-construct systems and interpersonal congruence. JOURNAL OF PERSONALITY, 1989, 57, 137-173.

Benjamin, L. T. A history of teaching machines. AMERICAN PSYCHOLOGIST, 1988, 43, 703-712.

Bennett, C. M. A Skinnerian view of human freedom. THE HUMANIST, 1990 (July/August), p. 18-20 & 30.

Bentler, P.M., Jackson, D.N., and Messick, S. Identification of content and style: A two-dimensional interpretation of acquiescence. PSYCHOLOGICAL BULLETIN, 1971, 76, 186-204.

Bexton, W., Heron, W. & Scott, T. The effects of decreased variation in the sensory environment. CANADIAN JOURNAL OF PSYCHOLOGY, 1954, 8, 70-76.

Bieri, J. Cognitive complexity—simplicity and predictive behavior. JOURNAL OF ABNORMAL AND SOCIAL PSYCHOLOGY, 1955, 51, 61-66.

Binswanger, L. BEING-IN-THE-WORLD, SELECTED PAPERS OF LUDWIG BINSWANGER. (J. Needleman, Trans.) New York: Harper and Row, 1963.

Binswanger, L. The case of Ellen West, An anthropological-clinical study. In R. May, E. Angel, and H.F. Ellenberger. (Eds.) EXISTENCE, A NEW DIMENSION IN PSYCHIATRY AND PSYCHOLOGY. New York: Basic Books, 1958, 237-364.

Blake, M.J.F. Relationship between circadian rhythm of body temperature and introversion-extraversion. NATURE, 1967, 215, 896-897.

Blake, M.J.F. Temperament and time of day. In

W.P. Colquhoun (Ed.), BIOLOGICAL RHYTHMS AND HUMAN PERFORMANCE. New York: Academic Press, 1971.

Block, J. THE Q-SORT METHOD IN PERSONALITY ASSESSMENT AND PSYCHIATRIC RESEARCH. Springfield, Illinois: Charles C. Thomas, 1961.

Block, J. & Ozer, D. Two types of psychologists: Remarks on the Mendelshon, Weiss, and Feimer Contribution. JOURNAL OF PERSONALITY AND SOCIAL PSYCHOLOGY, 1982, 42, 1171-1181.

Blum, G. The Blacky Test. GENETIC PSYCHOLOGY MONOGRAPHS, 1949, 39, 13-22.

Blum, G. THE BLACKY PICTURES: A TECHNIQUE FOR THE EXPLORATION OF PERSONALITY DYNAMICS. New York: Pychological Corporation, 1950.

Blum, G. The Blacky Test-Sections II, IV, and VII. In R. Birney & R. Teevan (Eds.), MEASURING HUMAN MOTIVATON. New York: Van Nostrand, 1962, 119-144.

Blum, G. PSYCHOANALYTIC THEORIES OF PERSONALITY. New York: McGraw-Hill, 1964.

Boring, E. A HISTORY OF EXPERIMENTAL PSYCHOLOGY (Second edition). New York: Appleton-Century-Crofts, Inc., 1957.

Bornstein, R. F. Radical behaviorism, internal states, and the science of psychology: A reply to Skinner. AMERICAN PSYCHOLOGIST, 1988, 43, 819-821.

Boss, M. PSYCHOANALYSIS AND DASEINSANALYSIS. (L.B. LeFebre, Trans.) New York: Basic Books, 1963.

Bosselman, B. C. SELF-DESTRUCTION: A STUDY OF THE SUICIDAL IMPULSE. Springfield, IL, 1958.

Bottome, P. ALFRED ADLER: APOSTLE OF FREEDOM. London: Faber & Faber, 1939.

Bowers, K. Situationalism in psychology: An analysis and a critique. PSYCHOLOGICAL REVIEW, 1973, 80, 307-336.

Bowlby, J. MATERNAL CARE AND MENTAL HEALTH. New York: Schocken Books, 1969.

Breuer, J. & Freud, S. STUDIES IN HYSTERIA. Boston: Beacon Press, 1985/1950.

Brigham, J. SOCIAL PSYCHOLOGY. Boston: Little, Brown & Co., 1986.

Brody, B. Freud's case-load. PSYCHOTHERAPY: THEORY, RESEARCH AND PRACTICE, 1970, 7, 8-12.

Bronfen, E. The lady vanishes: Sophie Freud and beyond the Pleasure Principle. THE SOUTH ATLANTIC QUARTERLY, 1989, 88 (Fall), 961-991.

Brunswick, E. Representative design and probabilistic theory in a functional psychology. PSYCHOLOGICAL REVIEW, 1955, 62, 193-217.

Buber, M. I AND THOU. (Second edition) New York: Scribners, 1958.

Bugental, J.F.T. The third force in psychology. JOURNAL OF HUMANISTIC PSYCHOLOGY, 1964, 4, 19-25.

Buhler, C. VALUES IN PSYCHOTHERAPY. New York: Free Press of Glencoe, 1962.

Buhler, C. Some observations on the psychology of the third force. JOURNAL OF HUMANISTIC PSYCHOLOGY, 1965, 5, 54-55.

Burks, H.F. MANUAL FOR BURKS' BEHAVIOR RATING SCALES. Huntington Beach, California: Arden Press, 1971.

Bullock, W. A. & Gilliland, K. Eysenck's arousal theory of introversion-extraversion: a converging measures investigation. JOURNAL OF PERSONALITY AND SOCIAL PSYCHOLOGY, 1993, 64, 113-123.

Burnell, G.M., & Solomon, G.F. Early memories and ego function. ARCHIVES OF GENERAL PSYCHIATRY, 1964, 11, 556-567.

Butcher, J.N. (Ed.) OBJECTIVE PERSONALITY ASSESSMENT. New York: Academic Press, 1972.

Butler, J.M., and Haigh, G.V. Changes in the relation between self-concepts and ideal concepts consequent upon client-centered counseling. In C.R. Rogers and R.F. Dymond. (Eds.) PSYCHOTHERAPY AND PERSONALITY CHANGE. Chicago: University of Chicago Press, 1954, 55-75.

Buttle, F. The social construction of needs. PSYCHOLOGY AND MARKETING, 1989, 6, 199-207.

Byrne, D. The Repression-Sensitization Scale: Rationale, reliability, and validity. JOURNAL OF PERSONALITY, 1961, 29, 334-349.

Cameron, N. THE PSYCHOLOGY OF THE

BEHAVIOR DISORDERS. Boston: Houghton Mifflin, 1947.

Campbell, D.P. MANUAL FOR THE STRONG-CAMPBELL INTEREST INVENTORY. (Revised edition) Stanford, California: Stanford University Press, 1977.

Campbell, D.T. On the conflicts between biological and social evolution and between psychology and moral tradition. AMERICAN PSYCHOLOGIST, 1975, 30, 1103-1126.

Campbell, D.T., & Fiske, D.W. Convergent and discriminant validation by the multitrait-multimethod matrix. PSYCHOLOGICAL BULLETIN, 1959, 56, 81-105.

Cannon, W.G. WISDOM OF THE BODY. New York: Norton, 1932.

Cantor, N. & Mischel, W. Traits as prototypes: Effects on recognition memory. JOURNAL OF PERSONALITY AND SOCIAL PSYCHOLOGY, 1977, 35, 38-48.

Cantor, N., Mischel, W. & Schwartz, J.C. A prototype analysis of psychological situations. COGNITIVE PSYCHOLOGY, 1982, 14, 45-77.

Carkhuff, R.R. HELPING AND HUMAN RELATIONS: A PRIMER FOR LAY AND PROFESSIONAL HELPERS. Vols. I and II. New York: Holt, Rinehart and Winston, 1969.

Carlson, R. Personality. In M.R. Rosensweig and L.W. Porter. (Eds.) ANNUAL REVIEW OF PSYCHOLOGY. Palo Alto, California: Annual Reviews, 1975, 26, 393-414.

Carlson, J. Brief therapy for health promotion. INDIVIDUAL PSYCHOLOGY, 1989, 45, 220-229.

Carlyn, M. An assessment of the Myers-Briggs Type Indicator. JOURNAL OF PERSONALITY ASSESSMENT, 1977, 41, 461-473.

Carskadon, T.G. Use of the Myers-Briggs Type Indicator in psychology courses and discussion groups. TEACHING OF PSYCHOLOGY, 1978, 5, 140-142.

Carson, R.C. INTERACTION CONCEPTS OF PERSONALITY. Chicago: Aldine, 1969.

Carson, R. C. & Butcher, J. N. ABNORNAL PSYCHOLOGY AND MODERN LIFE. New York: Harper Collins Publishers, 1992.

Catanzaro, S. J. & Mearns, J. Measuring generalized expectancies for negative mood regulation: Initial scale development and implications. JOURNAL OF PERSONALITY ASSESSMENT, 1990, 54, 546-563.

Cattell, R. B. "Is national intelligence declining?" EUGENICS REVIEW, 1936-1937, 28, 181-203.

Cattell, R.B. THE DESCRIPTION AND MEASUREMENT OF PERSONALITY. New York: World Book, 1946.

Cattell, R.B. THE SIXTEEN PERSONALITY FACTOR QUESTIONNAIRE. (First edition) Champaign, Illinois: Institute for Personality and Ability Testing, 1949.

Cattell, R.B. The nature and measurement of anxiety. SCIENTIFIC AMERICAN, 1963, 208, 96-104.

Cattell, R.B. PERSONALITY: A SYSTEMATIC, THEORETICAL AND FACTUAL STUDY. New York: McGraw-Hill, 1950.

Cattell, R.B. THE SCIENTIFIC ANALYSIS OF PERSONALITY. Baltimore, Maryland: Penguin Books, 1966 (1965).

Cattell, R.B. PERSONALITY AND MOOD BY QUESTIONNAIRE. San Francisco: Jossey-Bass, 1973.

Cattell, R.B. Raymond B. Cattell. In G. Lindzey (Ed.). A HISTORY OF PSYCHOLOGY IN AUTOBIOGRAPHY. Engelwood Cliffs, New Jersey: Prentice-Hall, 1974a.

Cattell, R.B. Travels in psychological hyperspace. In T.S. Krawiec (Ed.), Vol. 2, THE PSYCHOLOGISTS. New York: Oxford University Press, 1974b.

Cattell, R.B. STRUCTURED PERSONALITY-LEARNING THEORY: A WHOLISTIC MULTIVARIATE RESEARCH APPROACH. New York: Praeger, 1983.

Cattell, R.B. HUMAN MOTIVATION AND THE DYNAMIC CALCULUS. New York: Praeger, 1984a (1985).

Cattell, R.B. PERSONALITY AND LEARNING THEORY, Vols. 1 & 2. New York: Springer Publishing Co., 1979.

Cattell, R.B. The voyage of a laboratory, 1928-1984. MULTIVARIATE BEHAVIORAL RESEARCH, 1984b, 19, 121-174.

Cattell, R.B. & Brennan, J. The cultural types of modern nations, by two quantitative classification methods. SOCIOLOGY AND SOCIAL RESEARCH, 1984, 68, 208-235.

Cattell, R.B. The 16 PF personality structure and

Dr. Eysenck. JOURNAL OF SOCIAL BEHAVIOR AND PERSONALITY, 1986, 1, 153-160.

Cattell, R.B., Eber, H.W., & Tatsuoka, M.M. HANDBOOK FOR THE SIXTEEN PERSONALITY FACTOR QUESTIONNAIRE. Champaign, Illinois: Institute for Personality and Abiltiy Testing, 1970.

Cattell, R.B. & Kline, P. THE SCIENTIFIC ANALYSIS OF PERSONALITY AND MOTIVATION. New York: Academic Press, 1977.

Cattell, R.B., Rao, D. C., Schuerger, J. M. Heritability in the personality control system: Ego strength (C), super ego strength (G) and the self-sentiment (Q_3); by the MAVA mode, Q-data, and Maximun likelihood analyses. SOCIAL BEHAVIOR AND PERSONALITY, 1985, 13, 33-41.

Cattell, R.B. & Scheier, I.H. THE MEANING AND MEASUREMENT OF NEUROTICISM AND ANXIETY. New York: Ronald Press, 1961.

Cattell, R. B., Schuerger, J. M., & Klein, T. W. Heritabilities of ego strength (factor C), super ego strength (factor G), and self-sentiment (factor Q_3) by multiple abstract variance analysis. JOURNAL OF CLINICAL PSYCHOLOGY, 1982, 38, 769-779.

Cattell, R.B. & Warburton, F.W. OBJECTIVE PERSONALITY & MOTIVATION TESTS, A THEORETICAL INTRODUCTION AND PRACTICAL COMPENDIUM. Urbana: University of Illinois Press, 1967.

Cautela, J.R., & Upper, D. THE BEHAVIORAL INVENTORY BATTERY: THE USE OF SELF-REPORT MEASURES IN BEHAVIORAL ANALYSIS AND THERAPY. In M. Hersen & A.S. Bellack (Eds.), BEHAVIORAL ASSESSMENT: A PRACTICAL HANDBOOK. New York: Pergamon Press, 1976.

Cetola, H. & Prinkey, K. Introversion-extraversion and loud commercials. PSYCHOLOGY AND MARKETING, 1986, 3, 123-132.

Chapman, A. H. HARRY STACK SULLIVAN: HIS LIFE AND HIS WORK. New York: Putman, 1976.

Cherian, V. I. Birth order and academic achievement of children in Transkei. PSYCHOLOGICAL REPORTS, 1990, 66, 19-24.

Chomsky, N. A review of VERBAL BEHAVIOR by B. F. Skinner. LANGUAGE, 1959, 35, 26-58.

CHRISTIAN SCIENCE MONITOR. Editorial. December 4, 1978, p. 32.

Churchill, J. C. Broida, J. P. & Nicholson, N. L. Locus of control and self-esteem of adult children of alcoholics. JOURNAL OF STUDIES ON ALCOHOL, 1990, 51, 373-376.

Cialdini, R. B. INFLUENCE: SCIENCE AND PRACTICE. Glenview, IL: Scott, Foresman.

Ciminero, A.R., Calhoun, K.S., & Adams, H.E. (Eds.) HANDBOOK OF BEHAVIORAL ASSESSMENT. New York: Wiley, 1977.

Clark, K.B. The psychology of the ghetto. In DARK GHETTO. New York: Harper & Row, 1965, 63-80.

Cohen, D. PSYCHOLOGISTS ON PSYCHOLOGY. New York: Taplinger Publishing Co., 1977.

Collins, B. & Hoyt, M. Personal responsibility for consequences: An integration and extension of the "forced" compliance literature. JOURNAL OF EXPERIMENTAL SOCIAL PSYCHOLOGY, 1972, 8, 558-593.

Colm, H.N. The affirmation of distance and closeness in psychotherapy. REVIEW OF EXISTENTIAL PSYCHOLOGY AND PSYCHIATRY, 1961, 1, 33-43.

Combs, A.W. Some observations on self-concept research and theory. In M.D. Lynch, A.A. Norem-Hebeisen and K.J. Gergen. (Eds.) SELF-CONCEPT, ADVANCES IN THEORY AND RESEARCH. Cambridge, Massachusetts: Ballinger, 1981, 5-16.

Conn, J. H. & Kanner, L. Children's awareness of sex differences. JOURNAL OF CHILD PSYCHIATRY, 1947, 1, 3-57.

Conway, F. & Siegelman, J. SNAPPING, AMERICA'S EPIDEMIC OF SUDDEN PERSONALITY CHANGE. New York: Lippincott, 1978.

Corcoran, D.W.J. The relation between introversion and salivation. AMERICAN JOURNAL OF PSYCHOLOGY, 1964, 77, 298-300.

Corsini, R.J. CURRENT PSYCHOTHERAPIES. (Third edition) Itasca, Illinois: F.E. Peacock, 1984.

Cousins, N. ANATOMY OF AN ILLNESS AS PERCEIVED BY THE PATIENT. New York: Norton, 1979.

Cramer, P. WORD ASSOCIATION. New York: Academic Press, 1968.

Crandall, J. E. Adler's concept of social interest:

Theory, measurement, and implications for adjustment. JOURNAL OF PERSONALITY AND SOCIAL PSYCHOLOGY, 1980, 39, 481-495.

Cronbach, L.J. The two disciplines of scientific psychology. AMERICAN PSYCHOLOGIST, 1957, 12, 671-684.

Cronbach, L.J. ESSENTIALS OF PSYCHOLOGICAL TESTING. (Third edition) New York: Harper and Row, 1970.

Cronbach, L. J. A research worker's treasure chest. MULTIVARIATE BEHAVIORAL RESEARCH, 1984, 19, 223-240.

Crow, L., and Crow, A. (Eds.) READINGS IN GENERAL PSYCHOLOGY. New York: Barnes & Noble, 1954.

Crumbaugh, J., and Maholick, L. MANUAL OF INSTRUCTIONS FOR THE PURPOSE IN LIFE TEST. Munster, Indiana: Psychometric Affiliates, 1969.

Curran, C.A. PERSONALITY FACTORS IN COUNSELING. New York: Grune and Stratton, 1945.

Daly, M. & Wilson M. Is parent-offspring conflict sex-linked? Freudian and Darwinian models. JOURNAL OF PERSONALITY, 1990, 58, 163-190.

Damico, S.B. & Scott, E.S. Role of extracurricular activities in the promotion of cross-race contact by white students from high school to college. URBAN REVIEW, 1984, 16, 165-176.

Danto, A., & Morgenbesser, S. PHILOSOPHY OF SCIENCE. Cleveland:Meridan, 1960.

Darley, J. & Zanna, M. Making moral judgments. AMERICAN SCIENTIST, 1982, 70, 515-521.

Das, A.K. Beyond self-actualization. INTERNATIONAL JOURNAL FOR THE ADVANCEMENT OF COUNSELING, 1989, 12, 13-17.

Davidson, P.O., & Costello, C.G. (Eds.) N = 1: EXPERIMENTAL STUDIES OF SINGLE CASES. New York: Van Nostrand Reinhold, 1969.

Davis, W. & Phares, E. Parental antecedents of internal-external control of reinforcement. PSYCHOLOGICAL REPORTS, 1969, 24, 427-436.

Davison, G.C., and Neale, J.M. ABNORMAL PSYCHOLOGY, AN EXPERIMENTAL CLINICAL APPROACH. (3rd Ed.) New York: Wiley, 1982.

Dawidowicz, L. S. THE WAR AGAINST THE JEWS. New York: Bantam, 1975.

de Bonis, M., and Delgrange, C. A psycholinguistic approach to the measurement of anxiety. In C.D. Spielberger and I.G. Sarason, (Eds.), STRESS AND ANXIETY (Vol 4). New York: Wiley, 1977, 67-76.

DeCarvalho, R.J. Contributions to the history of psychology: LXIX. Gordon Allport on the problem of method in psychology. PSYCHOLOGICAL REPORTS, 1990, 67, 267-275.

DeCarvalho, R.J. Gordon Allport and humanistic psychology. JOURNAL OF HUMANISTIC PSYCHOLOGY, 1991, 31, 8-13.

deCharms, R., and Moeller, G.H. Values expressed in American children's readers: 1800-1950. JOURNAL OF ABNORMAL PSYCHOLOGY, 1962, 64,136-142.

deCharms, R. Personal causation training in the schools. JOURNAL OF APPLIED SOCIAL PSYCHOLOGY, 1972, 2, 95-113.

deCharms, R., and Muir, M.S. Motivation: Social approaches. In M.R. Rosenzweig and L.W. Porter, (Eds.), ANNUAL REVIEW OF PSYCHOLOGY (Vol 29). Palo Alto, California: Annual Reviews, 1978, 91-113.

Deci, E. INTRINSIC MOTIVATION. New York: Plenum, 1975.

Dement, W. C. SOME MUST WATCH WHILE SOME MUST SLEEP. New York: Norton, 1976

DePaulo, B. & Rosenthal, R. Telling lies. JOURNAL OF PERSONALITY AND SOCIAL PSYCHOLOGY, 1979, 37, 1713-1722.

Deutsch, H. THE PSYCHOLOGY OF WOMEN. Vol II. New York: Grune & Stratton, 1945.

Diener, E. & Wallbom, M. Effects of self-awareness on antinormative behavior. JOURNAL OF RESEARCH IN PERSONALITY, 1976, 10, 107-111.

Dinkmeyer, D. & Sherman, R. Brief Adlerian family therapy. INDIVIDUAL PSYCHOLOGY, 1989, 45, 148-158.

Dixon, N. SUBLIMINAL PERCEPTION: THE NATURE OF A CONTROVERSY. London: McGraw-Hill, 1971.

Doherty, W. Impact of divorce on locus of control orientation in adult women: A longitudial study. JOURNAL OF PERSONALITY AND

SOCIAL PSYCHOLOGY, 1983, 44, 834-840.

Dollard, J., Doob, L., Miller, N., Mowrer, O., & Sears, R. FRUSTRATION AND AGGRESSION. New Haven: Yale University Press, 1939.

Dollard, J. & Miller, N. PERSONALITY AND PSYCHOTHERAPY. New York: McGraw-Hill, 1950.

Dreikurs, R. Family counseling: a demonstration. JOURNAL OF INDIVIDUAL PSYCHOLOGY, 1972a, 28, 207-222.

Dreikurs, R. Technology of conflict resolution. JOURNAL OF INDIVIDUAL PSYCHOLOGY, 1972b, 28, 203-206.

Dry, A. THE PSYCHOLOGY OF JUNG: A CRITICAL INTERPRETATION. New York: Wiley, 1961.

Duval, S., & Wicklund, R.A. A THEORY OF OBJECTIVE SELF AWARENESS. New York: Academic Press, 1972.

Duval, S., & Wicklund, R.A. Effects of objective self awareness on attribution of causality. JOURNAL OF EXPERIMENTAL SOCIAL PSYCHOLOGY, 1973, 9, 17-31.

Eaves, L.J. & Eysenck, H.J. The nature of extraversion: A genetical analysis. JOURNAL OF PERSONALITY AND SOCIAL PSYCHOLOGY, 1975, 32, 102-112.

Eckardt, M.H. In K. Horney, THE ADOLESCENT DIARIES OF KAREN HORNEY. New York: Basic Books, 1980.

Ekman, P. & Friesen, W. Detecting deception from the body and face. JOURNAL OF PERSONALITY AND SOCIAL PSYCHOLOGY, 1974, 29, 288-298.

Ellenberger, H. THE DISCOVERY OF THE UNCONSCIOUS: THE HISTORY AND EVOLUTION OF DYNAMIC PSYCHIATRY. New York: Basic Books, 1970.

Ellis, A. RATIONAL-EMOTIVE THEORY. In A. Burton (Ed.), OPERATIONAL THEORIES OF PERSONALITY. New York: Brunner/Mazel, 1974a, pp. 308-344.

Ellis, A. Experience and rationality: The making of a Rational-Emotive therapist. PSYCHOTHERAPY: THEORY, RESEARCH AND PRACTICE, 1974b, 11, 194-198.

Endler, N.S. The person versus the situation—A pseudo issue? A response to Alker. JOURNAL OF PERSONALITY, 1973, 41, 287-303.

Endler, N.S. Persons, situations, and their interactions. In A.I. Rabin, J. Aronoff, A.M. Barclay & R.A. Zucker (Eds.), FURTHER EXPLORATIONS IN PERSONALITY. New York: Wiley-Interscience, 1981, 114-151.

Endler, N.S. Interactionism: A personality model, but not yet a theory. In M. Page & R. Dienstbier. NEBRASKA SYMPOSIUM ON MOTIVATION, 1982: PERSONALITY—CURRENT THEORY AND RESEARCH. Lincoln: University of Nebraska Press, 1983.

Endler, N.S. & Hunt, J. McV. S-R inventories of hostility and comparisons of the proportions of variance from persons, responses, and situations for hostility and anxiousness. JOURNAL OF PERSONALITY AND SOCIAL PSYCHOLOGY, 1968, 9, 309-315.

Endler, N.S. & Hunt, J. McV. Generalizability of contributions from sources of variance in the S-R Inventory of Anxiousness. JOURNAL OF PERSONALITY, 1969, 37, 1-24.

Endler, N.S., & Okada, M. A multidimensional measure of trait anxiety: The S-R Inventory of General Trait Anxiousness. JOURNAL OF CONSULTING AND CLINICAL PSYCHOLOGY, 1975, 43, 319-329.

Endler, N.S., Parker, J.D.A., Bagby. R.M. & Cox, B.J. Multidimensionality of state and trait anxiety: Factor structure on the Endler Multidimensional Anxiety Scales. JOURNAL OF PERSONALITY AND SOCIAL PSYCHOLOGY, 1991, 60, 919-926.

Engleman, E., BERGGASSE 19: SIGMUND FREUD'S HOME AND OFFICES, VIENNA 1938. New York: Basic Books, 1976.

Engelhard, G. Gender differences in performance on mathematics items: Evidence from the United States and Thailand. CONTEMPORARY EDUCATIONAL PSYCHOLOGY, 1990, 15, 13-26.

English, H.B., & English, A.C. A COMPREHENSIVE DICTIONARY OF PSYCHOLOGICAL AND PSYCHOANALYTICAL TERMS. New York: Longmans, Green and Company, 1958.

Epstein, L.H. Psychophysiological measurement in assessment. In M. Hersen & A.S. Bellack (Eds.), BEHAVIORAL ASSESSMENT, A PRACTICAL HANDBOOK. New York: Pergamon, 1976, 207-232.

Epstein, R. Skinner, creativity, and the problems of spontaneous behavior. PSYCHOLOGICAL SCIENCE, 1991, 2, 362-370.

Epstein, S. The nature of anxiety with emphasis upon its relationship to expectancy. In C.D. Spielberger, (Ed.), ANXIETY, CURRENT TRENDS IN THEORY AND RESEARCH (Vol. 2). New York: Academic Press, 1972, 291-337.

Epstein, S. Traits are alive and well. In D. Magnusson & N. Endler (Eds.), PERSONALITY AT THE CROSSROADS: CURRENT ISSUES IN INTERACTIONAL PSYCHOLOGY. Hillsdale, NJ: Erlbaum, 1977.

Erik Erikson: The quest for identity. (December 21), NEWSWEEK, 1970, pp. 84-89.

Erikson, E. CHILDHOOD AND SOCIETY. New York: W.W. Norton, 1950.

Erikson, E. Womanhood and the inner space. In E. H. Erikson. IDENTITY, YOUTH AND CRISIS. New York: Norton, 1968a, Pp. 261-294.

Erikson, E. Life cycle. In D. Sills (Ed.), INTERNATIONAL EXCYCLOPEDIA OF THE SOCIAL SCIENCES. New York: Macmillan & Free Press, 1968b, Vol. 9, 286-292.

Erikson, E. LIFE HISTORY AND THE HISTORICAL MOMENT, DIVERSE PRESENTATIONS. New York: Norton, 1975.

Estes, K. An experimental study of punishment. PSYCHOLOGICAL MONOGRAPHS, 1944, 47, No. 263, 40.

Evans, R.I. CONVERSATIONS WITH CARL JUNG, AND REACTIONS FROM ERNEST JONES. Princeton, New Jersey: Van Nostrand, 1964.

Evans, R.I. DIALOGUE WITH ERIK ERIKSON. New York: Harper & Row, 1967.

Evans. R.I. CARL ROGERS, THE MAN AND HIS IDEAS. New York: E.P. Dutton, 1975.

Evans, R.I. THE MAKING OF PSYCHOLOGY. New York: A.A. Knopf, 1976.

Eysenck, H.J. THE SCIENTIFIC STUDY OF PERSONALITY. New York: Macmillan, 1952.

Eysenck, H.J. SENSE AND NONSENSE IN PSYCHOLOGY. Baltimore, Maryland: Penguin Books, 1957.

Eysenck, H.J. MANUAL OF THE MAUDSLEY PERSONALITY INVENTORY. London: University of London Press, 1959.

Eysenck, H.J. THE MAUDSLEY PERSONALITY INVENTORY MANUAL. San Diego: Educational and Industrial Testing Service, 1962.

Eysenck, H.J. THE BIOLOGICAL BASIS OF PERSONALITY. Springfield, Illinois: Charles C. Thomas, 1967.

Eysenck, H.J. A dimensional system of psychodiagnosis. In A.R. Mahrer (Ed.), NEW APPROACHES TO PERSONALITY CLASSIFICATION. New York: Columbia University Press, 1970.

Eysenck, H.J. (Ed.) THE MEASUREMENT OF PERSONALITY. Baltimore, Maryland: University Park Press, 1976.

Eysenck, H.J. Hans Jurgen Eysenck. In G. Lindzey, A HISTORY OF PSYCHOLOGY IN AUTOBIOGRAPHY. (Vol. VII) San Francisco: W.H. Freeman, 1980, 153-187.

Eysenck, H.J. (Ed.) A MODEL FOR PERSONALITY. New York: Springer-Verlag, 1981.

Eysenck, H.J. Cattell and the theory of personality. MULTIVARIATE BEHAVIORAL RESEARCH, 1984, 19, 323-336.

Eysenck, H.J. Genetic and environmental contributions to individual differences: The three major dimensions of personality. JOURNAL OF PERSONALITY, 1990, 58, 245-261.

Eysenck, H.J. & Eysenck, S.B.G. PERSONALITY STRUCTURE AND MEASUREMENT. San Diego, California: Robert R. Knapp, 1969.

Eysenck, H.J. & Eysenck, S.B.G. PSYCHOTICISM AS A DIMENSION OF PERSONALITY. New York: Crane, Russak & Company, 1976.

Eysenck, S.B.G. & Eysenck, H.J. Salivary response to lemon juice as a measure of introversion. PERCEPTUAL AND MOTOR SKILLS, 1967, 24, 1047-1053.

Eysenck, S.B.G. & Eysenck, H.J. The measurement of psychoticism: A study of factor analytic stability and reliability. BRITISH JOURNAL OF SOCIAL AND CLINICAL PSYCHOLOGY, 1968, 7, 286-294.

Eysenck, S.B.G. & Eysenck, H.J. PERSONALITY STRUCTURE AND MEASUREMENT. New York: Crane, 1976.

Eysenck, H.J. & Levey, A. Conditioning, introversion-extraversion and the strength of the nervous system. In V.D. Nebylitsyn & J.A. Gray

(Eds.), BIOLOGICAL BASES OF INDIVID-UAL BEHAVIOR, New York: Academic Press, 1972, 206-220.

Falbo, T. Relationships between birth category, achievement and interpersonal orientation. JOURNAL OF PERSONALITY AND SOCIAL PSYCHOLOGY, 1981, 41, 121-131.

Falbo, T. & Polit, D. Quantitative review of the only child literature: Research evidence and theory development. PSYCHOLOGICAL BULLETIN, 1986, 100, 176-189.

Fairbairn, W.R.D. AN OBJECT-RELATIONS THEORY OF PERSONALITY. New York: Basic Books, 1954.

Farber, A. Freud's love letters: Intimations of psychoanalytic theory. THE PSYCHOANALYTIC REVIEW, 1978, 65, 167-189.

Farberow, N.L. A society by any other name. JOURNAL OF PROJECTIVE TECHNIQUES AND PERSONALITY ASSESSMENT, 1970, 34, 3-5.

Fenichel, O. THE PSYCHOANALYTIC THEORY OF NEUROSIS. New York: Norton, 1945.

Ferenczi, S. CONTRIBUTIONS TO PSYCHO-ANALYSIS. Boston: Badger, 1916.

Ferguson, E. D. Adler's motivational theory: An historical persepctive on belonging and the fundamental human striving. INDIVIDUAL PSYCHOLOGY, 1989, 45, 354-362.

Festinger, L. A theory of social comparison processes. HUMAN RELATIONS, 1954, 2, 117-114.

Festinger, L. & Carlsmith, J.M. Cognitive consequences of forced compliance. JOURNAL OF ABNORMAL AND SOCIAL PSYCHOLOGY, 1959, 58, 203-210.

Finchilescu, G. Interracial contact in South Aftica within the nursing context. JOURNAL OF APPLIED SOCIAL PSYCHOLOGY, 1988, 18, 1207-1221.

Findley, M. & Cooper, H. Locus of control and academic achievement: A literature review. JOURNAL OF PERSONALITY AND SOCIAL PSYCHOLOGY, 1983, 44, 419-427.

Fischer, W.F. THEORIES OF ANXIETY. New York: Harper and Row, 1970.

Fiske, D.W. MEASURING THE CONCEPTS OF PERSONALITY. Chicago: Aldine, 1971.

Fletcher, J. SITUATION ETHICS, THE NEW MORALITY. Philadelphia: Westminster Press, 1966.

Fliegel, Z. Half a century later: Current status of Freud's controversial view on women. THE PSYCHOANALYTIC REVIEW, 1982, 69, 7-28.

Frank, L.K. Projective methods for the study of personality. JOURNAL OF PSYCHOLOGY, 1939, 8, 389-413.

Frank, J.D. PERSUASION AND HEALING, A COMPARATIVE STUDY OF PSYCHOTHERAPY. New York: Schocken Books, 1961.

Frank, J.D. Therapeutic factors in psychotherapy. AMERICAN JOURNAL OF PSYCHOTHERAPY, 1971, 25, 350-361.

Frankl, V.E. Dynamics, existence and values. JOURNAL OF EXISTENTIAL PSYCHIATRY, 1961, 2, 5-16.

Frankl, V.E. THE DOCTOR AND THE SOUL, AN INTRODUCTION TO LOGOTHERAPY. New York: Knopf, 1960.

Frankl, V.E. PSYCHOTHERAPY AND EXISTENTIALISM, SELECTED PAPERS ON LOGOTHERAPY. New York: Simon and Schuster, Clarion Books, 1968.

Frankl, V.E. MAN'S SEARCH FOR MEANING, AN INTRODUCTION TO LOGOTHERAPY. New York: Washington Square Press, 1963.

Franz, C.E., McClelland, D.C., & Weinberger, J. Childhood antecedents of conventional social accomplishment in midlife adults: A 36-year prospective study. JOURNAL OF PERSONALITY AND SOCIAL PSYCHOLOGY, 1991, 60, 586-595.

Fredericksen, N. Toward a taxonomy of situations. AMERICAN PSYCHOLOGIST, 1972, 27, 114-123.

Fremont, T., Means, G.H. & Means, R.S. Anxiety as a function of task performance feedback and extraversion-introversion. PSYCHOLOGICAL REPORTS, 1970, 27, 455-458.

Freud, A. Changes in psychoanalytic practice and experience. INTERNATIONAL JOURNAL OF PSYCHO-ANALYSIS, 1976, 57, 257-260.

Freud, A. THE EGO AND THE MECHANISMS OF DEFENSE (Rev. Ed.). New York: International Univ. Press, 1936/1967.

Freud, E. (Ed.). LETTERS OF SIGMUND FREUD. New York: Basic Books, 1961.

Freud, S. THE EGO AND THE ID. London:

Hogarth, 1923.

Freud, S. THE PROBLEM OF ANXIETY. New York: Norton, 1923/1936.

Freud, S. MOSES AND MONOTHEISM. (K. Jones, Trans.) New York: Knopf, 1939a.

Freud, S. CIVILIZATION AND ITS DISCONTENTS. London: Hogarth, 1939b.

Freud S., AN OUTLINE OF PSYCHOANALYSIS. New York: Norton, 1940/1949.

Freud, S. CIVILIZATION AND ITS DISCONTENTS. (J. Riviere, Trans.) London: Hogarth, 1953.

Freud, S. Leonardo da Vinci and a memory of his childhood. In J. Strachey (Ed.), THE STANDARD EDITION OF THE COMPLETE PSYCHOLOGICAL WORKS OF SIGMUND FREUD, VOL. 11. London: Hogarth Press, 1910/1957.

Freud, S. THE INTERPRETATION OF DREAMS. New York: Basic Books, 1900/1958.

Freud, S. Some psychological consequences of the anatomical distinction between the sexes. In J. Strachey (Ed.), THE COLLECTED PAPER OF SIGUMND FREUD, Vol. 5, New York: Basic Books, 1925/1959, 186-197.

Freud, S. CIVILIZATION AND ITS DISCONTENTS. In Standard edition, Vol. XXI. London: Hogarth Press, 1930/1961.

Freud, S. Analysis of a phobia in a five-year-old boy. In S. Freud, THE SEXUAL ENLIGHTENMENT OF CHILDREN. New York: Collier, 1909/1963, 47-138.

Freud, S. THREE CASE HISTORIES. New York: Collier, 1963.

Freud, S. PSYCHOPATHOLOGY OF EVERYDAY LIFE. New York: Mentor (New American Library), 1901/1965.

Freud, S. NEW INTRODUCTORY LECTURES ON PSYCHOANALYSIS. New York: Norton, 1933/1965.

Freud, S. Why war? In E.I. Megargee and J.E. Hokanson. (Eds.) THE DYNAMICS OF AGGRESSION. New York: Harper and Row, 1970, 10-21. (Originally published in 1932.)

Freud, S. INTRODUCTORY LECTURES ON PSYCHOANALYSIS. New York: Norton, 1920/1977.

Freud, S. INHIBITION, SYMPTOMS AND ANXIETY. (translated by Alix Strachey and edited by James Strachey) New York: Norton, 1977

Freud, S., & Bullit, W.C. THOMAS WOODROW WILSON, A PSYCHOLOGICAL STUDY. New York: Avon, 1966.

Fromm, E. ESCAPE FROM FREEDOM. New York: Holt, Rinehart and Winston, 1941.

Fromm, E. MAN FOR HIMSELF, AN INQUIRY INTO THE PSYCHOLOGY OF ETHICS. New York: Holt, Rinehart and Winston, 1947.

Fromm, E. THE SANE SOCIETY. New York: Rinehart, 1955.

Fromm, E. THE ART OF LOVING. New York: Harper & Brothers, 1956.

Fromm, E. Values, psychology and human existence. In A.H. Maslow (Ed.), NEW KNOWLEDGE IN HUMAN VALUES. Harper & Brothers, 1959, 151-164.

Fromm, E. MAY MAN PREVAIL? Garden City, New York: Doubleday, Anchor Books, 1961.

Fromm, E. BEYOND THE CHAINS OF ILLUSION, MY ENCOUNTER WITH MARX AND FREUD. New York: Pocketbooks, 1962.

Fromm, E. THE HEART OF MAN, ITS GENIUS FOR GOOD AND EVIL. New York: Harper & Row, 1964.

Fromm, E. On the sources of human destructiveness. In L. Ng. (Ed.) ALTERNATIVES TO VIOLENCE. New York: Time-Life Books, 1968, 11-17.

Fromm, E. THE ANATOMY OF HUMAN DESTRUCTIVENESS. New York: Holt, Rinehart and Winston, 1973.

Fromm, E. TO HAVE OR TO BE? New York: Harper & Row, 1976.

Fromm, E. THE GREATNESS AND LIMITATIONS OF FREUD'S THOUGHT. New York: Harper and Row, 1980.

Fromm, E., and Maccoby, M. SOCIAL CHARACTER IN A MEXICAN VILLAGE, A SOCIOPSYCHOANALYTIC STUDY. Englewood Cliffs, New Jersey: Prentice-Hall, 1970.

Funder, D.C. & Ozer, D. Behavior as a function of the situation. JOURNAL OF PERSONALITY AND SOCIAL PSYCHOLOGY, 1983, 44, 107-112.

Funk, R. ERICH FROMM: THE COURAGE TO BE HUMAN. New York: Continuum, 1982.

Garfield, E. The hundred most cited authors. CURRENT CONTENTS, 1978, 45, 5-15.

Garrison, M. A new look at Little Hans. THE PSY-CHOANALYTIC REVIEW, 1978, 65, 523-532.

Gelman, D. & Hager, M. Finding the hidden Freud. NEWSWEEK, November, 30, 1981.

Gendlin, E.T. EXPERIENCING AND THE CREATION OF MEANING. New York: Free Press, 1962.

Gendlin, E.T. Experiencing: A variable in the process of therapeutic change. AMERICAN JOURNAL OF PSYCHOTHERAPY, 1961, 15, 2.

Gendlin, E.T., and Rychlak, J.F. Psychotherapeutic processes. In P.H. Mussen and M.R. Rosenzweig. (Eds.) ANNUAL REVIEW OF PSYCHOLOGY, 1970, 21, 155-190.

Gendlin, E.T. Carl Rogers (1902-1987). AMERICAN PSYCH0LOGIST, 1988, 43, 127-128.

Gendlin, E.T., and Tomlinson, T.M. The process conception and its measurement. In C.R. Rogers. (Ed.) THE THERAPEUTIC RELATIONSHIP AND ITS IMPACT: A STUDY OF PSYCHOTHERAPY WITH SCHIZOPHRENICS. Madison, Wisconsin: University of Wisconsin Press, 1967.

Gerard L. SIGMUND FREUD: THE MAN AND HIS THEORIES. New York:Fawcett, 1962.

Gibson, H.B. HANS EYSENCK, THE MAN AND HIS WORK. London: Peter Owen, 1981.

Gilberstadt, H., & Duker, J. A HANDBOOK FOR CLINICAL AND ACTUARIAL MMPI INTERPRETATION. Philadelphia: W.B. Saunders, 1965.

Gill, M. Special book review: A new perspective on Freud and psychoanalysis. THE PSYCHOANALYTIC REVIEW, 1981, 68, 343-347.

Gilligan, C. IN A DIFFERENT VOICE. Cambridge, MA: Harvard University Press, 1982.

Goble, F. G. THE THIRD FORCE: THE PSYCHOLOGY OF ABRAHAM MASLOW. New York: Brossman Publishers, 1970.

Goldberg, L.R. Language and individual differences: The search for universals in personality lexicons. In L. Wheeler (Ed.), REVIEW OF PERSONALITY AND SOCIAL PSYCHOLOGY, 1981, Beverly Hills,California: Sage, 141-165.

Goldstein, K. THE ORGANISM. New York: American Book Company, 1939.

Golub, S. Coping with cancer: Freud's experiences. THE PSYCHOANALYTIC REVIEW, 1981, 68, 191-200.

Gordon, J.E. Interpersonal prediction of repressors and sensitizers. JOURNAL OF PERSONALITY, 1957, 25, 686-698.

Gorlow, L., Simonson, N.R., and Krauss, H. An empirical investigation of the Jungian typology. BRITISH JOURNAL OF SOCIAL AND CLINICAL PSYCHOLOGY, 1966, 5, 108-117.

Gorman, C. Are gay men born that way? TIME, 9/9/1991, p. 60-61.

Gough, H.G., and Heilbrun, A.B., Jr. THE ADJECTIVE CHECK LIST MANUAL. (Revised edition) Palo Alto, California: Consulting Psychologists Press, 1980.

Gould, P. & White, R. MENTAL MAPS. Baltimore, Maryland: Penguin Books, 1974.

Graham, W.K., and Balloun, J. An empirical test of Maslow's need hierarchy theory. JOURNAL OF HUMANISTIC PSYCHOLOGY, 1973, 13, 97-108.

Gray, J.A. A critique of Eysenck's theory of personality. In H.J. Eysenck (Ed.) A MODEL FOR PERSONALITY, New York: Springer-Verlag, 1981, 246-276.

Gray, J.A. The psychophysiological basis of introversion-extraversion: A modification of Eysenck's theory. In V.D. Nebylitsyn & J.A. Gray (Eds.), THE BIOLOGICAL BASES OF INDIVIDUAL BEHAVIOR, New York: Academic Press, 1972, 182-205.

Green, C.W. Operationalizing contact theory: Measuring student attributes toward desegregation. Paper presented at the Annual Convention of the American Psychological Association, Los Angeles, August, 1981.

Greene, J. N.., Plank, R. E. & Fowler, D. G. Compu-grid: A program for computing, sorting, categorizing, and graphing multiple Bieri grid measurements of cognitive complexity. EDUCATIONAL AND PSYCHOLOGICAL MEASUREMENT, 1989, 49, 623-626.

Greenwald, A.G. New look 3: Unconscious cognition reclaimed. AMERICAN PSYCHOLOGIST, 1992, 47, 766-779.

Greever, K. B., Tseng, M. S. & Friedland, B. U. Development of the Social Interest Index. JOURNAL OF CONSULTING AND CLINICAL PSYCHOLOGY, 1973, 41, 454-458.

Gromly, J. Behaviorism and the biological veiwpoint of personality.BULLETIN OF THE PSYCHONOMIC SOCIETY, 1982, 20, 255-256.

Gross, O. Die zerebrale Sekundarfunktion. Leipzig, Germany: 1902. Referenced in H.J. Eysenck (Ed.) A MODEL FOR PERSONALITY, New York: Springer-Verlag, 1981.

Guilford, J.P. & Zimmerman, W.S. Fourteen dimensions of temperament. PSYCHOLOGICAL MONOGRAPHS, 1956, 70, Whole No. 417.

Guilford, J.P. PERSONALITY. New York: McGraw-Hill, 1959.

Guilford, J.P. THE NATURE OF HUMAN INTELLIGENCE. New York: McGraw-Hill, 1967.

Gupta, B.S. & Kaur, S. The effects of dextroamphetamine on kinesthetic figural after effects. PSYCHOPHARMACOLOGY, 1978, 56, 199-204.

Gurman, A.S., and Razin, A.M. (Eds.) EFFECTIVE PSYCHOTHERAPY, A HANDBOOK OF RESEARCH. New York, Pergamon Press, 1977.

Haan, N. Two moralities in action contexts. JOURNAL OF PERSONALITY AND SOCIAL PSYCHOLOGY, 1978, 36, 286-305.

Hafner, J.L., Fakouri, M.E., and Labrentz, H.L. First memories of "normal" and alcoholic individuals. INDIVIDUAL PSYCHOLOGY, 1982, 38, 238-244.

Hakmiller, K.L. Threat as a determinant of downward comparison. JOURNAL OF EXPERIMENTAL SOCIAL PSYCHOLOGY, 1966, Supplement No. 1, 32-39.

Hall, C. & Nordby, V.J. A PRIMER OF JUNGIAN PSYCHOLOGY. New York: Mentor Books, 1973.

Hall, C. & Van de Castle, R. An empirical investigation of the castration complex in dreams. JOURNAL OF PERSONALITY, 1965, 33, 20-29.

Hall, C.S., & Lindzey, G. THEORIES OF PERSONALITY. (Third edition) New York: Wiley, 1978.

Hall, E. A conversation with Erik Erikson. PSYCHOLOGY TODAY, June, 1983.

Hall, M. H. The psychology of universality. PSYCHOLOGY TODAY, 1968, 2, 34-37, 54-57.

Haney, D. O. Psychologist B. F. Skinner dies at 86. PEORIA JOURNAL STAR (ASSOCIATED PRESS), 1990 (August 20), P. B1.

Harlow, H.F. Love in monkeys. SCIENTIFIC AMERICAN, 1959, 200, 68-74.

Harlow, H.F. The nature of love. AMERICAN PSYCHOLOGIST, 1958, 13, 673-685.

Harlow, H.F., and Harlow, M.K. The young monkeys. In J.B. Maas, (Ed.). READINGS IN PSYCHOLOGY TODAY. (Third edition) Del Mar, California: CRM Books, 1974, 198-203.

Harper, H., Oei, T. P. S., Mendalgio, S. & Evans, L. Dimensionality, validity, and utility of the I-E scale with anxiety disorders. JOURNAL OF ANXIETY DISORDERS, 4, 1990, 89-98.

Harrington, D.M., Block, J.H., & Block, J. Testing aspects of Carl Rogers' theory of creative environments: Child-rearing antecedents of creative potential young adolescents. JOURNAL OF PERSONALITY AND SOCIAL PSYCHOLOGY, 1987, 52, 851-856.

Harris, M.E., and Greene, R.L. Students' perception of actual, trivial, and inaccurate personality feedback. JOURNAL OF PERSONALITY ASSESSMENT, 1984, 48, 179-184.

Hart, J.T., and Tomlinson, T.M. NEW DIRECTIONS IN CLIENT-CENTERED THERAPY. Boston: Houghton Mifflin, 1970.

Hartl, E., Monnelly, E. & Elderkin, R. PHYSIQUE AND DELINQUENT BEHAVIOR. New York: Academic Press, 1982.

Hartmann, H. EGO PSYCHOLOGY AND THE PROBLEM OF ADAPTATION. New York: International Universities Press,1958.

Haslam, D.R. & Thomas, E.A.C. An optimum interval in the assessment of pain threshold. QUARTERLY JOURNAL OF EXPERIMENTAL PSYCHOLOGY, 1967, 19, 54-58.

Haslam, D.R. Individual differences in pain threshold and level of arousal. BRITISH JOURNAL OF PSYCHOLOGY, 1967, 58, 139-142.

Hassatt, J. But that would be wrong. PSYCHOLOGY TODAY, November, 1981.

Hastorf, A.H., Schneider, D.J., & Polefka, J. PERSON PERCEPTION. Menlo Park, California: Addison-Wesley, 1970.

Hathaway, S.R., & McKinley, J.C. MANUAL FOR THE MINNESOTA MULTIPHASIC PERSONALITY INVENTORY. New York: Psychological Corporation, 1943.

Hathaway, S.R., & McKinley, J.C. THE MIN-NESOTA MULTIPHASIC PERSONALITY INVENTORY MANUAL. (Revised edition) New York: Psychological Corporation, 1967.

Hausdorff, D. ERIC FROMM. New York: Twayne Publishers, 1972.

Havassy-De Avila, B. A critical review of the approach to birth order research. THE CANADIAN PSYCHOLOGIST, 1971, 12, 282-305.

Hayes, C. Changes in MAACL Anxiety scale scores during 11 class meetings. Cited in M. Zuckerman and B. Lubin, MANUAL FOR THE MULTIPLE AFFECT ADJECTIVE CHECK LIST. San Diego, California: Educational and Industrial Testing Service, 1965,7-9.

Hayes, J. COGNITIVE PSYCHOLOGY, THINKING AND CREATING. Homewood, Illinois: Dorsey Press, 1978.

Hebb, D. O. THE ORGANIZATION OF BEHAVIOR. New York: John Wiley.

Heckhausen, H., and Krug, S. Motive modification. In A.J. Stewart, (Ed.), MOTIVATION AND SOCIETY. San Francisco: Jossey-Bass, 1982, 274-318.

Heidegger, M. AN INTRODUCTION TO METAPHYSICS. (R. Manheim, Trans.) New Haven: Yale University Press, 1959.

Heidegger, M. EXISTENCE AND BEING. Chicago: Henry Regnery, 1949.

Heider, F. THE PSYCHOLOGY OF INTERPERSONAL RELATIONS. New York:Wiley, 1958.

Hempel, C. & Oppenheim, P. Problems of the concept of general law. In A. Danto & S. Morgenbesser (Eds.), PHILOPSOHY OF SCIENCE, New York: World Publishing Co., 1960.

Henry, W.E. THE ANALYSIS OF FANTASY. New York: Wiley, 1974.

Hermann, B. P., Whitman, S. W., Wyler, A. R., Anton, M. T., & Vanderzwagg, R. Psychosocial predictors of psychopathology in epilepsy. BRITISH JOURNAL OF PSYCHIATRY, 1990, 156, 98-105.

Heron, W. The pathology of boredom. In S. Coopersmith (Ed.), FRONTIERS OF PSYCHOLOGICAL RESEARCH. San Francisco: W.H. Freeman and Company, 1966 (originally appeared in SCIENTIFIC AMERICAN, Jan.

1957).

Hersen, M., & Bellack, A.S. BEHAVIORAL ASSESSMENT: A PRACTICAL HANDBOOK. New York: Pergamon Press, 1976.

Heymans, G. Uber einige psychische Korrelationen. Z ANGEW PSYCHOLOGIE, 1908, 1, 313-381. Referenced in H.J. Eysenck (Ed.) A MODEL FOR PERSONALITY, New York: Springer-Verlag, 1981.

Hill-Hain, A. & Rogers, C. R. A dialogue with Carl Rogers: Cross-cultural challenges of facilitating person-centered groups in South Africa. JOURNAL OF SPECIALISTS IN GROUP WORK, 1988. 13, 62-69.

Hirsch, J. Genes and behavior: A reply. SCIENCE, 1964, 144, 891.

Hirsch, J. Jensenism: The bankruptcy of "science" without scholarship. EDUCATIONAL THEORY, 1975, 25 (1), 1-27.

Hirsch, J. To "unfrock the charlatans" SAGE RACE RELATIONS ABSTRACTS, 1981, 6, (May), 1-67.

Hoban, P. Psychodrama: The chilling story of how the Sullivanian cult turned a utopian dream into a nightmare. NEW YORK, (June 19, pp. 41-55), 1989.

Hoffman, E. THE RIGHT TO BE HUMAN. Los Angeles: Jeremy P. Tarcher, Inc., 1988.

Hogan, R. A socioanalytic theory of personality. In M. Page & R. Dienstbier, NEBRASKA SYMPOSIUM ON MOTIVATION, 1982: PERSONALITY—CURRENT THEORY AND RESEARCH. Lincoln: University of Nebraska Press, 1983.

Hogan, R. Moral conduct and moral character. PSYCHOLOGICAL BULLETIN, 1973, 79, 217-232.

Hogan, R. PERSONALITY THEORY, THE PERSONOLOGICAL TRADITION. Englewood Cliffs, New Jersey: Prentice-Hall, 1976.

Holland, J. & Skinner, B. THE ANALYSIS OF BEHAVIOR. New York: McGraw-Hill, 1961.

Hollander, J. & Yeostros, S. The effect of simultaneous variations of humidity and barometric pressure on arthritis. BULLETIN OF THE AMERICAN METEOROLOGICAL SOCIETY, 1963, 44, 489-494.

Holmes, T.H. & Masuda, M. Life change and illness susceptibility. SEPARATION AND

DEPRESSION, 1973, American Association for the Advancement of Science Publication No. 94, 161-186.

Holmes, T.H. & Rahe, R.H. The Social Readjustment Rating Scale. JOURNAL OF PSYCHOSOMATIC RESEARCH, 1967, 11, 213-218.

Holtzman, W. Thorpe, J. Swartz, J. & Herron, E. INKBLOT PERCEPTION AND PERSONALITY: HOLTZMAN INKBLOT TECHNIQUE. Austin: The Univ. of Texas Press, 1961.

Hopkins, E. The impact of B. F. Skinner. PEORIA JOURNAL STAR. 1990 (Sept. 11), p. A9.

Horney, K. The flight from womanhood: The masculinity complex in women as viewed by men and by women. INTERNATIONAL JOURNAL OF PSYCHO-ANALYSIS, 1926, 7, 324-329.

Horney, K. NEW WAYS IN PSYCHOANALYSIS. New York: Norton, 1939.

Horney, K. THE NEUROTIC PERSONALITY OF OUR TIME. New York: Norton, 1937.

Horney, K. SELF ANALYSIS. New York: Norton, 1942.

Horney, K. OUR INNER CONFLICTS, A CONSTRUCTIVE THEORY OF NEUROSIS. New York: Norton, 1945.

Horney, K. ARE YOU CONSIDERING PSYCHOANALYSIS? New York: Norton, 1946.

Horney, K. NEUROSIS AND HUMAN GROWTH, THE STRUGGLE TOWARD SELF-REALIZATION. New York: Norton, 1950.

Horney, K. FEMININE PSYCHOLOGY. New York: Norton, 1967,

Horney, K. THE ADOLESCENT DIARIES OF KAREN HORNEY. New York: Basic Books, 1980.

Houle, G. R. The diagnostic conference planning questionnaire for speech-language pathology. LANGUAGE, SPEECH, AND HEARING SERVICES IN SCHOOLS, 1990, 21, 118-119.

Huber, R.J., Widdifield, J. K., & Johnson, C. L. Frankenstein: An Adlerian Odyssey. INDIVIDUAL PSYCHOLOGY, 1989, 45, 267-278.

Hull, C.L. A BEHAVIOR SYSTEM. New Haven: Yale University Press, 1952.

Hull, C.L. Principles of Behavior. New York: Appleton-Century-Crofts, 1943.

Hunt, J. Mc V. Psychological development: Early experience. In Rosenzweig, M. & Porter, L.,

ANNUAL REVIEW, Vol. 30, 1979, pp. 103-144.

Husserl. E. IDEAS. (W.R. Boyce Gibson, Trans.) New York: Collier Books, 1961.

Hyer, L. Woods, M. G. & Boudewyns, P.A. Early recollections of Vietnam veterans with PTSD. INDIVIDUAL PSYCHOLOGY, 1989, 45, 300-312.

Inkeles, A. & Levinson, D. National character: The study of modal personality and sociocultural systems. In G. Lindzey & E. Aronson (Eds.), THE HANDBOOK OF SOCIAL PSYCHOLOGY (Second edition), 1969, 418-506.

Ionedes, N.S. Social interest psychiatry. INDIVIDUAL PSYCHOLOGY, 1989, 45, 416-422.

Ishiyama, F.I., Munson, P.A., & Chabassol, D.J. Birth order and fear of success among midadolescents. PSYCHOLOGICAL REPORTS, 1990, 66, 17-18.

Ittelson, W. & Kilpatrick, F. Experiments in perception. SCIENTIFIC AMERICAN, 1951, 185, 50-55.

Jackson, D.B., and Paunonen, S.V. Personality structure and assessment. In M.R. Rosenzweig and L.W. Porter (Eds.). ANNUAL REVIEW OF PSYCHOLOGY, 1980, 31, 503-551.

Jackson, D.N. PERSONALITY RESEARCH FORM MANUAL (3rd. ed.) Port Huron, MI: Sigma Assessment Systems, 1984.

Jackson, D.N. PERSONALITY RESEARCH FORM MANUAL. Goshen, New York: Research Psychologists Press, 1967.

Jackson, M., and Sechrest, L. Early recollections in four neurotic diagnostic categories. JOURNAL OF INDIVIDUAL PSYCHOLOGY, 1962, 18, 52-56.

Jacobi, J. THE PSYCHOLOGY OF C.G. JUNG. (Revised edition) New Haven: Yale University Press, 1962.

James, W. THE PRINCIPLES OF PSYCHOLOGY. VOLUMES I & II. New York: Dover Publications, 1890/1950.

James, W. THE VARIETIES OF RELIGIOUS EXPERIENCE. New York: Mentor Books, 1958.

Jankowicz, A.D. Whatever became of George Kelly? Applications and implications. AMERICAN PSYCHOLOGIST, 1987, 42, 481-487.

Jarman, T.L. THE RISE AND FALL OF NAZI

GERMANY. New York: Signet, 1961.

Jensen, A.R. How much can we boost IQ and scholastic achievement? HARVARD EDUCATIONAL REVIEW, 1969, 39, 1-123.

Jensen, A.R. Sir Cyril Burt in perspective. AMERICAN PSYCHOLOGIST, 1978, 33, 499-503.

Jones E. THE LIFE AND WORK OF SIGMUND FREUD. Garden City, N. Y.: Anchor Books, 1953/1963.

Jones E. THE LIFE AND WORK OF SIGMUND FREUD. Vol. II. New York: Basic Books, 1955.

Jones, B.M. Cognition performance of introverts and extraverts following acute alcohol ingestion. BRITISH JOURNAL OF PSYCHOLOGY, 1974, 65, 35-42.

Jones, B.M., Hatcher, E., Jones, M.K. & Farris, J.J. The relationship of extraversion and neuroticism to the effects of alcohol on cognitive performance in male and female social drinkers. In F.A. Seixas (Ed.), CURRENTS IN ALCOHOLISM, New York: Grune & Stratton, 1978.

Jordan, E.W., Whiteside, M.M., and Manaster, G.J. A practical and effective research measure of birth order. INDIVIDUAL PSYCHOLOGY, 1982, 38, 253-260.

Joseph, E. Presidential address: Clinical issues in psychoanalysis. INTERNATIONAL JOURNAL OF PSYCHO-ANALYSIS, 1980, 61, 1-9.

Joy, S. & Wise, P. Maternal employment, anxiety, and sex differences in college students' self-descriptions. SEX ROLES, 1983, 9, 519-525.

Jung, C.G. The association method. AMERICAN JOURNAL OF PSYCHOLOGY, 1910, 21, 219-269.

Jung, C. G. THE DEVELOPMENT OF PERSONALITY. (R.F.C. Hull, Trans.) New York: Pantheon Books, 1954

Jung, C.G. THE ARCHETYPES AND THE COLLECTIVE UNCONSCIOUS. (R.F.C. Hull, Trans.), Collected Works (Vol. IX, Part I). Princeton, New Jersey: Princeton University Press, 1959a.

Jung, C.G. THE ARCHETYPES AND THE COLLECTIVE UNCONSCIOUS. (R.F.C. Hull, Trans.), Collected Works (Vol. IX, Part 2). Princeton, New Jersey: Princeton University Press, 1959b.

Jung, C.G. MEMORIES, DREAMS, REFLECTIONS. (A. Jaffe, Ed.) New York: Pantheon Books, 1963.

Jung, C.G. MAN AND HIS SYMBOLS. New York: Dell, 1964.

Jung, C.G. PSYCHOLOGICAL TYPES. (R.F.C. Hull, Trans.) Collected Works (Vol. VI). Princeton, New Jersey: Princeton University Press, 1921/1971.

Jung, C.G. FLYING SAUCERS, A MODERN MYTH OF THINGS SEEN IN THE SKIES. (R.F.C. Hull, Trans.) Princeton, New Jersey: Princeton University Press, 1978.

Jung, J. UNDERSTANDING HUMAN MOTIVATION. New York: MacMillian Pub. Co., 1978.

Kal, E.F. Survey of contemporary Adlerian clinical practice. INDIVIDUAL PSYCHOLOGY, 1972, 28, 261-266.

Kanfer, F.H., & Goldstein, A.P. (Eds.) HELPING PEOPLE CHANGE, A TEXTBOOK OF METHODS. (Second edition) New York: Pergamon Press, 1980.

Kelley, H.H. Attribution theory in social psychology. In D. Levine (Ed.) NEBRASKA SYMPOSIUM ON MOTIVATION (Vol. 15). Lincoln: University of Nebraska Press, 1967.

Kelley, H.H. The process of causal attribution. AMERICAN PSYCHOLOGIST, 1973, 28, 107-128.

Kelly, G. A psychology of the optimal man. In A. W. Landfield and L. M. Leitner (Eds.), PERSONAL CONSTRUCT PSYCHOLOGY: PSYCHOTHERAPY AND PERSONALITY. New York: Wiley, 1980.

Kelly, G. A THEORY OF PERSONALITY: THE PSYCHOLOGY OF PERSONAL CONSTRUCTS. New York: Norton, 1963.

Kelly, G. THE PSYCHOLOGY OF PERSONAL CONSTRUCTS, (two vols.). New York: Norton, 1955.

Kelly, G. The autobiography of a theory. In B. Maher (Ed.), CLINICAL PSYCHOLOGY AND PERSONALITY: THE SELECTED PAPERS OF GEORGE KELLY. New York, 1969.

Kelman, H. Introduction. In K. Horney, FEMININE PSYCHOLOGY. New York: Norton, 1967.

Kendall, P. Anxiety: States, traits—situations? JOURNAL OF CONSULTING AND CLINI-

CAL PSYCHOLOGY, 1978, 46, 280-287.

Kendall, P.C., Finch, A., Auerbach, S., Hooke, J., & Mikulka, P. The state-trait anxiety inventory: A systematic evaluation. JOURNAL OF CONSULTING AND CLINICAL PSYCHOLOGY, 1976, 44, 406-412.

Kendler, H. H. Behavioral determinism: A strategic assumption? AMERICAN PSYCHOLOGIST, 1988, 43, 822-823.

Keniston, K. Remembering Erikson at Harvard. PSYCHOLOGY TODAY, June, 1983, p. 29.

Kerlinger, F.N. FOUNDATIONS OF BEHAVIORAL RESEARCH. (Second edition.) New York: Holt, Rinehart and Winston, 1973.

Kern, R.M. LIFE-STYLE SCALE. Coral Springs, FL: Communication and Motivation Training Institute, 1986.

Kierkegaard, S. FEAR AND TREMBLING, AND SICKNESS UNTO DEATH. (W. Lowrie, Trans.) Garden City, New York: Doubleday Anchor Books, 1954.

Kimble, G. HILGARD AND MARGUIS' CONDITIONING AND LEARNING. New York: Appleton-Century-Crofts, 1961.

Kinkade, K. Commune: A Walden-Two experiment. PSYCHOLOGY TODAY, 1973, 6, 35.

Kirschenbaum, H. & Henderson, V.L. (Eds.) The Carl Rogers Readers. Boston: Houghton Mifflin Co., 1989.

Kirschenbaum, H. ON BECOMING CARL ROGERS. New York: Delacorte Press, 1979.

Klein, G. PERCEPTIONS, MOTIVES AND PERSONALITY. New York: Knopf, 1970.

Klein, M. NARRATIVE OF A CHILD ANALYSIS. New York: Delta, 1961.

Klein, M. THE PSYCHOANALYSIS OF CHILDREN. London: Hogarth, 1932.

Kleinmuntz, B. PERSONALITY AND PSYCHOLOGICAL ASSESSMENT. New York: St. Martin's Press, 1982.

Kline, P. FACT AND FANTASY IN FREUDIAN THEORY. London: Methuen, 1972.

Klopfer, B., Meyer, M.M, & Brawer, F.B. (Eds.) DEVELOPMENTS IN THE RORSCHACH TECHNIQUE, VOL. III. New York: Harcourt Brace Jovanovich, 1970.

Knapp, R.R. HANDBOOK FOR THE PERSONAL ORIENTATION INVENTORY. San Diego: Edits Publishers, 1976.

Koestler, A. THE ROOTS OF COINCIDENCE. New York: Vintage, 1972.

Koffka, K. PRINCIPLES OF GESTALT PSYCHOLOGY. New York: Harcourt, 1935.

Kohlberg, L. A cognitive-developmental analysis of children's sex-role concepts and attitudes. In E.E. Maccoby (Ed.), THE DEVELOPMENT OF SEX DIFFERENCES, (Pp. 82-173) Stanford, CA: Stanford University Press, 1966.

Kohlberg, L. Moral stages and moralization. In T. Lickona (Ed.), MORAL DEVELOPMENT AND BEHAVIOR-THEORY RESEARCH, AND SOCIAL ISSUES. New York: Holt, 1976, 31-53.

Kohlberg, L. THE MEANING AND MEASUREMENT OF MORAL DEVELOPMENT. Worcester, Mass.: Clark University Press, 1981.

Kohlberg. L. Stage and sequence: The congitive-developmental approach to socialization. In D. Boslin (Ed.), HANDBOOK OF SOCIALIZATION THEORY AND RESEARCH. Chicago:Rand McNally, 1969.

Kohler, W. GESTALT PSYCHOLOGY: AN INTRODUCTION TO NEW CONCEPTS IN PSYCHOLOGY. New York: Liveright, 1947.

Kohn, A. The birth-order myth. HEALTH. 1990 (Jan.), pp. 34-35.

Kohut, H. THE ANALYSIS OF THE SELF. New York: International Universities Press, 1971.

Koppitz, E.M. THE BENDER GESTALT TEST FOR YOUNG CHILDREN, VOLUME II, RESEARCH AND APPLICATION, 1963-1973. New York: Grune and Stratton, 1975.

Kowaz, A.M. & Marcia, J.E. Development of and validation of a measure of Eriksonian industry. JOURNAL OF PERSONALITY AND SOCIAL PSYCHOLOGY, 1991, 60, 390-397.

Krane, R. & Wagner, A. Taste aversion learning with a delayed shock US: Implications for the "generality of the laws of learning." JOURNAL OF COMPARATIVE AND PHYSIOLOGICAL PSYCHOLOGY, 1975, 88, 882-889.

Kratochwill, T.R. (Ed.) SINGLE SUBJECT RESEARCH, STRATEGIES FOR EVALUATING CHANGE. New York: Academic Press, 1978.

Kretschmer, E. PHYSIQUE AND CHARACTER. W.J.H. Spratt (Trans.), New York: Harcourt,

1921/1925.

Krippner, S., Achterberg, J., Bugental, J. F. T., Banathy, B., Collen, A., Jaffe, D. T., Hales, S., Kremer, J., Stigliano, A., Giorgi, A., May, R., Michael, D. N., Salner, M. Whatever happened to Scholarly discorse? A reply to B. F. Skinner. AMERICAN PSYCHOLOGIST, 1988, 43, 819.

Kuhn, T.S. THE STRUCTURE OF SCIENTIFIC REVOLUTIONS. Chicago: University of Chicago Press, 1962.

Lamb, D.H. Anxiety. In H. London & J.E. Exner, Jr., (Eds.), DIMENSIONS OF PERSONALITY. New York: Wiley, 1978, 37-83.

Lamiell, J. Toward an idiothetic psychology of personality. AMERICAN PSYCHOLOGIST, 1981, 36, 276-289.

Langer, W.C. THE MIND OF ADOLPH HITLER, THE SECRET WARTIME REPORT. New York: Signet, 1972.

Latané, B. & Darley, J. THE UNRESPONSIVE BYSTANDER: WHY DOESN'T HE HELP? New York: Appleton-Century-Crofts, 1970.

Lawrence, A. The voice of Sigmund Freud, an audio tape. PSYCHOANALYTIC REVIEW, 1938.

Leak, G. K. & Williams, D. E. Relationship between Social Interest alienation, and psychological hardiness. INDIVIDUAL PSYCHOLOGY, 1989b, 45, 369-375.

Leak, G. K. & Williams, D. E. Relationship between Social Interest and perceived family environment. INDIVIDUAL PSYCHOLOGY, 1989a, 45, 362-368.

Lebowitz, M. Religious immoralism. THE KENYON REVIEW, 1990 (Spring), p. 154-156.

Lee, D.E., and Ehrlich, H.J. Sensory alienation and interpersonal constraints as correlates of cognitive structure, PSYCHOLOGICAL REPORTS, 1977, 40, 840-842.

Leupold-Lowenthal, H. The emigration of Freud's family. PARTISAN REVIEW, 1989, 56 (Winter), 57-64.

Leventhal, H. Findings and theory in the study of fear communications. In L. Berkowitz (Ed.), ADVANCES IN EXPERIMENTAL SOCIAL PSYCHOLOGY (Vol. 5, pp. 119-186). New York: Academic Press.

Levine, D. Why and when to test: The social context of psychological testing. In A.I. Rabin (Ed.), ASSESSMENT WITH PROJECTIVE TECHNIQUES. New York: Springer, 1981, 265-295.

Levinson, D. THE SEASONS OF A MAN'S LIFE. New York: Knopf, 1978.

Levy, M.R., & Fox, H.M. Psychological testing is alive and well. PROFESSIONAL PSYCHOLOGY, 1975, 6, 420-424.

Lewin, K. PRINCIPLES OF TOPOLOGICAL PSYCHOLOGY. New York: McGraw-Hill, 1936.

Lewis, A. Problems presented by the ambiguous word 'anxiety' as used in psychopathology. In G.D. Burrows and B. Elsevier/North-Holland Biomedical Press, 1980, 1-15.

Liddell, H.S. The role of vigilance in the development of animal neurosis. In P.H. Hoch & J. Zubin (Eds.), ANXIETY. New York: Hafner, 1964, 183-196.

Lifton, R.J. (Ed.) EXPLORATIONS IN PSYCHOHISTORY, THE WELLFLEET PAPERS. New York: Simon and Schuster, 1974.

Lilly, J.C. THE CENTER OF THE CYCLONE. New York: Bantam, 1973.

Lilly, J.C. THE DEEP SELF. New York: Warner Books, 1977.

Linder, D., Cooper, J., & Jones, E.E. Decision freedom as a determinant of the role of incentive magnitude in attitude change. JOURNAL OF PERSONALITY AND SOCIAL PSYCHOLOGY, 1967, 6, 245-254.

Lindzey, G.L. & Aronson, E. THE HANDBOOK OF SOCIAL PSYCHOLOGY (2nd edition). London: Addison-Wesley Publishing Co., Inc., 1969.

Lindzey, G.L. & Aronson, E. THE HANDBOOK OF SOCIAL PSYCHOLOGY (3rd edition). New York: Random House (dist. by Erlbaum), 1985.

Lindzey, G.L. (Ed.). THE HANDBOOK OF SOCIAL PSYCHOLOGY. London: Addison-Wesley Publishing Co., Inc., 1954.

Linville, P. The complexity-extremity effect and age-based stereotyping. JOURNAL OF PERSONALITY AND SOCIAL PSYCHOLOGY, 1982, 42, 293-311.

Loehlin, J. C. R. B. Cattell and behavior genetics. MULTIVARIATE BEHAVIORAL RESEARCH, 1984, 19, 337-343.

Loehlin, J. C., Horn, J. M. & Willerman, L. Heredity, environment, and personality change: Evidence from the Texas adoption project. JOURNAL OF PERSONALITY, 1990, 58, 221-244.

Loehlin, J.C. COMPUTER MODELS OF PERSONALITY. New York: Random House, 1968.

Lopez Ibor, J.J. Basic anxiety as the core of neuroses. In G.D. Burrows, B. Davies, (Eds.), HANDBOOK OF STUDIES ON ANXIETY. New York: Elsevier/North-Holland Biomedical Press, 1980, 17-20.

Lorenz, K. ON AGGRESSION. New York: Harcourt, Brace and World, 1966.

Lothane, Z. Special book review: A new perspective on Freud and psychoanalysis. THE PSYCHOANALYTIC REVIEW, 1981, 68, 348-361.

Loutitt, C.M., & Browne, C.G. Psychometric instruments in psychological clinics. JOURNAL OF CONSULTING PSYCHOLOGY, 1947, 11, 49-54.

Lubin, B., Wallis, R.R., & Paine, C. Patterns of psychological test usage in the United States: 1935-1969. PROFESSIONAL PSYCHOLOGY, 1971, 2, 70-74.

Lynch, M.D., Norem-Hebeisen, A.A., and Gergen, K.J. SELF-CONCEPT, ADVANCES IN THEORY AND RESEARCH. Cambridge, Massachusetts: Ballinger, 1981.

Lynn, R. & Eysenck, H.J. Tolerance for pain, extraversion and neuroticism. PERCEPTUAL AND MOTOR SKILLS, 1961, 12, 161-162.

MacDonald, A.P., Jr. Birth order and personality. JOURNAL OF CONSULTING AND CLINICAL PSYCHOLOGY, 1971, 36, 171-176.

Maddi, S. PERSONALITY THEORIES: A COMPARATIVE ANALYSIS. Homewood Illinois: The Dorsey Press, 1968.

Maier, N.R.F. FRUSTRATION: THE STUDY OF BEHAVIOR WITHOUT A GOAL. New York: McGraw-Hill, 1949.

Manaster, G.J., and Perryman, T.B. MANASTER-PERRYMAN MANIFEST CONTENT EARLY RECOLLECTION SCORING MANUAL. In H.A. Olson, 1979, 347-353.

Mandler, G., and Sarason, S.B. A study of anxiety and learning. JOURNAL OF ABNORMAL AND SOCIAL PSYCHOLOGY, 1952, 47, 166-173.

Mann, L. The baiting crowd in episodes of threatened suicide. JOURNAL OF PERSONALITY AND SOCIAL PSYCHOLOGY, 1981, 41, 703-709.

Mariotto, M.J., & Paul, G.L. A multimethod validation of the Inpatient Multidimensional Psychiatric Scale with chronically institutionalized patients. JOURNAL OF CONSULTING AND CLINICAL PSYCHOLOGY, 1974, 42, 497-509.

Martens, R., and Landers, D.M. Motor performance under stress: A test of the inverted-U hypothesis. JOURNAL OF PERSONALITY AND SOCIAL PSYCHOLOGY, 1970, 16, 29-37.

Martin, A.R. Karen Horney's theory in today's world. THE AMERICAN JOURNAL OF PSYCHOLOANALYSIS, 1975, 35, 297-302.

Maslow, A.H. Resistance to acculturation. JOURNAL OF SOCIAL ISSUES, 1951, 7, 26-29.

Maslow, A.H. MOTIVATION AND PERSONALITY. New York: Harper and Row, 1954.

Maslow, A.H. Psychological data and value theory. In A.H. Maslow (Ed.) NEW KNOWLEDGE IN HUMAN VALUES. New York: Harper and Row, 1959, 119-136.

Maslow, A.H. Lessons from the peak-experiences. JOURNAL OF HUMANISTIC PSYCHOLOGY, 1962, 2, 9-18

Maslow, A.H. EUPSYCHIAN MANAGEMENT. Homewood IL: The Dorsey Press, 1965.

Maslow, A.H. THE PSYCHOLOGY OF SCIENCE, A RECONNAISSANCE. New York: Harper and Row, 1966.

Maslow, A.H. A theory of metamotivation: The biological rooting of the value-life. JOURNAL OF HUMANISTIC PSYCHOLOGY, 1967, 7, 93-127.

Maslow, A.H. TOWARD A PSYCHOLOGY OF BEING. Princeton, NJ: D. Van Nostrand Co., Inc., 1968.

Maslow, A.H. Toward the study of violence. In L. Ng (Ed.), ALTERNATIVES TO VIOLENCE. New York: Time-Life Books, 1968, 34-37.

Maslow, A.H. Toward a humanistic biology. AMERICAN PSYCHOLOGIST, 1969, 24, 724-735.

Maslow, A.H. MOTIVATION AND PERSONALITY. (Second edition) New York: Harper and

Row, 1970.

Maslow, A.H. THE FARTHER REACHES OF HUMAN NATURE. New York: Viking Press, 1971.

Maslow, B.G. (Ed.) ABRAHAM H. MASLOW: A MEMORIAL VOLUME. Monterey, California: Brooks/Cole, 1972.

Masserman, J.H. BEHAVIOR AND NEUROSIS. Chicago: University of Chicago Press, 1943.

Massey, R. F. The philosophical compatability of Adler and Berne. INDIVIDUAL PSYCHOLOGY, 1989, 45, 323-334.

Masson, J. M. THE ASSAULT ON TRUTH. Toronto: Colins Publishers, 1984.

Mathes, E.W. FROM SURVIVAL TO THE UNIVERSE, VALUES AND PSYCHOLOGICAL WELL-BEING. Chicago: Nelson-Hall, 1981.

Mathes, E.W., Adams, H. & Daves, R. Jealousy: Loss of relationship rewards, loss of self-esteem, depression, anxiety and anger. JOURNAL OF PERSONALITY AND SOCIAL PSYCHOLOGY, 1985, 48, 1552-1556.

Mathes, E.W., Zevon, M.A., Roter, P.M., and Joerger, S.M. Peak experience tendencies: Scale development and theory testing. JOURNAL OF HUMANISTIC PSYCHOLOGY, 1982, 22, 92-108.

Matlin, M. W. & Foley, H.J. SENSATION AND PERCEPTION. Boston: Allyn & Bacon, 1992.

Matthews, G., Davies, D.R. & Lees, J.L. Arousal, extraversion, and individual differences in resource availability. JOURNAL OF PERSONALITY AND SOCIAL PSYCHOLOGY, 1990, 59, 150-168.

Matthews, G., Jones, D.M., & Chamberlin, A.G. Interactive effects of extraversion and arousal on attentional task performance: Multiple resources or encoding processes? JOURNAL OF PERSONALITY AND SOCIAL PSYCHOLOGY, 1989, 56, 629-639.

Maurer, A. Did Little Hans really want to marry his mother? JOURNAL OF HEALTH PROFESSIONS, 1964, 4, 139-148.

May, R. Contributions of existential psychotherapy. in R. May, E. Angel, and H.F. Ellenberger. (Eds.) EXISTENCE, A NEW DIMENSION IN PSYCHIATRY AND PSYCHOLOGY. New York: Basic Books, 1958, 37-91.

May, R. THE MEANING OF ANXIETY. New York: Ronald Press, 1950.

May, R., Angel, E., & Ellenberger, H.F. (Eds.) EXISTENCE, A NEW DIMENSION IN PSYCHIATRY AND PSYCHOLOGY. New York: Basic Books, 1958.

McAdams, D.P., Ruetzel, K. & Foley, J.M. Complexity and generativity at mid-life: Relations among social motives, ego development, and adults' plans for the future. JOURNAL OF PERSONALITY AND SOCIAL PSYCHOLOGY, 1986, 50, 800-807.

McCelland, D.C. THE ACHIEVING SOCIETY. New York: Free Press, 1961.

McEwan, K.L., and Devins, G.M. Is increased arousal in social anxiety noticed by others? JOURNAL OF ABNORMAL PSYCHOLOGY, 1983, 92, 417-421.

McGrath, J.E. SOCIAL AND PSYCHOLOGICAL FACTORS IN STRESS. New York: Holt, Rinehart and Winston, 1970.

McGraw-Hill Films. PERSONALITY. New York: CRM Educational Films Collection, 1971.

McGuire, T.R. & Hirsch, J. General intelligence (g) and heritability (H^2, h^2). In I. C. Uzgiris and F. Weizmann (Eds.), THE STRUCTURING OF EXPERIENCE. New York: Plenum, 1977, 25-72.

McGuire, W. (Ed.) THE FREUD/JUNG LETTERS. (R. Manheim & R.F.C. Hull, Trans.) Princeton, New Jersey: Princeton University Press, 1974.

McGuire, W., and Hull, R.F.C. (Eds.) C.G. JUNG SPEAKING, INTERVIEWS AND ENCOUNTERS. Princeton, New Jersey:Princeton University Press, 1977.

McIntosh, D. The empirical bearing of psychoanalytic theory. INTERNATIONAL JOURNAL OF PSYCHO-ANALYSIS, 1979, 60, 405-431.

Mead, M. BLACKBERRY WINTER, MY EARLIER YEARS. New York: PocketBooks, 1975.

Mead, M. On Freud's view of female psychology. In J. Strouse, WOMEN AND ANALYSIS: DIALOGUES ON PSYCHOANALYTIC VIEWS OF FEMININITY. New York: Grossman, 1974, 95-106.

Mearns, J. Coping with a breakup: Negative mood regulation expectancies and depression following the end of a romantic relationship. JOURNAL OF PERSONALITY AND SOCIAL PSYCHOLOGY, 1991, 60, 327-334.

Meehl, P.E. Wanted—A good cookbook. AMERICAN PSYCHOLOGIST, 1956, 11, 263-272.

Meltzoff, J. & Kornreich, M. RESEARCH IN PSYCHOTHERAPY. New York: Atherton Press, 1970.

Mendelsohn, G. Weiss, D. Feimer, N. Conceptual and empirical analysis of the typological implications of patterns of socialization and femininity. JOURNAL OF PERSONALITY AND SOCIAL PSYCHOLOGY, 1982, 42, 1157-1170.

Menninger, K. THE VITAL BALANCE, THE LIFE PROCESS IN MENTAL HEALTH AND ILLNESS. New York: Viking, 1963.

Menninger, W.C. PSYCHIATRY IN A TROUBLED WORLD. New York: Macmillan,1948.

Merleau-Ponty, M. THE STRUCTURE OF BEHAVIOR. (A.L. Fisher, Trans.) Boston: Beacon Press, 1963.

Merrens, M.R., & Richards, W.S. Acceptance of generalized versus "bona fide" personality interpretation. PSYCHOLOGICAL REPORTS, 1970, 27, 691-694.

Miley, C.H. Birth order research 1963-1967: Bibliography and index. JOURNAL OF INDIVIDUAL PSYCHOLOGY, 1969, 25, 64-70.

Milgram, S. OBEDIENCE TO AUTHORITY. New York: Harper & Row, 1974.

Miller, N. The frustration-aggression hypothesis. PSYCHOLOGICAL REVIEW, 1941, 48, 337-342.

Miller, P. C., Lefcourt, H. M., Holmes, J. G., Ware, E.E., & Saleh, W. E. Marital locus of control and marital problem solving. JOURNAL OF PERSONALITY AND SOCIAL PSYCHOLOGY, 1986, 51, 161-169.

Millon, T. On the Rennaissance of personality assessment and personality theory. JOURNAL OF PERSONALITY ASSESSMENT, 1984, 48, 450-466.

Mirels, H.L., and Garrett, J.B. The Protestant Ethic as a personality variable. JOURNAL OF CONSULTING AND CLINICAL PSYCHOLOGY, 1971, 36, 40-44.

Mischel, W. Convergences and challenges in the search for consistency. AMERICAN PSYCHOLOGIST, 1984, 39, 351-364.

Mischel, W. On the future of personality measurement. AMERICAN PSYCHOLOGIST, 1977, 32, 246-254.

Mischel, W. PERSONALITY AND ASSESSMENT. New York; Wiley, 1968.

Mischel, W. & Ebbesen, E. Selective atention to the self: Situational and dispositional determinants. JOURNAL OF PERSONALITY AND SOCIAL PSYCHOLOGY, 1973, 27, 129-142.

Mischel, W. Ebbesen, E. & Zeiss, A. Cognitive and attentional mechanisms in delay of gratification. JOURNAL OF PERSONALITY AND SOCIAL PSYCHOLOGY, 1972, 21, 204-218.

Mischel, W. & Peake, P. Analysing the construction of consistency in personality. In M. Page & R. Dienstbier. NEBRASKA SYMPOSIUM ON MOTIVATION, 1982: PERSONALITY—CURRENT THEORY AND RESEARCH. Lincoln: University of Nebraska Press, 1982a.

Mischel, W. & Peake, P. Beyond Deja Vu in the search for cross-situatonal consistnecy. PSYCHOLOGICAL REVIEW, 1982b, 89, 730-733.

Mischel, W. Toward a cognitive social learning reconceptualization of personality. PSYCHOLOGICAL REVIEW, 1973, 80, 252-283.

Mischel, W., Shoda, Y., & Rodriguez, M. L. Delay of gratification in children. SCIENCE, 1989, 933-938.

Mitchell, K.M., Bozarth, J.D., and Krauft, C.C. A reappraisal of the therapeutic effectiveness of accurate empathy, nonpossessive warmth and genuineness. In A.S. Gurman and A.M. Razin. (Eds.) EFFECTIVE PSYCHOTHERAPY, A HANDBOOK OF RESEARCH. New York: Pergamon, 1977, 482-499.

Moliere, J. LE BOURGEOIS GENTILHOMME. (1670) In I.A. Gregory (Ed.), THREE LAST PLAYS. New York: G.P. Putnam, 1928.

Morrow, L. "I spoke . . . as a brother." TIME, 1984, 123 (2), 26-33.

Mosak, H.H. Early recollections: Evaluation of some recent research. JOURNAL OF INDIVIDUAL PSYCHOLOGY, 1969, 25, 56-63.

Mosak, H.H., and Kopp, R.R. The early recollections of Adler, Freud, and Jung. JOURNAL OF INDIVIDUAL PSYCHOLOGY, 1973, 24,157-166.

Moss, P.D. & McEvedy, C.P. An epidemic of overbreathing among schoolgirls. BRITISH MEDICAL JOURNAL, 1966, 2, 1295-1300.

Motley, M. T. Slips of the tongue. SCIENTIFIC

AMERICAN, 1985 (March) 253, 116-127.

Motley, M. T. What I mean to say. PSYCHOLOGY TODAY, 1987 (February), 24-28.

Mowrer, O.H. On the dual nature of learning—a reinterpretation of "conditioning" and "problem solving." HARVARD EDUCATIONAL REVIEW, 1947, 17, 102-148.

Mullahy, P. (Ed.) THE CONTRIBUTIONS OF HARRY STACK SULLIVAN. New York: Science House, 1952.

Mullahy, P. OEDIPUS, MYTH AND COMPLEX. New York: Grove Press, 1948.

Mullahy, P. THE BEGINNINGS OF MODERN AMERICAN PSYCHIATRY, THE IDEAS OF HARRY STACK SULLIVAN. Boston: Houghton Mifflin, 1970.

Mummendey, H., Wilk, W. & Sturm, G. Die erfassung retrospektiver selbstbildanderungen erwachsener mit der Adjektiv-beschreibungs-technik (AGT). BIELEFELDER ARBEITEN ZUR SOZIALPSYCHOLOGIE, April, 1979.

Murray, H.A. THEMATIC APPERCEPTION TEST MANUAL. Cambridge: Harvard University Press, 1943.

Murray, H.A. EXPLORATIONS IN PERSONALITY. New York: Science Editions, 1938/1962.

Murray, H.A. Proposals for a theory of personality. In E.S. Shneidman (Ed.) ENDEAVORS IN PSYCHOLOGY: SELECTIONS FROM THE PERSONOLOGY OF HENRY A. MURRAY. New York: Harper & Row, 1981a, 125-203.

Murray, H.A. Jung: Beyond the hour's most exacting expectation. In E.S. Shneidman (Ed.) ENDEAVORS IN PSYCHOLOGY: SELECTIONS FROM THE PERSONOLOGY OF HENRY A. MURRAY. New York: Harper & Row, 1981b, 79-81.

Murray, H.A. A note on the possible clairvoyance of dreams. In E.S. Shneidman (Ed.) ENDEAVORS IN PSYCHOLOGY: SELECTIONS FROM THE PERSONOLOGY OF HENRY A. MURRAY. New York: Harper & Row, 1981c, 563-566.

Murray, H.A. A method for investigating fantasies: The Thematic Apperception Test (with Christiana D. Morgan). In E.S. Shneidman (Ed.) ENDEAVORS IN PSYCHOLOGY: SELECTIONS FROM THE PERSONOLOGY

OF HENRY A. MURRAY. New York: Harper & Row, 1981d, 390-408.

Murstein, B.I. (Ed.) HANDBOOK OF PROJECTIVE TECHNIQUES. New York: Basic Books, 1965.

Murstein, B.I. Normative written TAT responses for a college sample. JOURNAL OF PERSONALITY ASSESSMENT, 1972, 36, 109-147.

Murstein, B.I. THEORY AND RESEARCH IN PROJECTIVE TECHNIQUES: EMPHASIZING THE TAT. New York: Wiley, 1963.

Mussen, P., Conger, J. & Kagan J. CHILD DEVELOPMENT AND PERSONALITY. New York: Harper & Row, Publishers, 1979.

Myers, I.B. MYERS-BRIGGS TYPE INDICATOR MANUAL. Palo Alto, California: Consulting Psychologists Press, 1962.

Naisbett, J. MEGATRENDS. New York: Warner Books, 1984.

Nash, H. Thinking about thinking about the unthinkable. BULLETIN OF THE ATOMIC SCIENTISTS, 1983, 39 (October), 39-42.

Nay, W.R. MULTIMETHOD CLINICAL ASSESSMENT. New York: Gardner Press, 1979.

Needleman, H.L., Leviton, A. Bellinger, D. Lead-associated intellectual deficit. NEW ENGLAND JOURNAL OF MEDICINE, 1982, 306, 367.

Nesselroade, J.R. Concepts of intraindividual variability and change: Impressions of Cattell's influence on lifespan developmental psychology. MULTIVARIATE BEHAVIORAL RESEARCH, 1984, 19, 269-286.

Newman, L.S. Higgins, E.T. & Vookles, J. Self-guide strength and emotional vulnerability: Birth order as a moderator of self affect relations. PERSONALITY AND SOCIAL PSYCHOLOGY BULLETIN, 1992, 18, 402-411.

NEWSWEEK, Erik Erikson: The quest for identity, December 21, 1970, 84-89.

Nisbett, R.N. The trait construct in lay and professional psychology. In L. Festinger (Ed.), RETROSPECTIONS ON SOCIAL PSYCHOLOGY. New York: Oxford University Press, 1980.

Norman, W.T. Toward an adequate taxonomy of personality attributes: Replicated factor structure in peer nomination personality ratings. JOURNAL OF ABNORMAL AND SOCIAL PSYCHOLOGY, 1963, 66, 574-583.

Norton, H.W. Blood groups and personality traits. AMERICAN JOURNAL OF HUMAN GENETICS, 1972, 23, 225-226.

Nunnally, J.C. An investigation of some propositions of self-conception: The case of Miss Sun. JOURNAL OF ABNORMAL AND SOCIAL PSYCHOLOGY, 1955, 50, 87-92.

Ochse, R. & Plug C. Cross-Cultural investigation of the validity of Erikson's theory of personality development. JOURNAL OF PERSONALITY AND SOCIAL PSYCHOLOGY, 1986, 50, 1240-1252.

Olson, H.A. (Ed.) EARLY RECOLLETIONS, THEIR USE IN DIAGNOSIS AND PSYCHOTHERAPY. Springfield, Illinois: Charles C. Thomas, 1979.

Ormel, J. & Schaufeli, W. B. Stability and change in psychological distress and their relationship with self-esteem and locus of control: A dynamic equilibrium model. JOURNAL OF PERSONALITY AND SOCIAL PSYCHOLOGY, 1991, 60, 288-299.

Osgood, C.E., Suci, G.J., and Tannenbaum, P. THE MEASUREMENT OF MEANING. Urbana, Illinois: University of Illinois Press, 1957.

Ozer, E. M. & Bandura, A. Mechanisms governing empowerment effects: A self-efficacy analysis. PERSONALITY AND SOCIAL PSYCHOLOGY, 1990, 472-486.

Paige, K. E. Women learn to sing the menstrual blues. PSYCHOLOGY TODAY, 1973 (Sept.).

Parisi, T. Why Freud failed: Some implications for neurophysiology and sociobiology. AMERICAN PSYCHOLOGIST, 1987, 42, 235-245.

Parrish, T. S. Examining teachers' perceptions of children's support systems. THE JOURNAL OF PSYCHOLOGY, 1990, 124, 113-118.

Pasley, S. The Social Readjustment Rating Scale: A study of the significance of life events in age groups ranging from college freshmen to seventh grade. Unpublished paper, Chatham College, Pittsburgh, Pennsylvania, 1969.

Patterson, C.H. The self in recent Rogerian theory. JOURNAL OF INDIVIDUAL PSYCHOLOGY, 1961, 17, 5-11.

Paunonen, S.V., Jackson, D.N., & Keinonen, M. The structured nonverbal assessment of personality. JOURNAL OF PERSONALITY, 1990, 58, 481-502.

Pavlov, I.P. CONDITIONED REFLEXES. London: Oxford, 1927.

Pavlov, I.P. EXPERIMENTAL PSYCHOLOGY. New York: Philosophical Library, 1957.

Pearl, R.A. Some dangers of using personality questionnaires to study personality. PSYCHOLOGICAL BULLETIN, 1982, 92, 572-580.

Perls, F.S. GESTALT THERAPY VERBATIM. Lafayette, California: Real People Press, 1969.

Perry, H.S. PSYCHIATRIST OF AMERICA, THE LIFE OF HARRY STACK SULLIVAN. Cambridge: Harvard University Press, 1982.

Pervin, L.A. Personality: Current controversies, issues, and directions. In M.R. Rosenzweig and L.W. Porter, (Eds.), ANNUAL REVIEW OF PSYCHOLOGY, 1985, 36, 83-114.

Peterson, B. E., Doty, R. M., & Winter, D. G. Authoritarianism and attitudes toward contemporary social issues. PERSONALITY AND SOCIAL PSYCHOLOGY BULLETIN, 1993, 19, 174-184.

Phares, E. perceptual threshold decrements as a function of skill and chance expectancies. JOURNAL OF PSYCHOLOGY, 1962, 53, 399-407.

Phares, E. LOCUS OF CONTROL IN PERSONALITY. Morristown, N. J.: General Learning Press, 1976.

Phares, E.J., and Lamiell, J.T. Personality. In M.R. Rosenzweig and L.W. Porter, (Eds.), ANNUAL REVIEW OF PSYCHOLOGY, 1977, 28, 113-140.

Phillips, W.M., Watkins, J.T., and Noll, G. Self-actualization, self-transcendence, and personal philosophy. JOURNAL OF HUMANISTIC PSYCHOLOGY, 1974, 14, 53-73.

Piaget, J. THE MORAL JUDGMENT OF THE CHILD. Glencoe, Ill.: Free Press, 1948.

Pogrebin, L. GROWING UP FREE. New York: Bantam, 1980.

Potkay, C.R. THE RORSCHACH CLINICIAN, A NEW RESEARCH APPROACH AND ITS APPLICATION. New York: Grune and Stratton, 1971.

Potkay, C.R. The role of personal history data in clinical judgment: A selective focus. JOURNAL OF PERSONALITY ASSESSMENT, 1973, 37, 203-212.

Potkay, C.R. Using the word association test "to catch a thief." PROFESSIONAL PSYCHOLOGY, 1974, 5, 446-447.

Potkay, C.R. Current issues in projective and personality assessment in the schools. School Psychology in Illinois, NEWSLETTER OF THE ILLINOIS SCHOOL PSYCHOLOGISTS ASSOCIATION, 1982, 3, 9-11.

Potkay, C.R. & Allen, B.P. The Adjective Generation Technique (AGT): Assessment via Word Descriptions of Self and Others. In C.D. Spielberger and J.N. Butcher, ADVANCES IN PERSONALITY ASSESSMENT. Hillsdale, New Jersey: Lawrence Erlbaum Association, Publishers, 1988.

Potkay, C.R., Allen, B.P. & Merrens, M.R. Adjective Generation Technique descriptions of Kohoutek: A comet that fizzled. Paper presented at the annual convention of the American Psychological Association, Chicago, Illinois, September, 1975.

Potkay, C.R., and Merrens, M.R. Sources of male chauvinism in the TAT. JOURNAL OF PERSONALITY ASSESSMENT, 1975, 39, 471-479.

Potkay, C.R., Merrens, M.R., & Allen B.P. AGT descriptions of TAT figures: "Loving" females more favorable than "lonely" males. Paper presented at the Annual Meeting of the Midwestern Psychological Association, Chicago, 1979.

Potkay, C. E., Potkay, C. R., Boynton, G., & Klingbeil, J. Perceptions of male and female comic strip characters using the Adjective Generation Technique (AGT). SEX ROLES, 1982, 8, 185-200.

Powell, G.E. A survey of the effects of brain lesions upon personality. In H.J. Eysenck (Ed.), A MODEL FOR PERSONALITY, New York: Springer-Verlag, 1981, 65-87.

Purton, C. The person-centered Jungian. PERSON-CENTERED REVIEW, 1989, 4, 403-419.

Quinn, S. A MIND OF HER OWN: THE LIFE OF KAREN HORNEY. New York: Addison-Wesley Publishing Co., 1988.

Rabin, A.I. (Ed.) ASSESSMENT WITH PROJECTIVE TECHNIQUES. New York: Springer, 1981.

Rahe, R.H. Life changes and near-future illness reports. In L. Levi (Ed.), EMOTIONS—THEIR PARAMETERS AND MEASUREMENT. New York: Raven Press, 1975, 511-529.

Ram Dass. BE HERE NOW. New York: Crown, 1971.

Rank, O. WILL THERAPY AND TRUTH AND REALITY. New York: Knopf, 1945.

Raskin, R. & Shaw, R. Narcissism and the use of personal pronouns. JOURNAL OF PERSONALITY, 1988, 56, 393-404.

Ravizza, K. Peak experiences in sport. JOURNAL OF HUMANISTIC PSYCHOLOGY, 1977, 17, 35-40.

Revusky, S. & Garcia, J. Learned associations over long delays. In G. Bower (Ed.), THE PSYCHOLOGY OF LEARNING AND MOTIVATION (Vol. 4). New York: Academic Press, 1970.

Roazen, P. FREUD AND HIS FOLLOWERS. New York: Knopf, 1974.

Roazen, P. ERIK H. ERIKSON: THE POWER AND LIMITS OF A VISION. New York: The Free Press, 1976.

Roback, A.A. A HISTORY OF AMERICAN PSYCHOLOGY. (Revised edition) New York: Collier Books, 1964.

Robbins, A.D. Harry Stack Sullivan: Neo-Freudian or not? CONTEMPORARY PSYCHOANALYSIS, 1989, 25, 624-640.

Rodriquez, M. L. Mischel, W. & Shoda, Y. Cognitive variables in the delay of gratification of older children at risk. JOURNAL OF PERSONALITY AND SOCIAL PSYCHOLOGY, 1989, 57, 358-367.

Rogers, C.R. COUNSELING AND PSYCHOTHERAPY, NEWER CONCEPTS IN PRACTICE. Boston: Houghton Mifflin, 1942.

Rogers, C.R. Some observations on the organization of personality. AMERICAN PSYCHOLOGIST, 1947, 2, 358-368.

Rogers, C.R. The case of Mrs. Oak: A research analysis. In C.R. Rogers and R.F. Dymond (Eds.) PSYCHOTHERAPY AND PERSONALITY CHANGE. Chicago: The University of Chicago Press, 1954, 259-348.

Rogers, C.R. The necessary and sufficient conditions of therapeutic personality change. JOURNAL OF CONSULTING PSYCHOLOGY, 1957, 21, 95-103.

Rogers, C.R. A theory of therapy, personality, and

interpersonal relationships, as developed in the client-centered framework. In S. Koch (Ed.), PSYCHOLOGY: A STUDY OF A SCIENCE. New York: McGraw-Hill, 1959, 184-256.

Rogers, C.R. ON BECOMING A PERSON, A THERAPIST'S VIEW OF PSYCHOTHERAPY. Boston: Houghton Mifflin, 1961.

Rogers, C.R. FREEDOM TO LEARN: A VIEW OF WHAT EDUCATION MIGHT BECOME. Columbus, Ohio: Charles Merrill, 1969.

Rogers, C.R. CARL ROGERS ON ENCOUNTER GROUPS. New York: Harper and Row, Harrow Books, 1970.

Rogers, C.R. BECOMING PARTNERS: MARRIAGE AND ITS ALTERNATIVES. New York: Delacorte Press, 1972.

Rogers, C.R. My philosophy of interpersonal relationships and how it grew. JOURNAL OF HUMANISTIC PSYCHOLOGY, 1973, 13, 3-15.

Rogers, C.R. In retrospect: Forty-six years. AMERICAN PSYCHOLOGIST, 1974, 29, 115-123.

Rogers, C.R. In R.I. Evans. CARL ROGERS, THE MAN AND HIS IDEAS. New York: E.P. Dutton, 1975.

Rogers, C.R. CARL ROGERS ON PERSONAL POWER. New York: Delacorte Press, 1977.

Rogers, C.R. A WAY OF BEING. Boston: Houghton Mifflin, 1980.

Rogers, C.R. Personal communication, January 4, 1983.

Rogers, C.R. The foundations of the Person-Centered approach. EDUCATION, 1979, 100, 98-107. Reprinted in T.H. Carr and H.E. Fitzgerald (Eds.). PSYCHOLOGY 83/84. Guilford, Connecticut: Dushkin, 1983, 227-233.

Rogers, C.R. The underlying theory: Drawn from experience with individuals and groups. COUNSELING AND VALUES, 1987a, 32, 38-46.

Rogers, C.R. Inside the world of the Soviet professional. COUNSELING AND VALUES, 1987b, 32, 66.

Rogers, C.R. Comments on the issue of equality in psychotherapy. JOURNAL OF HUMANISTIC PSYCHOLOGY, 1987C, 27, 38-39.

Rogers, C.R. Steps Toward Peace, 1948-1986: Ten-

sion reduction in theory and practice. COUNSELING AND VALUES, 1987d, 32, 12-15.

Rogers, C.R. What I learned from two research studies. In H. Krischenbaum and V. L. Henderson (Eds.), THE CARL ROGERS READER. Boston: Houghton Mifflin Co., 1989a.

Rogers, C.R. A psychologist looks at nuclear war. In H. Krischenbaum and V.L. Henderson (Eds.), THE CARL ROGERS READER. Boston: Houghton Mifflin Co., 1989b.

Rogers, C.R., and Dymond, R.F. (Eds.) PSYCHOTHERAPY AND PERSONALITY CHANGE. Chicago: The University of Chicago Press, 1954.

Rogers, C.R. & Malcolm, D. The potential contribution of the behavioral scientist to world peace. COUNSELING AND VALUES, 1987, 32, 10-11.

Rogers, C.R. & Ryback, D. One alternative to nuclear planetary suicide. THE COUNSELING PSYCHOLOGIST, 1984, 12, 3-11.

Rogers, C.R. & Sanford, R. Reflections on our South African experience (January-February 1986). COUNSELING AND VALUES, 1987, 32, 17-20.

Rohrbaugh, J. WOMEN: PSYCHOLOGY'S PUZZLE. New York: Basic Books, 1979.

Roodin, P. & Hoyer, W. A framework for studying moral issues in later adulthood. Paper read at the American Psychological Association Convention, Washington, D.C., 1982.

Rorer, L.G., and Widiger, T.A. Personality structure and assessment. In M.R. Rosenzweig and L.W. Porter, (Eds.), ANNUAL REVIEW OF PSYCHOLOGY, 1983, 34, 431-463.

Rorschach, H. PSYCHODIAGNOSTICS, A DIAGNOSTIC TEST BASED ON PERCEPTION. New York: Grune and Stratton, 1942/1951.

Rosch, E. Principles of categorization. In E. Rosch & B.B. Lloyd (Eds.), COGNITION AND CATEGORIZATION. Hillsdale, New Jersey: Erlbaum, 1978.

Rosenhan, D.L. On being sane in insane places. SCIENCE, 1973, 179, 365-369.

Rosenthal, R. The "file drawer problem" and tolerance for null results. PSYCHOLOGICAL BULLETIN, 1979, 86, 638-641.

Ross, L. The intuitive psychologist and his shortcomings: Distortion in the attribution process. In L. Berkowitz (Ed.), ADVANCES IN EXPERIMENTAL SOCIAL PSYCHOLOGY, (Vol. 10). New York: Academic Press, 1977.

Rotter, J. SOCIAL LEARNING AND CLINICAL PSYCHOLOGY. New York: Prentice-Hall, Inc., 1954.

Rotter, J. Generalized expectancies for internal versus external control of reinforcement. PSYCHOLOGICAL MONOGRAPHS: GENERAL AND APPLIED, 1966, Vol 80, No. 1, Whole No. 609, 1-28.

Rotter, J. A new scale for the measurement of interpersonal trust. JOURNAL OF PERSONALITY, 1967, 35, 651-665.

Rotter, J. Some problems and misconceptions related to the construct of internal versus external control of reinforcement. JOURNAL OF CONSULTING AND CLINICAL PSYCHOLOGY, 1975, 43, 56-67.

Rotter, J. THE DEVELOPMENT AND APPLICATION OF SOCIAL LEARNING THEORY. New York: Praeger, 1982.

Rotter, J. Internal versus external control of reinforcement. AMERICAN PSYCHOLOGIST, 1990, 45, 489-493.

Royce, J.R., and Mos, L.P. HUMANISTIC PSYCHOLOGY, CONCEPTS AND CRITICISMS. New York: Plenum Press, 1981.

Ruble, D. N. Premenstrual symptoms: A reinterpretation. SCIENCE, 1977, 197, 291-292.

Rudman, F.W. & Ansbacher, H.L. Anti-war psychologists: Alfred Adler. PSYCHOLOGISTS FOR SOCIAL RESPONSIBILITY NEWSLETTER, 1989, 8(#4), p. 8.

Ryan, R.M. & Grolnick, W.S. Origins and pawns in the classroom: Self-report and projective assessments of individual differences in children's perceptions. JOURNAL OF PERSONALITY AND SOCIAL PSYCHOLOGY, 1986, 50, 550-558.

Rychlak, J.F. A PHILOSOPHY OF SCIENCE FOR PERSONALITY THEORY. Boston: Houghton-Mifflin, 1968.

Rychlak, J.F. Is a concept of "self" necessary in psychological theory? In A. Wandersman, P. Poppen, and D. Ricks. (Eds.) HUMANISM AND BEHAVIORISM: DIALOGUE AND GROWTH. New York: Pergamon Press, 1976,

121-143.

Rychlak, J. F. INTRODUCTION TO PERSONALITY AND PSYCYHOTHERAPY. Boston: Houghton Mifflin Company, 1981.

Sabatelli, R. Buck, R. & Dreyer, A. Locus of control, interpersonal trust, and nonverbal communication accuracy. JOURNAL OF PERSONALITY AND SOCIAL PSYCHOLOGY, 1983, 44, 399-409.

Salzinger, K. B. F. Skinner (1904-1990). OBSERVER (of the American Psychological Society). 1990 (Sept.), 3, pp. 1, 3, & 4.

Sanitioso, R., Kunda, Z. & Fong, G. T. Motivated recruitment of biographical memories. JOURNAL OF PERSONALITY AND SOCIAL PSYCHOLOGY, 1990, 59, 229-241.

Sapir, E. LANGUAGE, AN INTRODUCTION TO THE STUDY OF SPEECH. New York: Harcourt, Brace and Compan,. 1921.

Sarason, I.G. Anxiety and self-preoccupation. In C.D. Speilberger and I.G. Sarason, (Eds.), STRESS AND ANXIETY (Vol. 2). New York: Wiley, 1975, 27-44.

Sarason, I.G., Smith, R.E., & Diener, E. Personality research: Components of variance attributed to the person and the situation. JOURNAL OF PERSONALITY AND SOCIAL PSYCHOLOGY, 1975, 32, 199-204.

Sarbin, T. Metaphorical encounters of the fourth kind. Paper presented at the American Psychological Association Convention, Washington, D.C., 1982.

Sartre, J-P. BEING AND NOTHINGNESS, AN ESSAY ON PHENOMENOLOGICAL ONTOLOGY. (H. Barnes, Trans.) New York: Philosophical Library, 1956.

Sartre, J-P. EXISTENTIALISM AND HUMAN EMOTIONS. New York: Philosophical Library, 1957.

Scarr, S., Webber, P., Weinberg, R., Wittig, M. Personality resemblance among adolescents and their parents in biologically related and adoptive families. JOURNAL OF PERSONALITY AND SOCIAL PSYCHOLOGY, 1981, 40, 885-898.

Schafer, R. A NEW LANGUAGE FOR PSYCHOANALYSIS. New Haven: Yale University Press, 1976.

Schooler, C. Birth order effects: Not here, not now!

PSYCHOLOGICAL BULLETIN, 1972, 78, 161-175.

Schroeder, D.J. & Pendleton, M.G. The adjective generation technique: Consistency of self-description in psychiatric patients. JOURNAL OF PERSONALITY, 1983, 51, 631-639.

Schwartz, B. PSYCHOLOGY OF LEARNING AND BEHAVIOR. New York: Norton, 1978.

Sears, R.R. STUDIES IN PERSONALITY. New York: McGraw-Hill, 1942.

Sears, R.R. SURVEY OF OBJECTIVE STUDIES OF PSYCHOANALYTIC CONCEPTS. Bull. 51, New York: Social Science Research Council, 1943.

Sechrest, L. & Jackson, D. N. Social intelligence and accuracy of interpersonal predictions. JOURNAL OF PERSONALITY, 1961, 29, 167-182.

Seligman, M. HELPLESSNESS: ON DEPRESSION, DEVELOPMENT, AND DEATH. San Francisco: Freeman, 1975.

Seligman, M. On the generality of the laws of learning. PSYCHOLOGICAL REVIEW, 1970, 77, 406-418.

Selye, H. THE STRESS OF LIFE. (Revised edition) New York: McGraw-Hill, 1978.

Shaver, P. & Hazan, C. Being lonely and falling in love: Perspectives from attachment theory. In M. Hojat & R. Crandall (Eds.), Loneliness: theory, research and applications, a special issue of JOURNAL OF SOCIAL BEHAVIOR AND PERSONALITY, 1987, 2(2, Pt. 2), 105.

Shaver, P. Being lonely, falling in love: Perspectives from attachment theory, 1986 (August), Paper presented at the American Psychological Association Convention, Washington, D.C.

Sheehy, G. PASSAGES. New York: Bantam, 1977.

Sheldon, W.H. THE VARIETIES OF HUMAN PHYSIQUE: AN INTRODUCTION TO CONSTITUTIONAL PSYCHOLOGY. New York: Harper, 1940.

Shelley, M. W. FRANKENSTEIN: A MODERN PROMETHEUS. New York: Dell, 1965.

Sherrill, C., Gench, B., Hinson, M., Gilstrap, T., Richir, K. & Mastro, J. Self-actualization of elite blind athletes: An exploratory study. JOURNAL OF VISUAL IMPAIRMENT & BLINDNESS, 1990, 84, 55-60.

Shirer, W.L. THE RISE AND FALL OF THE THIRD REICH. Greenwich, Connecticut: Fawcett Crest, 1960.

Shlien, J.M. Phenomenology and personality. In J.T. Hart and T.M. Tomlinson. NEW DIRECTIONS IN CLIENT-CENTERED THERAPY. Boston: Houghton Mifflin, 1970, 95-128.

Shlien, J.M., and Zimring, F.M. Research directives and methods in client-centered therapy. In J.T. Hart and T.M. Tomlinson. NEW DIRECTIONS IN CLIENT-CENTERED THERAPY. Boston: Houghton Mifflin, 1970, 33-57.

Shneidman, E.S., Farberow, N.L. & Litman, R.E. THE PSYCHOLOGY OF SUICIDE. New York: Science House, 1970.

Shoda, Y., Mischel, W., & Peake, P.K. Predicting adolescent cognitive and self-regulatory competencies from preschool delay of gratificaiton: Identifying diagnostic conditions. DEVELOPMENTAL PSYCHOLOGY, 1990, 26, 978-986.

Shoda, Y., Mischel, W., & Wright, J.C. Intuitive interactionism in person perception: Effects of situation-behavior relations on dispositional judgments. JOURNAL OF PERSONALITY AND SOCIAL PSYCHOLOGY, 1989, 56, 41-53.

Shostrom, E. FREEDOM TO BE, EXPERIENCING AND EXPRESSING YOUR TOTAL BEING. New York: Bantam, 1972.

Shostrom, E.L. (Ed.) THREE APPROACHES TO PSYCHOTHERAPY: ROGERS, PERLS AND ELLIS. Orange, California: Psychological Films, 1965.

Shostrom, E.L. EITS MANUAL FOR THE PERSONAL ORIENTATION INVENTORY. San Diego: Educational and Industrial Testing Service, 1966.

Signell, K. Cognitive complexity in person perception and nation perception: A developmental approach. JOURNAL OF PERSONALITY, 1966, 34, 517-537.

Silva-Garcia, J. Fromm in Mexico: 1950-1973. CONTEMPORARY PSYCHOANALYSIS, 1989, 25, 244-257.

Silverman, L. An experimental technique for the study of unconscious conflict. BRITISH JOURNAL OF MEDICAL PSYCHOLOGY, 1971, 44, 17-25.

Silverman, L. Psychoanalytic theory: "The reports of my death are greatly exaggerated." AMERICAN PSYCHOLOGIST, 1976, 31, 621-637.

Simonton, O.C. & Simonton, S. Belief systems and management of the emotional aspects of malignancy. JOURNAL OF TRANSPERSONAL PSYCHOLOGY, 1975, 7, 29-48.

Singer, J. A. Affective responses to aubiographical memories and their relationship to long-term goals. JOURNAL OF PERSONALITY, 1990, 58, 535-563.

Singer, J. ANDROGENY, TOWARD A NEW THEORY OF SEXUALITY. Garden City, New York: Anchor Books, 1977.

Singer, J.L., and Singer, D.G. Personality. In P.H. Mussen and M.R. Rosenzweig, (Eds.), ANNUAL REVIEW OF PSYCHOLOGY, 1972, 23,375-412.

Skinner, B. F. WALDEN TWO. New York: McMillan, 1948.

Skinner, B. F. VERBAL BEHAVIOR. New York: Appleton-Century-Crofts, 1957.

Skinner, B. F. BEYOND FREEDOM AND DIGNITY. New York: Knopf, 1971.

Skinner, B. F. (Ed.) CUMMULATIVE RECORD: A SELECTION OF PAPERS THIRD EDITION. New York: Appleton-Century-Crofts, 1972.

Skinner, B. F. A lecture on "having" a poem. In B. Skinner (Ed.), CUMULATIVE RECORD : A SELECTION OF PAPERS THIRD EDITION. New York:Appleton-Century-Crofts, 1972a, 345-358.

Skinner, B. F. The design of cultures. In B. Skinner (Ed.), CUMULATIVE RECORD: A SELECTION OF PAPERS THRID EDITION. New York:Appleton-Century-crofts, 1972b, Pp. 39-50.

Skinner, B. F. Creating the creative artist. In B. Skinner (Ed.), CUMULATIVE RECORD : A SELECTION OF PAPERS THIRD EDITION. New York: Appleton-Century-Crofts, 1972c, 333-344.

Skinner, B. F. Freedom and the control of men. In B. Skinner (Ed.), CUMULATIVE RECORD: A SELECTION OF PAPERS THIRD EDITION. New York: Appleton-Century-Crofts, 1972d, 3-24.

Skinner, B. F. The operational analysis of psychological terms. In B. Skinner (Ed.), CUMULA-

TIVE RECORD: A SELECTION OF PAPERS THIRD EDITION. New York: Appleton-Century-Crofts, 1972e, 370-384.

Skinner, B. F. Baby in a box. In B. Skinner (Ed.), CUMULATIVE RECORD: A SELECTION OF PAPERS THIRD EDITION. New York: Appleton-Century-Crofts, 1972f, 567-573.

Skinner, B. F. "Superstition" in the pigeon. In B. Skinner (Ed.), CUMULATIVE RECORD: A SELECTION OF PAPERS THIRD EDITION. New York: Appleton-Century-Crofts, 1972g, 236-256

Skinner, B. F. Some relations between behavior modification and basic research. In B. Skinner (Ed.), CUMULATIVE RECORD: A SELECTION OF PAPERS THIRD EDITION. New York: Appleton-Century-Crofts, 1972h, 276-282.

Skinner, B. F. What is psychotic behavior? In B. Skinner (Ed.), CUMULATIVE RECORD: A SELECTION OF PAPERS THIRD EDITION. New York: Appleton-Century-Crofts, 1972i, 257-275.

Skinner, B. F. Reflection on a decade of teaching machines. In B. Skinner (Ed.), CUMULATIVE RECORD: A SELECTION OF PAPERS THIRD EDITION. New York: Appleton-Century-Crofts, 1972j, 194-207.

Skinner, B. F. Contingency management in the classroom. In B. Skinner (Ed.), CUMULATIVE RECORD: A SELECTION OF PAPERS THIRD EDITION. New York: Appleton-Century-Crofts, 1972k, 225-235.

Skinner, B. F. Why we need teaching machines. In B. Skinner (Ed.), CUMULATIVE RECORD: A SELECTION OF PAPERS THIRD EDITION. New York: Appleton-Century-Crofts, 1972l, 171-193.

Skinner, B. F. PARTICULARS OF MY LIFE. New York: Knopf, 1976a.

Skinner, B. F. ABOUT BEHAVIORISM. New York: Vintage Books, 1976b.

Skinner, B. F. THE SHAPING OF A BEHAVIORIST. New York: Knopf, 1979.

Skinner, B. F. Orgins of a behaviorist. PSYCHOLOGY TODAY, Sept, 1983a.

Skinner, B. F. A MATTER OF CONSEQUENCES. New York: Alfred A. Knopf, 1983b

Skinner, B. F. UPON FURTHER REFLECTION.

Englewood Cliffs, New Jersey: Prentice-Hall, 1987a.

Skinner, B. F. Whatever happened to psychology as the science of behavior? AMERICAN PSYCHOLOGIST, 1987b, 42, 780-786.

Skinner, B. F. The origins of cognitive thought. AMERICAN PSYCHOLOGIST, 1989, 44, 13-18.

Skinner, B.F. & M.E. Vaughan. ENJOY OLD AGE. New York: W. W. Norton, 1983.

Smith, B. On self-actualization: A transambivalent examination of a focal theme in Maslow's psychology. JOURNAL OF HUMANISTIC PSYCHOLOGY, 1973, 13, 17-33.

Smith, M.B. & Anderson, J.W. Henry A. Murray (1893-1988). AMERICAN PSYCHOLOGIST, 1989, 44, 153-154.

Smith, M.L. & Glass, G.V. Meta-analysis of psychotherapy outcome studies. AMERICAN PSYCHOLOGIST, 1977, 32, 752-760.

Smith, S.L. Extraversion and sensory threshold. PSYCHOPHYSIOLOGY, 1968, 5, 293-299.

Snyder, M. & Monson, T. Persons, situations, and the control of social behavior. JOURNAL OF PERSONALITY AND SOCIAL PSYCHOLOGY, 1975, 32, 637-644.

Snyder, M. The self-monitoring of expressive behavior. JOURNAL OF PERSONALITY AND SOCIAL PSYCHOLOGY, 1974, 30, 526-537.

Solomon, R. & Wynne, L. Traumatic avoidance learning: Acquisition in normal dogs. PSYCHOLOGICAL MONOGRAPHS, 1953, 67, No. 354, 19.

Spearman, C. ABILITIES OF MAN. New York: Macmillan, 1927.

Spearman, C. "General intelligence" objectively determined and measured. AMERICAN JOURNAL OF PSYCHOLOGY, 1904, 15, 201-293.

Speer, A. INSIDE THE THIRD REICH. New York: Avon, 1970.

Spence, J.T. (Ed.) ACHIEVEMENT AND ACHIEVEMENT MOTIVES, PSYCHOLOGICAL AND SOCIOLOGICAL APPROACHES. San Francisco: W.H. Freeman, 1983.

Spence, K.W. A theory of emotionally based drive (D) and its relation to performance in simple learning situations. AMERICAN PSYCHOLOGIST, 1958, 13, 131-141.

Spence, K.W. Anxiety (drive) level and performance in eyelid conditioning. PSYCHOLOGICAL BULLETIN, 1964, 61, 129-139.

Spence, K.W. BEHAVIOR THEORY AND CONDITIONING. New Haven: Yale University Press, 1956.

Spielberger, C.D. (Ed.) ANXIETY, CURRENT TRENDS IN THEORY AND RESEARCH. (Vol 1). New York: Academic Press, 1972.

Spielberger, C.D. Anxiety: State-trait-process. In C.D. Speilberger and I.G. Sarason, (Eds.), STRESS AND ANXIETY (Vol. 1). New York: Wiley, 1975, 115-143.

Spielberger, C.D., Gorsuch, R.L., and Lushene, R.E. MANUAL FOR THE STATE-TRAIT ANXIETY INVENTORY. Palo Alto, California: Consulting Psychologists Press, 1970.

Spitz, R.A. Hospitalism: An inquiry into the genesis of psychotic conditions in early chldhood. In PSYCHOANALYTIC STUDY OF THE CHILD. Vol. II. New York: International Universities Press, 1946.

Spivack, G., & Levine, M. The Devereux Child Behavior Rating Scales: A study of symptom behaviors in latency age atypical children. AMERICAN JOURNAL OF MENTAL DEFICIENCY, 1964, 68, 700-717.

Standal, S. The need for positive regard: A contribution to client-centered theory. Unpublished doctoral dissertation, University of Chicago, 1954.

Stanovich, K. E., HOW TO THINK STRAIGHT ABOUT PSYCHOLOGY (2nd ed.). Glenview, IL: Scott, Foresman and Company, 1989.

Station WQED, Pittsburgh. BECAUSE THAT'S MY WAY. (film) Lincoln: GPI Television Library, University of Nebraska, 1971.

Stelmack, R.M. Biological bases of extraversion: Psychopsychological evidence. JOURNAL OF PERSONALITY, 1990, 58, 291-311.

Stepansky, P.E. IN FREUD'S SHADOW, ADLER IN CONTEXT. Hillsdale, New Jersey: Erlbaum, 1983.

Stephenson, W. THE STUDY OF BEHAVIOR. Chicago: University of Chicago Press, 1953.

Stern, P.J. C.G. JUNG, THE HAUNTED PROPHET. New York: Delta, 1976.

Stevens, R. ERIK ERIKSON: AN INTRODUC-

TION. New York: St. Martin's Press, 1983.

Stolorow, R.D., and Atwood, G.E. FACES IN A CLOUD, SUBJECTIVITY IN PERSONALITY THEORY. New York: Jason Aronson, 1979.

Stuttaford, G. Review of "Freud on women: A reader" by Elisabeth Young-Bruehl. PUBLISHER'S WEEKLY, 237 (June), 1990, p. 54.

Sullivan, H.S. CONCEPTIONS OF MODERN PSYCHIATRY. New York: Norton, 1947.

Sullivan, H.S. PERSONAL PSYCHOPATHOLOGY. New York: Norton, 1972.

Sullivan, H.S. SCHIZOPHRENIA AS A HUMAN PROCESS. New York: Norton, 1962.

Sullivan, H.S. THE INTERPERSONAL THEORY OF PSYCHIATRY. (H.S. Perry & M.L. Gawel, Eds.) New York: Norton, 1953.

Sullivan, H.S. THE PSYCHIATRIC INTERVIEW. (H.S. Perry & M.L. Gawel, Eds.) New York: New York: Norton, 1954.

Sundberg, N.D. ASSESSMENT OF PERSONS. Englewood Cliffs: Prentice-Hall, 1977.

Sundberg, N.D. The practice of psychological testing in clinical services in the United States. AMERICAN PSYCHOLOGIST, 1961, 16, 79-83.

Sundberg, N.D., & Tyler, L.E. CLINICAL PSYCHOLOGY: AN INTRODUCTION TO RESEARCH AND PRACTICE. New York: Appleton-Century-Crofts, 1962.

Suomi, S.J., Collins, M.L., Harlow, H.F., and Ruppenthal, G.C. Effects of maternal and peer separations on young monkeys. JOURNAL OF CHILD PSYCHOLOGY AND PSYCHIATRY, 1976, 17, 101-112.

Suomi, S.J., and Harlow, H.F. Social rehabilitation of isolate-reared monkeys. DEVELOPMENTAL PSYCHOLOGY, 1972, 6, 487-496.

Super, D.E. Comment on Carl Rogers' Obituary. AMERICAN PSYCHOLOGIST, 1989, 44, 1162-1163.

Sutich, A.J. Transpersonal psychology: An emerging force. JOURNAL OF HUMANISTIC PSYCHOLOGY, 1968, 7, 77-78.

Suzuki, D.T. AN INTRODUCTION TO ZEN BUDDHISM. New York: Causeway, 1974.

Szasz, T.S. LAW, LIBERTY AND PSYCHIATRY. New York: Macmillan, 1963.

Szasz, T.S. The myth of mental illness. AMERICAN PSYCHOLOGIST, 1960, 15, 113-118.

Szent-Gyoergyi, A. Drive in living matter to perfect itself. SYNTHESIS, 1974, 12-24.

Tanner, O. STRESS. New York: Time-Life Books, 1976.

Taylor, J.A. The relationship of anxiety to the conditioned eyelid response. JOURNAL OF EXPERIMENTAL PSYCHOLOGY, 1951, 41, 81-92.

Taylor, J.A. A personality scale of manifest anxiety. JOURNAL OF ABNORMAL AND SOCIAL PSYCHOLOGY, 1953, 48, 285-290.

Taylor, J.A. Drive theory and manifest anxiety. PSYCHOLOGICAL BULLETIN, 1956, 53, 303-320.

Taylor, M. & Hall, J. Psychological androgyny: Theories, methods, and conclusions. PSYCHOLOGICAL BULLETIN, 1982, 92, 347-366.

Taylor, S.E. Adjustment to threatening events, A theory of cognitive adaptation. AMERICAN PSYCHOLOGIST, 1983, 38, 1161-1173.

Teplov, B. M. Problems in the study of general types of higher nervous activity in man and animals. In J. A. Gray (Ed.), PAVLOV'S TYPOLOGY (3-453). New York: Pergamon Press.

Thompson, G. George Alexander Kelly (1905-1967). JOURNAL OF GENERAL PSYCHOLOGY, 1968, 79, 19-24.

Thorne, F.C. CLINICAL JUDGMENT, A STUDY OF CLINICAL ERRORS. Brandon, Vermont: Journal of Clinical Psychology, 1961.

Thurstone, L.L. Primary mental abilities. PSYCHOMETRIC MONOGRAPHS, 1938, No. 1.

Tillich, P. THE COURAGE TO BE. New Haven: Yale University Press, 1952.

TIME. In the dock, The Popieluszko trial begins. January 7, 1985, p. 72.

Timnick, L. Chowchilla's kidnapped kids—Five years later. In Chicago SUNDAY SUN-TIMES, January 25, 1981, p. 52.

Toffler, A. FUTURE SHOCK. New York: Random House, 1970.

Toland, J. ADOLF HITLER. New York: Ballantine Books, 1976

Tomkins, S.S., and Izard, C.E. AFFECT, COGNITION AND PERSONALITY. New York: Springer, 1965.

Tosi, D.J., and Hoffman, S. A factor analysis of the Personal Orientation Inventory. JOURNAL

OF HUMANISTIC PSYCHOLOGY, 1972, 12, 86-93.

Triandis, H., Loh, W. & Levine, L. Race, status, quality of spoken English, and opinion about civil rights as determinants of imterpersonal attitudes. JOURNAL OF PERSONALITY AND SOCIAL PSYCHOLOGY, 1966, 3, 468-472.

Truax, C.B., and Carkhuff, R.R. TOWARD EFFECTIVE COUNSELING AND PSYCHOTHERAPY: TRAINING AND PRACTICE. Chicago: Aldine, 1967.

Truax, C.B., and Mitchell, K.M. Research on certain therapist interpersonal skills in relation to process and outcome. In A.E. Bergin and S.L. Garfield. (Eds.) HANDBOOK OF PSYCHOTHERAPY AND BEHAVIOR CHANGE: AN EMPIRICAL ANALYSIS. New York: Wiley, 1971, 299-344.

Tucibat, J. The effect of similarity of a braggart on self-esteem. Unpublished Masters Thesis, Department of Psychology, Western Illinois University, 1986.

Turco, R., Toon, T., Ackerman, T., Pollack, J. & Sagan, C. Nuclear winter: Global consequences of multiple nuclear explosions. SCIENCE, 1983, 222, 1283-1292.

Uhlemann, M.R., Lee, D.Y., & Hasse, R.F. The effects of cognitive complexity and arousal on client perception of counselor nonverbal behavior. JOURNAL OF CLINICAL PSYCHOLOGY, 1989, 45, 661-664.

Ullmann, L. & Krasner, L. (Eds.). CASE STUDIES IN BEHAVIOR MODIFICATION. New York: Holt, Rinehart and Winston, 1965.

Ulrich, R.E., Stachnik, T.J., & Stainton, N.R. Student acceptance of generalized personality interpretations. PSYCHOLOGICAL REPORTS, 1963, 20, 831-834.

Vaihinger, H. THE PHILOSOPHY OF 'AS IF' A SYSTEM OF THE THEORETICAL, PRACTICAL AND RELIGIOUS FICTIONS OF MANKIND. New York: Harcourt, Brace & Company, 1925.

Valins, S. & Nisbett, R. ATTRIBUTION PROCESSES IN THE DEVELOPMENT AND TREATMENT OF EMOTIONAL DISORDERS. Morristown, N. J.: General Learning Press, 1971.

Van Kaam, A. Existential psychology as a comprehensive theory of personality. REVIEW OF EXISTENTIAL PSYCHOLOGY AND PSYCHIATRY, 1963, 3, 11-26.

Van Kaam, A. Existential and humanistic psychology. REVIEW OF EXISTENTIAL PSYCHOLOGY AND PSYCHIATRY, 1965, 5, 291-296.

Van Kaam, A. EXISTENTIAL FOUNDATIONS OF PSYCHOLOGY. New York: Image Books, 1969.

VandeWoude, S., Richt, J. A., Zink, M.C., Rott, R., Narayan, O., Clements J. E. A borna virus cDNA encoding a protein recognized by antibodies in humans with behavioral diseases. SCIENCE, 1990, 250, 1278-1281.

Viney, L.L., Benjamin, Y.N., & Preston, C. Mourning and reminiscence: Parallel psychotherapeutic processes for elderly people. INTERNATIONAL JOURNAL OF AGING AND HUMAN DEVELOPMENT, 1989, 28, 239-249.

Vinokur, A. & Selzer, M.L. Desirable versus undesirable life events: Their relationship to stress and mental distress. JOURNAL OF PERSONALITY AND SOCIAL PSYCHOLOGY, 1975, 32, 329-337.

Vockell, E.L., Felker, D.W., and Miley, C.H. Birth order literature 1967-1971: Bibliography and index. JOURNAL OF INDIVIDUAL PSYCHOLOGY, 1973, 29, 39-53.

Wade, T.C., & Baker, T.B. Opinions and use of psychological tests: A survey of clinical psychologists. AMERICAN PSYCHOLOGIST, 1977, 32, 874-882.

Wallace, J. An abilities conception of personality: Some implications for personality measurement. AMERICAN PSYCHOLOGIST, 1966, 21, 132-138.

Watkins, M.M. WAKING DREAMS. New York: Harper Colophon Books, 1976.

Watson, D.L., & Tharp, R.G. SELF-DIRECTED BEHAVIOR, SELF-MODIFICATION FOR PERSONAL ADJUSTMENT. (Second edition) Monterey, California: Brooks/Cole, 1977.

Watson, J. BEHAVIORISM. Chicago: The University of Chicago Press, 1930.

Watson, J. & Rayner, R. Conditioned emotional reactions. JOURNAL OF EXPERIMENTAL PSYCHOLOGY, 1920, 3, 1-14.

Watts, A. PSYCHOTHERAPY EAST AND WEST. New York: Pantheon, 1961.

Weber, M. THE PROTESTANT ETHIC AND THE SPIRIT OF CAPITALISM. (T. Parsons, Trans.) New York: Scribner, 1904/1930.

Wehr, G. AN ILLUSTRATED BIOGRAPHY OF C. G. JUNG. Boston: Shambhala, 1989.

Weinberger, D.A., Schwartz, G.E., and Davidson, R.J. Low-anxious, high-anxious and repressive coping styles: Psychometric patterns and behavioral and physiological responses to stress. JOURNAL OF ABNORMAL PSYCHOLOGY, 1979, 88, 369-380.

Weiss, D. & Mendelsohn, G. & Feimer, N. Reply to the comments of Block and Ozer. JOURNAL OF PERSONALITY AND SOCIAL PSYCHOLOGY, 1982, 42, 1182-1184.

Weizmann, F., Wiener, N.I., Wiesenthal, D.L., & Ziegler, M. (1990). Differential K theory and racial hierarchies. *Canadian Psychology*, 31, 1-13.

Wessman, A.E., and Ricks, D.F. MOOD AND PERSONALITY. New York: Holt, Rinehart and Winston, 1966.

Wexler, D.A., and Rice, L.N. INNOVATIONS IN CLIENT-CENTERED THERAPY. New York: Wiley, 1974.

Wheeler, L. Motivation as a determinant of upward comparison. JOURNAL OF EXPERIMENTAL SOCIAL PSYCHOLOGY, 1966, Supplement No. 1,

Wheeler, L., Deci, E., Reis, H. & Zuckerman, Miron. INTERPERSONAL INFLUENCE. Boston: Allyn and Bacon, 1978.

White C., Flatley, D. & Janson, P. Moral reasoning in adulthood: Increasing consistency or contextual relativism? Paper presented at the American Psychological Association Convention, Washington, D. C., 1982.

White, D. E. Studies on Hysteria: Case histories and the case against history. MODERN LANGUAGE NOTES (MLN), 104 (Dec.) 1989, 1034-1048.

Wiedenfeld, S. A., O'Leary, A., Bandura, A., Brown, S., Levine, S., Raska, K. Impact of perceived self-efficacy in coping with stressors on components of the immune system. JOURNAL OF PERSONALITY AND SOCIAL PSYCHOLOGY, 1990, 39, 1082-1094.

Wiesel, E. NIGHT. New York: Pyramid Books, 1961.

Wiggins, J.S. Cattell's system from the perspective of mainstream personality theory. MULTIVARIATE BEHAVIORAL RESEARCH, 1984, 19, 176-190.

Will, O.A. Introduction. In H.S. Sullivan, 1954, pp. ix-xxiii.

Williams, D.E. & Page, Monte, M.M. A Multi-dimensional measure of Maslow's hierarchy of needs. JOURNAL OF RESEARCH IN PERSONALITY, 1989, 23, 192-213.

Williams, J. & Morland, J. Comment on Bank's "White preference in blacks: A paradigm in search of a phenomenon." PSYCHOLOGICAL BULLETIN, 1979, 86, 28-32.

Williams, J.H. PSYCHOLOGY OF WOMEN, BEHAVIOR IN A BIOSOCIAL CONTEXT. (Second edition) New York: Norton, 1983.

Wilson, G.D. Personality and social behavior. In H.J. Eysenck (Ed.), A MODEL FOR PERSONALITY, New York: Springer-Verlag, 1981, 210-245.

Wilson, S. & Barber, T. The fantasy prone personality: implications for understanding imagery, hypnosis, and parapsychological phenomena. In A. Sheikh (Ed.), IMAGERY: CURRENT THEORY, RESEARCH AND APPLICATION. New York: Wiley, 1982.

Wise, P. & Joy, S. Working mothers, sex differences, and self-esteem in college students' self-descriptions. SEX ROLES, 1982, 8, 785-790.

Wise, P., & Potkay, C. The KD-S: A technique in need of validation. In M.E. Sarbaugh, THE KINETIC DRAWING—SCHOOL TECHNIQUE. Monograph of the Illinois School Psychologists Association, 1983.

Wolff, P. THE DEVELOPMENTAL PSYCHOLOGIES OF JEAN PIAGET AND PSYCHOANALYSIS (Psychological Issues Monograph 5). New York: International Universities Press, 1960.

Wolman, B.B. CONTEMPORARY THEORIES AND SYSTEMS IN PSYCHOLOGY. (Second edition) New York: Plenum Press, 1981.

Wolpe, J. THE PRACTICE OF BEHAVIOR THERAPY. (Third edition) New York: Pergamon, 1982.

Wolpe, J., & Rachman, S. Psychoanalytic evidence: A critique based on Freud's case of Little Hans. JOURNAL OF NERVOUS AND MENTAL DISEASES, 1960, 131, 135-145.

Wong, P.T.P. & Weiner, B. When people ask "why" questions, and the heuristics of attributional search. JOURNAL OF PERSONALITY AND SOCIAL PSYCHOLOGY, 1981, 40, 650-663.

Wood, R. & Bandura, A. Impact of conceptions of ability on self-regulatory mechanisms and complex decision making. JOURNAL OF PERSONALITY AND SOCIAL PSYCHOLOGY, 1989, 56, 407-415.

Woodward, K.L. How they bend minds. NEWSWEEK, December 4, 1978, 92 (#23), 72-77.

Woody, R.H. ENCYCLOPEDIA OF CLINICAL ASSESSMENT, VOLUMES I AND II. San Francisco: Jossey-Bass, 1980.

Wortis, J. FRAGMENTS OF AN ANALYSIS WITH FREUD. New York: Charter, 1954.

Wright, J.C. & Mischel, W. Conditional hedges and the intuitive psychology of traits. JOURNAL OF PERSONALITY AND SOCIAL PSYCHOLOGY, 1988, 55, 454-469.

Wylie, R. THE SELF-CONCEPT, A REVIEW OF METHODOLOGICAL CONSIDERATIONS AND MEASURING INSTRUMENTS. Vol. I. (Revised edition). Lincoln, Nebraska: University of Nebraska Press, 1974.

Wylie, R. THE SELF-CONCEPT: THEORY AND RESEARCH ON SELECTED TOPICS. Vol. II. (Revised edition). Lincoln, Nebraska: University of Nebraska Press, 1979.

Young, P.T. The experimental analysis of appetite. PSYCHOLOGICAL BULLETIN, 1941, 38, 129-164.

Young, P.T. Appetite, palatability and feeding habit; A critical review. PSYCHOLOGICAL BULLETIN, 1948, 45, 289-320.

Young-Bruehl, E. FREUD ON WOMEN: A READER. New York: W. W. Norton and Company, 1990.

Zajonc, R. B. The decline and rise of the Scholastic Aptitude Scores: A prediction derived from the confluence model. AMERICAN PSYCHOLOGIST, 1986, 41, 862-867.

Zajonc, R. B. & Markus, G. B. Birth Order and intellectual development. PSYCHOLOGICAL REVIEW, 1975, 82, 74-88.

Zimbardo, P. The human choice: Individuation, reason, and order versus deindividuation, impulse, and chaos. In W. Arnold & D. Levine (Eds.), NEBRASKA SYMPOSIUM ON MOTIVATION. Lincoln, Nebraska: University of Nebraska Press, 1970.

Zuckerman, M. & Lubin, B. MANUAL FOR THE MULTIPLE AFFECT ADJECTIVE CHECK LIST. San Diego, California: Educational and Industrial Testing Service, 1965.

Zuckerman, M. (1990). Some dubious premises in research and theory on racial differences: Scientific, social, and ethical issues. *American Psychologist*, 12, 1297-1303.

Zuckerman, M. The distinction between trait and state scales is NOT arbitrary: Comments on Allen and Potkay's "On the Arbitrary distinction betyween tratis an states." JOURNAL OF PERSONALITY AND SOCIAL PSYCHOLOGY, 1983, 44, 1083-1086.

Zuckerman, Miron, and Wheeler, L. To dispel fantasies about the fantasy-based measure of fear of success. PSYCHOLOGICAL BULLETIN, 1975, 82, 932-946.

Zuroff, D.S. Person, situation, and person-by-situation interaction components in person perception. JOURNAL OF PERSONALITY, 1982, 50, 1-14.

Zuroff, D.S. Was Gordon Allport a trait theorist? JOURNAL OF PERSONALITY AND SOCIAL PSYCHOLOGY, 1986, 51, 993-1000.

Zweig, S. Wider horizons on Freud. In Gerard, L. SIGMUND FREUD: THE MAN AND HIS THEORIES. New York: Fawcett, 1962.

NAME INDEX

Hogan, R. 66
Holland, J. 366, 368, 370
Holmes, J. G. 309
Hopkins, E. 386
Horn, P. 447
Horney, K. 73, 77, 103–128,
    129–131, 145, 149, 150, 175,
    270, 391, 400
Houle, G. R. 256
Hoyt, M. 355
Huber, R. J. 88
Hussein, S. 199
Hull, C. 479
Hunt, J. McV 43
Husserl, M. 214
Huxley, A. 457
Hyer, L. 90, 92

Ionedes, N. S. 79
Ishiyama, O. 87

Jackson, D. N. 284, 399,
    407–408, 414
Jackson, Michael 61
Jackson, M. 92
Jacobi, J. 63, 71
James, W. 134, 229
Jim (Kelly constructs) 272–277
Jankowicz, A. D. 285, 288, 293
Joan (Kelly constructs) 272–277,
    286–288
Joerger, S.M. 259, 262
Johnson, C. L. 88
Jones, B. M. 446
Jones, D. M. 448
Jones, E. 24, 25
Jones, E. E. 355
Jordon, B. 161
Jordan, E. W. 96
Joseph, E. 79
Jung, C. 23, 53–75, 149, 159, 214,
    222, 229, 270, 278, 314, 379,
    383, 391, 394–395, 404, 420,
    455

Kagan, J. 384
Kal, E. F. 94
Kanner, L. 47

Katcher, A. 47
Kaur, S. 446
Keinonen, M. 399, 407
Kelly, G. 12, 267–297, 300, 302,
    316, 333, 391, 394, 453–454,
    457
Kendler, H. 385
Keniston, K. 156
Kerlinger, F.N. 424
Kierkegaard, S. 214
Kimble, G. 366, 383
King, M. L. 253, 354
Kinkade, K. 380
Kirschenbaum, H. 209–210, 211,
    216, 233
Klein, G. 45
Klein, T. W. 435, 436
Klotz, L. 441
Kobler, F. 98
Koffka, K. 478, 481
Kohlberg, L. 38, 47, 242
Kohler, W. 214
Kohn, A. 96
Kopp, R. R. 92
Kowaz, A.M. 313
Krasner, L. 382
Krauft, C. C. 233
Krauss, H. 68
Krippner, S. 385
Kunda, Z. 91

Labrentz, H. L. 92
Lamarck, C. de 72
Lamiell, J. 4
Lashley, K. 397
Latane, B. 353
Lawlis, G. F. 69
Lawrence, A. 42
Leak, G. K. 93
Lebowitz, M. 54, 64
Lee, D. Y. 285
Lees, J. 448
Lefcourt, H. M. 309
Leupold–Loewenthal, H. 25
Leventhal, H. 339
Levine, L. 472
Levine, S. 346
Levinson, D. 170–172, 175
Lewin, K. 300, 392

Linder, D. 355
Lindberg, C. 405
Lindzey, G. 204
Linville, P. 284
Little Anna 62
Little Hans 36
Loehlin, J.C. 422, 424, 447
Loh, W. 472
Lyer, L. 159
Lyle, W. H. 292–293

MacDonald, A. P. 96
Maddi, S. 43
Maholick, L. 260
Malcolm, D. 212, 232
Mann, L. 353
Manaster, G. J. 90, 96
Markus, G. B. 87, 97
Martin, J. 118
Marx, K. 181–182
Maslow, A. 66, 73, 189, 191, 209,
    213, 239–266, 270, 300, 303,
    314, 343, 391, 394, 396, 399,
    402, 428, 454–455
Masson, J. 47
Mastro, J. 502
Mathes, E.W. 119, 121, 259, 262
Matlin, M. 294, 332, 384
Matthews, G. 448
May, R. 214
McAdams, D. P. 174, 175
McCarthy, E. 185
McCarthy, J. 301
McClelland, D. C. 175
McDonald, F. 342
McEvedy, C. P. 447
McGuire, T. R. 423, 435, 436, 437
Mead, M. 105
Means, R. S. 446
Means, G. H. 446
Mearns, J. 312–313
Mendalgio, S. 305
Menninger, K. 216
Merleau–Ponty, M. 214
Merrens, M. 410
Miley, C. H. 87
Milgram, S. 353
Miller, N. 45, 330
Miller, P. C. 309

SUBJECT INDEX